Lecture Notes in Computer Science 4878

Commenced Publication in 1973
Founding and Former Series Editors:
Gerhard Goos, Juris Hartmanis, and Jan van Leeuwen

Eduardo Tovar   Philippas Tsigas
Hacène Fouchal (Eds.)

Principles of Distributed Systems

11th International Conference, OPODIS 2007
Guadeloupe, French West Indies, December 17-20, 2007
Proceedings

 Springer

Volume Editors

Eduardo Tovar
Polytechnic Institute of Porto (ISEP-IPP)
Department of Computer Engineering
Rua Dr. António Bernardino de Almeida 431, 4200-072 Porto, Portugal
E-mail: emt@dei.isep.ipp.pt

Philippas Tsigas
Chalmers University of Technology
Department of Computer Science & Engineering
412 96 Göteborg, Sweden
E-mail: tsigas@chalmers.se

Hacène Fouchal
GRIMAAG, Université des Antilles et de Guyane
97157 Pointe-à-Pitre, Guadeloupe, France
E-mail: Hacene.Fouchal@univ-ag.fr

Library of Congress Control Number: 2007940869

CR Subject Classification (1998): C.2.4, D.1.3, D.2.7, D.2.12, D.4.7, C.3

LNCS Sublibrary: SL 1 – Theoretical Computer Science and General Issues

ISSN   0302-9743
ISBN-10   3-540-77095-X Springer Berlin Heidelberg New York
ISBN-13   978-3-540-77095-4 Springer Berlin Heidelberg New York

Springer is a part of Springer Science+Business Media

springer.com

© Springer-Verlag Berlin Heidelberg 2007
Printed in Germany

Typesetting: Camera-ready by author, data conversion by Scientific Publishing Services, Chennai, India
Printed on acid-free paper   SPIN: 12199679   06/3180   5 4 3 2 1 0

Preface

It is our pleasure to welcome you to the 11th International Conference on Principles of Distributed Systems (OPODIS 2007), held during December 17–20, 2007, in Guadeloupe, French West Indies.

During the past years, OPODIS has established itself as one of the most important events related to principles of distributed computing, networks and systems. In this year's edition, we received 106 submissions in response to the call for papers. Papers were sought soliciting original research contributions to the theory, specifications, design and implementation of distributed systems, including: communication and synchronization protocols; distributed algorithms, multiprocessor algorithms; distributed cooperative computing; embedded systems; fault-tolerance, reliability, availability; grid and cluster computing; location- and context-aware systems; mobile agents and autonomous robot; mobile computing and networks; peer-to-peer systems, overlay networks; complexity and lower bounds; performance analysis of distributed systems; real-time systems; security issues in distributed computing and systems; sensor networks: theory and practice; specification and verification of distributed systems; testing and experimentation with distributed systems.

It was a hard task to select the 32 excellent papers that are compiled in this volume. All submissions received at least three reviews, resulting in an overall number of more than 350 reviews—involving more than 100 reviewers— being conducted. An important piece of the process was the Program Committee electronic meeting held during the week of September 10. It was definitely an outstanding performance by all 42 Program Committee members and their co-reviewers. We are convinced that a very good set of papers was selected for presentation at OPODIS 2007.

This year's edition also featured two exciting keynote talks by Moti Yung (Google Inc., USA) and Tarek Abdelzaher (University of Illinois at Urbana-Champaign, USA). We are grateful that those two distinguished speakers accepted our invitation to share with us their views.

It would not have been possible to set up this exciting program without the close cooperation and support of the General Chair, Hacène Fouchal, who deserves a big share of credit. We would also like to thank Thibault Bernard for his role as Publicity Chair and on managing both the electronic submission and reviewing system and OPODIS 2007 Web site, and to the other members of the Organizing Committee, Céline Butelle, Harry Gros-Désormeaux and Vincent Levorato.

December 2007

Eduardo Tovar
Philippas Tsigas

Conference Organization

OPODIS 2007 was organized by "Université des Antilles et de la Guyane" in Guadeloupe, French West Indies and APODIS "Association Pour la Diffusion Scientifique."

General Chair

Hacène Fouchal   Université des Antilles et de la Guyane, France

Program Co-chairs

Eduardo Tovar   Polytechnic Institute of Porto, Portugal
Philippas Tsigas   Chalmers University of Technology, Sweden

Program Committee

Tarek Abdelzaher	University of Illinois at Urbana-Champaign, USA
Mustaque Ahamad	Georgia Institute of Technology, USA
James Anderson	University of North Carolina at Chapel Hill, USA
Bjorn Andersson	Polytechnic Institute of Porto, Portugal
Alain Bui	University of Reims, France
Leandro Buss Becker	University of Santa Catarina, Brazil
Franck Cappello	LRI, France
Ajoy Datta	University of Nevada at Las Vegas, USA
Murat Demirbas	State University of New York at Buffalo, USA
Shlomy Dolev	Ben-Gurion University, Israel
Pascal Felber	University of Neuchatel, Switzerland
Gerhard Fohler	University of Kaiserslautern, Germany
Marisol Garcia Valls	UC3 Madrid, Spain
Christopher Gill	Washington University at St. Louis, USA
Rachid Guerraoui	EPFL, Switzerland
Maurice Herlihy	Brown University, USA
Ted Herman	University of Iowa, USA
Philippe Hunel	Université des Antilles et de la Guyane, France
Pierre Jansen	University of Twente, The Netherlands
Vana Kalogeraki	University of California at Riverside, USA
Anne-Marie Kermarrec	INRIA, France

Reviewers

Tarek Abdelzaher
Mustaque Ahamad
Murat Ali Bayir
James Anderson
Bjorn Andersson
Carlos Becker Westphall
Doina Bein
Thibault Bernard
Marin Bertier
Olga Brukman
Alain Bui
Leandro Buss Becker
John Calandrino
Franck Cappello
David Cash
Ioannis Chatzigiannakis
Tim Childress
Ajoy Datta
Seda Davtyan
Murat Demirbas
UmaMaheswari Devi
Stphane Devismes
Martin Dietzfelbinger
Shlomi Dolev
Ji (Adam) Dou
Yannis Drougas
Mahmoud Elhaddad
Sherif Fahmy
Gilles Fedak
Pascal Felber
Hen Fitoussi
Gerhard Fohler
Marisol Garcia Valls
Chris Gill
Sameh Gobrial
Maria Gradinariu
Harry Gros-Desormeaux
Maxim Gromov
Rachid Guerraoui

Arobinda Gupta
Kai Han
Nicolas Hanusse
Thomas Hérault
Maurice Herlihy
Ted Herman
Philippe Hunel
Muzammil Hussain
Mathieu Jan
Pierre Jansen
Rajeev Joshi
Vana Kalogeraki
Ronen Kat
Sotirios Kentros
Anne-Marie Kermarrec
Sherif Khattab
Ralf Klasing
Derrick Kondo
Herman Kopetz
Mimor Lahiani
Lawrence Larmore
Joao Leitao
Hennadiy Leontyev
Vasia Liagkou
Steve Liu
Lucia Lo Bello
Xuming Lu
Mihai Marin-Perianu
Charles Martel
Pau Marti
Rami Melhem
Yves Metivier
Maged Michael
Hugo Miranda
Jose Mocito
Peter Musial
Gil Neiger
Nicolas Nicolaou
Florent Nolot

Lucia Penso
Sylvain Peyronnet
Christian Poellabauer
Giuseppe Prencipe
Svetlana Prokopenko
Cyril Rabat
Raj Rajkumar
Krithi Ramamritham
Binoy Ravindran
Torvald Riegel
Luis Rodrigues
Rodrigo Rodrigues
Nasser Saheb
Nicola Santoro
Christian Scheideler
Andrey Shabaldin
Natalya Shabaldina
Marc Shapiro
Alex Shvartsman
Marcelo Sobral
Devan Sohier
Elaine Sonderegger
Onur Soysal
Paul Spirakis
Luiz-Angelo Steffenel
Pierre Sutra
Hisao Tamaki
Sebastien Tixeuil
Emanuele Toscano
Nir Tzachar
Nicolas Vidot
Zhijum Wang
Peter Widmayer
Ruibin Xu
Reuven Yagel
Masafumi Yamashita
Nina Yevtushenko

Sponsoring Institutions

UAG, Université des Antilles et de la Guyane
EPHE, l'Ecole Pratique des Hautes Etudes, Sorbonne, France
LaISC, Laboratoire d'Informatique et des Systèmes Complexes, France
GDR ARP du CNRS
INRIA, Institut National de la Recherche en Informatique et en Automatique

Table of Contents

A Decentralized, Scalable, and Autonomous Grid Monitoring System ... 1
Laurent Baduel and Satoshi Matsuoka

A Formal Analysis of the Deferred Update Technique 16
Rodrigo Schmidt and Fernando Pedone

ASAP: A Camera Sensor Network for Situation Awareness 31
Junsuk Shin, Rajnish Kumar, Dushmanta Mohapatra,
Umakishore Ramachandran, and Mostafa Ammar

Asynchronous Active Recommendation Systems 48
Baruch Awerbuch, Aviv Nisgav, and Boaz Patt-Shamir

Brute-Force Determination of Multiprocessor Schedulability for Sets of
Sporadic Hard-Deadline Tasks 62
Theodore P. Baker and Michele Cirinei

Byzantine Consensus with Few Synchronous Links 76
Moumen Hamouma, Achour Mostefaoui, and Gilles Trédan

Clock Synchronization in the Byzantine-Recovery Failure Model 90
Emmanuelle Anceaume, Carole Delporte-Gallet, Hugues Fauconnier,
Michel Hurfin, and Josef Widder

Computing Without Communicating: Ring Exploration by
Asynchronous Oblivious Robots 105
Paola Flocchini, David Ilcinkas, Andrzej Pelc, and Nicola Santoro

Deterministic Communication in the Weak Sensor Model 119
Antonio Fernández Anta, Miguel A. Mosteiro, and
Christopher Thraves

Deterministic Leader Election in Anonymous Sensor Networks Without
Common Coordinated System 132
Yoann Dieudonné and Franck Petit

Distance Sensitive Snapshots in Wireless Sensor Networks 143
Vinodkrishnan Kulathumani and Anish Arora

Distributed Approximation Algorithms for Finding 2-Edge-Connected
Subgraphs 159
Sven O. Krumke, Peter Merz, Tim Nonner, and Katharina Rupp

Does Clock Precision Influence ZigBee's Energy Consumptions? 174
Christian Groß, Holger Hermanns, and Reza Pulungan

From an Intermittent Rotating Star to a Leader 189
    Antonio Fernández Anta and Michel Raynal

Global Deadline-Monotonic Scheduling of Arbitrary-Deadline Sporadic
Task Systems 204
    Sanjoy Baruah and Nathan Fisher

LFTHREADS: A Lock-Free Thread Library 217
    Anders Gidenstam and Marina Papatriantafilou

Making Distributed Applications Robust 232
    Chi Ho, Danny Dolev, and Robbert van Renesse

Maximizing the Number of Broadcast Operations in Static Random
Geometric Ad-Hoc Networks 247
    *Tiziana Calamoneri, Andrea Clementi, Emanuele G. Fusco, and
    Riccardo Silvestri*

N-Consensus is the Second Strongest Object for $N + 1$ Processes 260
    Eli Gafni and Petr Kuznetsov

Non-Searchability of Random Power-Law Graphs 274
    Philippe Duchon, Nicole Eggemann, and Nicolas Hanusse

$O(\log n)$-Time Overlay Network Construction from Graphs with
Out-Degree 1 286
    James Aspnes and Yinghua Wu

On the Self-stabilization of Mobile Robots in Graphs 301
    Lélia Blin, Maria Gradinariu Potop-Butucaru, and Sébastien Tixeuil

Peer to Peer Multidimensional Overlays: Approximating Complex
Structures 315
    Olivier Beaumont, Anne-Marie Kermarrec, and Étienne Rivière

Secretive Birds: Privacy in Population Protocols 329
    *Carole Delporte-Gallet, Hugues Fauconnier, Rachid Guerraoui, and
    Eric Ruppert*

Self-stabilizing and Byzantine-Tolerant Overlay Network 343
    Danny Dolev, Ezra N. Hoch, and Robbert van Renesse

Separability to Help Parallel Simulation of Distributed Computations ... 358
    Philippe Mauran, Gérard Padiou, and Philippe Quéinnec

Small-World Networks: From Theoretical Bounds to Practical
Systems 372
    François Bonnet, Anne-Marie Kermarrec, and Michel Raynal

The Anonymous Consensus Hierarchy and Naming Problems 386
    Eric Ruppert

The Baskets Queue... 401
    Moshe Hoffman, Ori Shalev, and Nir Shavit

The Cost of Monotonicity in Distributed Graph Searching............. 415
    David Ilcinkas, Nicolas Nisse, and David Soguet

Timed Quorum Systems for Large-Scale and Dynamic Environments ... 429
    Vincent Gramoli and Michel Raynal

Worm Versus Alert: Who Wins in a Battle for Control of a Large-Scale
Network? 443
    James Aspnes, Navin Rustagi, and Jared Saia

Author Index 457

A Decentralized, Scalable, and Autonomous Grid Monitoring System

Laurent Baduel[1] and Satoshi Matsuoka[1,2]

[1] Tokyo Institute of Technology,
2-12-1 Ookayama, Meguro-ku, Tokyo 152-8552, Japan
[2] National Institut of Informatics,
2-1-2 Hitotsubashi, Chiyoda-ku, Tokyo, 101-8430, Japan
baduel@smg.is.titech.ac.jp, matsu@is.titech.ac.jp

Abstract. Grid monitoring systems collect a substantial amount of information on the infrastructure's status in order to perform various tasks, more commonly to provide a better use of the grid's entities. Modern computational and data grids have become very complex by their size, their heterogeneity, their interconnection. Monitoring systems as any other grid's tools have to adapt to this evolution. In this paper we present a decentralized, scalable, and autonomous grid monitoring system able to tackle the growths of scale and complexity. System's components communications are hierarchically organized on a peer-to-peer overlay network. Fresh information is efficiently propagated thanks to an *directed* gossip protocol that limits the number of message. Automation of key management operations eases system administration and maintenance. This approach provides scalability and adaptability. The main properties of our application are presented and discussed. Performance measurements confirm the efficiency of our system.

1 Introduction

Grid platforms with their ever-growing communication infrastructures and computing applications become larger and larger, which results in an exponential complexity in their engineering and maintenance operations. To efficiently handle such large and complex systems monitoring is necessary. By providing a global view of the system monitoring tools allow identifying performance problems and assisting in resources scheduling. Modern large scale systems do not allow anymore centralized organizations, with hand deployment, configuration, and administration. Automation of key operations must be introduced in such systems to free the administrators and programmers of many tiresome tasks.

After presenting related work, we propose a grid monitoring system built to address these challenges. It provides a scalable and portable monitoring of a wide range of entities connected in distributed systems. This decentralized tool achieves its communications thanks to a peer-to-peer overlay network. Peer-to-peer has become a popular way to communicate on grid thanks to its scalability, its decentralization, and its resistance to faults. It has already proved their efficiency in many aspects of distributed applications such as embarrassingly parallel computing, persistent and scalable storage, and especially in file sharing and dissemination. We use a gossip protocol to quickly spread

E. Tovar, P. Tsigas, and H. Fouchal (Eds.): OPODIS 2007, LNCS 4878, pp. 1–15, 2007.

information in the entire system. Components of the system are organized as a directed acyclic graph to guide information from their source to the bases storing the entire system state. This, combined to over-aged information filtering, reduces the amount of exchanged messages. Finally we have deployed a first implementation on a real grid and evaluated performance of our system.

In summary the contributions of this article are *(1)* the details of the conception of a decentralized and scalable grid monitoring system in which components are hierarchically organized through a directed acyclic graph on a peer-to-peer overlay network that provides a valuable communication layer thanks to a gossip multicast protocol, assures good performance on grids, and allows self-management of the system; *(2)* a performance evaluation of this system driven in a real large-sized grid. Speed of information dissemination, age of recorded information, impact of messages limitation, and dynamic adaptability are examined and discussed. This paper rather focuses on the fast and decentralized dissemination of information than on other aspects of monitoring such as sensors implementation or database organization.

The rest of this article is organized as follow: Section 2 describes the general properties of a monitoring system and insists on the specific requirements for grid environments. Then it presents related work. Section 3 introduces the architecture for monitoring system on which we based our implementation. Section 4 presents our original communication scheme based on peer-to-peer and what we name a *directed* gossip protocol. Then Section 5 details self-management mechanisms introduced in the system to help scalability and maintenance. Section 6 details the implementation and presents performance evaluations of the application. Finally Section 7 concludes the article and presents expected future works.

2   Grid Monitoring Systems

The activity of measuring significant resources parameters allows analyzing the usage, the behavior, and the performance of a cluster or a grid. It also provides Grid monitoring systems to collect a substantial amount of information on the infrastructure's status in order to perform various tasks, more commonly to provide a better use of the grid's entities.

Monitoring a system consists of observing events and communicating them to who are interested in that information. There are commonly two systems on a grid. According to [1], a *grid monitoring system* manages rapidly changing status information, such as the load of a CPU or the throughput of a network link. The high dynamicity of data that a grid monitoring system must handle makes it different from a *grid information system* which handles more static data, for instance the hardware configuration of a node. Although grid infrastructures can benefit a lot from a unified system that handles both roles. The global knowledge provided by a unified grid monitoring system helps resource scheduling, allocation and usage: reservation tools can be plugged in order to distribute resources and guarantee quality of service.

Monitoring dedicated to grids is subject to a growing interest. The recent large grids do not support anymore efficiently the existing monitoring tools. Most of existing solutions are adaptations of cluster oriented monitoring tools, and then lay to scalability and robustness issues. As detailed further the Network Weather Service is built around a centralized controller, and the Globus Monitoring and Discovery System suffers performance and scalability issues due to its LDAP architecture. On the contrary, the grid monitoring system we propose is adapted to the grid thanks to its scalability and fault tolerance ability, and also thank to its autonomous management.

The rest of this section presents a survey about grid monitoring systems and their potential autonomous mechanisms for configuration and adaptation.

2.1 Network Weather Service (NWS)

The Network Weather Service [2] is a distributed system that periodically monitors and dynamically forecasts the performance that various network and computational resources can deliver over a given time interval. The components of a NWS resource monitoring system are: a *name server*: a centralized controller that keeps a registry of all components and monitoring activities; *sensors* that produce resource observations; *memories* that store resource observations; and *forecasters* that process resource observations. Limits of the NWS architecture come from the presence of the name server. It introduces bottleneck, single point of failure, and does not embed security mechanism. Moreover the connections between sensors and the name server are manually managed by the administrator before starting the system. NWS is hardly applicable to a grid scale, mostly because of the absence of a real database.

2.2 Globus Monitoring and Discovery System (MDS)

The Monitoring and Discovery System [3] is the information services component of the Globus Toolkit and provides information about the available resources on the grid and their status. MDS is based on the Lightweight Directory Access Protocol (LDAP). The distributed nature of the LDAP architecture is appealing: information is organized hierarchically, and the resulting tree might be distributed over different servers. In a grid perspective, the hierarchy often reflects the organization of the grid: from continental networks to national networks to local networks. Leaves are single resource, like cluster of computers, single computer or storage element.

However, the LDAP architecture is appropriate to store static information, like the number of processors in a cluster, or the size of a disk partition. When data are more frequently changing, the LDAP architecture is a wrong choice: it is unsuitable to support frequent write operations. Indeed the LDAP Client Update Protocol is based on the assumption that "data changes, renames, and deletions of large subtrees are very infrequent" [4]. Under that condition LDAP architecture suffers serious performance and scalability problems.

2.3 Relational Grid Monitoring Architecture (R-GMA)

The Structured Query Language (SQL) allows manipulation of a relational database. Several implementations of this database are designed for extremely demanding applications. They offer a good compromise between the distributiveness, and the cost of query operations. In particular the database can be replicated in order to improve scalability and fault tolerance. The R-GMA [5] was developed to address those problems. The scalability of the architecture is improved by introducing components that combine data from the database and cache the results. R-GMA is an implementation of the GGF's GMA model (see Section 3) and is now developed as part of the *Enabling Grids for E-science in Europe* (EGEE) project. A strength of R-GMA is its ability to support queries which combine information across objects of different class (a *join* operation).

R-GMA focuses on the way data are stored, i.e. the relational database that is actually implemented by a virtual database distributed and accessible by hidden component named *mediator*. Concerns of easy deployment and adaptability are not the main issues of R-GMA.

2.4 Ganglia

Ganglia [6] is a scalable distributed monitoring system for high-performance computing systems such as clusters and Grids. It is based on a hierarchical design targeted at federations of clusters. It widely uses technologies such as XML for data representation, XDR[1] [7] for compact and portable data transport, and RRDtool[2] [8] for data storage and visualization. It uses carefully engineered data structures and algorithms to achieve low per-node overheads and high concurrency. The implementation has been ported to a large set of operating systems and processor architectures, and is currently in use on thousands of clusters around the world. It has been used to link clusters across university campuses and around the world and can scale to handle clusters with 2000 nodes.

Ganglia's implementation consists in the collaboration of two daemons. gmond running on every node provides local network monitoring by recording and communicating with multicast primitives. gmeta offers local networks federation by taking in charge the communication with other remote gmeta daemon. Ganglia is efficient and easy to deploy on small or medium sized clusters. However the copy on each node of the entire local network status may lead to scalability problem. Moreover some equipment with limited resources that may be present in a grid (such as personal digital assistant or various scientific equipments) may not be able to host a gmond daemon and its database. Finally the deployment and maintenance of double system gmond/gmeta require expertise from the administrators.

3   The Grid Monitoring Architecture

The Global Grid Forum (now known as Open Grid Forum) has introduced the Grid Monitoring Architecture (GMA) [9] which offers scalability and flexibility required by a grid monitoring system. This architecture simply identifies three kinds of component:

- the *producers* retrieve various information of a device and make them available to other GMA components; for instance a sensor reporting the CPU load of a computing node.

---

[1] XDR stands for eXternal Data Representation.
[2] RRD stands for Round Robin Database.

- the *consumers* request monitored information for which they have interest; for instance a resource broker that wants to locate suitable computing nodes.
- the *directory service* supports information publication and discovery of components as well as monitored information. A directory service is a place where producers advertise their data, and consumers advertise their needs.

In addition to those three basic components, the GMA lets room for *intermediate components*. Those components consist of both a consumer and a producer. They allow aggregation, filtering, forwarding, or broadcasting of the information received by other producers. Often monitoring tools use *aggregator* components. Those components help at the scalability of the system by avoiding communication bottlenecks between the producers and the directory service: the number of exchanged messages is reduced.

Scalability is assured by the separation of the publication, discovery, and query tasks. The GMA does not specify the way the components communicate among each others (message content or network protocol) or the format used by the directory service to store the information. Because of its flexibility and scalability we based our autonomic grid monitoring system on the GMA.

4 Decentralized and Scalable Communication Scheme

The priorities when building a grid tool is to ensure scalability and fault tolerance. Peer-to-peer networks and Gossip protocols scale very well thanks to their very decentralized organization. The decentralization of those systems also provides a good tolerance to faults by providing alternate paths of communication and replication of data.

4.1 A Peer-to-Peer Architecture

Grids and peer-to-peer have both an identical approach to the accomplishment of their goal: the use of overlay structures. However we can make an important distinction between the approaches of grids and peer-to-peer:

- *Grids* provide a large amount of services to moderated-sized communities with a generally high quality of service. Because of their hierarchical and static organizations grids are vulnerable to faults.
- In contrast *peer-to-peer systems* provide limited and specialized services to a very large amount of users. Peer-to-peer systems are strongly resistant to failure as a whole, but they do not provide a high quality of service. This limitation results from the fact the services are of nature as being provided in mass, and thus lead to various problems such as the node volatility, the best effort performance provided by the Internet, etc.

According to [10] the complementary nature of the strengths and weakness of the two approaches suggests that the interests of the two communities are likely to grow closer to each other. The main goals of current grids architecture are to increase their scalability and to provide a better handling of failures. Symmetrically peer-to-peer systems aim at improving the range of their services.

Current grids' component communications are fragile mainly because of static organizations and the absence of alternate paths of communication. They need to be sus-
tained by suitable overlays that are scalable and fault resilient. Peer-to-peer libraries are
the first stone to answers those concerns. As mentioned in Section 2 the main issue of
current monitoring systems is their centralized and static organization. Centralization
introduces weakness in a system because of the single point of failure problem and often leads to scalability issues by introducing bottleneck. A static organization makes the
maintenance of a large system specially challenging for the administrators.

As the GMA model does not specify communication mechanism for data transfer, we
decided to use peer-to-peer oriented communications. Figure 1 presents the structure of
a monitoring system using peer-to-peer interconnections. The producers are in contact
with aggregators. With regard to fast spreading of the information and fault-tolerance,
every producer keeps a contact with several aggregators (more details below). Similarly,
the aggregators communicate with the directory service. The directory service is made
of components that store information about the producers and the values they have
produced. We name those components *global storages*. For the same reasons as one
producer keeps contact with several aggregators, one aggregator keeps contact with
several global storages. Finally the consumers contact the directory service (i.e. the
global storages) to get the information it is interested in. A consumer may ask for the
location of the producer of a particular kind of event, and then contact the producer in
order to be directly notified of the information produced. A consumer may also ask for
the values stored in the global storage.

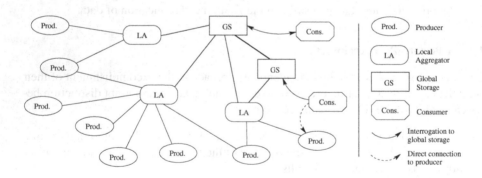

Fig. 1. Infrastructure

By introducing distribution, and indirect communication through a peer-to-peer network, we have to be careful regarding performance. The major challenge of our grid
monitoring system is to disseminate the information coming from the producers as fast
as possible to the global storages. Outdated information is useless since it is no more
relevant of the current node's status that may have radically changed. The monitoring
system has to be low resources consuming. Monitoring activities must not impact the
execution of other applications in the grid. CPU and bandwidth consumptions have to
be significantly low.

4.2   A Directed Gossip Protocol

The growth of large scale distributed applications is driving the need for scalable and reliable communications. Many network-level reliable multicast protocols are based on IP Multicast that is not widely deployed, resulting in a need for application-level broadcast protocol.

The communication model of our monitoring has to be scalable and low resource consuming. The system must spread the data as fast as possible in the entire system to ensure reactivity. On the other hand it is necessary to save bandwidth resource, for instance by avoiding multiple sending of the same data. We can not accept any component of the system emits several times the same info. Our solution is to use a *gossip protocol* [11] in order to broadcast the information. A pure gossip protocol takes place in rounds where in each round a participating process selects randomly another process and share information with it. In "push" gossip the process that initiates the gossip communicate its information to the selected target. It has been shown that in a group of n machines if one machine starts out with a new piece of information it takes $O(log\ n)$ rounds for every machine to become aware with that information [12].

The interest for using Gossip protocols on top peer-to-peer networks comes from two main points. *(1)* As mentioned before gossip protocols are very efficient to propagate information in large systems, like peer-to-peer systems. *(2)* Similarly to peer-to-peer systems, gossip protocols are totally decentralized and thus perfectly scalable.

In our system, we slightly modified the gossip protocol. All the nodes need not to get the information, but only the global storages. Thereby, the gossiping is performed only from producers to aggregators, from aggregators to global storages, and from global storages to global storages. This hierarchical structure, that is a directed acyclic graph from producers to global storages, provides a double benefit: by reducing the number of nodes to be informed it increases the scalability and reduces time and amount of messages required for all those nodes to be informed. As explained before, a challenge of our system is to spread information from one producer to all the global storages in the shortest time.

5   An Autonomous Monitoring System

Autonomic computing designates complex self-managed systems in which elements interact with each others in order to organize themselves and obtain a satisfactory general behavior. Modern large-scale computing systems widely distributed across multiple administrative domains have reached an unbelievable complexity. Autonomic computing offers to solve this problem through a smart and increased automation, freeing system administrators of many burdensome activities. Indeed, in modern large scale and distributed environments, and particularly grids, main difficulties has moved from application programming to configuration and maintenance.

As presented in [13] self-management falls in four categories: the *self-deployment* configures automatically the system; the *self-optimization* tunes the system to obtain the best performance; the *self-healing* detects, diagnostics, and fixes malfunctions; the *self-protection* defends the system against malicious attacks and cascading failures. In [14] we have presented the interests of using autonomic computing and how automatic behaviors can be implemented thanks to a peer-to-peer overlay network. The implementation of the four aspects of self-managed systems is based on the properties of peer-to-peer libraries, particularly the ability to dynamically find resources.

Self-configuration. When a new component enters into the system it has firstly to connect to the peer-to-peer network, then it may automatically retrieve some codes from other components in activity in the system, and finally it locates the components with which it will communicate. We will illustrate this procedure thanks to the producer component. A new producer firstly joins the peer-to-peer overlay network by searching for peers on the local network (broadcast) or by contacting a *bootstrap group* composed of nodes expected to be always online. Then as sensor's implementation for computational nodes may be quite similar, the producer may download the sensor's code from another producer already in activity. Finally the producer establishes contacts with a number of aggregators defined by the administrator. Those aggregators are selected regarding to the *round trip time* (RTT) that is the metric we use to express distance. A panel of aggregators with all RTTs is kept in order to uniformly spread information to "close" and "far" area of the network.

Self-optimization. Our policy for self-optimization is the dynamic dimensioning of the system size (number of components) according on the variation of its load. The size should be increase when the system gets overloaded and decrease in case of underload. In our system, the aggregators (and the global storages) have to adapt to the number of producer. Those components becomes overloaded when they receive more messages than they can handle or when they use more resources than they are supposed to do. An overloaded component takes the initiative to redirect some its producers to another component or, if no acceptable component is found, to create a new component. We consider an aggregator underloaded if during three successive evaluations the aggregator has received less than a fixed number of messages. The three evaluations allows smoothing the adaptation of the system and avoiding over-reactivity. We may also consider to observe the throughput, memory, or CPU usage of the component. Overtaking a certain threshold actions may be taken. Another aspect of the self-optimization may consist in regular observations of the system's performance. If the performance does not obey to constraints set by the administrator, the system may decide to take some measure. An example can be the momentary reduction of a communication frequency in order to eliminate network congestions.

Self-healing. A basic policy for self-healing can consist of the automatic detection of component's failure and the dynamic replacement of the failing component with the guaranty the system remains globally coherent. When an aggregator or a global storage fails, the failure is detected by the producers. If a producer does not succeed to communicate with a component, a failure is suspected. The producer broadcasts a message in the peer-to-peer network indicating the suspicion of a component failure, with the identity of the component. If one or more other producers confirm the failure of this component, an election mechanism decides where to restart the failed component. The election mechanism basically looks by a peer-to-peer search for the free host providing the more bandwidth, memory, and CPU power. In the case a failed component is not detected, the self-optimization mechanism may observe the overload of one component and decide the creation of a new one (c.f. self-optimization mechanism).

Self-protection. To make the system resistant to cascade failure we utilize the robust communication mechanism of some peer-to-peer networks that are able to re-route messages if a communication link falls and address peers that may have been disconnected during a while. We also rely on the replication of all aggregator and global storage components. The information aged x in one of those components is also present in another component with an age y, x and y beeing very similar. De facto there is no need to actively maintain consistency between those components.

6   Experimentations

This section presents some details of the implementation such as the peer-to-peer library we used and its particular features. Then it introduced the grid platform on which we performed experimentations. Relevant performance measurements are presented and discussed, proving the qualities of our monitoring in term of efficiency, scalability, and adaptability.

6.1   Implementation Details

JXTA [15] is a set of open and generalized peer-to-peer protocols that allow any connected device on the network to communicate and collaborate as peers. The JXTA protocols are independent of any programming language, and multiple implementations (called bindings) exist for different environments thus it is well adapted to the heterogeneous environments that compose a grid. JXTA has its own independent naming and addressing mechanism: a peer can move around the network, changes its transport protocol and network addresses, even being temporarily disconnected, and still addressable by other peers. This capability allows being resistant to the volatility of nodes in a grid. Moreover JXTA provides secure communication and access to resources following a role-based trust model. It provides also the possibility to cross firewall under the condition peers support HTTP. *Rendezvous peers* maintains a cache of advertissements and forward discovery requests to help other peers discover resources. Each rendezvous peer is like any other peer but keeps a list of other known rendezvous peers and a list of the peers that are using it as a rendezvous. *Relay peers* maintains information about the paths to other peers and routes messages to peers. They also forward messages on the behalf of peers that cannot directly address another peer (NAT environments). We configured those peers in order to connect peers from different sub-networks that compose a grid.

JXTA provides three levels of communication: *(1)* the *endpoint service* providing asynchronous, unidirectional, and unreliable static point-to-point communications; *(2)* the *pipes* providing asynchronous, unidirectional, and unreliable dynamic communications; and *(3)* the *JXTA sockets* adding reliability. We base our system on *BiDiPipes* that are pipes enhanced with bidirectional and (optinal) reliable communication. As exposed in [16] pipes provides better performance than sockets, moreover C/C++ implementation of JXTA does not provide the socket API. Indeed sockets are not part of the core specification of JXTA. In one direction bidipipes transport information from producer to aggregator, then to global storage; in the other direction the pipe is used to relay control signals for autonomic purposes. Control signals are for instance *RTT Request* and *Reply, Ping, Component failure suspicion, New component available* (for acquaintenances redirection), etc.

6.2 Performance Measures and Optimization

The *Grid'5000* project aims at building an experimental Grid platform gathering 9 sites geographically distributed in France combining up to 5000 processors. The plans are to assemble a physical platform featuring 16 clusters, each with an hundred to a thousand computers, connected by *Renater* the French Education and Research Network. Most sites are connected to Renater at 10 Gb/s (few of them still at 2.5 Gb/s). This high collaborative research effort is funded by the French ministry of education and research, INRIA, CNRS, the universities of all sites and several regional councils. Clusters composing the Grid'5000 platform are heterogeneous. To lead our experiments we used from 200 to 620 nodes (the number of nodes we used did not impact on the performance we observed cause each node was able to run the entire set of components we assigned to it). Multiple components were instanced on a same node, but for scalability reasons they were hosted in a unique Java Virtual Machine process. The collected information was limited to CPU and memory load.

The major point of interest in our system is to know how fresh the information in the global storages is, so our first experiment consists of observing the age of the information in a global storage. Each component gossips every 30 seconds. Our system being totally asynchronous we have no concern about possible time divergence between components: each component acts autonomously. At the beginning of the experiment the graph of components is already formed as follows. The ratios are arbitrarily set to 1 local aggregator for 100 producers and 1 global storage for 10 aggregators. Each producer is linked to 10 aggregators, each local aggregator is linked to 10 global storages, and each global storage is linked to 10 other global storages. The system ran one hour before being observed. Figure 2 presents the age of information in the global storages sorted by age. The instant of the observation is *age 0*.

Information in global storage is recent. The curves show peaks near the time of the observation. In a 20,000 producers system the peak is at -1.5 minute with 7.179% of the total information. In a 100,000 producers system the highest amount of information is aged 4.5 minutes with 3.697%. The average age of information is given in the following table (the size of the system is exposed in producers and age is exposed in minutes).

System size	20K	40K	60K	80K	100K
Average age	5.226	6.249	7.292	8.537	9.753

From Figure 2 we observe that half of the information, the older part, may be considered as useless. Indeed it is unnecessary to relay "old" information. Moreover it allows saving 50% of aggregators and storages' messages size. Figure 3 presents the age of information in the global storages sorted by age. In this experiment aggregators and storages only gossips the younger half of their information.

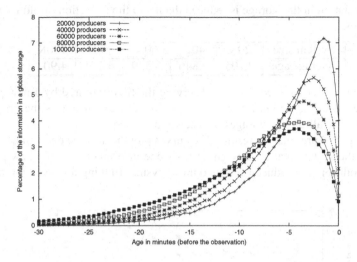

Fig. 2. Distribution of information by age

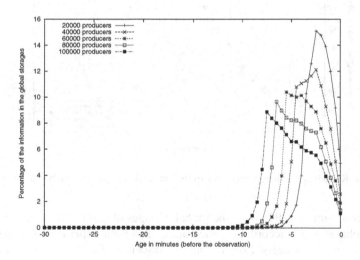

Fig. 3. Distribution of information by age with filtering of old information (50%)

We observe a reduction of the amount of older information, resulting in a higher percentage of younger information. The message reduction of course does not improve the efficiency of the system, it role is to reduce by almost half the amount of data transferred on the network.

Efficiency of the system seems to be very slightly impacted by the reduction of messages. Thanks to that observation we can imagine a dynamic adaptation of the age of information communicated each iteration in order to obtain the best trade-off between efficiency and bandwidth consumption. The following table shows the average

age of information in the storage is reduced thanks to the reduction of old information transmissions.

System size	20K	40K	60K	80K	100K
Average age	2.105	2.846	3.539	4.171	4.902

The second experiment consists of observing the time required by a new producer entering the system to be known by all the global storages. It means the propagation time required by all global storages to receive at least one information from the new producer. Figure 4 presents the results. The curves plot the average percentage of global storages in the system that already got at least one information from a new producer. The new producer is introduced at time 0 into a system running for several minutes.

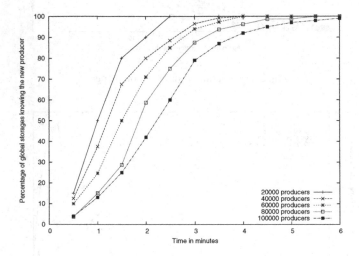

Fig. 4. Knowledge of a new producer in the entire system (i.e. all global storages)

In less than 4 minutes 92.0% of the global storages of a 100,001 producers system (i.e. 100 global storages according to the conditions of our experiment) have been informed of the new producers. Considering the abscence of point of centralization we consider the spreading of new information is very fast thanks to the gossip protocol. A first reason is that during one round the information is actually relayed three times: first from the producer to an aggregator, then in an aggregated form with other information from the aggregator to a global storage, and finally once again from the global storage to another global storage. Another reason is that our directed gossip protocol does not "broadcast" but "multicast" since only a subgroup of elements (the global storages) finally receives the information through the hierarchical architecture.

In our last experiment, we observe the adaptation of the number of aggregator regarding variation of producers in the system. From a 100 producers system, we add 10 new producers every 30 seconds, until the system reaches a size of 1,000 producers. Then number of producers remains stable for 7.5 minutes before we remove them gradually, 10 every 30 seconds. Producers cleanly exit: they notify their aggregators when

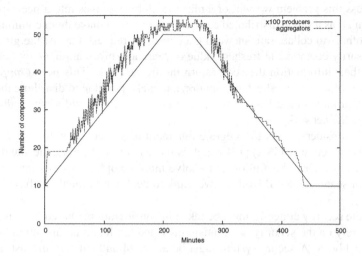

Fig. 5. Adaptation to the system size

they leave the system. During this experiment, we arbitrarily chose to declare an aggregator overloaded when it receives more than 100 information from the producers during three successive iterations. Similarly it is considered as underloaded if during three of its iterations it receives less than 80 information.

Figure 5 presents the number of aggregators and producers (by hundred), along the experiment. The curves remain close; it attests the quantity of aggregators increases in the same proportion as the producers. The ratio between aggregators and producers stays approximately the same over the time (average: 1 aggregator for 82.79 producers). The very fast growth of aggregators in the first minutes of the experiment results from the fact the system was already overloaded in its initial settings.

7   Conclusion and Perspectives

We presented a decentralized, scalable, and autonomous grid monitoring system able to tackle the growths of scale and complexity. The system's components are hierarchically organized on a peer-to-peer overlay network. A directed gossip protocol ensures efficient propagation of fresh information. Overproduction of messages is avoided by the organization of communication paths in DAG and by filtering on information depending on its age. Autonomic behaviors guarantee easy deployment and adaptability at runtime. The implementation was detailed as well as performance measurements that confirm the efficiency of our system. At this time the main advantages of our system are *(1)* its ability to be quickly and easily deploy; *(2)* its capacity to self-adapt; and *(3)* its fault-tolerance by information replication and alternative paths of communication. On the other hand, a drawback is to provide only "statistically" good quality of service: small probabilities remain to return a bad (too old) information.

To address this problem we will organize the global storages into a peer-group and access them all as a single distributed entity. The point is to make them communicating with each others to collaborate answering a consumer request. One of the global storages necessarily contains the freshest value of searched information, so by comparing the age of their information they can return the freshest one. This *peer-group service* guarantees to obtain the freshest information and make possible to distribute the global storages' information base leading to an improved scalability and a new reduction of messages on the network.

Our next consideration is to integrate our monitoring service with the Open Grid Software Architecture (OGSA) [17] which is more likely to become the standard way to access grid services. Also in order to solve more complex requests involving several fields of search, as R-GMA does, we think to deploy relational database in global storages.

Finally the security concerns must be taken in consideration. Our current implementation only rely on the security mechanism provided by the communication layer: the peer-to-peer library. A secure system must be aware of authentication, trust, and data integrity in order to prevent malicious attacks.

References

1. Zanikolas, S., Sakellariou, R.: A Taxonomy of Grid Monitoring Systems. Future Generation Computer Systems 21(1), 163–188 (2005)
2. Wolski, R., Spring, N., Hayes, J.: The Network Weather Service: A Distributed Resource Performance Forecasting Service for Metacomputing. Journal of Future Generation Computing Systems 15(5–6), 757–758 (1999)
3. Czajkowskiy, K., Fitzgeraldz, S., Foster, I., Kesselmany, C.: Grid Information Services for Distributed Resource Sharing. In: Proceedings of the 10th international symposium on High Performance Distributed Computing, San Francisco, California, USA, pp. 181–194 (August 2001)
4. Megginson, R., Smith, M., Natkovich, O., Parham, J.: Lightweight Directory Access Protocol: Client Update Protocol. In: IETF, vol. RFC3928 (October 2004)
5. Cooke, A.W., et al.: The Relational Grid Monitoring Architecture: Mediating Information about the Grid. Journal of Grid Computing 2(4), 323–339 (2004)
6. Massie, M.L., Chun, B.N., Culler, D.E.: The Ganglia Distributed Monitoring System: Design, Implementation, and Experience. Journal of Parallel Computing 30(7), 817–840 (2004)
7. Sun Microsystems Inc.: XDR: External Data Representation Standard. RFC1014, IETF (June 1987)
8. Oetiker, T., et al.: RDDtool, logging and graphing, http://oss.oetiker.ch/rrdtool/
9. Tierney, B., Aydt, R., Gunter, D., Smith, W., Swany, M., Taylor, V., Wolski, R.: A Grid Monitoring Architecture. Technical report, GGF (January 2002)
10. Foster, I., Iamnitchi, A.: On Death, Taxes, and the Convergence of Peer-to-Peer and Grid Computing. In: Kaashoek, M.F., Stoica, I. (eds.) IPTPS 2003. LNCS, vol. 2735, Springer, Heidelberg (2003)
11. Jenkins, K., Hopkinson, K., Birman, K.: A Gossip Protocol for Subgroup Multicast. In: ICDCS 2001. Proceedings of the 21st International Conference on Distributed Computing Systems, Phoenix, Arizona, USA (2001)
12. Pittel, B.: On Spreading a Rumor. SIAM Journal of Applied Mathematics 47(1), 213–223 (1987)

13. Kephart, J.O., Chess, D.M.: The Vision of Autonomic Computing. IEEE Computer 36(1), 41–52 (2003)
14. Baduel, L., Matsuoka, S.: A Peer-to-Peer Infrastructure for Autonomous Grid Monitoring. In: IPDPS 2007. Proceedings of the third International Workshop on Hot Topics in Peer-to-Peer Systems, Long Beach, California, USA (March 2007)
15. Gong, L.: Project JXTA: A Technology Overview. Technical report, Sun Microsystem, Inc (October 2002)
16. Antoniu, G., Jan, M., Noblet, D.A.: Enabling the P2P JXTA Platform for High-Performance Networking Grid Infrastructures. In: Nardi, D., Riedmiller, M., Sammut, C., Santos-Victor, J. (eds.) RoboCup 2004. LNCS (LNAI), vol. 3276, pp. 429–439. Springer, Heidelberg (2005)
17. Foster, I., Kesselman, C., Nick, J.M., Tuecke, S.: The physiology of the Grid. In: Grid Computing, Making the Global Infrastructure a Reality, pp. 217–249. John Wiley & Sons, Chichester (2003)

A Formal Analysis of the Deferred Update Technique*

Rodrigo Schmidt[1,2] and Fernando Pedone[2]

[1] École Polytechnique Fédérale de Lausanne, Switzerland
[2] University of Lugano, Switzerland

Abstract. The deferred update technique is a widely used approach for building replicated database systems. Its fame stems from the fact that read-only transactions can execute locally to any single database replica, providing good performance for workloads where transactions are mostly of this type. In this paper, we analyze the deferred update technique and show a number of characteristics and limitations common to any replication protocol based on it. Previous works on this replication method usually start from a protocol and then argue separately that it is based on the deferred update technique and satisfies serializability. Differently, ours starts from the abstract definition of a serializable database and gradually changes it into an abstract deferred update protocol. In doing that, we can formally characterize the deferred update technique and rigorously prove its properties. Moreover, our specification can be extended to create new protocols or used to prove existing ones correct.

1 Introduction

In the deferred update technique, a number of database replicas are used to implement a single serializable database interface. Its main idea consists in executing all operations of a transaction initially on a single replica. Transactions that do not change the database state can commit locally to the replica they executed, but other transactions must be globally certified and, if committed, have their update operations (those that change the database state) submitted to all database replicas. This technique is adopted by a number of database replication protocols in different contexts (e.g., [1,2,3,4,5]) for its good performance in general scenarios. The class of deferred update protocols is very heterogeneous, including algorithms that can optimistically apply updates of uncertified transactions [2], certify transactions locally to the database that executed them [1], execute all concurrent update transactions at the same database [3], reorder transactions during certification [4], and even cope with partial database replication [5]. However, all of them share the same basic structure, giving them some common characteristics and constraints.

Despite its wide use, we are not aware of any work that explored the inherent limitations and characteristics of deferred update database replication. Ours seems to be the first attempt in this direction. We specify a general abstract deferred update algorithm

---

* The work presented in this paper has been partially funded by the SNSF, Switzerland (project #200021-170824).

E. Tovar, P. Tsigas, and H. Fouchal (Eds.): OPODIS 2007, LNCS 4878, pp. 16–30, 2007.
© Springer-Verlag Berlin Heidelberg 2007

that embraces all the protocols we know of. This general specification allows us to isolate the properties of the *termination protocol* necessary to certify update transactions and propagate them to all database replicas. We show, for example, that the termination protocol must totally order globally committed transactions, a rather counter-intuitive result given that serializability itself allows transactions that operate on different parts of the database state to execute in any order. For example, according to serializability, if two transactions t_1 and t_2 update data items x and y, respectively, and have no other operations, it is correct to execute either t_1 before t_2 or t_2 before t_1. Therefore, one could expect that some databases would be allowed to execute t_1 followed by t_2 while others would execute t_2 followed by t_1. In deferred update protocols, however, all databases are obliged to execute t_1 and t_2 in exactly the same order, limiting concurrency.

Moreover, previous works considered that databases should satisfy a property called order-preserving serializability, which says that the commit order corresponds to a correct serialization of the committed transactions. This bears the question: Is order-preserving serializability necessary for deferred update replication? We show that databases can satisfy a weaker property, namely *active order-preserving serializability*, which we introduce. According to this property, found in some multiversion databases, the internal database serialization must satisfy the commit order only for transactions that change the database state, without further constraining read-only transactions.

In our approach, we start with a general serializable database and refine it to our abstract deferred update algorithm. Similarly, one can use our specification to ease designing and proving specific protocols. One can simply prove a protocol correct by showing that it implements ours through a refinement mapping [6]. Our specifications use atomic actions to define safety properties [7,8]. Due to the space limitations, we present only high-level specifications. Complete TLA$^+$ [9] specifications, which have been model checked for a finite subset of the possible execution scenarios, are given in our technical report [10].

2   A General Serializable Database

The consistency criterion for transactional systems in general is *Serializability*, which is defined in terms of the equivalence between the system's actual execution and a serial execution of the submitted transactions [11]. Traditional definitions of equivalence between two executions of transactions referred to the internal scheduling performed by the algorithms and their ordering of conflicting operations. This approach has led to different notions of equivalence and, therefore, different subclasses of Serializability [12]. In a distributed scenario, however, defining equivalence in terms of the internal execution of the scheduler is not straightforward since there is usually no central scheduler responsible for ordering transaction operations. To compare a serial centralized schedule with a general distributed one (e.g., in a replicated database), one has to create mappings between the operations performed in both schedules and extend the notion of conflicting operations to deal with sets of operations, since a single operation in the serial centralized schedule may be mapped to a set of operations executed on different sites in the distributed one [11]. This approach is highly dependent on the implemented protocol and, as explained in [13], does not generalize well.

Differently, we specify a general serializable database system, which responds to requests according to some internal serial execution of the submitted transactions. A database protocol satisfies serializability if it implements the general serializable database specification, that is, if its interface changes could be generated by the general serializable database. This sort of analysis is very common in distributed systems for its compromise between abstraction and rigorousness [8,9,13].

In our specification of serializability, we first define all valid state transitions for normal interactions between the clients and the database, without caring about the values returned as responses to issued operations, but rather storing them internally as part of the transaction state. The database is free to abort a transaction at any time during the execution of its operations. However, a transaction t can only be committed if its commit request was issued and there exists a sequential execution order for all committed transactions and t that corresponds to the results these transactions provided. We say the transaction is *decided* if the database has aborted or committed it. Operations issued for decided transactions get the final decision as its result.

We assume each transaction has a unique identifier and let Tid be the set of all identifiers. We call Op the set of all possible transaction operations, which execute over a database state in set $DBState$ and generate a result in set $Result$ and a new database state. We abstract the correct execution of an operation by the predicate $CorrectOp(op, res, dbst, newdbst)$, which is true iff operation op, when executed over database state $dbst$, may generate res as the operation result and $newdbst$ as the new database state. In this way, our specification is completely independent of the allowed operations, coping with operations based on predicates and even nondeterministic operations. As a simple example, one could define a database with two integer variables x and y with read and write operations for each variable. In this case, $DBstate$ corresponds to all possible combinations of values for x and y, Op is the combination of an identifier for x or y with a read tag or an integer (in case of a write), and $Result$ is the set of integers. $CorrectOp(op, res, dbst, newdbst)$ is satisfied iff $newdbst$ and res correspond to the results for the read or write operation op applied to $dbst$.

Two special requests, *Commit* and *Abort*, both not present in Op, are used to terminate a transaction, that is, to force a decision to be taken. Two special responses, *Committed* and *Aborted*, not present in $Result$, are used to tell the database user if the transaction has been committed or aborted. We also define *Decided* to equal the set $\{Committed, Aborted\}$, *Request* to equal $Op \cup \{Commit, Abort\}$, and *Reply* to equal $Result \cup Decided$.

During a transaction execution, operations are issued and responses are given until the client issues a *Commit* or *Abort* request or the transaction is aborted by the database for some internal reason. We represent the history of a transaction execution by a sequence of elements in $Op \times Result$, corresponding to the sequence of operations executed on the transaction's behalf and their respective results. We say that a transaction history h is *atomically correct* with respect to initial database state $initst$ and final database state $finalst$ iff it satisfies the recursive predicate defined below, where $THist$ is the set of all possible transaction histories and $Head$ and $Tail$ are the usual operators for sequences. Moreover, for notation simplicity, we identify the first and second elements of a tuple t in $Op \times Result$ by $t.op$ and $t.res$ respectively.

$CorrectAtomicHist(h \in THist, initst, finalst \in DBState) \triangleq$
  if $h = \langle \rangle$ **then** $initst = finalst$
        else $\exists ist \in DBState : CorrectOp(Head(h).op, Head(h).res, initst, ist) \land$
                $CorrectAtomicHist(Tail(h), ist, finalst)$

Intuitively, a transaction history is atomically correct with respect to *initst* and *finalst* iff there are intermediate database states so that all operations in the history can be executed in their correct order and generate their correct results.

During the system's execution, many transactions are started and terminated (possibly concurrently). We represent the current history of all transactions by a data structure called *history vector* (set *THistVector*) that maps each transaction to its current history. We say that a sequence *seq* of transactions and a history vector *thist* correspond to a correct serialization with respect to initial state *initst* and final state *finalst* iff the recursive predicate below is satisfied, where $Seq(S)$ represents the set of all finite sequences of elements in set S.

$CorrectSerialization(seq \in Seq(Tid), thist \in THistVector, initst, finalst \in DBState) \triangleq$
  if $seq = \langle \rangle$ **then** $initst = finalst$
        else $\exists ist \in DBState : CorrectAtomicHist(thist(Head(seq)), initst, ist) \land$
                $CorrectSerialization(Tail(seq), thist, ist, finalst)$

Intuitively, this predicate is satisfied iff there are intermediate database states so that all transactions in the sequence can be atomically executed in their correct order generating the correct results for their operations. We can now easily define a predicate *IsSerializable(S, thist, initst)* for a finite set of transaction id's S, history vector *thist*, and database state *initst*, satisfied iff there is a sequence *seq* containing exactly one copy of each element in S and a final database state *finalst* such that *Correct Serialization(seq, thist, initst, finalst)* is satisfied. Predicate *IsSerializable* indicates when a set of transactions can be serialized in some order, according to their execution history, so that every operation returns its correct result when the execution is started in a given database state.

We abstract the interface of our specification by the primitives *DBRequest(t, req)*, which represents the reception of a request *req* on behalf of transaction t, and *DBResponse(t, rep)*, which represents the database response to the last request on behalf of t with reply *rep*. The only restriction we make with respect to the database interface is that an operation cannot be submitted on behalf of transaction t if the last operation submitted for t has not been replied yet, which releases us from the burden of using unique identifiers for operations in order to match them with their results. Notice that the system still allows a high degree of concurrency since operations from different transactions can be submitted concurrently.

Our specification is based on the following internal variables:

thist: A history vector, initially mapping each transaction to an empty history.
tdec: A mapping from each transaction to its current decision status: *Unknown*, *Committed*, or *Aborted*. Initially, it maps each transaction to *Unknown*.
q: A mapping from each transaction to its current request or *NoReq* if no request is being executed on behalf of that transaction. Initially, it maps each transaction to *NoReq*.

ReceiveReq(t ∈ Tid, req ∈ Request)
   Enabled iff:
     – $DBRequest(t, req)$
     – $q[t] = NoReq$
   Effect:
     – $q[t] \leftarrow req$

ReplyReq(t ∈ Tid, rep ∈ Reply)
   Enabled iff:
     – $q[t] \in Request$
     – **if** $tdec[t] \in Decided$
         then $rep = tdec[t]$
         else $q[t] \in Op \wedge rep \in Result$
   Effect:
     – $DBResponse(t, rep)$
     – $q[t] \leftarrow NoReq$
     – **if** $tdec[t] \notin Decided$ **then**
         $thist[t] \leftarrow thist[t] \circ \langle q[t], rep \rangle$

DoAbort(t ∈ Tid)
   Enabled iff:
     – $tdec[t] \notin Decided$
   Effect:
     – $tdec[t] \leftarrow Aborted$

DoCommit(t ∈ Tid)
   Enabled iff:
     – $tdec[t] \notin Decided$
     – $q[t] = Commit$
     – $IsSerializable(committedSet \cup \{t\},$
                  $thist, InitialDBState)$
   Effect:
     – $tdec[t] \leftarrow Committed$

Fig. 1. The atomic actions allowed in our specification of a serializable database

Figure 1 presents the atomic actions of our specification. Action $ReceiveReq(t, req)$ is responsible for receiving a request on behalf of transaction t. Action $ReplyRep(t, rep)$ replies to a received request. It is enabled only if the transaction has been decided and the reply is the final decision or the transaction has not been decided but the current request is an operation (neither $Commit$ nor $Abort$) and the reply is in $Result$. This means that responses given after the transaction has been decided carry the final decision and requests to commit or abort a transaction are only replied after the transaction has been decided. Action $ReplyReq$ is responsible for updating the transaction history if the transaction has not been decided. It does that by appending the pair $\langle q[t], rep \rangle$ to $thist[t]$ (we use $\circ$ to represent the standard *append* operation for sequences). Action $DoAbort(t)$ simply aborts a transaction if it has not been decided yet. Action $DoCommit(t)$ commits t only if a t's commit request was issued and the set of all committed transactions (represented by $committedSet$) together with t is serializable with respect to the initial database state, denoted by the constant $InitialDBState$.

3   The Deferred Update Technique

3.1   Preliminaries

As mentioned before, deferred update algorithms initially execute transactions on a single replica. Transactions that do not change the database state (hereinafter called *passive*) may commit locally only, but *active* transactions (as opposed to passive ones) must be globally certified and, if committed, have their updates propagated to all replicas (i.e., operations that make them active). In order to correctly characterize the technique, we need to formalize the concepts of active and passive operations and transactions. An operation op is passive iff its execution never changes the database state, that is, iff the following condition is satisfied.

$$\forall st1, st2 \in DBState, rep \in Result : CorrectOp(op, rep, st1, st2) \Rightarrow st1 = st2 \quad (1)$$

An operation that is not passive is called active. Similarly, we define a transaction history h to be passive iff the condition below is satisfied.

$$\forall st1, st2 \in DBState : CorrectAtomicHist(h, st1, st2) \Rightarrow st1 = st2 \qquad (2)$$

Notice that a transaction history composed of passive operations is obviously passive, but the converse is not true. A transaction that adds and subtracts 1 to a variable is passive even though its operations are active.

The deferred update technique requires some extra assumptions about the system. Operations, for example, cannot generate new database states nondeterministically for this could lead different replicas to inconsistent states. The following assumption makes sure that operations do not change the database state nondeterministically but still allows nondeterministic results to be provided to the database user.

Assumption 1 (State-deterministic operations). *For every operation op, and database states st and st1, if there is a result res1 such that CorrectOp(op, res1, st, st1), then there is no result res2 and database state st2 such that st1 $\neq$ st2 $\wedge$ CorrectOp (op, res2, st, st2).*

As for the database replicas, one may wrongly think that simply assuming that they are serializable is enough to ensure global serializability. However, two replicas might serialize their transactions (local and global) differently, making the distributed execution non-serializable. Previous works on deferred update protocols assumed the notion of *order-preserving serializability*, originally introduced by Beeri et al. in the context of nested transactions [14]. In our model, order-preserving serializability ensures that the transactions' commit order represents a correct execution sequence, a condition satisfied by two-phase locking, for example. We show that this assumption can be relaxed since deferred update protocols can work with the weaker notion of *active order-preserving serializability* we introduce. Active order-preserving serializability ensures that there is an execution sequence of the committed transactions that generates their correct outputs and respects the commit order of all *active* transactions only. This notion is weaker than strict order-preserving serializability in that passive transactions do not have to provide results based on the latest committed state. Some multiversion concurrency control mechanisms [11] are active order-preserving but not strict order-preserving. Specifications of order-preserving and active order-preserving serializability can be derived from our specification in Figure 1 by just adding a variable *serialSeq*, initially equal to the empty sequence, and changing the *DoCommit* action. We show the required changes in Figure 2. The strict case (a) is simple and only requires that *serialSeq* $\circ$ *t* be a correct sequential execution of all committed transactions. The action automatically extends *serialSeq* with *t*. The active case (b) is a little more complicated to explain and requires some extra notation. Let *Perm(S)* be the set of all permutations of elements in finite set S (all the possible orderings of elements in S), and let *ActiveExtension(seq, t)* be *seq* if *thist*[*t*] is a passive history or *seq* $\circ$ *t* otherwise. The action is enabled only if there exists a sequence containing all committed transactions such that it represents a correct sequential execution and *ActiveExtension(seq, t)* is

$DoCommit(t \in Tid)$
   Enabled iff:
     – $tdec[t] \notin Decided$
     – $q[t] = Commit$
     – $\exists st \in DBState :$
         $CorrectSerialization(serialSeq \circ t, thist, InitialDBState, st)$
   Effect:
     – $tdec[t] \leftarrow Committed$
     – $serialSeq \leftarrow serialSeq \circ t$

(a)

$DoCommit(t \in Tid)$
   Enabled iff:
     – $tdec[t] \notin Decided$
     – $q[t] = Commit$
     – $\exists seq \in Perm(committedSet \cup \{t\}), st \in DBState :$
         $CorrectSerialization(seq, thist, InitialDBState, st) \wedge$
         $ActiveExtension(serialSeq, t)$ is a subsequence of seq
   Effect:
     – $tdec[t] \leftarrow Committed$
     – $serialSeq \leftarrow ActiveExtension(serialSeq, t)$

(b)

Fig. 2. $DoCommit$ action for (a) strict and (b) active order-preserving serializability

a subsequence of it.[1] In this action, $serialSeq$ is extended with t only if t is an active transaction.

3.2 Abstract Algorithm

We now present the specification of our abstract deferred update algorithm. It generalizes the ideas of a handful of deferred update protocols and makes it easy to think about sufficient and necessary requirements for them to work correctly. Our specification assumes a set $Database$ of active order-preserving serializable databases, and we use the notation $DB(d)!Primitive(\_)$ to represent the execution of interface primitive $Primitive$ (either $DBRequest$ or $DBResponse$) of database d. Since transactions must initially execute on a single replica only, we let $DBof(t)$ represent the database responsible for the initial execution of transaction t. One important remark is that these internal databases receive transactions whose id set is $Tid \times \mathbb{N}$, where $\mathbb{N}$ is the set of natural numbers. This is done so because a single transaction in the system might have to be submitted multiple times to a database replica in order to ensure that it commits locally. Recall that our definition of active order-preserving serializability does not force transactions to commit. Therefore, transactions that have been committed by the algorithm and submitted to the database replicas are not guaranteed to commit unless further assumptions are made. The only way around this is to submit these transactions multiple times (with different versions) until they commit. Besides the set of databases, we assume a concurrent termination protocol, fully explained in the next

---

[1] sequence $subseq$ is a subsequence of sequence seq iff it can be obtained by removing zero or more elements of seq.

section, responsible for committing active transactions and propagating their active operations to all databases.

The algorithm we present in the following orchestrates the interactions between the global database interface and the individual internal databases. It is mainly based on the following internal variables:

$thist$, q: Essentially the same variables as in the specification of a serializable database.

$dreq$: A mapping from each transaction t to the operation that is currently being submitted for execution on $DBof(t)$, or $NoReq$ if no operation is being submitted. This variable is used to implement the asynchronous communication that tells $DBof(t)$ to execute an operation of t. Initially all transactions are mapped to $NoReq$.

$dreply$: Similar to $dreq$, but mapping each transaction t to the last response given by $DBof(t)$.

$dcnt$: A mapping from each database d and transaction t to an integer representing the number of operations that executed on d for t. It counts the number of operations $DBof(t)$ has executed for t during t's initial execution and, if t is active, the number of active operations the other databases (or $DBof(t)$ if it does not manage to commit t directly after it is globally committed) have executed for t after it is globally committed. It is initially 0 for all databases and transactions.

$pdec$: A mapping like $tdec$ in the specification of a serializable database, used to tell whether the transaction was decided without being proposed for global termination either because it was prematurely aborted during its initial execution or because it was a passive transaction that committed on its execution database.

$vers$: A mapping from each database d and transaction t to an integer representing the current version of t being submitted to d. It is initially 0 for all databases and transactions.

$dcom$: A mapping from each database d and transaction t to a boolean telling whether t has been committed on d. It is initially false for all databases and transactions.

When a $Commit$ request is issued for a transaction whose history has been active, a decision must be taken on whether to commit or abort this transaction with respect to active transactions executed on other databases. In our specification, this is done separately by a termination protocol. The reason why we isolated this part of the specification is twofold. First, the nature of the rest of the algorithm is essentially local to the database that is executing a given transaction and it seems interesting to separate it from the part of the specification responsible for synchronizing active transactions executed on different databases. Second, the properties of the termination protocol, when isolated, can be related to properties of other agreement problems in distributed computing, which helps understand and solve it. The interface variables of the termination protocol used in our general specification are the following:

$proposed$: This is an input variable that keeps the set of all proposed transactions. It is initially empty.

$gdec$: An output variable that keeps a mapping like $pdec$ above, but managed by the termination protocol only. It tells whether a proposed transaction has already been decided or not.

learnedSeq: Another output variable mapping each database d to a sequence of globally committed active transactions. This sequence tells database d the order in which these active transactions must be committed to make the whole execution serializable. Initially, it maps each database to the empty sequence.

Our specification implements a serializable database, which can be proved by a refinement mapping from its internal variables to those of a general serializable database. Actually, the only internal variable of our specification of a serializable database not directly implemented in our abstract algorithm is *tdec*, given by joining the values of *pdec* and *gdec* in the following way:

$$tdec[t] \triangleq \textbf{if } t \in proposed \textbf{ then } gdec[t] \textbf{ else } pdec[t] \tag{3}$$

For simplicity, we use this definition of *tdec* in some parts of our specification. Another extra definition used in our algorithm is the $ActHist(t)$ operator that returns the subsequence of $thist[t]$ containing all its active operations. The atomic actions of our abstract algorithm, without the internal actions of the individual databases and the termination protocol, are shown in Figure 3.

Action *ReceiveReq* treats the receipt of a transaction request. If the transaction responsible for the operation has been decided (either for *pdec* or *gdec* according to the definition of *tdec* given above), then it only changes $q[t]$. Otherwise, it either proposes t for the termination protocol or sends the request to $DBof(t)$ through variable $dreq[t]$. Our complete specification allows passive transactions to be submitted for the termination protocol too and this is why we wrote "is active" between quotation marks. We allow that because sometimes it might not be possible to identify all passive transactions. Therefore, our specification also embraces algorithms that identify only a subset of the passive transactions as passive and conservatively propose the others for global termination.

Action *ReplyReq* replies a transaction request. It is very similar to the original *ReplyReq* action of our serializable database specification. The small differences only make sure that the value replied for a normal operation comes from $DBof(t)$ and, in this case, $dreq[t]$ is set back to *NoReq* to wait for the next operation. Actions *Premature Abort* and *PassiveCommit* abort or commit a transaction that has not been proposed for global termination. It can only be committed if a commit request was correctly replied by $DBof(t)$, which can only happen if t has a passive history.

Action *DBReq* submits a request to a database. There are three conditions that enable this action. The first one represents a normal request during the transaction's initial execution or a commit request for a passive transaction. The second one represents an operation request for an active transaction that has been proposed to the termination protocol. Notice that operations of proposed transactions can be optimistically submitted to the database before they commit or appear in some *learnedSeq*. Some algorithms do that to save processing time after the transaction is committed, reducing the latency for propagating transactions to the replicas. The third condition that enables this action represents a commit request for a transaction that has been committed by the termination protocol. For that to happen, the transaction must be present in $learnedSeq[d]$ and all transactions previous to it in the sequence must have been committed on that database. Moreover, all active operations of that transaction must have been applied to

$ReceiveReq(t \in Tid, req \in Request)$
Enabled iff:
  - $DBRequest(t, req)$
  - $q[t] = NoReq$
Effect:
  - $q[t] \leftarrow req$
  - if $tdec[t] \notin Decided$ then
      if $req = Commit \wedge thist[t]$ "is active"
        then $proposed \leftarrow proposed \cup \{t\}$
        else $dreq[t] \leftarrow req$

$ReplyReq(t \in Tid, rep \in Reply)$
Enabled iff:
  - $q[t] \in Request$
  - if $tdec[t] \in Decided$ then
      $rep = tdec[t]$
    else
      $q[t] \in Op \wedge rep \in Result \wedge$
      $dcnt[DBof(t)][t] > Len(thist[t]) \wedge$
      $rep = dreply[t]$
Effect:
  - $DBResponse(t, rep)$
  - $q[t] \leftarrow NoReq$
  - if $tdec[t] \notin Decided$ then
    • $thist[t] \leftarrow thist[t] \circ \langle q[t], rep \rangle$
    • $dreq[t] \leftarrow NoReq$

$PrematureAbort(t \in Tid)$
Enabled iff:
  - $t \notin proposed$
  - $pdec[t] \notin Decided$
Effect:
  - $pdec[t] \leftarrow Aborted$

$PassiveCommit(t \in Tid)$
Enabled iff:
  - $t \notin proposed$
  - $pdec[t] \notin Decided$
  - $dreply[t] = Committed$
Effect:
  - $pdec[t] \leftarrow Committed$

$DBReq(d \in Database, t \in Tid, req \in Request)$
Enabled iff **any** of the conditions below hold.

Condition 1: (external operation request)
  - $d = DBof(t)$
  - $dreq[t] = req$
  - $dcnt[d][t] = Len(thist[t])$

Condition 2: (operation after termination)
  - $t \in proposed$
  - $dcnt[d][t] < Len(ActHist(t))$
  - $req = ActHist(t)[dcnt[d][t] + 1].op$

Condition 3: (commit after termination)
  - $req = Commit$
  - $\exists i \in 1..Len(learnedSeq[d]) :$
    $learnedSeq[d][i] = t \wedge$
    $\forall j \in 1..i : dcom[d][learnedSeq[d][j]]$
  - **either** $d = DBof(t) \wedge vers[d][t] = 0$
    or $dcnt[d][t] = Len(ActHist(t))$

Effect:
  - $DB(d)!DBRequest(\langle t, vers[d][t]\rangle, req)$

$DBRep(d \in Database, t \in Tid, rep \in Reply)$
Enabled iff:
  - $DB(d)!DBResponse(\langle t, vers[d][t]\rangle, rep)$
Effect:
  - if $d = DBof(t)$ then $dreply[t] \leftarrow rep$
  - if $rep = Aborted \wedge t \in proposed$ then
    • $vers[d][t] \leftarrow vers[d][t] + 1$
    • $dcnt[d][t] \leftarrow 0$
  else
    • $dcnt[d][t] \leftarrow dcnt[d][t] + 1$
    • $dcom[d][t] \leftarrow rep = Committed$

Fig. 3. The atomic actions allowed in our specification of a serializable database

the database already, which is true if the database is the one originally responsible for the transaction and it has not changed the transaction version or the operations counter $dcnt[d][t]$ equals the number of active operations in the transaction history. Recall that, by the definition of a serializable database, a request can only be submitted if there is no pending request for the same transaction. This is actually an implicit pre-condition for $DBReq$ given by the specification of a serializable database.

Action $DBRep$ treats the receipt of a response coming from a database. If the database is the one responsible for initially executing the transaction, it sets $drepy[t]$ to the value returned. If the transaction is aborted but it has been proposed for global termination, it changes the version of that transaction on that database and sets the operation counter to zero so that the transaction's operations can be resubmitted for its new version; otherwise, it just increments the operation counter and sets $dcom$ accordingly.

3.3 Termination Protocol

The termination protocol gives a final decision to proposed transactions and, if they are committed, forwards them to the database replicas. It "reads" from variables *proposed* and *thist* (it relies on the transaction history to decide on whether to commit or abort it), and changes variables *gdec* and *learnedSeq*. As explained before, variable *gdec* simply assigns the final decision to a transaction; *learnedSeq*, however, represents the order in which each database should submit the active transactions committed by the termination protocol. These are the three safety properties the termination protocol must satisfy in order to ensure serializability:

Nontriviality. For any transaction t, t is decided ($gdec[t] \in Decided$) only if it was proposed.

Stability. For any transaction t, if t is decided at any time, then its decision does not change at any later time; and, for any database d, the value of $learnedSeq[d]$ at any time is a prefix of its value at all later times.

Consistency. There exists a sequence *seq* containing exactly one copy of every committed transaction (according to *gdec*) and a database state *st* such that *Correct Serialization(seq, thist, InitialDBState, st)* is true and, for every database d, $learnedSeq[d]$ is a prefix of *seq*.

The following theorem asserts that our complete abstract specification of a deferred update protocol is serializable. This result shows that every protocol that implements our specification automatically satisfies serializability. The proofs of our theorems can be found in [10].

Theorem 1. *Our abstract deferred update algorithm implements the specification of a serializable database given in Section 2.*

This theorem results in an interesting corollary, stated below. It shows that indeed databases are not required to be strict order-preserving serializable, an assumption that can be relaxed to our weaker definition of active order-preserving serializability.

Corollary 1. *Serializability is guaranteed by our specification if databases are active order-preserving serializable instead of strict order-preserving serializable.*

The three aforementioned safety properties are not strictly necessary to ensure serializability. Nontriviality can be relaxed so that non-proposed transactions may be aborted before they are proposed and Serializability is still guaranteed. However, we see no practical use of this since our algorithm already allows a transaction to be aborted at any point of the execution before it is proposed. Committing a transaction before proposing depends on making sure that the history of the transaction will not change and, in case it is active, on whether there are alternative sequences that ensure the Consistency properties if the transaction is committed or not, a rather complicated condition to be used in practice. Stability can be relaxed by allowing changes on suffixes of $learnedSeq[d]$ that have not been submitted to the database yet. However, keeping knowledge of what part of the sequence has already been submitted to the database and possibly changing the rest of it is equivalent to implementing our abstract algorithm with $learnedSeq[d]$ being the exact sequence locally submitted to the database. As a result, we see no practical advantage in relaxing Stability.

Consistency can be relaxed in a more complicated way. In fact, the different sequences $learnedSeq[d]$ can differ, as long as the set of intermediate states they generate (states in between transactions) are a subset of the intermediate states generated by some sequence seq containing all globally committed transactions and satisfying $CorrectSerialization(seq, thist, InitialDBState, st)$ for some state st. Ensuring this property without forcing the $learnedSeq$ sequences to prefix a common sequence is hard and may lead to situations in which committed transactions cannot be added to a sequence $learnedSeq[d]$ for they would generate states that are not present in any sequence that could satisfy our consistency criterion.

One might think, for example, that the consistency property can be relaxed to allow commuting transactions that are not related (i.e., operate on disjunct parts of the database state) in the sequences $learnedSeq[d]$. For that, however, we have to make some assumptions about the database state in order to define what we mean by disjunct parts of the database state. For simplicity, let us assume our database state is a mapping from objects in a set $Object$ to values in a set $Value$ and operations can read or write a single object value. We define the objects of a transaction history h, represented by $Obj(h)$, to be the set of objects the operations in h read or write. A consistency property based on the commutativity of transactions that have no intersecting object sets can be intuitively defined as follows:

Alternative Consistency. There exists a sequence seq containing exactly one copy of every committed transaction (according to $gdec$) and a database state st such that $CorrectSerialization(seq, thist, InitialDBState, st)$ is true and, for every database d, $learnedSeq[d]$ contains exactly one copy of some committed transactions (according to $gdec$) and, for every transaction t in $learnedSeq[d]$, the following conditions are satisfied:
  - Every transaction t' that precedes t in seq and shares some objects with t also precedes t in $learnedSeq[d]$, and
  - Every transaction t' that precedes t in $learnedSeq[d]$ either precedes t in seq or shares no objects with t.

Although this new consistency condition seems a little complicated, it is weaker than our original property for it allows the sequences $learnedSeq[d]$ differ in their order for transactions that operate on different objects. The following theorem shows that this property is not enough to ensure Serializability in our abstract algorithm.

Theorem 2. *Our abstract deferred update algorithm with the Consistency property for termination changed for the Alternative Consistency property defined above does not implement the specification of a serializable database given in Section 2.*

This result basically means that one cannot profit much from using Generic Broadcast [15] algorithms to propagate committed transactions. Our properties as originally defined seem to be the weakest practical conditions for ensuring Serializability in deferred update protocols. In fact, we are not aware of any deferred update replication algorithm whose termination protocol does not satisfy the three properties above.

So far, we have not defined any liveness property for the termination protocol. Although we do not want to force protocols to commit transactions in any situation (since this might rule out some deferred update algorithms that conservatively abort transactions), we think that a termination protocol that does not update the sequences *learnedSeq*[*d*] eventually, after having committed a transaction, is completely useless. Therefore, we add the following liveness property to our specification of the termination protocol:

Liveness. If *t* is committed at a given time, then *learnedSeq*[*d*] eventually contains *t*.

As it happens with agreement problems like Consensus, this property must be revisited in failure-prone scenarios, since it cannot be guaranteed for databases that have crashed. Independently of that, one can easily spot some similarities between the properties we have defined and those of Sequence Agreement as explained in [16]. Briefly, in the sequence agreement problem, a set of processes agree on an ever-growing sequence of commands, built out of proposed ones. The problem is specified in terms of proposer processes that propose commands to be learned by learner processes, where *learned*[*l*] represents the sequence of commands learned by learner *l*. Sequence Agreement is defined by the following properties:

Nontriviality. For any learner *l*, the value of *learned*[*l*] is always a sequence of proposed commands.
Stability. For any learner *l*, the value of *learned*[*l*] at any time is a prefix of its value at any later time.
Consistency. For any learners l_1 and l_2, it is always the case that one of the sequences *learned*[l_1] and *learned*[l_2] is a prefix of the other.
Liveness. If command *V* has been proposed, then eventually the sequence *learned*[*l*] will contain *V* as an element.

This problem is a sequence-based specification of the celebrated atomic broadcast problem [17]. The exact relation between the termination protocol and Sequence Agreement is given by the following theorem.

Theorem 3. *The four properties Nontriviality, Stability, Consistency, and Liveness above satisfy the safety and liveness properties of Sequence Agreement for transactions that commit.*

One possible way of reading this theorem is that any implementation of the termination protocol is free to abort transactions, but it must implement Sequence Agreement for the transactions it commits. As a consequence, any lower bound or impossibility result for atomic broadcast and consensus applies to the termination protocol.

4 Conclusion

In this paper, we have formalized the deferred update technique for database replication and stated some intrinsic characteristics and limitations of it. Previous works have only considered new algorithms, with independent specifications, analysis, and correctness proofs. To the best of our knowledge, our work is first effort to formally characterize this family of algorithms and establish its requirements. Our general abstraction can be used to derive other general limitation results as well as to create new algorithms and prove existing ones correct. Some algorithms can be easily proved correct by a refinement mapping to ours. Others may require an additional effort due to the extra assumptions they make, but the task seems still easier than with previous formalisms. In our personal experience, we have successfully used our abstraction to obtain interesting protocols and correctness proofs, which will appear elsewhere.

Finally, to increase the confidence in our results, we have model checked our specifications using the TLA$^+$ model checker (TLC). Our specifications have been extensively checked for consistency problems besides type safety and deadlocks. For that we used a database containing a small vector of integers with operations that could read and write the vector's elements. Our model considered a limited number of transactions (up to 10), each one containing a few operations. The automatic checking confirmed our results and allowed us to find a number of small mistakes in the TLA$^+$ translation of our ideas. We strongly believe these specifications can be extended or directly used in future works in this area.

References

1. Kemme, B., Alonso, G.: A new approach to developing and implementing eager database replication protocols. ACM Transactions on Database Systems 25(3), 333–379 (2000)
2. Patino-Martínez, M., Jiménez-Peris, R., Kemme, B., Alonso, G.: Scalable replication in database clusters. In: Herlihy, M.P. (ed.) DISC 2000. LNCS, vol. 1914, Springer, Heidelberg (2000)
3. Pedone, F., Frølund, S.: Pronto: A fast failover protocol for off-the-shelf commercial databases. In: SRDS 2000. Proceedings of the 19th IEEE Symposium on Reliable Distributed Systems, pp. 176–185. IEEE Computer Society Press, Los Alamitos (2000)
4. Pedone, F., Guerraoui, R., Schiper, A.: The database state machine approach. Journal of Distributed and Parallel Databases and Technology 14(1), 71–98 (2003)
5. Schiper, N., Schmidt, R., Pedone, F.: Optimistic algorithms for partial database replication. In: Shvartsman, A.A. (ed.) OPODIS 2006. LNCS, vol. 4305, pp. 81–93. Springer, Heidelberg (2006)
6. Abadi, M., Lamport, L.: The existence of refinement mappings. Theoretical Computer Science 82(2), 253–284 (1991)
7. Lamport, L.: A simple approach to specifying concurrent systems. Communications of the ACM 32(1), 32–45 (1989)
8. Lynch, N.: Distributed Algorithms. Morgan Kaufmann Publishers, Inc., San Mateo, CA, USA (1996)
9. Lamport, L. (ed.): Specifying Systems: The TLA+ Language and Tools for Hardware and Software Engineers. Addison-Wesley Longman Publishing Co., Inc., Boston, MA, USA (2002)
10. Schmidt, R., Pedone, F.: A formal analysis of the deferred update technique. Technical report, EPFL (2007)
11. Bernstein, P., Hadzilacos, V., Goodman, N.: Concurrency Control and Recovery in Database Systems. Addison-Wesley, Reading (1987)
12. Papadimitriou, C.H.: The serializability of concurrent database updates. Journal of the ACM 26(4), 631–653 (1979)

13. Lynch, N., Merrit, M., Weihl, W., Fekete, A.: Atomic Transactions. Morgan Kaufmann Publishers, Inc., San Mateo, CA, USA (1994)
14. Beeri, C., Bernstein, P.A., Goodman, N.: A model for concurrency in nested transaction systems. Journal of the ACM 36(2), 230–269 (1989)
15. Pedone, F., Schiper, A.: Handling message semantics with generic broadcast protocols. Distributed Computing 15(2), 97–107 (2002)
16. Lamport, L.: Generalized consensus and paxos. Technical Report MSR-TR-2005-33, Microsoft Research (2004)
17. Hadzilacos, V., Toueg, S.: Fault-tolerant broadcasts and related problems. In: Distributed systems, 2nd edn., pp. 97–145. ACM Press/Addison-Wesley Publishing Co., New York, NY, USA (1993)

ASAP: A Camera Sensor Network for Situation Awareness*

Junsuk Shin, Rajnish Kumar, Dushmanta Mohapatra,
Umakishore Ramachandran, and Mostafa Ammar

College of Computing, Georgia Institute of Technology, Atlanta GA, USA
{jshin,rajnish,dmpatra,rama,ammar}@cc.gatech.edu

Abstract. *Situation awareness* is an important application category
in cyber-physical systems, and *distributed video-based surveillance* is
a good canonical example of this application class. Such applications
are interactive, dynamic, stream-based, computationally demanding, and
needing real-time or near real-time guarantees. A *sense-process-actuate*
control loop characterizes the behavior of this application class. ASAP is
a scalable distributed architecture for a multi-modal sensor network that
caters to the needs of this application class. Features of this architecture
include (a) generation of *prioritization* cues that allow the infrastructure to pay *selective attention* to data streams of interest; (b) *virtual
sensor* abstraction that allows easy integration of multi-modal sensing
capabilities; and (c) dynamic redirection of sensor sources to distributed
resources to deal with sudden burstiness in the application. In both empirical and emulated experiments, ASAP shows that it scales up to a
thousand of sensor nodes (comprised of high bandwidth cameras and
low bandwidth RFID readers), significantly mitigates infrastructure and
cognitive overload, and reduces *false negatives* and *false positives* due to
its ability to integrate multi-modal sensing.

1 Introduction

Situation Awareness is both a property and an application class that deals with
recognizing when *sensed data* could lead to *actionable knowledge*. However, because of a huge increase in the amount of sensed data to be handled, providing
situation awareness has become a challenge. With advances in technology, it
is becoming feasible to integrate sophisticated sensing, computing, and communication in a single small footprint sensor platform. This trend is enabling
deployment of powerful sensors of different modalities in a cost-effective manner.
While Moore's law has held true for predicting the growth of processing power,
the volume of data that applications handle is growing similarly, if not faster.

There are three main challenges posed by data explosion for realizing situation awareness: overload on the infrastructure, cognitive overload on humans in
the loop, and dramatic increase in false positives and false negatives in identifying threat scenarios. Consider, for example, providing situation awareness in a

---

* ASAP stands for "Priority Aware Situation Awareness" read backwards.

E. Tovar, P. Tsigas, and H. Fouchal (Eds.): OPODIS 2007, LNCS 4878, pp. 31–47, 2007.

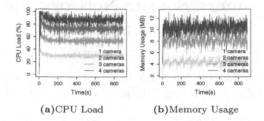

Fig. 1. Resource usage in a centralized camera network: cameras produce data at 5 fps with 320x240 resolution. Image processing happens on a 1.4GHz Pentium processor.

battlefield. It needs complex fusion of contextual knowledge with time-sensitive sensor data obtained from different sources to derive higher-level inferences. With an increase in the sensed data, a fighter pilot will need to take more data into account in decision-making leading to a cognitive overload and an increase in human errors (false positives and negatives). Also, to process and disseminate the sensed data, more computational and network resources are needed thus overloading the infrastructure.

The severity of infrastructure overload is more apparent for camera sensor networks because image dissemination and processing tasks are very resource intensive. Consider, for example, a simple surveillance system that does motion sensing and JPEG encoding/decoding. Figure 1 shows the processing requirements for such a system using a centralized set up: cameras produce data at 5 frames/second with a 320x240 resolution; image processing happens on a 1.4GHz Pentium processor. The results show that the above centralized setup cannot scale beyond four cameras (the CPU load is nearly 100%.) If we increase the video quality (frames/second and resolution), even a high-end computing resource will be unable to process more than a few cameras.

Clearly, scaling up to a large number of cameras (on the order of 100's or 1000's) warrants a distributed architecture. Further, to mitigate the challenges posed by the data explosion there is a need to add a *prioritize* step in the control loop for situation awareness. The ASAP architecture presented in this paper caters to the *sense-process-prioritize-actuate* control loop. Adding the prioritize step is expected to help not only in an effective use of the available resources, but also to achieve scalability and meet real-time guarantees in the data deluge.

ASAP provides features that are aimed to address the specific challenges posed by situation awareness application:

- It provides a framework for generating *priority cues* so that the system (and humans in the loop) can pay *selective attention* to specific data streams thus reducing both the infrastructure and cognitive overload.
- It consists of two *logical* networks, namely, *control* and *data*. The former generates priority cues and the latter provides processing functions (filtering and fusion) on the selected data streams. This tiered architecture enables the physical network consisting of cameras, sensors, and computational resources to be scaled up or down more easily. Further this logical separation aids in dealing with sudden burstiness in the sensed environment.

- It provides facilities for dynamic redirection of control and data streams to different computational resources based on the burstiness of the sensed environment.
- It provides an abstraction, *virtual sensor*, that allows sensors to operate multi-modally to reduce the ill effects of false positives and false negatives.
- It integrates hand-held devices (such as iPAQs) to enable flexible delivery of alerts and information digests.

The unique contributions of our work are as follows: (a) a systematic approach to help prioritize data streams, (b) a software architecture that ensures scalability and dynamic resource allocation, and (c) multi-model sensing cues to reduce false positives and false negatives.

The rest of the paper is organized as follows. Section 2 explores situation awareness applications to understand their requirements. Section 3 explains the ASAP architecture and its prioritization strategies. The implementation and evaluation of ASAP platform are presented in Sections 4 and 5, respectively. Related work is discussed in Section 6. Section 7 concludes the paper.

2   Understanding ASAP Requirements

2.1   Example Application: Video Based Surveillance

A video-based surveillance system is an attractive solution for threat identification and reduction. Cameras are deployed in a distributed fashion; the images from the cameras are filtered in some application-specific manner, and are fused together in a form that makes it easy for an end user (human or some program) to monitor the area. The compute intensive part may analyze multiple camera feeds from a region to extract higher-level information such as "motion", "presence or absence of a human face", or "presence or absence of any kind of suspicious activity". Security personnel can specify a set of security policies that must be adhered to, e.g. "only specified people are allowed to enter a particular area", and the system must continuously ensure that an alert is generated whenever any breach happens. Similarly, security personnel can do a search on all available camera streams for an event of interest, e.g. "show me the camera feed where there is a gas leak". To support the above two ways of deriving actionable knowledge, the extracted information from camera streams, e.g. motion or number of faces etc., may be the meta-data of importance for information prioritization. With a large number of surveillance cameras (e.g. 3K in New York [1] and 400K in London [2]), it becomes a more interesting issue.

2.2   Application Requirements

Applications such as video-based surveillance are capable of stressing the available computation and communication infrastructures to their limits. Fusion applications, as we refer to such applications in this paper have the many common needs that should be supported by the underlying ASAP platform:

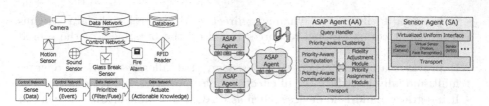

Fig. 2. Functional view of ASAP   **Fig. 3.** ASAP Software Architecture

1. High Scalability: The system should scale to large number of sensor streams and user queries. This necessarily means that the system should be designed to reduce infrastructure overload, cognitive overload, and false positives and false negatives. False positives refer to the actionable knowledge triggers generated by the system that turns out to be not really a security threat or an event of interest. False negatives refer to the security threat situations or interesting events that are missed by the system.

2. Query vs Policy-based interface: Situation awareness applications need to support both query- and policy-based user interfaces. A query-based interface will allow users to search streams of interest based on tags or information associated with the streams. On the other hand, a policy-based interface will allow users to specify conditions to monitor and to generate alerts based on the conditions. A set of policies can be specified by a security administrator to proactively monitor an area. A platform for situation awareness applications should provide both the query-based and policy-based mechanisms.

3. Heterogeneity and Extensibility: With advances in sensing technologies, it has become possible to deploy different types of sensors on a large scale to derive actionable knowledge. Further, since a single type of sensor may not be sufficient to provide accurate situational knowledge, there is a need to use different types of sensors to increase the accuracy of event detection. There is also a need to use different types of sensors, because a single sensing modality is often not sufficient to provide accurate situational knowledge. For use in diverse application scenarios, it is imperative that ASAP accommodate heterogeneity of sensing, while being flexible and extensible.

3   Architecture

Figure 2 shows the logical organization of the ASAP architecture into control and data network. The control network deals with low-level sensor specific processing to derive priority cues. These cues in turn are used by the data network to prioritize the streams and carry out further processing such as filtering and fusion of streams. It should be emphasized that this logical separation is simply a convenient vehicle to partition the functionalities of the ASAP architecture. The two networks are in fact overlaid on the same physical network and share the computational and sensing resources. For example, low bitrate sensing such as an RFID tag or a fire alarm are part of the control network. However, a high bitrate camera sensor while serving the video stream for the data network may also be used by the control network for discerning motion.

Figure 3 shows the software architecture of ASAP: it is a peer-to-peer network of ASAP agents (AA) that execute on independent nodes of the distributed system. The software organization in each node consists of two parts: *ASAP Agent (AA)* and *Sensor Agent (SA)*. There is one sensor agent per sensor, and a collection of sensor agents are assigned dynamically to an ASAP agent.

3.1   Sensor Agent

SA provides a *virtual sensor* abstraction that provides a uniform interface for incorporating heterogeneous sensing devices as well as to support multi-modal sensing in an extensible manner. This abstraction allows new sensor types to be added without requiring any change of the ASAP agent (AA). There is a potential danger in such a virtualization that some specific capability of a sensor may get masked from full utilization. To avoid such semantic loss, we have designed a minimal interface that serves the needs of situation awareness applications.

The virtual sensor abstraction allows the same physical sensor to be used for providing multiple sensing services. For example, a camera can serve not only as a video data stream, but also as a motion or a face detection sensor. Similarly, an SA may even combine multiple physical sensors to provide a multi-modal sensing capability. Once these different sensing modalities are registered with ASAP agents, they are displayed as a list of available features that users can select to construct a query for ASAP platform. ASAP platform uses these features as control cues for prioritization (see Section 3.2).

3.2   ASAP Agent

As shown in Figure 3, an AA is associated with a set of SAs. The association is dynamic, and is engineered at runtime in a peer-to-peer fashion among the AAs. The components of AA are shown in Figure 3.

Query Interface

ASAP agent provides a simple query interface with SQL-like syntax. Clients can pose an SQL query using control cues as attributes. Different cues can be combined using "AND" and "OR" operators to create multi-modal sensing queries. Here are some example queries which are self evident as to their intent: [1]

```
1) SELECT images FROM zone("Gate13")  WHERE RFIDTag = 'James'
2) SELECT images FROM zone("any")  WHERE FaceRecognition = 'Alice'
3) SELECT COUNT(Object) FROM zone("Concourse B")
```

False Positives and Negatives

Figure 2 shows that *sensed data* leads to *events*, which when filtered and fused ultimately leads to *actionable knowledge*. Unfortunately, individual sensors may often be unreliable due to environmental conditions (e.g., poor lighting conditions near a camera). Thus it may not always be possible to have high confidence

---

[1] It should be understood that the above queries are just a few examples. The interface is extensible to support different types of sensors, as well as, dispense both streams and digests of streams as the query output.

in the sensed data; consequently there is a danger that the system may experience high levels of false negatives and false positives. It is generally recognized that multi-modal sensors would help reduce the ill effects of false positives and negatives. The virtual sensor abstraction of ASAP allows multiple sensors to be fused together and registered as a new sensor. Unlike multi-feature fusion (*a la* face recognizer) where features are derived from the same (possibly noisy) image, multi-sensor fusion uses different sensing modalities. ASAP exploits a quorum system to make a decision. Even though a majority vote is implemented at the present time, AA may assign different weights to the different sensors commensurate with the error rates of the sensors to make the voting more accurate.

Prioritization Strategies

ASAP needs to continuously extract prioritization cues from all the cameras and other sensors (control network), and disseminate the selected camera streams (data network) to interested clients. ASAP extracts information from a sensor stream by invoking the corresponding SA. Since there may be many SAs registered at any time, invoking all SAs may be very compute intensive. ASAP needs to prioritize the invocations of SAs to scale well with the number of sensors. This leads to the need for *priority-aware computation* in the control network. Once a set of SAs that are relevant to client queries are identified, the corresponding camera feeds need to be disseminated to the clients. If the bandwidth required to disseminate all streams exceed the available bandwidth near the clients, network will end up dropping packets. This leads to the need for *priority-aware communication* in the data network. Based on these needs, the prioritization strategies employed by ASAP can be grouped into the following categories: Priority-aware computation and priority-aware communication.

Priority-aware Computation. The challenge is dynamically determining a set of SAs among all available SAs that need to be invoked such that overall value of the derived actionable knowledge (benefit for the application) is maximized. We use the term *Measure of Effectiveness (MOE)* to denote this overall benefit. ASAP currently uses a simple MOE based on clients' priorities.

The priority of an SA should reflect the amount of possibly "new" information the SA output may have and its importance to the query in progress. Therefore, the priority value is dynamic, and it depends on multiple factors, including the application requirements, and the information already available from other SAs. In its simplest form, priority assignment can be derived from the priority of the queries themselves. For instance, given two queries from an application, if the first query is more important than the second one, the SAs relevant to the first query will have higher priority compared to the SAs corresponding to the second query. More importantly, computations do not need to be initiated at all of SAs since (1) such information extracted from sensed data may not be required by any AA, and (2) unnecessary computation can degrade overall system performance. "WHERE" clause in SQL-like query is used to activate a specific sensing task. If multiple WHERE conditions exist, the lowest computation-intensive task is initiated first that activates the next task in turn. While it has a trade-off between latency and overhead, ASAP uses this for the sake of scalability.

(a)Axis 207MW   (b)RFID Antenna   (c)ASAP client on iPAQ

Fig. 4. Testbed building blocks

Priority-aware Communication. The challenge is designing prioritization techniques for communication on data network such that application specific MOE can be maximized. Questions to be explored here include: how to assign priorities to different data streams and how to adjust their *spatial* or *temporal* fidelities that maximizes the MOE?

In general, the control network packets are given higher priority than data network packets. Since the control network packets are typically much smaller than the data network packets, supporting a cluster of SAs with each AA does not overload the communication infrastructure.

4   Implementation

We have built an ASAP testbed with network cameras and RFID readers for object tracking based on RFID tags and motion detection. In implementing ASAP, we had three important goals: (1) platform neutrality for the "box" that hosts the AA and SA, (2) ability to support a variety of sensors seamlessly (for e.g., network cameras as well as USB cameras), and (3) extensibility to support a wide range of handheld devices including iPAQs and cellphones. Consequent to these implementation goals, we chose Java as the programming language for realizing the ASAP architecture. Java also provides Java Media Framework (JMF) API [3] that supports USB cameras on many platforms.

Table 1. Axis 207MW specifications

Specifications	
Video Compression	Motion JPEG, MPEG-4
Resolutions	15 resolutions up to 1280x1024
Frame Rate	Up to 14 fps up to 1280x720, Up to 12 fps in 1280x1024
Wireless interface	IEEE 802.11g 6-54 Mbps, IEEE 802.11b 1-11 Mbps

Figure 4 shows the building blocks of our testbed: a network camera, Axis 207MW from Axis Communication [4] and RFID antenna from Alien Technology [5]. The key specifications of the network camera are given in Table 1. Considering iPAQ[2] performance, we decided to use motion JPEG with 320x240

---

[2] At the time of writing, our implementation uses an iPAQ and/or a desktop for the GUI client. We plan to extend the implementation to include a cellphone through web service in the near future.

resolution, 5 fps, and 40 compression. Higher compression value (0–100) corresponds to lower quality and smaller image size. A JPEG frame requires 8–14 KBytes depending on the image content.

ASAP implementation consists of 3 main components: GUI Client, Sensor Agent, and ASAP Agent. GUI client has a simple interface to send a query. In a simple query, a user can select from drop-down lists for features such as RFID tag and motion detection, which tag needs to be tracked, and how many output streams he/she would like to receive. For a more complicated query such as tracking based on multiple tags and/or multiple features, SQL query is used. Then, the query is represented as an XML document and sent to the nearest ASAP Agent (either through the wired network or wirelessly depending on the connectivity of the client to the ASAP infrastructure). The client uses a *name server* to discover a nearby ASAP agent. In our current implementation, a text file at a well-known location serves the purpose of a name server. While there could be a debate about a scalability issue in this kind of naming service, the deployment of camera surveillance system is usually static, and AA keeps caches of topology information. Even in the case of dynamic deployment, ASAP can easily integrate DNS-like service which is not the focus of this work.

4.1 Sensor Agent

Sensor Agent needs to provide as simple as possible interface to alleviate the development of different types of sensors. This component requires frequent changes and updates due to the changes in detection algorithms or addition of sensors. The development of SA consists of 3 steps. The first step is the development of sensor functionality. It can be either physical sensor functions such as RFID tag reading or virtual sensor like motion detection or face recognition. The second step is the registration of sensor through a uniform interface. A control message handler is the last step. ASAP supports rich APIs to ease the second and third steps, and an application programmer can focus only on the first step. By having a tiered network architecture, Sensor Agent and ASAP Agent are functionally less dependent upon each other. This makes the ASAP software easy to understand, maintain, and extend with different sensors types.

The virtual sensor abstraction serves to make implementing new sensor functionality a cinch in ASAP. For e.g., given a camera, if the developer decides to implement two different functionalities (say, face recognition and motion detection) using the camera, then she would register each as a distinct sensor agent (SA) with the ASAP agent. This componentization of SAs allows modular extension to the overall architecture without any central control ensuring the scalability of the architecture.

For the testbed, we implemented camera, motion, and RFID sensors. In the case of camera sensors, ASAP supports USB cameras and Axis network cameras. JMF is used to support USB cameras, and it supports Windows, Linux, and Solaris. Axis supports HTTP API called VAPIX API. By sending HTTP request, camera features can be controlled, and images or streams can be retrieved. By sending a request, `http://[address]/axis-cgi/mjpg/video.cgi`, a camera is turned on and starts sending motion JPEG. With JMF, the camera URL is represented as following; `vfw://0` on Windows platform or `v41://1` on Linux platform. The last digit starts from 0 to the number of USB cameras attached exclusively. ASAP provides APIs for uniformly accessing cameras independent of their type. It implicitly figures out the camera type from the URL once again reducing the programming burden on the developer.

The data from the Sensor Agent may be directed dynamically to either the control network or the data network at the behest of the ASAP agent. The command from AA to SA specifies start/stop as well as periodicity (for periodic sensors, see Section 3.1). Alert sensors simply send a binary output. For instance, the RFID reader responds yes/no to a query for tracking a specific tag. It is possible for the user to control the amount of communication generated by an SA using the query interface. For example, if the user sets a threshold of motion, then this will be communicated by AA in a command to the SA. Upon receiving such a command, the associated SA for motion detection needs to send an alert only when the level of motion crosses the threshold specified by the AA. Even for a periodic stream (such as a video stream) communication optimization is possible from the query interface using the WHERE clause.

We implemented Java motion detection based on open source and RFID sensor using Alien Technology APIs. Since the ASAP agent is responsible for all command decisions regarding the granularity of operation of the SAs, it was easy to implement a variety of sensors (including multi-modal ones). Our experience validates our claim regarding the utility of the virtual sensor abstraction.

4.2 ASAP Agent

ASAP Agent (AA) is the core component of ASAP system. Not only does it handle multiple clients and Sensor Agents, but also communicates with other AAs in a distributed manner. ASAP Agent works as a delegate of a client. Since a client does not have global knowledge (e.g. how many cameras or RFID readers are deployed), it picks an ASAP Agent, and sends queries. AA should meet the following requirements: (1) efficient handling of multiple client queries, (2) efficient management of the control and data networks, and (3) dynamic load balancing via assignment of SAs to AAs.

Query Handler Module

Query handler module receives queries from multiple clients. An ASAP Agent that receives a query, interprets it, and decides on which peer AAs to activate on the control network. For example, a security guard may issue the following query to find where in Gate 11 "Ellice" is and request to receive one camera stream if she is in Gate 11.

```
SELECT images FROM zone('Gate 11') WHERE RFIDTag = 'Ellice'
```

As we mentioned in Section 3.2, each AA handles a cluster of SAs. There is no global knowledge of SA to AA association. A given AA knows the attributes of its peers (for e.g., which AA is responsible for SAs in Gate 11). Thus, upon receiving this query, the AA will forward the query to the appropriate AA using the control network. Upon receiving the forwarded query, the AA for Gate 11 will issue commands to its local SAs (if need be) to satisfy the query. If the AA already has the status of the SAs associated with it, then it can optimize by responding to the query without having to issue commands to its SAs.

Priority Assignment Module

The function of the priority assignment module is three-fold: 1) control message management, 2) relative priority assignment, and 3) data network management. Each of these functions is implemented by separate sub-modules.

Control message management sub-module maintains a *client request map*. Some of these requests may be from local clients, while others may be forwarded from peer AAs. If the request needs local resources, then it hands it to the relative priority assignment sub-module. If it requires remote resources, then it is forwarded as a control message to the peer AA. Communication is saved when a new client request can be satisfied by a pending remote request to the peer.

Relative priority assignment sub-module assigns priority values to various data streams. The priorities are assigned in the range {high,medium,low}. ASAP uses only three values for priority assignment due to a simple and efficient priority queue management and different streams are assigned to these queues. All streams belonging to the queue for one priority level are treated in the same way. This coarse grained priority assignment suits very well to ASAP. While more fine grained priority assignments are possible, they increase the complexity of implementation and overhead in queue managements.

The priority assignment happens over a series of steps and can take place in two different ways. The first is a top-down approach where a client query has a priority associated with it. In this case streams satisfying a query are assigned the priority associated with the query. If one stream satisfies the queries from multiple clients, the highest priority value among the queries is assigned to it. The accumulated or average priority among the queries can lead to a priority inversion. After a priority is assigned, streams are split into 3 groups for queues of different priority levels.

With a bottom-up approach, ASAP assigns a priority to a stream. Since there is no correlation among streams that meet distinct queries, this assignment occurs when a client requests for more than one stream or the conditions in a query are satisfied by multiple streams. In this situation AA assigns priority values ranging in {high,medium,low} to these streams. For instance, when a client requests a highest motion detection limited by 3 streams, a stream with the highest commotion will have {high} priority. As in a top-down approach, if a stream is requested by multiple clients, ASAP chooses the highest priority.

Data network management sub-module sends control messages to SAs indicating the data network to be turned on or off. The control messages also contain the priority assigned to the data network. The same scheme of control message management sub-module is used to manage request map of streams, and both control and data network are optimized to reduce redundant transmission.

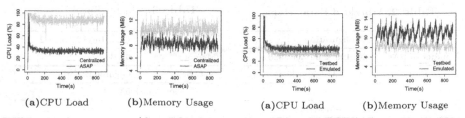

(a)CPU Load   (b)Memory Usage   (a)CPU Load   (b)Memory Usage

Fig. 5. Resource usage (Centralized vs. ASAP): A single object tracking system based on RFID tag. Cameras produce data (320x240 5 fps).

Fig. 6. Testbed vs. Emulated: A single object tracking system based on RFID tag with 4 cameras, 4 motion sensors, and 4 RFID readers

5   Evaluation

Before we go into the details of our scalability results, it is worth looking at how ASAP handles the concern that was raised in the introduction section. With a simple setup of 4 cameras, 4 motion sensors, 4 RFID readers, and a single client, we showed in Figure 1 that the CPU usage on a typical desktop system is close to 100%. Figure 5 shows the same setup using the prioritization strategy of ASAP and compares it with the 4-camera result from Figure 1. In this setup, ASAP uses a specific RFID tag as a control cue to decide the camera stream to be processed. As can be seen, use of control cues to select the camera stream results in a 60% improvement in CPU load. This establishes a baseline of expectation for performance improvement with the prioritization strategies of ASAP, and the promise ASAP offers for reducing the infrastructure overload. In the following subsections, we detail the experimental setup and the performance results of our scalability studies.

5.1   Experimental Setup

Since our current testbed has only a limited number of real cameras and RFID readers, the testbed is not enough for a large scale evaluation. Therefore, we developed emulated sensors support using the uniform virtual sensor interface discussed in Section 3. Due to the virtual sensor abstraction, an *ASAP Agent* does not distinguish whether data comes from an emulated sensor or a real sensor. The emulated camera sends JPEG images at a rate requested by a client. The emulated RFID reader sends tag detection event based on an event file, where different event files mimic different object movement scenarios.

To understand the impact of using emulated sensors on our results, we performed an experiment to compare the resource usage of emulated sensors with that of real sensors. Figure 6 shows the comparison. This experiment uses a network of 4 camera sensors, 4 RFID, and 4 motion detection, for a single object tracking. Because emulated sensors generate images and read from event files, they consume more CPU and memory resources than real sensors. However, the results show that the emulated setup is close enough to the real testbed thus validating our scalability studies with emulated sensors.

Table 2. Workload Parameters

Parameter	Configuration
Number of SAs	20, 125, 245, 500, 980
Image Format	M-JPEG 320x240 @ 5 fps
Number of Queries	1, 4, 8, 16, 32
Multi-Modality	1, 2, 3-Modality

Table 3. Cluster Specification

CPU	Dual Intel Xeon 3.2 GHz
Memory	6GB
Network	Gigabit Ethernet
Number of Nodes	53
OS	Linux (Kernel 2.6.9)

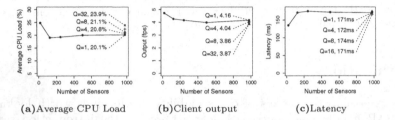

(a)Average CPU Load   (b)Client output   (c)Latency

Fig. 7. Scalability results: The solid line represents the effect of the number of SAs on different scalability metrics for a single query. The dotted lines point to the scalability results when the number of queries is varied from 1 ($Q = 1$) to 32 ($Q = 32$) for a setup with 980 SAs.

Workload

For the following experiments, *workload* used is as follows. An area is assumed to be made of a set of cells, organized as a grid. Objects start from a randomly selected cell, wait for a predefined time, and move to a neighbor cell. The number of objects, i.e. the number of RFID tags, the grid size, and the object wait time are workload parameters.

Table 2 summarizes the parameters used in our experiments. The number of SAs is varied from 20 to 980. An ASAP agent is assigned for every 20 SAs. For e.g., for a setup with 20 SAs, there will be one ASAP agent, and for a setup with 125 SAs, there will be 6 ASAP agents. Each ASAP agent runs on a distinct node of a cluster (see Table 3) of dual Intel Xeon 3.2 GHz processors with 6GB of RAM running Linux. A fixed experiment duration (15 minutes) is used through all performance evaluations. Other experimental parameters are explained below in the context of the specific experiments.

5.2   Scalability, Query Handling, and Latency

Figure 7 shows scalability results for tracking a single object when the number of SAs is increased. This corresponds to an application scenario wherein the movement of a suspicious individual carrying a boarding pass with a specific RFID is tracked in an airport. To handle the increase in the number of cameras and other sensors, more ASAP Agents are added (with 20:1 ratio between SAs and ASAP agent). Figure 7(a) shows the average CPU load over all the ASAP agents for a particular configuration. On each node, processing cycles are used for ASAP agent, SAs, and performance monitoring. With a single query, only one ASAP agent in the entire system has to do the heavy lifting. While there is processing cycles devoted to SAs and monitoring in each node of the distributed system despite the fact that there is just a single query, the prioritization architecture ensures that the CPU load due to the SAs on each node is pretty minimal. Since the Y-axis is the CPU load averaged over all the nodes, there is an initial drop in the average CPU load (from 25% to 19%) and then it remains the same at about 20%. The fact that the average CPU load remains the same despite the size of the deployment (with 980 sensors we use 49 nodes of the cluster) is confirmation of the scalability of the ASAP architecture. As a side note, the CPU load on each node due to performance monitoring is 7.5%.

For the maximum workload configuration of 980 SAs, Figure 7(a) also shows how ASAP scales with varying number of queries (clients). The multiple query experiment assumes the queries are independent of one other and are emanating from distinct clients. This corresponds to an application scenario wherein the movement of multiple suspicious individuals carrying boarding passes tagged with distinct RFIDs are tracked in an airport by different security personnel. Increasing the number of queries increases the average CPU load, but at a very low rate. For example, when the number of queries increases from one to 32, the average CPU usage per node increases only by 4%.

Figure 7(b) shows the scalability of ASAP for delivering output (video streams) to multiple clients. The workload (Table 2) fixes the camera data generation at 5 fps. Ideally, we would like to see this as the delivered frame rate to the clients. With the single node vanilla system that we discussed in the introduction (Section 1), we observed an output delivery rate of 3 fps (a companion measurement to Figure 1). As can be seen in Figure 7(b), the average output delivery rate is over 4.26 fps over the range of SAs we experimented with. The frame rate degrades gracefully as the size of the system is scaled up (along the x-axis). Even when the number of queries increase, the frames per second degrades gracefully, for e.g., with 32 queries, ASAP delivers (Figure 7(b)) on an average 3.87 fps over the range of SAs we experimented with.

Figure 7(c) shows the end-to-end latency measurement as the system size is scaled up (along the x-axis). The measured time is the elapsed time between receiving a frame at the SA associated with a camera to the time it is delivered to a client. This latency is 135 ms with a single AA. As the system is scaled up the source SA and the destination client may be associated with different nodes (i.e., different AAs as shown in Figure 3) requiring a forwarding of the data stream. However, as can be seen from Figure 7(c), the forwarding only slightly increases the end-to-end latency as the system is scaled up. On an average the latency is 170 ms over the range of SAs we experimented with. Similarly, the latency is not affected tremendously with the number of queries. In fact with 16 queries, there is even a reduction in the latency which may be attributed to perhaps the source SA and the destination client being collocated at an AA more often than not (thus reducing the forwarding messages incurred).

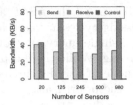

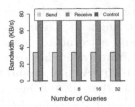

Fig. 8. Bandwidth usage: The number of SAs is varied from 20 to 980 with a single query

Fig. 9. Average Bandwidth: the number of queries is varied from 1 to 32 with the largest configuration of 980 SAs

5.3 Network Bandwidth

Another important resource to consider as we scale up the system size is the network bandwidth. Similar to the CPU load experiments in Section 5.2, we wish to understand how the network bandwidth requirement changes with increasing system size and increasing number of queries. As a point of reference, the observed raw bandwidth requirement per M-JPEG stream (from the Axis camera) is 40 KBytes/sec to 60 KBytes/sec (at 5 fps) depending on the contents of the image frame. There are three sources of demand on network bandwidth in the ASAP architecture: an AA *receiving* data streams from sensors via associated SAs (including forwarding to peer AAs), an AA *sending* data streams to clients, and AAs communicating control information with another. The first two are demands placed on the physical network by the data streams and the third by the control streams. Figure 8 shows the network bandwidth used for a single query when the system is scaled up. The *send* bandwidth remains roughly the same and tracks the frames/sec delivered to the clients in Figure 7(b). The *receive* bandwidth roughly doubles beyond one node and represents the data forwarding between AAs. However, it stays pretty much the same independent of the system size showing the scalability of the ASAP architecture. The reason for the doubling is due to the fact that the workload assumes random positioning of the object being tracked (over the 15 minute window of experimentation time); thus the larger the network the more the chance of data being forwarded between AAs. However, there is at most one hop of forwarding due to the peer-to-peer nature of the AA arrangement in the ASAP architecture. The control traffic (small black line which is almost invisible) is just 2% of the total bandwidth usage independent of the system size due to the variety of optimizations that we discussed in Section 4.2.

Figure 9 shows the average bandwidth usage for increasing number of queries. This experiment uses the maximum workload configuration of 980 SAs (Table 2). As with the CPU load experiments, each client query is tracking a different object. We do have results when all the clients request the same object to be tracked but have not presented them in this paper for space considerations. As may be expected such clustering of requests results in reducing the network requirements (specifically the receive and control traffic bandwidths are reduced).

5.4   Other Results

We have also conducted experiments to test false positives and false negatives. ASAP uses a dynamic voting mechanism to reduce the ill effects of false positive and false negatives. These mechanisms result in reduction in the range of 18%-64% for false-positives and -negatives. Due to space limitations, we do not present these experiments and results.

6   Related Works

There have been other interesting researches on architecture for camera sensor networks, which have motivated ASAP's two-tier approach of control and data networks. IrisNet [6] provides an architecture for a worldwide sensor web. It also shares commonalities with ASAP such as agent-based approach, two-tier network, and heterogeneous sensors support. The major difference lies in the main goal and target applications. IrisNet focuses on distributed database techniques for gathering sensor data and querying the collected data. The result of query in IrisNet is a digest of information culled from the collected data stored in the distributed databases. The focus of ASAP is to prioritize and prune data collection in an application-specific manner to deal with the data explosion so that irrelevant data is neither collected, nor processed, nor stored. Further, ASAP provides a continuous stream of information as the query result (which may be real-time data streams or digests of processing such real-time streams) satisfying the query constraints. The techniques for storing and retrieving data and maintaining consistency of the distributed databases, a forte of IrisNet project, is a nice complement to our work.

SensEye [7] is an architecture for multi-tier camera sensor network. SensEye uses three tier networks, and sense-actuate control loop exists from lowest tier (with low resolution cameras) to the highest (with higher resolution cameras). While SensEye focuses on the reduction of power consumption, having 3-tiered network can increase the complexity of software architecture. Tenet [8] also uses a tiered architecture. However, the focus of Tenet lies on the architecture support for simplifying application development and concurrent application, while ASAP focuses on how to query camera sensors in a scalable manner.

A natural way to think about managing resources in situation awareness applications is to leverage the application dataflow. For example, RF^2ID [9] is a middleware that uses the flow of tagged objects to create a group of nodes that can process the data generated from those objects. Similarly, the concept of flow is used to support QoS-aware routing [10]. In such situations, location-based correlation [11] can facilitate the desirable clustering of the nodes. Also, techniques from on-demand clustering [12] can be used to further reduce the amount of communication required to do reclustering in a dynamic environment. Finally, apart from using just location-based attributes, other attributes can also be used to achieve an application-aware clustering [13].

Supporting QoS in network layers has been an active area of research because of the growing popularity of cell phones and multimedia services. QoS-aware medium access control protocols have been proposed to handle different techniques to match with different data types, for e.g., IEEE 801.11e handles four different data classes for better QoS support [14]. To handle real-time requirements for QoS-aware routing, common techniques used are rate-control techniques at data sources and route adjustments by finding least-cost and delay-constrained links [15]. Similarly, rate control and congestion control mechanisms have been used to provide QoS-aware transport protocols [16]. Our application-layer approach to do the priority assignment is complementary to and fits on top of the above network layer techniques.

7   Conclusions

Situation awareness is an important application category in cyber-physical systems. Video-based surveillance is an example of this category of applications. There is an explosion in the amount of data that has to be dealt with in such applications, especially as the data sources scale up.

ASAP is a distributed systems architecture for camera based sensor networks that deals with this data deluge. The unique feature of ASAP is a systematic approach to prioritizing the data streams, and the subsequent processing of these streams using cues derived from a variety of sensory sources. Further, the peer-to-peer nature of the ASAP architecture ensures scalability to a large number of camera sources, and for the dynamic allocation of computational resources to hot spots in the application. Lastly, the system provides a systematic way for reducing false positives and false negatives using multi- modal sensing.

Acknowledgements

The work has been funded in part by an NSF ITR grant CCR-01-21638, NSF NMI grant CCR-03-30639, NSF CPA grant CCR-05-41079, and the Georgia Tech Broadband Institute. The equipment used in the experimental studies is funded in part by an NSF Research Infrastructure award EIA-99-72872, and Intel Corp. We thank the members of the Embedded Pervasive Lab at Georgia Tech (http://wiki.cc.gatech.edu/epl/) for their helpful feedback on our work.

References

1. Buckley, C.: New york plans surveillance veil for downtown. The New York Times (July 2007), http://www.nytimes.com/2007/07/09/nyregion/09ring.html
2. McCahill, M., Norris, C.: CCTV in London. Technical report, University of Hull (June (2002)
3. Java Media Framework API: http://java.sun.com/products/java-media/jmf
4. Axis Communication: http://www.axis.com/
5. Alien Technology: http://www.alientechnology.com/
6. Deshpande, A., Nath, S.K., Gibbons, P.B., Seshan, S.: Cache-and-query for wide area sensor databases. In: Proceedings of the 2003 ACM SIGMOD, pp. 503–514. ACM Press, New York (2003)

7. Kulkarni, P., Ganesan, D., Shenoy, P., Lu, Q.: Senseye: a multi-tier camera sensor network. In: MULTIMEDIA 2005, Hilton, Singapore, ACM, New York, NY, USA (2005)
8. Gnawali, O., Jang, K.-Y., Paek, J., Vieira, M., Govindan, R., Greenstein, B., Joki, A., Estrin, D., Kohler, E.: The tenet architecture for tiered sensor networks. In: SenSys 2006, Boulder, Colorado, USA, pp. 153–166. ACM, New York, NY, USA (2006)
9. Ahmed, N., Kumar, R., French, R., Ramachandran, U.: RF2ID: A reliable middleware framework for RFID deployment. In: IEEE IPDPS, March 2007, IEEE Computer Society Press, Los Alamitos (2007)
10. Apostolopoulos, G., Kama, S., Williams, D., Guerin, R., Orda, A., Przygienda, T.: QoS routing mechanisms and OSPF extensions. IETF Draft, RFC 2676 (1996)
11. Chen, B., Jamieson, K., Balakrishnan, H., Morris, R.: Span: An energy-efficient coordination algorithm for topology maintenance in ad hoc wireless networks. In: MOBICOM, pp. 85–96 (2001)
12. Chatterjee, M., Das, S., Turgut, D.: An on-demand weighted clustering algorithm (WCA) for ad hoc networks. In: Proceedings of IEEE Globecom, IEEE Computer Society Press, Los Alamitos (2000)
13. PalChaudhuri, S., Kumar, R., Baraniuk, R.G., Johnson, D.B.: Design of adaptive overlays for multi-scale communication in sensor networks. In: Prasanna, V.K., Iyengar, S., Spirakis, P.G., Welsh, M. (eds.) DCOSS 2005. LNCS, vol. 3560, Springer, Heidelberg (2005)
14. Fallah, Y.P., Alnuweiri, H.: A controlled-access scheduling mechanism for QoS provisioning in IEEE 802.11e wireless LANs. In: Proceedings of the 1st ACM international workshop on Quality of service & security in wireless and mobile networks, pp. 122–129. ACM Press, New York (2005)
15. Alghamdi, M.I., Xie, T., Qin, X.: PARM: a power-aware message scheduling algorithm for real-time wireless networks. In: WMuNeP 2005. Proceedings of the 1st ACM workshop on Wireless multimedia networking and performance modelin, ACM Press, New York (2005)
16. Cho, S., Bettati, R.: Improving quality of service of tcp flows in strictly prioritized network. In: ACST 2006. Proceedings of the 2nd IASTED international conference on Advances in computer science and technology

Asynchronous Active Recommendation Systems

(Extended Abstract)

Baruch Awerbuch[1,*], Aviv Nisgav[2], and Boaz Patt-Shamir[3,**]

[1] Dept. of Computer Science, Johns Hopkins University, Baltimore, MD 21218, USA
baruch@cs.jhu.edu
[2] School of Electrical Engineering, Tel Aviv University, Tel Aviv 69978, Israel
avivns@eng.tau.ac.il
[3] School of Electrical Engineering, Tel Aviv University, Tel Aviv 69978, Israel
boaz@eng.tau.ac.il

Abstract. We consider the following abstraction of recommendation systems. There are players and objects, and each player has an arbitrary binary preference grade ("likes" or "dislikes") for each object. The preferences are unknown at start. A player can find his grade for an object by "probing" it, but each probe incurs cost. The goal of a recommendation algorithm is to find the preferences of the players while minimizing cost. To save on cost, players post the results of their probes on a public "billboard" (writing and reading from the billboard is free). In asynchronous systems, an adversary controls the order in which players probe. Active algorithms get to tell players which objects to probe when they are scheduled. In this paper we present the first low-overhead algorithms that can provably reconstruct the preferences of players under asynchronous scheduling. "Low overhead" means that the probing cost is only a polylogarithmic factor over the best possible cost; and by "provably" we mean that the algorithm works with high probability (over internal coin tosses) for all inputs, assuming that each player gets some minimal number of probing opportunities. We present algorithms in this model for exact and approximate preference reconstruction.

1 Introduction

Recommendation systems are an important ingredient of modern life, where people must make decisions with partial information [7]. Everyday examples include buying books, going to a movie, choosing an on-line store etc. Computer-related examples include, among others, choosing peers in a potentially hostile peer-to-peer environment, or choosing a route in an unreliable network. The basic idea underlying such systems is that users can use the experience reported by others so as to improve their prediction of their own opinions. However, users may differ in their opinions either because they have different "tastes," or because their objectives may be different (e.g., in a peer-to-peer network some users may wish to destroy the system). Obviously, only users

---

* Partially supported by NSF grants CCF 0515080, ANIR-0240551, and CCR-0311795, and CNS-0617883.
** This research was supported in part by the Israel Science Foundation (grant 664/05) and by Israel Ministry of Science and Technology.

E. Tovar, P. Tsigas, and H. Fouchal (Eds.): OPODIS 2007, LNCS 4878, pp. 48–61, 2007.

whose preferences are similar to those of many others can enjoy the advantages of recommendation systems.

Most recommendation systems in use rely on various heuristics, trying to match a user with others of similar taste [6] or an item with similar items [8]. Recently, recommendation systems were looked at from the algorithmic viewpoint, using the following framework [5,4]. There are n users (also called "players"), and m products (a.k.a. "objects"), and each user has an unknown grade for each product. Each user can find his grade for each product by means of "probing" that product, but each probe incurs a unit cost (probing represents buying a book, or renting a movie etc.). The system provides a public "billboard" on which users post the results of their probes for the benefit of others.

Existing work. There are a few variants in the literature regarding the power of the algorithm and its goal. In this paper, we assume that the role of the algorithm is to tell the player which object to probe whenever the player gets a chance to probe. The goal is to correctly output all (or most) of the player's preferences, even though a player may probe only a negligible fraction of the object space. This problem has been studied before, and some previous solutions exist, each with its own drawback:

- *Committee.* Some algorithms (e.g., in [5,4]) require some players to probe all objects. This solution is problematic in practice both because it's unfair, and because it is vulnerable to malicious users, who may obstruct the selection of the committee, or may gain control over some committee members.
- *Separability assumptions.* Some algorithms (e.g., in [5]) work only if the preferences of the players admit a "low rank approximation," which translates to a severe restriction on the solvable inputs. These restrictions do not appear to apply in many cases.
- *Synchrony.* In [2,1], the algorithm is synchronous in the sense that time proceeds in global rounds. Each player probes once in each round; results from previous rounds are used to determine which objects to probe in the next round. Synchrony is hard to implement in practice, even if we assume that players are willing to follow the protocol: e.g., some players may wish to go much faster than others.

The first two disadvantages were removed recently [2,1].

Our contribution. In this paper, we take the next step by showing how to overcome the latter difficulty: we present an asynchronous algorithm to reconstruct the full preference vectors of players with similar tastes, regardless of the schedule in which they take probing steps. The total probing cost to a set of players with the same taste is larger than the best possible by only a *polylogarithmic* factor, provided that each player in the set makes some minimal number of probes, or that the number of similar players is at least a polylog fraction. We use a randomized scheduling methodology, which may be interesting in its own right.

More precisely, we assume that there is an arbitrary schedule that specifies a sequence of players so that at each step, the next player according to the schedule may take a probing action. The algorithm can control only which object does that player probe, based on the results posted on the billboard so far and random coin tosses. (We assume that the schedule is *oblivious*, i.e., the schedule is fixed ahead of time and may not depend on the outcome of coin tosses.) In this model the number of players that share a given taste is not very important: what counts is the total *volume* of probes done by players of a given taste. Therefore, our primary complexity measure is the total *work* by a given player set, i.e., the volume of probes performed by that set of users in a given schedule.

Clearly, the minimal amount of work that has to be done to find m grades is m probes, because each object must be probed at least once. In this paper we show that after the execution of $\tilde{O}(m)$ probes by the members of a single taste group, the correct vector appears as the output of one of the members, and thereafter it will propagate to all other members of the taste group in $\tilde{O}(n)$ additional probes (once they are given sufficiently many probing opportunities). We note that our algorithms does not terminate: rather, the output value is continuously updated, but once it has reached the correct output the output remains correct.

Our main result for exact type reconstruction is as follows ($\tilde{O}(\cdot)$ and $\tilde{\Omega}(\cdot)$ ignore polylogarithmic factors).

Theorem 1. *Fix a schedule where $\tilde{\Omega}(1)$ fraction of the first $\tilde{O}(m)$ probes are by players with identical preferences. Then with high probability, after $\tilde{O}(m)$ work by these players, their output stabilizes on their true preferences.*

A similar result holds for the approximate case.

Theorem 2. *Fix a schedule where $\tilde{\Omega}(1)$ fraction of the first $\tilde{O}(m)$ probes are by players with preferences at distance $D = \tilde{O}(1)$ from each other for some given D. Then with high probability, after $\tilde{O}(m)$ work by these players, their output is with distance $O(D)$ from their true preferences.*

Our algorithms consider only players performing some minimal work, which is unavoidable. To see that, consider executions where there are k tastes, and each taste group gets a $1/k$ fraction of the total number of probes. Symmetry considerations can be used to prove that $\Omega(k)$ probes are needed for a user just to figure out to which group he belongs (see [3] for a formal argument).

Organization. The remainder of this paper is organized as follows. We formally define the model and some notation in Section 2. In Section 3 we describe and analyze the algorithm for exact preference reconstruction. In Section 4 we present our algorithm for approximate reconstruction of the preference vectors. The analysis of the approximate algorithm is omitted from this extended abstract.

2   Preliminaries

Model. The input consists of n *players* and m *objects*. Each player p has an unknown binary *grade* for each object, and these grades are represented by a vector $v(p) \in \{0,1\}^m$ sometimes called the *preference vector*. An execution proceeds according to a *schedule*, which is an arbitrary infinite sequence of player identifiers. In a single step of an execution, the player selected by the schedule may *probe* a single object, i.e., learn its grade for that object. The identity of the object probed by the player is under the control of the local algorithm run by the player. We assume that the results of all previous probes by all players are available to everyone, and in particular they may be used by players to determine which object to probe next. The algorithm maintains, at each player p, an output vector $g(p)$, which is an estimate of the preference vector $v(p)$. The output vector changes over time. The goal of the algorithms in this work is to use similarity between players in order to minimize the total number of probes they perform. We consider two cases: in the *exact* reconstruction case, the goal is that $g(p)$ will stabilize on $v(p)$ exactly. In the *approximate* case, we are satisfied if from some point on, $g(p)$ differs from $v(p)$ in no more than D grades, for some given parameter D. In the former case, a player can rely only on other players with exactly the same preference vector, while in the latter case, a player may also "collaborate" with players whose preference vectors are close to his own.

Comments. First, for simplicity of presentation, we shall assume in the remainder of this paper that $m = n$. The extension to arbitrary number of objects is straightforward. Second, we note that it may be the case that some players do not report their true results. For our purposes, such players are not considered to be similar to honest players with the same preference vector.

Notation. Given a grade vector v and a set of coordinates (i.e., objects) O, let $v|_O$ denote the projection of v on O, i.e., the vector resulting from v by picking only the coordinates in O. For any two vectors u, v of the same length, we denote by $\text{dist}(v, u)$ the Hamming distance between u and v. For a set O of coordinates, we define $\text{dist}_O(v, u) = \text{dist}(v|_O, u|_O)$, i.e., the number of coordinates in O on which the two vectors differ.

Unless otherwise stated, all logarithms in this paper are to base 2. $\tilde{O}(\cdot)$ and $\tilde{\Omega}(\cdot)$ ignore polylogarithmic factors.

2.1 Building Block: Algorithm SELECT

One of the basic building blocks we use extensively in our algorithms is the operation of selection, defined as follows. The input to a player p consists of a set V of grade vectors for a set of objects O, and a distance bound D. It is assumed that $\min \{\text{dist}|_O(v(p), v) : v \in V\} \leq D$. The goal of the algorithm is to find the vector from V which is closest to $v(p)$ on O.

SELECT(V, D)

(1) Repeat
    (1a) Let $X(V)$ be set of coordinates on which some two vectors in V differ.
    (1b) Execute Probe on the first coordinate in X that has not been probed yet.
    (1c) Remove from V any vector with more than D disagreements with $v(p)$.
    Until all coordinates in $X(V)$ are probed or $X(V)$ is empty.
(2) Let Y be the set of coordinates probed by p throughout the algorithm. Find the set of vectors $U \subseteq V$ closest to $v(p)$ on Y, i.e., $U = \{v \in V : \forall u \in V : \text{dist}_Y(u, v(p)) \geq \text{dist}_Y(v, v(p))\}$.
(3) Return a randomly selected vector from U.

The main property of SELECT is summarized in the following lemma.

Lemma 1 ([1]). *If* $\text{dist}(v, v(p)) \leq D$ *for some* $v \in V$, *then the output of* SELECT(V, D) *by player* p *is the closest vector to* $v(p)$ *in* V. *The total number of probes executed in* SELECT(V, D) *is less than* $(D + 1)|V|$.

To aid readability, we write SELECT_EXACT(V) for SELECT$(V, 0)$.

2.2 Randomized Multiplexing

In our algorithms, we use a simple methodology for running multiple sequential tasks in parallel by a single player. In this extended abstract we only give an informal overview of the general framework.

The setup is as follows. Without getting into the details of the local computational model, let us assume that there is a well-defined notion of a sequential program, that consists of a sequence of atomic steps. Given the notion of a sequential program, we define the concept of a *task* recursively, as either an infinite-length sequential program, or a tuple $\mathrm{rmux}(p_1 : T_1, \ldots, p_n : T_n)$, where $n \geq 1$, and for all $1 \leq i \leq n$, T_i is a task and p_i is a positive real number called the *relative allocation* of T_i. It is required that $\sum_{i=1}^{n} p_i = 1$.

Graphically, a task can be visualized as a rooted tree, where edges are labeled by real numbers between zero and one, and leaves are labeled by sequential programs. For example, consider the task

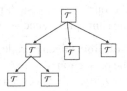

$$T_0 = \mathrm{rmux}(\tfrac{1}{3} : T_1, \tfrac{1}{2} : T_2, \tfrac{1}{6} : T_3),$$

where $T_1 = \mathrm{rmux}(\tfrac{1}{2} : T_{11}, \tfrac{1}{2} : T_{12})$, and each of the tasks T_2, T_3, T_{11} and T_{12} is a sequential program. This task is illustrated in Figure 1.

Fig. 1. Example of a multiplexing tree

The semantics of executing a task is like that of a multitasking operating system: each sequential program has its own state, called context. The sequential programs are executed in parallel, one step at a time. A time slot is allocated to a program at leaf ℓ with probability which is the product of the labels on the path leading from the root to ℓ. (In the figure, for example, the allocations of T_{11}, T_{12} and T_3 is $\tfrac{1}{6}$ each.). In each system step, a random leaf is chosen according to its probability, and a single instruction is executed in the context of that leaf's program; as a result, the context is updated (and possibly some global side effects take place). The contexts of all other leaf programs remain unchanged.

Using standard large deviations bounds, we have the following result for a set of players executing the same task asynchronously in parallel.

Theorem 3. *Consider an asynchronous schedule of T steps, and suppose all players execute the same task T. Let T_0 be a sequential program whose probability in T is p. Then for any $\delta > 0$: if $p \cdot T \geq 3 \log 2/\delta$, then with probability at least $1 - \delta$, the total number of steps of program T_0 done by all players together is $p \cdot T \cdot (1 + o(1))$ as $T \to \infty$.*

Intuitively, Theorem 3 says that if the expected number of steps that T should get is at least logarithmic, then with high probability the absolute deviation from the expected value is smaller than any positive constant factor.

The rmux construct is useful for stabilizing sequential programs, namely programs whose output stops changing after sufficient work was done. Even without explicit indication of stabilization, when programs with acyclic dependencies are run in parallel using rmux, their output will stabilize in a bottom-up fashion.

$$
\begin{pmatrix}
v_1^1 & \cdots & v_{n/2}^2 & & & \\
\vdots & \ddots & \vdots & & ? & \\
v_1^{n/2} & \cdots & v_{n/2}^{n/2} & & & \\
& & & v_{n/2+1}^{n/2+1} & \cdots & v_n^{n/2+1} \\
& ? & & \vdots & \ddots & \vdots \\
& & & v_{n/2+1}^{n} & \cdots & v_n^{n}
\end{pmatrix}
$$

Fig. 2. Matrix representation of the synchronous algorithm. Rows represent players and columns represent objects. After returning from the recursion, the entries in two quadrants are unknown.

3   Exact Preference Reconstruction

In this section we develop an algorithm for exact types. More formally, let P be any set of players with the same preference vector v_P. Each player p maintains an output vector $g(p)$. The goal of the algorithm is to minimize the total number of probes by players in P until their output vector stabilizes on v_P precisely. We start with some intuition and outline the general structure of the algorithm. In Section 3.1 we specify the algorithm, and in Section 3.2 we analyze it.

The synchronous algorithm. Our starting point is the synchronous algorithm $\mathcal{D}$ from [2]. To gain some intuition, we briefly review the way the synchronous algorithm works. First, it is assumed that a lower bound α on the relative frequency of players with exactly the same taste is given. The algorithm proceeds as follows. Given a set of players and a set of objects, the players and objects are split into two subsets each. Each half of the players recursively determines the values of half of the objects, and then the results are merged. Figure 2 gives a matrix representation of the situation after returning from the recursive call. Merging (i.e., filling in the missing entries) is done by applying SELECT_EXACT to the preference vectors that are sufficiently popular in the other half, where "sufficiently popular" means that the preference vector is supported by, say an $\alpha/2$ fraction of the players. This guarantees correctness, because with high probability, at least an $\alpha/2$ fraction of any large enough random player set are players of the given type (whose global frequency is at least α).

Asynchronous algorithm: basic structure and main ideas. Algorithm $\mathcal{D}$ does not work in the asynchronous case, because it is an adversarial schedule that controls which player gets to probe and when. Hence the number of players of a specific type that execute the algorithm at a given recursion level may be arbitrary, and the crucial popularity threshold becomes meaningless. If we try all possible vectors, the cost to a player increases to the trivial $\Theta(n)$.

Our approach to solve this difficulty can be intuitively described as based on the following ideas. Consider a specific type P. Clearly, the amount of work a single player $p \in P$ needs to do (on average) is inversely proportional to the amount of help he gets from other players of P. In our case, let us first assume that the *density* (i.e., fraction) of probes done by players of P in a given prefix of the execution is some known value

α (provided by an oracle to be implemented later). Note that even when we are given the density of the probes by players of P, we cannot readily apply the synchronous algorithm, because, for example, it may be the case that all these probes are allocated by the schedule to the same player, which, according to $\mathcal{D}$, is supposed to probe only a few objects. We cope with this problem using randomization as follows.

First, as a matter of convenience, we view the recursive partitioning of the object set as a complete binary tree, with the root corresponds to all objects, each of its two children to half of the objects etc. Each leaf corresponds to about $4/\alpha$ objects. In Algorithm $\mathcal{D}$, the players are arranged in a parallel tree, and the execution proceeds from the leafs toward the root level by level, where in each node each player executes SELECT_EXACT.

Here, we use spatial and temporal randomization to overcome the asynchronous schedule. By spatial randomness we mean that when a player gets a chance to probe, he effectively assumes the identity of a random player. This way the work is more-or-less evenly divided over the objects. By temporal randomness we mean that instead of going over the leaf-root path in an order, in our algorithm, after the player have chosen a random identity (and thus a leaf), he chooses a random node along the path from that leaf to the root. This ensures that all nodes will get their "right" amount of work— but not necessarily in the right order. To prove correctness, we show that node outputs stabilize to their correct values inductively, starting from the leaves and ending at the root. We note that this randomization increases the required number of probes by an $O(\log n)$ factor.

Two more ideas are used in the final algorithm. First, we eliminate the assumption that the density α of the probes by players of P is known by running multiple instances of the algorithm in parallel, using the rmux construct. Version i works under the assumption that $\alpha \geq 2^{-i}$. The player chooses among the various instances using SELECT_EXACT. Second, consider the case where some players wake up after most many players have already found the correct vector. To avoid duplicating the work, each player continuously looks for a good complete recommendation, by trying all possible output vectors generated by other players. We show that once the correct output appears as $g(p)$ for some player, it spreads quickly to all working players.

Finally, let us address the issue of the number of probes by a player. We note that the number of probes by a player in the synchronous algorithm is $O(\frac{\log n}{\alpha})$. In the asynchronous algorithm, only players doing $\Omega(\frac{\log^3 n}{\alpha})$ probes are useful for the algorithm. Another way to guarantee that sufficient work is useful is to require that the total work done by player of the given type is at least $\Omega(n \log^3 n/\alpha)$.

We present the algorithm in a bottom up fashion: first, we describe an algorithm that assume that the density of the probes by players of P is known, and then give the top-level algorithm.

3.1 The Algorithm

Algorithm for a given α. The objects are recursively divided into a tree structure as described above. Given a node v, $\mathrm{obj}(j)$ denotes the set of objects associated with v. If v is not a leaf, then it has two children denoted $c_1(v)$ and $c_2(v)$. Each node v has a list $G(v)$ of possible grade vectors, posted by the players.

The players work in elementary batches called *jobs*, where each job consists of $4/\alpha$ probes. Jobs are executed within the context of a single tree node. The goal of a job at node v is to append another vector to $G(v)$. The *job algorithm* at a node v is as follows.

JOB(v)   // $0 < \alpha \le 1$ *is a given parameter*
(1) If v is a leaf, probe all objects in $\mathrm{obj}(v)$ and post the results in $G(v)$.
(2) If v is an internal node:
    (2a) Read the list $G(c_1(v))$ and let B_1 be the set of the $2/\alpha$ most popular vectors in it (break ties arbitrarily). Similarly, construct a set B_2 of the $2/\alpha$ most popular vectors in $G(c_2(v))$.
    (2b) $g \leftarrow$ concatenation of SELECT_EXACT(B_1) and SELECT_EXACT(B_2); append g to $G(v)$.
    (2c) If v is the root, $g(p) \leftarrow$ SELECT_EXACT($\{g(p), g\}$).

Note that since the schedule is asynchronous, SELECT_EXACT in Step 2b is not done atomically (Step 2c consists of a single probe). Asynchrony has no effect on the output if v is a leaf (Step 1), because the set of objects probed in this case is always $\mathrm{obj}(v)$. But if v is an internal node, the situation is different: while the probing of Step 2b is carried out, the contents of the lists $G(c_1(v))$ and $G(c_2(v))$ may change. In our algorithm these lists are read once, at the beginning of the job (Step 2a) resulting in lists B_1 and B_2 whose contents is then frozen throughout the remainder of the execution of the job.

The algorithm for a given α is simply "execute jobs at random:"

Algorithm BASIC(α)
Repeat forever: pick a random node v and execute JOB(v).

Note that Algorithm BASIC(α) is a non-terminating sequential program. Its output is the vector $g(p)$ (written by a root job), which changes over time.

Algorithm for Unknown α. We now explain how to execute the algorithm without knowledge of α. Let P be a set of players with the same preference vector v_P. As we show later, BASIC(α) guarantees that for some player $p_0 \in P$, we will eventually have $g(p_0) = v_P$, provided that α is the relative density of probes by players of P. Thus, we need to solve two problems: how to choose the right value of α, and how to disseminate v_P to the other players of P, once v_P is discovered. Our approach is to solve both problems using the rmux construct. Choosing the right value of α is done by trying all $\log n$ powers of $1/2$ in parallel as possible values of α. To disseminate v_P, each player p repeatedly compares his own output $g(p)$ (which is common to all his instances of PULL and BASIC) with the output of a randomly chosen player. Formally, we define the following simple task:

Algorithm PULL(V, D)
Repeat forever:
    pick a random vector $v \in V$ and execute $g(p) \leftarrow$ SELECT($\{g(p), v\}, D$).

The main algorithm can now be specified as follows. Let $\alpha_{\min}$ be the smallest value of α for which the algorithm is designed, and define $I = \log(1/\alpha_{\min})$ (note that $I = O(\log n)$ if the schedule length is polynomial in n). We run I tasks in parallel, and the

PULL task. We note that the set of vectors sent to PULL changes over time: if $g(p')$ is chosen in PULL, its *current* value is copied over and sent to SELECT_EXACT.

Main Algorithm for Exact Reconstruction

rmux(
    1/2:   rmux $\left(\frac{1}{I} : \text{BASIC}(\frac{1}{2}),\ \frac{1}{I} : \text{BASIC}(\frac{1}{4}),\ \ldots,\ \frac{1}{I} : \text{BASIC}(\frac{1}{2I})\right)$,
    1/2:   PULL$(\{g(p') \mid p' \text{ is a player}\}, 0)$ *// the set sent to PULL is dynamic*
)

3.2 Analysis

We now analyze the main algorithm. Fix a specific set of players P with identical preference vector v_P. Below, we first do some straightforward accounting, and then analyze the instance of the basic algorithm that runs with the "correct" α value. We show that after $\tilde{O}(n)$ work in that instance, at least one player in P holds v_P in its output vector. We show that after this point, only $\tilde{O}(m)$ more work in total is needed until that output reaches all other players in P.

We start with some necessary notation. Fix an arbitrary schedule S. Define $T_P = 32In\log^2 n = \tilde{O}(n)$, and let S_0 be the shortest prefix of S that contains T_P probes by players in P. We denote $T_0 = |S_0|$. Let $\alpha_0 = T_P/T_0$. We assume that $\alpha_0 \geq 2^{-I}$. Finally, define $T_1 = T_0/2I$. As immediate corollaries of Theorem 3, we have the following.

Lemma 2. *With high probability, each instance of the basic algorithm gets $T_1(1+o(1))$ probes in S_0, of which an $\alpha_0(1 + o(1))$ fraction are executed by players in P.*

Lemma 3. *Consider an instance $A = \text{BASIC}(\alpha)$ run by the main algorithm. The number of probes executed at a given node of A in S_0 is, with high probability, $\frac{2T_1}{\alpha n}(1+o(1))$, of which an $\alpha_0(1 + o(1))$ fraction are done by players of P.*

Define $\alpha_1 = \frac{4nI\log n}{T_P}\alpha_0 = \frac{\alpha_0}{8\log n}$, and let $i_0 = \lceil \log 1/\alpha_1 \rceil$. Henceforth, we focus on the specific task executing $\text{BASIC}(2^{-i_0})$. Let us call this task A_{i_0}. We will use the following concept.

- A leaf ℓ is said to be *done at time* t if at least $\log n$ jobs were completed by players of P in ℓ in the time interval $(0, t]$.
- An internal node v at height $h > 0$ is said to be *done at time* t if there exists some time $t' < t$, such that both children of v are done by time t', and at least $\log n$ jobs of v were fully executed by players of P in the time interval $(t', t]$.

Note that *done* is a stable predicate: once a node is done, it is considered done throughout the remainder of the prefix of S containing T_0 probes. The significance of the notion is made apparent in the following key lemma.

Lemma 4. *Consider the execution of A_{i_0}. Suppose a node v is done at time t_0. Then at all times $t_0 \leq t \leq T_0$, at least $\alpha_1/2$ fraction of the vectors in $G(v)$ are the correct grade vectors of players in P for $\text{obj}(v)$.*

Proof: By induction on the height of v. For the base case, suppose that v is a leaf. By Lemma 3, the total number of probes at v at any given time is no more than $\frac{2T_1}{\alpha_1 n}(1 + o(1))$, and since each job contains $\frac{4}{\alpha_1}$ probes, the total number of jobs in a leaf v (and hence the size of $G(v)$) is at most $\frac{T_1}{2n}(1 + o(1))$. Therefore, once the total number of jobs by players of P in v exceeds $\frac{\alpha_1 T_1}{2n} = \frac{4nI \log n}{T_0} \cdot \frac{T_0}{2I} \cdot \frac{1}{2n} = \log n$, the number of vectors in $G(v)$ that are correct for P is at least an $\alpha_1/2$ fraction, as required.

For the induction step, assume that the lemma holds for height $h - 1$ and consider a node v at height h. Let u_1 and u_2 be the children of v. By definition and the induction hypothesis, we have that starting at the time t' when both u_1 and u_2 were done, all jobs at v had the correct vectors of them among their B_1 and B_2 lists (Step 2a of the job algorithm). By the correctness of SELECT_EXACT, each of these jobs will write the correct output in $G(v)$. Next, by Lemma 3, we have that the total number of probes in v is again at most $\frac{2T_1}{\alpha_1 n}(1 + o(1))$, which means that $|G(v)| \leq \frac{T_1}{2n}(1 + o(1))$, because each job at v consists of $4/\alpha_1$ probes. As in the base case, once at least $\frac{\alpha_1 T_1}{2n} = \log n$ jobs are completed at node v after its children are done, the correct vector for the players of P will be in the most popular vectors of v. ∎

The proof of Lemma 4 hints at the main argument of the theorem: we need to show that the nodes in the computation tree become gradually done. The remaining difficulty lies in the asynchrony: Lemma 3 talks about the total number of probes by players in P throughout the execution, while Lemma 4 talks about jobs, and at specific times. However, there is a logarithmic factor between α_0 used in Lemma 3 and α_1 used in Lemma 4; as we show next, this additional freedom, together with a guarantee on the minimum work done by each player, suffice to prove the result.

Lemma 5. *If each player in P executes at least $\frac{256I \log^2 n}{\alpha_0}$ probes, then with high probability, each player in P executes at least $2 \log n$ jobs in instance A_{i_0}.*

Proof: The size of each jobs is $\frac{4}{\alpha_1} = \frac{32 \log n}{\alpha_0}$. The expected number of probes by each player in P is at least $\frac{128 \log^2 n}{\alpha_0}$ in instance A_{i_0}. By Chernoff inequality the probability each player probes less than half of the expectation is at most $\exp(-\Omega(\frac{\log^2 n}{\alpha_0}))$. Since there are at most n players each of them probes, with high probability, at least $\frac{64 \log^2 n}{\alpha_0}$ times, i.e., $2 \log n$ jobs. ∎

Lemma 6. *If the number of probes in A_{i_0} by players in P is $\alpha_0 T_1 \geq 16n \log^2 n$, then at time T_0 the root node is done w.h.p.*

Proof: Consider only work done by players of P during the execution of A_{i_0}. Define time intervals inductively as follows: t_0 is the start of the schedule. Suppose that t_h is defined, for $0 \leq h < H$, where $H = \log \frac{\alpha n}{4}$ is the tree height. Define t_{h+1} to be the first time in which we have $\frac{\alpha_1 n \log n}{2^h}$ completed jobs that were executed at nodes at height h and started after t_h. Let us call these jobs "effective jobs."

To prove the lemma, it suffices to show that we can define these time points up to t_{H+1}, and that $t_{H+1} \leq T_0$: this implies that at time $t_{H+1} \leq T_0$, the root node is done. First, note that a job that starts in the interval $(t_h, t_{h+1}]$ may finish its execution outside that interval. However, for any given $h \geq 0$, a player may start at most one job in $[t_h, t_{h+1}]$ that doesn't finish in that interval. Since by Lemma 5, each player executes at least $2 \log n$ jobs, and since $H \leq \log n$, at least half of the jobs are fully executed within one time interval.

We now prove that $t_{H+1} \leq T_0$. Consider jobs executed within one time interval. In the first interval, half of the jobs are in leaves, so w.h.p., t_1 occurs before $2\alpha_1 n \log n(1 + o(1))$ such jobs are executed. Since the number of effective jobs is halved from one time interval to the next, and since the number of nodes in height h is half the number of nodes in height $h - 1$, in each interval there are at most $2\alpha_1 n \log n(1 + o(1))$ jobs, and t_{H+1} is before $2\alpha_1 H n \log n(1+o(1)) \leq 2\alpha_1 n \log^2 n$ jobs. Since by time T_0 $16n \log^2 n$ probes are executed by players in P, the number of jobs executed within single interval is at least $16n \log^2 n \frac{\alpha_1}{4} \cdot \frac{1}{2} \geq 2\alpha_1 n \log^2 n$, and it follows that $t_{H+1} \leq T_0$.

For any h, the $\frac{\alpha_1 n \log n}{2^h}$ effective jobs are distributed over $\frac{\alpha_1 n}{2^{h+2}}$ nodes. By Chernoff bound each node is associated with at least $\log n$ effective jobs with probability at least $1 - \frac{1}{n^{9/8}}$. As there are $\frac{\alpha_1 n}{2} = O(n/\log n)$ nodes then by time t_{H+1} all nodes in the computational tree are done with high probability.   ∎

By Lemma 2, the schedule for A_{i_0} consists of $\frac{16n \log^2 n}{\alpha_0}$ probes, of which an α_0 fraction are by players in P. Therefore, by Lemmas 6 and 4, by time T_0, the root node of A_{i_0} is done, and at least one player in P has $g(p) = v_p$. Next, we show that the PULL task allows players in P learn this vector in "epidemic" style. The key is that once a player $p \in P$ tests v_P in PULL, that player will eventually assign $g(p) \leftarrow v_P$, and furthermore, p will never change his $g(p)$ value ever again, because it will never find it to be inconsistent with his preferences. As more players assign v_P to their output vector, the probability of a player to choose it in PULL increases.

For the next lemma, call a probe by player $p \in P$ *non-stabilized* if $g(p) \neq v_P$ at the time of the probe.

Lemma 7. *Suppose that the root node of A_{i_0} is done at some point. Then after $O(n \log n)$ additional non-stabilized probes, we have $g(p) = v_P$ for all $p \in P$.*

Proof Sketch: Once A_{i_0} is done, at least one player $p_0 \in P$ executed JOB(root) when c_1(root) and c_2(root) are already done, and after that job is done we have $g(p_0) = v_P$. Let σ_l, for $l > 0$, be a random variable whose value is the number of non-stabilized probes done starting at the time that the lth player in P assigns v_P as its output, and ending at the time that the $(l + 1)$st such player assigned v_P as its output.

Consider σ_l: With probability $1/2$, the algorithm chooses a random player and examines its opinion. As there are l players holding v_P as their output, the probability of each probe to produce the right vector is $\frac{l}{2n}$, and hence the expected value of σ_l is $2n/l$. It follows that after expected $\sum_{l=1}^{|P|-1} \frac{2n}{l} < 2n \ln |P|$ non-stabilized probes, all $|P|$ players will have v_P as their output. Using standard arguments, it can also be shown that $O(n \log n)$ such probes are also sufficient w.h.p.   ∎

We can now conclude with the following theorem, which combines the previous results to show the full picture: if enough probes are done by players with the same preference vector, their output stabilizes on their true preference vector.

Theorem 4. *Let S be a schedule such that at least α fraction of the probes are by players with exactly the same preference vector v_P running the algorithm for exact reconstruction. Then with high probability, after total work of $(1 + \frac{8}{\alpha})33nI \log^2 n$, the output of all these players has stabilized on the correct value, where $I \geq \log(1/\alpha)$.*

Proof: Let P be the players with the same preference vector. Assume there are at least $(1 + \frac{8}{\alpha})33nI \log^2 n$ probes by players in P in S.

Consider the prefix T of the schedule in which $\frac{32 + 264/\alpha}{33 + 264/\alpha}\alpha|S| > (32 + \frac{264}{\alpha})nI \log^2 n$ probes are by players in P. The fraction of probes by players in P in this prefix is $\alpha' > \frac{32}{33}\alpha$. The number of players in P that don't make at least $\frac{256I \log^2 n}{\alpha'} < \frac{264I \log^2 n}{\alpha}$ probes is at most $|P| \leq n$. Therefore, at least $32nI \log^2 n$ probes are made by players who probe at least $\frac{256 \log^3 n}{\alpha'}$ times each. By Lemmas 6 and 4, the root node at A_{i_0} is done and at least one player in P has its preference vector as its opinion at the end of the prefix T. By Lemma 7, after at most $n \log n$ additional non-stabilized probes, all players in P learn their preference vector.   ∎

Theorem 1 is an immediate corollary of Theorem 4.

4 Approximate Preference Reconstruction

In Section 3 we presented an algorithm for reconstructing the preference vectors without any error (w.h.p.). One drawback of that algorithm was that collaboration took place only among players with identical preferences. In many cases, however, the number of players that share the exact same preferences may be small. In this section we extend on the results of Section 3 and present an asynchronous algorithm that allows players to use recommendations of any player whose preference vector differs from their own in no more than D objects, for some given parameter D. The output of the algorithm, at each player, may contain $O(D)$ errors. The total work done by the players of the similar preferences in our algorithm is $\tilde{O}\left(nD^{5/2}\right)$. The analysis of the algorithm is omitted from this extended abstract. For simplicity, we assume $D = O(\log n)$ here.

4.1 Algorithm

The asynchronous algorithm is based on the synchronous algorithm SMALL presented in [1]. The algorithm works as follows. Let P be set of players and $D \geq 0$ be such that $\text{dist}(v(p), v(p')) \leq D$ for any $p, p' \in P$. As in the exact reconstruction case, we first assume that the algorithm is given the density parameter α. Conceptually, the algorithm consists of three phases. In the first phase, the object set O is partitioned into $s = O(D^{3/2})$ random parts denoted $\{O_j\}_{j=1}^s$, and Algorithm BASIC(α) is run by all players on each O_j. Algorithm BASIC is guaranteed to succeed only if there are sufficiently many probes by players whose preferences on the objects of O_j are identical.

Fortunately, it can be shown that with probability at least $\frac{1}{2}$, a random partition of O will have, in each part, "many" players in P fully agreeing. Therefore, if K independent random partitions of O are used, then one of them will succeed in all parts with probability at least $1 - 2^{-K}$.

Typically, a player in P shares his exact preferences with sufficiently many other players in P and have correct output for BASIC(α) in some of the O_j parts, but in other parts, his result of BASIC(α) is unpredictable. To remedy this problem, in the second phase of the Algorithm, players adopt as their output, for each object part O_j, the closest of the most popular output vectors of Algorithm BASIC(α). In the full paper we show that concatenating these s partial vectors by a player in P results in a preference vector that contains no more than $5D$ errors.

Due to asynchrony, it may be the case that only a single player in P arrives at the correct vector in the second phase. The third phase of the algorithm disseminates this vector to other players using the PULL mechanism. This phase may introduce D more errors, so that the final output may contain up to $6D$ errors.

Asynchrony also implies that sequential execution of the phases cannot be guaranteed. We solve this problem by running all sequential programs in parallel, using the rmux construct. This ensures that at the price of polylogarithmic blowup in the number of probes, once the output of one phase has stabilized, it can be used as input to the next phase.

Finally, the assumption of a given parameter α is lifted by running a logarithmic number of possible α values in parallel. See the complete algorithm below.

Let $s = 100D^{3/2}$. The algorithm uses $K = O(\log n)$ random partitions of O: for $1 \leq k \leq K$, the kth partition is $O = O_1^k \cup O_2^k \cup \ldots \cup O_s^k$. The top level algorithm below uses the task PASTE$_{i,k}$, which pastes together all s components of the output corresponding to $\alpha = 2^{-i}$ in the kth partition.

Algorithm APPROX(D)

```
rmux(
        1/3: rmux(1/(K·s·I) : BASIC(2⁻ⁱ) on Oⱼᵏ, for randomly chosen 1 ≤ i ≤ I,
                             1 ≤ j ≤ s, 1 ≤ k ≤ K),
        1/3: rmux(1/(K·I) : PASTEᵢ,ₖ for randomly chosen 1 ≤ i ≤ I, 1 ≤ k ≤ K),
        1/3: rmux(PULL({g(p') | p' is a player}, 6D)
        )
```

Let $A_j^{i,k}$ be the k execution of the basic algorithm for $\alpha = 2^{-i}$ on the object set O_j^k, let the output of each such execution at given time be the 2^{i+1} most popular vectors in the root. Each player p maintains an output $g(p)$ which changes over time. Note this $g(p)$ isn't updated by the task JOB(root) as in the algorithm for exact reconstruction.

Operator PASTE : Algorithm PASTE, specified below, gets as input a partition index k, an α value 2^{-i} (repersented by i), and continuously updates the player's output vector for this case.

PASTE$_{i,k}$

Repeat forever:

(1) For each $j \in \{1, \ldots, s\}$:

Let V be the 2^{i+1} most popular vectors in $G(\text{root})$ of $A_j^{i,k}$

$u_j^{i,k} \leftarrow \text{SELECT}(V, D)$

(2) Let u be the concatenation of $u_j^{i,k}$ over all j.

Execute PULL$(\{u, g(p)\}, 5D)$.

As the output of $A_j^{i,k}$ might change over time, it is read once at the start of the procedure and frozen throughout the execution. Note that each execution of this operator takes $O(sD2^{i+1})$ probes.

The performance of the algorithm is summarized in the theorem below (proof omitted). Theorem 2 is an immediate corollary of Theorem 5 below.

Theorem 5. *Let P be a set of players such that* $\text{dist}(p, p') \leq D$ *for any* $p, p' \in P$. *Let* S *be a schedule with a prefix of length* $T = \Omega(\frac{nD^{5/2}I \log^3 n}{\alpha^2})$, *of which at least fraction* α *of the probes are by players of P executing Algorithm* APPROX. *By the end of the prefix, with high probability, there exists a player* $p_0 \in P$ *with* $\text{dist}(g(p_0), v(p_0)) \leq 5D$. *In* $O(Dn \log n)$ *additional work by players in P with* $\text{dist}(g(p), v(p)) > 6D$, *all these players will have, with high probability,* $\text{dist}(g(p), v(p)) \leq 6D$.

References

1. Alon, N., Awerbuch, B., Azar, Y., Patt-Shamir, B.: Tell me who I am: an interactive recommendation system. In: Proc. 18th Ann. ACM Symp. on Parallelism in Algorithms and Architectures, pp. 1–10. ACM Press, New York (2006)
2. Awerbuch, B., Azar, Y., Lotker, Z., Patt-Shamir, B., Tuttle, M.: Collaborate with strangers to find own preferences. In: SPAA 2005. Proc. 17th ACM Symp. on Parallelism in Algorithms and Architectures, pp. 263–269. ACM Press, New York (2005)
3. Awerbuch, B., Patt-Shamir, B., Peleg, D., Tuttle, M.: Adaptive collaboration in synchronous p2p systems. In: ICDCS 2005. Proc. 25th International Conf. on Distributed Computing Systems, pp. 71–80 (2005)
4. Awerbuch, B., Patt-Shamir, B., Peleg, D., Tuttle, M.: Improved recommendation systems. In: Proc. 16th Ann. ACM-SIAM Symp. on Discrete Algorithms, pp. 1174–1183. ACM Press, New York (2005)
5. Drineas, P., Kerenidis, I., Raghavan, P.: Competitive recommendation systems. In: STOC 2002. Proc. 34th ACM Symp. on Theory of Computing, pp. 82–90. ACM Press, New York (2002)
6. Resnick, P., Iacovou, N., Suchak, M., Bergstrom, P., Riedl, J.: Grouplens: an open architecture for collaborative filtering of netnews. In: CSCW 1994. Proc. 1994 ACM Conf. on Computer Supported Cooperative Work, pp. 175–186. ACM Press, New York (1994)
7. Resnick, P., Varian, H.R.: Recommender systems. Commun. ACM 40(3), 56–58 (1997)
8. Sarwar, B., Karypis, G., Konstan, J., Reidl, J.: Item-based collaborative filtering recommendation algorithms. In: Proc. 10th International Conf. on World Wide Web (WWW), pp. 285–295 (2001)

Brute-Force Determination of Multiprocessor Schedulability for Sets of Sporadic Hard-Deadline Tasks

Theodore P. Baker[1,*] and Michele Cirinei[2]

[1] Florida State University, Tallahassee, FL 32306, USA
baker@cs.fsu.edu
http://www.cs.fsu.edu/~baker
[2] Scuola Superiore Sant'Anna, Pisa, Italy
cirinei@gandalf.sssup.it

Abstract. This report describes a necessary and sufficient test for the schedulability of a set of sporadic hard-deadline tasks on a multiprocessor platform, using any of a variety of scheduling policies including global fixed task-priority and earliest-deadline-first (EDF). The contribution is to establish an upper bound on the computational complexity of this problem, for which no algorithm has yet been described. The compute time and storage complexity of the algorithm, which performs an exhaustive search of a very large state space, make it practical only for tasks sets with very small integer periods. However, as a research tool, it can provide a clearer picture than has been previously available of the real success rates of global preemptive priority scheduling policies and low-complexity sufficient tests of schedulability.

1 Introduction

This report describes a "brute force" algorithm for determining whether a hard-deadline sporadic task system will always be scheduled so as to meet all deadlines, for global preemptive priority scheduling policies on multiprocessor platforms. The algorithm is presented in a generic form, that can easily be applied to earliest-deadline-first, fixed-priority, least-laxity-first, earliest-deadline-zero-laxity, throwforward, and a variety of other scheduling policies.

Symmetric multiprocessor platforms have long been used for high performance real-time systems. Recently, with the introduction of low-cost multi-core microprocessor chips, the range of potential embedded applications of this kind of architecture as expanded rapidly.

The historically dominant approach to scheduling real-time applications on a multiprocessor has been partitioned; that is, to assign each task (statically) to a processor, and then apply a single-processor scheduling technique on each processor. The alternative is global scheduling; that is, to maintain a single queue of ready jobs and assign jobs

---

* This material is based upon work supported in part by the National Science Foundation under Grant No. 0509131, and a DURIP grant from the Army Research Office.

E. Tovar, P. Tsigas, and H. Fouchal (Eds.): OPODIS 2007, LNCS 4878, pp. 62–75, 2007.

from that queue dynamically to processors. Despite greater implementation overhead, the global approach is conceptually appealing in several respects.

Several sufficient tests have been derived for the schedulability of a sporadic task set on a multiprocessor using a given scheduling policy, such as global preemptive scheduling based on fixed task priorities (FTP) or deadlines (EDF) [1,2,3,5,6,7,10,14]. For example, it can be shown that a set of independent periodic tasks with deadline equal to period will not miss any deadlines if it is scheduled by a global EDF policy on m processors, provided the sum of the processor utilizations does not exceed $(m - 1)u_{max} + u_{max}$, where u_{max} is the maximum single-task processor utilization [14,10].

One difficulty in evaluating and comparing the efficacy of such schedulability tests has been distinguishing the causes of failure. That is, when one of these schedulability tests is unable to verify that a particular task set is schedulable there are three possible explanations:

1. The problem is with the task set, which is *not feasible*, *i.e.*, not able to be scheduled by any policy.
2. The problem is with the scheduling policy. The task set is *not schedulable* by the given policy, even though the task set is feasible.
3. The problem is with the test, which is *not able to verify* the fact that the task set is schedulable by the given policy.

To the best of our knowledge there are no previously published accounts of algorithms that can distinguish the above three cases, for global multiprocessor scheduling of sporadic task sets with arbitrary deadlines. The intent of this paper is to take one step toward closing this gap, by providing an algorithm that can distinguish case 2 from case 3.

The algorithm presented here is a simple one, based on modeling the arrival and scheduling processes of a sporadic task set as a finite-state system, and enumerating the reachable states. A task set is schedulable if and only if no missed-deadline state is enumerated. Although the computational complexity of this state enumeration process is too high to be practical for most real task systems, it still interesting, for the following reasons:

1. At least one prior publication [6] has incorrectly asserted that this problem can be solved by a simpler algorithm, based on the presumption that the worst-case scenario occurs when all tasks have jobs that arrive periodically, starting at time zero.
2. To the best of our knowledge, no other correct algorithm for this problem has yet been described.
3. This algorithm has proven to be useful as a research tool, as a baseline for evaluating the degree to which faster, but only sufficient, tests of schedulability fail to identify schedulable task systems, and for discovering interesting small examples of schedulable and unschedulable task sets.
4. Exposure of this algorithm as the most efficient one known for the problem may stimulate research into improved algorithms.

Section 2 reviews the formal model of sporadic task systems, and what it means for a task system to be schedulable. Section 3 describes a general abstract model of system states, and Sections 4 and 5 explain how to compute the state transitions in the model. Section 6 shows how this model fits several well known global multiprocessor scheduling policies. Section 7 describes a generic brute-force schedulability testing algorithm, based on a combination of depth-first and breadth-first search of the abstract system state graph. Section 8 provides a coarse estimate of the worst-case time and storage requirements of the brute-force algorithm. Section 10 summarizes, and indicates the direction further research on this algorithm is headed.

2   Sporadic Task Scheduling

A *sporadic task* $\tau_i = (e_i, d_i, p_i)$ generates a potentially infinite sequence of *jobs*, characterized by a *maximum (worst case) compute time requirement* e_i, a maximum response time (relative deadline) d_i , and a *minimum inter-arrival time* (period) p_i. It is assumed that $e_i \leq \min(d_i, p_i)$, since otherwise a task would be trivially infeasible. A *sporadic task system* τ is a set of sporadic tasks $\{\tau_1, \tau_2, \ldots, \tau_n\}$.

An *arrival time sequence* a_i for a sporadic task τ_i is a finite or infinite sequence of times $a_{i,1} < a_{i,2} < \cdots$ such that $a_{i,j+1} - a_{i,j} \geq p_i$, for $j = 1, 2, \ldots$. An *arrival time assignment* r for a task set is a mapping of arrival time sequences a_i to tasks τ_i, one for each of the tasks in τ. An arrival time assignment and a task set define a set of jobs.

An m-processor *schedule* for a set of jobs is a partial mapping of time instants and processors to jobs. It specifies the job, if any, that is scheduled on each processor at each time instant. For consistency, a schedule is required not to assign more than one processor to a job, and not to assign a processor to a job before the job's arrival time or after the job completes. For a job arriving at time a, the *accumulated compute time* at time b is the number of time units in the interval $[a, b)$ for which the job is assigned to a processor, and the *remaining compute time* is the difference between the total compute time and the accumulated compute time. A job is *backlogged* if it has nonzero remaining compute time. The *completion time* of a job is the first instant at which the remaining compute time reaches zero. The *response time* of a job is the elapsed time between the job's arrival time and its completion time. A job misses its absolute deadline if the response time exceeds its relative deadline.

The *laxity* (sometimes also known as slack time) of a job at any instant in time prior to its absolute deadline is the amount of time that the job can wait, not executing, and still be able to complete by its deadline. At any time t, if job J has remaining compute time e and absolute deadline d, its laxity is $\ell^J(t) \stackrel{\text{def}}{=} d - e$.

The jobs of each task are required to be executed sequentially. That is the earliest start time of a job is the maximum of its arrival time and the completion time of the preceding job of the same task. This earliest start time is also called the *ready time* of the job.

The decision algorithm described here is restricted to integer values for task periods, compute times, and deadlines. This is not a serious conceptual restriction, since in any actual system time is not infinitely divisible; the times of event occurrences and durations between them cannot be determined more precisely than one tick of the systems most precise clock. However, it is a practical restriction, since the complexity of the algorithm grows exponentially with the number of clock ticks in the task periods, compute times, and deadlines, as will be explained later. The notation $[a, b)$ is used for time intervals, as a reminder that the interval includes all of the time unit starting at a but does not include the time unit starting at b. These conventions allow avoid potential confusion around end-points and prevent impractical schedulability results that rely on being able to slice time at arbitrary points. They also permit exhaustive testing of schedulability, by considering all time values in a given range.

3   The Abstract State Model

Determining whether a sporadic task system τ can miss any deadlines if scheduled according to a given algorithm can be viewed as a reachability problem in a finite non-deterministic state transition graph. Given a start state in which no jobs have yet arrived, the problem is to determine whether the system can reach a state that represents a scheduling failure. A task set is schedulable if-and-only-if there is no sequence of valid transitions from the system start state to a failure state.

Ha and Liu [11] defined the concept of predictable scheduling policy, and showed that for all preemptive global fixed-task-priority and fixed-job-priority scheduling policies are predictable. As a consequence, for such scheduling policies, schedulability tests need only consider the case where each job's compute time requirement is equal to the worst-case compute time requirement of its generating task.

In order to reduce the time and storage complexity of determining schedulability, it is desirable to express the system state as simply as possible, and to eliminate from consideration as many states as possible.

Given a task system τ, an *abstract system state* S is defined to be an n-tuple of the form

$$((nat(S_1), rct(S_1)), \ldots, (nat(S_n), rct(S_n)))$$

The value $nat(S_i)$ denotes the earliest *next arrival time* for task τ_i, relative to the current instant, and the value $rct(S_i)$ denotes the *remaining compute time* of the job of τ_i that is currently contending for processor time.

If $rct(S_i)$ is zero there is no job of τ_i contending for processor time. That is, all the jobs of τ_i that have arrived so far have been completed. In this case the earliest time the next job of τ_i can arrive is $nat(S_i)$ time units from the present instant. That value cannot be negative, and it is zero only if a job of τ_i can arrive immediately.

If $rct(S_i)$ is positive, there is a job J of τ_i contending for processor time and J needs $rct(S_i)$ units of processor time to complete. In this case, $nat(S_i)$ is the offset in time, relative to the current instant, of earliest time that the next job of τ_i after J can arrive. If the value is negative, the earliest possible arrival time of the next job of τ_i after J is $nat(S_i)$ time units in the past.

It follows that the an abstract system state S determines the following information for each task in the system:

– Task τ_i has a ready job if-and-only-if $rct(S_i) > 0$.
– The remaining compute time of the current ready job of τ_i is $rct(S_i)$.
– The time to the arrival of the next job after the current ready job of τ_i is $nat(S_i)$.
– The *time to the next deadline* of the current ready job of task τ_i is

$$ttd(S_i) = nat(S_i) - (p_i - d_i) \tag{1}$$

– The *laxity* of the current ready job of τ_i is

$$laxity(S_i) = ttd(S_i) - rct(S_i) \tag{2}$$

There are two kinds of state transitions: (1) The passage of one instant of time is modeled by a *clock-tick* state transition, which is deterministic. (2) A job becoming ready is modeled by a *ready* state transition. Ready transitions are non-deterministic, because the sporadic task model allows a job to arrive at any time that is at least one period after the arrival time of the preceding job in the same task.

An abstract system state is *reachable* if it is reachable from the start state via a finite sequence of clock-tick and ready transitions.

The system *start state* is defined to be $((0,0),\ldots,(0,0))$. That is the state in which there are no tasks contending for processor time and all tasks are eligible to arrive.

An abstract state is a *failure state* if there is some task τ_i for which $laxity(S_i) < 0$, that is, if the remaining time to deadline is less than the remaining compute time of the current ready job of τ_i.

It follows from the construction of the model that a task system is schedulable to meet deadlines if-and-only-if no failure state is reachable from the start state. This can be tested using any finite graph reachability algorithm.

4   Clock-Tick Transitions

The clock-tick successor of a state S depends on the set $run(S)$ of tasks that the scheduling policy chooses to execute in the next instant. We assume that $run(S)$ includes only tasks τ_i that need to execute (that is, $rct(S_i) > 0$) and the number of tasks in $run(S)$ does not exceed the number of available processors.

The clock-tick successor $S' = Next(S)$ of any abstract system state S is computable as follows:

$$rct(S_i') \stackrel{\text{def}}{=} \begin{cases} rct(S_i) & \text{if } \tau_i \notin run(S) \\ rct(S_i) - 1 & \text{if } \tau_i \in run(S) \end{cases}$$

$$nat(S_i') \stackrel{\text{def}}{=} \begin{cases} \max(0, nat(S_i) - 1) & \text{if } rct(S_i) = 0 \\ nat(S_i) - 1 & \text{if } rct(S_i) > 0 \end{cases}$$

The reasoning behind the computation of $rct(S_i')$ is simple. S' represents a state that is one time unit further into the future than S, so on the transition from S to S' the remaining compute time is reduced by one time unit for those jobs that are scheduled to execute, and is unchanged for those jobs that are not scheduled to execute.

The reasoning behind the computation of $nat(S_i')$ involves two cases, based on whether there is a job of τ_i contending for processor time in S:
(i) If $rct(S_i) = 0$ then there is no job of τ_i contending for processor time, and the earliest time a job of τ_i can arrive is $nat(S_i)$ time units after S. If $nat(S_i) \leq 0$ the inter-arrival constraint permitted a job of τ_i to arrive at the time of S, but it did not arrive and so can still arrive at the time of S'; therefore $nat(S_i') = 0$. Otherwise, $nat(S_i) > 0$ and the time to next arrival in S' should be one time unit shorter than in S, so $nat(S_i') = nat(S_i) - 1$.

(ii) If $rct(S_i) > 0$ then there is a job J of τ_i contending for processor time in S, and if $d_i > p_i$, there may be one or more other backlogged jobs of τ_i that have arrived but are waiting for J to complete. Let J' be the next job of τ_i to arrive after J. The earliest time that J' could arrive is $nat(S_i)$ (positive or negative) time units from the time of S. Since S' represents a state one time unit later than S, the adjustment for the passage of one unit of time is $nat(S_i') = nat(S_i') - 1$.

At first it might seem that the value of $nat(S_i')$ could decrease without bound in case (ii) if $d_i > p_i$. That is not possible, so long as we stop as soon as we find a failure state. The deadline constraint provides a lower bound on how far negative $nat(S_i')$ can go without a job missing a deadline. That is, if S is a non-failure state and J has non-zero remaining compute time then the current time is certainly before J's deadline, the deadline of J' is at least p_i units in the future, and J' cannot arrive earlier than $\min(d_i - p_i, 0) + 1$ time units before S'. Therefore, the number of reachable non-failure states is finite.

5   Ready Transitions

The event of a new job becoming ready is modeled by a *ready* state transition. A job of a sporadic task may become ready any time that the preceding job of τ_i has completed execution and at least p_i time has elapsed since the preceding job arrived. In other words, a ready transition from state S for task τ_i is possible if-and-only-if $rct(S_i) = 0$ and $nat(S_i) \leq 0$.

For each task τ_i and each state S such that $rct(S_i) = 0$ and $nat(S_i) \leq 0$, the states S' to which a τ_i-*ready transition* is possible are all those that differ from S only in the values of $rct(S_i')$ and $nat(S_i')$ and satisfy the following:

$$rct(S_i') = e_i, \quad nat(S_i) + p_i \leq nat(S_i') \leq p_i$$

The reasoning is that a new job J' of τ_i does not become ready until the current job J of τ_i has been completed (indicated by $rct(S_i) = 0$), and the exact arrival time of J' does not matter until that instant. Then, the arrival time of J' can be chosen (non-deterministically) to be any instant from the present back to $nat(S_i')$ clock ticks into the past. It follows that the earliest arrival time of the next job of τ_i after J', relative to the present, can be any value between $nat(S_i) + p_i$ and p_i.

Ready transitions are non-deterministic, and are viewed as taking no time. Therefore, several of them may take place between one time instant and the next. $Ready(S)$ is the set of all states that can be reached by a sequence of one or more ready transitions from state S.

6   Specific Scheduling Policies

The basic abstract state model described above contains enough information to support the computation of $run(S)$ for several scheduling policies, including the following global multiprocessor scheduling policies:

Fixed task priority: Assuming the tasks are ordered by decreasing priority, choose the lowest-numbered tasks.

Shortest remaining-processing first: Choose tasks with the smallest nonzero values of $rct(S_i)$.

Earliest deadline first (EDF): Choose tasks with the shortest time to next deadline. The time to next deadline of each task can be computed using equation (1).

Least laxity first (LLF): Choose tasks with the smallest laxities. The laxity of each task can be computed using equation (2).

Throwforward [12]: Choose up to m tasks by the following algorithm: (i) Choose the task with shortest $ttd(S_i)$. Let $t \stackrel{\text{def}}{=} ttd(S_i)$ for this task. (ii) Choose the tasks with positive throwforward on the above task, where the throwforward $TF(S_i)$ of task τ_i in state S is defined as follows:

$$TF(S_i) \stackrel{\text{def}}{=} t - (ttd(S_i) - rct(S_i))$$

Our state model can also be applied to some hybrids of the above algorithms, including earliest-deadline zero-laxity (EDZL) and ED/LL [8]. EDZL was shown to be predictable in [13] and [9], and the proof in [9] applies also to ED/LL. Some more algorithms can also be supported, by adding information to the state. For example, to resolve priority ties in favor of the task that last executed on a given processor, it is sufficient to add one bit per task, indicating whether the task executed in the preceding time instant.

7   Generic Algorithm

It is clear that the set of all states reachable from the start state can be enumerated by breadth-first or depth-first search. Suppose the state set $Known$ starts out containing just the start state. The objective of the algorithm is to compute the closure of this set under all legal clock-tick and ready transitions, by iteratively *visiting* each member of the set, where visiting a state S involves: (a) determining the unique clock-tick successor, if there is one; (b) determining the set of states $Ready(S)$, including one state for each possible combination of new ready jobs. Each new state encountered in step (a) or step (b) is then added to the set of reachable states, $Known$. Thus, at any point in time the set $Known$ includes both all the states that have been visited and some unvisited states whose predecessors have been visited.

To keep track of which states have been visited, the set $Unvisited$ is introduced, which initially is the same as $Known$. When a new state is found, it is added to both $Known$ and $Unvisited$. States to visit are chosen from $Unvisited$, and they are removed once they have been visited. Depending on whether $Unvisited$ is organized as a stack or a queue, this results in either a depth-first or a breadth-first enumeration of reachable states. The algorithm terminates when either a failure state is found or there are no remaining states left in $Unvisited$.

```
BRUTE(τ)
 1   S ← ((0,0), ..., (0,0))
 2   Unvisited ← {S} ∪ Ready(S)
 3   Known ← Unvisited
 4   while Unvisited ≠ ∅ do {
 5      choose S ∈ Unvisited
 6      Unvisited ← Unvisited −{S}
 7      repeat
 8         if ∃i laxity(S, τᵢ) < 0 then return 0                    ▷ failure
 9         S ← Next(S)
10         if S ∉ Known then {
11            Known ← Known ∪ {S}
12            for S' ∈ Ready(S) do
13               if S' ∉ Known then {
14                  Known ← Known ∪ {S'}
15                  Unvisited ← Unvisited ∪ {S'}
16               }
17         } else  S ← undefined
18      until S = undefined
19   }
20   return 1                                                      ▷ success
```

Fig. 1. Pseudo-code for brute-force schedulability test

The algorithm BRUTE, whose pseudo-code is given in Figure 1, differs from the above abstract description by taking the following two shortcuts.

(i) Since there is a most one state that can be reached by clock-tick transition from any given state, the step of inserting clock-tick successors into *Unvisited* is skipped, and the clock-tick successor is visited immediately after its clock-tick predecessor. In this way, the algorithm proceeds depth-first along the (deterministic) clock-tick transitions, and queues up in *Unvisited* all the unknown states that can be entered via (non-deterministic) ready transitions from states encountered along the depth-first path. When the algorithm reaches a state from which no further clock-tick transitions are possible, it backtracks to the next unvisited state.

(ii) Since the set *Ready(S)* is closed under ready transitions, there is no need to enumerate further ready transitions from states in *Ready(S)*. Therefore, step (b) of visitation is skipped for states that are added via step (b) of visitation.

Note that the chain of states S' enumerated by the depth-first repeat-until loop at line (7) is completely determined by the state S chosen at line (5). There is a possibility that the chains of states for two different values of S may converge to a common state, after which the two chains will be the same. Such repetition of states entered on a clock-tick transition will be detected at line (10), terminating the repeat-until loop early via line (17) if S' is found in *Known*. This avoids re-traversal of convergent chains, and limits the aggregate number of iterations of the repeat-until loop (summed over all iterations of the while-loop) to one iteration per state reachable by a clock-tick transition.

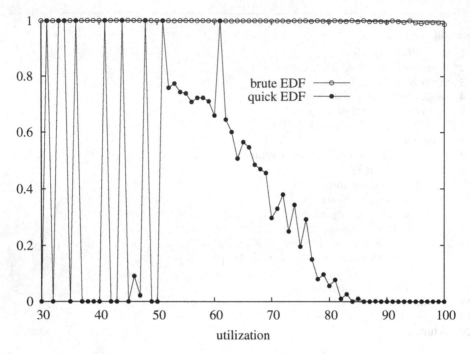

Fig. 2. Success of quick versus brute-force tests for global EDF scheduling, for task sets with integer periods in the range $1 \ldots 5$ and unconstrained deadlines

Algorithm *Brute* is just one of several state enumeration algorithms that would work. The combination of depth-first search for clock-tick transitions and breadth-first search for ready transitions was chosen because it seemed to result in failures being detected earlier, on the average, than with pure breadth-first or depth-first search.

8   Computational Complexity

It is clear that algorithm *Brute* visits each node and each edge of the state graph at most once, so the worst-case computation complexity can be bounded by counting the number of possible states.

Theorem 1. *The worst-case complexity of deciding schedulability on an abstract system-state graph for a task system τ of n tasks is $\mathcal{O}(N \cdot (1 + 2^n))$, and N is an upper bound on the number of system states, where*

$$N = \prod_{i=1}^{n} ((e_i + 1)(\min(0, d_i - p_i) + p_i + 1)) \tag{3}$$

Proof

Clearly, the range of values for $rct(S_i)$ is in the range $0 \ldots e_i$. From the definition of $nat(S_i)$ and the reasoning in the last paragraph of Section 4, it is clear that the range of

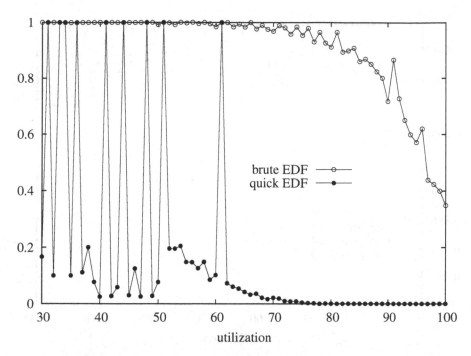

Fig. 3. Success of quick versus brute-force tests for global EDF scheduling, for task sets with integer periods in the range $1 \ldots 5$ and constrained deadlines

values for $nat(S_i)$ is in the range $\min(0, d_i - p_i) + 1 \ldots p_i$. Therefore, an upper bound on the number of nodes in the state graph is the value N given in (3).

The number of edges per node is at most $1 + 2^n$; that is, one for the clock-tick transition and at most 2^n for the various combinations of possible ready transitions. Therefore, the number of edges is grossly bounded by

$$E \leq N \times (1 + 2^n) \qquad (4)$$

The theorem follows. □

Theorem 1 gives an upper bound on the number of iterations of the innermost loop of algorithm BRUTE. The primitive operations on the set *Known* can be implemented in average-case $\mathcal{O}(n)$ time (to compare the n elements of a state) using a hash table, and the primitive operations on the set *Unvisited* can be implemented in time $\mathcal{O}(n)$ (to copy new states) using a stack. It follows that the worst-case complexity of the algorithm is at most $\mathcal{O}(n \cdot N \cdot (1 + 2^n))$, where N is the upper bound on the number of states derived in Theorem 1.

Assuming that e_i and p_i fit into a standard integer-sized word of memory, the storage size of one state is $\mathcal{O}(n)$ words, and so an upper bound on the storage complexity of the algorithm is $\mathcal{O}(n \cdot N)$,

These bounds grows very quickly, both with the number of tasks and the sizes of the task periods and deadlines. On the other hand, the bound is based on counting the entire domain of all possible states, and over-bounding the number of state transitions,

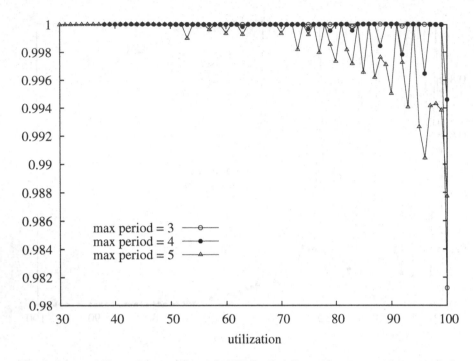

Fig. 4. Success of brute-force test for global EDF scheduling with respect to time granularity

whereas the algorithm considers only reachable states and terminates soon as it finds a failure state. Therefore, the actual numbers of states and transitions considered by the algorithm will be less than the upper bound.

9   Performance

We have implemented and tested algorithm BRUTE for all the specific scheduling policies mentioned as examples in Section 6. Because of the large storage and execution time requirements (especially storage), we have only been able to test it on small task sets. Nevertheless, the results are interesting. Due to the page limit of this conference, only the results of one experiment are provided here.

The experiments whose results are shown in Figures 2 through 5 are for global EDF scheduling of pseudo-randomly generated task sets, on two processors. The periods (p_i) are uniformly distributed in the range $1 \ldots p_{\max}$, for $p_{\max}$ in the range $3 \ldots 6$. (We ran out of memory for $p_{\max} = 6$.) The utilizations $(u_i = e_i/p_i)$ are exponentially distributed with mean 0.35. The deadlines (d_i) are uniformly distributed in the range $[u_i p_i, p_i]$ (constrained deadlines), or the range $[u_i p_i, 4 * p_i]$ (unconstrained deadlines).

Duplicate task sets were discarded, as were task sets that could be obtained from other task sets by re-ordering the tasks or scaling all the task parameters by an integer factor. In addition, task sets that were trivially schedulable by global EDF because $n \leq m$ or $\sum_{i=1}^{n} e_i / \min(d_i, p_i) \leq 1$, or obviously unschedulable by any algorithm because

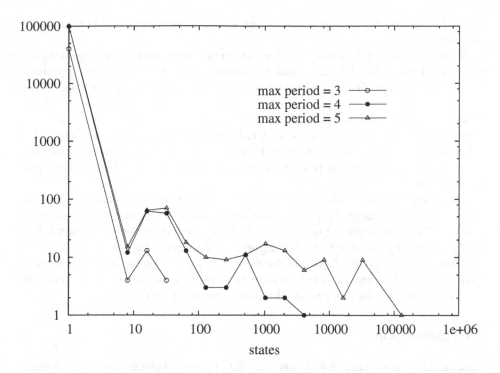

Fig. 5. Number of states examined by brute-force EDF test

maxmin load $> m$ [4] were also discarded. The experiment was run on 100,000 task sets that passed this initial screening.

The following tests were applied to each task set:

- Quick EDF: The sufficient schedulability test for global EDF scheduling of Bertogna, Cirinei, and Lipari[6] and the density test $\sum_{i=1}^{N} \frac{c_i}{\min\{d_i, T_i\}} \leq m$, (also described in [6]) were computed. Since task sets that passed either of these quick tests are schedulable, they were not subjected to the brute force test.
- Brute EDF: Algorithm BRUTE for global EDF scheduling was applied to the remaining task sets.

Figure 2 is a normalized histogram in which the X axis corresponds to a total processor utilization value (the value 100 corresponding to both of the two processors being fully utilized) and the Y axis corresponds to the ratio of the number of task sets that could be shown to be schedulable to the number of task sets tested (the value one corresponding to every task set being schedulable), for the utilization range $[X, X + 0.01)$. A Y-value of 1.0 indicates that all task sets were verified as being schedulable. The jaggedness of the graph is due primarily to the small range of integer values $(0 \ldots 5)$ permitted for periods and execution times, which produces only a small number of possible utilization values and makes some values more probable than others. The jaggedness is further exaggerated by the small sample size. This is especially apparent at utilization values below 50 percent, because very few such task sets passed through the filter for trivially schedulable test cases.

It can be seen that the quick EDF tests are rather pessimistic, especially at higher utilization levels. The EDF performance, according to the brute force test, appears to be near 100 percent. That may seem suspiciously good, considering that some of the task sets tested might be infeasible (not schedulable by EDF or any other algorithm). Part of the explanation is that rule for choosing unconstrained deadlines is strongly biased toward post-period deadlines. Such task sets tend to be feasible, and to be EDF-schedulable. The performance of global EDF was much worse on other experiments, shown in Figure 3, where the task deadlines were constrained to be less than or equal to the periods.

Part of the explanation also is that task sets with smaller integer periods tend to be more readily schedulable at high utilization levels than task sets with a larger range of periods. This is apparent in Figure 4, which shows the distribution of the number of states explored by the brute-force EDF algorithm for several values of p_{max}.

Figure 5 shows the distribution of the number of states explored by the brute-force EDF algorithm This makes it clear why the experiments were limited to task sets with very small integer values for periods, deadlines, and execution times.

10 Conclusion

Schedulability of sporadic task systems on a set of identical processors can be decided in finite time for several global preemptive priority-based scheduling policies, using a generic brute-force enumerative algorithm. Gross upper bounds have been derived for the time and storage complexity of this approach.

At least one prior publication has incorrectly asserted that schedulability of sporadic task systems under global EDF scheduling can be decided using a simpler algorithm, based on simulating execution when all tasks have jobs that arrive periodically, starting at time zero. To the best of our knowledge, ours is the first proposal of a correct algorithm for this problem. Moreover, it also applies to a variety of other global scheduling policies.

The algorithm has been implemented and tested on a variety of task sets, for several different scheduling policies. Exponential growth in the running time and storage, especially storage, limit the algorithm to small task sets. Nevertheless, it has proven to be useful as a research tool, for finding examples of task sets that are schedulable by one method and not by another, and in providing insight into the degree to which more efficient but only sufficient tests of schedulability err in the direction of conservatism.

We hope that, by publishing this simple brute-force algorithm, we may establish a base-line and stimulate further research into this important class of scheduling problems.

Acknowledgment

The authors are grateful to the anonymous referee who pointed out that the algorithm BRUTE is not limited to work-conserving scheduling policies.

References

1. Andersson, B., Baruah, S., Jonsson, J.: Static-priority scheduling on multiprocessors. In: Proc. 22nd IEEE Real-Time Systems Symposium, London, UK, pp. 193–202 (2001)
2. Baker, T.P.: An analysis of EDF scheduling on a multiprocessor. IEEE Trans. on Parallel and Distributed Systems 15(8), 760–768 (2005)
3. Baker, T.P.: An analysis of fixed-priority scheduling on a multiprocessor. Real Time Systems (2005)
4. Baker, T.P., Cirinei, M.: A necessary and sometimes sufficient condition for the feasibility of sets of sporadic hard-deadline tasks. In: Proc. 27th IEEE Real-Time Systems Symposium, Rio de Janeiro, Brazil, IEEE Computer Society Press, Los Alamitos (2006)
5. Baker, T.P., Fisher, N., Baruah, S.: Algorithms for determining the load of a sporadic task system. Technical Report TR-051201, Department of Computer Science, Florida State University, Tallahassee, FL (December 2005)
6. Bemrtogna, M., Cirinei, M., Lipari, G.: Improved schedulability analysis of EDF on multiprocessor platforms. In: Proc. 17th Euromicro Conference on Real-Time Systems, Palma de Mallorca, Spain, pp. 209–218 (July 2005)
7. Bertogna, M., Cirinei, M., Lipari, G.: New schedulability tests for real-time task sets scheduled by deadline monotonic on multiprocessors. In: Proc. 9th International Conf. on Principles of Distributed Systems, Pisa, Italy (December 2005)
8. Cho, S., Lee, S.-K., Han, A., Lin, K.-J.: Efficient real-time scheduling algorithms for multiprocessor systems. IEICE Trans. Communications E85-B(12), 2859–2867 (December 2002)
9. Cirinei, M., Baker, T.P.: EDZL scheduling analysis. In: Proc. EuroMicro Conference on Real-Time Systems, Pisa, Italy (to appear, July 2007)
10. Goossens, J., Funk, S., Baruah, S.: Priority-driven scheduling of periodic task systems on multiprocessors. Real Time Systems 25(2–3), 187–205 (2003)
11. Ha, R., Liu, J.W.S.: Validating timing constraints in multiprocessor and distributed real-time systems. In: Proc. 14th IEEE International Conf. Distributed Computing Systems, Poznan, Poland, pp. 162–171. IEEE Computer Society Press, Los Alamitos (1994)
12. Johnson, H.H., Maddison, M.S.: Deadline scheduling for a real-time multiprocessor. In: Proc. Eurocomp Conference, pp. 139–153 (1974)
13. Piao, X., Han, S., Kim, H., Park, M., Cho, Y., Cho, S.: Predictability of earliest deadline zero laxity algorithm for multiprocessor real time systems. In: Proc. 9th IEEE International Symposium on Object and Component-Oriented Real-Time Distributed Computing, Gjeongju, Korea, IEEE Computer Society Press, Los Alamitos (April 2006)
14. Srinivasan, A., Baruah, S.: Deadline-based scheduling of periodic task systems on multiprocessors. Information Processing Letters 84, 93–98 (2002)

Byzantine Consensus with Few Synchronous Links

Moumen Hamouma[1], Achour Mostefaoui[2], and Gilles Trédan[2]

[1] Département d'informatique, Université A. Mira, Béjaia 06000, Algeria
moumen.hamouma@univ-bejaia.dz
[2] IRISA, Université de Rennes 1, Campus de Beaulieu, 35042 Rennes, France
{achour,gtredan}@irisa.fr

Abstract. This paper tackles the consensus problem in asynchronous systems prone to byzantine failures. One way to circumvent the FLP impossibility result consists in adding synchrony assumptions (deterministic solution). In the context of crash failures (at most t processes may crash), the weakest partially synchronous system model assumes at least one correct process with outgoing links that eventually permit a bounded transmission delay with at least t neighbors (the set of neighbors may change over time).

Aguilera et al. provided the main result for systems where at most t processes may exhibit a byzantine behavior. They assume a correct process with all its outgoing and incoming links eventually timely. This paper considers a system model with at least one correct process connected with x privileged neighbors with eventually timely outgoing and incoming links. In this system model, a byzantine consensus protocol is proposed. It uses authentication and assumes $x \geq 2t$.

Keywords: Asynchronous distributed system, Byzantine process, Consensus, Distributed algorithm, Eventually timely link, Fault tolerance, Resilience.

1 Introduction

Context and motivation. In a distributed system a process is correct if it meets its specification during the whole execution. A process can, however, experience failures for different reasons (hardware, software, intrusion, etc.). The failure could be a simple crash. In this case, it simply stops its execution (fail-stop process). Otherwise a faulty process can exhibit an arbitrary behavior. Such a process is called *Byzantine*. This bad behavior can be intentional (malicious behavior due to intrusion) or simply the result of a transient fault that altered the local state of the process, thereby modifying its behavior in an unpredictable way. We are interested here in solving agreement problems (more precisely, the *Consensus* problem) in asynchronous distributed systems prone to Byzantine process failures whatever their origin.

In the Consensus problem, each process proposes a value, and the non-faulty processes have to eventually decide (termination property) on the same output value (agreement property) that should be a proposed value (validity property). This problem, whose statement is particularly simple, is fundamental in fault-tolerant distributed computing as it abstracts several basic agreement problems. Unfortunately, the Consensus problem has no deterministic solution in asynchronous distributed systems where even a single process can crash [13] (this is known as the FLP impossibility result). So, to

E. Tovar, P. Tsigas, and H. Fouchal (Eds.): OPODIS 2007, LNCS 4878, pp. 76–89, 2007.

solve Consensus, asynchronous distributed systems have to be enriched with additional power. Synchrony assumptions [12], Common coins [22], randomization [5], and unreliable failure detectors [8] are examples of such additions that make it possible to solve Consensus despite asynchrony and failures. When considering Byzantine processes, the Consensus validity property is stated as: if all correct processes propose the same value v then only v can be decided. Indeed, a Byzantine process may propose a wrong value.

Related work. To allow deterministic solutions to the Consensus problem [12], asynchronous systems need to be enriched with additional synchrony assumptions. In the context of crash failures, this approach has been abstracted in the notion of unreliable failure detectors [8]. A failure detector can be seen as a distributed oracle that gives (possibly incorrect) hints about which processes have crashed so far. Nearly all implementations of failure detectors consider that, eventually, the underlying system behaves in a synchronous way. More precisely, they consider the *partially synchronous system* model [8] which is a generalization of the models proposed in [12]. A partially synchronous system assumes there are bounds on process speeds and message transfer delays, but these bounds are not known and hold only after some finite but unknown time (called *Global Stabilization Time*).

The partially synchronous system model is considered by most of the works on Byzantine Consensus [3,16,7,10,11,17,18,20]. [16] and [10] build a muteness failure detector[1] that is then used to solve the Consensus problem. The Byzantine consensus algorithm proposed in [14] uses directly an eventually perfect muteness failure detector. Paxos-like protocols [6,20] first look for a stable leader before solving consensus or implementing state machine replication. Finally, [11,18] establish lower bounds relating resiliency and (very) fast decision. [11] gives a generic algorithm that can be parametrized (w/wo authentication, fast/very fast decision) by taking into account the maximum number of processes that may crash or have malicious behavior. These two papers divide processes into three categories proposers, acceptors and learners (each process can play different roles).

Other system models have been considered like the Trusted Timely Computing Base TTCB [9]. A TTCB is a special communication channel, also nicknamed *wormhole*, that guarantees timely behavior in an otherwise asynchronous byzantine environment. The idea is that this channel is used only by critical aspects of the application (e.g., a consensus protocol), where most of the system uses a standard asynchronous medium. Similarly to the works presented above, it is assumed that the wormhole allows timely communications between any pair of correct processes.

For a system composed of n partially synchronous processes [12] among which at most t may crash, many models [2,15,19] try to restrict the eventually synchronous property of communication to only a subset of links in contrast to the related works cited above which assume that the whole system is eventually synchronous. In this setting, a link between two processes is said to be timely at time τ if a message sent at time τ is received not later than $\tau + \delta$. The bound δ in not known and holds only after some finite but unknown time τ_{GST} (called *Global Stabilization Time*). A link is called

---

[1] A muteness failure detector is an oracle that allows to distinguish between a silent Byzantine process and a correct process that is slow or with which communication is slow.

eventually timely if it is timely at all times $\tau \geq \tau_{GST}$. The system model considered in [2] assumes at least one correct process with t outgoing eventually timely links (processes communicate using point-to-point communication primitives). Such a process is called an $\diamond t$-source (eventual t-source). On the other hand, the system model considered in [19] assumes a broadcast communication primitive and at least one correct process with t bidirectional but moving eventually timely links. These two models are not comparable [15]. In such a context, [2] proved that an $\diamond t$-source is necessary (and sufficient) to solve Consensus which means that it is not possible to solve Consensus if the number of eventually timely links is smaller than t or if they are not outgoing links of a same correct process.

In the context where the t faulty processes can exhibit a Byzantine behavior, Aguilera et al. [3] propose a system model with weak synchrony properties that allows to solve the consensus problem. Namely, the model assumes at least one correct process with all its outgoing and incoming links eventually timely (the other links of the system are asynchronous). Such a process is called an eventual bisource ($\diamond$ bisource). This means that the number of eventually timely links could be as low as $2(n - 1)$ links. Their protocol does not need authentication but they first build very costly communication procedures on top of point-to-point communication[2]. Their consensus protocol consists of a series of rounds each made up of 10 communication steps and $\Omega(n^3)$ messages.

Contribution. This paper first proposes a system model where processes are eventually synchronous and the communication model lies between the asynchronous model and the partially synchronous model. The assumed model considers that only few links are eventually synchronous. If all links are asynchronous the communication model is asynchronous. On the other hand, if all links are eventually synchronous, the system meets the partially synchronous model of [12]. It is thus stronger than the asynchronous model where the Consensus problem cannot be solved and is weaker than the partially synchronous model [12] where Byzantine Consensus can be solved if $t < n/3$ (with or without authentication[3]). The eventually synchronous links have to respect some pattern in order to be able to solve the Byzantine consensus. This pattern is captured by the notion of eventual bisource with a scope x. The eventual bisource assumed by [3] has a maximal scope ($x = n - 1$). Informally, an eventual x-bisource is a correct process where the number of privileged neighbors is x instead of $n - 1$. In this system model, a byzantine consensus protocol is proposed. It uses authentication and assumes an $\diamond 2t$-bisource. We assume $t < n/3$ meeting the resiliency lower bound byzantine consensus [12]. The proposed protocol enjoys the nice property of being very simple compared to other paxos like algorithms and elegant in its design. Moreover, in good settings, the decision is reached within 5 communication steps whatever is the behavior of byzantine processes. Good settings occur when the first coordinator is a $2t$-bisource.

This is a very interesting property as under a normal setting, the communication system is mainly synchronous (having an $\diamond 2t$-bisource is very likely to happen) and failures

---

[2] These communication procedures are similar to the consistent broadcast and the authenticated broadcast procedures [24].

[3] Byzantine Consensus can be solved with $t < n/2$ only if the processes are partially synchronous and communication are synchronous.

seldom occur. A Consensus algorithm designed for the proposed model terminates as soon as some (even unknown) part of the system enjoys the $2t$-bisource property. Of course, if the system is completely synchronous, the decision can be reached faster. Contrarily, one asynchronous link over the $(n-1)^2$ links of the system can prevent an algorithm designed for a partially synchronous model from terminating.

Paper structure. This paper is made up of five parts. Section 2 defines the computation and failure model and the byzantine consensus problem. Section 3 presents the consensus protocol we propose and Section 4 proves its correctness. Section 5 discusses the cost of the protocol and makes a conjecture with the intuition that sustains it. Finally, Section 6 concludes the paper.

2 Computation Model and the Consensus Problem

2.1 Computation Model

The system model is patterned after the partially synchronous system described in [12]. The system is made up of a finite set Π of n $(n > 1)$ fully-connected processes, namely, $\Pi = \{p_1, \ldots, p_n\}$. Moreover, up to t processes can exhibit a *Byzantine* behavior, which means that such a process can behave in an arbitrary manner. This is the most severe process failure model: a Byzantine process can crash, fail to send or receive messages, send arbitrary messages, start in an arbitrary state, send different values to different processes, perform arbitrary state transitions, etc. A process that exhibits a Byzantine behavior is called *faulty*. Otherwise, it is *correct*.

Communication network. The communication network is reliable in the sense that a message sent by a correct process to another correct process will be received exactly once within a finite time. Messages are not altered by the link and the receiver knows who the sender is. In other words, we are using authenticated asynchronous links. Such a communication network can be built atop of fair lossy links (in fair lossy links, a message can be lost a finite number of times). As advocated in [15], advanced techniques like [1] or [4] could be adopted here. They prove that even a simple retransmission until acknowledgment protocol suffices to implement a reliable link between correct processes. Using these techniques, a message that was initially lossy will eventually be received by its destinator. Note that the simulation preserves the timeliness of the messages sent on timely fair-lossy links.

Synchrony properties and bisource. Every process executes an algorithm consisting of atomic computing steps (send a message, receive a message or execute local computation). We assume that processes are partially synchronous, in the sense that every correct process takes at least one step every θ steps of the fastest correct process (θ is unknown). Instead of real-time clocks, time is measured in multiples of the steps of the fastest process like in [12]. In particular, the (unknown) transfer delay bound δ is such that any process can take at most δ steps while a timely message is in transit. Hence, we can use simple step-counting for timing out messages. Hereafter, we rephrase the definition of [15] to define more formally a timely link and a bisource.

Definition 1. *A link from a process p to any process q is timely at time τ if (1) no message sent by p at time τ is received at q after time $(\tau + \delta)$ or (2) process q is not correct.*

Definition 2. *A process p is an x-bisource at time τ if:*
- (1) p is correct
- (2) There exists a set X of processes of size x, such that: for any process q in X, both links from p to q and from q to p are timely at time τ. The processes of X are said to be privileged neighbors of p.

Definition 3. *A process p is an $\diamond x$-bisource if there is a time τ such that, for all $\tau' \geq \tau$, p is an x-bisource at τ'.*

For the rest of the paper, we consider a partially synchronous system where the only assumed synchrony properties are those needed by the $\diamond x$-bisource. This means that all the links that do not participate in the $\diamond x$-bisource could be asynchronous.

Authentication. A process may be Byzantine and disseminate a wrong value (different from the value it would have obtained if it behaved correctly). To prevent such a dissemination, the protocol uses certificates. This implies the use of application level signatures (public key cryptography such as RSA signatures). A straightforward implementation of certificates would consist of including a set of signed messages as a certificate. For example, process p has to relay a value (say v) it has received from process q. Process q signs its message and sends it to p. Process p cannot relay v' if it cannot forge q's signature. Of course p can say that it received no value from q (no one can check whether this is true or not) but if it relays a value from q, it is necessarily the value it actually received from q. This means that in our model we assume that Byzantine processes are not able to subvert the cryptographic primitives. Now, suppose that p has to send to all processes the majority value among all the values it has received. The certificate, will consist of the set of received signed messages (any process can check that the value p has sent is really the majority value).

A certificate for a message m sent by p contains at least $(n - t)$ messages p has received, such that these messages led p to send m according to the protocol. Certificates do not prevent all the bad behaviors of Byzantine processes. As in many asynchronous protocols, during an all-to-all exchange, a process waits for at most $n - t$ messages otherwise it may block forever (of course a process can receive more than $n - t$ messages). In a general case, two different sets of $n - t$ messages can have a different majority value (each of the them can be certified). A Byzantine process that receives more than $(n - t)$ messages can send different certified majority values to different processes (in this case the certificate only means that the sent value is a possible value).

2.2   The Consensus Problem

The Consensus problem has been informally stated in the introduction. This paper considers *multivalued* Consensus (no bound on the cardinality of the set of proposable values): every process p_i *proposes* a value v_i and all correct processes have to eventually *decide* on some value v in relation with the set of proposed values. Let us observe that, in a byzantine failure context, one must not choose a consensus definition that is too strong. For example, it is not possible to force a faulty process to decide as a correct process, since a byzantine process can decide whatever it wants. Similarly, it is not always possible to decide a proposed value since a faulty process can initially propose different values to distinct processes and consequently the notion of "proposed value" is not defined for byzantine processes. Thus, in such a context, the consensus problem is defined by the following three properties:

- **Termination**: Every correct process eventually decides.
- **Agreement**: No two correct processes decide different values.
- **Validity**: If all the correct processes propose the same value v, then only the value v can be decided.

3   The Byzantine Protocol

The proposed protocol (Figure 1) uses authentication and assumes an $\diamond 2t$-bisource. Each process p_i manages a local variable est_i which contains its current estimate of the decision value. The init phase (lines 1-3) consists of an all-to-all message exchange that allows to initializes the variable est_i to a value it has received at least $(n - 2t)$ times if any[4]. Otherwise, est_i is set v_i the value proposed by p_i. This phase establishes the validity property as if all correct processes propose the same value v, all processes will receive v at least $(n - 2t)$ times and the only value that can be received at least $(n - 2t)$ times is v (in this case, v is the only certified value). From line 5, all messages exchanged during each phase are signed, and include as certificate $(n - t)$ messages the emitting process has received during the previous exchange phase.

> **Message validity** Each process has an underlying daemon that filters the messages it receives. For example, the daemon will discard all duplicate messsages (necessarily sent by byzantine processes as we assume reliable send and receive operations between correct processes). The daemon, will also discard all messages that are not syntactically correct, or that do not comply with the text of the protocol (e.g. a process that sends two different messages with the same type within the same round, a process that sends a QUERY(r,*) message to a process that is not the coordinator of round r, etc.). Of course a message that do not comply with the associated certified is also discarded.

After the init phase, the protocol procedes in consecutive asynchronous rounds. Each process manages a variable r_i (initially set to 0). Each round r is coordinated by a predetermined process p_c (*e.g.*, c can be defined according to the round robin order). So, the protocol uses the well-known *rotating coordinator* paradigm. Each round is composed of four communication phases.

First phase of a round r (lines 5-7). Each process that starts a round (including its coordinator) first sends its own estimate (with the associated certificate) to the coordinator

---

[4] This phase does not use certificates as there is no prior communication.

(p_c) of the current round and sets a timer to $(\Delta_i[c])$. Δ_i is an array of time-outs (one per process) managed by p_i. When the timer times out while waiting the response from a process p_j, $\Delta_i[j]$ is incremented. This allows to eventually reach the bound on the round trip between p_i and p_j if p_i and p_j are privileged neighbors. Moreover, this prevents p_i from blocking while waiting (line 6) for the response of a faulty coordinator. When the coordinator of round r receives a valid QUERY message (perhaps from itself) containing an estimate est for the first time at line 19[5], it sends sends a COORD(r, est) messages to all processes.

The COORD message is sent from another parallel task because the coordinator of round r could be stuck in previous rounds and if it does not respond quickly, the sender on the QUERY message may time out. This is why, whatever is the coordinator doing, as soon as it receives a valid QUERY message for a round it coordinates, it sends the included estimate to all processes (this allows a coordinator to coordinate a round with a certified value it has received even if it is itself lying far behind).

If the current coordinator is a $2t$-bisource it has at least $2t$ privileged neighbors among which at least t are correct process. Consequently, at least $(t + 1)$ correct processes (the t correct neighbors and the coordinator itself) got the value v of the coordinator and thus set their variable aux to v $(\neq \perp)$. If the current coordinator is byzantine, it can send nothing to some processes and perhaps send different certified values to different processes (in such a case, necessarily none of these values has been decided in a previous round as we will see later). If the current coordinator is not a $2t$-bisource or if Byzantine, the three next phases allow correct processes to behave in a consistent way. Either none of them decides or if some of them decide a value v, then the only certified value for the next round will be v and thus preventing Byzantine processes from introducing other values.

Second phase of a round r (lines 8-10). This phase aims to extend the scope of the $2t$-bisource. Indeed, if the current coordinator is a $2t$-bisource then at least $(t + 1)$ correct processes set their variable aux_i to the same non-$\perp$ value (say v). During the second phase, all processes relay the value they got from the coordinator (with its certificate) or $\perp$ if they timed out (all-to-all message exchange). Each process collects $(n - t)$ valid messages (the values carried by these messages are stored into a set V_i - of course each value appears at most once in V_i as V_i is a set). If the coordinator is a $2t$-bisource then any correct process will get at least one message from the set of $(t+1)$ correct processes that got the value of the coordinator because $(n - t) + (t + 1) > n$. Otherwise, this phase has no particular effect. The condition $(V_i - \{\perp\} = \{v\})$ of line 10 means that if there is only one non-$\perp$ value v in V_i then this value is kept in aux_i (otherwise, aux_i is set to $\perp$).

Third phase of a round r (lines 11-13). This phase has no particular effect if the coordinator is correct. Its aims is to avoid the situations where the coordinator is Byzantine. Indeed, in such a case two different correct processes may have set their aux_i variables

---

[5] For any round, the coordinator will receive at least $(n - t)$ QUERY messages but it will send COORD messages only once and will ignore subsequent QUERY messages related to the same round.

to different values. Phase three is a filter, it ensures that at the end of this phase, at most one non-$\perp$ value can be kept in the aux variables. In other words, if p_i and p_j are correct processes and if $aux_i \neq \perp$ and $aux_j \neq \perp$ then necessarily, $aux_i = aux_j$ whatever is the behavior of the byzantine processes. This phase consists of an all-to-all message exchange. Each process collects $(n - t)$ valid messages the values of which are stored in a set V_i. If all received messages contains the same value v ($V_i = \{v\}$) then v is kept in aux_i otherwise aux_i is set to the default value $\perp$. At the end of this phase, there is at most one (or none) certified value v ($\neq \perp$).

Fourth phase of a round r (lines 14-17). This phase is the decision phase. Its aim is to ensure that the Agreement property will never be violated. This prevention is done in the following way: if a correct process p_i decides v during this round then if some processes progress to the next round, then v is the only certified value. After an all-to-all message exchange, processes collect $(n - t)$ valid messages and stores the values in V_i. If the set V_i of p_i contains a unique non-$\perp$ value v, p_i decides v. Indeed among the $(n - t)$ values v received by p_i, at least $t + 1$ have been sent by correct processes. Recall that after phase three, there is at most one certified values. This means that all processes receive at least one value equal to v (the other values could be v or $\perp$). Consequently any set of $(n - t)$ valid signed messages of this phase, will certify a unique value v. If a process p_j has received only $\perp$ values, it is sure that no process decides during this phase and thus it can keep the value it already has stored in est_j (the certificate composed of the $(n - t)$ valid signed messages containing $\perp$ values, allow p_j to keep its previous values).

Before deciding (line 16), a process first sends to all other processes a signed message DEC that contains the decision value (and the associated certificate). This will prevent the processes that progress to the next round from blocking because some correct processes have already decided. When a process p_i receives a valid DEC message at line 20, it first relays is to all other processes and then decides. Indeed, task T_3 is used to implement a reliable broadcast to disseminate the eventual decision value preventing some correct processes from blocking while others decide (not all processes decide necessarily during the same round).

4 Correctness of the Protocol

Remark: A message exchange is the combination of a send to all operation and a message collect operation issued by every process. Let us note that, as there are at most t byzantine processes. Each correct process collects $(n - t)$ messages since only the byzantine processes could be silent (only message delivered by the communication daemon described in the previous section are considered).

There are four such exchanges: lines 1-2, lines 8-9, lines 11-12 and lines 14-15.

Lemma 1. *Let V_i and V_j be the sets of messages collected by two correct processes p_i and p_j respectively after a message exchange. We have:*

$$V_i \cap V_j \neq \emptyset$$

Function Consensus(v_i)

Init: $r_i \leftarrow 0$; $\Delta_i[1..n] \leftarrow 1$;

Task $T1$:   % basic task %

————————————————————————— init phase ——————————————————————

(1)   *send* INIT(r_i, v_i) to all;
(2)   **wait until** (INIT($r_i, *$) received from at least $(n-t)$ distinct processes);
(3)   **if** ($\exists v$: received at least $(n-2t)$ times) **then** $est_i \leftarrow v$ **else** $est_i \leftarrow v_i$ **endif**;

  repeat forever
(4) $c \leftarrow (r_i \mod n) + 1$; $r_i \leftarrow r_i + 1$;

——————————————————————————— round r_i ——————————————————————

(5)   *send* QUERY(r_i, est_i) to p_c; *set_timer*($\Delta_i[c]$);
(6)   **wait until** (COORD(r_i, est) received from p_c or *time-out*) **store value** in aux_i; % *else* $\perp$ %
(7)   **if** (*timer times out*)) **then** $\Delta_i[c] \leftarrow \Delta_i[c] + 1$ **else** *disable_timer* **endif**;

(8)   *send* RELAY(r_i, aux_i) to all;
(9)   **wait until** (RELAY($r_i, *$) received from at least $(n-t)$ distinct processes) **store values** in V_i;
(10)   **if** ($V_i - \{\perp\} = \{v\}$) **then** $aux_i \leftarrow v$ **else** $aux_i \leftarrow \perp$ **endif**;

(11)   *send* FILT1(r_i, aux_i) to all;
(12)   **wait until** (FILT1($r_i, *$) received from at least $(n-t)$ distinct processes) **store values** in V_i;
(13)   **if** ($V_i = \{v\}$)   **then** $aux_i \leftarrow v$ **else** $aux_i \leftarrow \perp$ **endif**;

(14)   *send* FILT2(r_i, aux_i) to all;
(15)   **wait until** (FILT2($r_i, *$) received from at least $(n-t)$ distinct processes) **store values** in V_i;
(16)   **case** ($V_i = \{v\}$)   **then** *send* DEC(v) to all; **return**(v);
(17)   ($V_i = \{v, \perp\}$)   **then** $est_i \leftarrow v$;
(18)   **endcase**;

  end repeat

Task $T2$:   % coordination task %
(19) **upon** *receipt* of QUERY(r, est) for the first time for round r: *send* COORD(r, est) to all;

Task $T3$:
(20) **upon** *receipt* of DEC(est): *send* DEC(est) to all; **return**(est);

Fig. 1. The Byzantine Consensus Protocol (assumes a $2t$-bisource)

Proof. The proof is by contradiction. Suppose that $\mathcal{V}_i \cap \mathcal{V}_j = \emptyset$ and let S be the set of all messages p_i and p_j can receive during the message exchange (i.e. messages sent to p_i and p_j).

We have $|S| = |\mathcal{V}_i| + |\mathcal{V}_j|$. Thus, $|S| = 2 \times (n-t)$ as each process waits for $(n-t)$ messages during the collect phase of an exchange.

Moreover, let f be the actual number of byzantine processes ($f \leq t$). Since, the $(n-f)$ correct processes send (according to the protocol) the same message to both processes and the f byzantine processes can send a different message to them, we have $|S| \leq 1 \times (n-f) + 2 \times f = (n+f)$ and hence, $|S| \leq (n+t)$ as $f \leq t$.

We have, $|S| \geq 2 \times (n-t)$ and $|S| \leq (n+t)$. This leads to $(n+t) \geq 2 \times (n-t)$ i.e. $n \leq 3t$ a contradiction as we assume $n > 3t$ □

Lemma 2. *After the message exchange lines 11-12, at most one non-$\perp$ value can be certified.*

Proof. Let us consider a run where a process p_i collects only messages carrying values v. Process p_i keeps the value v (the collected messages constitute the certificate of v). By Lemma 1, no other process p_j can exhibit a set of $(n - t)$ that all carry w values as the two sets need to intersect and hence, no certificate can be exhibited for another value. $\qquad\square$

Corollary 1. *If a process decides a certified value v during a round, then only v can be decided in the same or in the next rounds (no other value than v can no more be certified).*

Proof. Let us consider the first message exchange that led a process p_i to decide a certified value v (p_i received only v values during the exchange). As p_i received a certified value v then, by Lemma 2 v is the only certified value. Thus all valid messages either carry v or $\perp$. By Lemma 1, we have: $\forall j, V_i \cap V_j \neq \emptyset$. As p_i received only v values, all possible sets of messages of size $(n - t)$ (i.e. certificates for the next round) include at least one one message carrying the value v. If a process decides, it decides v. If it does not decide, it has to set its local variable est_j to v for the next round (v will be the only certified value as even $\perp$ is not certified). $\qquad\square$

Theorem 1 (agreement). *No two correct processes decide differently.*

Proof. If a correct process decides at line 20, it decides a certified value decided by another process. Let us consider the first round where a process decides at line 16. By Corollary 1, if a process decides a certified value during the same round, it decides the same value. If a process decides after receiving a DEC message at line 20 it decides the same value. Any process that starts the next round with its local variable $est_i \neq v$ will see its messages rejected (no value different from v could be certified). $\qquad\square$

Lemma 3. *If no process decides a certified value during $r' \leq r$, then all correct processes start $r + 1$.*

Proof. Let us first note that a correct process cannot be blocked forever in the init phase. Moreover, it cannot be blocked at line 6 because of the time-out.

The proof is by contradiction. Suppose that no process has decided a certified value during a round $r' \leq r$, where r is the smallest round number in which a correct process p_i blocks forever. So, p_i is blocked at lines 9, 12 or 15.

Let us first examine the case where p_i blocks at line 9. In that case, as r is the smallest round number in which a correct process p_i blocks forever, and as line 9 is the first statement of round r where a process can block forever this means that all correct processes (they are at least $(n - t)$) eventually execute line 8. Consequently as communication is reliable between correct processes the messages sent by correct processes will eventually arrive and p_i that blocks forever at line 9. It follows that if p_i does not decide, it will proceed to the next round. A contradiction. $\qquad\square$

Theorem 2 (termination). *If there is a $\diamond 2t$-bisource in the system, then all correct processes decide eventually.*

Proof. If a correct process decides then, due to the sending of DEC messages at line 16, any correct process will receive such a message and decide accordingly (line 20).

So, suppose that no process decides. The proof is by contradiction. By hypothesis, there is a time τ after which there is a process p_x that is a $2t$-bisource. Let p_j be a correct process and one of the $2t$ privileged neighbors of p_x. As no process decides, the time-out on the round-trip delay (from p_j to p_x plus the local computation time on p_x plus the transmission delay back to p_j) as computed by p_j will continuously increase (line 7) until it bypasses the bound imposed by the system model. Consequently, there is a time τ' after which the respective timers of all the privileged neighbors of p_x will never expire. Let r be the first round that starts after τ' and that is coordinated by p_x. As by assumption no process decides, due to Lemma 3, all the correct processes eventually start round r.

All correct processes (and possibly some byzantine processes) p_i start round r and send a QUERY message to p_x (line 5). When the coordinator p_x of round r receives the first QUERY message (line 19), it sends a COORD message to all processes. If we consider any privileged neighbor p_i of p_x the COORD message will be sent by p_x at the latest when the QUERY message from p_i is received by p_x. This means that no one of the correct privileged neighbors of p_x will time-out. They all will receive the COORD message.

In the worst case, there are t byzantine processes among the $2t + 1$ privileged neighbors of p_x. A byzantine process can either relay the value of p_x or relay $\perp$ during the next phase (these are only two certified values). This allows to conclude that the value v sent by p_x is relayed (line 8) at least by the $t + 1$ correct privileged neighbors of p_x (the only other possible value is $\perp$). Since each process collects at least $(n - t)$ RELAY messages we can conclude that *all* processes will get at least one message RELAY containing the value v of p_x. It is important to notice that even byzantine processes cannot lie about the fact they received p_x's value at line 10 as any set of $(n - t)$ messages contains at least one value v and possibly $\perp$ values.

During the third phase (lines 11-13), as the value v of p_x is the only certified value, *all* the processes that emit a certified message (byzantine processes can stay mute) emit v. This allows to conclude that all processes will have to set their aux value to v value line 13. By the same way, all processes that emit certified messages will emit v at line 14. From there we can conclude that correct processes will all decide at line 16, which proves the theorem.   □

Theorem 3 (validity). *If all correct processes propose v, then only v could be decided.*

Proof. Let v the only proposed value by correct processes. Since all correct processes propose v, v is sent at least $(n - t)$ times at line 1. Since processes discard at most t messages, we can conclude that at line 3 any process will receive at least $(n - 2t)$ times the value v. Moreover, any value proposed by byzantine processes will be received at most t times. As $n > 3t$, we have $t < n - 2t$. Consequently, the only certified value is v.   □

5   Discussion

5.1   On the Efficiency of the Protocol

The number of rounds executed by the protocol is unbounded but finite. Each round in composed four all-to-all message exchanges. Each message exchange needs $\Omega(n^2)$ messages if the links are reliable (we do not include messages sent by the byzantine processes as they can sent any number of messages).

If we consider synchronous runs (we assume accurate values for the time-outs) and no process exhibits a malicious behavior, the protocol terminates after the first round (four communication steps) and the init phase (one communication step). The protocol thus terminates in 5 communication steps.

Let us now consider synchronous links and $f \leq t$ processes exhibit malicious behavior. In the worst cat case, the first f coordinators are Byzantine. This means that the protocol will terminate at the latest after round $f + 1$ (and the init phase). The total number of communication steps is thus $(4f + 5)$. Which is the worst case.

5.2   On the Minimality of the $\diamond 2t$-bisource

If we consider the partially synchronous model we defined in Section 2 (extension of [12]), we conjecture that an $\diamond 2t$-bisource in the weakest timing assumption that allows to solve the Byzantine Consensus problem if at most t processes can exhibit a Byzantine behavior.

The intuition that underlies this conjecture is the following. The $\diamond 2t$-bisource and its privileged neighbors can be seen as a cluster. Inside this cluster, communication is eventually synchronous as the bisource (1) is a correct process, (2) has timely links with all other processes of the cluster and thus can serve as a router between processes that will provide eventually timely communication between any pair of processes. We suppose that processes are partially synchronous. Moreover, if we assume that communication is synchronous then it has been proved in [12] that the size of the cluster needs to be at least $2t + 1$ if authentication is used to be able to solve synchronous Byzantine Consensus inside the cluster. In our case communication is only partially synchronous but we still only need a size of $2t + 1$ for the cluster for the following reason.

The whole set of processes can be used for agreement preserving will trying all possible clusters. Let us imagine a protocol that executes a series of rounds each coordinated by a preselected cluster (a rotating coordination among all possible clusters of size $2t + 1$). Necessarily, it will select the good cluster infinitely often if the algorithm executes an infinite number of rounds. During the first phase of a round, the processes of the selected cluster execute a limited scope synchronous Byzantine Consensus and each of them broadcasts its decision value to the whole set of processes of the system. Indeed, if the communication between the processes of the cluster is synchronous, the correct processes that compose it will all decide the same value otherwise the processes of the cluster will terminate the synchronous Byzantine consensus with different values. In the latter case, the whole processes of the system need to execute all-to-all message exchanges to preserve the overall agreement property (at most one value). In the case where the correct process of the cluster have all decided the same value, in order to be able to extend the agreement among the processes of the "good" cluster to the whole system, it is necessary for the cluster to be enough big. This minimal size is also $2t + 1$ as this implies that there are at least $t + 1$ correct processes of the cluster that will send the decided value and hence any process from outside the cluster that collects messages from the cluster will get at least one response from a correct process.

In this sketch, we can see that $2t + 1$ is used twice. The first time to reach among the processes of the cluster (the minimal size is $2t + 1$) and the second time, the cluster needs to be large enough in order to be able to extend the decision to the whole system such that any process is sure to hear from at least one correct process of the cluster.

6 Conclusion

This paper has presented a protocol for solving Consensus in distributed systems prone to Byzantine failures. The protocol assumes a relaxed partially synchronous distributed system but where at least $4t$ communication links are eventually synchronous. These links connect the same process ($2t$ incoming links and $2t$ outgoing links). The proposed protocol has very simple design principles. In favorable setting, it can reach decision in only 5 communication steps and needs only $\Omega(n^2)$ messages in each step. Of course this protocol uses authentication.

The major contribution of this paper is to show that Byzantine Consensus is possible with very fewtimelyy links ($4t$ eventually synchronous links) versus $2n$ links for the best known protocol. Moreover, we conjecture that this is a lower bound.

Acknowledgments

The authors would like to thank Corentin Travers for the fruitful discussions on Byzantine Consensus.

References

1. Aguilera, M.K., Chen, W., Toueg, S.: Heartbeat: a timeout-free failure detector for quiescent reliable communication. In: Mavronicolas, M. (ed.) WDAG 1997. LNCS, vol. 1320, pp. 126–140. Springer, Heidelberg (1997)
2. Aguilera, M.K., Delporte-Gallet, C., Fauconnier, H., Toueg, S.: Communication-efficient leader election and consensus with limited link synchrony. In: PODC 2004. Proc. 23nd ACM Symposium on Principles of Distributed Computing, ACM Press, New York (2004)
3. Aguilera, M.K., Delporte-Gallet, C., Fauconnier, H., Toueg, S.: Consensus with byzantine failures and little system synchrony. In: DSN 2006. Proc. International Conference on Dependable Systems and Networks, Philadelphia (2006)
4. Basu, A., Charron-Bost, B., Toueg, T.: Crash failures vs. crash + link failures. In: PODC 1996. Proc 15th ACM Symposium on Principles of Distributed Computing, Philadelphia, Pennsylvania (1996)
5. Ben-Or, M.: Another Advantage of Free Choice: Completely Asynchronous Agreement Protocols. In: PODC 1983. Proc. 2nd ACM Symposium on Principles of Distributed Computing, pp. 27–30. ACM Press, New York (1983)

6. Boichat, B., Dutta, P., Frölund, S., Guerraoui, G.: Deconstructing paxos. SIGACT News in Distributed Computing 34(1), 47–67 (2003)
7. Castro, M., Liskov, B.: Practical Byzantine fault tolerance. In: Proc. of the 3rd Symposium on Operating Systems Design and Implementation, New Orleans, USA (February 1999)
8. Chandra, T.D., Toueg, S.: Unreliable Failure Detectors for Reliable Distributed Systems. Journal of the ACM 43(2), 225–267 (1996)
9. Correia, M., Neves, N.F., Lung, L.C., Verissimo, P.: Low Complexity Byzantine-Resilient Consensus. Distributed Computing 17, 13 (2004)
10. Doudou, A., Garbinato, B., Guerraoui, R.: Encapsulating Failure Detection: from Crash to Byzantine Failures. In: Proc. International Conference on Reliable Software Technologies, Vienna (Austria) (2002)
11. Dutta, P., Guerraoui, R., Vukolic, M.: Best-case complexity of asynchronous byzantine consensus. Technical Report EPFL/IC/200499, EPFL (February 2005)
12. Dwork, C., Lynch, N.A., Stockmeyer, L.: Consensus in the presence of partial synchrony. Journal of the ACM 35(2), 288–323 (1988)
13. Fischer, M.J., Lynch, N., Paterson, M.S.: Impossibility of Distributed Consensus with One Faulty Process. Journal of the ACM 32(2), 374–382 (1985)
14. Friedman, R., Mostefaoui, A., Raynal, M.: Simple and efficient oracle-based consensus protocols for asynchronous byzantine systems. IEEE Transactions on Dependable and Secure Computing 2(1), 46–56 (2005)
15. Hutle, M., Malkhi, D., Schmid, U., Zhou, L.: Chasing the Weakest System Model for Implementing Omega and Consensus. Research Report 74/2005, Technische Universität Wien, Institut für Technische Informatik (July 2006)
16. Kihlstrom, K.P., Moser, L.E., Melliar-Smith, P.M.: Solving Consensus in a Byzantine Environment Using an Unreliable Fault Detector. In: OPODIS 1997. Proc. of the Int. Conference on Principles of Distributed Systems, pp. 61–75 (1997)
17. Kursawe, K.: Optimistic Byzantine agreement. In: SRDS 2002 Workshops. Proc. of the 21st IEEE Symposium on Reliable Distributed Systems (2002)
18. Lamport, L.: Lower bounds for asynchronous consensus. Distributed Computing 19(2), 104–125 (2006)
19. Malkhi, D., Oprea, F., Zhou, L.: Ω meets paxos: Leader election and stability without eventual timely links. In: Fraigniaud, P. (ed.) DISC 2005. LNCS, vol. 3724, pp. 26–29. Springer, Heidelberg (2005)
20. Martin, J.P., Alvisi, L.: Fast Byzantine paxos. In: DSN 2005. Proc. International Conference on Dependable Systems and Networks, Yokohama, Japan, pp. 402–411 (2005)
21. Pease, L., Shostak, R., Lamport, L.: Reaching Agreement in Presence of Faults. Journal of the ACM 27(2), 228–234 (1980)
22. Rabin, M.: Randomized Byzantine Generals. In: FOCS 1983. Proc. 24th IEEE Symposium on Foundations of Computer Science, pp. 403–409. IEEE Computer Society Press, Los Alamitos (1983)
23. Schneider, F.B.: Implementing Fault-Tolerant Services Using the State Machine Approach: A Tutorial. ACM Computing Surveys 22(4), 299–319 (1990)
24. Srikanth, T.K., Toueg, S.: Simulating authenticated broadcasts to derive simple fault-tolerant algorithms. Distributed Computing 2(2), 380–394 (1987)

Clock Synchronization in the Byzantine-Recovery Failure Model

Emmanuelle Anceaume[1], Carole Delporte-Gallet[2], Hugues Fauconnier[2], Michel Hurfin[1], and Josef Widder[3,4,*]

[1] IRISA, Campus de Beaulieu, Rennes (France)
[2] LIAFA / Paris VII, Paris (France)
[3] Technische Universität Wien, Vienna (Austria)
[4] École Polytechnique, Palaiseau (France)

Abstract. We consider the problem of synchronizing clocks in synchronous systems prone to transient and dynamic process failures, i.e., we consider systems where all processes may alternate correct and Byzantine behaviors. We propose a clock synchronization algorithm based on periodical resynchronizations which is based on the assumption that no more than $f < n/3$ processes (with n the number of processors in the system) are simultaneously faulty. Both, accuracy (clocks being within a linear envelope of real-time) and precision (maximum deviation between clocks) perpetually hold for processes which sufficiently long follow their algorithm. We provide expressions for both the recovery time and the failure turn-over rates. Both expressions are independent of f, and are less than the time needed to execute 3 resynchronizations.

1 Introduction

Tightly synchronized and accurate clocks among the members of a distributed system is a fundamental service as it allows, e.g., to perform synchronized actions or estimate the behavior of the environment in a control system. One way to ensure reliable and tight synchronization among local clocks is the use of a clock synchronization algorithm. Essentially such an algorithm overcomes clock drift, variations of transmission delays and failures. It guarantees that the maximum deviation between (correct) local clocks is bounded (precision) and that these clocks are within a linear envelope of real-time (accuracy).

There is considerable literature devoted to the design and implementation of clock synchronization algorithms; see [1,2,3,4,5] for an overview. Some algorithms are specified for environments in which processes may crash [6], may suffer timing failures [7], or may execute arbitrarily bad operations [1,8,9,10]. The last type of behavior, called Byzantine, is the most severe type of process failures. It captures all causes of failures, ranging from accidental memory bit flips to malicious attacks on a system. Therefore this model seems appropriate for a large range of distributed applications.

Another kind of fault tolerance is self-stabilization. Here it is assumed that the system behaves arbitrarily (including, e.g., that the assumed threshold of faults is temporarily

---

* Partially supported by the Austrian FWF project *Theta* (proj. no. P17757).

E. Tovar, P. Tsigas, and H. Fouchal (Eds.): OPODIS 2007, LNCS 4878, pp. 90–104, 2007.

violated) but if eventually all processes behave according to the algorithm the system stabilizes to a good state (where in our case the clock synchronization properties hold). A highly interesting work is with respect to joining the two approaches: Self-stabilizing clock synchronization algorithms that work in the presence of permanent Byzantine faults are given in [11,12]. However, these solutions share some properties which seem inherent to the problem of fault-tolerant self-stabilization: First, even processes that always follow their algorithm are not guaranteed to remain synchronized to each other (this is clearly due to well known bounds on resilience [1] which are violated during unstable periods) and second, resynchronization of recovered processes takes $O(f)$ time.

This paper is based on the idea, that permanent failures are too optimistic for certain applications, while fault-tolerant self-stabilization might be too pessimistic, or the provided properties too weak. We therefore explore under which conditions clock properties can be provided permanently in the presence of transient and dynamic Byzantine faults, where processes recover from "bad periods" with an arbitrary state and just start following their algorithm. We, however, limit the number of components which may suffer from faults simultaneously.

This Byzantine-recovery failure model has been previously investigated in [13,14] (both work will be discussed in Section 6). In [14], the work is motivated by security schemes for which a clock synchronization algorithm under this failure model is more robust than others. However, our motivation for this failure model comes from long-lived applications in the space domain. There, transient and repeated bit-flips phenomena, caused by single event upsets (SEU), may impact processors of the computing system. In addition, mission times can be extremely long, rendering unrealistic the hypothesis that there is a limitation on the number of faults that may occur during the application life, and that only a subset of the processors can be affected by these faults. To deal with such strong requirements, complex checking procedures are designed, and reconfiguration and/or correcting mechanisms are applied on the altered components. Such mechanisms ensure that altered processors recover some operational state, mainly they recover a correct execution code. Clearly, recovering an operational state does not mean recovering a safe state, i.e., having the clock synchronized, for example. To summarize, the notion of faulty and correct processors does not make sense in the Byzantine-recovery failure model, "correct" in the sense that a processor is correct for the whole mission. Rather, processors alternate between periods of time during which they are faulty, and periods of time during which they follow their prescribed protocol.

Contribution. We propose a clock synchronization algorithm tolerant to moving Byzantine failures. In particular our algorithm guarantees that in presence of up to f "moving" and concurrent Byzantine failures, correctly behaving processes (that is at least $n - f$ processes, with $n \geq 3f + 1$, and n the number of processors in the system) have synchronized logical clocks. Our algorithm is a variation of Srikanth and Toueg's clock synchronization algorithm [9], in which the classic notion of "correct process" is assumed. The challenge of the present work is the guarantee that correctly behaving processes are never corrupted by recovering processes, and that clocks of recovering processes get quickly tightly synchronized with those of correctly behaving processes. We provide an expression for the recovery time (i.e., the period of time after which a recovered process is synchronized with the other processes). This bound is independent of f, and is roughly equal to the time needed to execute two resynchronizations. We derive an expression for the failure turn-over rate, i.e., the maximal allowable frequency at which processes may enter (and leave) faulty periods. This rate is also independent of f, and is roughly equal to the time needed to execute three resynchronizations.

2   System Model and Problem Statement

Network and Clock Model. The system consists of a finite set of $n \geq 3f + 1$ processes, where f is a parameter which is used below for our failure assumption. Processes communicate and synchronize with each other by sending and receiving messages over a (logically) fully connected reliable point-to-point network. The system is synchronous, as that there exists known upper and lower bounds on processing speeds; every process has access to a hardware clock with bounded drift with respect to Newtonian real-time; and there is a known upper bound on messages transmission delays. More precisely, we assume the following:

1. The rate of drift of physical clocks from real-time is bounded by a known constant $\varrho > 0$. That is, if $H_p(t)$ is the reading of the hardware clock of process p at real-time t, then for all $t_2 \geq t_1$:

$$\frac{t_2 - t_1}{1 + \varrho} \leq H_p(t_2) - H_p(t_1) \leq (1 + \varrho)(t_2 - t_1)$$

    The rate of drift between clocks is consequently bounded by $dr = \varrho \cdot \frac{2+\varrho}{1+\varrho}$.

2. There is an upper bound δ on the time required for a message to be prepared by a process, sent to a process and processed by the recipient of the message.

Failure Model. As written above, we want to model transient and dynamic process failures, i.e., processes may temporarily (permanent process failures are just a special case) deviate from the specified behavior. For example, such a process may arbitrarily change its local state, omit to send messages, may change the content of its messages or may even generate spurious messages. Note however, that we exclude masquerading by our logical point-to-point assumption. Further we want to model recovery such that process p reaches an operational state whenever p recovers a correct code, and makes steady progress in its computation, i.e., follows its algorithm. Note that p's execution context may be still altered (similar to self-stabilization), and thus p may still be perceived as faulty as long as it has not reached a safe state, i.e., an internal state that satisfies problem specific invariants (e.g., having its logical clock synchronized). The time needed to reach a safe state from an operational one is called the *recovery time*, and is denoted in the following by j.

Definition 1 (Obedient Processes). *We denote by Obedient(t_1, t_2) the set of processes that follow their algorithm during the whole real-time interval $[t_1, t_2]$, and by $\mathcal{P}_\Delta(t)$ the set in Obedient$(max\{0, t - \Delta\}, t)$, with Δ being some constant real-time interval.*

Definition 2 (Fault Model). *For every real-time $t > 0$ it holds that*

$$|\mathcal{P}_m(t)| \geq n - f \qquad (1)$$

with m being some constant real-time (the fault turn-over interval), and $n \geq 3f + 1$. Initially, at time $t = 0$, all processes are in an initial (i.e., correct) state.

This definition states that in a sliding window of length m, the number of processes that can concurrently exhibit faulty behavior is no more than f, with $n \geq 3f + 1$. With $m = \infty$ there are at least $n - f$ "correct" processes, while at most f may fail during an execution: We get similar restrictions as in the classic Byzantine fault model [15,16].

Problem Statement. As previously said, a clock synchronization algorithm allows processes to update their local clocks to overcome drifts and failures. Process p's local clock (also called in the literature p's logical clock) at real-time t, denoted $C_p(t)$, follows its hardware clock $H_p(t)$ with periodic re-adjustment. A Δ-Clock Synchronization algorithm has to satisfy the following two properties:

(π) *Precision.* At any real-time $t \geq 0$ and for any two processes $p, q \in \mathcal{P}_\Delta(t)$ it holds for some constant $D_{\max}$ that

$$|C_p(t) - C_q(t)| \leq D_{\max}$$

(α) *Accuracy.* For any process p and for any two real-times s and e with $p \in Obedient$ $(s, e) \wedge (e - s) > \Delta$ it must hold for any two real-times $t_1, t_2 \in [s + \Delta, e], t_1 < t_2$, for some constants a, b, c, and d that

$$\frac{t_2 - t_1}{a} - b \leq C_p(t_2) - C_p(t_1) \leq (t_2 - t_1)c + d$$

Precision ensures that the maximum deviation between logical clocks of any two processes that are obedient for at least Δ real-time units is bounded. Accuracy guarantees that the logical clock of a process obedient for at least Δ real-time units remains in the linear envelope of real-time.

3 The Algorithm

Algorithm 1 is a variant of the non-authentication clock synchronization algorithm by Srikanth and Toueg [9]. Its rules (starting with "*on*") are executed atomically. There are several data structures, namely *Buffer* and *timestamps*, where *Buffer$_p$[q]* contains the last resynchronization message sent by q that p received, and *timestamps$_p$[q]*, p's local time at which p received that resynchronization message. The algorithm relies on several parameters. The (local) interval P between two executions of the resynchronization protocol, the delete interval parameter R which is the time interval during which resynchronization messages are locally kept within *Buffer*, and the adjustment parameter A guaranteeing that logical clocks of processes which are obedient for sufficiently long are not set back. All these parameters are computed from the estimation of system parameters δ and ϱ. They have to satisfy the following solvable set of constraints, constraints that will be discussed in the remainder:[1]

$$A \geq r \cdot (1 + \varrho) \qquad P > (3 \cdot \delta) \cdot (1 + \varrho) + A + R \cdot (1 + \varrho)$$
$$R = r \cdot (1 + \varrho) \qquad r = (P - A) \cdot dr + 3 \cdot \delta$$

After discussing the general principles of our algorithm, we will show that it solves Δ-Clock Synchronization under the failure assumption of Definition 2 for $\Delta = j$ and m as follows (with an infinitesimally small ε):

$$j \geq 2 \cdot r + P \cdot (1 + \varrho) \qquad m \geq j + R \cdot (1 + \varrho) + \delta + \varepsilon$$

Srikanth and Toueg's Algorithm [9]. We briefly discuss the principles of their algorithm. It is based on processes which are either "correct" or "faulty" permanently. The resynchronization proceeds in rounds, a period of time during which processes exchange messages and update their logical clocks: When the logical clock of some correct process shows time $k \cdot P$, with $k \geq 1$, this process sends a message to all, indicating that it is ready to resynchronize. When a correct process receives $f + 1$ such messages, it knows that at least one was sent by a correct process, and thus that at least one correct process is ready to resynchronize. Therefore it also sends such a message to all. Upon receipt of a resynchronization message from $n - f \geq 2f + 1$ processes, process p knows that all correct processes will receive at least $n - 2f \geq f + 1$ of these messages within bounded time, and will therefore send their resynchronization messages to all, such that in turn every correct process receives $n - f$ such messages within bounded time. Thus, p "accepts" this message and resynchronizes its logical clock to $k \cdot P + A$.

Our Algorithm. Intuitively, the main problem in the dynamic fault model is that a process has to get rid of messages which it receives from a, then faulty, process for "future" rounds, i.e., for too large values of k. In the static failure model this is simpler to overcome since such messages are sent just by the at most f faulty processes during the whole execution, while in the dynamic model such messages may be sent by every process at times it does not follow its algorithm.

The structure of our algorithm is similar to [9]. Resynchronizations are triggered periodically (line 7), and if properly relayed, and agreed by sufficiently many processes resynchronization is applied by all the processes in $\mathcal{P}_j(t)$ (line 25). To prevent too much bad information from being present in *Buffer*, invalid messages are deleted from *Buffer* (line 11). A message is invalid if it belongs to *Buffer* for more than R logical time units, or if its reception time is in the future; R corresponds to the maximal time needed to properly complete a resynchronization phase. To prevent incorrect resynchronizations,

---

[1] The constraints are given here as required for the proofs. At first sight there seem to be cyclic dependencies. However, by simple arithmetical manipulation one can derive that A does in fact only depend on δ and ϱ while P must be greater than A plus a term depending again on δ and ϱ. The system is sound if $\varrho < 0.32$, which is in practice given as hardware clocks have drift rates between 10^{-6} and 10^{-4}.

Algorithm 1. Clock Synchronization Algorithm

```
 1: variables
 2:     k ← 1                                                    // round number
 3:     vector of integers: Buffer[1 . . . n] ← ⊥
 4:     vector of real: timestamps[1 . . . n] ← 0
 5:     real: C(t) ← 0
 6:     sent ∈ {TRUE, FALSE} ← FALSE

 7: on C(t) = k · P do
 8:     if sent = FALSE then
 9:         send (TICK, k) to all
10:         sent ← TRUE

11: on ((timestamps[q] < C(t) − R) ∨ (C(t) < timestamps[q])) ∧ (Buffer[q] ≠ ⊥) do
12:     Buffer[q] ← ⊥

13: on receipt of message (TICK, ℓ) sent by process q do
14:     Buffer[q] ← ℓ
15:     timestamps[q] = C(t)
16:     if |{r : Buffer[r] = ℓ}| ≥ f + 1 ∧ ℓ = k then
17:         if sent = FALSE then
18:             send (TICK, ℓ) to all
19:             sent ← TRUE
20:     if |{r : Buffer[r] = ℓ}| ≥ n − f then
21:         for all r ∈ Π do
22:             timestamps[r] ← timestamps[r] + (ℓ · P + A − C(t))
23:             if Buffer[r] = ℓ then
24:                 Buffer[r] ← ⊥
25:         C(t) ← ℓ · P + A
26:         k ← ℓ + 1                                            // set round number
27:         sent ← FALSE
```

process p relays a (TICK, k) message only if it makes sense for itself, i.e., (1) p is sure that at least one process with a "good" internal state wants to resynchronize, (2) both q and p agree on the resynchronization round (line 16), and (3) p has not already sent (TICK, k).

The presence of $n - f$ (TICK, k) messages in p's buffer is sufficient to resynchronize its clock, i.e., to set it to $k \cdot P + A$. This also allows a recovering process p to resynchronize its clock. Note that this resynchronization need not be based on "real" messages, as p may still have bad information in its buffer that is due to the time when it did not follow its algorithm, and thus it may synchronize to a wrong clock. However, the algorithm guarantees that at the end of the next resynchronization, p will have cleaned its buffer, and will be able to resynchronize its clock with all the other correct processes. We did not explicitly handle overruns of the round number k or the clock variables. With assumptions on the mission duration, variables can be dimensioned sufficiently large, such that overruns only happen due to local faults such that variables can be reset safely.

4 Properties of the Algorithm

In this section we give the main lines of the correctness proofs. (See [17] for the complete proofs.) We begin by defining some intensively used notations.

If some process $p \in \mathcal{P}_j(t)$ takes some step s at real-time t then we say that p *properly executes* s and if some process $p \in \mathcal{P}_j(t)$ sends some message m at real-time t we say that p *properly sends* m. If p properly executes line 26, then p *terminates* round ℓ. Moreover, we will heavily use t_{del} which is defined to be 2δ. We now give some preliminary definitions, the first of which are similar to [9].

Definition 3. *For each round k, the instant the first process properly sends (TICK, k) is denoted by $ready^k$. The time the $f + 1^{st}$ process properly sends (TICK, k) is denoted go^k. The time the $n - f^{th}$ process properly sends (TICK, k) is called fast-go^k. Finally, the time the first (or last) process properly terminates round k and sets its clock to $kP + A$ is denoted beg^k (or end^k, resp.). Further, based on these times we define:*

$$\mathcal{O}_k = Obedient(ready^k, fast\text{-}go^k + \delta)$$
$$\mathcal{C}_k = Obedient(ready^k - r, fast\text{-}go^k + \delta)$$
$$\mathcal{S}_k = Obedient(ready^k - j, fast\text{-}go^k + \delta)$$

The following properties form a central part of the analysis. Essentially these properties impose constraints on local structures at the start of a resynchronization period. In this section, we assume initial synchronization, i.e., we assume that the properties hold for $k = 1$. A large part of the analysis is then devoted to prove that the properties are in fact invariants of the algorithm. On these invariants we later build our proofs for (π) and (α). We discuss in Section 5 how and under which assumptions initial synchronization can be achieved.

Invariant 1. *With respect to round $k \geq 1$, we define:*

(S) Synchronized Start. *fast-go^k $-$ $ready^k \leq t_{\text{del}} + (P - A) \cdot dr$.*
(N) Consistent round numbers. *At $ready^k - \varepsilon$ (for an infinitesimally small ε) all processes in $\mathcal{P}_j(ready^k)$ have a round number equal to k and sent $=$ FALSE.*
(B) Clean buffer. *At real-time $ready^k - \varepsilon$ all processes in $\mathcal{P}_j(ready^k)$ have Buffer$[p] = \bot$ and there are no messages in transit on outgoing links of processes $p \in \mathcal{P}_j(ready^k)$.*
(C) $|\mathcal{S}_k| \geq n - f$.
(T) *No process has properly sent a message (TICK, ℓ) for $\ell \geq k$ before $ready^k$.*

In the case of classic, i.e., static Byzantine faults, a consequence of the model is, that at no time, a correct process has received messages by more than f faulty processes. In our case, we neither have the notion of a correct nor of a faulty process. In order to achieve clock synchronization—and thus to circumvent the lower bound in [1]—we have to ensure that not too much bad information is present at processes which should ensure properties (π) and (α).

Recall that the fault turn-over interval m (see Definition 2) satisfies the following relation: $m \geq j + R \cdot (1 + \varrho) + \delta + \varepsilon$, with an infinitesimally small ε, and the recovery time j is such that $j = 2 \cdot r + P \cdot (1 + \varrho)$. Intuitively, m must be greater than the recovery time j (otherwise the adversary could corrupt all the processes in the system by moving fast enough from one to another one), and must face situations in which some process p that recovered a safe state at time t (i.e., p enters $\mathcal{P}_j(t)$) may have sent "wrong" messages right before t. Thus buffers have to be cleaned (which takes $\delta + R \cdot (1 + \varrho) + \varepsilon$ real time units) before the adversary is allowed to break into new processes. Then we have:

Lemma 1 (Clean State). *At all times t, any process $p \in \mathcal{P}_j(t)$ has less than or equal to f values different from $\perp$ in the vector Buffer which were not received via properly sent messages.*

Proof. Suppose by way of contradiction that p has more than f values in his vector *Buffer* which it wrote in line 14 due to a message sent by some process q at some time $t' \leq t$ such that $q \notin \mathcal{P}_j(t')$. By line 11, no values which are older than R are kept in p's vector *Buffer*. Thus messages by more than f distinct processes must have been sent at some times t' such that these processes where not in $\mathcal{P}_j(t')$ and $t - R \cdot (1 + \varrho) - \delta \leq t' \leq t$.

As $|\mathcal{P}_m(t)| \geq n - f$ and $m \geq j + R \cdot (1 + \varrho) + \delta + \varepsilon$ it follows that $\mathcal{P}_j(t') \supseteq \mathcal{P}_m(t)$. Consequently, $|\bigcup_{t'} p \notin \mathcal{P}_j(t')| \leq f$ which provides the required contradiction to p having received messages by more than f distinct processes. $\qquad\square$

We now investigate properties of the round structure. We show two basic properties of our algorithm, which are named after similar properties of the broadcasting primitive in [9,18], i.e., unforgeability and correctness.

Lemma 2 (Unforgeability). *If a process properly terminates round k at time t, then at least one process properly has sent (TICK, k) at some time $t' \in [t - R \cdot (1 + \varrho) - \delta, t]$.*

Proof. Assume by contradiction that $q \in \mathcal{P}_j(t')$ terminates round k at time t', although no message (TICK, k) was properly sent in the given interval. Due to line 20, it does so because it has at least $n - f \geq f + 1$ entries in *Buffer* for round k. By Lemma 1 no more than f of these are due to processes not in $\mathcal{P}_j(t'')$ when they send (TICK, k) at time t'', with $t'' \leq t'$. Thus at least one process must have properly sent (TICK, k) within the interval (otherwise it would have been deleted by time t in line 11) which provides the required contradiction. $\qquad\square$

Lemma 3. *The first process that properly sends (TICK, k) does so in line 9.*

Lemma 4. *No process properly terminates round k at some time $t' < \text{go}^k$.*

Lemma 5. *For every k, if (S) then (C).*

Proof. By Definition 2, $|\mathcal{P}_m(t)| \geq n - f$, for all t. Consequently, it suffices to show that $m \geq \text{fast-go}^k + \delta - \text{ready}^k + j$. By (S), $\text{fast-go}^k + \delta - \text{ready}^k + j \leq \delta + (P - A) dr + t_{\text{del}} + j = r + j$. Further, $m = j + R(1 + \varrho) + \delta + \varepsilon$ such that it follows that $m > \text{fast-go}^k + t_{\text{del}} - \text{ready}^k + j$ which concludes the proof. $\qquad\square$

We now present some lemmas which are all built upon properties (S), (N), (B), (C), and (T). These lemmas are used in the induction proof of Theorem 2.

Lemma 6. *Suppose (S), (N), (B), (C), and (T) hold for round k. Then process $p \in \mathcal{O}_k$ does not remove any messages that are sent within $[\text{ready}^k, \text{fast-go}^k + \delta]$ within this interval via line 11.*

Proof. Only messages older than R on p's logical clock are removed (in line 11). The minimum real-time duration for R is $\frac{R}{1+\varrho}$ which is r. Consequently only messages sent before $\text{fast-go}^k + \delta - r$ are removed. By (S), $\text{fast-go}^k + \delta - r < \text{ready}^k$ which concludes the proof. $\qquad\square$

Lemma 7. *Suppose (S), (N), (B), and (C), and (T) hold for round k. Then no process in S_k sends a (TICK, ℓ), with $\ell \neq k$, message within $[ready^k, fast\text{-}go^k + \delta]$.*

Lemma 8. *Suppose (S), (N), (B), (C), and (T) hold for round k. Then let some process $p \in \mathcal{O}_k$ receive (TICK, k) messages by at least $n - f$ distinct processes in S_k within $[ready^k, t]$, with $ready^k \leq t \leq fast\text{-}go^k + \delta$.*

1. *p terminates round k within $[ready^k, t]$.*
2. *After terminating round k within $[ready^k, t]$, p does not terminate round ℓ for some $\ell \neq k$ by $go^k + t_{\mathrm{del}}$.*

Lemma 9 (Correctness). *Suppose (S), (N), (B), (C), and (T) hold for round k. Then every process in $\mathcal{O}_k$ terminates round k within $[ready^k, go^k + t_{\mathrm{del}}]$.*

Proof. By go^k, $f + 1$ processes properly send (TICK, k). These messages are received by all processes in S_k (which have a clean *Buffer* due to Lemma 1) such that by time $go^k + \delta$ at least $f + 1$ messages are in their buffer. These processes send (TICK, k) by time $fast\text{-}go^k \leq go^k + \delta$ due to line 18. Thus the messages by these at least $n - f$ distinct processes are received by all processes in $\mathcal{O}_k$ within $[ready^k, fast\text{-}go^k + \delta]$. By Lemma 8, our lemma follows. $\qquad\square$

Lemma 10. *Suppose (S), (N), (B), (C), and (T) hold for round k. Then:*

1. *Every $p \in \mathcal{C}_k$ terminates round k exactly once within $[go^k, go^k + t_{\mathrm{del}}]$.*
2. *At time $go^k + t_{\mathrm{del}}$, p has at most f messages for round k sent by processes in S_k and at most f messages which where not sent properly in Buffer.*

Proof. As processes in $\mathcal{C}_k$ follow their algorithm at least r before $ready^k$, they have deleted all messages they had in their *Buffer* that were due to a time where they possibly did not follow their algorithm in line 11.

Due to Lemma 9 and by similar reasoning with which one can show Lemma 4, every process $p \in \mathcal{C}_k$ terminates round k at some time $t \in [go^k, go^k + t_{\mathrm{del}}]$ at least once. To prove (1), let p do so such that it removes all messages from *Buffer* for round k in line 24. It does so based on $n - f$ received messages, i.e., at least $n - 2f$ messages by processes in S_k. Only one[2] (TICK, k) message sent by each process in S_k is received such that no more than f messages from processes in S_k can be received after t. Consequently, p cannot reach the $n - f > 2f$ threshold necessary to execute line 26 (and terminate round k) within $[t, go^k + t_{\mathrm{del}}]$.

The first part of (2) is a consequence of the proof of (1), while the second part of the proof is identical to the proof of Lemma 1. $\qquad\square$

Let in the remainder of this section e^k be the time the last process in $\mathcal{C}_k$ terminates round k within $[go^k, go^k + t_{\mathrm{del}}]$ and also fix the real-time $\tau = e^k + (P - A)(1 + \varrho)$.

Lemma 11. *For every process $p \in \mathcal{P}_j(\tau)$ it holds that $p \in \mathcal{C}_k$.*

---

[2] Processes follow their algorithm, i.e., cannot terminate a round other than k within the time window, consequently they cannot set their round number to k (and set *sent* to FALSE) which would be required to re-send a message.

Proof. First we have to show that $\tau - j \leq ready^k - r$. According to its definition, $j = 2 \cdot r + P \cdot (1 + \varrho)$. We have to show that $\tau - ready^k \leq r + P \cdot (1 + \varrho)$, i.e.,

$$e^k - ready^k \leq (P - A) \cdot dr + \delta + t_{\text{del}} + A(1 + \varrho) \tag{2}$$

By property (S), $fast\text{-}go^k - ready^k \leq t_{\text{del}} + (P - A) \cdot dr$ and by Lemma 8, $e^k \leq fast\text{-}go^k + \delta$. Consequently, we know that $e^k - ready^k \leq 3\delta + (P - A) \cdot dr$ which — by the size of A — proves Equation (2).

Second we have to show that $fast\text{-}go^k + \delta \leq \tau$, i.e., that

$$fast\text{-}go^k + \delta \leq e^k + (P - A)(1 + \varrho). \tag{3}$$

Since by definition of P, $P - A > (3 \cdot \delta) \cdot (1 + \varrho) + R(1 + \varrho)$, we can prove Equation (3) by showing that $fast\text{-}go^k \leq e^k + 2\delta$.

By Lemma 4, $go^k \leq beg^k$. Since by time $go^k + \delta$ all processes in $\mathcal{S}_k$ receive $f + 1$ (TICK, k) messages and therefore send (TICK, k) it follows that $fast\text{-}go^k \leq go^k + \delta$ since $|\mathcal{S}_k| \geq n - f$. As $go^k \leq beg^k \leq e^k$ it follows that $fast\text{-}go^k \leq e^k + \delta$ and thus our lemma follows. □

Lemma 12. *If (S), (N), (B), (C), and (T) hold for round k, then no messages are properly sent within $[beg^k + t_{\text{del}}, ready^{k+1}]$, for any $k > 0$.*

Proof. Lemma 11 in conjunction with Lemma 10 shows that all processes $p \in \mathcal{P}_j(\tau)$ update their round number once to $k + 1$ within t_{del}. By Lemma 10(2), there are not sufficiently many messages in transit such that p can execute line 18 before the first process in $\mathcal{C}_k$ has properly sent (TICK, $k + 1$), while there are also not sufficiently many messages (i.e., less than $n - f$) to execute line 25 before the first process in $\mathcal{C}_k$ has sent a message. Thus processes properly execute no rule (except line 11) before the first clock of a process in $\mathcal{C}_k$ properly reaches $(k + 1) \cdot P$ which is not before $beg^k + \frac{P-A}{1+\varrho}$ which thus is a lower bound for $ready^{k+1}$. □

Lemma 13 (Monotony). *Suppose (S), (N), (B), (C), and (T) hold for round k. If $p \in \mathcal{P}_j(\tau)$ terminates round k within $[ready^k, beg^k + t_{\text{del}}]$, then at no time t, $beg^k + t_{\text{del}} < t \leq \tau$, p terminates round k.*

Proof. Suppose $p \in \mathcal{P}_j(\tau)$ terminates round k within $[ready^k, beg^k + t_{\text{del}}]$. By Lemma 12, from $beg^k + t_{\text{del}}$ on, no process properly sends (TICK, k). Within $[ready^k, beg^k + t_{\text{del}}]$, no process properly sends (TICK, ℓ), with $\ell < k$ (Lemma 7). By an argument similar to the one used for Lemma 2, the lemma follows. □

After all these preliminary lemmas, we finally arrive at our major theorem. If initial synchronization is given one may set $\sigma = 0$. For our initialization algorithm, however, σ will be 2.

Theorem 2. *Algorithm 1 ensures that for all $k \geq \sigma$ the properties (S), (N), (B), (C), and (T) as well as $e^k - beg^k \leq t_{\text{del}}$ are satisfied given that the properties (S), (N), (B), (C), and (T) hold for some round $\sigma \geq 0$.*

Proof. The proof is by induction on k. For $k = \sigma$, (S), (N), (B), (C), and (T) hold since the properties of initial synchronization are assumed to hold. By Lemma 10 the base case follows.

Now assume that (S), (N), (B), (C), and (T) hold for all ℓ, with $\sigma \leq \ell < k + 1$ and $e^\ell - beg^\ell \leq t_{\text{del}}$. We have to show that they hold for round $k + 1$. Relation $e^{k+1} - beg^{k+1} \leq t_{\text{del}}$ then follows directly from Lemma 10.

(S) All processes $p \in \mathcal{P}_j(\tau)$ send $(\text{TICK}, k + 1)$ at the latest by $e^k + (P - A)(1 + \varrho)$ which constitutes an upper bound for *fast-go*$^{k+1}$. From the induction assumptions and Lemma 10 it follows that $e^k - beg^k \leq t_{\text{del}}$. Thus *fast-go*$^{k+1}$ − *ready*$^{k+1}$ $\leq t_{\text{del}} + (P - A)\,dr$ which proves (S) for $k + 1$.

(N) Since no rules (except line 11) are executed after processes in $\mathcal{P}_j(\tau)$ have set their round number to $k + 1$, their round number remains unchanged and *sent* = FALSE as it is set to this value when the round number is updated.

(B) As no rules (except line 11) are properly executed by processes in $\mathcal{C}_k$ between e^k and *ready*$^{k+1}$, no messages are sent by processes in $\mathcal{P}_j(ready^{k+1})$ in this interval, and all messages they have sent before are received by $e^k + \delta$. Thus between time $beg^k + t_{\text{del}} + \delta$ and time *ready*$^{k+1}$, no properly sent message from p can be received in q's buffer, with $q \in \mathcal{P}_j(ready^{k+1})$. By time $beg^k + t_{\text{del}} + \delta + R(1 + \varrho)$, q's buffer is empty (line 11). We have to show that (1) $beg^k + t_{\text{del}} + \delta + R(1 + \varrho) < ready^{k+1}$. The lower bound for *ready*$^{k+1}$ is obtained as follows. Let p be the first process that properly terminates round k and let it be the process with the fastest clock. It will send $(\text{TICK}, k + 1)$ when its clock reads $(k + 1) P$. Consequently, *ready*$^{k+1} \geq beg^k + \frac{P-A}{1+\varrho}$. From (1), we have to show that $t_{\text{del}} + \delta + r < \frac{P-A}{1+\varrho}$. From constraints on P, and A it follows that we have to show that $t_{\text{del}} + \delta + r < \frac{(t_{\text{del}}+\delta)\cdot(1+\varrho)+R(1+\varrho)}{1+\varrho} = t_{\text{del}} + \delta + R$ which is obvious from the definition of R.

(C) Straightforward from Lemma 5.

(T) As no rules (except line 11) are properly executed by processes in $\mathcal{C}_k$ between e^k and *ready*$^{k+1}$, no messages are sent by processes in $\mathcal{P}_j(ready^{k+1})$ within this interval. By Lemma 7, no process properly sends a (TICK, ℓ) message, with $\ell \neq k + 1$, within $[ready^k, fast\text{-}go^k + \delta]$. Finally by the induction assumptions, no process has properly sent a message (TICK, ℓ) for $\ell \geq k$ before *ready*^{k}. □

Lemma 14. *For every round k it holds that $e^{k+1} - ready^k \leq j$.*

Theorem 3. *For every round k it holds that $end^k - beg^k \leq t_{\text{del}}$.*

Proof. From Lemma 14 it follows that if $p \in \mathcal{P}_j(t)$ it holds that $p \in \mathcal{O}_k$ for the latest resynchronization period with $e^k \leq t$. Process p's round number is thus greater than k at time t and if it follows its algorithm until e^ℓ for some $\ell > k$ it sets its round number to $\ell + 1$ by then (Lemma 10) and thus, after e^k has a round number greater than k as long it remains obedient. Thus, it never again properly sends (TICK, k) after e^k, such that by Lemma 2 and Lemma 13 no process properly terminates round k after e^k; by the definition of *end*^{k} the theorem follows. □

We have seen that the collective update of the round numbers is ensured which is fundamental for round based clock synchronization algorithms. Based upon it one can show the following properties of the local bounded drift clocks.

Algorithm 2. Initialization Algorithm

```
1: variables
2:    Buffer⁰[n] ← FALSE
3:    sent⁰ ∈ {TRUE, FALSE} ← FALSE

4: on external start event do
5:    if sent⁰ = FALSE then
6:        send (START) to all
7:    sent⁰ ← TRUE

8: on receipt of message (START) sent by process q do
9:    Buffer⁰[q] ← TRUE
10:   if |{r : Buffer⁰[r]}| ≥ f + 1 then
11:       if sent⁰ = FALSE then
12:           send (START) to all
13:       sent⁰ ← TRUE
14:   if |{r : Buffer⁰[r]}| ≥ n − f then
15:       C(t) ← A
16:       k ← 1                                      // start clock
```

Theorem 4 (Precision). *For all real-times t and for any two processes $p, q \in \mathcal{P}_j(t)$ it holds that*
$$|C_p(t) - C_q(t)| \leq D_{\max}, \text{ with } D_{\max} \triangleq \frac{P}{1+\varrho} \cdot dr + \frac{A}{(1+\varrho)^2} + \frac{t_{\text{del}}(1+\varrho(2+\varrho))}{1+\varrho}$$

Theorem 5 (Accuracy). *For any process p and for any two real-times s and e with $p \in Obedient(s, e) \wedge (e - s) > j$ it must hold for any two real-times $t_1, t_2 \in [s + j, e]$, $0 \leq t_1 < t_2$, that*

$$\frac{t_2 - t_1}{a} - b \leq C_p(t_2) - C_p(t_1) \leq (t_2 - t_1)c + d$$

with

$$a = 1 + \varrho \qquad\qquad b = 0$$
$$c = \frac{P(1+\varrho)}{P - A - t_{\text{del}}(1+\varrho)} \qquad d = P - \frac{P - A - t_{\text{del}}(1+\varrho)}{(1+\varrho)^2}$$

5 Initialization

For initial synchronization, it is usually assumed that all processes of the system are up and listening to the network when the algorithm is started [9,10]. In systems where processes boot at unpredictable times, it was shown in [19] that this assumption can be dropped. In this paper, we consider the classic case and propose an initialization protocol which requires that there are sufficiently many processes following their protocol during the initialization phase.

Definition 4 (Failure Model for Initialization). *Let t be the maximum real-time at which a process $p \in Obedient(0, t)$, properly starts initialization. Then it holds that $|Obedient(0, t_b)| \geq n - f$ with $t_b = t + 2\delta + 2 \cdot (P - A)(1 + \varrho)$, and $\forall t' > t_b : |\mathcal{P}_m(t')| > n - f$.*

Algorithm 2 presents a protocol which established initial synchronization, i.e., ensures Invariant 1 when used in conjunction with Algorithm 1 for $k = 2$: All processes in

$\mathcal{P}_j(t_b)$ properly terminate round 0 within t_{del} of each other. However, since these processes may start synchronization whenever they want, the initial synchronization period is is not bounded in size. This is only given for the first resynchronization such that starting with the second resynchronization (which can be shown to terminate before t_b) our properties (S), (N), (B), (C), and (T) hold. (More detailed analysis is given in [17].)

6   Related work

From the failure model perspective, the problem we solve is different from the Byzantine-tolerant self-stabilization version of clock synchronization [11,12]. There, all the processes start with a possibly corrupted state, and eventually converge toward a safe state in which all processes have a synchronized clock. From the properties our algorithm achieves, we provide precise expressions on how many faults may occur in the system such that still perpetual clock synchronization is possible, which is in sharp contrast with self-stabilization.

The closest work to ours is the one of Barak et al. [14]. Their synchronization algorithm assumes that processes alternate between correct behaviors and faulty ones, and that no more than f processes can fail during sliding window of length θ. Differently from our solution, their resynchronization algorithm uses a convergence function similar to the differential fault-tolerant midpoint function of Fetzer and Cristian [20]. Maximal drift of logical clocks, ϱ, is very close to the one of hardware clocks, which shows the adequacy of that convergence function for maximizing logical clock accuracy. However, the weakness of their algorithm lies in the way clock synchronization is achieved. Whenever some process p decides to start a resynchronization phase, p asks all the processes to send their current clock values, which enables p to estimate the "system time". It is not hard to see that in case of Byzantine failures, resynchronizations can be invoked infinitely often with the main consequence of overloading processors and communication links which makes it difficult to guarantee some upper-bound on communication delays, as well as on the maximal error reading estimates, which has clearly a dramatic impact of convergence functions, and thus on the clock synchronization algorithm as the achievable precision depends on the timing uncertainty of the system [21]. Modifying their algorithm to prevent such behavior does not seem trivial. An idea would be to reject/ignore too early clock synchronization messages, but this would postpone recovery, and probably would have severe impact on the correctness proof. In contrast to their solution, ours does not compute a new clock based on the clock values of other processes but based on the receipt of a minimum number of synchronization messages; some of which must have been sent by "correct" processes, preventing thus abusive release clock resynchronizations. Finally, regarding fault turn-over rate, we improve the results by Barak et al. [14] by a factor of approximately 3.

Anceaume et al. [13] present an ad-hoc solution to the clock synchronization problem for the particular case where $f = 1$ and $n \geq 4$. The present work is a generalization of that result by considering an unvalued variable f.

Open Problems. We proposed (simple) mechanisms to transform a clock synchronization algorithm tolerant to permanent Byzantine failures into an algorithm in which all processes may recover after Byzantine failures. This transformation takes advantage of the inherent properties of the problem we address, namely, data have a limited duration of validity, or can be refreshed periodically. We conjecture that it is possible to design automatic transformations for all distributed algorithms that manipulate evanescent variables.

References

1. Dolev, D., Halpern, J.Y., Strong, H.R.: On the possibility and impossibility of achieving clock synchronization. Journal of Computer and System Sciences 32, 230–250 (1986)
2. Simons, B., Welch, J., Lynch, N.: An overview of clock synchronization. In: Simons, B., Spector, A. (eds.) Fault-Tolerant Distributed Computing. LNCS, vol. 448, pp. 84–96. Springer, Heidelberg (1990)
3. Schneider, F.B.: Understanding protocols for Byzantine clock synchronization. Technical Report 87-859, Cornell University, Dept. of Computer Science (1987)
4. Anceaume, E., Puaut, I.: Performance evaluation of clock synchronisation algorithms. Technical Report 3526, INRIA (1998)
5. Schmid, U.(ed.): Special Issue on The Challenge of Global Time in Large-Scale Distributed Real-Time Systems. J. Real-Time Systems 12(1–3) (1997)
6. Guzella, R., Zatti, S.: The accuracy of clock synchronization achieved by Tempo in Berkeley Unix 4.3BSD. IEEE Transactions on Software Engineering 15(7), 847–853 (1989)
7. Cristian, F., Aghili, H., Strong, R.: Clock synchronization in the presence of omission and performance failures, and joins. In: Proc. of the 15th Int'l Symposium on Fault Tolerant Computing, IEEE Computer Society Press, Los Alamitos (1986)
8. Halpern, J., Simons, B., Strong, R., Dolev, D.: Fault-tolerant clcok synchronization. In: Proceedings of the 3rd ACM Symposium on Principles of Distributed Computing, pp. 89–102. ACM Press, New York (1984)
9. Srikanth, T.K., Toueg, S.: Optimal clock synchronization. Journal of the ACM 34(3), 626–645 (1987)
10. Welch, J.L., Lynch, N.: A new fault tolerant algorithm for clock synchronization. Information and Computation 77(1), 1–36 (1988)
11. Daliot, A., Dolev, D., Parnas, H.: Linear time byzantine self-stabilizing clock synchronization. In: Papatriantafilou, M., Hunel, P. (eds.) OPODIS 2003. LNCS, vol. 3144, pp. 7–19. Springer, Heidelberg (2004)
12. Dolev, S., Welch, J.L.: Self-stabilizing clock synchronization in the presence of byzantine faults. Journal of the ACM 51(5), 780–799 (2004)
13. Anceaume, E., Delporte-Gallet, C., Fauconnier, H., Hurfin, M., Lann, G.L.: Designing modular services in the scattered byzantine failure model. In: 3rd International Symposium on Parallel and Distributed Computing, pp. 262–269 (2004)
14. Barak, B., Halevi, S., Herzberg, A., Naor, D.: Clock synchronization with faults and recoveries (extended abstract). In: Proceedings of the nineteenth annual ACM symposium on Principles of distributed computing, pp. 133–142. ACM Press, New York (2000)
15. Lamport, L., Shostak, R., Pease, M.: The Byzantine generals problem. ACM Transactions on Programming Languages and Systems 4(3), 382–401 (1982)
16. Lamport, L., Melliar-Smith, P.M.: Synchronizing clocks in the presence of faults. Journal of the ACM 32(1), 52–78 (1985)

17. Anceaume, E., Delporte-Gallet, C., Fauconnier, H., Hurfin, M., Widder, J.: Clock synchronization in the Byzantine-recovery failure model. Technical Report 59/2007, Technische Universität Wien, Institut für Technische Informatik (2007)
18. Srikanth, T.K., Toueg, S.: Simulating authenticated broadcasts to derive simple fault-tolerant algorithms. Distributed Computing 2, 80–94 (1987)
19. Widder, J., Schmid, U.: Booting clock synchronization in partially synchronous systems with hybrid process and link failures. Distributed Computing 20(2), 115–140 (2007)
20. Fetzer, C., Cristian, F.: An optimal internal clock synchronization algorithm. In: Proceedings of the 10th Annual Conference on Computer Assurance, pp. 187–196 (1995)
21. Lundelius, J., Lynch, N.: An upper and lower bound for clock synchronization. Information and Control 62, 190–240 (1984)

Computing Without Communicating: Ring Exploration by Asynchronous Oblivious Robots

Paola Flocchini[1], David Ilcinkas[2], Andrzej Pelc[3], and Nicola Santoro[4]

[1] SITE, University of Ottawa, Canada
flocchin@site.uottawa.ca
[2] CNRS, LaBRI, Université Bordeaux I, France
david.ilcinkas@labri.fr
[3] Département d'informatique, Université du Québec en Outaouais, Canada
pelc@uqo.ca
[4] School of Computer Science, Carleton University, Canada
santoro@scs.carleton.ca

Abstract. We consider the problem of exploring an anonymous unoriented ring by a team of k identical, oblivious, asynchronous mobile robots that can view the environment but cannot communicate. This weak scenario is standard when the spatial universe in which the robots operate is the two-dimensional plane, but (with one exception) has not been investigated before. We indeed show that, although the lack of these capabilities renders the problems considerably more difficult, ring exploration is still possible.

We show that the minimum number $\rho(n)$ of robots that can explore a ring of size n is $O(\log n)$ and that $\rho(n) = \Omega(\log n)$ for arbitrarily large n. On one hand we give an algorithm that explores the ring starting from any initial configuration, provided that n and k are co-prime, and we show that there always exist such k in $O(\log n)$. On the other hand we show that $\Omega(\log n)$ agents are necessary for arbitrarily large n. Notice that, when k and n are not co-prime, the problem is sometimes unsolvable (i.e., there are initial configurations for which the exploration cannot be done). This is the case, e.g., when k divides n.

1 Introduction

1.1 Framework

Recently a lot of attention has been devoted to the computational and complexity issues arising in systems of autonomous mobile entities located in a spatial universe $\mathcal{U}$. The entities have storage and processing capabilities, exhibit the same behavior (i.e., execute the same protocol), can move in $\mathcal{U}$ (their movement is constrained by the nature of $\mathcal{U}$), and are asynchronous in their actions. Depending on the context, the entities are sometimes called *agents*, other times *robots*; in the following, we use the latter. The research concern is on determining what tasks can be performed by such entities, under what conditions, and at what cost. In particular, a central question is to determine what minimal hypotheses allow a given problem to be solved.

E. Tovar, P. Tsigas, and H. Fouchal (Eds.): OPODIS 2007, LNCS 4878, pp. 105–118, 2007.
© Springer-Verlag Berlin Heidelberg 2007

Depending on the nature of $\mathcal{U}$, there are two basic settings in which autonomous mobile entities are being investigated. The first setting, called sometimes *continuous universe*, is when $\mathcal{U}$ is the two-dimensional plane (e.g., [1,9,10,19,27,29,30]). The second setting, sometimes called *graph world* or *discrete universe*, is when $\mathcal{U}$ is a simple graph (e.g., [3,4,7,12,20,21]). In both settings, each robot is viewed as operating in a *Look - Compute - Move* cycle. The robot observes the environment (Look), then, based on this observation, it decides to stay idle or to move (Compute), and in the latter case it moves towards its destination (Move).

Interestingly, in spite of the common features of the two settings, the researchers investigating them usually operate under two radically different assumptions on the robots' capabilities.

(1) *Communication vs Vision* - In the investigations in a graph world, the robots are assumed to communicate with each other directly; e.g., by means of tokens [6,7], or whiteboards [12,20], or when they meet [20]. Instead, in the studies on a continuous universe, the robots do not communicate in any explicit way; they however see the position of the other robots and can acquire knowledge from this information (e.g., see [1,9,10,19,26,27,29,30]).

(2) *Persistency vs Obliviousness* - In addition to its program, each robot has a local memory (sometimes called notebook or workspace), used for computations and to store different amount of information obtained during the cycles. In all the investigations in a graph world, the local memory is possibly limited (e.g., each robot is a finite-state automaton) but almost always *persistent*: unless explicitly erased by the robot, all the information contained in the workspace will persist throughout the robot's cycles. Instead, in the majority of the studies on a continuous universe, the robots are *oblivious*: all the information contained in the workspace is *cleared* at the end of each cycle. In other words, the robots have *no* memory of past actions and computations, and the computation is based solely on what has been determined in the current cycle. The importance of obliviousness comes from its link to *self-stabilization* and *fault-tolerance*.

Let us point out that there is nothing inherent in the nature of $\mathcal{U}$ that forces these differences in the assumptions. In other words, there is no reason why robots in a graph should not be oblivious; on the contrary, an oblivious solution would be highly desirable ensuring fault-tolerance and self stabilization. Similarly, there is nothing in the continuous domain that forbids robots from communicating explicitly; indeed, in the recent investigations on mobile sensor networks, the robots do communicate wirelessly [24].

Surprisingly, nobody has investigated how to solve problems in the discrete universe if the robots have the capabilities and limitations standard in the continuous one. In fact, with one exception, there are no studies on how a collection of asynchronous oblivious robots endowed with vision can perform a non-trivial task without any communication. The only exception is the recent investigation of the *gathering* problem in the ring [23].

In this paper, we continue this investigation and focus on a basic primitive problem in a graph world: *Exploration*, that is the process by which every node of the graph is visited by at least one robot, and we study this problem in a *ring*.

1.2 Our Results

We consider the problem of exploring an anonymous ring of size n by k oblivious anonymous asynchronous robots scattered in the ring. The robots are endowed with vision but they are unable to communicate. Within finite time and regardless of the initial placement of the robots, each node must be visited by a robot and the robots must be in a configuration in which they all remain idle.

We first show that this problem is unsolvable if $k|n$. We then prove that, whenever $gcd(n, k) = 1$, for $k \geq 17$, the robots can explore the ring terminating within finite time. The proof is constructive: we present a terminating protocol that explores the ring starting from an arbitrary initial configuration, and prove its correctness.

Finally, we consider the minimum number $\rho(n)$ of robots that can explore a ring of size n. As a consequence of our positive result we show that $\rho(n)$ is $O(\log n)$. We also prove that $\rho(n) = \Omega(\log n)$ for arbitrarily large n. More precisely, there exists a constant c such that, for arbitrarily large n, we have $\rho(n) \geq c \log n$.

1.3 Related Work

Algorithms for graph exploration by mobile entities (robots) have been intensely studied in recent literature. Several scenarios have been considered. Most of the research is concerned with the case of a single robot exploring the graph. In [2,6,7,14,18] the robot explores strongly connected directed graphs and it can move only in the direction from head to tail of an edge, not vice-versa. In particular, [14] investigates the minimum time of exploration of directed graphs, and [2,18] give improved algorithms for this problem in terms of the deficiency of the graph (i.e., the minimum number of edges to be added to make the graph Eulerian). Many papers, e.g., [15,16,17,22,25] study the scenario where the explored graph is undirected and the robot can traverse edges in both directions. In [15] the authors investigate the problem of how the availability of a map influences the efficiency of exploration. In [25] it is shown that a graph with n nodes and e edges can be explored in time $e + O(n)$. In some papers, additional restrictions on the moves of the robot are imposed. It is assumed that the robot has either a restricted tank [5,8], forcing it to periodically return to the base for refueling, or that it is tethered, i.e., attached to the base by a rope or cable of restricted length [17].

Exploration of anonymous graphs presents different difficulties. In this case it is impossible to explore arbitrary graphs by a single robot if no marking of nodes is allowed. Hence the scenario adopted in [6,7] allows the use of *pebbles* which the robot can drop on nodes to recognize already visited ones, and then remove them and drop in other places. The authors concentrate attention on the minimum number of pebbles allowing efficient exploration and mapping of arbitrary directed n-node graphs. (In the case of undirected graphs, one pebble suffices for efficient exploration.) In [7] the authors compare exploration power of one robot with a constant number of pebbles to that of two cooperating robots, and give an efficient exploration algorithm for the latter scenario. In [6] it is shown that one pebble is enough if the robot knows an upper bound on the size of the graph, and $\Theta(\log \log n)$ pebbles are necessary and sufficient otherwise.

In all the above papers, except [7], exploration is performed by a single robot. Exploration by many robots has been investigated mostly in the context when moves of the robots are centrally coordinated. In [21], approximation algorithms are given for the collective exploration problem in arbitrary graphs. In [3,4] the authors construct approximation algorithms for the collective exploration problem in weighted trees. On the other hand, in [20] the authors study the problem of distributed collective exploration of trees of unknown topology. However, the robots performing exploration have memory and can directly communicate with each other.

To the best of our knowledge, the very weak assumption of asynchronous identical robots that cannot send any messages and communicate with the environment only by observing it, has not been previously used in the context of graph exploration. It has been used, however in the case of robots moving freely in the plane (e.g., see [1,9,10,11,19,26,30]), where the robots were oblivious, i.e., it was assumed that they do not have any memory of past observations. Oblivious robots operate in Look-Compute-Move cycles, similar to those described in our scenario. The differences are in the amount of synchrony assumed in the execution of the cycles. In [13,30] cycles were executed synchronously in rounds by all active robots, and the adversary could only decide which robots are active in a given cycle. In [9,10,11,19,26] they were executed asynchronously: the adversary could interleave operations arbitrarily, stop robots during the move, and schedule Look operations of some robots while others were moving.

Our scenario has been recently introduced in [23] to study the gathering problem in the ring. This scenario is very similar to the asynchronous model used in [19,26]. The only difference with respect to [19,26] is in the execution of Move operations. All possibilities of the adversary concerning interleaving operations performed by various robots as well as the characteristics of the robots are the same as in the model from [19,26].

2   Preliminaries

2.1   Terminology and Definitions

The network we consider is a ring of n nodes, $u_0, u_1, \ldots, u_{n-1}$; i.e., u_i is connected[1] to both u_{i-1} and u_{i+1}. The indices are used for notation purposes; in fact, the nodes are anonymous (i.e., identical) and the ring is unoriented. Operating in the ring are k identical robots; initially, at time $t = 0$, there is at most one robot in each node. During the exploration, robots move, and at any time they occupy some nodes of the ring.

We shall indicate by $d_i(t)$ the multiplicity of robots present at node u_i at time t; more precisely $d_i(t) = 0$ indicates that there are no robots, $d_i(t) = 1$ indicates that there is exactly one robot, and $d_i(t) = 2$ indicates that there is more than one robot at u_i at time t. If $d_i(t) = 2$, we will say that there is a *tower* in u_i at time t.

Let $\delta^{+j}(t)$ denote the sequence $\delta^{+j}(t) = < d_j(t) \ d_{j+1}(t) \ \ldots d_{j+n-1}(t) >$, and let $\delta^{-j}(t)$ denote the sequence $\delta^{-j}(t) = < d_j(t) \ d_{j-1}(t) \ \ldots \ d_{j-(n-1)}(t) >$. The unordered pair[2] of sequences $\delta^{+j}(t)$ and $\delta^{-j}(t)$ describes the configuration of the

---

[1] Here and in the following, all operations on the indices are modulo n.

[2] Since the ring is not oriented, agreement on only one of the two sequences might be impossible, and the pair cannot be ordered.

system at time t viewed from node u_j. Let $\Delta^+(t) = \{\delta^{+j}(t) : 0 \leq j < n\}$ and $\Delta^-(t) = \{\delta^{-j}(t) : 0 \leq j < n\}$.

We will denote by $\delta_{max}(t)$ the lexicographically maximum sequence in $\Delta^+(t) \cup \Delta^-(t)$. It is immediate to verify that there is at most one maximal sequence in each of $\Delta^+(t)$ and $\Delta^-(t)$. A configuration is said to be *symmetric* if the maximal sequences in $\Delta^+(t)$ and $\Delta^-(t)$ are equal, and *asymmetric* otherwise.

Each robot operates in Look-Compute-Move cycles described in section 1.1. Cycles are performed asynchronously for each robot: the time between Look, Compute, and Move operations is finite but unbounded, and is decided by the adversary for each action of each robot. The only constraint is that moves are instantaneous, as in [23], and hence any robot performing a Look operation sees all other robots at nodes of the ring and not on edges. However, a robot $\mathcal{R}$ may perform a Look operation at some time t, perceiving robots at some nodes, then Compute a target neighbor at some time $t' > t$, and Move to this neighbor at some later time $t'' > t'$ in which some robots are in different nodes from those previously perceived by $\mathcal{R}$ because in the meantime they performed their Move operations. Hence robots may move based on significantly outdated perceptions. We assume that the robots can perceive, during the Look operation, if there is one or more robots in a given location; this ability, called *multiplicity detection* is a standard assumption in the continuous model [9,23,26]. We now describe formally what a robot perceives when performing a Look operation. Consider a robot $\mathcal{R}$ that, at time t is at node u_j and performs a Look; the result of this operation, called the *view* of $\mathcal{R}$ at time t, is precisely the unordered pair of sequences $\{\delta^{+j}(t), \delta^{-j}(t)\}$, that is, the configuration of the system at time t viewed from node u_j. We order all views as follows: order each pair $\{\delta^{+j}(t), \delta^{-j}(t)\}$ lexicographically and then use the lexicographic order on these pairs. From its view, the robot can determine $\delta_{max}(t)$, decide whether or not it is unique, and compute views of all other robots.

Let robot $\mathcal{R}$ perform in the same cycle a Look operation at time t' and a Move operation at time $t'' > t'$. We will say that $\mathcal{R}$ is *engaged to move* (or, simply *engaged*) in the open interval (t', t''); that is, $\mathcal{R}$ is engaged at any time t, where $t' < t < t''$.

One final precision has to be added, concerning the decisions of robots made during the Compute action. Every such decision is based on the snapshot obtained during the last Look action. However it may happen that both edges incident to a node v currently occupied by the deciding robot look identical in this snapshot, i.e., v lies on a symmetry axis of the configuration. In this case if the robot decides to take one of these edges, it may take any of the two. We assume the worst-case decision in such cases, i.e., that the actual edge among the identically looking ones is chosen by an adversary.

We say that exploration of a n-node ring is possible with k robots, if there exists an algorithm which, starting from any initial configuration of the k robots without towers, allows the robots to explore the entire ring and brings all robots to a configuration in which they all remain idle. Obviously, if $n = k$, the exploration is already accomplished, hence we always assume that $k < n$.

2.2   Basic Restriction

Lemma 1. *Let $k < n$. If $k|n$ then the exploration of a n-node ring with k robots is not possible.*

Proof. By contradiction, let P be a solution protocol. Choose as the initial configuration an equidistant placement of the k robots in the ring (it exists since $k|n$). Thus, initially the states of all robots are identical, say $\sigma(0)$. Clearly this state is not a terminal state. Otherwise, since $k < n$, P would terminate without exploring the ring, thus contradicting the correctness of P. Consider now an adversary that uses a synchronous scheduler and a consistent orientation of the ring. Then, at each time step t, the states of all robots continue to be identical, say $\sigma(t)$, and furthermore they are the same as those of previous steps; i.e., $\sigma(t) = \sigma(0)$ for all t. Hence the robots will never enter a terminal state, contradicting the fact that P leads within finite time to a configuration in which all robots remain idle. □

In the following we will consider the case when $gcd(n, k) = 1$, and design an algorithm that allows $k \geq 17$ robots to explore a n-node ring whenever $gcd(n, k) = 1$. Observe that if $gcd(n, k) = 1$, the configuration is either asymmetric or it is symmetric with respect to a single axis of symmetry. Therefore at most two robots can have the same view. In the symmetric case, the adjective symmetric will be used with respect to this unique axis of symmetry. Note that symmetric robots have the same view.

3   Exploration of a Ring

3.1   Overview of the Algorithm

The overall structure of the algorithm can be seen as a sequence of three distinct phases: *Set-Up*, *Tower-Creation*, and *Exploration*.

The purpose of the *Set-Up* phase is to transform the (arbitrary) initial configuration into one from a predetermined set of configurations (called *no-towers-final*) with special properties. More precisely, in the *Set-Up* phase, the robots create a configuration where there is a single set of consecutive nodes occupied by robots, or two such sets of the same size (called *blocks*). When the configuration is *no-towers-final*, the next phase begins.

The purpose of the *Tower-Creation* phase is to transform the *no-towers-final* configuration created in the previous phase, into one from a predetermined set of configurations (called *towers-completed*) in which everything is prepared for exploration to begin. More precisely, in the *Tower-Creation* phase, one or two towers are created inside each block (the number depending on the parity of the size of the block); furthermore a number of robots become uniquely identified as explorers. As soon as the configuration is *towers-completed*, the next phase begins.

During the *Exploration* phase, the ring is actually being explored. The configuration reached upon exploration depends solely on the configuration at the beginning of this phase. The set of these special *exploration-completed* configurations is uniquely identified, and once in a configuration of this type, no robots will make any further move.

The *Set-Up* phase is by far the most complicated part of the algorithm, hence we describe it in a detailed way. To simplify the presentation, the next two phases are described in detail only in the case when k is odd. The case of k even can be described and analyzed using similar techniques and is omitted.

Since the robots are oblivious (i.e., they have no recollection of actions and computations made in previous cycles), there is no explicit way for them to record which phase is the current one. This information is derived by a robot solely based on the configuration currently observed (i.e., the one obtained as a result of the Look operation). Since the determination of the phase should be non-ambiguous, each reachable configuration should be assigned to exactly one phase.

For any possible configuration we will identify a set of *players*, which are the robots deciding to move if they perform a Look operation in this configuration, and corresponding *destinations*, i.e., target neighbors. The exploration algorithm (which contains the rules describing the Compute actions in the robot's cycle) can be succinctly formulated as follows.

Algorithm RING EXPLORATION

If I am a *player*
  move to my *destination*

3.2 Set-Up Phase

The first phase of the protocol is the *Set-Up*. The fact of being in this phase is easily recognizable by the robots since, unlike those of the other phases, the configurations of this phase contain no towers. Precisely because they contain no towers, any configuration of this phase can be an initial configuration.

We define the *interdistance* of a configuration as the minimum distance taken over all pairs of distinct robots in the configuration. Given an arbitrary configuration of interdistance d, a *block* is a maximal set of robots, of size at least 2, forming a line with a robot every d nodes. The *size* of a block is the number of robots it contains. The *border* of a block are the two nodes occupied by the two extremal robots of the block. A robot not in a block is said to be *isolated*. A robot is said to be a *neighbor* of a block/robot if in at least one direction there is no robot between itself and the block/robot. A *leader* of a configuration is a robot from which the view is the maximal in the configuration, with respect to the order defined in Section 2.1. A block containing a leader is called a *leading block*. Otherwise it is called a *non-leading block*.

The *Set-Up* phase is described by identifying four types of configurations that form a disjoint partition of all possible configurations without towers. For each type we indicate the players and their destinations.

Type A. A configuration of *type A* is a configuration of interdistance $d \geq 1$ with at least one isolated robot. Consider an arbitrary configuration of type A and let S be the maximum among the sizes of the blocks that are neighbors of at least one isolated robot. Let $\mathcal{I}$ be the set of isolated robots that are neighbors of a block of size S such that no other isolated robot is closer to a block of size S. The players in a configuration of type A are all the robots in $\mathcal{I}$. The destination of a player is its adjacent node in the direction of the closest neighboring block of size S.

Type B. A configuration of *type B* is a configuration of interdistance $d \geq 1$, without isolated robots, and containing at least one non-leading block. More precisely, if all blocks have the same size then the configuration is of type $B1$. Otherwise, it is of type $B2$.

Consider an arbitrary configuration of type $B1$. If there is only one leader, then the player is the leader and its destination is its adjacent node outside the block it belongs to. From now on, we assume that there are two leaders. This implies that the configuration is symmetric. There are two cases. The first case is when the blocks are of size 2. Since $k \geq 17$, there are at least 9 blocks and hence there exist two symmetric blocks separated by at least three blocks on each side. (Observe that this property does not hold for $k = 16$.) The players in such a configuration are the robots of such two blocks, having the smallest view. The destination of a player is its adjacent node outside the block it belongs to. We consider now the second case, that is when the blocks are of size larger than 2. The players in such a configuration are the pair of symmetric robots that are the closest to each other among the robots at the border of a block and such that these two robots are not neighbor. The destination of a player is the adjacent node outside the block it belongs to.

Consider an arbitrary configuration of type $B2$ and let s be the minimum size of a block in the configuration. Let S be the maximum among the sizes of the blocks that are neighbors of a block of size s and let d be the minimal distance between a block of size s and a block of size S. We define T as the set of robots belonging to a block of size s, neighbors of a block of size S, and at distance d from it. The players in a configuration of type $B2$ are the robots in T with the largest view. The destination of a player is its adjacent node in the direction of its neighboring block of size S.

Type C. A configuration of *type C* is a configuration of interdistance $d \geq 2$, without isolated robots, and such that each of its blocks is a leading block. Note that this implies that either all robots are in the same block or the robots are divided in two blocks of the same size. Moreover, there are exactly two leaders because the configuration is symmetric. The players in a configuration of type C are the two leaders. The destination of a player is its adjacent node in the direction of the block it belongs to. (This is not ambiguous because leaders are always located at the border of a block).

Type D. A configuration of *type D* is a configuration of interdistance $d = 1$, without isolated robots, and such that each of its blocks is a leading block. Type D is the set of configurations *no-towers-final*. When such a configuration is reached, the *Set-Up* phase ends and the *Tower-Creation* phase begins.

Note that types A, B, C and D form a partition of all possible initial configurations (when $gcd(n, k) = 1$).

The general idea of the *Set-Up* phase is to create few compact blocks (interdistance 1). Each decrease of interdistance is accomplished by first decreasing the number of blocks. The following lemmas show how this progress is achieved. The proofs of most of them are ommitted due to lack of space. Theorem 1 shows that a *no-towers-final* configuration is always reached at the end.

Lemma 2. *Assume that at some time t the configuration is of type A and that the only engaged robots are isolated robots engaged to move toward a neighboring block. Then* *after finite time, the configuration is of type B, C or D, of the same interdistance as in time t, and no robots are engaged.*

Lemma 3. *Assume that at some time t the configuration is asymmetric, of type B1, and that no robots are engaged. Then after finite time, the configuration is of type B2, of the same interdistance as in time t, no robots are engaged, and there is one block less than at time t.*

Lemma 4. *Assume that at some time t the configuration is symmetric, of type B1, with blocks of size 2, and that no robots are engaged. Then after finite time, the configuration is of type C or D, of the same interdistance as in time t, and no robots are engaged.*

Lemma 5. *Assume that at some time t the configuration is symmetric, of type B1, with blocks of size $s \geq 3$, and that no robots are engaged. Then after finite time, the configuration is of type B2, C or D, of the same interdistance as in time t, no robots are engaged, and there are fewer blocks than at time t.*

Lemma 6. *Assume that at some time t the configuration is of type B2 and that no robots are engaged. Then after finite time, the configuration is of type B, C or D, of the same interdistance as in time t, no robots are engaged, and there are fewer blocks than at time t.*

Lemma 7. *Assume that at some time t the configuration is of type C, of interdistance $d \geq 2$, and that no robots are engaged. Then at some time $t' > t$ one of the two following situations occurs:*

- *The configuration is of type A, of interdistance $d - 1$, and the only engaged robots are isolated robots engaged to move toward a block.*
- *The configuration is of type B, of interdistance $d - 1$, and no robots are engaged.*

Proof. Assume that at some time t the configuration is of type C, of interdistance $d \geq 2$, and no robots are engaged. The players are the two leaders. After finite time, at least one will move. Consider the moment t_1 where the first moves. At this moment the configuration changes to type A. If the other player moved at the same time or is not engaged, we are done because the configuration is of type A, of interdistance $d - 1$, and no robots are engaged.

Thus we assume that the other player $\mathcal{R}$ is engaged at time t_1. By the definition of type C configurations and the fact that $k \geq 17$, it is engaged to move toward an isolated robot $\mathcal{R}'$ that is at distance exactly d. Note that until $\mathcal{R}$ moves, there is only one block (of interdistance $d - 1$) and $\mathcal{R}$ is a neighbor of it (its other neighbor is $\mathcal{R}'$). Moreover, $\mathcal{R}$ is isolated and no robots will move toward it to make a block because no other robot is engaged at the moment and because a player in a configuration of type A never moves toward an isolated robot. Therefore, the configuration will remain of type A while $\mathcal{R}$ does not move.

Consider now the time t_2 where $\mathcal{R}$ makes its move. If this move does not make it belong to a block, then the configuration is of type A, of interdistance $d - 1$, and the only engaged robots are isolated robots engaged to move toward a block. Assume now that the move of $\mathcal{R}$ makes it belong to a block. Then necessarily it is a new block, of size two, and formed with robot $\mathcal{R}'$. If $\mathcal{R}'$ is not engaged then we are at a time t' satisfying the lemma. Indeed if there are isolated robots then the first situation occurs, and if there are not then the other block is larger, of size $k - 2$, and thus the second situation occurs. If $\mathcal{R}'$ is engaged at time t_2, then there are no isolated robots because there is none between $\mathcal{R}$ and the other block (in the segment excluding $\mathcal{R}'$) and there is none between $\mathcal{R}'$ and the other block (in the segment excluding $\mathcal{R}$) since $\mathcal{R}'$ got engaged as an isolated robot and thus was engaged to move toward a block. Therefore, we are in the following situation: there are two blocks of sizes $k - 2$ and 2, at distances at least $d + 1$ (on both sides); exactly one robot of the smaller block is engaged to move toward the other block, and no other robots are engaged. Thus the configuration is of type $B2$ and after some finite time, one of the two robots of the smaller block will move. At this moment, the first situation occurs, which concludes the proof of the lemma. $\square$

Theorem 1. *Any initial configuration is transformed after finite time into a configuration of type D (i.e. no-towers-final) without engaged robots.*

Proof. Let Φ be the property that the only engaged robots (if any) in a given configuration are isolated ones and they are engaged to move toward a neighboring block. For any configuration c of type A, B or C define the triple $T(c) = (d, t, x)$, where d is the interdistance of c, t is the type of c, i.e., t is A, B or C, and x is the number of blocks in c. Order all triples lexicographically, assuming that $C < B < A$. Lemmas $2 - 7$ imply that any configuration c of type A, B or C satisfying property Φ is transformed after finite time either in a configuration c' of type A, B or C satisfying property Φ, such that $T(c') < T(c)$, or in a configuration of type D with no robots engaged. Since any initial configuration satisfies property Φ, this concludes the proof. $\square$

Figure 1 ilustrates the progress of configurations toward type D.

3.3   Tower-Creation Phase

The second phase of the protocol is *Tower-Creation*. This phase begins with a configuration of type D, i.e., one of the configurations *no-towers-final*. The goal of this phase

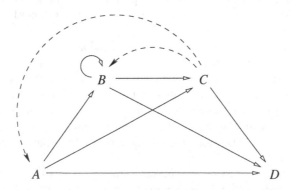

Fig. 1. Progress toward type D. Dashed arrows correspond to transitions where the interdistance decreases. The loop corresponds to a transition where the number of blocks decreases.

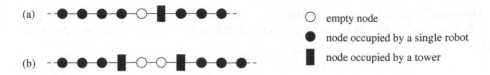

Fig. 2. Transformed blocks (a) of odd size (b) of even size

is to create one or two towers in each block (depending on the parity of the number of robots per block). More precisely, in a block of odd size there will be one tower, and in a block of even size there will be two towers. In a block of odd size the tower is formed by the central robot moving to its adjacent node containing the robot with the larger view. In a block of even size the two towers are formed by the two central robots moving to their other neighbors. The obtained configuration is called *towers-completed*. This is easily recognizable as each block of a *no-towers-final* configuration is transformed as follows. A block of odd size $2a + 1$ is transformed into a segment of a consecutive robots followed by an empty node, followed by a tower, followed by a segment of $a - 1$ consecutive robots. A block of even size $2a$ is transformed into a segment of $a - 2$ consecutive robots followed by a tower, followed by two empty nodes followed by a tower, followed by a segment of $a - 2$ consecutive robots (see Figure 2).

Since we limit our detailed description to the case of k odd, the only possibility is that the *no-towers-final* configuration starting the *Tower-Creation* phase consists of one block of odd size. In this case the phase consists of one move of the central robot. This robot moves to the neighbor decided by the adversary, as the configuration is symmetric.

3.4 Exploration Phase

Exploration starts when towers in the preceding phase are created. Note that the empty nodes adjacent to towers have already been explored, so the segments of empty nodes between the transformed blocks are the only ones possibly not yet explored. Each of these segments is explored in the current phase using one or two robots closest to the segment. If k is even, such a segment must lie between two segments of consecutive robots of equal size, and it is explored by the two border robots that meet in the middle of the segment (either at the extremities of the central edge, or in the central node). The obtained configuration is called *exploration-completed*.

We describe exploration in detail for k odd. In this case the configuration starting *Exploration* phase is a single transformed block of odd size, with $a = (k-1)/2$ (hence in particular $a \geq 3$), see Figure 2 (a). The unique player is the robot in the segment of $a-1$ consecutive robots, farthest from the tower. This robot moves to its empty neighbor node. In a resulting configuration with a single isolated robot, the player is this robot and it moves toward the segment of a consecutive robots. When the configuration contains $a + 1$ consecutive robots followed by an empty node, followed by a tower, followed by a segment of $a - 2$ consecutive robots, all robots remain idle. At this point exploration is completed.

From Theorem 1 describing the conclusion of the *Set-Up* phase and from the properties of *Tower-Creation* and *Exploration* phases we get the following result.

Theorem 2. *Let* $17 \leq k < n$. *Algorithm* RING EXPLORATION *allows a team of* k *robots to explore a* n-*node ring and enter a terminal state within finite time, provided* $gcd(n, k) = 1$.

4   Size of the Minimum Team

In this section we show that the minimum number of robots that can explore a n-node ring regardless of their initial position, is logarithmic in n. More precisely, we have the following result.

Theorem 3. *The minimum number* $\rho(n)$ *of robots that can explore a* n-*node ring has the following properties:*

1. $\rho(n) \in O(\log n)$;
2. *there exists a constant* c *such that, for infinitely many* n, *we have* $\rho(n) \geq c \log n$.

Proof. Let p_j denote the j-th prime, and let $p_j \#$ denote the p_j-*primorial*, that is

$$p_j \# = \Pi_{i=1}^{j} \ p_i \tag{1}$$

An important property of the primorial is the following [28]:

$$\lim_{j \to \infty} (p_j \#)^{\frac{1}{p_j}} = e . \tag{2}$$

We will now prove each part of the theorem separately.

Part 1

Let $f(n)$ be the smallest integer coprime with n and larger than 16. Thus, by Theorem 2, exploration is possible with $f(n)$ agents. Hence, $\rho(n) \leq f(n)$.

Take j such that $\frac{p_j \#}{13\#} \leq n < \frac{p_{j+1}\#}{13\#}$. We have $f(n) \leq p_{j+1}$. (Otherwise, all primes in $\{17, \ldots, p_{j+1}\}$ divide n and hence $n \geq \frac{p_{j+1}\#}{13\#}$, contradiction.) By property (2) we have $2 \leq (p_j \#)^{\frac{1}{p_j}}$, for sufficiently large j. Hence $2^{p_j} \leq p_j \#$, and thus $p_j \leq \log(p_j \#)$. Hence $p_{j+1} \leq \log(p_{j+1}\#) \leq \log(p_j \#) + \log p_j$. Since $p_{j+1} \leq p_j \# + 1 \leq 2 \cdot 13\# \cdot n$, we have $\rho(n) \leq f(n) \leq p_{j+1} \leq \log(2 \cdot 13\# \cdot n) + \log n$, which is at most $3 \log n$, for sufficiently large n.

Part 2

Let n be the least common multiple of integers $1, 2, \ldots, m$. Let $g(n)$ be the smallest integer not dividing n. By Lemma 1 we have $\rho(n) \geq g(n)$. We have $g(n) \geq m + 1$. The Prime Number Theorem implies $\frac{\ln n}{m} \to 1$. Hence $\ln n \leq 2m$, for sufficiently large m. This implies the existence of a constant c such that $\rho(n) \geq g(n) \geq m + 1 > m \geq \frac{\ln n}{2} \geq c \log n$. $\square$

It should be noted that for some specific values of n, the number $\rho(n)$ is constant. For example, if $n > 17$ is prime, then Theorem 2 shows that 17 robots can explore the n-node ring, hence $\rho(n) \leq 17$.

5   Conclusion

In this paper we have analyzed the exploration problem in rings by asynchronous robots when they are oblivious and can see the environment but cannot communicate. This is a further step in the understanding of how these robots' capabilities, standard in continuous universes, can be exploited in the discrete ones. These results open several interesting problems and pose intriguing questions. First, the complete characterization of couples (n, k) for which exploration of the ring is solvable remains open. Next, the problem of exploring other topologies and arbitrary graphs is a natural extension of this work. Moreover, since the robots cannot communicate, they have to be able to observe the environment; an immediate question is what happens if the robots can only see within a fixed distance. Accuracy of vision as well as fault-tolerance are issues that should be addressed by future research.

Acknowledgment. This work was done during the stay of David Ilcinkas at the Research Chair in Distributed Computing at the Université du Québec en Outaouais and at the University of Ottawa, as a postdoctoral fellow. Andrzej Pelc was partially supported by the Research Chair in Distributed Computing at the Université du Québec en Outaouais, Paola Flocchini was partially supported by the University Research Chair of the University of Ottawa. This work was supported in part by the Natural Sciences and Engineering Research Council of Canada under Discovery grants.

References

1. Agmon, N., Peleg, D.: Fault-Tolerant Gathering Algorithms for Autonomous Mobile Robots. SIAM J. Comput. 36(1), 56–82 (2006)
2. Albers, S., Henzinger, M.R.: Exploring unknown environments. SIAM J. Comput. 29, 1164–1188 (2000)
3. Averbakh, I., Berman, O.: A heuristic with worst-case analysis for minimax routing of two traveling salesmen on a tree. Discr. Appl. Math. 68, 17–32 (1996)
4. Averbakh, I., Berman, O.: $(p - 1)/(p + 1)$-approximate algorithms for p-traveling salesmen problems on a tree with minmax objective. Discr. Appl. Mathematics 75, 201–216 (1997)
5. Awerbuch, B., Betke, M., Rivest, R., Singh, M.: Piecemeal graph learning by a mobile robot. In: Proc. 8th Conf. on Comput. Learning Theory, pp. 321–328 (1995)
6. Bender, M.A., Fernandez, A., Ron, D., Sahai, A., Vadhan, S.: The power of a pebble: Exploring and mapping directed graphs. In: STOC 1998. Proc. 30th Ann. Symp. on Theory of Computing, pp. 269–278 (1998)
7. Bender, M.A., Slonim, D.: The power of team exploration: Two robots can learn unlabeled directed graphs, Proc. 35th Ann. In: FOCS 1994. Symp. on Foundations of Computer Science, pp. 75–85 (1994)
8. Betke, M., Rivest, R., Singh, M.: Piecemeal learning of an unknown environment. Machine Learning 18, 231–254 (1995)
9. Cieliebak, M., Flocchini, P., Prencipe, G., Santoro, N.: Solving the Robots Gathering Problem. In: Baeten, J.C.M., Lenstra, J.K., Parrow, J., Woeginger, G.J. (eds.) ICALP 2003. LNCS, vol. 2719, Springer, Heidelberg (2003)
10. Cohen, R., Peleg, D.: Robot convergence via center-of-gravity algorithms. In: Kralovic, R., Sýkora, O. (eds.) SIROCCO 2004. LNCS, vol. 3104, pp. 79–88. Springer, Heidelberg (2004)

11. Czyzowicz, J., Gasieniec, L., Pelc, A.: Gathering few fat mobile robots in the plane. In: Asano, T. (ed.) ISAAC 2006. LNCS, vol. 4288, pp. 744–753. Springer, Heidelberg (2006)
12. Das, S., Flocchini, P., Kutten, S., Nayak, A., Santoro, N.: Map construction of unknown graphs by multiple agents. Theoretical Computer Science (to appear 2007)
13. Défago, X., Konagaya, A.: Circle formation for oblivious anonymous mobile robots with no common sense of orientation. In: Workshop on Principles of Mobile Computing, pp. 97–104 (2002)
14. Deng, X., Papadimitriou, C.H.: Exploring an unknown graph. Journal of Graph Theory 32, 265–297 (1999)
15. Dessmark, A., Pelc, A.: Optimal graph exploration without good maps. In: Möhring, R.H., Raman, R. (eds.) ESA 2002. LNCS, vol. 2461, pp. 374–386. Springer, Heidelberg (2002)
16. Diks, K., Fraigniaud, P., Kranakis, E., Pelc, A.: Tree exploration with little memory. In: SODA 2002. Proc. 13th Ann. ACM-SIAM Symp. on Discrete Algorithms, pp. 588–597. ACM Press, New York (2002)
17. Duncan, C.A., Kobourov, S.G., Kumar, V.S.A.: Optimal constrained graph exploration. In: SODA 2001. Proc. 12th Ann. ACM-SIAM Symp. on Discrete Algorithms, pp. 807–814. ACM Press, New York (2001)
18. Fleischer, R., Trippen, G.: Exploring an unknown graph efficiently. In: Brodal, G.S., Leonardi, S. (eds.) ESA 2005. LNCS, vol. 3669, pp. 11–22. Springer, Heidelberg (2005)
19. Flocchini, P., Prencipe, G., Santoro, N., Widmayer, P.: Hard tasks for weak robot. In: Aggarwal, A.K., Pandu Rangan, C. (eds.) ISAAC 1999. LNCS, vol. 1741, pp. 93–102. Springer, Heidelberg (1999)
20. Fraigniaud, P., Gasieniec, L., Kowalski, D., Pelc, A.: Collective tree exploration. In: Farach-Colton, M. (ed.) LATIN 2004. LNCS, vol. 2976, pp. 141–151. Springer, Heidelberg (2004)
21. Frederickson, G.N., Hecht, M.S., Kim, C.E.: Approximation algorithms for some routing problems. SIAM J. Comput. 7, 178–193 (1978)
22. Gasieniec, L., Pelc, A., Radzik, T., Zhang, X.: Tree exploration with logarithmic memory. In: SODA 2007. Proc. 18th Annual ACM-SIAM Symp. on Discrete Algorithms, New Orleans, Louisiana, USA (January 2007)
23. Klasing, R., Markou, E., Pelc, A.: Gathering asynchronous oblivious mobile robots in a ring. In: Asano, T. (ed.) ISAAC 2006. LNCS, vol. 4288, Springer, Heidelberg (2006)
24. Li, X., Santoro, N.: An Integrated self-deployment and coverage maintenance scheme for mobile sensor networks. In: Cao, J., Stojmenovic, I., Jia, X., Das, S.K. (eds.) MSN 2006. LNCS, vol. 4325, Springer, Heidelberg (2006)
25. Panaite, P., Pelc, A.: Exploring unknown undirected graphs. Journal of Algorithms 33, 281–295 (1999)
26. Prencipe, G.: On the feasibility of gathering by autonomous mobile robots. In: Pelc, A., Raynal, M. (eds.) SIROCCO 2005. LNCS, vol. 3499, pp. 246–261. Springer, Heidelberg (2005)
27. Prencipe, G., Santoro, N.: Distributed algorithms for mobile robots. In: TCS 2006. Proc. 5th IFIP Int. Conf. on Theoretical Computer Science, pp. 47–62 (2006)
28. Ruiz, S.M.: A Result on Prime Numbers. Math. Gaz. 81, 269 (1997)
29. Souissi, S., Défago, X., Yamashita, M.: Gathering asynchronous mobile robots with inaccurate compasses. In: Shvartsman, A.A. (ed.) OPODIS 2006. LNCS, vol. 4305, pp. 333–349. Springer, Heidelberg (2006)
30. Suzuki, I., Yamashita, M.: Distributed anonymous mobile robots: formation of geometric patterns. SIAM J. Comput. 28(4), 1347–1363 (1999)

Deterministic Communication
in the Weak Sensor Model

Antonio Fernández Anta, Miguel A. Mosteiro, and Christopher Thraves

LADyR, GSyC, Universidad Rey Juan Carlos, 28933 Móstoles, Madrid, Spain
anto@gsyc.es, mosteiro@cs.rutgers.edu, cbthraves@gmail.com

Abstract. In Sensor Networks, the lack of topology information and the availability of only one communication channel has led research work to the use of randomization to deal with collision of transmissions. However, the scarcest resource in this setting is the energy supply, and radio communication dominates the sensor node energy consumption. Hence, redundant trials of transmission as used in randomized protocols may be counter-effective. Additionally, most of the research work in Sensor Networks is either heuristic or includes unreallistic assumptions. Hence, provable results for many basic problems still remain to be given. In this paper, we study upper and lower bounds for deterministic communication primitives under the harsh constraints of sensor nodes.

1 Introduction

The Sensor Network is a well-studied simplified abstraction of a radio-communication network where nodes are deployed at random over a large area in order to monitor some physical event. Sensor Networks is a very active research area, not only due to the potential applications of such a technology, but also because well-known techniques used in networks cannot be straightforwardly implemented in sensor nodes, due to harsh resource limitations.

Sensor Networks are expected to be used in remote or hostile environments. Hence, random deployment of nodes is frequently assumed. Although the density of nodes must be big enough to achieve connectivity, precise location of specific nodes cannot be guaranteed in such scenario. Consequently, the topology of the network is usually assumed to be unknown, except perhaps for bounds on the total number of nodes and the maximum number of neighbors of any node. In addition, given that in Sensor Networks only one channel of communication is assumed to be available, protocols must deal with collision of transmissions.

Most of the Sensor Network protocols use randomness to deal with collisions and lack of topology information. Randomized protocols are fast and resilient to failures, but frequently rely on redundant transmissions. Given that the most restrictive resource in a Sensor Network is energy and that the dominating factor in energy consumption is the radio communication, deterministic algorithms may yield energy-efficient solutions. In this paper, deterministic communication primitives are studied under the harsh restrictions of sensor nodes.

Model. We model the potential connectivity of nodes as a *Geometric Graph* where n nodes are deployed in $\mathbb{R}^2$, and a pair of nodes is connected by an undirected edge if and

E. Tovar, P. Tsigas, and H. Fouchal (Eds.): OPODIS 2007, LNCS 4878, pp. 119–131, 2007.
© Springer-Verlag Berlin Heidelberg 2007

only if they are at an Euclidean distance of at most a parameter r. It is important to stress that this topology models the *potential* connectivity of nodes. However, upon deployment, two neighboring nodes still have to establish a communication link in order to be neighbors in terms of the communication network. The geometric graph model implies a circular-range assumption, which in practice may not be true. However, whenever this is the case, the minimum radius may be taken without extra asymptotic cost.

Although random, deployment is not the result of an uncontrolled experiment where any outcome has a positive probability. Hence, we assume that the network is connected and that the maximum degree, i.e., the maximum number of nodes located within a radius of r of any node, is a known value $k - 1 < n$. Each node knows only the total size of the network n, its unique identifier in $\{1, \dots, n\}$ and the maximum degree $k - 1$.

Regarding sensor node limitations, we use the comprehensive Weak Sensor Model [12] unless otherwise stated. The following assumptions are included in this model. Time is assumed to be slotted and all nodes have the same clock frequency, but no global synchronizing mechanism is available. Furthermore, nodes are activated adversarially. The communication among neighboring nodes is through broadcast on a shared channel where a node receives a message only if exactly one of its neighbors transmits in a time slot. If more than one message is sent in the same time slot, a collision occurs and no collision detection mechanism is available. Sensor nodes cannot receive and transmit in the same time slot. The channel is assumed to have only two states: transmission and silence/collision. The memory size of each sensor node is bounded by $O(1)$ words of $O(\log n)^1$ bits. We assume that sensor nodes can adjust their power of transmission but only to a constant number of levels. Other limitations include: limited life cycle due to energy constraints, short transmission range, only one channel of communication, no position information, and unreliability.

In a time slot, a node can be in one of three states, namely *transmission*, *reception*, or *inactive*. A node that is in the transmission or reception state is *active*. We denote a temporal sequence of states of a node as a *schedule of transmissions*, or simply a *schedule* when the context is clear.

Problem Definition. An expected application of Sensor Networks is to continuously monitor some physical phenomena. Hence, in this paper, the problem we address is to guarantee that each active node can communicate with all of its neighboring active nodes infinitely many times. The actual use of such a capability will depend of course on the availability of messages to be delivered. Our goal is to give guarantees on the energy cost and the time delay of the communication only, leaving aside the overhead due to queuing or other factors.

In Radio Networks, messages are successfully delivered by means of non-colliding transmissions. Non-colliding transmissions in single-hop Radio Networks are clearly defined: the number of transmitters must be exactly one. However, in a multi-hop scenario such as Sensor Networks the same transmission may be correctly received by some nodes and collide with other transmissions at other nodes. Thus, a more precise definition is necessary. If in a given time slot exactly one of the adjacent neighbors of a node x transmits, and x itself is not transmitting, we say that there was a *clear*

---

[1] Througout this paper, log means $\log_2$ unless otherwise stated.

reception at x in that time slot. Whereas, in the case where a node transmits a message in a given time slot, and no other node within *two* hops of the transmitter transmits in the same time slot, we say that there was a *clear transmission*. Notice that when a clear transmission is produced by a node, all its neighbors clearly receive at the same time. Of course, in a single-hop network both problems are identical.

In this paper, our goal is to guarantee that each node communicates with all of its at most $k - 1$ neighbors. Hence, a closely-related communication primitive known as *selection* is relevant for our purposes. In the selection problem, each of k *active* nodes of a single-hop Radio Network hold a different message that has to be delivered to all the active nodes. Once its message is successfully transmitted, a node becomes inactive. Given that we want to guarantee communication forever, in this paper, we give upper and lower bounds for generalizations of the selection problem that we define as follows.

Definition 1. *Given a single-hop Radio Network of n nodes where k of them are activated possibly at different times, in order to solve the* Recurring Selection *problem every active node must clearly transmit infinitely many times.*

Definition 2. *Given a Sensor Network of n nodes and maximum degree $k - 1$, where upon activation, possibly at different times, nodes stay active forever, in order to solve the* Recurring Reception *problem every active node must clearly receive from all of its active neighboring nodes infinitely many times.*

Definition 3. *Given a Sensor Network of n nodes and maximum degree $k - 1$, where upon activation, possibly at different times, nodes stay active forever, in order to solve the* Recurring Transmission *problem every active node must clearly transmit to all of its active neighboring nodes infinitely many times.*

Given that protocols for such problems run forever, we need to establish a metric to evaluate energy cost and time efficiency. Let $R_u^i(v)$ be the number of transmissions of u between the $(i - 1)^{th}$ and the ith clear receptions from u at v, and $R_u(v) = \max_i R_u^i(v)$. In order to measure time we denote $\Delta R_u^i(v)$ the time (number of time slots) that are between the $(i - 1)^{th}$ and the ith clear receptions from u at v, and $\Delta R_u(v) = \max_i \Delta R_u^i(v)$. Similarly, Let $T^i(u)$ be the number of transmissions from u between the $(i - 1)^{th}$ and the ith clear transmissions from u, and $T(u) = \max_i T^i(u)$; and let $\Delta T^i(u)$ be the time between the $(i - 1)^{th}$ and the ith clear transmission from u, and $\Delta T(u) = \max_i \Delta T^i(u)$.

We define the *message complexity* of a protocol for Recurring Reception as $\max_{(u,v)} R_u(v)$, over all pairs (u, v) of adjacent nodes; and for Recurring Transmission as $\max_u T(u)$ over all nodes u. We define the *delay* of a protocol for Recurring Reception as $\max_{(u,v)} \Delta R_u(v)$, over all pairs (u, v) of adjacent nodes; and for Recurring Transmission as $\max_u \Delta T(u)$ over all nodes u. Any of these definitions is valid for the Recurring Selection problem since clear transmissions and clear receptions are the same event in a single-hop network.

Unless otherwise stated, throughout the paper we assume the presence of an adversary that gets to choose the time step of activation of each node. Additionally, for Recurring Selection, the adversary gets to choose which are the active nodes; and for Recurring Reception and Recurring Transmission, given a topology where each node has at most $k - 1$ adjacent nodes, the adversary gets to choose which is the identity of each node. In other words, the adversary gets to choose which of the n schedules is assigned to each node.

Constraints such as limited life cycle and unreliability imply that nodes may power on and off many times. If such a behaviour were adversarial, the delay of any protocol could be infinite. Therefore, we assume that active nodes that become inactive are not activated back.

Related Work. In [1], Alon, Bar-Noy, Linial and Peleg gave a deterministic distributed protocol to simulate the message passing model in radio networks. Using this technique, each node receives a transmission of all its neighbors after $O(k^2 \log^2 n / \log(k \log n))$ steps. Unfortunately, simultaneous wake-up and $\omega(\log n)$ memory size is required. In the same paper, lower bounds for this problem are also proved by showing bipartite graphs that require $\Omega(k \log k)$ rounds. Bipartite graphs with maximum degree $\omega(1)$ are not embeddable in geometric graphs therefore these bounds do not apply to our setting.

The question of how to diseminate information in Radio Networks has led to different well-studied important problems such as *Broadcast* [2, 20] or *Gossiping* [21, 4]. However, deterministic solutions for these problems [8, 6, 10, 5] include assumptions such as simultaneous startup or the availability of a global clock, which are not feasible in Sensor Networks.

The selection problem previously defined was studied [19] in *static* and *dynamic* versions. In static selection all nodes are assumed to start simultaneously, although the choice of which are the active nodes is adversarial. Instead, in the dynamic version, the activation schedule is also adversarial. For static selection, Komlos and Greenberg showed in [18] a non-constructive upper bound of $O(k \log(n/k))$ to achieve *one* successful transmission. More recently, Clementi, Monti, and Silvestri showed for this problem in [9] a tight lower bound of $\Omega(k \log(n/k))$ using intersection-free families. For k distinct successful transmissions, Kowalski presented in [19] an algorithm that uses $(2^{\ell-1}, 2^{\ell}, n)$-selectors for each ℓ. By combining this algorithm and the existence upper bound of [3] a $O(k \log(n/k))$ is obtained. Using Indyk's constructive selector, a $O(k \text{ polylog } n)$ is also proved. These results take advantage of the fact that in the selection problem nodes turn off upon successful transmission. For dynamic selection, Chrobak, Gąsieniec and Kowalski [7] proved the existence of $O(k^2 \log n)$ for dynamic 1-selection. Kowalski [19] proved $O(k^2 \log n)$ and claimed $\Omega(k^2 / \log k)$ both by using the probabilistic method, and $O(k^2 \text{ polylog } n)$ using Indyk's selector.

A related line of work from combinatorics is (k, n)-*selective families*. Consider the subset of nodes that transmit in each time slot. A family $\mathcal{R}$ of subsets of $\{1, \ldots, n\}$ is (k, n)-selective, for a positive integer k, if for any subset Z of $\{1, \ldots, n\}$ such that $|Z| \leq k$ there is a set $S \in \mathcal{R}$ such that $|S \cap Z| = 1$. In terms of Radio Networks, a set of n sequences of time slots where a node transmits or receives is (k, n)-selective if for any subset Z of k nodes, there exists a time slot in which exactly one node in the subset transmits. In [17] Indyk gave a constructive proof of the existence of (k, n)-selective families of size $O(k \text{ polylog } n)$. A natural generalization of selective families follows. Given integers m, k, n, with $1 \leq m \leq k \leq n$, we say that a boolean matrix M with t rows and n columns is a (m, k, n)-*selector* if any submatrix of M obtained by choosing arbitrarily k out of the n columns of M contains at least m distinct rows of the identity matrix I_k. The integer t is the size of the (m, k, n)-selector. In [11] Dyachkov and Rykov showed that (m, k, n)-selectors must have a size $\Omega(\min\{n, k^2 \log_k n\})$ when $m = k$. Recently in [3], De Bonis, Gąsieniec and Vaccaro showed that (k, k, n)-selectors must have size $t \geq (k - 1)^2 \log n/(4 \log(k - 1) + O(1))$ using superimposed codes. In the same paper, it was shown the existence of (k, k, n)-selectors of size $O(k^2 \ln(n/k))$.

Regarding randomized protocols, an optimal $O(D + k)$-algorithm for gossiping in a Sensor Network of diameter D was presented in [14]. The algorithm includes a preprocessing phase that allows to achieve global synchronism and to implement a collision detection mechanism. After that, nodes transmit their message to all neighboring nodes within $O(k + \log^2 n \log k)$ steps with high probabiliy. The expected message complexity of such phase is $O(\log n + \log^2 k)$. A non-adaptive randomized algorithm that achieves one clear transmission for each node w.h.p. in $O(k \log n)$ steps was shown in [13]. The expected message complexity of such a protocol is $O(\log n)$. In the same paper it was shown that such a running time is optimal for fair protocols, i.e., protocols where all nodes are assumed to use the same probability of transmission in the same time slot.

Our Results. Our objective is to find deterministic algorithms that *minimize the message complexity* and, among those, algorithms that attempt to minimize the delay. As in [18], we say that a protocol is *oblivious* if the sequence of transmissions of a node does not depend on the messages received. Otherwise, we call the protocol *adaptive*. We study deterministic oblivious and adaptive protocols for Recurring Selection, Recurring Reception and Recurring Transmission. These problems are particularly difficult due to the arbitrary activation schedule of nodes. In fact, the study of oblivious protocols is particularly relevant under adversarial wake-up, given their simplicity as compared with adaptive protocols where usually different phases need to be synchronized. If we were able to weaken the adversary assuming that all nodes are activated simultaneously, as it is customary in the more general Radio Network model, the following well-known oblivious algorithm would solve these problems optimally.

> *For each node i,*
> *node i transmits in time slot $t = i + jn, \forall j \in \mathbb{N} \cup \{0\}$.*

The message complexity for this algorithm is 1 which of course is optimal. To see why the delay of n is optimal for a protocol with message complexity 1, assume that there is an algorithm with smaller delay. Then, there are at least two nodes that transmit in the same time slot. If these nodes are placed within one-hop their transmissions will collide, hence increasing the message complexity.

We first study oblivious protocols. We show that the message complexity of any oblivious deterministic protocol for these problems is at least k. Then, we present a message-complexity optimal protocol, which we call Primed Selection, with delay $O(kn \log n)$. We then evaluate the time efficiency of such a protocol studying lower bounds for these problems. Since a lower bound for Recurring Selection is also a lower bound for Recurring Reception and Recurring Transmission, we concentrate on the first problem. By giving a mapping between (m, k, n)-selectors and Recurring Selection, we establish that $\Omega(k^2 \log n/ \log k)$ is a lower bound for the delay of any protocol that solves Recurring Selection. Maintaining the optimal message complexity may be a good approach to improve this bound. However, the memory size limitations motivates the study of protocols with some form of periodicity. Using a simple argument we show that the delay of any protocol that solves Recurring Selection is in $\Omega(kn)$, for the important class of *equiperiodic protocols* , i.e., protocols where each node transmits with a fixed frequency. Finally, we show that choosing appropriately the periods that nodes use, for $k \leq n^{1/6 \log \log n}$ Primed Selection is also optimal delay wise for equiperiodic protocols. Given that most of the research work in Sensor Networks assumes a logarithmic one-hop density of nodes, Primed Selection is optimal in general for most of the values of k and the delay is only a logarithmic factor from optimal for arbitrary graphs.

Moving to adaptive protocols, we show how to implement a preprocessing phase using Primed Selection so that the delay is reduced to $O(k^2 \log k)$.

To the best of our knowledge, no message-complexity lower bounds for recurring communication with randomized oblivious protocols have been proved. Nevertheless, the best algorithm known to solve Recurring Selection w.h.p. is to repeatedly transmit with probability $1/k$ which solves the problem with delay $O(k \log n)$ and expected message complexity in $O(\log n)$. Therefore, deterministic protocols outperform this randomized algorithm for $k \in o(\log n)$ and for settings where the task has to be solved with probability 1.

Roadmap. Oblivious and adaptive protocols are studied in Sections 2 and 3 respectively. Lower bounds are studied for message complexity in Section 2.1 and for the delay in Section 2.3. The Primed Selection oblivious protocol is presented and analyzed in Section 2.2. An improvement of this algorithm for most of the values of k is shown in Section 2.4 whereas an adaptive protocol that uses Primed Selection is given in Section 3. We finish with some acknowledgements.

2   Oblivious Protocols

2.1   Message-Complexity Lower Bound

A lower bound on the message complexity of any protocol that solves Recurring Selection is also a lower bound for Recurring Reception and Recurring Transmission. To see why, we map Recurring Selection into Recurring Reception and viceversa. A similar argument can be given for Recurring Transmission.

Consider a single-hop Radio Network N_S where Recurring Selection is solved and a Sensor Network N_R where Recurring Reception is solved. Consider the set of k active nodes in N_S. There is at least one node i with degree $k-1$ in N_R. Map any of the active nodes in N_S to i and the remaining $k-1$ active nodes in N_S to the neighbors of i in N_R. The adversarial choice of which are the k active nodes in N_S is equivalent to the adversarial choice of which schedules of the protocol are assigned to i and its neighbors in N_R.

Now, for the sake of contradiction, assume that for any protocol that solves Recurring Selection, the message complexity is at least s but there is a protocol $\mathcal{P}$ that solves Recurring Reception with message complexity $r < s$. Then, we can use $\mathcal{P}$ to solve Recurring Selection as follows. Consider a network N_R that contains a clique of size k. $\mathcal{P}$ must solve Recurring Reception in this network. Consider nodes u and i that belong to the clique in N_R. By definition of Recurring Reception, it is guaranteed that i receives from u every r transmissions of u. Hence, every r transmissions of u there is at least one transmission of u that does not collide with any other node adjacent to i. Since this is true for each of the nodes adjacent to i, Recurring Selection can be solved with message complexity r which is a contradiction.

Theorem 1. *Any oblivious deterministic algorithm that solves the Recurring Selection problem, on an n-node single-hop Radio Network where k nodes are activated, perhaps at different times, has a message complexity of at least k.*

Proof. Assume for the sake of contradiction that there exists a protocol such that some node i achieves a non-colliding transmission every $t < k$ transmissions. But then, an adversary can activate each of the other $k - 1$ nodes in such a way that at least one transmission collides with each transmission of i within an interval of t transmissions, which is a contradiction.

2.2 A Message-Complexity-Optimal Protocol: Primed Selection

In the following sections we present our *Primed Selection* protocol for deterministic communication. Such a protocol solves Recurring Selection, Recurring Reception and Recurring Transmission with the same asymptotic cost. For clarity, we first analyze the protocol for Recurring Selection, then we extend the analysis to Recurring Reception and finally we argue why Recurring Transmission is solved with the same asymptotic cost.

A static version of the Recurring Selection problem, where k nodes are activated simultaneously, may also be of interest. For the case $k = 2$, a $(k \log_k n)$-delay protocol can be given recursively applying the following approach. First, evenly split the nodes in two subsets. Then, in the first step one subset transmits and the other receives and in the next one the roles are reversed. Finally, recursively apply the same process to each subset.

Recurring Selection. We assume that the choice of which are the active nodes and the schedule of activations is adversarial. In principle, k different schedules might suffice to solve the problem. However, if only s different schedules are used, for any $s < n$ there exists a pair of nodes with the same schedule. Then, since the protocols are oblivious, if the adversary activates that pair at the same time the protocol would fail. Instead, we define a set of schedules such that each node in the network is assigned a different one.

We assume that, for each node with ID i, a prime number $p(i)$ has been stored in advance in its memory so that $p(1) = p_j < p(2) = p_{j+1} \ldots p(n) = p_{j+n-1}$. Where p_ℓ denotes the ℓ-th prime number and p_j is the smallest prime number bigger than k. Notice that the biggest prime used is $p(n) < p_{n+k} \in O(n \log n)$ by the prime number theorem [16]. Hence, its bit size is in $O(\log n)$. Thus, this protocol works in a small-memory model. The algorithm, which we call *Primed Selection* is simple to describe.

> *For each node i with assigned prime number $p(i)$,*
> *node i transmits with period $p(i)$.*

Theorem 2. *Given a one-hop Radio Network with n nodes, where k nodes are activated perhaps at different times, Primed Selection solves the Recurring Selection problem with delay in $O(kn \log n)$ and the message complexity per successful transmission is k, which is optimal as shown in Theorem 1.*

Proof. If no transmission collides with any other transmission we are done, so let us assume that there are some collisions. Consider a node i whose transmission collides with the transmission of a node $j \neq i$ at time t_c. Since $p(i)$ and $p(j)$ are coprimes, the next collision among them occurs at $t_c + p(i)p(j)$. Since $p(i)p(j) > p(i)k$, j does not collide with i within the next $kp(i)$ steps. Node i transmits at least k times within the interval $(t_c, t_c + kp(i)]$. There are at most $k - 1$ other active nodes that can collide with i. But, due to the same reason, they can collide with i only once in the interval $[t_c, t_c + kp(i)]$. Therefore, i transmits successfully at least once within this interval. In the worst case, $i = n$ and the delay is in $O(kp(n)) \in O(kn \log n)$. Since every node transmits successfully at least once every k transmissions, the message complexity is k.

Recurring Reception. A protocol for Recurring Selection may be used to solve the Recurring Reception problem. However, two additional issues appear: the restrictions of sensor nodes and the interference among one-hop neighborhoods. As mentioned, Primed Selection works under the constraints of the Weak Sensor Model. We show in this section that interference is also handled.

Recall that in the Recurring Reception problem n nodes of a Sensor Network are activated, possibly at different times, the maximum number of neighbors of any node is bounded by some value $k - 1 < n$, and every active node must receive from all of its active neighboring nodes periodically forever. The non-active nodes do not participate in the protocol. We assume the choice of which are the active nodes and the schedule of activations to be adversarial.

Theorem 3. *Given a Sensor Network with n nodes, where the maximum number of nodes adjacent to any node is $k - 1 < n$, Primed Selection solves the Recurring Reception problem with delay in $O(kn \log n)$ and the message complexity per reception is k, which is optimal as shown in Theorem 1.*

Proof. Consider any node u and the set of its adjacent nodes $N(u)$. If u receives the transmissions of all its neighbors without collisions we are done. Otherwise, consider a pair of nodes $i, j \in N(u)$ that transmit –hence, collide at u– at time t_c. Since $p(i)$ and $p(j)$ are coprimes, the next collision among them at u occurs at time $t_c + p(i)p(j)$. Since $p(i)p(j) > p(i)k$, j does not collide with i at u within the next $kp(i)$ steps. Node i transmits at least k times within this interval. There are at most $k - 2$ other nodes adjacent to u that can collide with i at u, and of course u itself can collide with i at u. But, due to the same reason, they can collide with i at u only once in the interval $[t_c, t_c + kp(i)]$. Therefore, i transmits without collision at u at least once within this interval and the claimed delay follows. The transmission of every node is received by some neighboring node at least once every k transmissions.

Recurring Transmission. Observe that Primed Selection solves the Recurring Transmission problem also, modulo an additional factor of 7 in the analysis, because any two-hop neighborhood has at most $7k$ nodes, by a simple geometric argument based on the optimality of an hexagonal packing [15].

2.3 Delay Lower Bounds

De Bonis, Gąsieniec and Vaccaro have shown [3] a lower bound of $((k - m + 1) \lfloor (m - 1)/(k - m + 1) \rfloor^2 / (4 \log(\lfloor (m - 1)/(k - m + 1) \rfloor) + O(1))) \log(n/(k - m + 1))$ on the size of (k, m, n)-selectors when $1 \leq m \leq k \leq n, k < 2m - 2$. When $m = k > 2$, this lower bound gives a lower bound of $\Omega(k^2 \log n / \log k)$ for the delay of any protocol that solves Recurring Selection. To see why, recall that a (k, m, n)-selector is defined as follows

Definition 4. *[3] Given integers k, m, and n, with $1 \leq m \leq k \leq n$, we say that a boolean matrix M with t rows and n columns is a (k, m, n)-selector if any submatrix of M obtained by choosing k out of n arbitrary columns of M contains at least m distinct rows of the identity matrix I_k. The integer t is the size of the (k, m, n)-selector.*

Now, assume that there exists a protocol $\mathcal{P}$ for Recurring Selection with delay in $o(k^2 \log n / \log k)$. Recall that a protocol for Recurring Selection is a set of schedules of transmissions. Assuming that all nodes start simultaneously, consider such a set of schedules. By definition of Recurring Selection, for each choice of k schedules of $\mathcal{P}$, i.e., active nodes, there exists a positive integer $t \in o(k^2 \log n / \log k)$ such that in every time interval of length t each active node must achieve at least one non-colliding transmission.

Representing a transmission with a 1 and a reception with a 0, the set of schedules can be mapped to a matrix M where each time step is a row of M and each schedule is a column of M. The arbitrary choice of k active nodes is equivalent to choose k arbitrary columns of M. The time steps where each of the k active nodes achieve non-colliding transmissions gives the $m = k$ distinct rows of the identity matrix I_k in M. Therefore, there exists a (k, k, n)-selector of size in $o(k^2 \log n / \log k)$ which violates the aforementioned lower bound. Thus, $\Omega(k^2 \log n / \log k)$ is a lower bound for the delay of any protocol that solves Recurring Selection and, as shown before, a lower bound for Recurring Selection is a lower bound for Recurring Reception and Recurring Transmission.

Recall that our main goal is to minimize the message complexity. Hence, this lower bound might be improved if we maintain the constraint of k message complexity. Nevertheless, in order to obtain a better lower bound, we will use the memory size constraint present in the Weak Sensor Model (and any Radio Network for that matter) which leads to protocols with some form of periodicity.

We define an *equiperiodic protocol* as a set of schedules of transmissions where, in each schedule, every two consecutive transmissions are separated by the same number of time slots. A simple lower bound of $\Omega(kn)$ steps for the delay of any equiperiodic protocol that solves Recurring Selection can be observed as follows. n different periods are necessary otherwise two nodes can collide forever. At least k transmissions are necessary within the delay to achieve one reception successfully as proved in Theorem 1. Therefore, there exist a node with delay at least kn, which we formalize in the following theorem.

Theorem 4. *Any oblivious equiperiodic protocol that solves Recurring Selection in a one-hop Radio Network with n nodes, where k of them are activated possibly at different times, has delay at least kn.*

2.4 A Delay-Optimal Equiperiodic Protocol for $k \leq n^{1/6 \log \log n}$

In Primed Selection, the period of each node is a different prime number. However, in order to achieve optimal message complexity as proved in Theorem 1, it is enough to use a set of n periods such that, for each pair of distinct periods u, v, it holds that $v/\gcd(u, v) \geq k$ and $u/\gcd(u, v) \geq k$. In this section, we define such a set of periods so that, when used as periods in Primed Selection, gives optimal delay for equiperiodic protocols when $k \leq n^{1/6 \log \log n}$.

The idea is to use a set of composite numbers each of them formed by $\log \log n$ prime factors taken from the smallest $\log n$ primes bigger than k. More precisely, we define a *compact set* C as follows. Let p_ℓ denote the ℓ-th prime number. Let p_μ be a prime number such that $p_\mu = 2$ if $k \leq 2$, and $p_{\mu-1} < k \leq p_\mu$ otherwise. Let P be the set of prime numbers $P = \{p_\mu, p_{\mu+1}, \ldots, p_{\mu+\log n-1}\}$. Let $\mathcal{F}$ be a family of sets such that $\mathcal{F} = \{F | (F \subset P) \wedge (|F| = \log \log n)\}$. Make C a set of composite numbers such that $C = \{c_F | c_F = (\prod_{i \in F} i) \wedge (F \in \mathcal{F})\}$. The following lemma shows that the aforementioned property holds in a compact set.

Lemma 1. *Given a positive integer $k \leq n$ and a compact set C defined as above, $\forall u, v \in C, u \neq v$ it holds that $v/\gcd(u, v) \geq k$ and $u/\gcd(u, v) \geq k$.*

Proof. For the sake of contradiction, assume that there exists a pair $u, v \in C, u \neq v$ such that either $v/\gcd(u, v) < k$ or $u/\gcd(u, v) < k$. Let $U = \{u_1, u_2, \ldots, u_{\log \log n}\}$ and $V = \{v_1, v_2, \ldots, v_{\log \log n}\}$ be the sets of prime factors of u and v respectively. Given that the prime factorization of a number is unique and that $|U| = |V|$, there must exist $u_i \in U$ and $v_j \in V$ such that $u_i \notin V$ and $v_j \notin U$. But then $u/\gcd(u, v) \geq u_i \geq k$ and $v/\gcd(u, v) \geq v_i \geq k$. ∎

We assume that, for each node with ID i, a number $P(i) \in C$ has been stored in advance in its memory so that no two nodes have the same number. It can be derived that $|C| = \binom{\log n}{\log \log n} \geq n$ for large enough values of n. Hence, C is big enough as to assign a different number to each node.

In order to show the delay-optimality of this assignment it remains to be proved that the biggest period is in $O(n)$ when $k \leq n^{1/6 \log \log n}$, which we do in the following lemma.

Lemma 2. *Given a positive integer $k \leq n^{1/6 \log \log n}$ and a compact set C defined as above, $\max_{c \in C}\{c\} \in O(n)$.*

Proof. Consider the prime number $p_{k+\log n}$. Using the prime number theorem, it can be shown that the number of primes in the interval $[k, p_{k+\log n}]$ is bigger than $\log n$. Hence, in order to prove the claim, it is enough to prove $(p_{k+\log n})^{\log \log n} \in O(n)$. Thus, using the prime number theorem, for some constants α, β we want to prove

$$(\beta(k + \log n) \log(k + \log n))^{\log \log n} \leq \alpha n.$$

Replacing $k \leq n^{1/6 \log \log n}$, the inequality is true for large enough values of n. ∎

Now we are in conditions to state the main theorem for Recurring Selection which can be proved using Lemmas 1 and 2 and Theorems 1 and 4, and can be extended to Recurring Reception and Recurring Transmission.

Theorem 5. *Given a one-hop Radio Network with n nodes, where $k \leq n^{1/6 \log \log n}$ nodes are activated perhaps at different times, using a compact set of periods Primed*

Selection solves the Recurring Selection problem with optimal message complexity k and $O(kn)$ delay, optimal for equiperiodic protocols.

The good news is that this value of k is actually very big for most of the applications of Sensor Networks, where a logarithmic density of nodes in any one-hop neighborhood is usually assumed.

3   Adaptive Protocols: Reduced Primed Selection

The same technique used in Primed Selection yields a reduced delay if we use only $O(k)$ coprime periods in the whole network as long as we guarantee that, for every node u, every pair of nodes $i, j \in N(u) \cup \{u\}$ use different coprimes. However, given that the topology is unknown, it is not possible to define an oblivious assignment that works under our adversary.

We show now how to reduce the delay introducing a pre-processing phase in which nodes self-assign those primes appropriately. Given that in this protocol it is necessary to maintain two sets of k primes, we relax the Weak Sensor Model assuming that the memory size of each node is bounded only by $O(k + \log n)$ bits. We further assume that nodes are deployed densely enough so that if we reduce the radius of transmission by a constant factor the network is still connected. This assumption introduces only an additional constant factor in the total number of nodes to be deployed n and the maximum degree $k - 1$.

The intuition of the protocol follows. As before, we use prime numbers bigger than k but, additionally, the smallest k of them are left available. More precisely, each node with ID $i \in 1, \ldots, n$ is assigned a *big* prime number $p(i)$ so that $p(1) = p_{j+k} < p(2) = p_{j+k+1} \ldots p(n) = p_{j+k+n-1}$. Where p_ℓ is the ℓ-th prime number and p_j is the first prime number bigger than k. Again, given that $k \leq n$, the size in bits of the biggest prime is still in $O(\log n)$.

Using their big prime as a period of transmission nodes first compete for one of the k *small* primes left available. Once a node chooses one of these small primes, it announces its choice with period its big prime and transmits its messages with period its small prime. If at a given time slot these transmissions coincide, it is equivalent to the event of a collision of the transmissions of two different nodes, hence, we do nothing.

In order to prevent two nodes from choosing the same small prime, each node maintains a counter. A node chooses an available small prime upon reaching a final count. When a node reaches its final count and chooses, it is guaranteed that all neighboring nodes lag behind enough so that they receive the announcement of its choice before they can themselves choose a small prime.

In order to ensure the correctness of the algorithm, no two nodes within two hops should choose the same small prime. Therefore, we use a radius of $r/2$ for message communication[2] and r for small-prime announcements.

We omit the details of the algorithm in this extended abstract for brevity. The analysis follows. It was shown before that the delay of Primed Selection is in $O(kn \log n)$. For clarity of the presentation, we denote this value as T.

---

[2] The choice of small radius $r/2$ is arbitrary. Any radius in $\Theta(r)$ strictly smaller than r would work with the same asymptotic cost.

Let us call a node that has chosen a small prime a *decided* node and *undecided* otherwise. In order to prove correctnes, we have to prove that every node becomes decided and that no pair of neighboring nodes choose the same prime.

Lemma 3. *Given any node u that becomes decided in the time slot t, the counter of every undecided node $v \in N(u)$ is at most T in the time slot t.*

Proof. Consider a node u that becomes decided at time t. For the sake of contradiction, assume there is an undecided node $v \in N(u)$ whose counter is greater than T at t. By the definition of the algorithm, v did not receive a bigger counter for more than T steps before t, and u did not receive a bigger counter for $2T$ steps before t. In the interval $[t - T, t]$ the local counter of u is larger than the local counter of v. As shown in Theorem 3, v must receive from u within T steps. But then, v must have been reset in the interval $[t - T, t]$.

Theorem 6. *Given a Sensor Network with n nodes, where the maximum degree is $k - 1 < n$, if nodes run Reduced Primed Selection, no pair of neighboring nodes choose the same small prime and every node becomes decided within $O(Tn^2)$ steps after starting running the algorithm.*

Proof. The first statement is a direct conclusion of Lemma 3 and Theorem 3. For the second statement, if a node u is not reset within T steps no neighbor of u has a bigger counter and u will become decided within $2T$ steps. Thus, it takes at most $(n+1)T$ steps for the first node in the network that becomes decided. By definition of the algorithm, a decided node does not reset the counter of any other node. Applying the same argument recursively the claim follows.

Theorem 7. *Given a Sensor Network with n nodes, where the maximum degree is $k - 1 < n$, after the pre-processing, the delay of Reduced Primed Selection is $O(k^2 \log k)$ and the message complexity is k.*

Proof. As in Theorem 3.

Acknowledgements. We thank Dariusz Kowalski for useful discussions and David Peleg for pointing out an important reference. This research was supported in part by EU Marie Curie European Reintegration Grant IRG 210021; Comunidad de Madrid grant S-0505/TIC/0285; Spanish MEC grant TIN2005-09198-C02-01; NSF grants CCF0621425, CCF 05414009, and CCF 0632838; and Universidad de Chile, Mecesup fellowship and Anillo en Redes.

References

1. Alon, N., Bar-Noy, A., Linial, N., Peleg, D.: Single round simulation in radio networks. Journal of Algorithms 13, 188–210 (1992)
2. Bar-Yehuda, R., Goldreich, O., Itai, A.: On the time-complexity of broadcast in multi-hop radio networks: An exponential gap between determinism and randomization. Journal of Computer and System Sciences 45, 104–126 (1992)

3. Bonis, A.D., Gąsieniec, L., Vaccaro, U.: Generalized framework for selectors with applications in optimal group testing. In: Proc. of 30th International Colloquium on Automata Languages and Programming (2003)
4. Chlebus, B., Gąsieniec, L., Lingas, A., Pagourtzis, A.: Oblivious gossiping in ad-hoc radio networks. In: Proc. of 5th International Workshop on Discrete Algorithms and Methods for Mobile Computing and Communications (2001)
5. Chlebus, B.S., Gąsieniec, L., Gibbons, A., Pelc, A., Rytter, W.: Deterministic broadcasting in unknown radio networks. Distributed Computing 15, 27–38 (2002)
6. Chlebus, B.S., Gąsieniec, L., Östlin, A., Robson, J.M.: Deterministic radio broadcasting. In: Proc. of 27th International Colloquium on Automata Languages and Programming (2000)
7. Chrobak, M., Gąsieniec, L., Kowalski, D.: The wake-up problem in multi-hop radio networks. In: Proc. of the 15th Annual ACM-SIAM Symposium on Discrete Algorithms (2004)
8. Chrobak, M., Gąsieniec, L., Rytter, W.: Fast broadcasting and gossiping in radio networks. In: Proc. of the 41st IEEE Annual Symp. on Foundation of Computer Science (2000)
9. Clementi, A., Monti, A., Silvestri, R.: Selective families, superimposed codes, and broadcasting on unknown radio networks. In: Proc. of the 12th Annual ACM-SIAM Symposium on Discrete Algorithms (2001)
10. Czumaj, A., Rytter, W.: Broadcasting algorithms in radio networks with unknown topology. In: Proc. of the 44th IEEE Annual Symp. on Foundation of Computer Science (2003)
11. Dyachkov, A., Rykov, V.: A survey of superimposed code theory. Problems Control and Inform. Theory 12 (1983)
12. Farach-Colton, M., Fernandes, R.J., Mosteiro, M.A.: Bootstrapping a hop-optimal network in the weak sensor model. In: Brodal, G.S., Leonardi, S. (eds.) ESA 2005. LNCS, vol. 3669, pp. 827–838. Springer, Heidelberg (2005)
13. Farach-Colton, M., Mosteiro, M.A.: Initializing sensor networks of non-uniform density in the weak sensor model. In: Proc. of 10th International Workshop on Algorithms and Data Structures (to appear, 2007)
14. Farach-Colton, M., Mosteiro, M.A.: Sensor network gossiping or how to break the broadcast lower bound. Manuscript (2007)
15. Fejes-Tóth, L.: Über einen geometrischen Satz. Mathematische Zeitschrift 46, 83–85 (1940)
16. Hardy, G.H., Wright, E.M.: An introduction to the theory of numbers. Oxford University Press, Oxford (1979)
17. Indyk, P.: Explicit constructions of selectors and related combinatorial structures, with applications. In: Proc. of the 13th Annual ACM-SIAM Symposium on Discrete Algorithms (2002)
18. Komlòs, J., Greenberg, A.: An asymptotically nonadaptive algorithm for conflict resolution in multiple-access channels. IEEE Trans. Inf. Theory 31, 303–306 (1985)
19. Kowalski, D.R.: On selection problem in radio networks. In: Proceedings 24th Annual ACM Symposium on Principles of Distributed Computing (2005)
20. Kushilevitz, E., Mansour, Y.: An $\Omega(D \log(N/D))$ lower bound for broadcast in radio networks. SIAM Journal on Computing 27, 702–712 (1998)
21. Liu, D., Prabhakaran, M.: On randomized broadcasting and gossiping in radio networks. In: Ibarra, O.H., Zhang, L. (eds.) COCOON 2002. LNCS, vol. 2387, pp. 340–349. Springer, Heidelberg (2002)

Deterministic Leader Election in Anonymous Sensor Networks Without Common Coordinated System

Yoann Dieudonné and Franck Petit

LaRIA, CNRS
Université de Picardie Jules Verne
Amiens, France

Abstract. We address the Leader Election (LE) problem in networks of anonymous sensors sharing no kind of common coordinate system. The contribution of this paper is twofold: First, assuming n anonymous sensors agreeing on a common *handedness* (*chirality*) of their own coordinate system, we provide a complete characterization on the sensors positions to deterministically elect a leader. Our result holds for any $n > 1$, even if the n sensors have unlimited visibility and regardless of their capabilities, unbounded memory, mobility, and communication settings. Second, we show that this statement also holds assuming sensors without chirality provided that n is odd.

Keywords: Distributed Leader Election, Sense of Direction, Chirality, Sensor Networks.

1 Introduction

In distributed settings, many problems that are hard to solve otherwise become easier to solve with a *leader* to coordinate the system. The problem of electing a leader among a set of computing units is then one of the fundamental tasks in distributed systems. The *Leader Election* (LE) Problem consists in moving the system from an initial configuration were all entities are in the same state into a final configuration were all entities are in the same state, except one, the leader. The leader election problem is covered in depth in many books related to distributed systems, *e.g.*, [13,16].

The distributed systems considered in this paper are *sensor networks*. Sensor networks are dense wireless networks that are used to collect (to sense) environmental data such as temperature, sound, vibration, pressure, motion, etc. The data are either simply sent toward some data collectors or used as an input to perform some basic cooperative tasks. Wireless Sensor Networks (WSN) are emerging distributed systems providing diverse services to numerous applications in industries, manufacturing, security, environment and habitat monitoring, healfcare, traffic control, etc. WSN aim for being composed of a large quantity of sensors as small, inexpensive, and low-powered as possible. Thus, the interest has shifted towards the design of distributed protocols for very weak sensors, *i.e.*, sensors requiring very limited capabilities, *e.g., uniformity* (or, *homogeneity* — all the sensors follow the same program —, *anonymity* — the sensors are *a priori* indistinguishable —, *disorientation* — the sensors share no kind of coordinate system nor common sense of direction.

E. Tovar, P. Tsigas, and H. Fouchal (Eds.): OPODIS 2007, LNCS 4878, pp. 132–142, 2007.
© Springer-Verlag Berlin Heidelberg 2007

However, in weak distributed environments, many tasks have no solution. In particular, in uniform anonymous general networks, the impossibility of breaking a possibly symmetry in the initial configuration makes the leader election unsolvable deterministically [1]. In this paper, we investigate the leader election problem with sensors having minimal capabilities, *i.e.*, they are anonymous, uniform and disoriented. We come up with the following question: *"Given a set of such weak sensors scattered on the plane, what are the (minimal) geometric conditions to be able to deterministically agree on a single sensor?"*

Related Works. Similar questions are addressed in [2,9,10]. In the former, the authors address the problem of *Localization* in sensor networks. This problem is to reconstruct the positions of a set of sensors with a *Limited Visibility*, *i.e.*, sensors which are able to locate of other sensors within a certain distance $v > 0$. The authors show that no polynomial-time algorithm can solve this problem in general. In [9,10], the authors address the *Pattern Formation* problem for sensors having the additional capability of *mobility*. Such mobile sensors are often referred to as *robots* or *agents*. The Pattern Formation problem consists in the design of protocols allowing autonomous mobile robots to form a specific class of patterns, *e.g.*, [18,9,10,4,11,6,7,8]. In [9], the authors discuss whether the pattern formation problem can be solved or not according to the capabilities the robots are supposed to have. They consider the ability to agree on the direction and orientation of one axis of their coordinate system (North) (Sense of Direction) and a common *handedness* (*Chirality*). Assuming sense of direction, chirality, and *Unlimited Visibility* — each robot is able to locate all the robots —,, they show that the robots can form any arbitrary pattern. Then, they show that with the lack of chirality, the problem can solved in general with an odd number of robots only. With the lack of both sense of direction and chirality, the pattern formation problem is unsolvable in general.

In [10], the authors show the fundammental relationship between the Pattern Formation problem and the Leader Election problem. They show that under sense of Direction and chirality, the Leader Election problem can be solved by constructing a total order over the coordinates of all the agents. With sense of direction and lack of chirality, the Leader Election is solvable if and only if the number of robots is odd. Informally, the results in [9,10] comes from the fact that starting from some symmetric configurations, no robot can be distinguished if the number of robots is even. In other words, they show that even if the robots have sense of direction and unlimited visibility, the lack of chirality prevents from breaking symmetry in a deterministic way.

Contribution. In this paper, we address the leader election problem under very weak assumptions: the sensors share no kind of common coordinate system. More precisely, they are not required to share any unit measure, common orientation or direction. However, even under such an assumption, they can agree on a common handedness or not.

The contribution of this paper is twofold. Assuming a set of n anonymous sensors with chirality, we first provide a complete characterization (necessary and sufficient conditions) on the sensors positions to deterministically elect a leader. Our result holds for any $n > 1$, even if the sensors have unlimited visibility and regardless of their capabilities, unbounded memory, mobility, and communication settings. The sufficient condition is shown by providing a deterministic algorithm electing a leader.

The proof is based on the ability for the sensors to construct a *Lyndon word* from the sensors' positions as an input. A Lyndon word is a non-empty word strictly smaller in the lexicographic order than any of its suffixes, except itself and the empty word. Lyndon words have been widely studied in the combinatorics of words area [12]. However, only a few papers consider Lyndon words addressing issues in other areas than word algebra, *e.g.*, [3,5,17,7]. In [7], we already shown the power of Lyndon words to built an efficient and simple deterministic protocol to form a regular n-gon. However, the results in [7] hold for a prime number n of robots only.

The second fold of our contribution addresses the lack of chirality. We show that our characterization still holds if and only if the number of sensors is odd. Again, we give a deterministic algorithm that shows the sufficient condition.

In the next section (Section 2), we formally describe the distributed model and the words considered in this paper. Both results are presented in Section 3. Finally, we conclude this paper in Section 4.

2 Preliminaries

In this section, we define the distributed system considered in this paper. Next, we review some formal definitions and basic results on words and Lyndon words

2.1 Model

Consider a set of n *sensors* (or *agents*, *robots*) arbitrarily scattered on the plane such that no two sensors are located at the same position. The sensors are *uniform* and *anonymous*, i.e, they all execute the same program using no local parameter (such that an identity) allowing to differentiate any of them. However, we assume that each sensor is a computational unit having the ability to determine the positions of the n sensors within an infinite decimal precision. We assume no kind of communication medium. Each sensor has its own local x-y Cartesian coordinate system defined by two coordinate axes (x and y), together with their *orientations*, identified as the positive and negative sides of the axes.

In this paper, we discuss the influence of *Sense of Direction* and *Chirality* in a sensor network.

Definition 1 (Sense of Direction). *A set of n sensors has sense of direction if the n sensors agree on a common direction of one axis (x or y) and its orientation. The sense of direction is said to be* partial *if the agreement relates to the direction only —i.e., they are not required to agree on the orientation.*

In Figure 1, the sensors have sense of direction in the cases (a) and (b), whereas they have no sense of direction in the cases (c) and (d).

Given an x-y Cartesian coordinate system, the *handedness* is the way in which the orientation of the y axis (respectively, the x axis) is inferred according to the orientation of the x axis (resp., the y axis).

Definition 2 (Chirality). *A set of n sensors has chirality if the n sensors share the same handedness.*

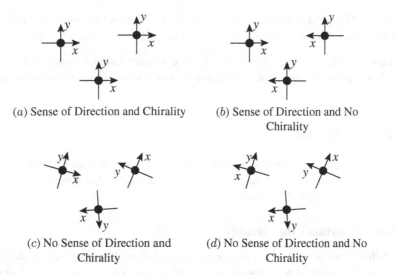

(a) Sense of Direction and Chirality

(b) Sense of Direction and No Chirality

(c) No Sense of Direction and Chirality

(d) No Sense of Direction and No Chirality

Fig. 1. Four examples showing the relationship between Sense of Direction and Chirality

In Figure 1, the sensors have chirality in the cases (a) and (c), whereas they have no chirality in the cases (b) and (d).

2.2 Words and Lyndon Words

Let an ordered alphabet A be a finite set of letters. Denote $\prec$ an order on A. A non empty *word* w over A is a finite sequence of letters $a_1, \ldots, a_i, \ldots, a_l$, $l > 0$. The *concatenation* of two words u and v, denoted $u \circ v$ or simply uv, is equal to the word $a_1, \ldots, a_i, \ldots, a_k, b_1, \ldots, b_j, \ldots, b_l$ such that $u = a_1, \ldots, a_i, \ldots, a_k$ and $v = b_1, \ldots, b_j, \ldots, b_l$. Let ϵ be the *empty word* such that for every word w, $w\epsilon = \epsilon w = w$. The *length* of a word w, denoted by $|w|$, is equal to the number of letters of w—$|\epsilon| = 0$.

A word u is *lexicographically* smaller than or equal to a word v, denoted $u \preceq v$, iff there exists either a word w such that $v = uw$ or three words r, s, t and two letters a, b such that $u = ras$, $v = rbt$, and $a \prec b$.

Let k and j be two positive integers. The kth *power* of a word w is the word denoted s^k such that $s^0 = \epsilon$, and $s^k = s^{k-1}s$. A word u is said to be *primitive* if and only if $u = v^k \Rightarrow k = 1$. Otherwise ($u = v^k$ and $k > 1$), u is said to be *strictly periodic*. The *reversal* of a word $w = a_1 a_2 \cdots a_n$ is the word $\tilde{w} = a_n \cdots a_1$. The jth *rotation* of a word w, notation $R_j(w)$, is defined by:

$$R_j(w) \overset{\text{def}}{=} \begin{cases} \epsilon & \text{if } w = \epsilon \\ a_j, \ldots, a_l, a_1, \ldots, a_{j-1} & \text{otherwise } (w = a_1, \ldots, a_l, \, l \geq 1) \end{cases}$$

Note that $R_1(w) = w$.

Lemma 1 ([12]). *Let w and $R_j(w)$ be a word and a rotation of w, respectively. The word w is primitive if and only if $R_j(w)$ is primitive.*

A word w is said to be *minimal* if and only if $\forall j \in 1, \ldots, l, \, w \preceq R_j(w)$.

Definition 3 (Lyndon Word). *A word w ($|w| > 0$) is a Lyndon word if and only if w is nonempty, primitive and minimal, i.e., $w \neq \epsilon$ and $\forall j \in 2, \ldots, |w|, \ w \prec R_j(w)$.*

For instance, if $A = \{a, b\}$, then a, b, ab, aab, abb are Lyndon words, whereas aba, and $abab$ are not— aba is not minimal ($aab \preceq aba$) and $abab$ is not primitive ($abab = (ab)^2$).

3   Leader Election

The *leader election* problem considered in this paper is stated as follows: Given the positions of n sensors in the plane, the n sensors are able to deterministically agree on the same position L called the leader.

3.1   Leader Election with Chirality

In this subsection, we assume a sensor networks having the property of chirality. A *configuration* π of the sensor network is a set of positions $p_1, \ldots, p_n$ ($n > 1$) occupied by the sensors. Given a configuration π, SEC denotes the *smallest enclosing circle* of the positions in π. The center of SEC is denoted O. In any configuration π, SEC is unique and can be computed in linear time [14,19]. It passes either through two of the positions that are on the same diameter (opposite positions), or through at least three of the postions in π. Note that if $n = 2$, then SEC passes both sensors and no sensor can be located inside SEC, in particular at O. Since the sensors have the ability of chirality, they are able to agree on a common orientation of SEC, denoted $\circlearrowright$.

Given a smallest enclosing circle SEC, the radii are the line segments from the center O of SEC to the boundary of SEC. Let $\mathcal{R}$ be the finite set of radii such that a radius r belongs to $\mathcal{R}$ iff at least one sensor is located on r but O. Denote $\sharp\mathcal{R}$ the number of radii in $\mathcal{R}$. In the sequel, we will abuse language by considering radii in $\mathcal{R}$ only. Given two distinct positions p_1 and p_2 located on the same radius r ($\in \mathcal{R}$), $d(p_1, p_2)$ denotes the Euclidean distance between p_1 and p_2.

Definition 4 (Radius Word). *Let $p_1, \ldots, p_k$ be the respective positions of k robots ($k \geq 1$) located on the same radius $r \in \mathcal{R}$. Let w_r be the word such that*

$$w_r \overset{\text{def}}{=} \begin{cases} 0 \text{ if there exists one sensor at } O \\ a_1, \ldots, a_k \text{ with } a_1 = d(O, p_1) \text{ and } \forall i \in [2, k], a_i = d(p_{i-1}, p_i) \text{, otherwise} \end{cases}$$

Note that all the distances are computed by each sensor with respect to its own coordinate system, *i.e., proportionally* to its own measure unit. Let RW be the set of radius words built over $\mathcal{R}$, computed by any sensor s. The lexicographic order $\preceq$ on RW is naturally built over the natural order $<$ on the set of real numbers.

Remark 1. If there exists one sensor on O ($n > 2$), then for every radius $r \in \mathcal{R}, w_r = 0$.

Let r be a radius in $\mathcal{R}$. The successor of r, denoted by $Succ(r, \circlearrowright)$, is the next radius in $\mathcal{R}$, according to $\circlearrowright$. The ith successor of r, denoted by $Succ_i(r, \circlearrowright)$, is the radius such that $Succ_0(r, \circlearrowright) = r$, and $Succ_i(r, \circlearrowright) = Succ(Succ_{i-1}(r, \circlearrowright), \circlearrowright)$. Given r and its successor $r' = Succ(r, \circlearrowright)$, $\sphericalangle(rOr')$ denotes the angle between r and r'.

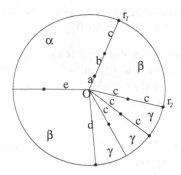

Fig. 2. Computation of Configuration words — the sensors are the black bullets

Definition 5 (Configuration Word Set)
Given an orientation $\circlearrowright$, let $CW^{\circlearrowright}$ be the set of configuration words, computed by any sensor s, build over $\mathcal{R}$ such that for each radius $r \in \mathcal{R}$, the associated configuration word $W(r)$ is equal to $(0,0)$ if $w_r = 0$, otherwise $W(r)$ is equal to the word $a_1, \ldots, a_k$ such that $k = \sharp\mathcal{R}$ and $\forall i \in [1, k]$, $a_i = (Succ_{i-1}(r, \circlearrowright), \triangleleft(Succ_{i-1}(r, \circlearrowright) 0Succ_i(r, \circlearrowright)))$.

Remark 2. The three following propositions are equivalent:

1. There exists one sensor on O
2. For every radius $r \in \mathcal{R}$, $W(r) = (0,0)$
3. $CW^{\circlearrowright} = \{(0,0)\}$

In Figure 2, if $\circlearrowright$ is the clockwise orientation, then: $W(r_1) = (abc, \beta)(c^2, \gamma)^2(c, \gamma)$ $(d, \beta)(e, \alpha)$ and $W(r_2) = (c^2, \gamma)^2(c, \gamma)(d, \beta)(e, \alpha)(abc, \beta)$.

If $\circlearrowright$ is the counterclockwise orientation, then: $W(r_1) = (abc, \alpha)(e, \beta)(d, \gamma)(c, \gamma)$ $(c^2, \gamma)(c^2, \beta)$ and $W(r_2) = (c^2, \beta)(abc, \alpha)(e, \beta)(d, \gamma)(c, \gamma)(c^2, \gamma)$.

Remark 3. Let $W(r_1)$ and $W(r_2)$ be two words in $CW^{\circlearrowright}$, r_1 and r_2 belong to $\mathcal{R}$. Then, $W(r_1)$ (respectively, $W(r_2)$) is a rotation of $W(r_2)$ (resp. $W(r_1)$) — refer to Figure 2.

Let $A_{CW^{\circlearrowright}}$ be the set of letters over $CW^{\circlearrowright}$. Let (u, x) and (v, y) be any two letters in $A_{CW^{\circlearrowright}}$. Define the order $\lessdot$ over $A_{CW^{\circlearrowright}}$ as follows:

$$(u, x) \lessdot (v, y) \Longleftrightarrow \begin{cases} u \ngeqq v \\ \text{or} \\ u = v \text{ and } x < y \end{cases}$$

The lexicographic $\preceq$ order over $CW^{\circlearrowright}$ is naturally built over $\lessdot$.

Remark 4. Each sensor having its own unit measure, given $r \in \mathcal{R}$, the word $W(r)$ computed by any sensor s can be different to the one computed by another sensor s'. However, all the distances are computed by each sensor proportionally to its own measure unit. So, if $W(r) \preceq W(r')$ for one sensor s, then $W(r) \preceq W(r')$ for every sensor s'. In particular, if $W(r)$ is a Lyndon word for one sensor s, then $W(r)$ is a Lyndon word for every sensor s'.

Lemma 2. *If there exists two distinct radii r_1 and r_2 in $\mathcal{R}$ such that both $W(r_1)$ and $W(r_2)$ are Lyndon words, then $CW^\circlearrowleft = \{(0,0)\}$.*

Proof. Assume by contradiction that there exists two distinct radii r_1 and r_2 such that both $W(r_1)$ and $W(r_2)$ are Lyndon words and $CW^\circlearrowleft \neq \{(0,0)\}$. By Remark 2, there exists no sensor located at 0. By Remark 3, $W(r_1)$ (respectively, $W(r_2)$) is a rotation of $W(r_2)$ (resp. $W(r_1)$). So, by Definition 3, $W(r_1) \prec W(r_2)$ and $W(r_2) \prec W(r_1)$. A contradiction.

Lemma 3. *If there exists $r \in \mathcal{R}$ such that $W(r)$ is a Lyndon word, then the n sensors are able to determiniscally agree on the same sensor L.*

Proof. Directly follows from Lemma 2 and Remark 4: If there is a sensor s located on 0, then the n sensors are able to agree on $L = s$. Otherwise, there exists a single $r \in \mathcal{R}$ such that $W(r)$ is a Lyndon word. In that case, all the sensors are able to agree on the sensor on r which is the nearest one from 0.

Lemma 4. *If there exists no radius $r \in \mathcal{R}$ such that $W(r)$ is a Lyndon word, then there exists no deterministic algorithm allowing the n sensors to agree on the same sensor L.*

Proof. Assume by contradiction that no radius $r \in \mathcal{R}$ exists such that $W(r)$ is a Lyndon word and there exists an algorithm A allowing the n sensors to deterministically agree on the same sensor L. Let $minW$ be a word in $CW^\circlearrowleft$ such that $\forall r \in \mathcal{R}$, $minW \preceq W(r)$. That is, $minW$ is minimal. Assume first that $minW$ is primitive. Then, $minW$ is a Lyndon word which contradicts the assumption. So, $minW$ is a strictly periodic word (there exists u and $k > 1$ such that $minSC = u^k$) and, from Lemma 1, we deduce that for all $r \in \mathcal{R}$, $W(r)$ is also strictly periodic. Thus, for every $r \in \mathcal{R}$, there exists at least one radius $r' \in \mathcal{R}$ such that $r \neq r'$ and $W(r) = W(r')$. So, for every radius $r \in \mathcal{R}$, there are $k > 1$ radii in $\mathcal{R}$ on which the sensors can have the same view of π. It is the case if the sensors have the same measure unit and their y axis meet the

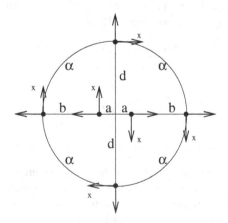

Fig. 3. A counter example showing Lemma 4

radius on which they are located — refer to Figure 3. In that case, A cannot allow the n sensors to deterministically agree on the same sensor L.

The following theorem follows from Lemmas 3 and 4:

Theorem 1. *Given a configuration π of any number $n \geq 2$ sensors with chirality scattered on the plane, the n sensors are able to deterministically agree on the same sensor L if and only if there exists a radius $r \in \mathcal{R}$ such that $W(r)$ is a Lyndon Word.*

3.2   Leader Election Without Chirality

Without chirality, the sensors are not able to agree on a common orientation of SEC. Define $\circlearrowright$ (respectively, $\circlearrowleft$) the clockwise (resp., counterclockwise) orientation. Obviously, with respect to their handedness, some of the n sensors choose to orient SEC according to $\circlearrowright$, whereas some other to $\circlearrowleft$. In this subsection, we use same definition of radius word (Definition 4) as in Subsection 3.1. Since the sensors have no chirality, for each radius $r \in \mathcal{R}$, there are two configuration words w.r.t. the orientation of SEC, denoted by $W(r)^{\circlearrowright}$ and $W(r)^{\circlearrowleft}$. Let CW be the set of all the configuration words, computed by any sensor s, in both clockwise and counterclockwise orientations.

We now show that the statement of Theorem 1 also holds assuming no chirality if n is odd.

Lemma 5. *Given an orientation $\circ$ of SEC in $\{\circlearrowright, \circlearrowleft\}$, if there exists two distinct radii r_1 and r_2 in $\mathcal{R}$ such that both $W(r_1)^{\circ}$ and $W(r_2)^{\circ}$ are Lyndon words, then $CW^{\circ} = \{(0,0)\}$.*

Proof. The proof is similar to that of Lemma 2.

Let $\mathcal{R}_L$ be the subset of radius $r \in \mathcal{R}$ such that $W(r)$ is a Lyndon word in the clockwise or in the counterclockwise orientation. Denote $\sharp \mathcal{R}_L$ the number of radii in $\mathcal{R}_L$.

Lemma 6. *If $\sharp \mathcal{R}_L > 2$, then for any orientation $\circ$ of SEC in $\{\circlearrowright, \circlearrowleft\}$, $\forall r \in \mathcal{R}$, $W(r)^{\circ} = (0,0)$.*

Proof. Assume by contradiction that $\sharp \mathcal{R}_L > 2$ and there exists $\circ \in \{\circlearrowright, \circlearrowleft\}$ and $r \in \mathcal{R}$ such that $W(r)^{\circ} \neq (0,0)$. Since $\sharp \mathcal{R}_L > 2$, there exists at least two distinct radii r_1 and r_2 such that either $W(r_1)^{\circlearrowright}$ and $W(r_2)^{\circlearrowright}$ are Lyndon words or $W(r_1)^{\circlearrowleft}$ and $W(r_2)^{\circlearrowleft}$ are Lyndon words. Without loss of generality, assume that $W(r_1)^{\circlearrowright}$ and $W(r_2)^{\circlearrowright}$ are Lyndon words. By, Lemma 5, $CW^{\circlearrowright} = \{(0,0)\}$. By Remark 2, $\forall r \in \mathcal{R}$, $W(r)^{\circlearrowright} = (0,0)$ and $W(r)^{\circlearrowleft} = (0,0)$. Hence, there exists no $r \in \mathcal{R}$ such that $W(r)^{\circ} \neq (0,0)$. A contradiction.

Lemma 7. *If n is odd and $\sharp \mathcal{R}_L \geq 1$, then the n sensors are able to deterministically agree on the same sensor L.*

Proof. Since n is odd, $n \geq 3$. From Lemma 6, there are three cases to consider:

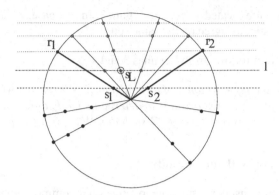

Fig. 4. An example showing the construction in the proof of Lemma 7

1. $\sharp \mathcal{R}_L > 2$. Then, $\forall r \in \mathcal{R}$ and for any orientation $\circ$ of SEC in $\{\circlearrowright, \circlearrowleft\}$, $W(r)^\circ = (0,0)$. Thus, there exists one sensor s located at 0. The n sensors are then able to agree on s.
2. $\mathcal{R}_L = \{r\}$. If $W(r)$ the leader is the nearest sensor to 0, on r.
3. $\mathcal{R}_L = \{r_1, r_2\}$. Again, there are two subcases :
   (a) $W(r_1)^\circlearrowright = (0,0)$. The leader is the sensor at the center of SEC.
   (b) $W(r_1)^\circlearrowright \neq (0,0)$. From Lemma 5 again, if $W(r_1)^\circlearrowright$ (respectively $W(r_1)^\circlearrowleft$) is a Lyndon word, then $W(r_2)^\circlearrowright$ (resp. $W(r_2)^\circlearrowleft$) is a Lyndon word. Without loss of generality, assume that $W(r_1)^\circlearrowright$ and $W(r_2)^\circlearrowright$ are Lyndon words. We have two subsubcases :
      i. $W(r_1)^\circlearrowright \neq W(r_2)^\circlearrowright$. Without loss of generality again, assume that $W(r_1)^\circlearrowright \prec W(r_2)^\circlearrowright$. The leader is the nearest sensor to 0 on r_1.
      ii. $W(r_1)^\circlearrowright = W(r_2)^\circlearrowright$. In that case, note that r_1 and r_2 divide SEC into two parts, π_1 and π_2, where n_1 and n_2 are the number of robots inside π_1 and π_2, respectively. Since $W(r_1)^\circlearrowright = W(r_2)^\circlearrowright$, the number x of sensors located on r_1 is equal to the number of robots located on r_2. So, the total number of sensors located on r_1 and r_2 is equal to $2x$ (because there is no sensor at the center of SEC). Thus, $n_1 + n_2 = n - 2x$ because no sensors located on r_1 and r_2 is in π_1 or π_2. Since $n - 2x$ is odd (n is odd), there exists one part of SEC with an even number of robots, and one part of SEC with an odd number of sensors. Without loss of generality, assume that n_1 is odd. Let s_1 and s_2 be the nearest sensors to 0 on r_1 and r_2, respectively. Consider P the set of lines passing through the sensors in π_1 which are parallel to the line (s_1, s_2) — refer to Figure 4. Since n_1 is odd, there exists at least one line in P with an odd number of sensors located on it. Among those lines, choose the unique line which is the nearest from both 0 and the line (s_1, s_2). Denote this line by l and the number of sensors located on it in π_1 by n_l. Therefore, the leader is the unique sensor s_L which is the median sensor among the sensor on l and π_1, i.e., the $(\lfloor \frac{n_l}{2} \rfloor + 1)^{\text{th}}$ sensor starting indifferently from the left or the right of l in π_1.

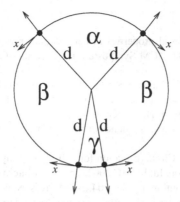

Fig. 5. A counter example showing that the statement of Theorem 2 does not hold if n is even

Lemma 8. *If there exists no radius $r \in \mathcal{R}$ such that either $W(r)^{\circlearrowright}$ or $W(r)^{\circlearrowleft}$ is a Lyndon word, then there exists no algorithm allowing the n sensors to deterministically agree on the same sensor L.*

Proof. The proof is similar as to that of Lemma 4.

The following theorem follows from Lemmas 7 and 8:

Theorem 2. *Given a configuration π of any number $n \geq 2$ sensors without chirality scattered on the plane, the n sensors are able to deterministiscally agree on the same sensor L if and only if n is odd and there exists a radius $r \in \mathcal{R}$ such that $W(r)$ is a Lyndon Word.*

Note that the equivalence does not work with an even number of sensors. A counter example is shown in Figure 5. For any orientation in $\{\circlearrowright, \circlearrowleft\}$, there exists one Lyndon word equal to $(d, \alpha)(d, \beta)(d, \gamma)(d, \beta)$. However, the symetry of the configuration does not allow to choose any sensor as a leader.

4 Conclusion

We studied the leader election problem in networks of anonymous sensors sharing no kind of common coordinate system. Assuming anonymous sensors with chirality, we used properties of Lyndon words to give a complete characterization on the sensors positions to deterministically elect a leader for any number $n > 1$ of sensors. We also showed that our characterization still holds with sensors without chirality if and only if the number of sensors is odd.

Our future work will concentrate to find a similar characterization for an even number of sensors without chirality. A more general problem is to find the minimal geometrical conditions to deterministiscally solve other collaborative tasks in mobile sensor networks such as pattern formation for which we know that no solution exists in general if the sensors do not agree on a sense of direction [15].

References

1. Angluin, D.: Local and global properties in networks of processors. In: STOC 1980. Proceedings of the 12th Annual ACM Symposium on Theory of Computing, pp. 82–93. ACM Press, New York (1980)
2. Aspnes, J., Goldengerg, D., Yang, Y.R.: On the computational complexity of sensor network localization. In: Nikoletseas, S.E., Rolim, J.D.P. (eds.) ALGOSENSORS 2004. LNCS, vol. 3121, pp. 32–44. Springer, Heidelberg (2004)
3. Chemillier, M.: Periodic musical sequences and lyndon words. Soft Computing 8(9), 611–616 (2004)
4. Defago, X., Konagaya, A.: Circle formation for oblivious anonymous mobile robots with no common sense of orientation. In: POMC 2002. 2nd ACM International Annual Workshop on Principles of Mobile Computing, pp. 97–104. ACM Press, New York (2002)
5. Delgrange, O., Rivals, E.: Star: an algorithm to search for tandem approximate repeats. Bioinformatics 20(16), 2812–2820 (2004)
6. Y Dieudonné, Y., Labbani, O., Petit, F.: Circle formation of weak mobile robots. In: Datta, A.K., Gradinariu, M. (eds.) SSS 2006. LNCS, vol. 4280, pp. 262–275. Springer, Heidelberg (2006)
7. Y Dieudonné, Y., Petit, F.: Circle formation of weak robots and Lyndon words. Information Processing Letters 104(4), 156–162 (2007)
8. Dieudonné, Y., Petit, Y.: Swing words to make circle formation quiescent. In: Prencipe, G., Fales, S. (eds.) SIROCCO 2007. LNCS, vol. 4474, pp. 166–179. Springer, Heidelberg (2007)
9. Flocchini, P., Prencipe, G., Santoro, N., Widmayer, P.: Hard tasks for weak robots: The role of common knowledge in pattern formation by autonomous mobile robots. In: ISAAC 1999. 10th Annual International Symposium on Algorithms and Computation, pp. 93–102 (1999)
10. Flocchini, P., Prencipe, G., Santoro, N., Widmayer, P.: Pattern formation by autonomous robots without chirality. In: SIROCCO 2001. VIII International Colloquium on Structural Information and Communication Complexity, pp. 147–162 (2001)
11. Katreniak, B.: Biangular circle formation by asynchronous mobile robots. In: Pelc, A., Raynal, M. (eds.) SIROCCO 2005. LNCS, vol. 3499, pp. 185–199. Springer, Heidelberg (2005)
12. Lothaire, M.: Combinatorics on words. Addison-Wesley, Reading (1983)
13. Lynch, N.: Distributed algorithms. Morgan Kaufmann, San Francisco (1996)
14. Megiddo, N.: Linear-time algorithms for linear programming in r^3 and related problems. SIAM Journal on Computing 12(4), 759–776 (1983)
15. Prencipe, G.: Distributed Coordination of a Set of Autonomous Mobile Robots. PhD thesis, Dipartimento di Informatica, University of Pisa (2002)
16. Santoro, N.: Design and Analysis of Distributed Algorithms. John Wiley & Sons, Inc., Chichester (2007)
17. Siromoney, R., Mathew, L.: A public key cryptosystem based on lyndon words. Information Processing Letters 35(1), 33–36 (1990)
18. Suzuki, I., Yamashita, M.: Distributed anonymous mobile robots - formation of geometric patterns. SIAM Journal of Computing 28(4), 1347–1363 (1999)
19. Welzl, E.: Smallest enclosing disks (balls and ellipsoids). In: Maurer, H.A. (ed.) New Results and New Trends in Computer Science. LNCS, vol. 555, pp. 359–370. Springer, Heidelberg (1991)

Distance Sensitive Snapshots in Wireless Sensor Networks

Vinodkrishnan Kulathumani and Anish Arora

Department of Computer Science and Engineering, The Ohio State University
{vinodkri,anish}@cse.ohio-state.edu

Abstract. Global state snapshots are a fundamental primitive for wireless networks that sense and control real environments. Consistent and timely snapshots are potentially costly. Cost reduction is often realized by gathering only a "delta" from previous snapshots. In this paper, we explore an alternative form of efficiency by generalizing the notion of a snapshot to satisfy *distance sensitivity* properties, wherein the state of nearby nodes is available with greater resolution, speed, and frequency than that of farther away nodes. Our algorithms are memory efficient and do not require global time synchronization or localization.

For pedagogical reasons, we describe our solutions for the case of perfect 2-d grid topologies first, and then show how to extend them for higher dimensions, for network with irregular density, arbitrary sized holes, networks and non unit disk radios. We also discuss how different control applications can exploit these generalized snapshots.

1 Introduction

Sensor networks have found significant adoption in continuous observation applications and are now progressively being incorporated in distributed control applications, for instance, pursuer evader tracking [1, 2] and control of distributed parameter systems such as flexible structures [3, 4]. These applications often require information from network nodes to be periodically delivered to one or more observer/controller nodes in the network in a consistent and timely manner. For example, in pursuer evader tracking, pursuer objects require ongoing knowledge of other pursuer/evader locations in order to maintain an optimum assignment. In distributed vibration control of flexible structures, controllers need to (re)estimate the modes of vibration using samples from across the network in order to optimally assign controllers for each mode and to use the optimal control parameters. Thus global state snapshots are fundamental for wireless networks that sense and control real environments.

Although consistency, timeliness, and reliability have traditionally been the main design considerations for periodic snapshots, their efficiency becomes essential when considering resource constrained wireless sensor networks. The standard way to realize efficiency is to communicate the "delta" from previous readings or from model-driven predictions, possibly in compressed form. In this paper, we explore a complementary form of efficiency based on the observation that many applications can accommodate generalized forms of snapshots, wherein the information delivered across the network is not necessarily consistent but satisfies certain *distance sensitive* properties: The state of

E. Tovar, P. Tsigas, and H. Fouchal (Eds.): OPODIS 2007, LNCS 4878, pp. 143–158, 2007.

nearby nodes has greater resolution (*distance sensitive resolution*), arrives faster (*distance sensitive rate*) and with higher speed (*distance sensitive latency*). By way of example, consider: (1) In pursuer evader tracking, information about nearer objects are required at a faster rate and lower latency that that of farther objects for guaranteeing optimal pursuit [1,5]. (2) In scale based control [6] used for vibration control of flexible structures, different controllers are assigned to different modes (frequencies) of vibration; in this case, estimating characteristics of lower frequencies requires information from a wider area but that can be sampled at a slower rate and coarser resolution than that for nearer areas.

While collecting snapshots at a central base station has been a common pattern in sensor networks, delivering snapshots to nodes in-network is desirable from an efficiency and correctness perspective in large scale networks used for applications such as object tracking [5] and distributed control and is also an emerging pattern in applications involving mobile users. In this paper we focus on in-network delivery of snapshots.

Informal problem statement: Given is a connected wireless sensor network with N nodes embedded in an f dimensional space. Each node periodically generates m bits of information, can communicate at W bits per second, and is memory constrained.

Design efficient snapshots of the network state that are distance sensitive in resolution, latency, and rate for periodic delivery at (some or all) nodes.

Contributions: In this paper, we systematically design wireless sensor network algorithms that periodically deliver distance sensitive snapshots to all nodes in the network. Our algorithms are easily adapted to allow snapshots to be delivered only to a subset of nodes as opposed to all nodes. They are memory efficient, requiring only $O(3^f * log(N^{\frac{1}{f}}) * m)$ bits per node. They are readily realized in networks with irregular density, networks with arbitrary sized holes, imperfect clustering, and non unit disk radios. We quantify the maximum rate at which information can be generated at each node so that snapshots are periodically delivered across the network, the algorithms can of course be operated at lower rates than these. For our services, global time synchronization is not required; a local notion of time however is needed to ensure fair scheduling of transmission of nodes.

Overview of algorithms and main results: Consider an ideal network where nodes are embedded in a virtual 2-d grid such that there is exactly one node at each grid location and that each grid node can reliably reach each of its neighbors in the grid and no others. Snapshots with distance sensitive latency may be realized in these grids, firstly, by scheduling each node to transmit its local view of the network so as to not interfere with its neighbors and, secondly, by ensuring that the schedules all nodes to transmit at the same rate. In order to ensure uniform latency, we introduce a single level of clustering to regulate the flow of information in all directions by proceeding in rounds. Intuitively, a round is a unit of time when information is exchanged between any level 1 cluster and all its neighboring clusters. Our scheduling and other protocol actions at each step are such that information is propagated across the network in a pipelined manner; by this, new information can be generated at a node as soon as previous information has been dispersed only to its local neighborhood as opposed to the entire network.

In this first algorithm, in a snapshot S of the network delivered to all nodes the staleness of the state of a node i in S is $O(3^f * N * m * d)$, where $d = dist(i, j)$, and the average network communication cost is as high as $O(N^2 * m)$ for N samples (one from each node).

To add distance sensitive resolution, instead of dispersing the individual state of each node, we map the state of nodes into aggregate values of non-overlapping regions. We then deliver snapshots across the network such in a snapshot delivered to a node j, the size of a region into which a node i is mapped increases as $dist(i, j)$ increases. Thus, the resolution with which i is represented in the snapshot decreases as $dis(i, j)$ increases. To achieve this kind of snapshot delivery, we refine the clustering of nodes into a hierarchical one with a logarithmic number of levels as the network size. The basic idea is that a clusterhead at each level compresses data from all nodes in that level into m bits. Thus, the data aggregated at each level is represented by the same number of bits. At higher levels, the data is summarized with a coarser resolution as these levels contain more nodes.

In this second algorithm, in a snapshot S of the network delivered to node j the resolution of the state of a node i in S decreases as $O(d^f)$, the staleness of the state of a node i in S is $O(3^{2f} * m * log(n) * d)$ and the average network communication cost for N samples is $O(3^f * log(n) * N * m)$.

To achieve distance sensitive rate, we schedule the delivery of aggregated information at each level such that information of higher levels is delivered over a larger interval as opposed to lower levels. We do this in two ways. In the first solution, we allocate an exponentially increasing number of bits per message to lower level aggregates so that they are delivered at a faster rate. In the second solution, we allocate more time for aggregation and dispersion of lower level data.

In the first of these two algorithms, the average communication cost per N samples (one from each node) is $O(3^f * N * (m + log(n/m)))$. In the second, the average communication cost per N samples (one from each node) in the second algorithm is $O(N * m)$, but the staleness of the received states grows as $O(d^f)$.

Our algorithms allow for a user-pluggable aggregation function. We require only that the function, say f, be idempotent and satisfy the following *decomposability* property: $\forall a, b, f(a \cup b) = f(f(a) \cup f(b))$. Examples of such functions are average, max, min, count and wavelet functions.

We then relax our regularity assumptions and describe how our algorithms handle the cases of non uniform density, non uniform radio range and holes of arbitrary sizes in the network. The case of over density is modeled as certain virtual grid locations containing more than 1 node. In the case of holes in the network, we show that our algorithms achieve distance sensitivity in terms of the shortest communication path between any two nodes as opposed to the physical distance.

Outline of the paper: In Section 2, we present the system model. In Section 3, we design a snapshot service that has the property of *distance sensitive latency*. In Section 4, we design a snapshot service that has the additional property of *distance* *sensitive resolution.* In Section 5, we refine our snapshot service so that snapshots are delivered with a *distance sensitive rate* property. In Section 6, we consider irregular networks. We discuss related work in Section 7 and make concluding remarks in Section 8.

2   Model and Specification

In this section, we present the system model and a generalization of the concept of snapshots based on distance sensitive properties.

Network model: A sensor network consists of N nodes that are embedded in an f-dimensional space. We let n abbreviate $N^{\frac{1}{f}}$. The nodes induce a connected network where each communicate at W bits per second. Nodes are synchronized in time. Each node j periodically generates m bits of (sensor) information, and maintains a data structure comprising the most recent state of nodes (or partitions of nodes) and a timestamp associated with that state.

In the next three sections (3-5), for ease of exposition, we restrict our attention to sensor networks that form a 2 dimensional grid with a node at every grid location. We further assume that node communication follows an idealized disk model: specifically, each node can communicate reliably with all its neighbors in the grid and with no others. We define the neighbors of node j to be the ones to its north, east, west, and south and also to its northeast, northwest, southeast, or southwest that exist in the grid; we denote these (up to 8) neighbors as $j.n$, $j.e$, $j.w$, $j.s$, $j.ne$, $j.nw$, $j.se$ and $j.sw$ respectively. In Section 6, we remove each of these restrictive assumptions.

Definition 1 (Snapshot S). *A snapshot S is a mapping from each node in the network to a state value and a timestamp associated with that state value.*

A consistent snapshot is one where the timestamps associated with each state value are all the same. The *staleness* of a state value in S is the time elapsed between its timestamp and the current time. We now consider a generalization where state values do not necessarily correspond to the same instant of time but their staleness enjoys a distance sensitive property.

Definition 2 (Snapshots with distance sensitive latency). *A snapshot S received by a node j has* distance sensitive latency *if the staleness in the state of each node i in S decreases as $dist(i, j)$ decreases.*

We now further generalize the notion of snapshots so that state is associated with partitions p of the network as opposed to individual nodes. Let P be a partitioning of the network.

Definition 3 (Snapshot S of P). *A snapshot S of P is a mapping from each partition p in P to a state value and a timestamp associated with that state value.*

The generalized definition is useful even if P is not a total but a partial partition, i.e., not all nodes are represented in the snapshot. The state and timestamp of each p in S intuitively represent the aggregate state of all nodes in the partition and the aggregate timestamp. We assume that the timestamp of recording the state of all nodes in any partition p is the same, and refer to this common value as the aggregate timestamp. Note that the aggregate timestamp of different partitions may be different.

As there may not exist a mapping from the aggregate state of a partition to the exact state of individual nodes that was recorded for the purpose of computing the aggregate, the latter may be estimated using some function of the state of the partition. The *resolution* of the state of a node in a snapshot is an inverse measure of the error between the state of the node that was recorded and the aggregate state of the partition p that it belongs to.

We are interested in snapshots where the increase in the error in the state of a node is bounded by the size of the partition p to which it belongs. This leads us to consider a generalization where the resolution of the state of a node increases as distance decreases.

Definition 4 (Snapshots with distance sensitive resolution). *A snapshot S of P received by a node j has* distance sensitive resolution *if the resolution of the state of each node i covered by P increases as $dist(i, j)$ decreases.*

Informally speaking, the size of the partition to which the state of node i is mapped into in a snapshot received at j increases as $dist(i, j)$ increases. Therefore the resolution with which i is represented in S decreases with distance.

Finally, we consider a generalization where the rate at which state of the nodes is reported to a node decreases as the distance of the nodes increase.

Definition 5 (Snapshots with distance sensitive rate). *A node j receives snapshots of P with* distance sensitive rate *if the rate at which the state of each node i covered by P is updated in snapshots received by j increases as $dist(i, j)$ decreases.*

3 Distance Sensitive Latency Snapshots

In this section, we describe a snapshot service that has distance sensitive latency. Moreover, by introducing a single level of clustering, we also achieve information flow with uniform latency in all directions. Uniformity is a desirable property especially when aggregation needs to be performed.

Clustering: In order to achieve uniform latency, we create a single level of clustering. The grid is partitioned in 3 by 3 sub-grids of nodes, with the center node in each sub-grid cluster being its clusterhead. We call the clusterhead a level 1 node and the rest of the nodes in the cluster as level 0 nodes. This kind of clustering is illustrated in Fig. 1.

Schedule: We schedule the nodes to transmit in rounds. A round is a unit of time in which information is exchanged between a level 1 clusterhead and all of its 8 neighboring level 1 clusterheads. Each round is divided into multiple slots. In the first slot, all level 1 clusterheads transmit. In the remaining slots, all level 0 nodes in each cluster transmit twice. The second transmission by a node within a round takes place after all its 8 neighbors have transmitted at least once. Intuitively speaking, during the first turn for a node, information is communicated outwards from the clusterhead. In the next turn for the node, information is communicated to the level 1 clusterhead that the node belongs to. A simple non-interference schedule that satisfies these constraints is one where all level 0 nodes take turns in a round robin manner. Each round thus consists of 17 slots.

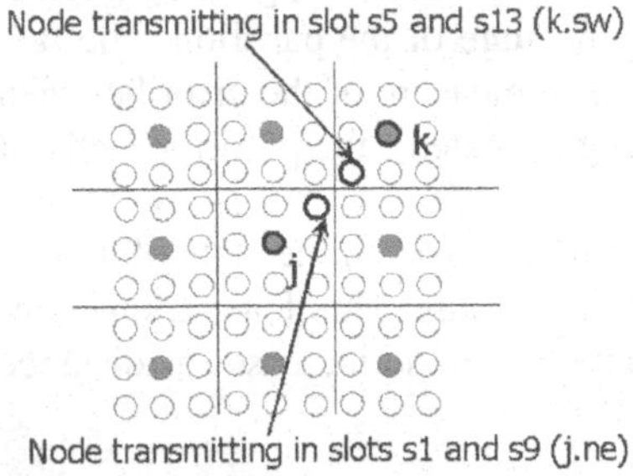

Node transmitting in slot s5 and s13 (k.sw)

Node transmitting in slots s1 and s9 (j.ne)

Fig. 1. 1 level clustering

Algorithm $S1$: In slot 0 of every round, the level 1 nodes update their own state in the local data structure and transmit the entire data structure. The level 0 nodes in each cluster update their local data structure as follows: wlog, node $j.ne$ copies the state of all nodes in its own cluster and the state of nodes in all level 1 clusters that are not north east of j.

To explain the actions in other slots, without loss of generality, consider level 1 nodes j and k and level 0 nodes $j.ne$ and $k.sw$, as shown in Fig. 1.

- In the first slot for node $j.ne$, $j.ne$ transmits its local data structure which contains the updates that were heard from j. Node $k.sw$ updates the state of all nodes in clusters that are southwest of k.
- In the second slot for node $j.ne$, $j.ne$ transmits its local data structure which contains the updates sent from k and $k.sw$, heard via $k.sw$. Node j updates the state of all nodes in clusters that are north east of j. □

In the remaining slots, the states are exchanged along the other axes around j. In algorithm $S1$, information flows between any 2 nodes through paths defined by level 1 clusters. Moreover, by the rules of updating a unique path is maintained for communicating state from a node to any other node [7]. Within a round, information is fully exchanged in a level 1 neighborhood. Thus, the latency involved in moving information between a pair of nodes depends on the number of level 1 clusters in their path, and this is uniform in all directions. Note also that between a pair of level 1 nodes, information is exchanged in 17 slots and the length of the path through level 1 nodes is proportional to d. We now state the following lemmas, the proofs of which have been relegated to the technical report for reasons of space.

Lemma 1. *In S1, the maximum staleness in the state of a node i received by a snapshot at node j is $O(N * m * d)$ where $d = dist(i,j)$.* □

Lemma 2. *In S1, the average communication cost to deliver a global snapshot to all nodes per sample from each node is $O(N^2 * m)$.* □

4 Distance Sensitive Resolution Snapshots

To incorporate the property of distance sensitive resolution, we refine the partitioning of the network into a hierarchical one with a logarithmic number of levels, which are numbered $0..(log_3n)$. A 3 by 3 set of 9 level r clusters form a cluster at level $r + 1$, as illustrated in Fig. 2. Each node belongs to one cluster at each level, and each cluster has a clusterhead which is the center node of that cluster. A clusterhead at level r is also a clusterhead at levels $0..r - 1$.

Overview of algorithm $S2$**:** The basic idea is that a clusterhead at each level compresses data from all nodes in that level into m bits. Thus, aggregated data at each level is represented by the same number of bits. At higher levels, data is summarized into a coarser resolution as the levels contain more nodes. The aggregated data is then dispersed to all nodes at that level. This solution suffers from a multi-level boundary problem however: two nodes could be neighbors but belong to a common cluster only at level $r \gg 1$. Thus despite being neighbors, both nodes get a summary of the other at a much coarser resolution than desired. The multi-level boundary problem is illustrated in Fig. 2, where nodes j and k are neighbors at level 0 but belong to a common cluster only at level 3. To avoid this problem, we disperse a summary computed at level r not only to nodes in level r cluster, but also to nodes in all neighboring level r clusters. We now describe a pipelined implementation of this algorithm.

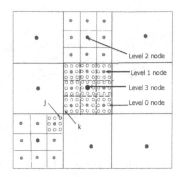

Fig. 2. Hierarchical clustering

Notations: Let $j.L$ be the highest level for which j is clusterhead. Note that there are at most 8 neighbors at each level for each node in the grid topology. We implement virtual trees along the structure at each level. To describe these trees, we will need the following definitions.

Definition 6 $(tree(k, j))$**.** $tree(k, j)$, where j is a level k clusterhead, is a level k tree formed with j as root and spanning all nodes in the level k cluster of j and all level k clusters that are its neighbors.

Definition 7 $(j.in(k, y))$**.** For each $tree(k, y)$ that j belongs to, $j.in(k, y)$ is j's parent towards root y.

Definition 8 $(j.out(k, y))$**.** For each $tree(k, y)$ that j belongs to, $j.out(k, y)$ is the set of j's descendants on the tree.

Definition 9 $(M(k, y))$**.** $M(k, y)$ is the level k summary computed by a level k clusterhead y.

In Fig. 3, a level 1 tree rooted at j is shown as an illustration. The level 1 tree extends up to all level 0 nodes in its own cluster and level 0 nodes in the 8 neighboring level 1 clusters. The trees represent the distance up to which an aggregate at any level is propagated.

Schedule: In the first slot of a round, level 1 clusterheads transmit. In the remaining slots, all the level 0 nodes per cluster take turns and transmit twice such that the second transmission occurs after all its 8 neighbors have transmitted at least once, as described in algorithm $S1$.

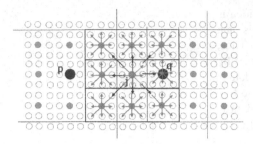

Fig. 3. Illustrating level 1 tree rooted at j

Local storage: Each node i stores the most recent value of $M(x, y)$ received by i for each $tree(x, y)$ that i belongs to. The state of any node j is obtained as a function of $M(x', y')$ where x' is the smallest level that contains information about j. Recall that the resolution of the state of j decreases as the number of nodes in the aggregate $M(x', y')$ increases.

Algorithm $S2$: We describe the actions executed by the nodes.

- In slot 0 of each round nodes with $j.L > 0$ compute the summary $M(r, j)$ for each level $1 \leq r \leq j.L$ that they are a clusterhead of based on the corresponding lower level information received in the previous round. The computed summary at each level is transmitted to the children on the respective tree rooted at j. Thus $M(r, j)$ is sent to $j.out(r, j)$ for $1 \leq r \leq j.L$.
- To explain the actions of level 0 nodes, without loss of generality, consider level 1 nodes j and k and level 0 nodes $j.ne$ and $k.sw$ as shown in Fig. 1.

  - In first slot for $j.ne$, for each $tree(x, y)$ that $j.ne$ belongs to but is not a leaf of, transmit $M(x, y)$ as heard in slot 0 from $j.in(x, y)$ to $j.out(x, y)$. Also, transmit its own information $M(0, j.ne)$ to children in the level 0 tree rooted at $j.ne$.
  - In second slot for $j.ne$, for each $tree(x, y)$ that $j.ne$ belongs to but not a leaf of, transmit $M(x, y)$ as heard in slots 2 to 8 from $j.in(x, y)$ to $j.out(x, y)$.

- The action at any node j upon receiving a message from i is as follows: for each $tree(x, y)$ that j belongs to, store $M(x, y)$ if $i = j.in(x, y)$. ☐

In summary, aggregates computed at each level are copied only going downwards along a tree. This is sufficient for a level r node to compute aggregates from level $r - 1$ nodes, because a tree at level $r - 1$ extends up to all level 0 nodes in neighboring level $r - 1$ clusters. And one of the neighboring level $r - 1$ node is a level r node. Thus, when a computed aggregate by any node is being dispersed to nodes in its own cluster and the neighboring clusters, it is also being sent *in* to a higher level node to compute an aggregate. In Fig. 3, nodes p and q are level 2 clusterheads. Note that the level 1 tree rooted at j reaches the level 2 clusterhead q that j belongs to. Since a level r node is equidistant from all level $r - 1$ nodes and because of the uniform latency property, the computed summaries are synchronous.

Lemma 3. *In $S2$, the slot width s_W needed is $\frac{(9*log(n)-7)*m}{W}$ bits per second.*

Proof. Note that, at most 9 trees at levels $1..log(n) - 1$ can pass through each node. There is only one level $logn$ tree. Also j belongs to only one level 0 tree for which it is not a leaf. Hence the maximum message length needed per slot is $(9 * log(n) - 7) * m$ bits [7]. The result follows. ☐

Lemma 4. *In $S2$, the maximum staleness in the state of a node i received by a snapshot at node j is $O(log(n) * m * d)$ where $d = dist(i, j)$.*

Proof. Consider a node p at level r. To compute a summary at level r, level $r - 1$ summaries are needed. $dist(p, q) = 3^{r-1}$, where q is any node in the set $p.nbr(r)$. A level $r - 1$ summary is computed based a level $r - 2$ summary, and so on until level 0. Upon summation, the staleness of a level 0 (individual node) state information in a level r summary is equal to $(17/2) * 3^{r-1} * s_w$ [7]. The maximum distance traveled by a level r summary is $(3/2) * 3^r$ with latency bounded by $(17/2) * 3^r * s_w$. The minimum distance between j and i for which a level r summary is the smallest level that contains information about j is 3^{r-1}. The result follows.   □

Lemma 5. *In $S2$, the resolution of state of a node i in a snapshot received at node j is $\Omega(\frac{1}{d^2})$ where $d = dist(i, j)$.*

Proof. In a level r summary, the state of 9^r nodes is compressed into m bits. We thus regard the error in the state of each node in that summary to be $O(9^r)$. The minimum distance between i and j at which j gets a level r summary of i but not a level $r - 1$ summary of i is 3^{r-1}. Thus, the error in the state of i in a snapshot received at j is $O(d^2)$ and the resolution of state of i in a snapshot received at j is $\Omega(\frac{1}{d^2})$, where $d = dist(i, j)$.

Lemma 6. *In $S2$, the average communication cost in the network to deliver a snapshot of one sample from each node to all nodes is $O(N * log(n) * m)$.*

Proof. To deliver a snapshot with a sample from each node, every node communicates $O(m * log(n))$ bits n times. And to deliver a snapshot with y samples from each node, every node communicates $O((n + y) * (m * log(n)))$ bits, since all the y samples are pipelined. Hence, if y is large and $y = \Omega(n)$, the average communication cost at each node to deliver a snapshot of a sample from each node to all nodes is $O(m * log(n))$. The average communication cost over N nodes is $O(N * (m * log(n)))$.   □

Lemma 7. *In $S2$, the memory requirement per node is $O(log(n) * m)$ bits.*

Proof. Recall that the data structure maintained at each node is the most recent value of $M(x, y)$ received by i for each $tree(x, y)$ that i belongs to. Nodes do not buffer information to be forwarded over multiple rounds. The maximum number of trees through any node is $O(log(n))$, with m bits of information flowing along each tree. The result follows.

Extending to other dimensions: In an f dimensional structure, nodes are divided into clusters with 3^f nodes per cluster. Thus there are $3^f - 1$ level 0 nodes per cluster. Each round consists of $2 * 3^f - 1$ slots and thus the number of slots per round increases proportional to 3^f. Further, there can be at most $3^f - 1$ neighbors at each level. Thus, there can be $O(3^f * log(n))$ trees passing through each node. Using these, we can generalize Lemmas for performance of $S2$ [7]. We summarize our results for all algorithms in Fig. 4 in Section 5.

5   Distance Sensitive Rate Snapshots

In this section, we describe two algorithms in which nodes receive snapshots that are distance sensitive in latency, resolution and also distance sensitive in rate.

5.1   Distance Sensitive Rate by Data Division

We partition the network hierarchically into clusters and schedule nodes to transmit in rounds exactly as we did in algorithm $S2$. However, instead of transmitting m bits for each level of data in every round, we allocate the number of bits hierarchically. Accordingly, a message transmitted by a node in any given round consists of m bits for each level 0 information, $m/3$ bits for each level 1 information, and 1 bit for each level from $log(m)$ to $log(n)$.

Algorithm $S3a$: By way of refining algorithm $S2$, consider a level 0 node with $j.L = r$. A level r summary is computed by this node once every 3^r rounds based on the most recent level $r - 1$ summaries it receives. This summary $M(r, j)$, which consists of m bits, is transmitted in slot 0 of each round with $max(1, \frac{m}{3^r})$ bits per round. Thus, a level r summary is sent over $min(3^r, m)$ rounds. The actions for forwarding nodes remain the same except for the change that each node now only receives a fraction of $M(x, y)$ in every round for each $tree(x, y)$ that it belongs to, and it forwards only that fraction in the next round. We now state the latency and communication cost of algorithm $S3a$.

Lemma 8. *In $S3a$, the maximum message length needed per slot in algorithm is $11 * \frac{m}{2} + 9 * log(\frac{n}{m})$ bits.*   □

Lemma 9. *In $S3a$, the maximum interval between when a node j receives the state of node i is $O((m + log(n/m)) * d)$, where $d = dist(i, j)$.*   □

Lemma 10. *In $S3a$, the maximum staleness in the state of a node i received by a snapshot at node j is $O((m + log(n/m)) * d)$ where $d = dist(i, j)$.*   □

Lemma 11. *In $S3a$, the average communication cost to deliver a snapshot of one sample from each node to all nodes is $O(N * (m + log(n/m)))$.*   □

5.2   Distance Sensitive Rate by Time Division

Again, we hierarchically partition the network into clusters and schedule nodes to transmit in rounds exactly as in algorithm $S2$. However, instead of allocating exponentially increasing number of bits per level in each round, we allocate each round to a particular level and the information corresponding to that level is propagated only in that round. The frequency at which a round is allocated to a particular level increases exponentially as level decreases.

Algorithm $S3b$: Consider level $r > 0$. Let the rounds be numbered starting from 1. All rounds enumerated by $2^{r-1} + i \times 2^r$ for $i > 0$ are allocated to round r, where $r > 0$. A level 0 information is carried in all rounds. Consider a round s that belongs to level $r_s > 0$. A node j with level $j.L \geq r_s$ computes the summary only corresponding to level r_s. The computed summary at each level is transmitted to the children on the respective tree rooted at j. Level 0 nodes forward information only pertaining to level r_s in round s.

Lemma 12. *In* $S3b$, *the maximum message length needed per slot is* $10 * m$ *bits.*

Lemma 13. *In* $S3b$, *the maximum staleness in the state of a node* i *received by a snapshot at node* j *is* $O(m * d^2)$ *where* $d = dist(i, j)$.   □

Lemma 14. *In* $S3b$, *the maximum interval between when a node* j *receives the state of node* i *is* $O(m * d)$.   □

Lemma 15. *In* $S3b$, *the average communication cost to deliver a snapshot of one sample from each node to all nodes is* $O(N * m)$.   □

Lemma 16. *In* $S3a$ *and* $S3b$, *the memory requirement per node is* $O(log(n) * m)$.

Both algorithms $S3a$ and $S3b$ can be generalized to f dimensions just as algorithm $S2$ is [7]. We summarize all our results in Fig. 4.

Algorithm	Staleness	Communication cost	Resolution	Interval	Memory
$S1$	$O(3^f * N * m * d)$	$O(N^2 * m)$	$full$	independent of d	$N * m$
$S2$	$O(3^{2f} * log(n) * m * d)$	$O(3^f * N * m * log(n))$	$\Omega(\frac{1}{d})$	independent of d	$3^f * log(n) * m$
$S3a$	$O(3^{2f} * (m + log(n/m)) * d)$	$O(3^f * N * (m + log(n/m)))$	$\Omega(\frac{1}{d})$	$O(3^f * (m + log(n/m)) * d)$	$3^f * log(n) * m$
$S3b$	$O(3^{2f} * m * d^2)$	$O(3^f * N * m)$	$\Omega(\frac{1}{d})$	$O(m * d * 3^f)$	$3^f * log(n) * m$

Fig. 4. Summary of results for snapshot algorithms

6   Irregular Networks

In this section, we show how our algorithms continue to yield distance sensitive snapshots in the following cases: non uniform density, holes of arbitrary sizes within the connected network, non unit disk radios and imperfect clustering.

Clustering Model CM: We assume the existence of a clustering layer that partitions the general but connected network, as modeled in Section 2, into hierarchical clusters such that every network node belongs to one cluster at each level. As perfect (i.e., regular and symmetric) clustering may no longer be possible, we weaken that assumption to: each level 1 cluster includes all nodes that are 1 hop away but may also include nodes that are up to some bounded number of hops, z, from it. Likewise, all higher level clusterheads also have the same radius range as opposed to a uniform radius.

More formally, our clustering assumption is stated as follows. For simplicity we specify the model for a 2 dimensional network that can be generalized to f dimensions. In this model, we refer to distance in terms of communication *hop* distances.

– ($C1$) All nodes within hop distance $\frac{3^k - 1}{2}$ from a level k clusterhead belong to that cluster.
– ($C2$) The maximum hop distance of a node from its level k clusterhead is $z^k \times \frac{3^k - 1}{2}$.

- (C3) There exists a path from each clusterhead to all nodes in that cluster containing only nodes belonging to that cluster.
- (C4) At all levels $k > 0$, there is at least one and at most 8 neighboring level k clusters for each level k clusterhead and there exists a path between any two neighboring clusterheads.

We note that the existence of such clustering solutions has been validated in previous research [8] and also been used in the context of object tracking.

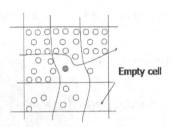

Fig. 5. Virtual grid

Once the network has been partitioned into clusters, we impose a virtual grid on the network, as shown in Fig. 5. Each level 0 node belongs to some cell, but now each cell in the virtual grid may contain any number of nodes. In particular, cells may be empty and empty cells may be contiguous; we call sets of contiguous empty cells the *holes* of the network.

Over density cells: In the virtual grid, each cell gets a slot to transmit as described in algorithm $S2$. When a cell has more than one node, each node in the cell gets a turn over multiple rounds to send its data, resulting in time sharing between nodes of a cell to transmit its own data. However, once data is sent out from the source, the forwarding of the data does not incur this extra delay despite going through denser cells. This is because any node in the dense cell that gets a turn in a given round can forward the data heard in the previous round from neighboring cells.

Under density cells, holes, and imperfect clustering: We first describe the changes needed in the scheduling to handle clusters of non uniform size. We then describe how distance sensitivity is preserved.

Scheduling scheme (FS): Recall that a *round* is a unit of time in which information is exchanged between a level 1 clusterhead and all its neighboring level 1 clusterheads. In the general model, a level 1 cluster can cover up to a z hop neighborhood. Accordingly, the basic round scheduling introduced in Section 3 is adapted to have $O(3^z)$ level 0 slots that fulfill the function of a round. Some slots may not be utilized because the cells may be empty.

Distance sensitivity: Recalling the clustering specifications stated above, consider any two nodes i and j in the network. Let the shortest path between these two nodes in the presence of holes be hop distance p.

Lemma 17. *Under clustering model CM, if k is the smallest level at which i and j are neighbors then $p > 3^{k-1}$.*

Proof. Note that i and j are not neighbors at level $k - 1$. And if $p \leq 3^{k-1}$, then a level $k - 1$ cluster cannot exist between i and j since from property $C1$, a level $k - 1$ cluster has a minimum radius of $\frac{3^{k-1}-1}{2}$. □

Theorem 1. *Under model CM, algorithms $S2$, $S3a$ and $S3b$ yield snapshots that retain their distance sensitive properties.*

Proof. From the previous lemma, the minimum distance between two nodes i and j for which level k is the smallest level at which i and j are neighbors is 3^{k-1}.

Despite the fact the trees are not formed along the regular grid pattern, it still holds that not more than 9 trees per level pass through any node. This is because there at most 8 neighboring level k clusters for any level k cluster. Moreover, the maximum degree of any node in all trees is still 8, by imposing the virtual grid for level 0. Therefore, the slot width allocations in algorithms $S2$, $S3a$ and $S3b$ are sufficient to transmit all information. □

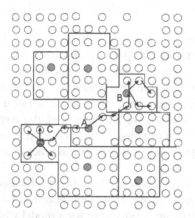

Fig. 6. Handling holes in dense networks

Fig. 6 illustrates how snapshots are communicated in irregular networks. The figure shows a level 1 cluster with a clusterhead A that has 7 neighboring level 1 clusters. The small unfilled circles represent cells of the virtual grid; these may contain one or more level 0 nodes. The level 1 clusters cover up to a 2 hop neighborhood. The figure also shows a level 1 tree rooted at A and extending up to clusters B and C.

Non-uniform radio range: If communication range were relaxed to radio interference range varying from 1 to s hops, the basic scheduling for each round would need to take into account this additional interference. This would result in longer round lengths proportional to the size of interference region.

Implementation considerations: We now highlight considerations for implementing our snapshot services in wireless sensor networks. The snapshot services that we consider in this paper are high density operations and TDMA [9] is naturally suited for such scenarios as interference can be avoided. But we do not need global time synchronization in the network. Nodes in their network can learn their TDMA slots by knowing their relative position to that of a clusterhead and locally scheduling in a non interference manner. Note that our snapshot services are continuous and we do not recover a *lost* message. On the other hand we avoid message losses by interference free scheduling.

Another issue to consider is that of localization. For our snapshot services, information is communicated only along a tree structure that is rooted at clusterheads of different levels. Knowledge of location is not needed in the protocol actions; only knowledge of which trees a node belongs to is sufficient. Also it is sufficient for the nodes to be scheduled in a non interference manner, not particularly in any order. Thus localization is not required for our snapshot services.

7   Related Work

Communicating periodic global state snapshots is a well studied problem in distributed systems [10] and consistency, timeliness and reliability have been the main design considerations in those studies. But efficiency becomes essential when considering periodic snapshots for resource constrained wireless sensor networks. To the best of our knowledge algorithms for delivering periodic snapshots across a wireless sensor network have not been studied before.

A common approach to achieving compression for efficiency is to exploit the temporal and spatial correlation of data being shared. For example, in [11], the authors propose a framework for a one time all-to-all broadcast of sensor data assuming the data is spatially correlated. Instead, in this paper we do not require data to be correlated. At the same time, our algorithms can be used in conjunction with other forms of compression.

Fractionally cascaded information [12] is a form of distance sensitive resolution that is widely used in computational geometry community for speeding up data structures. Recently, fractional cascading has been used for sensor networks as an efficient storage mechanism [13, 14]. Data is first stored at multiple resolutions across the network, which is then used to efficiently answer aggregate queries about a range of locations without exploring the entire area. In contrast, we have considered a model where information is generated and consumed on an ongoing basis. At the same time these services can be used in range based querying as well as in several other control applications.

An algorithm for creating the multi-resolution data structure based on probabilistic gossip mechanism has been discussed in [14]. In [14], the algorithm described is for a one shot dispersion and proceeds in stages while our services are for a model where information is consumed on an ongoing basis and accordingly we describe a pipelined implementation that is based on scheduling. In [14], the aggregation oprations are duplicate insensitive and global time synchronization is assumed while we do not require either of these properties. Our comunication costs and latency are lower than those in [14] and we also describe services that additionally have distance sensitive rate properties. But we note that while we assume hierarchical clustering in our solutions, the algorithm in [14] does not.

The idea of *distance sensitive rate* has also arisen in other contexts. Fisheye state routing is a proactive routing protocol [15] that reduces the frequency of topology updates to distant parts of the network.

Recently algorithms for bulk data collection in sensor networks have been proposed. In [16] data is collected from one node at a time, while [17] performs concurrent, pipelined exfiltration of data using TDMA schedules. Our algorithms can be specialized for the case of bulk convergecast and we additionally emphasize on efficiency using distance sensitive properties.

8   Conclusion

We have generalized the basic notion of snapshots using distance sensitive notions and accordingly designed efficient wireless sensor network algorithms that periodically deliver them. We achieve compression by forming hierarchical clusters and aggregating information at clusterheads. To communicate the snapshots, we embed logical trees rooted at clusterheads that extend up to all neighboring clusters at the corresponding level. Aggregate information at each level is then propagated downwards along the respective tree and this is sufficient for higher level clusterheads to compute respective aggregates. Our algorithm actions are such that information propagates in a pipelined manner; by this, new information can be generated as soon as previous information has been dispersed to a local neighborhood as opposed to the entire network. We achieve further compression in our algorithms by exponentially decreasing the bandwidth allocated to aggregates at higher levels.

Our algorithms are memory efficient and realizable in networks with irregular density, with arbitrary sized holes, and imperfect clustering. We have quantified the maximum rate at which information can be generated at each node so that snapshots are periodically delivered across the network; the algorithms can be operated at lower rates. We have specified the allowable aggregation functions in abstract terms, allowable functions include average, max, min and wavelet functions. Our algorithms neither require global time synchronization nor localization.

We expect to implement our snapshot algorithms in the context of applications such as pursuer evader tracking and vibration control, and study their performance and trade-offs more exhaustively in the future.

References

1. Cao, H., Ertin, E., Kulathumani, V., Sridharan, M., Arora, A.: Differential games in large scale sensor actuator networks. In: IPSN, pp. 77–84. ACM Press, New York (2006)
2. Sinopoli, B., Sharp, C., Schenato, L., Schaffert, S., Sastry, S.: Distributed control applications within sensor networks. Proceedings of the IEEE 91, 1235–1246 (2003)
3. Challenge problem description for network embedded software technology (nest). Boeing Tech Report, The Boeing Company, St. Louis, MO 63166 (April 2002)
4. Kim, Y.M., Arora, A., Kulathumani, V.: On Effect of Faults in Vibration Control of Fairing Structures. In: MSNDC 2005 (2005)
5. Kulathumani, V., Demirbas, M., Arora, A.: Trail: A Distance Sensitive WSN Service for Distributed Object Tracking. In: European Conference on Wireless Sensor Networks (2007)
6. Chou, K., Flamm, D., Guthart, G.: Multiscale Approach to the Control of Smart Structures. In: SPIE, vol. 2721, pp. 94–105 (1996)
7. Kulathumani, V., Arora, A.: Distance Sensitive Snapshots in Wireless Sensor Networks. Technical Report OSU-CISRC-7/07-TR51, The Ohio State University (2007)
8. Mittal, V., Demirbas, M., Arora, A.: Loci: Local clustering service for large scale wireless sensor networks. Technical Report OSU-CISRC-2/03-TR07, The Ohio State University (2003)
9. Kulkarni, S., Arumugam, U.: TDMA service for Sensor Networks. In: ICDCS, vol. 4, pp. 604–609 (2004)
10. Chandy, M., Lamport, L.: Distributed snapshots: determining global states of distributed systems. ACM Transacttions on Computer Systems 3(5), 63–75 (1985)
11. Servetto, S.: Sensing LENA - Massively Distributed Compression of Sensor Images. In: IEEE ICIP (2003)
12. Dehne, F., Ferreira, A., Rau-Chaplin, A.: Parallel fractional cascading on hypercube multi-processors. In: Computational Geometry Theory Applications, vol. 2, pp. 144–167 (1992)
13. Gao, J., Guibas, L.J., Hershberger, J., Zhang, L.: Fractionally cascaded information in a sensor network. In: IPSN, pp. 311–319 (2004)

14. Sarkar, R., Zhu, X., Gao, J.: Hierarchical Spatial Gossip for MultiResolution Representations in Sensor Networks. In: IPSN, pp. 311–319 (2007)
15. Pei, G., Gerla, M., Chen, T.-W.: Fisheye State Routing in Mobile Adhoc Networks. In: ICDCS Workshop on Wireless Networks, pp. 71–78 (2000)
16. Kim, S.: Sensor networks for structural health monitoring. Master's thesis, University of California, Berkeley (2005)
17. Naik, V., Arora, A.: Harvest: A reliable bulk data collection service for large scale wireless sensor networks. Technical Report OSU-CISRC-4/06-TR37, The Ohio State University (2006)

Distributed Approximation Algorithms for Finding 2-Edge-Connected Subgraphs

Sven O. Krumke[1], Peter Merz[2], Tim Nonner[3, *], and Katharina Rupp[1,**]

[1] Department of Mathematics, University of Kaiserslautern, Kaiserslautern, Germany
[2] Department of Computer Science, University of Kaiserslautern, Kaiserslautern, Germany
[3] Department of Computer Science, Albert-Ludwigs-University Freiburg,
Freiburg im Breisgau, Germany
`tim.nonner@informatik.uni-freiburg.de`

Abstract. We consider the distributed construction of a minimum weight 2-edge-connected spanning subgraph (2-ECSS) of a given weighted or unweighted graph. A 2-ECSS of a graph is a subgraph that, for each pair of vertices, contains at least two edge-disjoint paths connecting these vertices. The problem of finding a minimum weight 2-ECSS is NP-hard and a natural extension of the distributed MST construction problem, one of the most fundamental problems in the area of distributed computation. We present a distributed $\frac{3}{2}$-approximation algorithm for the unweighted 2-ECSS construction problem that requires $O(n)$ communication rounds and $O(m)$ messages. Moreover, we present a distributed 3-approximation algorithm for the weighted 2-ECSS construction problem that requires $O(n\log n)$ communication rounds and $O(n\log^2 n + m)$ messages.

1 Introduction

The robustness of a network subject to link failure is often modeled by the edge connectivity of the associated graph. On the other hand, in order to construct a communication-efficient backbone of the network, it is crucial to find a spanning subgraph with low weight, where the weight of an edge represents for example bandwidth or latency. Hence, the construction of highly-connected subgraphs with low weight is a fundamental problem in network design. Due to the distributed nature of a network, it is important to decentralize such a task. However, mostly non-distributed algorithms have been proposed. From the vast area of non-distributed connectivity algorithms, the papers [1,2,3] are the most related to this work. The best investigated problem in our context is probably the distributed minimum spanning tree (MST) construction problem. Starting with the seminal paper of Gallagher et al. [4] which introduced the first distributed algorithm with a non-trivial time and message complexity, there has been a line of improvements concerning the time complexity [5,6]. However, the failure of one edge already disconnects a MST. Therefore, we consider a natural extension of this problem, the distributed construction of a minimum weight *2-edge-connected spanning subgraph (2-ECSS)* of a

* Corresponding Author. Supported by DFG research program No 1103 *Embedded Microsystems*.
** Supported by the *Landesexzellenzcluster* DASMOD of the state Rhineland-Palatinate.

E. Tovar, P. Tsigas, and H. Fouchal (Eds.): OPODIS 2007, LNCS 4878, pp. 159–173, 2007.
© Springer-Verlag Berlin Heidelberg 2007

given graph $G = (V, E)$. That is, a subgraph such that for each pair of vertices, there exist at least two edge-disjoint paths connecting them. A 2-ECSS is hence resilient against the failure of a single edge.

Let $n = |V|$ and $m = |E|$. The problem of computing a minimum weight 2-ECSS of a given graph is known to be NP-hard, even in the unweighted case. This follows by a reduction from the Hamiltonian cycle problem: a graph has a Hamiltonian cycle if and only if it has a 2-ECSS of the size of the number of vertices in the graph. Furthermore, the problem is MAX-SNP-hard [7]. We therefore consider distributed approximation algorithms for the weighted and unweighted version of this problem. To simulate bandwidth limitation, we restrict messages to $O(\log n)$ bits in size, thus meeting the *CONGEST* model described in [8]. This restriction is important, since if we allow messages of arbitrary size, we can solve every distributed optimization problem in $O(n)$ rounds by collecting the whole network topology in one vertex. But if we restrict the size, this trivial approach requires $\Omega(nm)$ rounds and messages if we assume that we need $\Omega(\log n)$ bits to represent an edge.

1.1   Contributions

For the unweighted 2-ECSS construction problem, we present a distributed $\frac{3}{2}$- approximation algorithm using $O(n)$ communication rounds and $O(m)$ messages. The approximation ratio is based on a result by Khuller and Vishkin [1]. For the weighted 2-ECSS construction problem, we give a distributed 3-approximation algorithm that requires $O(n \log n)$ communication rounds and $O(n \log^2 n + m)$ messages. The approximation ratio of the latter algorithm meets the best known approximation ratio which was introduced by Khuller and Thurimella [3]. Our algorithm has the same basic structure as the algorithm described in [3], but a different implementation, since the proposed reduction to the computation of a minimum directed spanning tree does not work in the more restrictive distributed model. Moreover, the best known distributed algorithm for the computation of a minimum directed spanning tree requires $\Omega(n^2)$ communication rounds [9]. Hence, our algorithm beats such a straightforward approach. Observe that $O(n \log n)$ communication rounds correspond to the running time of the best known non-distributed algorithm for the computation of a minimum weight directed spanning tree which was introduced by Gabow [10]. It is worth noting that our results show that more complex connectivity problems than the MST construction problem can be efficiently approximated in the distributed context.

1.2   Further Related Work

In other words, this paper discusses the distributed construction of a minimum weight subgraph that does not contain *bridges*, where a bridge is an edge whose removal disconnects the graph. Hence, a bridge-finding algorithm can be used to verify a 2-ECSS. An optimal distributed algorithm for this task is given in [11]. Another related problem is the distributed construction of a sparse *k-connectivity certificate* [12], that is a sparse k-connected subgraph. However, the paper [12] does not deal with the approximation of an optimal 2-connectivity certificate. In the distributed context, labeling schemes can be quite helpful for various tasks. The vertex-connectivity labeling scheme described in [13] is the most related to our context.

1.3 Model

Consider an undirected graph $G = (V, E)$ with an associated non-negative edge-weight function ω. In the unweighted case, the function ω is constant. Each vertex hosts a processor with "unlimited computational power". Hence, the terms "vertex" and "processor" are synonyms in this context. All vertices begin with distinct identifiers. Initially, the vertices do neither know the network size nor the identities of their neighbors, but have a fixed list of incident edges including the weight of these edges. Finally, to distributively solve the 2-ECSS construction problem, each vertex needs to have a sublist of this list such that the union of these sublists defines the 2-ECSS. The only way to achieve information about their neighborhood is to communicate via elementary messages that can be sent along incident edges. Communication takes place in synchronous rounds: in each round, each vertex is allowed to exchange a message with each neighbor and do some local computation. A single vertex, named *leader*, initiates the algorithm. This model, where all elementary messages are $O(\log n)$ bits in size, is called *CONGEST* [8]. In addition to the number of rounds, also called the *time complexity*, the *message complexity*, that is the total number of messages sent, is also often used to measure the performance of an algorithm.

1.4 Outline and Definitions

In Sect. 2 and 3, we describe distributed approximation algorithms for the unweighted and weighted 2-ECSS construction problem, respectively. Both algorithms use the same straightforward strategy to find a 2-ECSS: compute a rooted spanning subtree T, and then solve a *tree augmentation problem* for T, i.e., find an augmentation of T with minimum weight. An *augmentation* of a spanning subtree T is a 2-ECSS A of G that contains T, and the weight of A is the sum of the weights of the edges in A that do not belong in T. We refer to all edges in T as *tree edges* and to all other edges in G as *back edges*. We say that a back edge $\{u, w\} \in E$ *covers* a vertex $v \in V$ if and only if v lies on the unique simple path from u to w in T. Moreover, we say that a back edge $e \in E$ covers a tree edge $e' \in E$ if both endpoints of e' are covered by e. Hence, to get an optimal augmentation of T, we need to find a set of back edges with minimum weight that covers all tree edges. This is the major problem in the distributed context, since it is not possible for a vertex to decide whether to add an adjacent edge or not only on local information.

For a vertex $v \in V$, we denote by T_v the subtree of T rooted in v. A vertex $v \in V$ is an *ancestor* of a vertex $u \in V$ if and only if $u \in T_v$. The *depth* of a vertex $v \in V$ is the distance from v to the root of T with respect to the hop-metric. We denote the depth of a vertex v by $\text{depth}(v)$. The *depth* of T is the maximum depth of a vertex in T. All logarithms are base 2. For an integer i, let $[i] := \{1, \ldots, i\}$. We do not distinguish in between a path P and its vertex set $V(P)$. Hence, $|P|$ denotes the number of vertices on P.

We assume that G is 2-connected. To ensure this, we can first run a biconnectivity check [11]. To avoid degenerated cases, we assume that any shortest path does not contain loops of weight 0. We use the terms *broadcast* and *convergecast* to abstract standard tasks in the design of distributed algorithms. In a broadcast, we distribute information top-down in a tree. A convergecast is the inverse process, where we collect information bottom-up.

2   The Unweighted Case

The following algorithm $\mathscr{A}_{card}$ is basically a distributed version of the algorithm described in [1]. As already mentioned in Sect. 1.4, we first compute a rooted spanning tree T of G. In this case, we choose T to be a DFS-tree. Such a tree T can be straightforward computed in $O(n)$ time with $O(m)$ messages and has the nice property that for every back edge $\{u, w\} \in E$, either u is an ancestor of w or w is an ancestor of u in T. As a byproduct of the DFS-computation, each vertex $v \in V$ knows its DFS-index in T. Next, we determine for each vertex $v \in V$ the back edge $\{u, w\} \in E$ that covers $\{v, p(v)\}$ such that $\min\{\text{depth}(u), \text{depth}(w)\}$ is minimal, where $p(v)$ is the parent of v. We denote this edge by $\text{sav}(v)$. Clearly, if all tree edges in T_v are already covered, the back edge $\text{sav}(v)$ is the "best choice" to cover the edge $\{v, p(v)\}$, since besides covering $\{v, p(v)\}$, it covers the most edges above. We can easily implement a convergecast in T such that afterwards, each vertex $v \in V$ knows $\text{sav}(v)$ and additionally the depth of both endpoints of $\text{sav}(v)$. Then, to cover T, we use the following bottom-up process in T which can be implemented as a convergecast in T: when a vertex v is reached by the convergecast, v checks whether the back edges added by the vertices in T_v cover the edge $\{v, p(v)\}$ as well. To this end, v only needs to know the minimum depth of a vertex covered by the edges that have been added by the vertices in T_v. This information can be easily aggregated during the convergecast. If $\{v, p(v)\}$ is not covered, then $\{v, p(v)\}$ is a bridge, and hence v adds the back edge $\{u, w\} = \text{sav}(v)$. This is the critical point, since there is no global control to address, but v has to tell both endpoints u, w to add $\text{sav}(v)$ to the their list of adjacent edges. A straightforward approach would be for v to send a request message addedge(u, w) to u and w. Note that we can route such a request on the shortest path in T by using the DFS-indices of the vertices in an interval routing scheme [14]. However, this approach requires $\Omega(n^2)$ time and messages. We show that the strategy to send only one request message addedge(u, w) to the *nearest* of the two endpoints u and w is much more efficient. Specifically, v sends addedge(u, w) to u if $|\text{depth}(u) - \text{depth}(v)| \leq |\text{depth}(w) - \text{depth}(v)|$, and to w, otherwise. This endpoint then informs the other endpoint by sending a message over the edge $\{u, w\}$.

Theorem 1. *Algorithm $\mathscr{A}_{card}$ has time complexity $O(n)$ and message complexity $O(m)$.*

Proof. Clearly, the only critical part is the adding of edges. To add an edge $\{u, w\}$, a vertex v needs to send a request message addedge(u, w) either to u or to w. We will show that the number of elementary messages needed for this process is $O(n)$. Hence, the time complexity is $O(n)$ as well.

Let E' be the back edges added to T in algorithm $\mathscr{A}_{card}$, and let $e_1, e_2, \ldots, e_r$ be an ordering of E' such that if the endpoint of e_j with the smaller depth in T is an ancestor of the endpoint of e_i with the smaller depth in T, then $j < i$. For a back edge $e_i = \{u, w\}$ with u is an ancestor of w, let P_i be the unique simple path from u to w in T. Let then $V_i := \sum_{j=1}^{i} P_j$. In contrast to the adding of edges, we count the number of messages top-down in T. Let $a(i)$ be the total number of elementary messages needed to add the back edge e_i. We will show that $a(i) \leq |V_i| - |V_{i-1}|$. Hence, $\sum_{1}^{r} a(i) \leq n$. The claim follows.

For a back edge e_i with a path $P_i = (v_1, v_2, \ldots, v_s)$, let $v_k \in P_i$ be the vertex that discovered that $\{v_k, p(v_k)\}$ is a bridge, where $p(v_k)$ is the parent of v_k, and hence decided to add the edge e_i. Then $e_i = \{v_1, v_s\} = \text{sav}(v_k)$ and $v_1 \neq v_k$. For contradiction, assume that $v_k \in V_{i-1}$. Then there exists at least one path $P_j = (u_1, u_2, \ldots, u_t)$ with $j < i$ such that $v_k \in P_j$ and u_1 is an ancestor of v_1. Hence, the edge $e_j = \{u_1, u_t\}$ covers $\{v_k, p(v_k)\}$. Therefore, the edge e_i was added before e_j, because otherwise, $\{v_k, p(v_k)\}$ would have already been covered by e_j. Hence, $u_1 \neq v_1$, since otherwise, there would have been no need to add e_j. But then, the edge e_j would have been a better choice than e_i for v_k to add. Hence, $v_k \notin V_{i-1}$.

The vertex v_k has either sent a request message addedge(v_1, v_s) to v_1 or to v_s, depending on which of these vertices is closer. The number of elementary messages needed to deliver this request is therefore the distance to the closest vertex. Hence, we need to distinguish two cases. First, if v_s is closer, i.e., $s - k < k - 1$, then we need $s - k \leq |V_i| - |V_{i-1}|$ messages, since $v_k \notin V_{i-1}$, and hence $V_i \backslash V_{i-1}$ contains at least the vertices on the subpath $(v_k, v_{k+1}, \ldots, v_s)$ of P_i. Second, if v_1 is closer, i.e., $k - 1 \leq s - k$, then we need $k - 1 \leq s - k \leq |V_i| - |V_{i-1}|$ messages for the same reason. Therefore, in both cases, $a(i) \leq |V_i| - |V_{i-1}|$. □

Theorem 2. *[1] Algorithm $\mathscr{A}_{card}$ is a distributed $\frac{3}{2}$-approximation algorithm for unweighted 2-ECSS construction problem.*

3 The Weighted Case

The weighted case is much more involved than the unweighted case, since we can not simply follow the description of a known non-distributed algorithm. In contrast to the unweighted case, we first compute a rooted MST T. For example, we can use the well-known algorithm of Gallager et al. [4] for this task that requires $O(n \log n)$ time and messages. Note that since the weight of T and the weight of an optimal augmentation of T are both smaller than the weight of an optimal 2-ECSS of G, a distributed α-approximation algorithm for the weighted tree augmentation problem yields a distributed $(1 + \alpha)$-approximation algorithm for the weighted 2-ECSS construction problem.

This section is organized as follows. For the sake of exposition, we first consider the case that T is a *chain*, i.e., T has only one leaf, in Sect. 3.1. We use here that the tree augmentation problem for a chain is equivalent to a shortest path problem. Second, we extend the obtained algorithm to the general case in Sect. 3.2. The high-level idea is to decompose a general spanning tree T in paths in order to compute one shortest path for each path in the decomposition with a modified weight function. Altogether, these shortest paths result in a 2-approximation of an optimal augmentation of T. In combination with the distributed MST construction, this yields a distributed 3-approximation algorithm for the weighted 2-ECSS construction problem. Note that although the basic structure of this algorithm is the same as the algorithm described in [3], we can not use the same simple proof to obtain the approximation ratio of 2.

3.1 The Chain Case

Assume that T is a chain, and let then $v_1, v_2, \ldots, v_n$ be an ordering of V such that depth$(v_i) = i - 1$. Consider the following orientation $G^* = (V, E^*)$ of G: for each tree

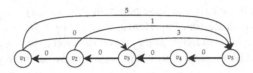

Fig. 1. The orientation G^* of G

edge $\{v_i, v_{i+1}\} \in E$, $(v_{i+1}, v_i) \in E^*$, and for each back edge $\{v_i, v_j\} \in E$ with $i < j$, $(v_i, v_j) \in E^*$. We use the notion of back and tree edges in G^* analogously to G, but define the weights of the edges E^* as follows: the back edges in E^* have the same weight as the corresponding back edges in E, but the tree edges in E^* have weight 0. The following observation motivates this construction.

Observation 3. *Let A be the shortest path from v_1 to v_n in G^*. Then adding all edges in G that correspond to the back edges on A to T yields an optimal augmentation of T.*

For example, consider a graph G with five vertices v_1, v_2, v_3, v_4, v_5. Assume that we have four additional back edges $\{v_1, v_3\}, \{v_1, v_5\}, \{v_2, v_5\}, \{v_3, v_5\}$ of weight $0, 5, 1, 3$, respectively. The graph G^* is depicted in Fig. 1. The shortest path from v_1 to v_5 in G^* contains the two back edges (v_1, v_3) and (v_2, v_5). The corresponding edges in G are $\{v_1, v_3\}$ and $\{v_2, v_5\}$. Adding these edges to T yields an optimal augmentation of T.

According to Observation 3, we only need to distributively compute the shortest path from v_1 to v_n in G^*. Clearly, we can use the well-known distributed single-source shortest path algorithm of Bellman and Ford for this task [15]. In this algorithm, each vertex v_i needs to hold two variables $\text{dist}(v_i)$ and $\text{next}(v_i)$, where $\text{dist}(v_i)$ stores the length of the shortest path to v_n currently known, and $\text{next}(v_i)$ stores the first edge in this path. Since these variables need to be updated n times, this algorithm requires $O(n)$ rounds and $O(nm)$ messages. Because we can not transfer this algorithm to the general case described in Sect. 3.2 and the number of messages is quite high, we will describe a modification of this algorithm that takes $O(n \log n)$ time and messages.

For simplicity, assume that n is a power of 2. Then, by iteratively halving the path $P := (v_1, v_2, \ldots, v_n)$, we can construct a binary tree of depth $\log n$ with ordered children whose vertices with depth i are a fragmentation of the path P in subpaths of length $n/2^i$. We call this tree without the vertices with depth $\log n$ that represent subpaths containing a single vertex the *hierarchical fragmentation* of P and denote it by $F(P)$. For a subpath $Q \in F(P)$ with $Q = (v_s, v_{s+1}, \ldots, v_r)$, we refer to the subpaths $(v_s, v_{s+1}, \ldots, v_t)$ and $(v_{t+1}, v_{t+2}, \ldots, v_r)$ with $t = (r - s + 1)/2$ as the *left* and *right half* of Q, respectively. We say that a back edge $(u, w) \in E^*$ *belongs* to a subpath $Q \in F(P)$ if u and w lie on the left and right half of Q, respectively. The following algorithm is based on an *inverse inorder-traversal* of the tree $F(P)$. In an inverse inorder-traversal, the right and left child of a vertex are processed before and after this vertex, respectively.

For example, the sequence $(v_3, v_4), (v_1, v_2, v_3, v_4), (v_1, v_2)$ is an inverse inorder-traversal of $F(v_1, v_2, v_3, v_4)$, that is the hierarchical fragmentation of the path (v_1, v_2, v_3, v_4).

Algorithm $\mathscr{A}_{sp}$

1. Set $dist(v_n) := 0$, and for each $i \in [n-1]$, set $dist(v_i) := \infty$.
2. Let $Q_1, Q_2, \ldots, Q_k$ be an inverse inorder-traversal of $F(P)$. For $l = 1, \ldots, k$, *process the subpath $Q_l = (v_s, v_{s+1}, \ldots, v_r)$ twice with the following two distance update steps:*
   (a) For each back edge $(v_i, v_j) \in E^*$ that belongs to Q_l, if it holds that $dist(v_j) + \omega(v_i, v_j) < dist(v_i)$, then set $dist(v_i) := dist(v_j) + \omega(v_i, v_j)$ and $next(v_i) := (v_i, v_j)$.
   (b) For $i = s, \ldots, r-1$, if $dist(v_i) < dist(v_{i+1})$, then set $dist(v_{i+1}) := dist(v_i)$ and $next(v_{i+1}) := (v_{i+1}, v_i)$.
3. Return $next(v_1), next(v_2), \ldots, next(v_n)$.

To analyze algorithm $\mathscr{A}_{sp}$, we need the following two simple observations.

Observation 4. *Each back edge in G^* belongs to exactly one subpath in $F(P)$.*

Observation 5. *Let A be the shortest path from v_1 to v_n in G^*. Then, for each subpath $Q \in F(P)$, A contains at most two back edges that belong to Q.*

Lemma 1. *Algorithm $\mathscr{A}_{sp}$ is a single-source shortest path algorithm, i.e., it holds for the next-variables returned by $\mathscr{A}_{sp}$ that for each vertex v_i, $next(v_i)$ is the first edge on the shortest path from v_i to v_n in G^*.*

Proof. For each $i \in [k]$, let $K_i := \{e \in E^* \mid e \text{ belongs to } Q_i\}$, and let $G_i^* = (V, E_T^* \cup \bigcup_{j=1}^i K_j)$ be a subgraph of G^*, where E_T^* are the tree edges in E^*.
   We prove via induction on the index j that after a subpath Q_j is processed, it holds for each vertex v_i that $dist(v_i)$ contains the distance from v_i to v_n in G_j^*. Since the next-variables are updated according to the dist-variables and $G^* = G_k^*$, the claim follows. Assume that the induction hypothesis holds after Q_j is processed. For a vertex v_i, let R be the shortest path from v_i to v_n in G_{j+1}^* if such a path exists. If there is no such path, then the distance from v_i to v_n in G_{j+1}^* is ∞, and hence we are done. Assume now that the path R contains no back edge from K_{j+1}. Then R is the shortest path from v_i to v_n in G_j^* as well, and hence, by the induction hypothesis, we are done. Therefore, we only have to consider the case that R contains at least one back edge from K_{j+1}. By Observation 5, there are at most two such edges. Since the case that there is only one such edge works analogously, assume that there are exactly two such edges, say $(u, w), (u', w') \in K_{j+1}$, and (u, w) appears before (u', w') on R. Let R' be the subpath of R from w' to v_n. Since R' does not contain an edge from K_{j+1}, the induction hypothesis implies that $dist(w')$ contains the distance from w' to v_n in G_j^* before the processing of Q_{j+1}. Note that during the processing of Q_{j+1}, we run the distance update steps twice. Since the distance $dist(w')$ "travels" through G^* during the distance updates, $dist(w) = dist(w') + \omega(u', w')$ after the first round. For the same reason, $dist(v_i) = dist(w') + \omega(u, w) + \omega(u', w')$ after the second round. Hence, $dist(v_i)$ contains the weight of the path R after the processing of Q_{j+1}. This proves the induction. $\square$

Having algorithm $\mathscr{A}_{sp}$, it is easy to define an augmentation algorithm $\mathscr{A}_{chain}^{seq}$ for T: run algorithm $\mathscr{A}_{sp}$, use the returned next-variables to compute the shortest path A from v_1 to v_n in G^*, and add the edges in G corresponding to the back edges on A to T. The following theorem follows immediately from Observation 3 and Lemma 1.

Theorem 6. *Algorithm $\mathscr{A}_{chain}^{seq}$ computes an optimal augmentation of T.*

To turn algorithm $\mathscr{A}_{chain}^{seq}$ into a distributed algorithm, we need to show how to distributively "emulate" an inverse inorder-traversal. We can assume that each vertex v_i knows its index i and the size n of the graph G. Hence, for each index $t \in [k]$, it is clearly possible for a vertex to determine the two indices s, r with $Q_t = (v_s, v_{s+1}, \dots, v_r)$ and vice versa. Using this, we can simulate a loop through the range $1, 2, \dots, k$ by sending a message around that carries the current position in this loop. Specifically, when a vertex v_i receives such a message with a current position t, it is able to determine whether v_i is the first vertex on the subpath Q_t, i.e., $Q_t = (v_s, v_{s+1}, \dots, v_r)$ and $i = s$. If yes, then v_i *marks* itself and releases a message with the current position $t + 1$. Otherwise, v routes the received message towards the first vertex on the subpath Q_t. This process terminates when the first vertex on Q_k is marked. Observe that the first vertices on the subpaths $Q_1, Q_2, \dots, Q_k$ are marked in exactly this order. Hence, this process emulates an inverse inorder-traversal.

Note that using this emulation of an inorder-traversal, we can easily distribute algorithm $\mathscr{A}_{chain}^{seq}$, since each edge in G^* directly corresponds to an edge in G. Hence, we can use these edges to update distances as in the distributed Bellman-Ford algorithm. Moreover, for a current subpath $Q_t = (v_s, v_{s+1}, \dots, v_r)$, each vertex v_i on the left half of Q_t is able to check for each outgoing edge (v_i, v_j) if v_j lies on the right half of Q_t by comparing j, s and r. Therefore, for each such subpath $(v_s, v_{s+1}, \dots, v_r)$, we only need to broadcast the indices s and r once in this subpath before processing it. We refer to the resulting distributed algorithm as $\mathscr{A}_{chain}$.

Theorem 7. *Algorithm $\mathscr{A}_{chain}$ has time complexity $O(n \log n)$ and message complexity $O(n \log n + m)$.*

Proof. First, we count the number of messages sent over the tree edges in G. Since for each tree edge $e \in E$, the corresponding edge in E^* belongs to $\lceil \log n \rceil$ many subpaths in $F(P)$, e has to pass $O(\log n)$ messages during the emulation. Because there are $n - 1$ tree edges, we get $O(n \log n)$ messages for the tree edges in G in total. The time complexity follows.

By Observation 4, each back edge in G^* belongs to exactly one subpath in $F(P)$. Hence, each back edge is used only once to update a distance, and therefore, for each such edge, the corresponding edge in G needs to pass only a constant number of messages. This results in $O(m)$ messages for the distance updates with the back edges in G^*. The claim follows. □

3.2 The General Case

In this subsection, we first show how to adapt algorithm $\mathscr{A}_{chain}^{seq}$ to the general case. Afterwards, we turn the result into a distributed algorithm. We first need to state some definitions.

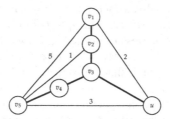

Fig. 2. A sample graph G

For each vertex $v \in V$, we name the child u of v in T such that $|T_u|$ is maximal the *heavy child* of v. Ties are broken arbitrarily. Let w be the root of T. Then, for each vertex $v \in V \setminus \{w\}$, let $\mathcal{T}_v := T_v \setminus T_u$, where u is the heavy child of v. If v is a leaf of T, then let $\mathcal{T}_v := T_v$. In other words, $\mathcal{T}_v$ is the subtree of T rooted in v without the subtree rooted in its heavy child u. Moreover, let $\mathcal{T}_w := T_u$, where u is the heavy child of the root w. Using the notion of a heavy child, we can unambiguously define a decomposition of T in a sequence of *heavy paths* $P_1, P_2, \ldots, P_k$ with the following four properties: First, $\cup_{i=1}^{k} P_i = V$. Second, Each path P_i *descending*, i.e., it holds for two consecutive vertices $u, w \in P_i$ that depth(u) < depth(w). Third, for each path P_i, we denote the first and last vertex on P_i by p_i and l_i, respectively, and for each vertex $v \in P_i \setminus \{p_i, l_i\}$, it holds for the heavy child u of v as well that $u \in P_i$. Fourth, each path P_i has maximal length subject to the constraint that for two paths P_i, P_j with $i \neq j$, either $P_i \cap P_j = \emptyset$ or $P_i \cap P_j = \{p_i\}$ and $i > j$. In the latter case, we call the path P_j the *father path* of P_i and P_i a *child path* of P_j. Hence, we can think of this decomposition as a tree of paths. Observe that p_1 is the root of T and the vertices $l_1, l_2, \ldots, l_k$ are the leaves of T.

For example, consider the graph G depicted in Fig. 2. The thickened edges are the edges belonging to the spanning tree T rooted in v_1, and the back edges are labeled with their weight. Since $|T_{v_4}| > |T_u|$, v_4 is the heavy child of v_3. Hence, we decompose T in paths P_1, P_2 with $P_1 = (v_1, v_2, v_3, v_4, v_5)$ and $P_2 = (v_3, u)$. Consequently, P_1 is the father path of P_2, and P_2 is the child path of P_1.

For a vertex $v \in V$ and a heavy path P_i, we name the closest vertex to v on P_i in T with respect to the hop-metric the *projection* of v to P_i. Moreover, by projecting the two endpoints of an edge $e \in E$ to P_i, we get a new edge to which we refer as the *projection* of e to P_i. Then, for each heavy path P_i, let E_i' be the projections of all edges E to P_i, and let $G_i' := (P_i, E_i')$ be an undirected graph. Since the subtree of T induced by P_i is a spanning tree of G_i' and a chain, we can construct an orientation $G_i = (P_i, E_i)$ of G_i' analog to the construction of the orientation G^* of G as described in Sect. 3.1. Each edge in a graph G_i corresponds to an edge in G_i', and each edge in G_i' corresponds to an edge in G. Hence, each edge in G_i corresponds to an edge in G as well. Additionally, we say that two edges $e \in E_i$ and $e' \in E_j$ with $i \neq j$ *correspond* to each other if they both correspond to the same edge in G. We associate each graph G_i with an edge-weight function ω_i. The weight functions $\omega_1, \omega_2, \ldots, \omega_k$ are recursively defined as follows: for each tree edge $e \in E_i$, let $\omega_i(e) := 0$. Let now $e = (u, w) \in E_i$ be a back edge, and let $e' = \{u', w'\} \in E$ be the corresponding edge in G with u and w are the projections of u' and w' to P_i, respectively. Assume that the weight functions $\omega_{i+1}, \omega_{i+2}, \ldots, \omega_k$ are already known, and let R be the path in T from w to w'. We travel along this path to compute a value $\Delta(w,w')$. Initially, we set $\Delta(w,w') := 0$. For each path P_j with $j > i$ that path R enters, we subtract the distance from p_j to l_j in G_j from $\Delta(w,w')$, and for each path P_j with $j > i$ that path R leaves at a vertex $v \in P_j$, we add the distance from v to l_j in G_j to $\Delta(w,w')$. Let then $\omega_i(e) := \Delta(w,w') + \omega(e')$. Observe that $\Delta(w,w') \leq 0$. The intuition behind this construction is that the edge $\{u',w'\}$ does not only cover vertices on the path P_i, but it might also cover vertices on some paths $P_{i+1}, P_{i+2}, \ldots, P_k$. Hence, adding the edge (u,w) might have a higher benefit. To this end, we decrease the weight of the edge (u,w) by adding the value $\Delta(w,w')$ that represents the additional benefit of the edge (u,w). We chose $\Delta(w,w')$ such that we get a constant approximation ratio. Finally, if G_i contains parallel edges, remove all edges except the one with the smallest weight with respect to the weight function ω_i. Now, we are ready to adapt algorithm $\mathscr{A}_{chain}^{seq}$ to the general case.

For example, consider again the graph G depicted in Fig. 2. The projection of u to P_1 is v_3, and hence the projection of the back edge $\{v_1,u\}$ to P_1 is $\{v_1,v_3\}$. Note that the graph G_1 is exactly the graph illustrated in Fig. 1. Assume that we want to compute the weight $\omega_1(e)$ of the edge $e = (v_1,v_3) \in E_1$. To this end, we first need to compute the value $\Delta(v_3,u)$. The graph G_2 only contains the back edge $e' = (v_3,u) \in E_2$, and since the projection of u to P_2 is u again, $\omega_2(e') = 2$. Let R be the path of length 1 from v_3 to u. The only path R enters is P_2, and the shortest path from $p_2 = v_3$ to $l_2 = u$ in G_2 is exactly the edge e'. Hence, $\Delta(e') = -2$, and therefore $\omega_1(e) = 0$.

Algorithm $\mathscr{A}^{seq}$

1. Let A_1 be the shortest path from p_1 to l_1 in G_1.
2. For $i = 2,\ldots,k$, do the following steps:
   (a) Let P_j be the father path of P_i.
   (b) If A_j contains an incoming edge $(u,p_i) \in E_j$ of p_i and the edge $(p_i,w) \in E_i$ corresponding to (u,p_i) is not a loop, i.e., $w \neq p_i$, then let A_i be the concatenation of the edge (p_i,w) with the shortest path from w to l_i in G_i. Note that we can interpret an edge as a path of length 1. Otherwise, let A_i be the shortest path from p_i to l_i in G_i. Use algorithm $\mathscr{A}_{chain}^{seq}$ to calculate these shortest paths.
3. Augment T with all edges in G that correspond to the back edges on the paths $A_1,A_2,\ldots,A_k$.

To illustrate Step 2b of algorithm $\mathscr{A}^{seq}$, consider again the graph G depicted in Fig. 2. Then the shortest path A_1 from p_1 to l_1 contains the edge $(v_1,v_3) \in E_1$, and the corresponding edge $(v_3,u) \in E_2$ is not a loop. Hence, A_2 is a concatenation of the edge (v_3,u) and the shortest path from u to l_2 in G_2. But since $u = l_2$, $A_2 = (v_3,u)$. Due to space limitations, we have to omit the quite technical proof of the following theorem.

Theorem 8. *Algorithm $\mathscr{A}^{seq}$ is a 2-approximation algorithm for the weighted tree augmentation problem.*

When it comes to turn algorithm $\mathscr{A}^{seq}$ into a distributed algorithm, the main problem is the computation of the paths $A_1,A_2,\ldots,A_k$. Unfortunately, we can not apply a straightforward modification of algorithm $\mathscr{A}_{chain}$ described in Sect. 3.1, since the back edges in a graph G_i do not *directly correspond* to edges in G, i.e., the back edge in G corresponding to a back edge in G_i might have different endpoints. Hence, these edges are virtual and can therefore not be used to pass messages. However, there is a close relationship which can be exploited to simulate the edges in G_i. We need one more ingredient: to give the vertices in G a geometric orientation in the tree T, we initially compute an ancestor labeling scheme for T. As a consequence, each vertex $v \in V$ holds an ancestor label, and knowing the ancestor labels of two vertices $u, w \in V$, it is possible to determine whether u is an ancestor of w in T simply by comparing these ancestor labels. We can for example use the ancestor labeling scheme of size $O(\log n)$ described in [16] whose computation requires $O(n)$ rounds and messages. In the following, we identify each vertex in G with its ancestor label, i.e., whenever we send a message that contains a vertex as a parameter, we represent this vertex by its ancestor label.

Now, we are ready to describe the simulation of edges. Similar to algorithm $\mathscr{A}_{chain}$, each vertex $v \in V$ holds some variables $\text{dist}_1(v), \text{dist}_2(v), \ldots, \text{dist}_k(v)$ and $\text{next}_1(v)$, $\text{next}_2(v), \ldots, \text{next}_k(v)$. Initially, each vertex $v \in V$ sets $\text{dist}_i(v) := \infty$ for each $i \in [k]$. Afterwards, each vertex l_i sets $\text{dist}_i(l_i) := 0$. Recall that the vertices $l_1, l_2, \ldots, l_k$ are the leaves of T. For a graph G_i, let $e = (u, w) \in E_i$ be a back edge, and let $e' = \{u', w'\} \in E$ be the edge in G that corresponds to e with u and w are the projections of u' and w' to P_i, respectively. If $u \neq u'$ or $w \neq w'$, then e does not directly correspond to e'. To apply algorithm $\mathscr{A}_{chain}$, assume that during the inverse inorder-traversal of $F(P_i)$, the back edge e needs to be used to update the distance of u, but since it is virtual, we can not directly use it. Assume as well that we have already computed all shortest distances in the graphs $G_{i+1}, G_{i+2}, \ldots, G_k$, i.e., for each heavy path P_j with $j > i$ and each vertex $v \in P_j$, $\text{dist}_j(v)$ contains the distance from v to l_j in G_j. In this case, by the definition the value $\Delta(w, w')$, the vertex w can initiate a broadcast in $\mathscr{T}_w$ such that afterwards, the vertex w' knows about $\Delta(w, w')$. Such a broadcast simply adds up distances top-down. We need to distinguish two cases. First, let $u \in P_i \setminus \{p_i\}$ as depicted in Fig. 3. Then, w broadcasts its current distance $\text{dist}_i(w)$ in the subtree $\mathscr{T}_w$. Once w' has received $\text{dist}_i(w)$, it sends $\text{dist}_i(w)$ and $\Delta(w, w')$ to its neighbor u'. Note that w' can locally decide whether $u' \in \mathscr{T}_u$ by comparing the ancestor labels of u and u'. If $\text{dist}_i(w) + \Delta(w, w') + \omega(u', w') < \text{dist}_i(u')$, then u' sets $\text{dist}_i(u') := \text{dist}_i(w) + \Delta(w, w') + \omega(u', w')$. Recall that $\omega_i(u, w) = \Delta(w, w') + \omega(u', w')$. Finally, u collects $\text{dist}_i(u')$ by a convergecast in $\mathscr{T}_u$ and sets $\text{dist}_i(u) := \text{dist}_i(u')$. Hence, a distance update with the edge (u, w) can be simulated by a broad- and convergecast in $\mathscr{T}_w$ and $\mathscr{T}_u$, respectively. It is easy to see that we can parallelize this simulation for all edges that belong to a subpath $Q \in F(P_i)$ such that each vertex $v \in Q$ needs to initiate only constantly many broad- and convergecasts in $\mathscr{T}_v$ during the processing of Q. We refer to this processing of Q as the *new processing*.

Second, let $u = p_i$. Then let $(u, w) \in E_i$ be an outgoing edge of u, and let $\{u', w'\} \in E$ be the corresponding edge in G with u and w are the projections of u' and w' to P_i, respectively. The problem is that there is no vertex $u \in P_i \setminus \{p_i\}$ such that $u' \in \mathscr{T}_u$, and therefore, we can not efficiently reach u' by a convergecast. But we can exploit the following simple observation.

Observation 9. *Let R be the shortest path from a vertex $v \in P_i$ to l_i in G_i. If $p_i \in R$, then all edges on R ahead p_i are tree edges.*

By Observation 9, it suffices to update distances with the outgoing edges of p_i only once after the inverse inorder-traversal of $F(P_i)$, and then update distances with all tree edges in G_i again. This can be implemented by constantly many broad- and convergecasts in $\mathcal{T}_{p_i}$. Note that using the ancestor labels, we can locally decide for a vertex u' whether $u' \notin \mathcal{T}_{p_i}$. We call this the *finalization* of G_i.

Now, we are ready to describe the distributed algorithm $\mathcal{A}$. This algorithm has two phases. Phase 1 works as follows. As in the sequential algorithm $\mathcal{A}^{seq}$, we process the heavy paths $P_1, P_2, \ldots, P_k$ bottom-up. This can be implemented by a convergecast in T. Once we are done with all child paths of a heavy path P_i, we start to compute all shortest distances in G_i by using algorithm $\mathcal{A}_{chain}$ in combination with the new processing of a subpath and the finalization of G_i as described above. This immediately gives us the following lemma.

Lemma 2. *After Phase 1, for each heavy path P_i and each vertex $v \in P_i$, $\text{next}_i(v)$ contains an orientation of the edge in G that corresponds to the first edge on the shortest path from v to l_i in G_i.*

Phase 2 resembles the adding of edges in algorithm $\mathcal{A}_{card}$ described in Sect. 2. Initially, each vertex $v \in V$ marks itself as *uncovered*. Then the root vertex v of T marks itself as *covered* and *adds* the edge $\{u, w\} \in E$ to the augmentation, where $(u, w) = \text{next}_1(v)$. Recall that the edges contained in the next-variables are orientations of edges in G. The adding of edges works similar to algorithm $\mathcal{A}_{card}$: when a vertex $v \in V$ wants to add an edge $\{u, w\} \in E$ to the augmentation, where $(u, w) = \text{next}_i(v)$ for a $i \in [k]$, it sends a message addedge(u, w) to w to request w to add the edge $\{u, w\}$ to its list of adjacent edges. Then w informs its neighbor u to act similarly. To distinguish the two endpoints, here it is important that the next-variables contain directed edges. Since we use ancestor labels to identify the vertices, we can easily route such a message through T. Note that we also allow messages to travel upwards in T. In contrast to algorithm $\mathcal{A}_{card}$, such a message spawns new messages on its way to its destination. Specifically, assume that a vertex $v \in V$ receives a message addedge(u, w) from its parent. If $w \neq v$, then the message branches towards a child c of v. Specifically, the message branches towards the child c with $w \in T_c$. In this case, c marks itself as *covered*. Let C be the children of v that have not been marked as covered. For each child $c \in C$, v adds the edge $\text{next}_i(v)$, where P_i is the heavy path with $\{v, c\} \subseteq P_i$, and marks all children in C as covered as well. Clearly, after this process, each vertex in G is marked as covered. It is easy to see that this process corresponds to the computation of shortest paths in the sequential algorithm: for each graph G_i, a sequence of messages "travels" along

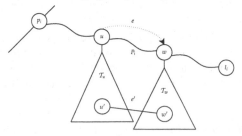

Fig. 3. The edge e' and its projection e

the path A_i. Hence, this process yields the same augmentation as algorithm $\mathscr{A}^{seq}$. The following theorem follows immediately.

Theorem 10. *Algorithm $\mathscr{A}$ is a distributed 2-approx. algorithm for the weighted tree augmentation problem.*

Since all messages contain at most a constant number of ancestor labels and a path length, the message size is $O(\log n)$. To analyze the time and message complexity, we need the following definition. We call a subsequence $P_{a(1)}, P_{a(2)}, \ldots, P_{a(s)}$ of $P_1, P_2, \ldots, P_k$ a *monotone sequence of heavy paths* if $a(1) = 1$ and for each $i \in [s-1]$, $P_{a(i)}$ is the father path of $P_{a(i+1)}$. For each $v \in V$, let then $h(v)$ be the depth of $\mathscr{T}_v$. In the following, For each $i \in [k]$, we abbreviate $\mathscr{T}_{p_i}$ by $\mathscr{T}_i$ and $h(p_i)$ by $h(i)$. We need the following preliminary lemma.

Lemma 3. *For each monotone sequence of heavy paths $P_{a(1)}, P_{a(2)}, \ldots, P_{a(s)}$,*

$$\sum_{i=1}^{s} h(a(i)) \leq n.$$

Proof. We show that for each $i \in [s-1]$, $|\mathscr{T}_{a(i)}| \geq |\mathscr{T}_{a(i+1)}| + h(a(i))$. Since $|\mathscr{T}_{a(1)}| \leq n$ and $|\mathscr{T}_{a(s)}| \geq h(a(s))$, the claim follows by using this inequation inductively.

Let $v \in \mathscr{T}_{a(i)}$ be a vertex with maximal depth in $\mathscr{T}_{a(i)}$, and let P be the path from $p_{a(i)}$ to v in T. Hence, $h(a(i)) = |P| - 1$. We need to distinguish two cases. First, if $v \notin \mathscr{T}_{a(i+1)}$, then $P \cap \mathscr{T}_{a(i+1)} \subseteq \{p_{a(i+1)}\}$. Hence, $|\mathscr{T}_{a(i)}| \geq |\mathscr{T}_{a(i+1)}| + h(a(i))$. Second, if $v \in \mathscr{T}_{a(i+1)}$, then let u be the child of $p_{a(i+1)}$ with $v \in T_u$, and let $w \neq u$ be the heavy child of $p_{a(i+1)}$. Let P' be the subpath of P from u to v. By the definition of the heavy path decomposition, $|T_w| \geq |T_u| \geq |P'|$. Clearly, $|\mathscr{T}_{a(i)}| \geq |\mathscr{T}_{a(i+1)}| + |P \setminus P'| + |T_w| - 1$. Hence, $|\mathscr{T}_{a(i)}| \geq |\mathscr{T}_{a(i+1)}| + h(a(i))$. Therefore, in both cases, $|\mathscr{T}_{a(i)}| \geq |\mathscr{T}_{a(i+1)}| + h(a(i))$. □

Theorem 11. *Algorithm $\mathscr{A}$ has time complexity $O(n \log n)$.*

Proof. First, we analyze the number of rounds needed for Phase 1. There are two time-critical parts for each path P_i. First, we need to emulate an inverse inorder-traversal of the hierarchical fragmentation $F(P_i)$ of P_i. As already explained in the proof of Theorem 7, this can be done in $O(|P_i| \log |P_i|)$ rounds. Second, to simulate the edges in G_i, for each vertex $v \in P_i \setminus \{p_i\}$, we need $\lceil \log |P_i| \rceil$ broad- and convergecasts in $\mathscr{T}_v$, where each takes $2 \cdot h(v)$ rounds. For each $i \in [k]$, let $t(i)$ be total number of rounds passed until we are done with path P_i. Hence, the number of rounds needed for Phase 1 is $t(1)$. Let $P_{a(1)}, P_{a(2)}, \ldots, P_{a(s)}$ be a monotone sequence of paths such that for each $i \in [s-1]$, if $P_{a(i)}$ has a child path, we chose $P_{a(i+1)}$ to be the child path of $P_{a(i)}$ such that $t(a(i+1))$ is maximal. Consequently, the time needed for this sequence dominates all other sequences. We separately count the number of rounds needed for the two time-critical parts for this sequence. Then $t(1)$ is the sum of rounds of theses two parts. Because $\sum_{i=1}^{s} |P_{a(i)}| \leq n + s - 1$, the rounds needed for the first time-critical part is

$$O(\sum_{i=1}^{s} |P_{a(i)}| \log |P_{a(i)}|) = O(n \log n).$$

Since no vertex is counted twice

$$\sum_{i=1}^{s-1} \sum_{v \in P_{a(i)} \setminus \{P_{a(i)}, P_{a(i+1)}\}} h(v) \leq n.$$

Hence, by Lemma 3, the time needed for the second time-critical part is

$$O(\sum_{i=1}^{s} \sum_{v \in P_{a(i)} \setminus \{P_{a(i)}\}} \log |P_{a(i)}| \cdot h(v)) = O(n \log n).$$

Note here that $\sum_{v \in P_{a(s)} \setminus \{P_{a(s)}\}} h(v) = 0$, because $P_{a(s)}$ has no child path.

In Phase 2, we send addedge-messages around. Observe that each vertex receives at most two such messages from its parent and one from its heavy child. Hence, since then each vertex passes a constant number of messages, we need $O(n)$ time for this phase. The claim follows.   □

Theorem 12. *Algorithm $\mathscr{A}$ has message complexity $O(n \log^2 n + m)$.*

Proof. As already explained in the proof of Theorem 11, we need $O(n)$ messages for Phase 2. Hence, we only have to analyze Phase 1. We do this by counting the number of messages passed by an edge $e \in E$. We need to distinguish two cases. First, let e be a tree edge. Hence, $e = \{v, p(v)\}$ for a vertex $v \in V$, where $p(v)$ is the parent of v. The heavy paths above v form a monotone sequence of heavy paths. Clearly, by the definition of the heavy path decomposition, the length of a monotone sequence of heavy paths is $\leq \lceil \log n \rceil$. For each such path P_i, the edge e needs to pass one message for each broad- or convergecast the projection u of v to P_i initiates in $\mathscr{T}_u$. Since each vertex $u \in P_i$ initiates $O(\log |P_i|)$ many broad- and convergecasts in $\mathscr{T}_u$, the edge e has to pass $O(\log^2 n)$ messages. Second, let e be a back edge. Clearly, there is at most one heavy path P_i such that the projection of e to P_i is not adjacent to p_i. Consequently, the edge e is used only once during the simulation of edges to pass messages. Hence, each back edge has to pass $O(1)$ messages. The claim follows by summing up all messages.   □

4   Conclusion

In this paper, we presented distributed approximation algorithms for the weighted and unweighted 2-ECSS construction problem, where the main building blocks were distributed tree augmentation algorithms. The major open problem is to establish lower bounds as for the distributed MST construction problem [17].

References

1. Khuller, S., Vishkin, U.: Biconnectivity approximations and graph carvings. J. ACM 41(2), 214–235 (1994)
2. Jothi, R., Raghavachari, B., Varadarajan, S.: A 5/4-approximation algorithm for minimum 2-edge-connectivity. In: SODA 2003: Proceedings of the fourteenth annual ACM-SIAM symposium on Discrete algorithms, Philadelphia, PA, USA, Society for Industrial and Applied Mathematics, pp. 725–734 (2003)

3. Khuller, S., Thurimella, R.: Approximation algorithms for graph augmentation. J. Algorithms 14(2), 214–225 (1993)
4. Gallager, R.G., Humblet, P.A., Spira, P.M.: A distributed algorithm for minimum-weight spanning trees. ACM Trans. Program. Lang. Syst. 5(1), 66–77 (1983)
5. Awerbuch, B.: Optimal distributed algorithms for minimum weight spanning tree, counting, leader election, and related problems. In: STOC 1987: Proceedings of the nineteenth annual ACM conference on Theory of computing, pp. 230–240. ACM Press, New York (1987)
6. Elkin, M.: A faster distributed protocol for constructing a minimum spanning tree. In: SODA 2004: Proceedings of the fifteenth annual ACM-SIAM symposium on Discrete algorithms, pp. 359–368 (2004)
7. Fernandes, C.G.: A better approximation ratio for the minimum k-edge-connected spanning subgraph problem. In: SODA 1997: Proceedings of the eighth annual ACM-SIAM symposium on Discrete algorithms, Philadelphia, PA, USA. Society for Industrial and Applied Mathematics, pp. 629–638 (1997)
8. Peleg, D.: Distributed Computing, A Locality-Sensitive Approach. Siam, Philadelphia (2000)
9. Humblet, P.A.: A distributed algorithm for minimum weight directed spanning trees. IEEE Trans. Comm. 31(6), 756–762 (1983)
10. Gabow, H., Galil, Z., Spencer, T., Tarjan, R.E.: Efficient algorithms for finding minimum spanning trees in undirected and directed graphs. Combinatorica 6(2), 109–122 (1986)
11. Pritchard, D.: Robust network computation. Master's thesis, Massachusetts Institute of Technology (August 2005)
12. Thurimella, R.: Sub-linear distributed algorithms for sparse certificates and biconnected components (extended abstract). In: PODC 1995: Symposium on Principles of Distributed Computing, pp. 28–37 (1995)
13. Korman, A.: Labeling schemes for vertex connectivity. In: Arge, L., Gachin, C., Jurdzinshi, T., Taoledci, A. (eds.) ICALP 2007. LNCS, vol. 4596, Springer, Heidelberg (2007)
14. Gavoille, C.: A survey on interval routing. Theor. Comput. Sci. 245(2), 217–253 (2000)
15. Bellman, R.: On a routing problem. Quart. Appl. Math. 16, 87–90 (1958)
16. Alstrup, S., Gavoille, C., Kaplan, H., Rauhe, T.: Nearest common ancestors: a survey and a new distributed algorithm. In: SPAA 2002: Proceedings of the fourteenth annual ACM symposium on Parallel algorithms and architectures, pp. 258–264. ACM Press, New York (2002)
17. Peleg, D., Rubinovich, V.: A near-tight lower bound on the time complexity of distributed minimum-weight spanning tree construction. SIAM Journal on Computing 30(5), 1427–1442 (2000)

Does Clock Precision Influence ZigBee's Energy Consumptions?*

Christian Groß[1],[**], Holger Hermanns[2], and Reza Pulungan[2]

[1] comlet Verteilte Systeme GmbH, Amerikastraße 21,
D-66482, Zweibrücken, Germany
[2] Department of Computer Science, Saarland University
Fax: +49 (681) 302-5636, D-66123, Saarbrücken, Germany
christian.gross@comlet.de, {hermanns,pulungan}@cs.uni-sb.de

Abstract. Wireless embedded sensor networks are predicted to provide attractive application possibilities in industry as well as at home. IEEE 802.15.4 and ZigBee are proposed as standards for such networks with a particular focus on pairing reliability with energy efficiency, while sacrificing high data rates.

IEEE 802.15.4 is configurable in many aspects, including the synchronicity of the communication, and the periodicity in which battery-powered sensors need to wake up to communicate. This paper develops a formal behavioral model for the energy implications of these options. The model is modularly specified using the language MODEST, which has an operational semantics mapping on stochastic timed automata. The latter are simulated using a variant of discrete-event simulation implemented in the tool MÖBIUS. We obtain estimated energy consumptions of a number of possible communication scenarios in accordance with the standards, and derive conclusions about the energy-optimal configuration of such networks. As a specific fine point, we investigate the effects of drifting clocks on the energy behavior of various application scenarios.

Keywords: Sensor networks, formal modelling, distributed coordination, power-aware design, clock drift.

1 Introduction

Quantitative analyses of ad hoc and wireless networks have in the past been concentrating on scalability and routing questions [6]. The predominantly applied techniques are based on simulation using enhanced tools such as GloMoSim or NS-2 [23,5], Omnet [21] or commercially available simulation tools, such as Opnet. Another approach is based on instruction-level simulation of the actual microcontroller codes [22,20].

The credibility of simulation results obtained using the above enhanced modelling tools seems not to be free of doubts. Such studies generally suffer from (1) unclarities of how simulation models are obtained from the modelling language, (2) the sheer number

---

* This work is supported by the German Research Council (DFG) as part of the Transregional Collaborative Research Center "Automatic Verification and Analysis of Complex Systems" (SFB/TR 14 AVACS). See www.avacs.org for information.
** Part of this work was done while at Saarland University.

E. Tovar, P. Tsigas, and H. Fouchal (Eds.): OPODIS 2007, LNCS 4878, pp. 174–188, 2007.

of parameters with non-obvious effects adjustable by the user, some of them having hidden effects on the simulation outcomes, (3) excessive simulation times needed to simulate the ensemble of many protocol stacks and states, and (4) the impossibility to validate simulation results through reproducible real-life experiments.

As a matter of fact, some recent articles have criticized the extremely poor quality and reproducibility of simulation-based experimentations with ad hoc or wireless networks [13,6]. Indeed, this questions the validity of simulation-based predictions for this area as a whole.

The work presented in this paper is among the few which attempt to attack the above mentioned principal problems. Other loosely similar approaches include [16,12]. While we still rely on discrete-event simulation as our analytic workhorse, we proceed in a drastically different way. The main difference is that (1) we use a language with a strictly formal semantics, which is equipped with well-established abstraction techniques. Consequently, the underlying stochastic model for simulation is well-defined and the obtained simulation results are trustworthy. (2) We expose all assumptions explicitly, since they are part of the formal system specification. (3) We do not model entire protocol stacks, but work with well-justified abstractions of lower layer effects. We consider worst-case scenarios, if no other information is available. But (4) we do not yet provide real-life experiments to back up our simulation results.

The model is modularly specified using the language MODEST, which has an operational semantics mapping on stochastic timed automata. The latter are simulated using a variant of discrete-event simulation implemented in the tool MÖBIUS. In this paper, that approach is applied to the IEEE 802.15.4 and ZigBee standards. This is a protocol family dedicated to low-bandwidth sensor networks operating on battery. IEEE 802.15.4 is configurable in many aspects, including the synchronicity of the communication, and the periodicity in which battery-powered sensors need to wake up to communicate. The particular configuration chosen has obvious – and non-obvious – implications on the lifetime of battery-powered devices. An obvious rule of thumb is, for instance, that battery-operated devices can survive longer timespans if they need to wake up less often. This paper investigates the non-obvious rules.

We obtain estimated energy consumptions of a number of possible communication scenarios in accordance with the standards, and derive conclusions about the energy-optimal configuration of such networks. In particular, we investigate the effects of time-slotted and unslotted medium access techniques, and their interplay with drifting clocks. Our observations allow us to establish rules of the following kind: (1) Unslotted CSMA/CA is more favourable w.r.t. energy saving than slotted CSMA/CA. (2) If devices using GTSs and CSMA/CA coexist, those operating in GTSs expend considerably less energy. (3) Small clock drifts can have far overproportional effects on energy consumption, but with only minor adverse effects on battery lifetimes. For sure, power consumption does not only depend on clock drift and synchronization policy. It also depends on many other factors, such as link quality and other environmental conditions. For our studies, these are assumed constant, since we see no way to include them in our studies without loosing focus. Further, we do not include comparison with experimental measurements. The reason is that (1) controlling physical clock drifts is virtually impossible with available hardware, and (2) real-life experiments would take several months or years to show measurably distinct effects on battery lifetimes. The main contribution of this paper is that it pioneers a model-based analysis of the interplay of clock drift and energy cost in sensor networks.

The paper is organized as follows: Section 2 provides a brief introduction to ZigBee and IEEE 802.15.4. In Section 3, the modelling formalism we employ is described together with the tool chain supporting it. Section 4 describes the modelling of ZigBee and IEEE 802.15.4 in MODEST. We also clarify the modelling assumptions we make and discuss in detail a particular model representative. In Section 5, we describe and discuss the simulation experiments and their results. Section 6 concludes the paper.

2   ZigBee and IEEE 802.15.4

This section provides a general introduction to ZigBee and IEEE 802.15.4, focussed on the characteristics and features that are important for the scope of the paper. For more detailed information, the interested reader is invited to consult the standard documents [3,2].

ZigBee is a wireless communications standard for low-cost and low-power consumption networks. It is a layered architecture. Both physical and medium access control (MAC) layers are defined in IEEE 802.15.4 standard. The ZigBee standard, on the other hand, provides the definition of the Network layer and the framework for the Application layer. ZigBee supports star, tree and mesh network topologies. In all these topologies, a device called ZigBee coordinator controls the network, but per-to-peer communication is allowed in mesh topology.

IEEE 802.15.4 is an open standard for ultra-low complexity, cost, power consumption and low data rate wireless connectivity among inexpensive devices in wireless personal area networks (WPAN) [2]. Devices participating in WPAN can be distinguished into full-function devices (FFD) and reduced-function devices (RFD). Communication between FFDs and RFDs is possible, but RFDs cannot directly communicate with each other. An FFD may become a personal area network (PAN) coordinator, a coordinator, or a device. There are two topologies in which a WPAN can operate: star and peer-to-peer.

The functional characteristic of low-rate PAN can be distinguished into beacon-enabled and nonbeacon-enabled networks. The simplest manner of operation is nonbeacon-enabled, where the network operates by using the (unslotted) Carrier Sense Multiple Access with Collision Avoidance (CSMA/CA). CSMA/CA is a multiple access protocol similar to CSMA/CD. As opposed to CSMA/CD, which operates by listening to the channel while sending in order to detect collisions, CSMA/CA tries to avoid collisions by listening to the channel for a predetermined amount of time prior to transmissions.

In beacon-enabled mode, on the other hand, the coordinator periodically emits beacon signals, which provide a frame of reference for a time-slotted access to the medium. More precisely, a so-called superframe structure, which is defined by the coordinator, is used. Inside of the superframe structure, communication can be carried out with a guaranteed time slot (GTS) mechanism or with slotted CSMA/CA mechanisms. Devices using GTS and those using CSMA/CA may coexist, as we will explain below.

The structure of a superframe is shown in Fig. 1. The coordinator broadcasts network beacons regularly. These beacons mark the beginnings and the ends of superframes. The beacons can be used for synchronization purpose, to identify the PAN, to describe the structure of the superframe, as well as to announce the GTS allocations.

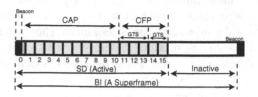

Fig. 1. The Superframe Structure

The coordinator can divide a superframe into an active and an inactive portion. The active portion is further divided into 16 equally sized slots. The coordinator may decide to allocate up to 7 of these slots as GTSs. These GTSs form the Contention-Free Period (CFP) and must appear at the end of the active portions. The rest of the slots forms the Contention-Access Period (CAP), in which devices compete using a slotted CSMA/CA mechanism.

The length of a superframe (Beacon Interval–BI) is determined by the coordinator by varying Beacon Order (BO) which influences the length exponentially:

$$\texttt{BI} = \texttt{aBaseSuperframeDuration} \times 2^{\texttt{BO}}, 0 \leq \texttt{BO} \leq 14,$$

where $\texttt{aBaseSuperframeDuration} = 960$ symbols. The duration of active portion (Superframe Duration–SD) is set by varying Superframe Order (SO):

$$\texttt{SD} = \texttt{aBaseSuperframeDuration} \times 2^{\texttt{SO}}, 0 \leq \texttt{SO} \leq \texttt{BO} \leq 14.$$

3 MODEST and Supporting Tools

The *Modelling and Description Language for Stochastic and Timed Systems* (MODEST) [8] is a specification formalism for stochastic real-time systems. The language is rooted in classical process algebra, *i.e.* the specification of models is compositional. Basic activities are expressed with atomic actions, more complex behavior with constructs for sequential composition, non-deterministic choice, parallel composition with CSP-style synchronization, looping and exception handling. A special construct exists to describe probabilistic choice. Clocks, variables and random variables are used to describe stochastic real-time aspects.[1]

In order to facilitate the analysis of the different models, tool support is indispensable. The MODEST Tool Environment (MOTOR) is a software tool that implements the MODEST semantics and is the central vehicle in the multi-solution analysis of MODEST models. The by now most mature backend of MOTOR is provided by a link to the MÖBIUS evaluation environment. MÖBIUS has been developed independently from MODEST and MOTOR at the University of Illinois at Urbana-Champaign [14]. From a user perspective, the MOTOR/MÖBIUS tandem enables one to perform simulation of MODEST models, and to gather performance and dependability estimates.

---

[1] MODEST also supports for modelling time variation, especially time non-determinism, but this feature is not used in this case study.

Simulation-based analysis covers the largest language fragment of MODEST: the only concept that cannot be supported by simulation is non-determinism, in particular of delay durations and non-deterministic choice between actions. We exclude the former by assuming maximal-progress with respect to delays. We do not restrict action non-determinism, since it is a convenient modelling instrument. However, no mechanisms, like a well-specified-check [15], is implemented yet to ensure the validity of the simulation statistics in the presence of action non-determinism.

MOTOR and its connection to MÖBIUS is mature and has been tested in a number of non-trivial case studies. In [18], it has been used for reliability analysis of the upcoming European Train Control System standard. In [9], it has been applied to the analysis of an innovative plug-and-play communication protocol, which has led to a patent application of our industrial partner. In [10], MOTOR has been used for the optimization of production schedules, in combination with timed automata-based schedule synthesis with UPPAAL.

4   Modelling

We model ZigBee/IEEE 802.15.4-compliant personal area networks in a star topology. Each network consists of a single PAN coordinator and a number of stations or devices. We assume that the PAN coordinator has continuous power supply, while the stations do not. A station can be either an FFD or an RFD, attached to a sensor. Periodically, a station communicates with the PAN coordinator, either to transmit its gathered sensor data or to receive instructions, but a station cannot communicate with other stations.

Two separate models, beacon and nonbeacon-enabled PAN models, are built. The simpler, nonbeacon-enabled model is parameterized by BI, but this is not used to signal beacons. Instead, BI is used to indicate the arrival of messages to each station from its sensor. Each station, in both models, is assumed to always have a message to send: almost one slot-length of data every beacon interval.

In the beacon-enabled PAN model, some of the stations use the CAP for CSMA/CA communications, and some use GTS in the CFP, the detailled scenarios considered are described later. The model is parameterized by BI, the beacon interval. We set the superframes to have the same duration as BI, hence there is no inactive period. Every BI-equivalent time units, the PAN coordinator broadcasts a beacon, and all stations must be ready to receive it. Henceforth, the coordinator is ready to receive transmissions from the stations. The stations which are not assigned any GTSs compete with other similar stations to send their messages by using slotted CSMA/CA, while the stations with assigned GTSs wait for their turns.

To save energy, a station goes to sleep mode whenever it has a chance to. For instance, a station sleeps while waiting for its GTS turn or when performing backoff or whenever it has no messages to transmit. However, a station must always wake up before its turn to transmit or before the beacon is transmitted.

We abstain from modelling the PAN initialization. We instead concentrate on the typical operations of the PAN, when the stations are transmitting messages. The physical layer of IEEE 802.15.4 is not modelled either. For instance, we assume that there is no significant propagation delay and no channel selection procedure. Nevertheless, those physical layer constants which affect the timing of the communication, such as the duration of CCAs (Clear Channel Assessments), are taken into account. Furthermore, we assume the PAN to operate in 2.4 GHz band, hence all devices transmit at 62.5 ksymbols/s. The medium is assumed uniform, in the sense that all participants have complete knowledge of it.

4.1 Models

The model of the PAN in beacon-enabled mode is described in this section, focusing on slotted CSMA/CA, which is more complex and interesting than the GTS case. Complete details are available as a tutorial-style modelling guide [4]. The model consists of two distinct process definitions: `coordinator()` and `station()`, modelling the behaviors of a PAN coordinator and a station, respectively. In all experiments, we set `macMaxCSMABackoff` (the maximum number of backoff attempts before declaring a channel access failure) to 5 and `macMinBE` (the minimum value of the backoff exponent) to 2.

The System. The model of the overall system is depicted in MODEST model 1. The system consists of 11 process instances, one coordinator and ten stations, run in parallel.

This is achieved by using the parallel composition construct `par{}`. Processes inside of a parallel composition construct run concurrently and synchronize on their common actions, if existing. The operator

MODEST **model 1** : The complete system

```
01 par{
02   ::coordinator()
03   ::relabel {...} by {...} station(1)
..   ...
12   ::relabel {...} by {...} station(10)
13 }
```

`relabel {} by {} p()` relabels actions in the first set by the actions in the second in a particular instance of process `p()`. This allows multiple instantiations of process definition `station()`.

The Coordinator. A simple model of the PAN coordinator is shown in MODEST model 2, especially to highlight some of the clock manipulation features of MODEST. The coordinator has two clock variables: `btimer` modelling the time progress between beacons, and clock `c` modelling the transmission time of a beacon. In MODEST, clocks increase linearly with time and can only be reset to zero. The coordinator process begins by immediately sending a beacon (action `sendb_start`).All beacons are of length

MODEST **model 2** : The coordinator

```
01 process coordinator() {
02   clock btimer, c;
03   sendb_start {= bintheair=true =} ;
04   when(c==52) sendb_end {= bintheair=false =} ;
05   do{::when(btimer==binterval) sendb_start {= c=0, btimer=0, bintheair=true =} ;
06        when(c==52) sendb_end {= bintheair=false =}
07   }}
```

$52\mu s$ (lines 04 & 06), namely the duration of the smallest possible beacon. Action `sendb_end` signals the end of the beacon's transmission. From then on, the coordinator waits until clock `btimer` is equal to the value of `binterval` (line 05). At this point, a beacon interval has expired and the coordinator broadcasts a new beacon. The coordinator proceeds thus continuously, broadcasting beacons every time a beacon interval expires.

The process makes use of two global variables, *i.e.* variables accessible to all processes in the model. They are `binterval`, of type integer, which represents the time it takes for a BI according to the standard; and `bintheair`, a boolean variable used to indicate to the whole system that a beacon is being transmitted. Delimiters {= =} wrap a set of variable assignments. Such assignments are executed atomically at the time instant of the action preceeding them.

The Stations. The model of the station is shown in MODEST model 3 and 4. In the beginning, a station waits until a new beacon is transmitted (line 10). At the same time, it resets its main clock and sets `ttosend` (the duration of the remaining data to send). Once the beacon finishes, the station aligns its backoff boundary with the superframe slot boundary by waiting until a multiple of the backoff period (line 16) expires since the beginning of the previous beacon (line 14). The station then performs backoff and attempts to transmit. This is repetitively done as long as there is still something to send and enough time to do so (line 13), otherwise (line 12) the station just waits for the next beacon.

The maximum length of messages submittable to the physical layer is 133 bytes, which takes 4256 μs to transmit in 2.4 GHz band. Thus the remaining data is split accordingly (line 14). Line 16 is a placeholder for the code for the random selection of variable r.

MODEST **model 3** : The station (Part 1)

```
01 process station(int id) {
.. ...
10    do{::when(bintheair) beacon_received {= mainclock=0, ttosend=sendingtime =} ;
11        when(!bintheair) start_waiting ;
12    do{::when(ttosend==0 || !enoughtime) do_nothing {= enoughtime=true =} ; break
13        ::when(ttosend>0 && enoughtime) start_csmaca
14        {= NB=0, CW=2, BE=2, attosend=(ttosend>=4256)?4256:ttosend =} ;
15        when(mainclock%320==0)
16        do{::choose_random {= c=0, r=//Uniform(0,2^BE-1), backofftime=r*320 =} ;
.. ...
```

As shown in MODEST model 4, once the duration of the backoff delay is determined, the backoff is performed only if there is still enough time to complete the backoff together with a CCA before the contention-access period ends (line 19). CCA detection time is equal to 8 symbols period, namely 128 μs in 2.4 GHz band. If there is not enough time, the station stops and waits until the next beacon comes (line 18). A CCA is carried out immediately after the backoff finishes (line 20 & 21). There are three possible outcomes of the CCA: a busy channel, an idle channel with enough time to send the current portion of the message and an idle channel but not enough time. The outcome of a CCA is determined by the value of global variable `sending`. This variable indicates the number of stations currently transmitting. A station about to transmit increases this variable and decreases it again once the transmission finishes.

MODEST **model 4** : The station (Part 2)

```
. . . . . .
17 alt{
18   ::when(mainclock>=CAP-backofftime-ccatime) {= enoughtime=false =} ; break
19   ::when(mainclock<CAP-backofftime-ccatime)
20   when(c==backofftime) {= c=0 =} ;
21   do{::when(c==ccatime)
22       alt{::when(sending>0)
23           alt{::when(NB<=maxbackoff) channel_busy {=CW=2,NB=NB+1,BE=(BE<6)?BE+1:6=};break
24           ::when(NB>maxbackoff) {= restart=true =} ; break }
25       ::when(sending==0 && mainclock<CAP-attosend-960) count_down_CW {= CW=CW-1 =} ;
26       alt{::when(CW==0) wait_for_boundary ;
27           when (c==320) send_message_start {= sending+=1, c=0 =} ;
28           when (c==attosend) send_message_end
29               {= ttosend-=attosend, sending-=1, restart=true =} ; break
30       ::when(CW>0) wait_for_boundary ;
31           when(c==320) {= c=0 =} }
32   :when(sending==0 && mainclock>=CAP-attosend-960)
33       {= enoughtime=false, restart=true =} ; break }
34   } ; alt{::when(restart) {= restart=false =} ; break
35       ::when(!restart)
36       } } } } } }
```

A busy channel triggers another backoff if the number of backoff so far does not exceed the maximum allowed – maxbackoff – (line 22 & 23), otherwise the whole CSMA/CA procedure must be restarted to transmit the current portion of the message (line 24). When the channel is idle but there is not enough time to complete the transmission (line 32) the station escapes the CSMA/CA procedure and waits for the next beacon for further attempts.

In a beacon-enabled PAN, two CCAs are required after backoffs before the transmission of the message. Hence, when the channel is idle and there is enough time to complete the transmission (line 25), the transmission is only commenced if $CW = 0$ (line 26), namely when two consecutive CCAs find the channel idle. The transmission, which starts at the next backoff boundary, is announced to all other devices by increasing the global variable sending, and it takes the amount of time to send the portion of the message, namely attosend.

Once the portion of the message is transmitted, the station decreases the variable sending and updates the remaining portions of the message to transmit by changing ttosend (line 29). Henceforth, the station restarts the CSMA/CA procedure to transmit the remaining message, without waiting for a new beacon.

4.2 Energy Consumption

In modelling the energy consumption of a station, we use the technical specification of CC2420 [1]. CC2420 is a 2.4 GHz ZigBee/IEEE 802.15.4-compliant radio frequency (RF) transceiver produced by Chipcon AS. Fig. 2 summarizes the specification relevant for this paper. During its operation, the transceiver can be in four modes: shutdown, idle, transmitting or receiving modes. The rate of energy consumption while occupying these modes [11] are $0.144, 712, 30672$ and 35280 μW, respectively. A small amount of energy is required during the shutdown mode to power clock and to witness power-ups.

Furthermore, the transitions from mode s to i, from mode i to t, and from mode i to r do not happen instantaneously, but take $970, 194$ and 194 μs to complete, respectively. During these transitions [11], the transceiver is considered to be still in the original mode, while consuming energy at the level of the destination mode. This reflects that the transceiver requires time (and power) to turn on its transmitting and receiving devices. All other transitions, namely those with dotted edges in the figure, take no time to complete.

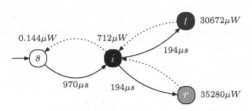

Fig. 2. Energy Modes of CC2420

When the PAN coordinator broadcasts a beacon, all stations must be in receiving mode. That means, some time beforehand, they must have woken up and proceeded to the idle and then to the receiving mode. If a station is assigned GTSs, it immediately changes to shutdown mode upon the completion of the beacon. However, the station must already be in transmitting mode, when its assigned GTSs begin. To anticipate this, the station must leave the shutdown mode 1164 (namely 970+194) μs before the GTSs. After finishing the transmission in the GTSs, the station moves to idle mode. If there is still 'enough' time before the next beacon, it changes further to shutdown mode.

A station without assigned GTSs must compete with similar stations by using slotted or unslotted CSMA/CA to gain access to the medium. Immediately after the end of a beacon, the station enters the CSMA/CA procedure. Depending on the duration of the backoff delay, the station may transition to idle or shutdown mode. If the backoff delay is long enough, the station may sleep and wake up 1164 μs before it must perform a CCA, and be ready in receiving mode. If two consecutive CCAs result in idle channel, the station changes to transmitting mode and sends the message portion. This is performed continuously until the whole message is sent. Afterwards, the station may move to shutdown mode if there is enough time to do so before the next beacon.

To incorporate the energy consumption to the PAN models, each instant of station changes variables time_in_s_mode, time_in_i_mode, time_in_t_mode and time_in_r_mode every time it spends some portions of time in s, i, t, and respectively r mode. The framework models are annotated accordingly and the four variables are turned into four global variable arrays, that each instant of station accesses through its id. The amount of energy consumed by a station during a beacon interval is the sum of the amount of time it spends in each mode weighted by the rate of the energy consumption of the mode.

Referring back to MODEST models 3 and 4, the background color of each line number of the model corresponds to the energy mode as depicted in Fig. 2. Those line numbers with two background colors indicates the case where the station is deciding whether to enter idle or shutdown mode based on the progress of its main clock so far.

4.3   Clock Precision

Clock precision is important to ensure the correct functioning of ZigBee/IEEE 802.15.4-compliant PANs. In the case of PANs which provide CFPs, it is crucial that stations with assigned GTSs transmit exactly in their allocated period of time. Similarly with PANs employing the slotted CSMA/CA mechanism, the ability to correctly determine the backoff boundaries, which requires a precise clock, is necessary to avoid collisions.

Quarz-based clocks are generally used for electronic devices. Such clocks suffer from inaccuracy due to aging and temperature variations. Usually, the manufacturers guarantee a certain upper bound inaccuracy for their clock products. Assuming this upper bound to be constant is actually not realistic. However, we do so in our models. Hence, a clock with a guaranteed accuracy may deviate from the real time within a given time interval based on the accuracy and exhibit at different times a different deviation from the real time.

Clock inaccuracy is usually expressed in 'parts per million' (ppm), referring to the maximum difference (in time units) one may witness relative to perfect time, within a million time units. In the models, we assume that a physical clock with a guaranteed accuracy of p ppm may show at time t, a clock value within the interval:

$$[t - p \cdot 10^{-6} \cdot t, t + p \cdot 10^{-6} \cdot t].$$

A station, however, does not know the exact value of the deviation. Nevertheless, it must be able to precisely observe the deadlines, for instance the arrival of a beacon. Therefore, it counts on the maximum inaccuracy and be ready for the beacon even before the actual time. It is also assumed that the stations synchronize their clocks to the PAN coordinator's, while receiving the beacons.

We model the effect of clock inaccuracy to energy consumption in the following way. Assume that a station must wait for W time units to be ready for some event. The clock of the station has inaccuracy p ppm. The actual waiting time W' for the station is:

$$W' = W - W \cdot p \cdot 10^{-6} + W \cdot p' \cdot 10^{-6}, \tag{1}$$

where $W \cdot p \cdot 10^{-6}$ is the maximum deviation of the clock given the clock inaccuracy and $W \cdot p' \cdot 10^{-6}$ is the actual deviation. The actual inaccuracy p' is a value in the interval $[-p, p]$. The models can be parametrized by the actual deviation. In full generality, a clock's inaccuracy may be time-dependent, in which case the above formula involves integration.

5   Simulations

In this section, we describe the simulations of the MODEST models presented in the previous section. The simulation was done with discrete-event simulator of MÖBIUS, and we only present an excerpt of several thousand simulation runs we performed. First, the experimental setups are described. The result of the experiments is presented afterwards, followed by its analyses and discussions.

Experiments. In all experiments, the system is a personal area network, which consists of a single PAN coordinator and 10 stations with star topology. The network uses 2.4 GHz band and all durations appearing in the standard which are defined by amount of symbols are adapted accordingly. The networks do not use any inactive periods, thus the beacon interval is always the same as the superframe duration (BI=SD).

The experiments cover BO $= 0, \cdots, 10$, which means a beacon interval ranges from 15360 μs to 15728640 μs. Similarly the length of a slot ranges from 960 μs to

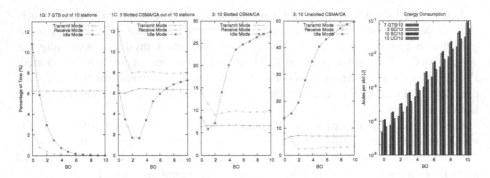

Fig. 3. Percentage of time per energy mode and energy consumption for perfect clocks

983040 μs. In all experiments, a station always has about a slot-length message to transmit during the duration between two beacons. A station using GTS mode can transmit the whole message continuously. On the other hand, a station using slotted or unslotted CSMA/CA can only transmit 133 bytes at a time, which takes 4256 μs to transmit.

The simulation time of each experiment spans 10 beacon intervals. For instance, when BO = 7, a beacon interval takes 1966080 μs. Therefore, the simulation is run for around 20 seconds (19660800 μs). Simulations are carried out to estimate the mean values of some measures of interest, such as the time a station spends in shutdown mode. The simulation is repeated until the mean values of all measures of interest converge with relative confidence interval 0.1 and confidence level 95%. MÖBIUS allows users to adjust these settings as desired.

As mentioned earlier, we consider worst-case scenarios whenever appropriate. For clock inaccuracy, the worst scenarios occur when the clock of the PAN coordinator is progressing as slow as possible within its inaccuracy bounds, while the clock of a station is in its fastest possible progress. Referring to Eqn. 1, the clock of a station is fastest when $p' = -p$. Then the station, which needs to wake up some time before the actual deadlines, actually wakes up even earlier because its clock is too fast. We proved this situation to be worst case by analytical means, which is backed up by simulation.

All simulations are conducted on a PC with a Pentium 4 3.0 GHz processor with 1 GB RAM running Linux 2.6.17-2.686. The CPU time per experiment series ranges from around 5.2 seconds to 15429 seconds (about 4.25 hours).

Results. The graphs in Fig. 3 summarize our experimental results when clocks are perfect. The leftmost graph shows the percentage of the time spent in transmit, receive and idle modes for the 7 stations assigned with GTSs in experiment series 1 (we denote this as series 1G). While the portion of time spent in transmit mode is constant for all BO's, the portions in receive and idle modes diminish as the beacon intervals get larger, and become less than 1% after BO = 5. This is because the actual time spent in receive and idle modes remains constant for all beacon intervals, thus their percentages decrease as the beacon intervals get longer. They are constant because a station only goes to receive mode while receiving beacons and to idle mode prior to the arrivals of beacons and before the transmissions of the messages.

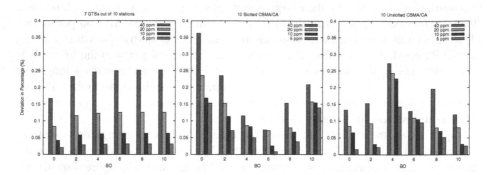

Fig. 4. Increase of energy consumptions when clocks drift, relative to perfect clocks

The second graph in the figure depicts the same percentage distribution for the 3 stations using slotted CSMA/CA in experiment series 1 (denoted as series 1C). The portion of time spent in the transmit mode remains almost constant and around 0.25% higher throughout than the previous case. The percentage of time spent in receive mode is also almost constant at around 8%, which is higher than in series 1G. The percentage increase in receive mode is due to the CCAs, and since the number of CCAs to be performed is proportional to the length of the message, the percentage is steady for most BO values. The time spent in the idle mode, on the other hand, increases with the length of beacon intervals. The longer the beacon interval, the longer a slot-length message. However, since the length of message portion transmittable is restricted, the more often slotted CSMA/CA procedure is repeated to send the whole message. Hence the station spends more percentage of time in idle mode.

The third and fourth graphs in the figure show similar percentage distribution for experiment series 2 and 3, namely 10 stations using slotted and unslotted CSMA/CA, respectively. Compared to series 1C, the percentage of time spent in receive mode is higher in series 2. This is due to the fact that there are 10 stations for 15 CAP slots in series 2 compared to 3 stations for 8 CAP slots in series 1C. Thus stations perform more CCAs and spend more percentage of time in receive mode. Similar reason applies to the percentage of idle mode. In series 3, however, the percentage of time spent in receive mode is lower than series 1C and 2 because the stations perform only one CCA in every CSMA/CA cycle. Between themselves, the stations in experiment series 3 spend more time in idle mode compared to those in series 2. This can be explained by the absence of beacons in unslotted CSMA/CA. Once a station finishes transmitting the whole message, it has no estimation when the next message will be available and thus must stay idle. The station enters the shutdown mode when performing backoff.

The rightmost graph in Fig. 3 depicts the amount of energy consumed by a station during a beacon interval time for each value of BO and for each of the formerly described series. Note that the y-axis of the graph is in logarithmic scale. The largest energy consumption is around 0.096946940587 Joules per beacon interval when BO = 10. We can observe that for all values of BO, a station using GTSs consumes the least amount of energy. A station using the unslotted CSMA/CA consumes more energy that that using GTSs but less than the energy consumption of a station using slotted CSMA/CA.

A question arises as to why the energy consumption of a station in series 1C is lower than that in series 2, considering the fact that the former has more CAP-slots per station. The reason is in series 1C, a station spends more time in shutdown mode, namely during the CFP period. This can also be observed from the second graph in the figure. It is also worth noting that the differences between the energy consumptions amongst the series are significant, even though they are not apparent due the logarithmic scale. For instance, a station in series 2 consumes almost thrice the energy of a station in series 1G and almost twice of a station in series 3.

Fig. 4 shows the influence of worst-case clock drifts on the energy consumptions of stations in series 1G, 2 and 3, respectively. Consistently, clock drifts increase the amount of energy consumed for all experiments. The graphs in the figure show the increase in energy expended relative to the amount of energy needed in the precise clock setting. The first graph depicts the deviations for a station in series 1G with clock inaccuracies 40, 20, 10 and 5 ppm for $BO = 0, 2, 4, 6, 8, 10$. We observe a linear correlation between the clock inaccuracies and the deviations in the graph. For instance, for most of BO values, a station with clock inaccuracy 40 and 20 ppm spends approximately 0.25% and respectively 0.125% more energy than a station with precise clock. The second and third graphs in Fig. 4 depicts the deviations for a station in series 2 and 3, respectively. We abstain from explaining the precise patterns exhibited by these plots for increasing BO due to space constraints. However, the effects of the level of clock inaccuracies are obvious. In both graphs, higher clock inaccuracy tends to cause higher energy consumption level.

Overall, a deviation of 0.25% or 0.125% may seem small. If extrapolated, it amounts to about half a day per year decrease in lifetime of a battery. However, a clock drift of 40 ppm is – percentwise – only 0.004%, and we thus conclude that such a clock drift may be amplified by a factor of 62.5 when looking at the excess in energy consumption caused.

6   Conclusion

This paper has advocated a rigorous approach to modelling and simulation of energy-aware networked embedded systems. In this approach, MODEST, a language with a strictly formal semantics is used to specify the system under study. Since all assumptions are exposed explicitly in the specification, the underlying stochastic model is well-defined and the obtained simulation results are trustworthy. This is different from many other simulation-based results lately published in the networking literature. The simulation is carried out via the tools MOTOR and MÖBIUS. MOTOR is available as source code from http://www.purl.org/net/motor under the GPL license. MÖBIUS is freely available for educational and research purposes from http://www.mobius.uiuc.edu/. MOTOR can be installed as an add-on package to the MÖBIUS installation.

We applied the proposed approach to the modelling of crucial medium access mechanisms in IEEE 802.15.4, with a particular emphasis on energy specific configuration relevant to ZigBee operation. When investigating the effects of time-slotted (*i.e.*, beacon-enabled) and unslotted medium access techniques, we observed that slotted

CSMA/CA is clearly inferior to unslotted CSMA/CA w.r.t. energy efficiency. In slotted mode, devices using GTSs use considerably less energy than those using CSMA/CA.

Our studies of drifting clocks reveal some interesting observations. Most of them are consistent with what one might expect – but we did not see them published elsewhere. However interesting, they only show minor quantitative effects. The IEEE standard limits the allowed clock drift to 40 ppm, and this appears to be caused by correctness concerns. (One can show that with 64 ppm the clock boundaries could drift apart to an extent that the protocol could desynchronize and thus malfunction). In the worst case we estimate that a clock drift of 40 ppm induces a shortage in battery life of about half a day per year. While this amplifies the clock drift by a factor of about 60, we think it is not particularly significant, leading us to finally negate the question in the title of this paper.

References

1. CC2420 Product Information. Chipcon AS (2005),
   http://www.chipcon.com/index.cfm?kat_id=2&subkat_id=12&dok_id=115
2. IEEE 802.15.4: Wireless Medium Access Control (MAC) and Physical Layer (PHY) Specifications for Low-Rate Wireless Personal Area Networks (2003)
3. ZigBee Specification Version 1.0. ZigBee Alliance (2004),
   http://www.zigbee.org/en/spec_download/download_request.asp
4. MoDeST Tutorial: development of a complex model in MoDeST. Dependable Systems and Software, Saarland University, Germany (2006),
   http://depend.cs.uni-sb.de/modesttutorial/index.html
5. The network simulator – ns-2 website (2007), http://www.isi.edu/nsnam/ns/
6. Andel, T.R., Yasinac, A.: On the credibility of Manet simulations. IEEE Computer 39(7), 48–54 (2006)
7. Bengtsson, J., Larsen, K.G., Larsson, F., Pettersson, P., Yi, W.: Uppaal – a tool suite for automatic verification of real-time systems. In: Hybrid Systems III, pp. 232–243. Springer, Heidelberg (1995)
8. Bohnenkamp, H.C., D'Argenio, P.R., Hermanns, H., Katoen, J.-P.: MoDeST: A compositional modeling formalism for hard and softly timed systems. IEEE Trans. Soft. Eng. 32(10), 812–830 (2006)
9. Bohnenkamp, H.C., Gorter, J., Guidi, J., Katoen, J.-P.: Are you still there? - A lightweight algorithm to monitor node presence in self-configuring networks. In: DSN 2005, pp. 704–709. IEEE CS Press, Los Alamitos (2005)
10. Bohnenkamp, H.C., Hermanns, H., Klaren, R., Mader, A., Usenko, Y.S.: Synthesis and stochastic assessment of schedules for lacquer production. In: QEST 2004, pp. 28–37. IEEE CS Press, Los Alamitos (2004)
11. Bougard, B., Catthoor, F., Daly, D.C., Chandrakasan, A., Dehaene, W.: Energy efficiency of the IEEE 802.15.4 standard in dense wireless microsensor networks: Modeling and improvement perspectives. In: DATE 2005, pp. 196–201. IEEE CS Press, Los Alamitos (2005)
12. Cadilhac, M., Hérault, T., Lassaigne, R., Peyronnet, S., Tixeuil, S.: Evaluating complex MAC protocols for sensor networks with APMC. Elect. Notes Theor. Comput. Sci. 185, 33–46 (2007)
13. Cavin, D., Sasson, Y., Schiper, A.: On the accuracy of MANET simulators. In: POMC 2002, pp. 38–43. ACM Press, New York (2002)

14. Daly, D., Deavours, D.D., Doyle, J.M., Webster, P.G., Sanders, W.H.: Möbius: An extensible tool for performance and dependability modeling. In: Haverkort, B., Bohnenkamp, H.C., Smith, C.U. (eds.) TOOLS 2000. LNCS, vol. 1786, pp. 332–336. Springer, Heidelberg (2000)

15. Deavours, D.D., Sanders, W.H.: An efficient well-specified check. In: PNPM 1999, pp. 124–133. IEEE CS Press, Los Alamitos (1999)

16. Fruth, M.: Probabilistic model checking of contention resolution in the IEEE 802.15.4 low-rate wireless Personal Area Network protocol. In: ISoLA 2006 (2006)

17. Garavel, H., Lang, F., Mateescu, R.: An overview of CADP 2001. EASST Newsletter 4, 13–24 (2001)

18. Hermanns, H., Jansen, D.N., Usenko, Y.S.: From StoCharts to MoDeST: a comparative reliability analysis of train radio communications. In: WOSP 2005, pp. 13–23. ACM Press, New York (2005)

19. Kwiatkowska, M.Z., Norman, G., Parker, D.: PRISM: Probabilistic symbolic model checker. In: Field, T., Harrison, P.G., Bradley, J., Harder, U. (eds.) TOOLS 2002. LNCS, vol. 2324, pp. 200–204. Springer, Heidelberg (2002)

20. Landsiedel, O., Wehrle, K., Götz, S.: Accurate prediction of power consumption in sensor networks. In: EmNetS-II, pp. 37–44 (2005)

21. Pongor, G.: OMNeT: Objective modular network testbed. In: MASCOTS 1993, pp. 323–326 (1993)

22. Titzer, B.L., Lee, D.K., Palsberg, J.: Avrora: Scalable sensor network simulation with precise timing. In: IPSN 2005, pp. 477–482 (2005)

23. Zeng, X., Bagrodia, R., Gerla, M.: GloMoSim: A library for parallel simulation of large-scale wireless networks. In: WPDS 1998, pp. 154–161 (1998)

From an Intermittent Rotating Star to a Leader

Antonio Fernández Anta[1]   and   Michel Raynal[2]

[1] LADyR, GSyC, Universidad Rey Juan Carlos, 28933 Móstoles, Spain
anto@gsyc.escet.urjc.es
[2] IRISA, Université de Rennes 1, Campus de Beaulieu, 35042 Rennes, France
raynal@irisa.fr

Abstract. Considering an asynchronous system made up of n processes and where up to t of them can crash, finding the weakest assumptions that such a system has to satisfy for a common leader to be eventually elected is one of the holy grail quests of fault-tolerant asynchronous computing. This paper is a step in such a quest. It has two main contributions. First, it proposes an asynchronous system model, in which an eventual leader can be elected, that is weaker and more general than previous models. This model is captured by the notion of *intermittent rotating t-star*. An x-star is a set of $x + 1$ processes: a process p (the center of the star) plus a set of x processes (the points of the star). Intuitively, assuming logical times rn (round numbers), the *intermittent rotating t-star* assumption means that there are a process p, a subset of the round numbers rn, and associated sets $Q(rn)$ such that each set $\{p\} \cup Q(rn)$ is a t-star centered at p, and each process of $Q(rn)$ receives from p a message tagged rn in a timely manner or among the first $(n - t)$ messages tagged rn it ever receives. The star is called *t-rotating* because the set $Q(rn)$ is allowed to change with rn. It is called *intermittent* because the star can disappear during finite periods. This assumption, not only combines, but generalizes several synchrony and time-free assumptions that have been previously proposed to elect an eventual leader (e.g., eventual t-source, eventual t-moving source, message pattern assumption). Each of these assumptions appears as a particular case of the *intermittent rotating t-star* assumption. The second contribution of the paper is an algorithm that eventually elects a common leader in any system that satisfies the *intermittent rotating t-star* assumption. That algorithm enjoys, among others, two noteworthy properties. Firstly, from a design point of view, it is simple. Secondly, from a cost point of view, only the round numbers can increase without bound. This means that, be the execution finite or infinite, be links timely or not (or have the corresponding sender crashed or not), all the other local variables (including the timers) and message fields have a finite domain.

Keywords: Assumption coverage, Asynchronous system, Distributed algorithm, Eventual t-source, Eventual leader, Failure detector, Fault-tolerance, Message pattern, Moving source, Omega, Partial synchrony, Process crash, System model, Timely link.

1 Introduction

1.1 Leader Oracle: Motivation

A failure detector is a device (also called oracle) that provides the processes with guesses on which processes have failed (or not failed) [3,21]. According to the

E. Tovar, P. Tsigas, and H. Fouchal (Eds.): OPODIS 2007, LNCS 4878, pp. 189–203, 2007.

properties associated with these estimates, several failure detector classes can be defined. It appears that failure detector oracles are at the core of a lot of fault-tolerant protocols encountered in asynchronous distributed systems. Among them, the class of *leader* failure detectors is one of the most important. This class, also called the class of leader oracles, is usually denoted Ω. (When clear from the context, the notation Ω will be used to denote either the oracle/failure detector class or an oracle of that class.) Ω provides the processes with a *leader* primitive that outputs a process id each time it is called, and such that, after some finite but unknown time, all its invocations return the same id, that is the identity of a correct process (a process that does not commit failures). Such an oracle is very weak: (1) a correct leader is eventually elected, but there is no knowledge on when it is elected; (2) several (correct or not) leaders can co-exist before a single correct leader is elected.

The oracle class Ω has two fundamental features. The first lies on the fact that, despite its very weak definition, it is powerful enough to allow solutions to fundamental problems such as the consensus problem [4]. More precisely, it has been shown to be the weakest class of failure detectors that allows consensus to be solved in message-passing asynchronous systems with a majority of correct processes (let us remind that, while consensus can be solved in synchronous systems despite Byzantine failures of less than one third of the processes [14], it cannot be solved in asynchronous distributed systems prone to even a single process crash [7]). Basically, an Ω-based consensus algorithm uses the eventual leader to impose a value to all the processes, thereby providing the algorithm liveness. Leader-based consensus protocols can be found in [9,13,18]. The second noteworthy feature of Ω lies on the fact that it allows the design of *indulgent* protocols [8]. Let P be an oracle-based protocol that produces outputs, and PS be the safety property satisfied by its outputs. P is *indulgent with respect to its underlying oracle* if, whatever the behavior of the oracle, its outputs never violate the safety property PS. This means that each time P produces outputs, they are correct. Moreover, P always produces outputs when the underlying oracle meets its specification. The only case where P can be prevented from producing outputs is when the implementation of the underlying oracle does not meet its specification. (Let us notice that it is still possible that P produces outputs despite the fact that its underlying oracle does not work correctly.) Interestingly, Ω is a class of oracles that allows designing indulgent protocols [8,9]. More precisely, due to the very nature of an *eventual* leader, it cannot be known in advance when that leader is elected; consequently, the main work of an Ω-based consensus algorithm is to keep its safety property, i.e., guarantee that no two different values can be decided before the eventual leader is elected.

Unfortunately, Ω cannot be implemented in pure asynchronous distributed systems where processes can crash. (Such an implementation would contradict the impossibility of solving consensus in such systems [7]. Direct proofs of the impossibility to implement Ω in pure crash-prone asynchronous systems can be found in [2,19].) But thanks to indulgence, this is not totally bad news. More precisely, as Ω makes it possible the design of indulgent protocols, it is interesting to design "approximate" protocols that do their best to implement Ω on top of the asynchronous system itself. The periods during which their best effort succeeds in producing a correct implementation of the oracle (i.e., there is a single leader and it is alive) are called "good" periods (and then, the upper layer Ω-based protocol produces outputs and those are correct). During the other periods (sometimes called "bad" periods, e.g., there are several leaders or the leader is a crashed process), the upper layer Ω-based protocol never produces erroneous outputs. The only bad thing that can then happen is that this protocol can be prevented from producing outputs, but when a new long enough good period appears, the upper layer Ω-based protocol can benefit from that period to produce an output.

A main challenge of asynchronous fault-tolerant distributed computing is consequently to identify properties that are at the same time "weak enough" in order to be satisfied "nearly always" by the underlying asynchronous system, while being "strong enough" to allow Ω to be implemented during the "long periods" in which they are satisfied.

1.2 Existing Approaches to Implement Ω

Up to now, two main approaches have been investigated to implement Ω in crash-prone asynchronous distributed systems. Both approaches enrich the asynchronous system with additional assumptions that, when satisfied, allow implementing Ω. These approaches are orthogonal: one is related to timing assumptions, the other is related to message pattern assumptions.

The eventual timely link approach. The first approach considers that the asynchronous system eventually satisfies additional *synchrony* properties. Considering a reliable communication network, the very first papers (e.g., [15]) assumed that all the links are *eventually timely*[1]. This assumption means that there is a time τ_0 after which there is a bound δ -possibly unknown- such that, for any time $\tau \geq \tau_0$, a message sent at time τ is received by time $\tau + \delta$.

This approach has then been refined to obtain weaker and weaker assumptions. It has been shown in [1] that it is possible to implement Ω in a system where communication links are unidirectional, asynchronous, and lossy, provided that there is a correct process whose $n - 1$ output links are eventually timely (n being the total number of processes). This assumption has further been weakened in [2] where it is shown that Ω can be built as soon as there is a correct process that has only t eventually timely links (where t is a known upper bound on the number of processes that can crash); such a process is called an *eventual t-source*. (Let us notice that, after the receiver has crashed, the link from a correct process to a crashed process is always timely.)

Another time-based assumption has been proposed in [16] where the notion of *eventual t-accessibility* is introduced. A process p is eventual t-accessible if there is a time τ_0 such that, at any time $\tau \geq \tau_0$, there is a set $Q(\tau)$ of t processes such that $p \notin Q(\tau)$ and a message broadcast by p at τ receives a response from each process of $Q(\tau)$ by time $\tau + \delta$ (where δ is a bound known by the processes). The very important point here is that the set $Q(\tau)$ of processes whose responses have to be received in a timely manner is not fixed and can be different at distinct times.

The notions of eventual t-source and eventual t-accessibility cannot be compared (which means that none of them can be simulated from the other). In a very interesting

---

[1] Actually, the Ω protocol presented in [15] only requires that the output links of the correct process with the smallest identity to be eventually timely.

way these two notions have been combined in [11] where is defined the notion of *eventual t-moving source*. A process p is an eventual t-moving source if there is a time τ_0 such that at any time $\tau \geq \tau_0$ there is a set $Q(\tau)$ of t processes such that $p \notin Q(\tau)$ and a message broadcast by p at τ is received by each process in $Q(\tau)$ by time $\tau + \delta$. As we can see, the *eventual t-moving source* assumption is weaker than the *eventual t-source* as the set $Q(\tau)$ can vary with τ.

Other time-based approaches are investigated in [5,12]. They consider weak assumptions on both the initial knowledge of processes and the network behavior. Protocols building Ω are presented [5,12] that assume the initial knowledge of each process is limited to its identity and the fact that identities are totally ordered (so, a process knows neither n nor t). An unreliable broadcast primitive allows the processes to communicate. One of the protocols presented in [5] is communication-efficient (after some time a single process has to send messages forever) while, as far as the network behavior is concerned, it only requires that each pair of correct processes be connected by fair lossy links, and there is a correct process whose output links to the rest of correct processes are eventually timely. It is shown in [12] that Ω can be built as long as there is one correct process that can reach the rest of the correct processes via eventually timely paths.

The message pattern approach. A totally different approach to build Ω has been introduced in [17]. That approach does not rely on timing assumptions and timeouts. It states a property on the *message exchange pattern* that, when satisfied, allows Ω to be implemented. The statement of such a property involves the system parameters n and t.

Let us assume that each process regularly broadcasts queries and, for each query, waits for the corresponding responses. Given a query, a response that belongs to the first $(n - t)$ responses to that query is said to be a *winning* response. Otherwise, the response is a *losing* response (then, that response is slow, lost or has never been sent because its sender has crashed). It is shown in [19] that Ω can be built as soon as the following behavioral property is satisfied: "There are a correct process p and a set Q of t processes such that $p \notin Q$ and eventually the response of p to each query issued by any $q \in Q$ is always a winning response (until -possibly- the crash of q)." When $t = 1$, this property becomes: "There is a link connecting two processes that is never the slowest (in terms of transfer delay) among all the links connecting these two processes to the rest of the system." A probabilistic analysis for the case $t = 1$ shows that such a behavioral property on the message exchange pattern is practically always satisfied [17].

This *message pattern* approach and the *eventual timely link* approaches cannot be compared. Interestingly, the message pattern approach and the eventual t-source approach have been combined in [20]. This combination shows that Ω can be implemented as soon as there is a correct process p and a time τ_0 after which there is a set Q of t processes q such that $p \notin Q$ and either (1) each time a process $q \in Q$ broadcasts a query, it receives a winning response from p, or (2) the link from p to q is timely. As it can be seen, if only (1) is satisfied, we obtain the *message pattern* assumption, while, if only (2) is satisfied, we obtain the *eventual t-source* assumption. More generally, here, the important fact is that the message pattern assumption and the timely link assumption are combined at the "finest possible" granularity level, namely, the link level.

1.3   Content of the Paper: Towards Weaker and Weaker Synchrony Assumptions

A quest for a fault-tolerant distributed computing holy grail is looking for the *weakest synchrony assumptions* that allow implementing Ω. Differently from the quest for the weakest information on failures that allows solving the consensus problem (whose result was Ω [4]), it is possible that this quest be endless. This is because we can envisage lots of base asynchronous computation models, and enrich each of them with appropriate assumptions that allow implementing Ω in the corresponding system. Such a quest should be based on a well-formalized definition of a low level asynchronous model, including all the models in which Ω can be implemented. There is no guarantee that such a common base model exists.

So, this paper is only a step in that direction. It considers the classical asynchronous computing model where processes can crash. They communicate through a reliable network [3,7]. (Fair lossy links could be used instead of reliable links[2] but we do not consider that possibility in order to keep the presentation simple.) The paper shows that it is possible to implement Ω in an asynchronous system from a synchrony assumption weaker than any of the previous ones, namely, *eventual t-source*, *eventual t-moving source*, or the *message pattern* assumption. Interestingly, these specific assumptions become particular cases of the more general (and weaker) assumption that is proposed. In that sense, the paper not only proposes a weaker assumption, but has also a generic dimension.

The proposed behavioral assumption (that we denote $\mathcal{A}$) requires that each process regularly broadcasts ALIVE(rn) messages, where rn is an increasing round number (this can always be done in an asynchronous system). The sending of ALIVE(rn) messages by the processes can be seen as an *asynchronous round*, each round number defining a new round.

To make easier the presentation we describe first an assumption $\mathcal{A}^+$ of which $\mathcal{A}$ is a weakening. $\mathcal{A}^+$ is as follows. There is a correct process p and a round number RN_0 such that, for each $rn > RN_0$, there is a set $Q(rn)$ of t processes such that $p \notin Q(rn)$ and for each process $q \in Q(rn)$ either (1) q has crashed, or (2) the message ALIVE(rn) sent by p is received by q at most δ time units after it has been sent (the corresponding bound δ can be unknown), or (3) the message ALIVE(rn) sent by p is received by q among the first $(n - t)$ ALIVE(rn) messages received by q (i.e., it is a winning message among ALIVE(rn) messages received by q). It is easy to see, that if only (1) and (2) are satisfied, $\mathcal{A}^+$ boils down to the eventual t-moving source assumption, while if only (1) and (3) are satisfied, it boils down to a *moving* version of the message pattern assumption (because the set $Q()$ can change over time). The set of processes $\{p\} \cup Q(rn)$ defines a star centered at p. As it must have at least t points (links), we say it is a *t-star*. Moreover, as $Q(rn)$ can change at each round number, we say that p is the *center* of an *eventual*

---

[2] This can easily be done by using message acknowledgments and piggybacking: a message is piggybacked on the next messages until it has been acknowledged. So, a message sent by the underlying communication protocol can be made up of several messages sent by the upper layer algorithm. It is nevertheless important to remark that such a piggybacking + acknowledgment technique is viable only if the size of the messages sent by the underlying communication protocol remains manageable.

rotating t-star ("eventual" because there is an arbitrary finite number of round numbers during which the requirement may not be satisfied).

While $\mathcal{A}^+$ allows implementing Ω, it appears that a weakened form of that assumption is sufficient. This is the assumption $\mathcal{A}$. It is sufficient that p be the center of an eventual rotating t-star only for a subset of the round numbers. More precisely, $\mathcal{A}$ requires that there is an infinite sequence $S = s_1, s_2, \ldots$ of (not necessarily consecutive) round numbers, and a bound D (not necessarily known), such that, $\forall k \geq 1, s_{k+1} - s_k \leq D$, and there is a process p that is the center of a rotating t-star when we consider only the round numbers in S. We call such a configuration an *eventual intermittent rotating t-star* (in fact, the "eventual" attribute could also be seen as being part of the "intermittent" attribute).

Basically, the difference between $\mathcal{A}^+$ and $\mathcal{A}$ is related to the notion of observation level [10]. While $\mathcal{A}^+$ considers a base level including all the round numbers, $\mathcal{A}$ provides an abstraction level (the sequence S) that eliminates the irrelevant round numbers. Of course, as it is not known in advance which are the relevant round numbers (i.e., S), an $\mathcal{A}$-based algorithm has to consider a priori all the round numbers and then find a way to dynamically skip the irrelevant ones.

After having introduced $\mathcal{A}^+$ and $\mathcal{A}$, the paper presents, in an incremental way, an $\mathcal{A}^+$-based algorithm and an $\mathcal{A}$-based algorithm that build a failure detector oracle of the class Ω. The $\mathcal{A}$-based algorithm enjoys a noteworthy property, namely, in an infinite execution, only the round numbers increase forever. All the other local variables and message fields remain finite. This means that, among the other variables, all the timeout values (be the corresponding link eventually timely or not) eventually stabilize. From an algorithmic mechanism point of view, the proposed algorithm combines new ideas with mechanisms also used in [2,5,11,17,20].

All the proofs and additional technical developments can be found in [6].

2   Definitions

2.1   Basic Distributed System Model

We consider a system formed by a finite set Π of $n \geq 2$ processes, namely, $\Pi = \{p_1, p_2, \ldots, p_n\}$. Process identifiers are totally ordered. Without loss of generality we assume that $ID(p_i) < ID(p_j)$, when $i < j$, and use $ID(p_i) = i$. We sometimes use p and q to denote processes. A process executes steps (a step is the reception of a set of messages with a local state change, or the sending of messages with a local state change). A process can fail by *crashing*, i.e., by prematurely halting. It behaves correctly (i.e., according to its specification) until it (possibly) crashes. By definition, a *correct* process is a process that does not crash. A *faulty* process is a process that is not correct. As previously indicated, t denotes the maximum number of processes that can crash $(1 \leq t < n)$.

Processes communicate and synchronize by sending and receiving messages through links. Every pair of processes (p, q) is connected by two directed links, denoted $p \rightarrow q$ and $q \rightarrow p$. Links are assumed to be reliable: they do not create, alter, or lose messages. In particular, if p sends a message to q, then eventually q receives that message unless one of them fails. There is no assumption about message transfer delays (moreover, the links are not required to be FIFO).

Processes are synchronous in the sense that there are lower and upper bounds on the number of processing steps they can execute per time unit. Each process has also a local clock that can accurately measure time intervals. The clocks of the processes are not synchronized. To simplify the presentation, and without loss of generality, we assume in the following that the execution of the local statements take no time. Only the message transfers consume time.

In the following, $AS_{n,t}[\emptyset]$ denotes an asynchronous distributed system as just described, made up of n processes among which up to $t < n$ can crash. More generally, $AS_{n,t}[P]$ will denote an asynchronous system made up of n processes among which up to $t < n$ can crash, and satisfying the additional assumption P (so, $P = \emptyset$ means that the system is a *pure* asynchronous system).

We assume the existence of a global discrete clock. This clock is a fictional device which is not known by the processes; it is only used to state specifications or prove protocol properties. The range of clock values is the set of real numbers.

2.2 The Oracle Class Ω

Ω has been defined informally in the introduction. A leader oracle is a distributed entity that provides the processes with a function leader() that returns a process id each time it is invoked. A unique correct process is eventually elected but there is no knowledge of when the leader is elected. Several leaders can coexist during an arbitrarily long period of time, and there is no way for the processes to learn when this "anarchy" period is over. A leader oracle satisfies the following property [4]:

– Eventual Leadership: There is a time τ and a correct process p such that any invocation of leader() issued after τ returns the id of p.

Ω-based consensus algorithms are described in [9,13,18] for asynchronous systems where a majority of processes are correct ($t < n/2$). These algorithms can then be used as a subroutine to solve other problems such as atomic broadcast (e.g., [3,13]).

As noticed in the introduction, whatever the value of $t \in [1, n - 1]$, Ω cannot be implemented in $AS_{n,t}[\emptyset]$. Direct proofs of this impossibility can be found in [2,19] ("direct proofs" means that they are not based on the impossibility of asynchronously solving a given problem such as the consensus problem [7]).

3   The Additional Assumption $\mathcal{A}$

This section defines a system model, denoted $AS_{n,t}[\mathcal{A}]$ ($AS_{n,t}[\emptyset]$ enriched with the assumption $\mathcal{A}$) in which failure detectors of the class Ω can be built. (Said differently, this means that Ω can be implemented in all the runs of $AS_{n,t}[\emptyset]$ that satisfy $\mathcal{A}$.)

Process behavior requirement. The assumption $\mathcal{A}$ requires that each process p_i *regularly* broadcasts ALIVE(rn) messages (until it possibly crashes). The parameter rn is a round number that, for each process p_i, takes the successive values $1, 2, \ldots$

Let $send\_time(i, rn)$ be the time at which p_i broadcasts ALIVE(rn). The words "regularly broadcasts" means that the duration separating two broadcasts by the same process is bounded. More formally, there is a bound β (not necessarily known by the processes) such that, for any round number rn and any process p_i (until it possibly crashes), we have $0 < send\_time(i, rn+1) - send\_time(i, rn) \leq \beta$. It is important to notice that, given two different processes, there is no relation linking $send\_time(i, rn)$ and $send\_time(j, rn)$. It is easy to see that this broadcast mechanism can be implemented in $AS_{n,t}[\emptyset]$.

In the text of the algorithms, "**repeat regularly** ST" means that two consecutive executions of the statement ST are separated by at most β time units.

Definitions. According to the time or the order in which it is received, an ALIVE(rn) message can be δ-*timely* or *winning*. These notions are central to state the assumptions $\mathcal{A}^+$ and $\mathcal{A}$. It is important to remark that they are associated with messages, not with links. Let δ denote a bounded value.

Definition 1. *A message* ALIVE(rn) *is δ-timely if it is received by its destination process at most δ time units after it has been sent.*

Definition 2. *A message* ALIVE(rn) *is winning if it belongs to the first $(n - t)$* ALIVE *(rn) messages received by its destination process.*

System model $AS_{n,t}[\mathcal{A}^+]$. The additional assumption $\mathcal{A}^+$ is the following: There is a correct process p, a bound δ, and a finite round number RN_0, such that for any $rn \geq RN_0$, there is a set of processes $Q(rn)$ satisfying the following properties:

- A1: $p \notin Q(rn)$ and $|Q(rn)| \geq t$ (i.e., $\{p\} \cup Q(rn)$ is a t-star centered at p), and
- A2: For any $q \in Q(rn)$ (i.e., any point of the star), one of the following properties is satisfied: (1) q has crashed, or (2) the message ALIVE(rn) is δ-timely, or (3) the message ALIVE(rn) is winning.

It is important to see that p, δ, and RN_0 are not known in advance, and can never be explicitly known by the processes. As said in the introduction, the process p that satisfies $\mathcal{A}^+$ is the center of an eventual rotating t-star.

$\mathcal{A}^+$ includes several dynamicity notions. One is related to the fact that the sets $Q()$ are not required to be the same set, i.e., $Q(rn_1)$ and $Q(rn_2)$ can be different for $rn_1 \neq rn_2$. This is the *rotating* notion (first introduced in [11,16] under the name *moving* set). A second dynamicity notion is the fact that two points of the star $\{p\} \cup Q(rn)$ (e.g., $p \to q1$ and $p \to q2$), are allowed to satisfy different properties, one satisfying the "δ-timely" property, while the other satisfying the "winning" property. Finally, if the point q appears in $Q(rn_1)$ and $Q(rn_2)$ with $rn_1 \neq rn_2$, it can satisfy the "δ-timely" property in $Q(rn_1)$ and the "winning" property in $Q(rn_2)$.

It is important to notice that the assumption $\mathcal{A}^+$ places constraints only on the messages tagged ALIVE. This means that, if an algorithm uses messages tagged ALIVE plus messages with other tags, there is no constraint on the other messages, even if they use the same links as the ALIVE messages.

System model $AS_{n,t}[\mathcal{A}]$. As indicated in the introduction, $\mathcal{A}$ is a weakening of $\mathcal{A}^+$ that allows the previous properties to be satisfied by only a subset of the round numbers. (None of the previous assumptions proposed so far have investigated such an assumption weakening.)

The additional assumption $\mathcal{A}$ is the following: There is a correct process p, a bound δ, a bound D, and a finite round number RN_0, such that:

- There is an infinite sequence S of increasing round numbers $s_1 = RN_0, s_2, \ldots, s_k,$ $s_{k+1}, \ldots$, such that $s_{k+1} - s_k \leq D$, (so, the round numbers in S are not necessarily consecutive), and
- For any $s_k \in S$ there is a set of processes $Q(s_k)$ satisfying the properties A1 and A2 previously stated.

When $D = 1$, $\mathcal{A}$ boils down to $\mathcal{A}^+$. So, $\mathcal{A}$ weakens $\mathcal{A}^+$ by adding another dynamicity dimension, namely, a dimension related to time. It is sufficient that the rotating t-star centered at p appears from time to time in order Ω can be built. This is why we say that $\mathcal{A}$ defines an *intermittent rotating t-star*. The limit imposed by $\mathcal{A}$ to this dynamicity dimension is expressed by the bound D.

4 An $\mathcal{A}^+$-Based Leader Algorithm

This section presents and proves an algorithm that builds a failure detector of the class Ω in $AS_{n,t}[\mathcal{A}^+]$. This algorithm will be improved in the next sections to work in $AS_{n,t}[\mathcal{A}]$ (Section 5), and then to have only bounded variables (Section 6).

4.1 Principles and Description of the Algorithm

The algorithm is based on the following idea (used in one way or another in several leader protocols -e.g., [2,17]-): among all the processes, a process p_i elects as its current leader the process it suspects the least to have crashed (if several processes are the least suspected, p_i uses their ids to decide among them).

Local variables. To attain this goal each process p_i uses the following local variables:

- s_rn_i and r_rn_i are two round number variables. s_rn_i is used to associate a round number with each ALIVE() message sent by p_i. When $s\_rn_i = a$, p_i has executed up to its ath sending round.
  r_rn_i is the round number for which p_i is currently waiting for ALIVE() messages. When $r\_rn_i = b$, p_i is currently executing its bth receiving round.
  Sending rounds and receiving rounds are not synchronized (separate tasks are associated with them).
- $timer_i$ is p_i's local timer.
- $susp\_level_i[1..n]$ is an array such that $susp\_level_i[j]$ counts, from p_i's point of view, the number of rounds during which p_j has been suspected to have crashed by at least $(n - t)$ processes.
- $rec\_from_i[1..]$ is an array such that $rec\_from_i[rn]$ keeps the ids of the processes from which p_i has received an ALIVE(rn) message while $rn \geq r\_rn_i$ (if $rn < r\_rn_i$ when the message arrives, then it is too late and is consequently discarded).

- $suspicions_i[1.., 1..n]$ is an array such that $suspicions_i[rn, j]$ counts, as far as the receiving round rn is concerned, how many processes suspect that p_j has crashed.

Process behavior. The algorithm for a process p_i is described in Figure 1. It is made up of two tasks. The task $T1$ (Lines 1-3) is the sending task. In addition to its round number, each ALIVE() message carries the current value of the array $susp\_level_i$ (this gossiping is to allow the processes to converge on the same values for those entries of the array that stop increasing).

The task $T2$ is the main task. When leader() is locally invoked, it returns the id of the process that locally is the least suspected (Lines 19-21). If several processes are the least suspected, their ids are used to decide among them[3]. When an ALIVE(rn, sl) message is received, $T2$ updates accordingly the array $susp\_level_i$, and $rec\_from_i[rn]$ if that message is not late (i.e., if $r\_rn_i \geq rn$). The core of the task $T2$ is made up of the other two sets of statements.

- Lines 8-12. The timer $timer_i$ is used to benefit from the "δ-timely message" side of the assumption $\mathcal{A}^+$, while the set $rec\_from_i[r\_rn_i]$ is used to benefit from its "winning message" side. At each receiving phase r_rn_i, p_i waits until both the timer has expired and it has received $(n - t)$ ALIVE($rn, *$) messages with $rn = r\_rn_i$.

When this occurs, as far as the receiving phase r_rn_i is concerned, p_i suspects all the processes p_k from which it has not yet received ALIVE($r\_rn_i, *$) message. It consequently informs all the processes about these suspicions (associated with the receiving phase r_rn_i) by sending to all a SUSPICION($r\_rn_i, suspects$) message (Line 10). Then, p_i proceeds to the next receiving phase (Line 12). It also resets the timer for this new (r_rn_ith) waiting phase (Line 11).

The timer has to be reset to a value higher than the previous one when p_i discovers that it has falsely suspected some processes because its timer expired too early[4]. A way to ensure that the timeout value increases when there are such false suspicions, is adopting a conservative approach, namely, systematically increasing the timeout value. So, a correct statement to reset the timer (at Line 11) could be "**set** $timer_i$ **to** s_rn_i" (or to r_rn_i) as these round numbers monotonically increase.

It appears (see the proof) that $susp\_level_i[j]$ is unbounded if p_i is correct and p_j is faulty. So, another possible value to reset $timer_i$ is $\max(\{susp\_level_i[j]\}_{1 \leq j \leq n})$.

The reason to reset $timer_i$ that way (instead of using s_rn_i or r_rn_i) will become clear in the last version of the algorithm (Section 6) where we will show that all the $susp\_level_i[j]$ variables can be bounded, and so all the timeout values will

---

[3] Let X be a non-empty set of pairs (integer, process id). The function $\min(X)$ returns the smallest pair in X, according to lexicographical order. This means that $(sl1, i)$ is smaller than $(sl2, j)$ iff $sl1 < sl2$, or $(sl1 = sl2) \wedge (i < j)$.

[4] Let us remark that an ALIVE($rn, *$) message that arrives after the timer has expired, but belongs to the first $(n - t)$ ALIVE($rn, *$) messages received by p_i, is considered by the algorithm as if it was received before the timer expiration. So, such a message cannot give rise to an erroneous suspicion.

init: **for_each** $rn \geq 1$ **do** $rec\_from_i[rn] \leftarrow \{i\}$ **end_do**;
  for_each $rn \geq 1, 1 \leq j \leq n$ **do** $suspicions_i[rn, j] \leftarrow 0$ **end_do**;
  $s\_rn_i \leftarrow 0$; $r\_rn_i \leftarrow 1$; $susp\_level_i \leftarrow [0, \ldots, 0]$; **set** $timer_i$ **to** 0;

task $T1$:
(1) **repeat regularly**:
  % Two consecutive repeats are separated by at most β time units %
(2) $s\_rn_i \leftarrow s\_rn_i + 1$;
(3) **for_each** $j \neq i$ **do** *send* ALIVE$(s\_rn_i, susp\_level_i)$ *to* p_j **end_do**

task $T2$:
(4) **upon reception** ALIVE(rn, sl) **from** p_j:
(5) **for_each** k **do** $susp\_level_i[k] \leftarrow \max(susp\_level_i[k], sl[k])$ **end_do**;
(6) **if** $rn \geq r\_rn_i$ **then** $rec\_from_i[rn] \leftarrow rec\_from_i[rn] \cup \{j\}$
(7) **end_if**

(8) **when** ($timer_i$ has expired) $\wedge$ ($|rec\_from_i[r\_rn_i]| \geq n - t$):
(9) **let** $suspects = \Pi \setminus rec\_from_i[r\_rn_i]$;
(10) **for_each** j **do** *send* SUSPICION$(r\_rn_i, suspects)$ *to* p_j **end_do**;
(11) **set** $timer_i$ **to** $\max(\{susp\_level_i[j]\}_{1 \leq j \leq n})$;
(12) $r\_rn_i \leftarrow r\_rn_i + 1$

(13) **upon reception** SUSPICION$(rn, suspects)$ **from** p_j:
(14) **for_each** $k \in suspects$ **do**
(15) $suspicions_i[rn, k] \leftarrow suspicions_i[rn, k] + 1$;
(16)   **if** ($suspicions_i[rn, k] = n - t$)
(17)   **then** $susp\_level_i[k] \leftarrow susp\_level_i[k] + 1$ **end_if**
(18) **end_do**

(19) **when** leader() **is invoked by the upper layer**:
(20) **let** ℓ **such that** $(susp\_level_i[\ell], \ell) = \min(\{(susp\_level_i[j], j)\}_{1 \leq j \leq n})$;
(21) **return** (ℓ)

Fig. 1. Algorithm for process p_i in $AS_{n,t}[\mathcal{A}^+]$

also be bounded (while the round numbers cannot be bounded). Let us notice that bounded timeout values can allow reducing stabilization time.

– Lines 13-18. When it receives a SUSPICION$(rn, suspects)$ message, p_i increases $suspicions_i[rn, k]$ for each process p_k such that $k \in suspects$ (Line 15). Moreover, if p_k is suspected by "enough" processes (here, $n - t$) during the receiving phase rn, p_i increases $susp\_level_i[k]$ (Lines 16-17)[5].

---

[5] It is worth noticing that the system parameter t is never explicitly used by the algorithm. This means that $(n - t)$ could be replaced by a parameter α. For the algorithm to work, α has to be a lower bound on the number of the correct processes.

4.2   Proof of the Algorithm

Lemma 1. *Let p_i be a correct process and p_j a faulty process. $susp\_level_i[j]$ increases forever.*

Lemma 2. *Let p_ℓ be a correct process that is the center of an eventual rotating t-star (i.e., it makes true $\mathcal{A}^+$). There is a time after which, for any process p_i, $susp\_level_i[\ell]$ is never increased at Line 17.*

Theorem 1. *The algorithm described in Figure 1 implements Ω in $AS_{n,t}[\mathcal{A}^+]$.*

5   An $\mathcal{A}$-Based Leader Algorithm

5.1   From $\mathcal{A}^+$ to $\mathcal{A}$

The difference between $\mathcal{A}^+$ and $\mathcal{A}$ lies on the fact that the properties A1 and A2 that define an eventual rotating t-star, have no longer to be satisfied by each round number starting from some unknown but finite number RN_0, but only by the round numbers of an infinite sequence $S = s_1, s_2, \ldots, s_k, s_{k+1}, \ldots$, that (1) starts at RN_0 (i.e., $s_1 = RN_0$), and (2) is such that $\forall k$, $s_{k+1} - s_k \leq D$, where D is a (possibly unknown) constant.

This means that, when compared to an $\mathcal{A}^+$-based algorithm, an Ω $\mathcal{A}$-based algorithm has to filter the round numbers in order to skip the irrelevant ones, i.e., the round numbers that do not belong to S. In a very interesting way, this can be attained by adding a single line (more precisely, an additional test) to the $\mathcal{A}^+$-based algorithm described in Figure 1. The corresponding $\mathcal{A}$-based algorithm is described in Figure 2 where the new line is prefixed by "$*$".

The variable $susp\_level_i[k]$ must no longer be systematically increased when there is a round number rn such that $suspicion_i[rn, k] = n - t$. This is in order to prevent such increases when rn is a round number that does not belong to the sequence S. But,

---

─────────────── The Lines 1-12 are the same as in Figure 1 ───────────────

(13) **upon reception** SUSPICION($rn, suspects$) **from** p_j:
(14)   **for_each** $k \in suspects$ **do**
(15) $suspicions_i[rn, k] \leftarrow suspicions_i[rn, k] + 1$;
(16)   **if** $(suspicions_i[rn, k] = n - t)$
  $*$ $\wedge\ (\forall x : rn - susp\_level_i[k] < x < rn : suspicions_i[x, k] \geq n - t)$
(17)   **then** $susp\_level_i[k] \leftarrow susp\_level_i[k] + 1$ **end_if**
(18)   **end_do**

─────────────── The Lines 19-21 are the same as in Figure 1 ───────────────

Fig. 2. Algorithm for process p_i in $AS_{n,t}[\mathcal{A}]$

on the other side, $susp\_level_i[k]$ has to be forever increased if p_k has crashed. To attain these "conflicting" goals, the variables $susp\_level_i[k]$ and $suspicion_i[rn, k]$ are simultaneously used as follows: $susp\_level_i[k]$ is increased if $suspicion_i[rn, k] = n - t$ and, $\forall x$ such that $rn - susp\_level_i[k] < x < rn$, we have $suspicion_i[x, k] \geq n - t$. When it is satisfied, this additional condition means that p_k has been continuously suspected during "enough" rounds in order $susp\_level_i[k]$ to be increased. The exact meaning of "enough" is dynamically defined as being the round number window $[rn - susp\_level_i[k] + 1, rn]$, thereby allowing not to explicitly use the bound D (that constraints the sequence S) in the text of the algorithm.

5.2 Proof of the Algorithm

The statements of the lemmas and theorem that follow are the same as in Section 4. As $\mathcal{A}$ is weaker than $\mathcal{A}^+$ their proofs are different.

Lemma 3. *Let p_i be a correct process and p_j a faulty process. $susp\_level_i[j]$ increases forever.*

Lemma 4. *Let p_ℓ be a correct process that is the center of an eventual rotating t-star (i.e., it makes true $\mathcal{A}$). There is a time after which, for any process p_i, $susp\_level_i[\ell]$ is never increased at Line 17.*

Theorem 2. *The algorithm described in Figure 2 implements Ω in $AS_{n,t}[\mathcal{A}]$.*

6   A Bounded Variable $\mathcal{A}$-Based Leader Algorithm

When we examine the $\mathcal{A}$-based leader algorithm described in Figure 2, it appears that, for each process p_i, the size of its variables is bounded, except for variables s_rn_i, r_rn_i, and $susp\_level_i[j]$ in some cases (e.g., when p_j crashes). Since the current value of $\max(\{susp\_level_i[j]\}_{1 \leq j \leq n})$ is used by p_i to reset its timer, it follows that all the timeout values are potentially unbounded (e.g., this occurs as soon as one process crashes).

We show here that each local variable $susp\_level_i[j]$ can be bounded whatever the behavior of p_j and the time taken by the messages sent by p_j to p_i. Consequently, all the variables (except the round numbers) are bounded, be the execution finite or infinite. It follows that all the timeout values are bounded, whatever the fact that processes crash or not, and the links are timely or not. This is a noteworthy property of the algorithm. (Of course, it remains possible to use s_rn_i or r_rn_i if, due to specific application requirements, one needs to have increasing timeouts.)

6.1 Bounding all the Variables $susp\_level_i[k]$

Let us observe that if $susp\_level_i[k]$ is not the smallest value of the array $susp\_level_i$, p_i does not currently considers p_k as the leader. This means that it is not necessary to increase $susp\_level_i[k]$ when $susp\_level_i[k] \neq \min(\{susp\_level_i[j]\}_{1 \leq j \leq n})$. The proof shows that this intuition is correct.

(13) **upon reception** SUSPICION($rn, suspects$) **from** p_j:
(14)   **for each** $k \in suspects$ **do**
(15) $suspicions_i[rn, k] \leftarrow suspicions_i[rn, k] + 1$;
(16)   **if** $(suspicions_i[rn, k] = n - t)$
* $\wedge\ (\forall x : rn - susp\_level_i[k] < x < rn : suspicions_i[x, k] \geq n - t)$
** $\wedge\ (susp\_level_i[k] = \min(\{susp\_level_i[j]\}_{1 \leq j \leq n}))$
(17)   **then** $susp\_level_i[k] \leftarrow susp\_level_i[k] + 1$ **end if**
(18)   **end do**

Fig. 3. Algorithm with bounded variables for process p_i in $AS_{n,t}[\mathcal{A}]$

Let B be the final smallest value in the array $susp\_level_i[1..n]$, once the eventual leader has been elected. The previous observation allows us to conclude that no value in this array will ever be greater than $B + 1$, and consequently, all the values are bounded.

As for the previous algorithm (Figure 2), The resulting algorithm can be attained by adding a single line (more precisely, an additional test) to the $\mathcal{A}^+$-based algorithm described in Figure 1. This new test is described in Figure 3 where it appears at the line marked "**".

6.2   Proof and Properties of the Algorithm

Lemma 5. *Let p_ℓ be a correct process that makes true the assumption $\mathcal{A}$. There is a time after which, for any process p_i, $susp\_level_i[\ell]$ is never increased at Line 17.*

Definition 3. *Let B_j be the greatest value (or $+\infty$ if there is no such finite value) ever taken by a variable $susp\_level_i[j]$, $\forall i \in [1..n]$. Let $B = \min(B_1, \ldots, B_n)$ or $+\infty$ if all B_j are equal to $+\infty$.*

Lemma 6. *Let p_i be a correct process and p_j a faulty process. We eventually have $susp\_level_i[j] > B$.*

Theorem 3. *The algorithm described in Figure 3 implements Ω in $AS_{n,t}[\mathcal{A}]$.*

Lemma 7. $\forall\ p_i$, $\max(\{susp\_level_i[x]\}_{1 \leq x \leq n}) - \min(\{susp\_level_i[x]\}_{1 \leq x \leq n}) \leq 1$ *is always satisfied.*

Theorem 4. *No variable $susp\_level_i[j]$ is ever larger than $B + 1$.*

7   Conclusion

Combining the result of [3,4] with this paper we obtain the following theorem:

Theorem 5. *Consensus can be solved in any message-passing asynchronous system that has (1) a majority of correct processes ($t < n/2$), and (2) an intermittent rotating t-star.*

References

1. Aguilera, M.K., Delporte-Gallet, C., Fauconnier, H., Toueg, S.: On Implementing Omega with Weak Reliability and Synchrony Assumptions. In: 22th ACM Symposium on Principles of Distributed Computing (PODC 2003), pp. 306–314 (2003)
2. Aguilera, M.K., Delporte-Gallet, C., Fauconnier, H., Toueg, S.: Communication Efficient Leader Election and Consensus with Limited Link Synchrony. In: 23th ACM Symp. on Principles of Distributed Computing (PODC 2004), pp. 328–337 (2004)
3. Chandra, T.D., Toueg, S.: Unreliable Failure Detectors for Reliable Distributed Systems. Journal of the ACM 43(2), 225–267 (1996)
4. Chandra, T.D., Hadzilacos, V., Toueg, S.: The Weakest Failure Detector for Solving Consensus. Journal of the ACM 43(4), 685–722 (1996)
5. Fernández, A., Jiménez, E., Raynal, M.: Eventual Leader Election with Weak Assumptions on Initial Knowledge, Communication Reliability, and Synchrony. In: Proc. Int'l IEEE conference on Dependable Systems and Networks (DSN 2006), pp. 166–175 (2006)
6. Fernández, A., Raynal, M.: From an Intermittent Rotating Star to a Leader. Tech Report 1810, IRISA, Rennes (2006)
7. Fischer, M.J., Lynch, N., Paterson, M.S.: Impossibility of Distributed Consensus with One Faulty Process. Journal of the ACM 32(2), 374–382 (1985)
8. Guerraoui, R.: Indulgent Algorithms.In: 19th ACM Symposium on Principles of Distributed Computing (PODC 2000), pp. 289–298 (2000)
9. Guerraoui, R., Raynal, M.: The Information Structure of Indulgent Consensus. IEEE Transactions on Computers 53(4), 453–466 (2004)
10. Hélary, J.-M., Mostéfaoui, A., Raynal, M.: Interval Consistency of Asynchronous Distributed Computations. Journal of Computer and System Sciences 64(2), 329–349 (2002)
11. Hutle, M., Malkhi, D., Schmid, U., Zhou, L.: Chasing the weakest system model for implementing Ω and consensus. In: Datta, A.K., Gradinariu, M. (eds.) SSS 2006. LNCS, vol. 4280, pp. 576–577. Springer, Heidelberg (2006)
12. Jiménez, E., Arévalo, S., Fernández, A.: Implementing unreliable failure detectors with unknown membership. Information Processing Letters 100(2), 60–63 (2006)
13. Lamport, L.: The Part-Time Parliament. ACM Trans. on Comp. Systems 16(2), 133–169 (1998)
14. Lamport, L., Shostak, R., Pease, L.: The Byzantine General Problem. ACM Transactions on Programming Languages and Systems 4(3), 382–401 (1982)
15. Larrea, M., Fernández, A., Arévalo, S.: Optimal Implementation of the Weakest Failure Detector for Solving Consensus.In: Proc. 19th IEEE Int'l Symposium on Reliable Distributed Systems (SRDS 2000), pp. 52–60 (2000)
16. Malkhi, D., Oprea, F., Zhou, L.: Ω Meets Paxos: Leader Election and Stability without Eventual Timely Links. In: Fraigniaud, P. (ed.) DISC 2005. LNCS, vol. 3724, pp. 199–213. Springer, Heidelberg (2005)
17. Mostéfaoui, A., Mourgaya, E., Raynal, M.: Asynchronous Implementation of Failure Detectors.In: Proc. Int'l IEEE Conf. on Dependable Systems and Networks, pp. 351–360 (2003)
18. Mostéfaoui, A., Raynal, M.: Leader-Based Consensus. Parallel Processing Letters 11(1), 95–107 (2000)
19. Mostéfaoui, A., Raynal, M., Travers, C.: Crash-resilient Time-free Eventual Leadership.In: Proc. 23th Int'l IEEE Symposium on Reliable Distributed Systems, pp. 208–217 (2004)
20. Mostéfaoui, A., Raynal, M., Travers, C.: Time-free and timer-based assumptions can be combined to get eventual leadership. IEEE Transactions on Parallel and Distributed Systems 17(7), 656–666 (2006)
21. Raynal, M.: A short Introduction to Failure Detectors for Asynchronous Distributed Systems. ACM SIGACT News, Distributed Computing Column 36(1), 53–70 (2005)

Global Deadline-Monotonic Scheduling of Arbitrary-Deadline Sporadic Task Systems*

Sanjoy Baruah[1] and Nathan Fisher[2]

[1] The University of North Carolina at Chapel Hill
baruah@cs.unc.edu
[2] Wayne State University
fishern@cs.wayne.edu

Abstract. The multiprocessor Deadline-Monotonic scheduling of sporadic task systems is studied. A new sufficient schedulability test is presented and proved correct. It is shown that this test offers non-trivial quantitative guarantees, including a processor speedup bound.

Keywords: Multiprocessor scheduling; real-time systems; sporadic tasks; arbitrary deadlines; global scheduling; Deadline Monotonic; schedulability analysis.

1 Introduction

A real-time system is often modelled as a finite collection of independent recurring tasks, each of which generates a potentially infinite sequence of *jobs*. Every job is characterized by an arrival time, an execution requirement, and a deadline, and it is required that a job complete execution between its arrival time and its deadline. Different formal models for recurring tasks place different restrictions on the values of the parameters of jobs generated by each task. One of the more commonly used formal models is the *sporadic task model* [1,2], which is described in Section 2.1

In this paper, we consider real-time systems that are modeled by the sporadic task model and implemented upon a platform comprised of several identical processors. We assume that the platform

- is fully *preemptive*: an executing job may be interrupted at any instant in time and have its execution resumed later with no cost or penalty.
- allows for *global* inter-processor migration: a job may begin execution on any processor and a preempted job may resume execution on the same processor as, or a different processor from, the one it had been executing on prior to preemption.
- forbids *intra-task parallelism*: each task may have at most one job executing on at most one processor at each instant in time, regardless of how many jobs of the task are awaiting execution and how many processors are idle.

We study the behavior of the well-known and very widely-used *Deadline Monotonic* scheduling algorithm [3] when scheduling systems of sporadic tasks upon such preemptive platforms. (We describe the Deadline Monotonic algorithm is Section 2.3.) We

---

* Supported in part by NSF Grant Nos. CNS-0408996, CCF-0541056, and CCR-0615197, ARO Grant No. W911NF-06-1-0425, and funding from the Intel Corporat.

E. Tovar, P. Tsigas, and H. Fouchal (Eds.): OPODIS 2007, LNCS 4878, pp. 204–216, 2007.

will refer to Deadline Monotonic scheduling with global inter-processor migration as *global* DM (or simply DM).

Our results, and significance. We present a new test for determining whether a given sporadic task system is guaranteed to meet all deadlines upon a specified computing platform, when scheduled using global DM. We prove the correctness of this test, and provide several different quantitative characterizations of its performance. For instance, we show that any sporadic task system that is feasible (i.e., can be scheduled using an optimal clairvoyant algorithm) is identified as being DM-schedulable by our test upon a platform in which each processor is approximately four times as fast.

Previous tests for determining whether sporadic task systems can be successfully scheduled using DM have been applicable only to task systems in which every sporadic task generates a job only after the deadline of its previous job has elapsed (such task systems are called constrained-deadline task systems – see Section 2.1). Since (as stated above) our machine model forbids the simultaneous execution of multiple jobs of the same task, getting rid of this restriction turns out to be surprisingly challenging. We believe that one of the major contributions of the research represented in this paper is the discovery of general techniques for dealing with task systems in the absence of this restriction, thereby enabling the analysis of the behavior of scheduling algorithms on sporadic task systems that are not constrained-deadline.

Organization. The remainder of this paper is organized as follows. In Section 2 we formally define the task and machine models used, and provide some additional useful definitions. In Section 3 we derive, and prove the correctness of, a new global DM schedulability test. In Section 4 we provide a quantitative characterization of the efficacy of this new schedulability test in terms of the resource augmentation metric.

2 Model and Definitions

In this section, we describe in greater detail the task (Section 2.1) and machine (Section 2.2) models used in this research. We also briefly discuss the Deadline Monotonic scheduling algorithm (Section 2.3), and motivate and describe the *speedup* metric which we use to evaluate the goodness of the schedulability test that will be derived (Section 2.4). We briefly list some related research in Section 2.5.

2.1 Task Model

A *sporadic task* $\tau_i = (C_i, D_i, T_i)$ is characterized by a *worst-case execution requirement* C_i, a *(relative) deadline* D_i, and a *minimum inter-arrival separation* parameter T_i, also referred to as the *period* of the task. Such a sporadic task generates a potentially infinite sequence of jobs, with successive job-arrivals separated by at least T_i time units. Each job has a worst-case execution requirement equal to C_i and a deadline that occurs D_i time units after its arrival time. We refer to the interval, of size D_i, between such a job's arrival instant and deadline as its *scheduling window*. A *sporadic task system* is comprised of several such sporadic tasks. A task system is said to be a *constrained-deadline* sporadic task system if it is guaranteed that each task in the system has its relative deadline parameter no larger than its period. A task system that is not constrained-deadline is said to be an *arbitrary-deadline* task system.

Throughout this paper, τ denotes an arbitrary-deadline sporadic task comprised of the n tasks $\tau_1, \tau_2, \ldots, \tau_n$. We assume that these tasks are indexed in order or non-decreasing relative deadline parameters: $D_i \leq D_{i+1}$ for all i, $1 \leq i < n$.

We now introduce some definitions and notation used in the remainder of this paper.

Definition 1 (density; largest density). *The density δ_i of a task τ_i is the ratio $(C_i / \min (D_i, T_i))$ of its execution requirement to the smaller of its relative deadline and its period. For each k, $1 \leq k \leq n$, $\delta_{\max}(k)$ denotes the largest density from among the tasks $\tau_1, \tau_2, \ldots, \tau_k$:*

$$\delta_{\max}(k) \stackrel{def}{=} \max_{i=1}^{k}(\delta_i)$$

□

That is, $\delta_{\max}(k)$ denotes the density of the task of greatest density among the k tasks with the smallest values of the relative deadline parameters.

The concepts of *demand bound function* and *load* find widespread use in real-time schedulability analysis. We provide formal definitions below; for further detail, consult, e.g., [4].

Definition 2 (DBF). *For any $t > 0$, the **demand bound function** DBF(τ_i, t) of a sporadic task τ_i bounds the maximum cumulative execution requirement by jobs of τ_i that both arrive in, and have deadlines within, any interval of length t.*   □

It has been shown [2] that

$$\mathrm{DBF}(\tau_i, t) = \max\left(0, \left(\left\lfloor \frac{t - D_i}{T_i} \right\rfloor + 1\right) C_i\right)$$

Definition 3 (load). *For each k, $1 \leq k \leq n$, a **load** parameter is defined as follows:*

$$\mathrm{LOAD}(k) \stackrel{def}{=} \max_{t>0}\left(\frac{\sum_{i=1}^{k} \mathrm{DBF}(\tau_i, t)}{t}\right)$$

□

Efficient algorithms have been designed for computing LOAD both exactly in pseudo-polynomial time, and approximately to any arbitrary desired degree of accuracy in polynomial time — see, e.g., [5,6].

The following Lemma relates the density of a task to its DBF:

Lemma 1. *For all tasks τ_i and for all $t \geq 0$,*

$$t \times \delta_i \geq \mathrm{DBF}(\tau_i, t) .$$

Proof Sketch: This lemma is easily validated informally by sketching $\text{DBF}(\tau_i, t)$ as a function of t, and comparing this with the graph for $t \times \delta_i$, a straight line of slope $(C_i / \min(D_i, T_i))$ through the origin. $\text{DBF}(\tau_i, t)$ is a step function comprised of steps of height C_i, with the first step at $t = D_i$ and successive steps exactly T_i time units apart. It is seen that the graph of δ_i lies above the plot for $\text{DBF}(\tau_i, t)$, for all t. (For $D_i < T_i$, the graph for δ_i touches the plot for $\text{DBF}(\tau_i, t)$ at $t = D_i$; for $D_i = T_i$, the two touch at all integer multiples of T_i; and for $D_i > T_i$ the two plots never touch.)   □

In constrained task systems — those in which $D_i \leq T_i \; \forall i$ — a job becomes eligible to execute upon arrival, and remains eligible until it completes execution[1]. In systems with $D_i > T_i$ for some tasks τ_i, we require that at most one job of each task be eligible to execute at each time instant. We assume that jobs of the same task are considered in first-come first-served order; hence, a job only becomes eligible to execute after both these conditions are satisfied: *(i)* it has arrived, and *(ii)* all previous jobs generated by the same task that generated it have completed execution. This gives rise to the notion of an active task: briefly, a task is active at some instant if it has some eligible job awaiting execution at that instant. More formally,

Definition 4 (active task). *A task is said to be* active *in a given schedule at a time-instant t if some job of the task is eligible to execute at time-instant t. That is, (i) $t \geq$ the greater of the job's arrival time and the completion time of the previous job of the same task, and (ii) the job has not completed execution prior to time-instant t.*   □

2.2 Processor Model

In this paper, we study the scheduling of sporadic task systems upon a platform comprised of m identical processors, where m is an integer ≥ 1. For the most part (except, e.g., in Lemmas 4 and 5), we assume that all processors are of unit computing capacity: a job completes one unit of execution by executing upon a processor for one unit of time. We assume that the platform is fully *preemptive* — an executing job may be interrupted at any instant in time and have its execution resumed later with no cost or penalty. We assume that the platform allows for *global* inter-processor migration – a job may begin execution on any processor, and a preempted job may resume execution on the same processor as, or a different processor from, the one it had been executing on prior to preemption. (However, each task may have at most one job executing on at most one processor at each instant in time.)

2.3 Deadline Monotonic Scheduling

Priority-driven scheduling algorithms operate as follows: at each instant in time they assign a priority to each job that is awaiting execution, and choose for execution the jobs with the greatest priority. The **Deadline Monotonic** (DM) scheduling algorithm [3] is a priority-driven scheduling algorithm that assigns priority to jobs according to the relative-deadline parameter of the task that generates them: the smaller the relative deadline, the greater the priority.

---

[1] Or its deadline has elapsed, in which case the system is deemed to have failed.

Recall that we are assuming that tasks are indexed in order of non-decreasing deadlines; henceforth, we assume that DM assigns jobs of τ_i priority over jobs of τ_{i+1}, for all i.

2.4   Processor Speedup Bounds

With respect to a given platform, a given sporadic task system is said to be *feasible* if there exists a schedule meeting all deadlines, for every collection of jobs that may be generated by the task system. A given sporadic task system is said to be *(global)* DM *schedulable* if DM meets all deadlines for every collection of jobs that may be generated by the task system. While every DM-schedulable task system is trivially feasible, it is known that not all feasible task systems are DM-schedulable. A *schedulability test* for DM scheduling accepts as input the specifications of a sporadic task system and an identical multiprocessor platform, and determines whether the system is DM-schedulable upon the platform. Such a test is *exact* if is correctly identifies all DM-schedulable systems, and *sufficient* if it identifies some, but not necessarily all, DM-schedulable systems (however, it must not incorrectly declare some non DM-schedulable system to be DM-schedulable).

Processor speedup bounds are one metric that may be used for quantifying the quality of sufficient schedulability tests. A sufficient schedulability test is said to have a processor speedup bound of c if

- Any task system deemed schedulable by the test is guaranteed to actually be so; and
- For any task system that is not deemed schedulable by the test, it is the case that the task system is actually not schedulable upon a platform in which each processor is $\frac{1}{c}$ times as fast.

Intuitively speaking, a processor speedup bound of c for a sufficient schedulability test implies that the inexactness of the test penalizes its user by at most a speedup factor of c when compared to an exact test. The smaller the processor speedup bound, the better the sufficient schedulability test: a processor speedup bound of 1 would mean that the test is in fact an exact one.

2.5   Related Work

The Deadline Monotonic scheduling algorithm has been widely studied in the context of uniprocessor systems (see, e.g., [7,8,9,4]), and is arguably one of the most widely-used real-time scheduling algorithms. However, not much research has been done on global DM scheduling upon multiprocessor platforms. Baker [10] and Bertogna et al. [11] have presented, and evaluated via simulation, sufficient schedulability tests for multiprocessor global DM that are essentially formulae involving the parameters of all the tasks in the system under consideration. Our own recent research [12,13] has attempted to obtain speedup bounds for DM; however, our results thus far only apply to constrained-deadline sporadic task system. To our knowledge, this paper contains the first non-trivial speedup bounds for global DM of arbitrary-deadline sporadic task systems.

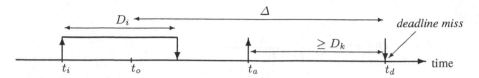

Fig. 1. Notation. A job of task τ_k arrives at t_a. Task τ_k is is not active immediately prior to t_a, and is continually active over $[t_a, t_d)$.

3 A DM **Schedulability Test**

In this section, we derive (Theorem 1) a DM-schedulability test for arbitrary sporadic task systems.

Consider any legal sequence of job requests of task system τ, on which DM misses a deadline. Suppose that a job J_k of task τ_k is the one to first miss a deadline, and that this deadline miss occurs at time-instant t_d (see Figure 1).

Discard from the legal sequence of job requests all jobs of tasks with priority lower than τ_k's, and consider the DM schedule of the remaining (legal) sequence of job requests. Since lower-priority jobs have no effect on the scheduling of greater-priority ones under preemptive DM, it follows that a deadline miss of τ_k occurs at time-instant t_d (and this is the earliest deadline miss), in this new DM schedule. We will focus henceforth on this new DM schedule.

Let t_a denote the earliest time-instant prior to t_d, such that τ_k is continuously active[2] over the interval $[t_a, t_d]$. It must be the case that t_a is the arrival time of some job of τ_k since τ_k is, by definition, not active just prior to t_a and becomes active at t_a.

It must also be the case that $t_a \leq t_d - D_k$. This follows from the observation that the job of τ_k that misses its deadline at t_d arrives at $t_d - D_k$. If $D_k < T_k$, then t_a is equal to this arrival time of the job of τ_i that misses its deadline at t_d. If $D_k \geq T_k$, however, t_k may be the arrival-time of an earlier job of τ_k.

Let $\mathcal{C}$ denote the cumulative execution requirement of all jobs of τ_k that arrive $\geq t_a$, and have deadline $\leq t_d$. By definition of DBF and Lemma 1, we have

$$\mathcal{C} \leq \mathrm{DBF}(\tau_k, t_d - t_a) \leq \delta_k \times (t_d - t_a) \, . \tag{1}$$

We now introduce some notation: for any time-instant $t \leq t_a$,

– let $W(t)$ denote the total amount that all jobs, other than those generated by task τ_k that arrive $\geq t_a$, and have deadline $\leq t_d$, execute over the interval $[t, t_d)$ in this new DM schedule, plus $\mathcal{C}$. (Informally, $W(t)$ denotes the amount of work that DM needs –but fails– to execute over $[t, t_d)$.)

– Let $\Omega(t)$ denote $W(t)$ normalized by the interval-length: $\Omega(t) \overset{\mathrm{def}}{=} W(t)/(t_d - t)$.

Since jobs of τ_k receive strictly less than $\mathcal{C}$ units of execution over $[t_a, t_d)$, all m processors must be executing jobs of tasks other than τ_k for a total duration greater than $(t_d - t_a - \mathcal{C})$ over this interval. Hence it must be the case that

$$W(t_a) > (t_d - t_a - \mathcal{C})m + \mathcal{C}$$

---

[2] See Definition 4 to recall the definition of an active task.

i.e.,

$$\Omega(t_a) > \frac{(t_d - t_a - C)m + C}{t_d - t_a}$$

$$= m - (m - 1)\frac{C}{t_d - t_a}$$

$$\geq m - (m - 1)\frac{(\delta_k \times (t_d - t_a))}{t_d - t_a} \quad \text{(By Equation 1)}$$

$$= m - (m - 1)\delta_k$$

Let

$$\mu_k \stackrel{\text{def}}{=} m - (m - 1)\delta_k \tag{2}$$

Let t_o denote the smallest value of $t \leq t_a$ such that $\Omega(t) \geq \mu_k$. Let $\Delta \stackrel{\text{def}}{=} t_d - t_o$ (see Figure 1).

Now the work that needs to be done by DM over $[t_o, t_d)$ (which we denote as $W(t_o)$) arises from two sources: those jobs that arrive at or after t_o, and those that arrive prior to t_o but have not completed execution in the DM schedule by time-instant t_o. We will refer to jobs arriving prior to t_o that need execution over $[t_o, t_d)$ as **carry-in jobs.** (The job of τ_i arriving at time-instant t_i in Figure 1 is an example of a carry-in job, provided it is still active at time-instant t_o.)

For *constrained* sporadic task systems — those in which $D_i \leq T_i (\forall i)$ — a bound can be obtained on the number of carry-in jobs. Unfortunately, extending this bound directly to arbitrary-deadline sporadic task systems yields a bound that is too pessimistic to be useful. However, similar reasoning can be applied to bound the number of distinct <u>tasks</u> contributing carry-in jobs (although each such task may contribute multiple carry-in jobs).

Lemma 2. *The number of tasks that have carry-in jobs is bounded from above by* $\lceil \mu_k \rceil - 1$.

Proof: Let ϵ denote an arbitrarily small positive number. By definition of the instant t_o, $\Omega(t_o - \epsilon) < \mu_k$ while $\Omega(t_o) \geq \mu_k$; consequently, strictly fewer than μ_k jobs must have been executing at time-instant t_o. And since $\mu_k \leq m$ (as can be seen from Equation 2 above), it follows that some processor was idled over $[t_o - \epsilon, t_o)$, implying that all tasks with jobs awaiting execution at this instant would have been executing. This allows us to conclude that there are strictly fewer than μ_k – equivalently, at most $(\lceil \mu_k \rceil - 1)$ – tasks with carry-in jobs. □

Lemma 3. *The total remaining execution requirement of all the carry-in jobs of each task τ_i (that has carry-in jobs at time-instant t_o) is* $< \Delta \times \delta_{\max}(k)$.

Proof: Let us consider some task τ_i that has carry-in jobs. By definition of carry-in jobs, it must be the case that τ_i is active at time-instant t_o. Let $t_i < t_o$ denote the earliest time-instant such that τ_i is active throughout the interval $[t_i, t_o]$. Observe that t_i is necessarily the arrival time of some job of τ_i. If $D_i < T_i$, then t_i is the arrival time of the (sole) carry-in job of τ_i, as illustrated in Figure 1. If $D_i \geq T_i$, however, t_i may be the arrival-time of a job that is not a carry-in job — see Figure 2.

Let $\phi_i \stackrel{\text{def}}{=} t_o - t_i$ (see Figure 1). All the carry-in jobs of τ_i have their arrival-times and their deadlines within the $(\phi_i + \Delta)$-sized interval $[t_i, t_o)$, and consequently their cumulative execution requirement is $\leq \text{DBF}(\tau_i, \phi_i + \Delta)$; in what follows, we will quantify how much of this must have been completed prior to t_o (and hence cannot contribute to the carry-in). We thus obtain an upper bound on the total work that all the carry-in jobs of τ_i contribute to $W(t_o)$, as the difference between $\text{DBF}(\tau_i, \phi_i + \Delta)$ and the amount of execution received by τ_i over $[t_i, t_o)$.

By definition of t_o as the earliest time-instant $t \leq t_a$ at which $\Omega(t) \geq \mu_k$, it must be the case that $\Omega(t_i) < \mu_k$. That is,

$$W(t_i) < \mu_k(\Delta + \phi_i) \tag{3}$$

On the other hand, $\Omega(t_o) \geq \mu_k$, meaning that

$$W(t_o) \geq \mu_k \Delta \tag{4}$$

From Inequalities 3 and 4 and the definition of $W(\cdot)$, it follows that the amount of work done in the EDF schedule over $[t_i, t_o)$ is <u>less than</u> $\mu_k \phi_i$. Let y_i denote the amount of time over this interval $[t_i, t_o)$, during which some job of τ_i is executing. All m processors must be executing jobs from tasks other than τ_i for the remaining $(\phi_i - y_i)$ time units, implying that the total amount of work done in the DM schedule over $[t_i, t_o)$ is <u>at least</u> $m(\phi_i - y_i) + y_i$. From these upper and lower bounds, we have

$$\begin{aligned}
m(\phi_i - y_i) + y_i &< \mu_k \phi_i \\
\equiv m\phi_i - (m-1)y_i &< (m - (m-1)\delta_k)\phi_i \\
\Rightarrow m\phi_i - (m-1)y_i &< (m - (m-1)\delta_{\max}(k))\phi_i \\
\equiv y_i &> \phi_i \delta_{\max}(k) \tag{5}
\end{aligned}$$

As argued above, the total amount of work contributed to $W(t_o)$ by all the carry-in jobs of τ_i is bounded from above by $\text{DBF}(\tau_i, \phi_i + \Delta)$ minus the amount of execution received by jobs of τ_i over $[t_i, t_o)$. This is bounded from above by

$$\begin{aligned}
&\text{DBF}(\tau_i, \phi_i + \Delta) - y_i \\
&< \text{DBF}(\tau_i, \phi_i + \Delta) - \phi_i \, \delta_{\max}(k) \text{ (by Inequality 5 above)} \\
&\leq (\phi_i + \Delta)\delta_i - \phi_i \, \delta_{\max}(k) \text{ (from Lemma 1)} \\
&\leq (\phi_i + \Delta)\delta_{\max}(k) - \phi_i \, \delta_{\max}(k) \\
&= \Delta \, \delta_{\max}(k)
\end{aligned}$$

as claimed in the lemma.   □

A pointed out previously, $W(t_o)$ — the amount of work that the DM schedule needs (but fails) to execute over $[t_o, t_d)$ — arises from two sources: the carry-in jobs, and those jobs that arrived at or after t_o.

- First, consider the work contributed by the carry-in jobs: by Lemmas 2 and 3, there are at most $(\lceil \mu_k \rceil - 1)$ distinct tasks with carry-in jobs, with the total carry-in work for all the jobs of each task bounded from above by $\Delta \, \delta_{\max}(k)$ units of work. Therefore their total contribution to $W(t_o)$ is bounded from above by $(\lceil \mu_k \rceil - 1)\Delta \, \delta_{\max}(k)$.

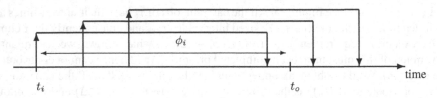

Fig. 2. Example: defining t_i for a task τ_i with $D_i \geq T_i$. Three jobs of τ_i are shown. Task τ_i is not active prior to the arrival of the first of these 3 jobs, and the first job completes execution only after the next job arrives. This second job does not complete execution prior to t_o. Thus, the task is continuously active after the arrival of the first job shown, and t_i is hence set equal to the arrival time of this job.

- All other jobs that contribute to $W(t_o)$ arrive within the Δ-sized interval $[t_o, t_d)$, and hence have their deadlines within $[t_o, t_d + D_k)$, since their relative deadlines are all $\leq D_k$. Their total execution requirement is therefore bounded from above by $(\Delta + D_k) \times \text{LOAD}(k)$.

Considering both sources together, we obtain the following bound on $W(t_o)$:

$$W(t_o) \leq (\Delta + D_k)\text{LOAD}(k) + (\lceil \mu_k \rceil - 1)\Delta\, \delta_{\max}(k) \tag{6}$$

Since, by the definition of t_o, it is required that $\Omega(t_o)$ be at least as large as μ, we must have

$$\left(1 + \frac{D_k}{\Delta}\right)\text{LOAD}(k) + (\lceil \mu_k \rceil - 1)\delta_{\max}(k) \geq \mu_k$$

as a necessary condition for DM to miss a deadline; equivalently, the negation of this condition is sufficient to ensure DM-schedulability:

$$\left(1 + \frac{D_k}{\Delta}\right)\text{LOAD}(k) + (\lceil \mu_k \rceil - 1)\delta_{\max}(k) < \mu_k$$
$$\Leftarrow \text{ (since } D_k \leq \Delta)$$
$$2\,\text{LOAD}(k) + (\lceil \mu_k \rceil - 1)\delta_{\max}(k) \leq \mu_k$$

This immediately yields the following sufficient schedulability condition for global DM:

Theorem 1. *Sporadic task system τ is global-DM schedulable upon a platform comprised of m unit-capacity processors, provided that for all k, $1 \leq k \leq n$,*

$$2\,\text{LOAD}(k) + (\lceil \mu_k \rceil - 1)\delta_{\max}(k) < \mu_k , \tag{7}$$

where μ_k is as defined in Equation 2 above: $\mu_k = m - (m-1)\delta_k$. □

4   A Processor Speedup Bound

Theorem 1 can be used to determine whether any sporadic task system is DM-schedulable upon a platform of m unit-capacity processors. To our knowledge, this is the first DM-schedulability test that is applicable to arbitrary-deadline sporadic task systems. In this section, we obtain a processor speedup bound for this DM-schedulability test. Our approach is as follows. We will identify (Lemma 5) the smallest value of $x \leq 1$ for which we can prove that *any sporadic task system not deemed* DM-*schedulable upon m speed-1 processors by the test of Theorem 1 is infeasible upon m speed-x processors.* By taking the contra-positive, we may conclude that $\frac{1}{x}$ is a processor speedup bound for the test of Theorem 1.

We first obtain the following corollary to Theorem 1:

Corollary 1. *Sporadic task system τ is global-DM schedulable upon a platform comprised of m unit-capacity processors, provided that for all k, $1 \leq k \leq n$,*

$$\text{LOAD}(k) \leq \frac{1}{2}(m - (m-1)\delta_k)(1 - \delta_{\max}(k)) \tag{8}$$

Proof: From Theorem 1, we know that τ_k meets its deadline provided for all k, $1 \leq k \leq n$,

$$2\,\text{LOAD}(k) + (\lceil \mu_k \rceil - 1)\delta_{\max}(k) \leq \mu_k$$
$$\equiv \text{LOAD}(k) \leq \frac{\mu_k - (\lceil \mu_k \rceil - 1)\delta_{\max}(k)}{2}$$
$$\Leftarrow \text{Since } \lceil \mu_k \rceil - 1 < \mu_k$$
$$\text{LOAD}(k) \leq \frac{1}{2}\,\mu_k\,(1 - \delta_{\max}(k))$$
$$\equiv \text{LOAD}(k) \leq \frac{1}{2}(m - (m-1)\delta_k)(1 - \delta_{\max}(k))$$

which is as claimed in the corollary.   □

We are almost ready to obtain a processor speedup bound. But first, we need another technical lemma.

Lemma 4. *Any sporadic task system τ that is feasible upon a multiprocessor platform comprised of m speed-x processors must satisfy*

$$\delta_{\max}(k) \leq x \text{ and } \text{LOAD}(k) \leq mx \tag{9}$$

for all k, $1 \leq k \leq n$.

Proof Sketch: Suppose that task system τ is feasible upon m speed-x processors. To prove that $\delta_{\max}(k) \leq x$, consider each task τ_i separately:

– In order to be able to meet all deadlines of τ_i if τ_i generates jobs exactly T_i time units apart, it is necessary that $C_i/T_i \leq x$.
– Since any individual job of τ_i can receive at most $D_i \times x$ units of exccution by its deadline, we must have $C_i \leq D_i \times x$; i.e., $C_i/D_i \leq x$.

Putting both conditions together, we get $(C_i/\min(T_i, D_i)) \leq x$. Taken over all the tasks $\tau_1, \tau_2, \ldots, \tau_k$, this observation yields the condition that $\delta_{\max}(k) \leq x$.

Since any individual job of τ_i can receive at most $D_i \times x$ units of execution by its deadline, we must have $C_i \leq D_i \times x$; i.e., $C_i/D_i \leq x$. Taken over all tasks in τ, this observation yields the first condition.

To prove that LOAD(k) $\leq mx$, recall the definition of LOAD(k) from Section 1. Let t' denote some value of t which defines LOAD(k):

$$t' \overset{\text{def}}{=} \arg\max_{t>0} \left(\frac{\sum_{i=1}^{k} \text{DBF}(\tau_i, t)}{t} \right).$$

Suppose that all tasks in $\{\tau_1, \tau_2, \ldots, \tau_k\}$ generate a job at time-instant zero, and each task τ_i generates subsequent jobs exactly T_i time-units apart. The total amount of execution that is available over the interval $[0, t')$ on this platform is equal to mxt'; hence, it is necessary that LOAD(k) $\leq mx$ if all deadlines are to be met.   □

Using Corollary 1 and Lemma 4, we obtain below a bound on the processor speedup that is sufficient in order for the test of Theorem 1 to identify DM-schedulability:

Lemma 5. *Any sporadic task system that is feasible upon a multiprocessor platform comprised of m speed-x processors platform is determined to be global-DM schedulable on m unit-capacity processors by the DM-schedulability test of Theorem 1, provided*

$$x \leq \frac{(4m - 1) - \sqrt{12m^2 - 8m + 1}}{2(m - 1)} \tag{10}$$

Proof: Suppose that τ is feasible upon a platform comprised of m speed-x processors. From Lemma 4, it must be the case that LOAD(k) $\leq mx$ and $\delta_{\max}(k) \leq x$ for all k. For τ to be determined to be DM-schedulable upon m unit-capacity processors by the test of Theorem 1, it follows from Corollary 1 that it is sufficient that for all k, $1 \leq k \leq n$:

$$\text{LOAD}(k) \leq \frac{1}{2}(m - (m - 1)\delta_k)(1 - \delta_{\max}(k))$$

$$\Leftarrow mx \leq \frac{1}{2}(m - (m - 1)x)(1 - x)$$

$$\equiv (m - 1)x^2 - (4m - 1)x + m \geq 0$$

Solving for x using standard techniques for the solution of quadratic inequalities yields Equation 10.   □

Lemma 5 bounds from above the values of x such that task systems feasible on speed-x processors are correctly identified as being DM-schedulable by the test of Theorem 1. From the definition of processor speedup (Section 2.4), it can be seen that the processor speedup bound for the schedulability test of Theorem 1 is obtained by taking the multiplicative inverse of this x:

Theorem 2. *The DM-schedulability test of Theorem 1 has a processor speedup bound of*

$$\frac{2(m - 1)}{(4m - 1) - \sqrt{12m^2 - 8m + 1}} \tag{11}$$

□

Equation 11 expresses the processor speedup bound as a function of the number of processors m in the platform. The computed values for selected example values of m are

Table 1. The processor speedup bound as a function of m

m:	3	4	5	10	20	30	50	100	1000
speedup:	2.246	2.595	2.812	3.261	3.494	3.572	3.636	3.684	3.727

listed in Table 1 above. As seen from this table, the bound increases with increasing m, apparently approaching some upper bound as m becomes very large. Standard algebraic techniques may be used to show that it is indeed the case that the bound of Equation 11 increases with increasing m, asymptotically approaching $(2 + \sqrt{3})$ as $m \to \infty$:

Corollary 2. *The* DM-*schedulability test of Theorem 1 has a processor speedup bound of* $(2 + \sqrt{3})$ *(≈ 3.73).* $\square$

Discussion. It is known that global DM is not an optimal scheduling algorithm upon uni- or multi-processors, in the sense that there are feasible arbitrary-deadline sporadic task systems upon which DM misses deadlines. It is also easy to show that the schedulability test of Theorem 1 is not an exact one, in that there are DM-schedulable systems that this test fails to correctly identify as being so. The significance of the processor speedup result in Corollary 2 lies in what it tells us about the "goodness" of the conjunction of global DM and our schedulability test: in essence, it is asserting that a processor speedup of $(2 + \sqrt{3})$ compensates for *both* the non-optimality of global DM *and* the inexactness of our schedulability test.

5 Conclusions

We have derived a new sufficient schedulability test for determining whether a given sporadic task system is DM-schedulable upon a preemptive multiprocessor platform, when global inter-processor migration is permitted. To our knowledge, this is the first non-trivial DM schedulability test that may be be applied to the analysis of arbitrary-deadline sporadic task systems.

We have also obtained a processor speedup bound for our test. This speedup bound of $(2 + \sqrt{3}) \approx 3.73$ tells us that any arbitrary-deadline sporadic task system that is feasible upon a multiprocessor platform is correctly identified by our test as being DM-schedulable upon a platform in which each processor is 3.73 times as fast.

References

1. Mok, A.K.: Fundamental Design Problems of Distributed Systems for The Hard-Real-Time Environment. PhD thesis, Laboratory for Computer Science, Massachusetts Institute of Technology (1983), Available as Technical Report No. MIT/LCS/TR-297
2. Baruah, S., Mok, A., Rosier, L.: Preemptively scheduling hard-real-time sporadic tasks on one processor. In: Proceedings of the 11th Real-Time Systems Symposium, Orlando, Florida, pp. 182–190. IEEE Computer Society Press, Los Alamitos (1990)

3. Leung, J., Whitehead, J.: On the complexity of fixed-priority scheduling of periodic, real-time tasks. Performance Evaluation 2, 237–250 (1982)
4. Buttazzo, G.C.: Hard Real-Time Computing Systems: Predictable Scheduling Algorithms and Applications, Second edn. (2005)
5. Baker, T.P., Fisher, N., Baruah, S.: Algorithms for determining the load of a sporadic task system. Technical Report TR-051201, Department of Computer Science, Florida State University (2005)
6. Fisher, N., Baker, T., Baruah, S.: Algorithms for determining the demand-based load of a sporadic task system. In: Proceedings of the International Conference on Real-time Computing Systems and Applications, Sydney, Australia, IEEE Computer Society Press, Los Alamitos (2006)
7. Klein, M., Ralya, T., Pollak, B., Obenza, R., Harbour, M.G.: A Practitioner's Handbook for Real-Time Analysis: Guide to Rate Monotonic Analysis for Real-Time Systems. Kluwer Academic Publishers, Boston (1993)
8. Audsley, N.C., Burns, A., Davis, R.I., Tindell, K.W., Wellings, A.J.: Fixed priority preemptive scheduling: An historical perspective. Real-Time Systems 8, 173–198 (1995)
9. Sha, L., Abdelzaher, T., Årzén, K.E., Cervin, A., Baker, T., Burns, A., Buttazzo, G., Caccamo, M., Lehoczky, J., Mok, A.K.: Real-time scheduling theory: A historical perspective. Real-Time Systems: The International Journal of Time-Critical Computing 28(2–3), 101–155 (2004)
10. Baker, T.P.: An analysis of fixed-priority schedulability on a multiprocessor. Real-Time Systems: The International Journal of Time-Critical Computing 32(1–2), 49–71 (2006)
11. Bertogna, M., Cirinei, M., Lipari, G.: New schedulability tests for real-time tasks sets scheduled by deadline monotonic on multiprocessors. In: Proceedings of the 9th International Conference on Principles of Distributed Systems, Pisa, Italy, IEEE Computer Society Press, Los Alamitos (2005)
12. Fisher, N., Baruah, S.: Global static-priority scheduling of sporadic task systems on multiprocessor platforms. In: Proceeding of the IASTED International Conference on Parallel and Distributed Computing and Systems, Dallas, TX, IASTED (November 2006)
13. Baruah, S.: Schedulability analysis of global deadline-monotonic scheduling (submission, 2007)

LFTHREADS: A Lock-Free Thread Library

Anders Gidenstam[1] and Marina Papatriantafilou[2]

[1] Algorithms and Complexity, Max-Planck-Institut für Informatik,
66123 Saarbrcken, Germany
andersg@mpi-inf.mpg.de
[2] Computer Science and Engineering, Chalmers University of Technology,
SE-412 96 Göteborg, Sweden
ptrianta@cs.chalmers.se

Abstract. LFTHREADS is a thread library entirely based on lock-free methods, i.e. no spin-locks or similar synchronization mechanisms are employed in the implementation of the multithreading. Since lock-freedom is highly desirable in multiprocessors/multicores due to its advantages in parallelism, fault-tolerance, convoy-avoidance and more, there is an increased demand in lock-free methods in parallel applications, hence also in multiprocessor/multicore system services. This is why a lock-free multithreading library is important. To the best of our knowledge LFTHREADS is the first thread library that provides a lock-free implementation of blocking synchronization primitives for application threads. Lock-free implementation of objects with blocking semantics may sound like a contradicting goal. However, such objects have benefits: e.g. library operations that block and unblock threads on the same synchronization object can make progress in parallel while maintaining the desired thread-level semantics and without having to wait for any "slow" operations among them. Besides, as no spin-locks or similar synchronization mechanisms are employed, processors are always able to do useful work. As a consequence, applications, too, can enjoy enhanced parallelism and fault-tolerance. The synchronization in LFTHREADS is achieved by a new method, which we call *responsibility hand-off* (RHO), that does not need any special kernel support.

Keywords: lock-free, multithreading, multiprocessors, multicores, synchronization, shared memory.

1 Introduction

Multiprogramming and threading allow the processor(s) to be shared efficiently by several sequential threads of control. This paper studies synchronization algorithms for realizing standard thread-library operations and objects (create, exit, yield and mutexes) based entirely on *lock-free* methods. Lock-freedom implies that no spin-locks or similar locking synchronization is used in the implementation of the operations/objects and guarantees that in a sct of concurrent operations at least one of them makes progress when there is interference and thus operations eventually completes.

The rationale in LFTHREADS is that processors should always be able to do useful work when there are runnable threads available, regardless of what other processors do;

E. Tovar, P. Tsigas, and H. Fouchal (Eds.): OPODIS 2007, LNCS 4878, pp. 217–231, 2007.

i.e. despite other processors simultaneously accessing shared objects related with the implementation of the LFTHREADS-library operations and/or suffering stop failures or delays (e.g. from I/O or page-fault interrupts).

Even a lock-free thread library needs to provide blocking synchronization objects, e.g. for mutual exclusion in legacy applications and for other applications where threads might need to be blocked, e.g. to interact with some external device. Our new synchronization method in LFTHREADS implements a mutual exclusion object with the standard blocking semantics for application threads but *without enforcing mutual exclusion among the processors* executing the threads.We consider this an important part of the contribution in this paper. It enables library operations blocking and unblocking threads on the same synchronization object to make progress in parallel, while maintaining the desired thread-level semantics, without having to wait for any "slow" operation among them to complete. This is achieved via a new synchronization method, which we call *responsibility hand-off* (RHO), which may also be useful in lock-free synchronization constructions in general. Roughly speaking, the RHO method handles cases where processors need to perform sequences of atomic actions on a shared object in a consistent and lock-free manner, for example a combination of (i) checking the state of a mutex, (ii) blocking if needed by saving the current thread state and (iii) enqueuing the blocked thread on the waiting queue of the mutex; or a combination of (i) changing the state of the mutex to unlocked and (ii) activating a blocked process if there is any. "Traditional" ways to do the same use locks and are therefore vulnerable to processors failing or being delayed, which the RHO method is not. The method is lock-free and manages thread execution contexts without needing special kernel or scheduler support.

Related and motivating work. A special kernel-level mechanism, called *scheduler activations*, has been proposed and studied [1,2], to enable user-level threads to offer the functionality of kernel-level threads with respect to blocking and also leave no processor idle in the presence of ready threads, which is also LFTHREADS's goal. It was observed that application-controlled blocking and interprocess communication can be resolved at user-level without modifications to the kernel while achieving the same goals as above, but multiprogramming demands and general blocking, such as for page-faults, seem to need scheduler activations. The RHO method and LFTHREADS complement these results, as they provide thread synchronization operation implementations that do not block each other unless the application blocks within the same level (i.e. user- or kernel-level). LFTHREADS can be combined with scheduler activations for a hybrid thread implementation with minimal blocking.

To make the implementation of blocking mutual exclusion more efficient, operating systems that implement threads at the kernel level may split the implementation of the mutual exclusion primitives between the kernel and user-level. This is done in e.g. Linux [3] and Sun Solaris [4]. This division allows the cases where threads do not need to be blocked or unblocked, to be handled at the user-level without invoking a system call and often in a non-blocking way by using hardware synchronization primitives. However, when the calling thread should block or when it needs to unblock some other thread, an expensive system call must be performed. Such system calls contain, in all cases we are aware of, critical sections protected by spin locks.

Although our present implementation of LFTHREADS is entirely at the user-level, its algorithms are also suited for use in a kernel - user-level divided setting. With our method a significant benefit would be that there is no need for spin locks and/or disabling interrupts in either the user-level or the kernel-level part.

Further research motivated by the goal to keep processors busy doing useful work and to deal with preemptions in this context includes: mechanisms to provide some form of control on the kernel/scheduler to avoid unwanted preemption (cf. e.g. [5,6]) or the use of some application-related information (e.g. from real-time systems) to recover from it [7]; [8] and subsequent results inspired by it focus on scheduling with work-stealing, as a method to keep processors busy by providing fast and concurrent access to the set of ready threads; [9] aims at a similar direction, proposing thread scheduling that does not require locking (essentially using lock-free queuing) in a multithreading library called Lesser Bear; [10] studied methods of scheduling to reduce the amount of spinning in multithreaded mutual exclusion; [11] focuses on demands in real-time and embedded systems and studies methods for efficient, low-overhead semaphores; [12] gives an insightful overview of recent methods for mutual exclusion.

There has been other work at the operating system kernel level [13,14,15,16], where basic kernel data structures have been replaced with lock-free ones with both performance and quality benefits. There are also extensive interest and results on lock-free methods for memory management (garbage collection and memory allocation, e.g. [17,18,19,20,21,22]).

The goal of LFTHREADS is to implement a common thread library interface, including operations with blocking semantics, in a lock-free manner. It is possible to combine LFTHREADS with lock-free and other non-blocking implementations of shared objects, such as the NOBLE library [23] or software transactional memory constructions (cf. e.g. [24,25]).

2 Preliminaries

System model. The system consists of a set of processors, each having its own local memory as well as being connected to a shared memory through an interconnect network. Each processor executes instructions sequentially at an arbitrary rate. The shared memory might not be uniform, that is, for each processor the latency to access some part of the memory is not necessarily the same as the latency for any other processor to access that part. The shared memory supports atomic read and write operations of any single memory word, and also stronger single-word synchronization primitives, such as Compare-And-Swap (CAS) and Fetch-And-Add (FAA) used in the algorithms in this paper. These primitives are either available or can easily be derived from other available primitives [26,27] on contemporary microprocessor architectures.

Lock-free synchronization. *Lock-freedom* [28] is a type of non-blocking synchronization that guarantees that in a set of concurrent operations at least one of them makes progress each time operations interfere and thus some eventually completes. Other types of non-blocking synchronization are wait-freedom and obstruction-freedom. The correctness condition for atomic non-blocking operations is *linearizability* [29]. An execution is *linearizable* if it guarantees that even when operations overlap in time, each of them appears to take effect at an atomic time instant that lies within its respective time duration, such that the effect of each operation is consistent with the effect of its corresponding operation in a sequential execution in which the operations appear in the same order.

Non-blocking synchronization is attractive as it offers advantages over lock-based synchronization, w.r.t. priority inversion, deadlocks, lock convoys and fault tolerance. It has also been shown, using well-known parallel applications, that *lock-free* methods imply at least as good performance as lock-based ones in several applications, and often significantly better [30,31]. Wait-free algorithms, as they provide stronger progress guarantees, are inherently more complex and more expensive than lock-free ones. Obstruction freedom implies weak progress guarantees and can be used e.g. for reference purposes, for studying parallelization.

In LFTHREADS the focus is on *lock-free synchronization* due to its combined benefits in progress, fault-tolerance and efficiency potential.

The problem and LFTHREADS**'s API.** The LFTHREADS library defines the following procedures for thread handling[1]:
create(thread,main): creates a new thread which starts in the procedure main; *exit*: terminates the calling thread and if this was the last thread of the application/process the latter is terminated as well;
yield: causes the calling thread to be put on the ready queue and the (virtual) processor that running it to pick a new thread to run from the ready queue.

For blocking mutual exclusion-based synchronization between threads LFTHREADS provides a mutex object supporting the operations:
lock(mutex): attempts to lock the mutex. If it is locked already the calling thread is blocked and enqueued on the waiting queue of the mutex;
unlock(mutex): unlocks the mutex if there are no waiting threads in the waiting queue, otherwise the first of the waiting threads is made runnable and becomes the owner of the mutex (only the thread owning the mutex may call *unlock*);
trylock(mutex): tries to lock the mutex. Returns true on success, otherwise false.

3   Detailed Description of the LFTHREADS Library

3.1   Data Structures and Fundamental Operations

We assume a data type, context_t, that can store the CPU context of an execution (i.e. thread) and some operations to manipulate such contexts (cf. Fig. 1). These operations, available in many operating systems[2], are:
(i) *save*(ctx) stores the state of the current CPU context in the supplied variable and switches the processor to a special system context. There is one such context for each processor. The return value from *save* is true when the context is stored and false when the context is restored.

---

[1] The interface we present here was chosen for brevity and simplicity. Our actual implementation aims to provide a POSIX threads compliant (IEEE POSIX 1003.1c) interface.

[2] In systems supporting the Single Unix Specification v2 (*SUSv2*), e.g. GNU/Linux, getcontext(2), setcontext(2) and makecontext(3) can be used; in other Unix systems setjump(3) and longjmp(3) or similar.

type context_t **is** record ⟨implementation defined⟩;
function save(ctx : **out** context_t): **boolean**;
/* Saves the current CPU context and switches to a
 * system context. The call returns **true** when
 * the context is saved; **false** when it is restored. */
procedure restore(ctx : **in** context_t);
/* Replaces the current CPU context with a
 * previously stored CPU context.
 * The current context is destroyed. */
procedure make_context(ctx : **out** context_t;
        main : **in pointer to** procedure);
/* Creates a new CPU context which will wakeup
 * in a call to the procedure main when restored. */

type thread_t **is** record
    uc : context_t;

type lf_queue_t **is** record ⟨implementation defined⟩;
procedure enqueue(q : **in out** lf_queue_t;
        thread : **in pointer to** thread_t);
/* Appends the TCB thread to q. */
function dequeue(q : **in out** lf_queue_t;
        thread : **out pointer to** thread_t): **boolean**;
/* If the queue is not empty the first thread_t pointer
 * in the queue is dequeued and **true** is returned.
 * Returns **false** if the queue is empty. */
function is_empty(q : **in out** lf_queue_t): **boolean**;
/* Returns **true** if q is empty, **false** otherwise. */

function get_cpu_id(): **cpu_id_t**
/* Returns the ID of the current CPU (an int). */

/* Global shared variables. */
Ready_Queue : lf_queue_t;

/* Private per-processor persistent
 * variables. */
Current$_p$: **pointer to** thread_t;

/* Local temporary variables. */
next : **pointer to** thread_t;
old_count : **integer**;
old : **cpu_id_t**;

procedure create(thread : **out** thread_t;
        main : **in pointer to** procedure)
C1 make_context(thread.uc, main);
C2 enqueue(Ready_Queue, thread);

procedure yield()
Y1 **if not** is_empty(Ready_Queue) **then**
Y2   **if** save(Current$_p$.uc) **then**
Y3   enqueue(Ready_Queue, Current$_p$);
Y4   cpu_schedule();

procedure exit()
E1 cpu_schedule();

procedure cpu_schedule()
Cl1 **loop**
Cl2   **if** dequeue(Ready_Queue, Current$_p$)
        then
Cl3   restore(Current$_p$.uc);

Fig. 1. The basic thread operations and shared data in LFTHREADS

(ii) *restore*(ctx) loads the supplied stored CPU context onto the processor. The restored context resumes execution in the (old) call to *save*, returning false. The CPU context that made the call to *restore* is lost (unless it was saved before).

(iii) *make_context*(ctx,main) creates a new CPU context. The new context starts in a call to the procedure main when it is loaded onto a processor with *restore*.

Each thread in the system will be represented by a thread control block (TCB) of type thread_t, containing a context_t field for storing the thread's state when it is not being executed on one of the processors.

Further, we assume we have a lock-free queue data structure (like e.g. [32]) for pointers to thread control blocks; the queue supports three lock-free and linearizable operations: *enqueue*, *dequeue* and *is_empty* (each with its intuitive semantics). The lock-free queue data structure is used as a building block in the implementation of LFTHREADS. However, as we will see in detail below, additional synchronization methods are needed to make operations involving more than one queue instance lock-free and linearizable.

3.2   Thread Operations in LFTHREADS

The general thread operations and variables used are shown in Fig. 1. The variables consist of the global shared Ready_Queue[3], which contains all runnable threads not

---

[3] The Ready_Queue here is a lock-free queue, but e.g. work-stealing [8] could be used.

currently being executed by any processor, and the per-processor persistent variable Current, which contains a pointer to the TCB of the thread currently being executed on that processor.

In addition to the public thread operations *create*, *exit* and *yield*, introduced above, there is an internal operation, *cpu_schedule*, used for selecting the next thread to load onto the processor. If there are no threads available in the Ready_Queue, the processor is idle and waits for a runnable thread to appear.

3.3   Blocking Thread Synchronization and the RHO Method

To facilitate blocking synchronization among application threads, LFTHREADS provides a mutex primitive, mutex_t. While the operations on a mutex, *lock*, *trylock* and *unlock* have their usual semantics for application threads, they are lock-free with respect to the processors in the system. This implies improved fault-tolerance properties against stop and timing faults in the system compared to traditional spin-lock-based implementations, since even if a processor is stopped or delayed in the middle of a mutex operation all other processors are still able to continue performing operations, *even on the same mutex*. However, note that an application thread trying to lock a mutex is blocked if the mutex is locked by another thread. A faulty application can also dead-lock its threads. It is the responsibility of the application developer to prevent such situations.[4]

Mutex operations in LFTHREADS.   The mutex_t structure (cf. Fig. 2) consists of three fields: (i) an integer counter, which counts the number of threads that are in or want to enter the critical section protected by the mutex; (ii) a lock-free queue, where the TCBs of blocked threads that want to lock the mutex is stored; and (iii) a hand-off flag, whose role and use will be described in detail below.

The operations on the mutex_t structure are shown in Fig. 2. In rough terms, the *lock* operation locks the mutex and makes the calling thread its owner. If the mutex is already locked the calling thread is blocked and the processor switches to another thread. The blocked thread's context will be activated and executed later when the mutex is released by its previous owner.

In the ordinary case a blocked thread is activated by the thread releasing the mutex by invoking *unlock*, but due to fine-grained synchronization, it may also happen in other ways. In particular, note that checking whether the mutex is locked and entering the mutex waiting queue are distinct atomic operations. Therefore, the interleaving of thread-steps can e.g. cause a thread A to find the mutex locked, but later by the time it has entered the mutex queue the mutex has been released, hence A should not remain blocked in the waiting queue. The "traditional" way to avoid this problem is to ensure that at most one processor modifies the mutex state at a time by enforcing mutual exclusion among the processors, e.g. by using a spin-lock. In the lock-free solution proposed here, the synchronization required for such cases is managed with a new method, which

---

[4] I.e. here lock-free synchronization guarantees deadlock-avoidance among the operations implemented in lock-free manner, but an *application* that uses objects with blocking semantics (e.g. mutex) of course needs to take care to avoid deadlocks due to *inappropriate use* of the blocking operations by its threads.

we call the *responsibility hand-off* (RHO) method. In particular, the thread/processor releasing the mutex is able, using appropriate fine-grained synchronization steps, to detect whether such a situation may have occurred and, in response, "hand-off" the ownership (or responsibility) for the mutex to some other processor.

By performing a *responsibility hand-off*, the processor executing the *unlock* can finish this operation and continue executing threads without waiting for the concurrent *lock* operation to finish (and vice versa). As a result, the mutex primitive in LFTHREADS tolerates arbitrary delays and even stop failures inside mutex operations without affecting the other processors' ability to do useful work, including operations on the same mutex. The details of the *responsibility hand-off* method are given in the description of the operations, below:

The lock operation: Line L1 atomically increases the count of threads that want to access the mutex using Fetch-And-Add. If the old value was 0 the mutex was free and is now locked by the thread. Otherwise the mutex is likely to be locked and the current thread has to block. Line L3 stores the context of the current thread in its TCB and line L4 enqueues the TCB on the mutex's waiting queue. From now on, this invocation of *lock* is not associated with any thread.

However, the processor cannot just leave and do something else yet, because the thread that owned the mutex might have unlocked it (since line L1); this is checked by line L6 to L8. If the token read from m.hand-off is not null then an *unlock* has tried to unlock the mutex but found (line U2) that although there is a thread waiting to lock the mutex, it has not yet appeared in the waiting queue (line H2). Therefore, the *unlock* has set the hand-off flag (line H5). However, it is possible that the hand-off flag was set after the thread enqueued by this *lock* (at line L4) had been serviced. Therefore, this processor should only attempt to take responsibility of the mutex if there is a thread available in the waiting queue. This is ensured by the *is_empty* test at line L7 and the CAS at line L8 which only succeeds if no other processor has taken responsibility of the mutex since line L6. If the CAS at line L8 succeeds, *lock* is now responsible for the mutex again and must find the thread wanting to lock the mutex. That thread (it might not be the same as the one enqueued by this *lock*) is dequeued from the waiting queue and this processor will proceed to execute it (line L9-L10). If the conditions at line L7 are not met or the CAS at line L8 is unsuccessful, the mutex is busy and the processor can safely leave to do other work (line L11).

To avoid ABA-problems (i.e. cases where CAS succeeds because the variable has been modified from its old value A to some value B and back to A) m.hand-off should, in addition to the processor id, include a per-processor sequence number. This is a well-known method in the literature, easy to implement and has been excluded from the presented code to make the presentation clearer.

The trylock operation: The operation will lock the mutex and return true if the mutex was unlocked. Otherwise it does nothing and returns false. The operation tries to lock the mutex by increasing the waiting count on line TL1. This will only succeed if the mutex was unlocked and there were no ongoing *lock* operations. If there are ongoing *lock* operations or some thread has locked the mutex, *trylock* will attempt to acquire the hand-off flag. If the *trylock* operation succeeds in acquiring the hand-off flag it becomes the owner of the mutex and increases the waiting count at line TL3 before returning true. Otherwise *trylock* returns false.

The unlock operation: If there are no waiting threads *unlock* unlocks the mutex. Otherwise one of the waiting threads is made owner of the mutex and enqueued on the Ready_Queue. The operation begins by decreasing the waiting count at line U1, which was increased by this thread's call to *lock* or *trylock*. If the count becomes 0, there are no waiting threads and the *unlock* operation is done. Otherwise, there are at least one thread wanting to acquire the mutex and the *do_hand-off* procedure is used to either find the thread or hand-off the responsibility for the mutex. If the waiting thread has been enqueued in the waiting queue, it is dequeued (line H2) and moved to the Ready_Queue (line H3) which completes the *unlock* operation. Otherwise, a *responsibility hand-off* is initiated to get rid of the responsibility for the mutex (line H5):

- The responsibility hand-off is successful and terminates if: (i) the waiting queue is still empty at line H6; in that case either the offending thread has not yet been enqueued there (in which case, it has not yet checked for hand-offs) or it has in fact already been dequeued (in which case, some other processor took responsibility for the mutex); or if (ii) the attempt to retake the hand-off flag at line H8 fails, in which case, some other processor has taken responsibility for the mutex. After a successful hand-off the processor leaves the *unlock* procedure (line H7 and H9).
- If the hand-off is unsuccessful, i.e. the CAS at line H8 succeeds, the processor is again responsible for the mutex and must repeat the hand-off procedure. Note that when a hand-off is unsuccessful, at least one other concurrent *lock* operation made progress, namely by completing an enqueue on the waiting queue (otherwise this *unlock* would have completed at lines H6-H7). Note further that since the CAS at line H8 succeeded, none of the concurrent *lock* operations have executed line L6-L8 since the hand-off began.

Fault-tolerance. Regarding *processor failures*, the procedures enable the highest achievable level of fault-tolerance for a mutex. Note that even though a *processor failure* while the *unlock* is moving a thread from the m.waiting queue to the Ready_Queue (between line H2 and H3) could cause the loss of two threads (i.e. the current one and the one being moved), the system behaviour in this case is indistinguishable from the case when the processor fails before line H2. In both cases the thread owning the mutex has failed before releasing ownership. At all other points a *processor failure* can cause the loss of at most one thread.

4   Correctness of the Synchronization in LFTHREADS

To prove the correctness of the thread library we need to show that the mutex primitive has the desired semantics. We will first show that the mutex operations are lock-free and linearizable with respect to the processors and then that the lock-free mutex implementation satisfies the conditions for mutual exclusion with respect to the application threads. First we (i) define some notation that will facilitate the presentation of the arguments and (ii) establish some lemmas that will be used later to prove the safety,

```
type mutex_t is record
    waiting : lf_queue_t;
    count : integer := 0;
    hand-off : cpu_id_t := null;

procedure lock(m : in out mutex_t)
L1  old_count := FAA(&m.count, 1);
L2  if old_count ≠ 0 then
        /* The mutex was locked.
        * Help or run another thread. */
L3      if save(Current_p.uc) then
L4          enqueue(m.waiting, Current_p);
L5          Current_p := null;
            /* The thread is now blocked. */
L6          old := m.hand-off;
L7          if old ≠ null and
            not is_empty(m.waiting) then
L8              if CAS(&m.hand-off, old, null)
                then /* We now own m; */
                /* ... run a blocked thread */
L9                  dequeue(m.waiting, Current_p);
L10                 restore(Current_p); /* Done. */
L11             cpu_schedule(); /* Done. */

function trylock(m : in out mutex_t): boolean
TL1 if CAS(&m.count, 0, 1) then return true;
TL2 else if GrabToken(&m.hand-off) then
TL3     FAA(&m.count, 1);
TL4     return true;
TL5 return false;
```

```
procedure unlock(m : in out mutex_t)
U1  old_count := FAA(&m.count, −1);
U2  if old_count ≠ 1 then
        /* There is a waiting thread. */
U3      do_hand-off(m);

procedure do_hand-off(m : in out mutex_t)
H1  loop /* We own the mutex. */
H2      if dequeue(m.waiting, next) then
H3          enqueue(Ready_Queue, next);
H4          return; /* Done. */
        else
            /* The waiting thread isn't ready! */
H5          m.hand-off := get_cpu_id();
H6          if is_empty(m.waiting) then
                /* Some concurrent operation will
                * see/or has seen the hand-off. */
H7              return; /* Done. */
H8          if not CAS(&m.hand-off,
                get_cpu_id(), null) then
                /* Some concurrent operation
                * acquired the mutex. */
H9              return; /* Done. */

function GrabToken(loc : pointer to cpu_id_t)
    : boolean
GT1 old := *loc;
GT2 if old = null then return false;
GT3 return CAS(loc, old, null);
```

Fig. 2. The lock-free mutex protocol in LFTHREADS

liveness, fairness and atomicity properties of the algorithm. Due to space constraints the full proofs can be found in [33].

Definition 1. *A thread's call to a blocking operation Op is said to be* completed *when the processor executing the call leaves the blocked thread and goes on to do something else (e.g. executing another thread). The call is said to have* returned *when the thread (after becoming unblocked) continues its execution from the point of the call to Op.*

Definition 2. *A mutex m is* locked *when* **m.count** > 0 *and* **m.hand-off** = null. *Otherwise it is* unlocked.

Definition 3. *When a thread τ's call to* lock *on a mutex m returns we say that thread τ has* locked *or acquired the mutex m. Similarly, we say that thread τ has* locked *or acquired the mutex m when the thread's call to* trylock *on the mutex m returns* True. *Further, when a thread τ has acquired a mutex m by a* lock *or successful* trylock *operation and not yet released it by calling* unlock *we say that the thread τ is the* owner *of the mutex m (or that τ owns m).*

Lock-freedom. The lock-free property of the thread library operations will be established with respect to the processors. An operation is lock-free if it is guaranteed to complete in a bounded number of steps unless it is interfered with an unbounded number of times by other operations and every time operations interfere, at least one of them is guaranteed to make progress towards completion.

Theorem 1. *The mutex operations lock, trylock and unlock are all lock-free.*

The lock-freedom of *trylock* and *unlock* with respect to application threads follows from their lock-freedom with respect to the processors, as they do not contain context switches. The operation *lock* is neither non-blocking nor lock-free for application threads, since a call to *lock* on a locked mutex should block.

Linearizability. Linearizability guarantees that the result of any concurrent execution of operations is identical to a sequential execution where each operation takes effect atomically at a single point in time (its *linearization point*) within its duration in the original concurrent execution.

Theorem 2. *The mutex operations lock, trylock and unlock are linearizable.*

Mutual exclusion properties. The mutual exclusion properties of the new mutex protocol are established with respect to application threads.

Theorem 3 (Safety). *For any mutex m and at any time t there is at most one thread τ such that τ is the owner of m at time t.*

Theorem 4 (Liveness I). *A thread τ waiting to acquire a mutex m eventually acquires the mutex once its lock operation has enqueued τ on the m.waiting queue.*

Theorem 5 (Liveness II). *A thread τ wanting to acquire a mutex m can only be starved if there is an unbounded number of lock operations on m performed by threads on other processors.*

Theorem 6 (Fairness). *A thread τ wanting to acquire a mutex m only has to wait for the threads enqueued on the m.waiting queue before τ was enqueued.*

5 Experimental Study

The primary contribution of this work is to enhance qualitative properties of thread library operations, such as the tolerance to delays and processor failures. However, since lock-freedom may also imply performance/scalability benefits with increasing number of processors, we also wanted to observe this aspect. We made an implementation of the mutex object and the thread operations on the GNU/Linux operating system. The implementation is written in the C programming language and was done entirely at the user-level using "cloned"[5] processes as *virtual processors* for running the threads. The implementation uses the lock-free queue in [32] for the mutex waiting queue and the Ready_Queue. To ensure sufficient memory consistency for synchronization variables, memory barriers surround all CAS and FAA instructions and the writes at lines L6 and H5. The lock-based mutex implementation uses a test and test-and-set spin-lock

---

[5] "Cloned" processes share the same address space, file descriptor table and signal handlers etc and are also the basis of Linux's native pthread implementation.

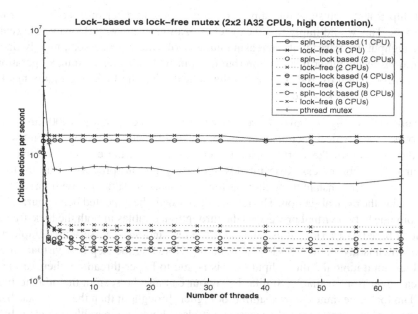

Fig. 3. Mutex performance in LFTHREADS and pthreads at high contention

to protect the mutex state. Unlike the use of spin-locks in an OS kernel, where usually neither preemptions nor interrupts are allowed while holding a spin-lock, our virtual processors can be interrupted by the OS kernel due to such events. This behaviour matches the asynchronous processors in our system model.

The experiments were run on a PC with two Intel Xeon 2.80GHz processors (acting as 4 due to hyper-threading) using the GNU/Linux operating system with kernel version 2.6.9. The microbenchmark used for the experimental evaluation consists of a single critical section protected by a mutex and a set of threads that each try to enter the critical section a fixed number of times. The contention level on the mutex was controlled by changing the amount of work done outside the critical section. We evaluated the following configurations experimentally:

- The lock-free mutex using the protocol presented in this paper, using 1, 2, 4 and 8 virtual processors to run the threads.
- The spin-lock based mutex, using 1, 2, 4 and 8 virtual processors.
- The platform's standard pthreads library and a standard pthread mutex. The pthreads library on GNU/Linux use kernel-level "cloned" processes as threads, which are scheduled on all available processors, i.e. the pthreads are at the same level as the virtual processors in LFTHREADS. The difference in scheduling makes it difficult to interpret the pthreads results with respect to the others; i.e. the pthreads results are primarily for reference.

Each configuration was run 10 times; the diagrams present the mean.

High contention. Fig. 3 shows the results when no work is done outside the critical section, i.e. the contention on the mutex is high. The desired result here is that throughput for an implementation stays the same regardless of the number of threads or (virtual) processors. This would imply that the synchronization scales well. However, in reality the throughput decreases with increasing number of virtual processors, mainly due to preemptions inside the critical section (but for spin-locks also inside mutex operations) and synchronization overhead. The results indicate that the lock-free mutex has less overhead than the lock-based.

Low contention. Fig. 4 shows the results when the threads perform 1000 times more work outside the critical section than inside, making the contention on the mutex low. With the majority of the work outside the critical section, the expected behaviour is a linear throughput increase over threads until all (physical) processors are in use by threads, thereafter constant throughput as the processors are saturated with threads running outside the critical section. The results agrees with the expected behaviour; we see that from one to two virtual processors the throughput doubles in both the lock-free and spin-lock based cases. (Recall that the latter is a test-and-test-and-set-based implementation, which is favoured under low contention). Note that the step to 4 virtual processors does not double the throughput — this is due to hyper-threading, there are not 4 physical processors available. Similar behaviour can also be seen in the pthread-based case. The lock-free mutex shows similar or higher throughput than the spin-lock-based for the same number of virtual processors; it also shows comparable and even better performance than the pthread-based when the number of threads is large and there are more virtual processors than physical.

Summarizing, we observe that LFTHREADS's lock-free mutex protocol implies comparable or better throughput than the lock-(test-and-test-and-set-)based implementation, both in high- and in low-contention scenario for the same number of virtual processors,

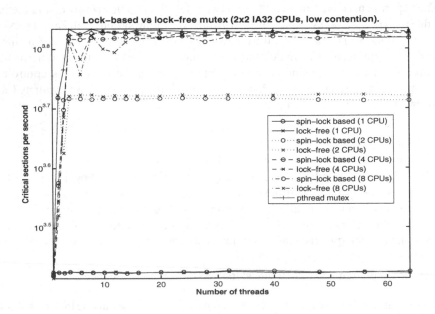

Fig. 4. Mutex performance in LFTHREADS and pthreads at low contention

besides offering the qualitative advantages in tolerance against slow, delayed or crashed threads, as discussed earlier in the paper.

6 Conclusion

This paper presented the LFTHREADS library and the responsibility hand-off (RHO) method. Besides supporting a thread-library interface with lock-free implementation of a blocking synchronization primitive and fault-tolerance properties, the RHO method can be regarded as a conceptual contribution, which can be useful in lock-free synchronization in general.

The present implementation of LFTHREADS is done entirely at the user-level, but the algorithms are well suited for use also in a kernel - user-level divided setting. A significant benefit of the new method there is that neither modifications to the operating system kernel nor spin-locks and/or disabling of interrupts are needed in the user-level or the kernel-level part. LFTHREADS constitutes a proof-of-concept of lock-free implementation of the blocking mutex introduced in the paper and serves as basis for an experimental study of its performance. The experimental study performed here, using a mutex-intensive microbenchmark, shows positive figures. Moreover, the implementation can also serve as basis for further development, for porting the library to other multiprocessors and experimenting with parallel applications such as the Spark98 matrix kernels or the SPLASH-2 suite.

Acknowledgements. We thank the anonymous reviewers for useful comments.

References

1. Anderson, T., Bershad, B., Lazowska, E., Levy, H.: Scheduler Activations: Effective Kernel Support for the User-Level Management of Parallelism. In: ACM Trans. on Computer Systems, pp. 53–79. ACM Press, New York (1992)
2. Feeley, M.J., Chase, J.S., Lazowska, E.D.: User-level threads and interprocess communication. Technical Report TR-93-02-03, University of Washington, Department of Computer Science and Engineering (1993)
3. Franke, H., Russell, R., Kirkwood, M.: Fuss, futexes and furwocks: Fast userlevel locking in linux. In: Proc. of the Ottawa Linux Symp, pp. 479–494 (2002)
4. Multithreading in the solaris operating environment. Technical report, Sun Microsystems
5. Kontothanassis, L.I., Wisniewski, R.W., Scott, M.L.: Scheduler-conscious synchronization. ACM Trans. Computer Systems 15(1), 3–40 (1997), doi:10.1145/244764.244765
6. Holman, P., Anderson, J.H.: Locking under pfair scheduling. ACM Trans. Computer Systems 24(2), 140–174 (2006)
7. Devi, U.C., Leontyev, H., Anderson, J.H.: Efficient synchronization under global edf scheduling on multiprocessors. In: Proc. of the 18th Euromicro Conf. on Real-Time Systems, pp. 75–84. IEEE Computer Society, Los Alamitos (2006)
8. Blumofe, R.D., Leiserson, C.E.: Scheduling multithreaded computations by work stealing, In: Proc. of the 35th Annual Symp. on Foundations of Computer Science (FOCS), 356–368 (1994)

9. Oguma, H., Nakayama, Y.: A scheduling mechanism for lock-free operation of a lightweight process library for SMP computers. In: Proc. of the 8th Int. Conf. on Parallel and Distributed Systems (ICPADS), 235–242 (2001)
10. Zahorjan, J., Lazowska, E.D., Eager, D.L.: The effect of scheduling discipline on spin overhead in shared memory parallel processors. IEEE Trans. on Parallel and Distributed Systems 2(2), 180–198 (1991)
11. Zuberi, K.M., Shin, K.G.: An efficient semaphore implementation scheme for small-memory embedded systems. In: Proc. of the 3rd IEEE Real-Time Technology and Applications Symp (RTAS), IEEE, pp. 25–37. IEEE Computer Society Press, Los Alamitos (1997)
12. Anderson, J.H., Kim, Y.J., Herman, T.: Shared-memory mutual exclusion: major research trends since 1986. Distributed Computing 16(2-3), 75–110 (2003)
13. Massalin, H., Pu, C.: A lock-free multiprocessor OS kernel. Technical Report CUCS-005-91 (1991)
14. Massalin, H.: Synthesis: An Efficient Implementation of Fundamental Operating System Services. PhD thesis, Columbia University (1992)
15. Greenwald, M., Cheriton, D.R.: The synergy between non-blocking synchronization and operating system structure. In: Operating Systems Design and Implementation, 123–136 (1996)
16. Greenwald, M.B.: Non-blocking synchronization and system design. PhD thesis, Stanford University (1999)
17. Valois, J.D.: Lock-free linked lists using compare-and-swap. In: Proc. of the 14th ACM Symp. on Principles of Distributed Computing (PODC), ACM, pp. 214–222. ACM Press, New York (1995)
18. Michael, M.M., Scott, M.L.: Correction of a memory management method for lock-free data structures. Technical Report TR599, University of Rochester, Computer Science Department (1995)
19. Michael, M.: Scalable lock-free dynamic memory allocation. In: Proc. of SIGPLAN 2004 Conf. on Programming Languages Design and Implementation, ACM Press, ACM SIG-PLAN Notices (2004)
20. Gidenstam, A., Papatriantafilou, M., Sundell, H., Tsigas, P.: Practical and efficient lock-free garbage collection based on reference counting. In: Proc. of the 8th Int. Symp. on Parallel Architectures, Algorithms, and Networks (I-SPAN), pp. 202–207. IEEE Computer Society Press, Los Alamitos (2005)
21. Gidenstam, A., Papatriantafilou, M., Tsigas, P.: Allocating memory in a lock-free manner. In: Proc. of the 13th Annual European Symp. on Algorithms (ESA), pp. 242–329. Springer, Heidelberg (2005)
22. Herlihy, M., Luchangco, V., Martin, P., Moir, M.: Nonblocking memory management support for dynamic-sized data structures. ACM Trans. on Computer Systems 23(2), 146–196 (2005)
23. Sundell, H., Tsigas, P.: NOBLE: A non-blocking inter-process communication library. In: Sundell, H., Tsigas, P. (eds.) Proc. of the 6th Workshop on Languages, Compilers and Runtime Systems for Scalable Computers, Springer, Heidelberg (2002)
24. Marathe, V.J.I.W.N.S., Scott, M.L: Adaptive software transactional memory. In: Proc. of the 19th Int. Conf. on Distributed Systems (DISC), Springer, pp. 354–368. Springer, Heidelberg (2005)
25. Shavit, N., Touitou, D.: Software transactional memory. In: Proc. of the 14th ACM Symp. on Principles of Distributed Computing (PODC), pp. 204–213. ACM Press, New York (1995)
26. Jayanti, P.: A complete and constant time wait-free implementation of CAS from LL/SC and vice versa. In: Proc. of the 12th Int. Symp. on Distributed Computing (DISC), pp. 216–230. Springer, Heidelberg (1998)

27. Moir, M.: Practical implementations of non-blocking synchronization primitives. In: Proc. of the 16th annual ACM Symp. on Principles of Distributed Computing, pp. 219–228. ACM Press, New York (1997), citeseer.ist.psu.edu/moir97practical.html
28. Herlihy, M.: A methodology for implementing highly concurrent data objects. ACM Trans. on Programming Languages and Systems 15(5), 745–770 (1993)
29. Herlihy, M.P., Wing, J.M.: Linearizability: A correctness condition for concurrent objects. ACM Trans. on Programming Languages and Systems 12(3), 463–492 (1990), http://www.acm.org/pubs/toc/Abstracts/0164-0925/78972.html
30. Sundell, H.: Efficient and Practical Non-Blocking Data Structures. PhD thesis, Chalmers University of Technology (2004)
31. Tsigas, P., Zhang, Y.: Evaluating the performance of non-blocking synchronisation on shared-memory multiprocessors. In: Proc. of the ACM SIGMETRICS 2001/Performance 2001, pp. 320–321. ACM Press, New York (2001)
32. Tsigas, P., Zhang, Y.: A simple, fast and scalable non-blocking concurrent fifo queue for shared memory multiprocessor systems. In: Proc. 13th ACM Symp. on Parallel Algorithms and Architectures, pp. 134–143. ACM Press, New York (2001)
33. Gidenstam, A., Papatriantafilou, M.: LFthreads: A lock-free thread library. Technical Report MPI-I-2007-1-003, Max-Planck-Institut für Informatik, Algorithms and Complexity (2007)

Making Distributed Applications Robust*

Chi Ho[1], Danny Dolev[2], and Robbert van Renesse[1]

[1] Dept. of Computer Science
Cornell University, Ithaca, NY
{chho,rvr}@cs.cornell.edu
[2] School of Engineering and Computer Science
The Hebrew University of Jerusalem, Israel
dolev@cs.huji.ac.il

Abstract. We present a novel translation of systems that are tolerant of crash failures to systems that are tolerant of Byzantine failures in an asynchronous environment, making weaker assumptions than previous approaches. In particular, we assume little about how the application is coded. The translation exploits an extension of the Srikanth-Toueg protocol, supporting ordering in addition to authentication and persistent delivery. We illustrate the approach by synthesizing a version of the Castro and Liskov Practical Byzantine Replication protocol from the Oki and Liskov Viewstamped Replication protocol.

Keywords: Byzantine Fault Tolerance, Ordered Broadcast.

1 Introduction

Developing applications that span multiple administrative domains is difficult if the environment is asynchronous and machines may exhibit arbitrary failures. Yet, this is a problem that many software developers face today. While we know how to build replicated data stores that tolerate Byzantine behavior (*e.g.*, [4]), most applications go well beyond providing a data store. Tools like Byzantine consensus may help developing such applications, but most software developers find dealing with arbitrary failures extremely challenging. They often make simplifying assumptions like a crash failure model, relying on careful monitoring to detect and fix problems that occur when such assumptions are violated.

We are interested in techniques that automatically transform crash-tolerant applications into Byzantine-tolerant applications that do not require careful monitoring and repair.

This paper makes the following contributions. First we present a novel ordered broadcast protocol that we will use as a building block. The protocol is an extension of the Srikanth and Toueg authenticated broadcast protocol often used in Byzantine consensus protocols [11], adding consistent ordering for messages from the same sender

---

* This work is supported by AFOSR grants FA9550-07-1-0304, FA8750-06-2-0060, FA9550-06-1-0019, FA9550-06-1-0244, the National Science Foundation under grant 0424422, and ISF, ISOC, and CCR. Any opinions expressed in this publications are those of the authors and do not necessarily reflect the views of the funding agencies.

E. Tovar, P. Tsigas, and H. Fouchal (Eds.): OPODIS 2007, LNCS 4878, pp. 232–246, 2007.
© Springer-Verlag Berlin Heidelberg 2007

even in the face of Byzantine behavior. Second, we present a new way of translating a distributed application that is tolerant of crash failures into one that tolerates the same number of Byzantine failures, while imposing fewer restrictions on how the application is constructed than previous approaches. Third, we show how a version of the Castro and Liskov Practical Byzantine Replication protocol [4] can be derived from the Oki and Liskov Viewstamped Replication protocol [10] using our translation technique, something not possible with previous approaches.

We present background in Sect. 2. After describing a system model in Sect. 3, we introduce three mechanisms used for translation: Authenticated Reliable broadcast (Sect. 4), Ordered Authenticast Reliable broadcast (Sect. 5), and the translation mechanism itself (Sect. 6). Correctness proofs for these appear in the appendix. In Sect. 7 we demonstrate the translation mechanism.

2 Background

The idea of automatically translating crash-tolerant systems into Byzantine systems can be traced back to the mid-eighties. Gabriel Bracha used a translation similar to ours to generate a consensus protocol tolerant of t Byzantine failures out of $3t + 1$ hosts [3]. Brian Coan also presents a translation [6] that is similar to Bracha's. The most important restriction in these approaches is that input protocols are required to have a specific style of execution, and in particular they have to be round-based with each participant awaiting the receipt of $n - t$ messages before starting a new round. These requirements exclude, for example, protocols that designate roles to senders and receivers such as the primary role used in Viewstamped Replication [10]. Our approach makes no such assumptions, and we will demonstrate our approach for Viewstamped Replication.

Toueg, Neiger and Bazzi worked on an extension of Bracha's and Coan's approaches for translation of synchronous systems [9,2,1]. Their approach takes advantage of synchrony to detect faulty hosts and eliminate them from the protocol. The extension can be applied to our scheme as well.

Most recently, Mpoeleng et al. [8] present a translation that is intended for synchronous systems, and transforms Byzantine faults to so-called *signal-on-failure* faults. They replace each host with a pair, and assume only one of the hosts in each pair may fail. They require $4t + 2$ hosts, but the system may break with as few as two failures no matter how large t is chosen.

3 System Model

In order to be precise we present a simple model to talk about machines, processes, and networks. The model consists of *agents* and *links*. An agent is an active entity that maintains state, receives messages on incoming links, performs some processing based on this input and its state, possibly updating its state and producing output messages on outgoing links.

Links are abstract unidirectional FIFO channels between two agents. Agents can interact across links only. In particular, an agent can *enqueue* a message on one of its outgoing links, and it can *dequeue* messages from one of its incoming links (assuming a message is available there).

We use agents and links to model various activities and interactions. Processes that run on hosts are agents, but the network is also an agent—one that forwards messages from its incoming links to its outgoing links according to some policy. Agents are named by lower-case Greek letters $\alpha, \beta, \ldots$. For agents that are processes, we will use subscripts on names to denote which hosts they run on. For example, β_i is an agent that runs on host h_i.

Hosts are containers for agents, and they are also the unit of failure. Hosts are either *honest*, executing programs as specified, or *Byzantine* [7], exhibiting arbitrary behavior. We also use the terms *correct* and *faulty*, but not as alternatives to honest and Byzantine. A correct host is honest and always eventually makes progress. A faulty host is a Byzantine host or an honest host that has crashed or will eventually crash. Honest and Byzantine are mutually exclusive, as are correct and faulty. However, a host can be both honest and faulty.

We do not assume timing bounds on execution of agents. Latency in the network is modeled as execution delay in a network agent. Note that this prevents hosts from accurately detecting crashes of other hosts.

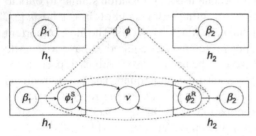

Fig. 1. An agent model and a refinement

Figure 1 depicts an example of an agent model and a *refinement*. Agents are represented by circles, links by arrows, and hosts by rectangles. The top half models two application agents β_1 and β_2 running on two hosts h_1 and h_2 communicating using a FIFO network agent ϕ. The bottom half refines the FIFO network using an unreliable network agent ν and two protocol agents ϕ_1^s and ϕ_2^R that implement ordering and retransmission using sequence numbers, timers, and acknowledgment messages. This kind of refinement will be a common theme throughout this paper.

4   The ARcast Mechanism

The first mechanism we present is Authenticated Reliable broadcast (ARcast). This broadcast mechanism was suggested by Srikanth and Toueg, and they present an implementation that does not require digital signatures in [11]. Their implementation requires $n > 3t$. As shown below, it is also possible to develop an implementation that uses digital signatures, in which case n only has to be larger than $2t$.

4.1   ARcast Definition

Assume $\beta_i, \ldots$ are agents communicating using ARcast on hosts $h_i, \ldots$. Then ARcast provides the following properties:

1. *bc-Persistence.* If two hosts h_i and h_j are correct, and β_i sends a message m, then β_j delivers m from β_i;

2. *bc-Relay.* If h_i is honest and h_j is correct, and β_i delivers m from β_k, then β_j delivers m from β_k (host h_k is not necessarily correct);
3. *bc-Authenticity.* If two hosts h_i and h_j are honest and β_i does not send m, then β_j does not deliver m from β_i.

Informally, ARcast ensures that a message is reliably delivered to all correct receivers in case the sender is correct (bc-Persistence) or in case another honest receiver has delivered the message already (bc-Relay). Moreover, a Byzantine host cannot forge messages from an honest host (bc-Authenticity).

4.2   ARcast Implementation

x We assume there is a single sender β_i on h_i. We model ARcast as a network agent ξ_i, which we refine by replacing it with the following agents (see Fig. 2):

ξ_i^s *sender* agent that is in charge of the sending side of the ARcast mechanism;
ξ_*^R *receiver* agents that are in charge of the receive side;
ϕ *FIFO network* agent that provides point-to-point authenticated FIFO communication between agents.

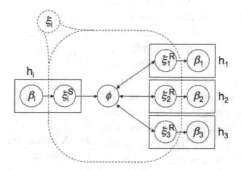

Fig. 2. Architecture of the ARcast implementation if the sender is on host h_i

The mechanism has to be instantiated for each sender. The sending host h_i runs the ARcast sender agent ξ_i^s. Each receiving host h_j runs a *receiver* agent ξ_j^R. There have to be at least $2t + 1$ receiving hosts, one of which may be h_i. When ξ_i^s wants to ARcast a message m, it sends $\langle \text{echo } m, i \rangle_i$, signed by h_i using its public key signature, to all receivers. A receiver that receives such an echo message for the first time forwards it to all receivers. On receipt of $t+1$ of these correctly signed echoes for the same m from different receivers (it can count an echo from itself), a receiver delivers m from i.

Due to space considerations, we omit the (simple) correctness proof.

5   The OARcast Mechanism

ARcast does not provide any ordering. Even messages from a correct sender may be delivered in different orders at different receivers. Next we introduce a broadcast mechanism that is like ARcast, but adds delivery order for messages sent by either honest or Byzantine hosts.

5.1   OARcast Definition

OARcast provides, in addition to the ARcast properties, the following:

4. *bc-FIFO*. If two hosts h_i and h_j are honest and β_i sends m_1 before m_2, and β_j delivers m_1 and m_2 from β_i, then β_j delivers m_1 before m_2;
5. *bc-Ordering*. If two hosts h_i and h_j are honest and β_i and β_j both deliver m_1 from β_k and m_2 from β_k, then they do so in the same order (even if h_k is Byzantine).

As a result of bc-Ordering, even a Byzantine sender cannot cause two honest receivers to deliver OARcast messages from the same source out of order. bc-FIFO ensures that messages from honest hosts are delivered in the order sent. OARcast does not guarantee any order among messages from different sources, and is thus weaker than consensus.

5.2   OARcast Implementation

We describe how OAR-cast may be implemented using ARcast. Again, we show the implementation for a single sender β_i on host h_i. With multiple senders, the implementation has to be instantiated for each sender separately. We refine the OARcast network agent ω_i by replacing it with the following agents (see Fig. 3):

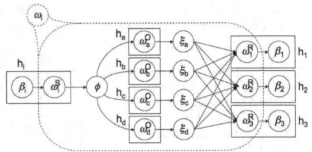

Fig. 3. Architecture of the OARcast implementation if the sender is on host h_i

ω_i^S *sender* agent that is in charge of the sending side of the OARcast mechanism;
ω_*^O *orderer* agents that are in charge of ordering;
ω_*^R *receiver* agents that are in charge of the receive side;
ϕ *FIFO network* agent that provides point-to-point authenticated FIFO communication from the sender agent to each orderer agent;
ξ_* *ARcast network* agents each provides ARcast from a particular orderer agent to all receiver agents.

We need to run $3t + 1$ orderers on separate hosts, of which no more than t may fail. A host may end up running a sender, a receiver, as well as an orderer. A receiver ω_j^R maintains a sequence number c_j, initially 0. An orderer ω_k^O also maintains a sequence number, t_k, initially 0.

To OARcast a message m, ω_i^S sends m to each orderer via ϕ. When an orderer ω_k^O receives m from ω_i^S, it ARcasts $\langle order\ m, t_k, i \rangle$ to each of the receivers, and increments t_k. A receiver ω_j^R awaits $2t + 1$ messages $\langle order\ m, c_j, i \rangle$ from different orderers before delivering m from ω_i^S. After doing so, the receiver increments c_j.

We prove the correctness of this implementation in Appendix A.

6   The Translation Mechanism

In this section, we describe how an *arbitrary* protocol tolerant only of crash failures can be translated into a protocol that tolerates Byzantine failures.

6.1 Definition

Below we use the terms *original* and *translated* to distinguish the system before and after translation, respectively. The original system tolerates only crash failures, while the translated system tolerates Byzantine failures as well. The original system consists of n hosts, each of which runs an *actor agent*, $\alpha_1, \ldots, \alpha_n$. Each actor α_i is a state machine that maintains a running state s^i, initially s_0^i, and, upon receiving an input message m, executes a deterministic *state transition function* F^i: $(\overline{m_o}, s_{c+1}^i) := F^i(m, s_c^i)$ where

- c indicates the number of messages that α_i has processed so far;
- s_c^i is the state of α_i before processing m;
- s_{c+1}^i is the next state of s_c^i as a result of processing m (called $F^i(m, s_c^i)$.next);
- $\overline{m_o}$ is a finite, possibly empty set of output messages (called $F^i(m, s_c^i)$.output).

The state transition functions process one input message at a time and may have no computational time bound.

Actors in the original system communicate via a FIFO network agent ϕ. Each actor maintains a pair of input-output links with the FIFO network agent. When an actor α_i wants to send a message m to another actor α_j (may be itself), α_i formats m (detailed below) and enqueues it on α_i's output link. We call this action α_i *sends m to α_j*. ϕ dequeues m from the link and places it into the message buffer that ϕ maintains. Eventually ϕ removes m from its buffer and enqueues m on the input link of α_j. When α_j dequeues m we say that α_j *delivers m from α_i*. The original system assumes the following of the network:

1. *α-Persistence.* If two hosts h_i and h_j are correct and α_i sends m to α_j, then α_j delivers m from α_i.
2. *α-Authenticity.* If two hosts h_i and h_j are honest and α_i does not send m to α_j, then α_j does not deliver m from α_i.
3. *α-FIFO.* If two hosts h_i and h_j are honest and α_i sends m_1 before m_2, and α_j delivers m_1 and m_2 from α_i, then α_j delivers m_1 before m_2;

Note that in the original system all hosts are honest. However, for the translation we need to be able to generalize these properties to include Byzantine hosts.

Messages in the original system are categorized as internal or external. *Internal messages* are sent between actors and are formatted as $\langle d, i, j \rangle$, where d is the data (or payload), i indicates the source actor, and j indicates the destination actor. *External messages* are from clients to actors and are formatted as $\langle d, \bot, j \rangle$, similar to the format of internal messages except the source actor is empty ($\bot$). Internal and external messages are in general called α-*messages*, or simply *messages* when the context is clear.

In the original system all actors produce output messages by making transitions based on input as specified by the protocol. We call such output messages *valid*. We formalize validity below.

External messages are assumed to be valid. For example, we may require that clients sign messages. An internal message m sent by actor α_i is valid if and only if there exists a sequence of valid messages $m_1^i, \ldots, m_c^i$ delivered by α_i such that $m \in F^i(m_c^i, F^i(m_{c-1}^i, F^i(\ldots, F^i(m_1^i, s_0^i).\text{next} \ldots).\text{next}).\text{next}).\text{output}$. The

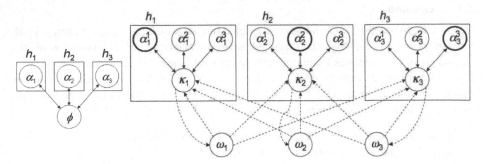

Fig. 4. Translation: the original system (left) is simulated at each host in the translated system (right). Dark circles are master actors. Dashed lines represent OARcast communication.

expression means that actor α_i sends m after it has processed the first c input messages, be they internal or external. Note that external input forms the base case for this recursive definition, as actors produce no internal messages until at least one delivers an external message.[1]

In order for the original system to work correctly, each actor needs to make transitions based on valid input. More formally,

4. *α-Validity.* If h_i is honest and α_i delivers m from α_j, then m is valid.

The property is granted to the original system by default, because it is in an environment where faulty hosts follow the protocol faithfully until they crash.

Besides the four α–properties, the original system requires no other assumptions about communication among actors. However, the original system may require non-communication assumptions such as "up to t hosts can fail."

The Translation mechanism transforms a crash-tolerant system in which all hosts require the four α-properties into a Byzantine-tolerant system that preserves the α-properties.

6.2   Implementation

In the original system, each actor α_i runs on a separate host h_i. In the translated system each host simulates the entire original system (see Fig. 4). That is, a host runs a replica of each of the n actors and passes messages between the actors internally using a simulated network agent, called *coordinator*, that runs on the host. We denote the coordinator running on host h_i as κ_i.

To ensure that the different hosts stay synchronized, the coordinators agree on the order in which messages are delivered to replicas of the same actor. The replica of α_i on host h_j is called α_j^i. We designate α_i^i as the *master* replica and α_j^i ($i \neq j$) as *slave* replicas. On honest hosts, the replicas of each actor start in the same initial state.

Each coordinator replaces ϕ of the original system by OARcast, i.e., OARcast is used to send messages. OARcast guarantees that coordinators agree on the delivery of messages to replicas of a particular actor. Coordinators wrap each α-message

---

[1] We model periodic processing not based on input by external *timer* messages.

in a κ-*message*. κ-messages have the form $\langle tag\ m, i \rangle$, where tag is either internal or external, m is an α-message, and i indicates the destination actor.

Each coordinator maintains an unordered *message bag* and n per-actor-replica *message queues*. By B_i we denote the message bag at host i and by Q_i^j we denote the message queue for actor α_i^j at host i (see Fig. 5). The pseudocode for a coordinator κ_i appears in Fig. 6. κ_i intercepts messages from local actors, and it receives messages from remote coordinators. κ_i places α-messages sent by local actor replicas in B_i, and places α-messages received within κ-messages from κ_j in Q_i^j. When there is a match between a message m in the bag and the head of a queue, the coordinator enqueues m for the corresponding actor.

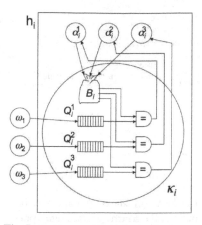

Fig. 5. Anatomy of host h_i in the translated system

```
// Message from external client
On receipt of msg m = ⟨x, ⊥, i⟩:
   κ_i.send(⟨external m, i⟩);

// Message from actor j to actor k
On α_i^j.send(⟨d, j, k⟩):
   B_i.add(⟨d, j, k⟩);
   if k = i then
       κ_i.send(⟨internal ⟨d, j, i⟩, i⟩);

// κ-message from j
On κ_i.deliver(⟨tag m, j⟩):
   Q_i^j.enqueue(m);

// Head of queue matches msg in bag
When ∃j : Q_i^j.head() ∈ B_i:
   m = Q_i^j.dequeue();
   B_i.remove(m);
   α_i^j.deliver(m);

// Head of message queue is external
When ∃j, d : Q_i^j.head() = ⟨d, ⊥, j⟩:
   m = Q_i^j.dequeue();
   α_i^j.deliver(m);
```

Fig. 6. Pseudo-code of the Translation Mechanism for coordinator κ_i

The translated system guarantees α-Persistence, α-Authenticity, α-FIFO, and α-Validity to all master actors on honest hosts. Appendix B contains a proof of correctness.

7   Illustration: BFT

In 1999 Castro and Liskov published "Practical Byzantine Fault Tolerance," a paper about a replication protocol (BFT) for a Byzantine-tolerant NFS file system [4]. The paper shows that BFT is indeed practical, adding relatively little overhead to NFS. In this section we show, informally, that a protocol much like BFT can be synthesized from the Viewstamped Replication protocol by Oki and Liskov [10] and the transformations of the current paper. The main difference is that our protocol is structured, while BFT is largely monolithic. In our opinion, the structure simplifies understanding and enhances the ability to scrutinize the protocol. The BFT paper addresses several practical issues and possible optimizations that can be applied to our scheme as well, but omitted for brevity.

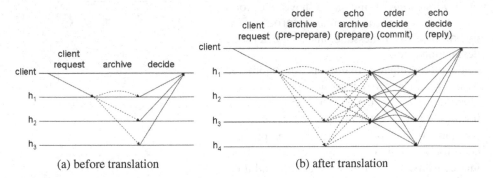

Fig. 7. A normal case run of (a) the original system and (b) the translated system. Dashed arrows indicate the `archive` message from the primary. Between brackets we indicate the corresponding BFT message types.

Viewstamped Replication is a consensus protocol. A normal case execution is shown in Fig. 7(a).[2] A client sends a request to a server that is elected primary. The primary server sends an `archive` message to each server in the system. If a quorum responds to the client, the request is completed successfully. In the case of failures, a possibly infinite number of rounds of this consensus protocol may be necessary to reach a decision.

If we were to apply translation literally as described, we would end up with a protocol that sends significantly more messages than BFT. The reason for this is two-fold. First, our translation does nothing to group related information from a particular sender to a particular receiver in single messages. Instead, all pieces of information go out, concurrently, in separate small messages. While explicit optimizations could eliminate these, FIFO protocols like TCP automatically aggregate concurrent traffic between a pair of hosts into single messages for efficiency, obviating the need for any explicit optimizations. Note that while these techniques reduce the number of messages, the messages become larger and the number of rounds remains the same.

Second, the translation would produce a protocol that solves *uniform Byzantine consensus* [5], guaranteeing that if two honest servers decide on an update, they decide on the same update. In a Byzantine environment, one may argue that this property is stronger than needed. We only need that if two *correct* servers decide on an update, they decide the same update. The reason for this is that clients of the system have to deal with the results from Byzantine servers, and because Byzantine and crashing hosts are both counted towards t it is not usually a problem that an honest server makes a "mistake" before crashing. Such servers would be outvoted by correct servers.

BFT does not provide uniform consensus, but Viewstamped Replication does. Our translation maintains uniformity. This arises in the bc-Relay property, which requires that if an honest host delivers a message, then all correct hosts have to do the same. For our purposes, it would be sufficient to require that if a correct host delivers a message, all correct hosts have to follow suit.

---

[2] Slightly optimized for our purpose by sending `decide` messages back to the client instead of the primary.

If we revisit the ARcast implementation, we see that the protocol maintains the original uniform bc-Relay property by having a receiver await $t + 1$ copies of a message before delivery. Doing so makes sure that one of the copies was sent by a correct receiver that forwards a copy to all other correct receivers as well. For non-uniform bc-Relay this is unnecessary because the receiver itself, if correct, is guaranteed to forward the message to all other correct receivers, and thus a receiver can deliver the message as soon as the first copy is received. The `echo` traffic can be piggybacked on future traffic.

Using this modification, Fig. 7(b) demonstrates a normal run of the translated system for $t = 1$. The figure only shows the traffic that is causally prior to the reply received by the client and thus essential to the latency that the client experiences. In this particular translation we used t additional hosts for OARcast only, but a more faithful translation would have started with $3t + 1$ servers. Nevertheless, the run closely resembles that of a normal run of BFT (see Figure 1 of [4]).

8 Conclusion

We presented a mechanism to translate a distributed application that tolerates only crash failures into one that tolerates Byzantine failures. Few restrictions are placed on the application, and the approach is applicable not only to consensus but to a large class of distributed applications. The approach makes use of a novel broadcast protocol. We have illustrated how the approach may be used to derive a version of the Castro and Liskov Practical Byzantine Replication protocol, showing that our translation mechanism is pragmatic and more powerful than previous translation approaches.

References

1. Bazzi, R.A.: Automatically increasing fault tolerance in distributed systems. PhD thesis, Georgia Institute of Technology, Atlanta, GA, USA (1995)
2. Bazzi, R.A., Neiger, G.: Simplifying fault-tolerance: providing the abstraction of crash failures. J. ACM 48(3), 499–554 (2001)
3. Bracha, G.: Asynchronous byzantine agreement protocols. Inf. Comput. 75(2), 130–143 (1987)
4. Castro, M., Liskov, B.: Practical Byzantine Fault Tolerance. In: Proc. of the 3rd Symposium on Operating Systems Design and Implementation (OSDI), New Orleans, LA (February 1999)
5. Charron-Bost, B., Schiper, A.: Uniform consensus is harder than consensus. Journal of Algorithms 51(1), 15–37 (2004)
6. Coan, B.A.: A compiler that increases the fault tolerance of asynchronous protocols. IEEE Transactions on Computers 37(12), 1541–1553 (1988)
7. Lamport, L., Shostak, R., Pease, M.: The Byzantine generals problem. Trans. on Programming Languages and Systems 4(3), 382–401 (1982)
8. Mpoeleng, D., Ezhilchelvan, P., Speirs, N.: From crash tolerance to authenticated byzantine tolerance: A structured approach, the cost and benefits. In: Int. Conf. on Dependable Systems and Networks (2003)
9. Neiger, G., Toueg, S.: Automatically increasing the fault-tolerance of distributed systems. In: PODC 1988: Proceedings of the Seventh Annual ACM Symposium on Principles of Distributed Computing, pp. 248–262. ACM Press, New York (1988)

10. Oki, B.M., Liskov, B.H.: Viewstamped replication: A general primary-copy method to support highly-available distributed systems. In: Proc. of the 7th ACM Symp. on Principles of Distributed Computing,Toronto, Ontario, ACM SIGOPS-SIGACT, pp. 8–17 (August 1988)
11. Srikanth, T.K., Toueg, S.: Simulating authenticated broadcasts to derive simple fault-tolerant algorithms. Distributed Computing 2(2), 80–94 (1987)

A   Correctness of OARcast

Lemma 1. *Say h_i and h_j are honest and m is the cth message that ω_j^R delivers from ω_i^s, then m is the cth message that ω_i^s sent.*

Proof. Say m is not the cth message sent by ω_i^s, but it is the cth message delivered by ω_j^R. ω_j^R must have received $2t+1$ messages of the form $\langle \text{order } m, c-1, i \rangle$ from different orderers. Because only t hosts may fail, and because of bc-Authenticity of ARcast, at least one of the order messages comes from a correct orderer. Because communication between ω_i^s and this orderer is FIFO, and because the sender does not send m as its cth message, it is not possible that the orderer sent $\langle \text{order } m, c-1, i \rangle$.   □

Lemma 2. *Say m is the cth message that a correct sender ω_i^s sends. Then all correct receivers receive at least $2t+1$ messages of the form $\langle \text{order } m, c-1, i \rangle$ from different orderers.*

Proof. Because the sender is correct, each of the correct orderers will deliver m. As all links are FIFO and m is the cth message, it is clear that for each orderer ω_k^o, $t_k = c-1$. Each correct orderer ω_k^o therefore sends $\langle \text{order } m, c-1, i \rangle$ to all receivers. Because at least $2t+1$ of the orderers are correct, and because of ARcast's bc-Persistence, each correct receiver receives $2t+1$ such order messages.   □

Theorem 1. *OARcast satisfies bc-Persistence.*

Proof. Assume the sending host, h_i, is correct, and consider a correct receiving host h_j. The proof proceeds by induction on c, the number of messages sent by ω_i^s. Consider the first message m sent by ω_i^s. By Lemma 2, ω_j^R receives $2t+1$ messages of the form $\langle \text{order } m, 0, i \rangle$. By Lemma 1 it is not possible that the first message that ω_j^R delivers is a message other than m. Therefore, $c_j = 0$ when ω_j^R receives the order messages for m and will deliver m.

Now assume that bc-Persistence holds for the first c messages from ω_i^s. We show that bc-Persistence holds for the $(c+1)^{st}$ message sent by ω_i^s. By Lemma 2, ω_j^R receives $2t+1$ messages of the form $\langle \text{order } m, c, i \rangle$. By the induction hypothesis, ω_j^R will increment c_j at least up to c. By Lemma 1 it is not possible that the cth message that ω_j^R delivers is a message other than m. Therefore, $c_j = c$ when ω_j^R receives the order messages for m and will deliver m.   □

Theorem 2. *OARcast satisfies bc-Authenticity.*

Proof. This is a straightforward corollary of Lemma 1.   □

Theorem 3. *OARcast satisfies bc-Relay.*

Proof. By induction on the sequence number. Say some correct receiver ω_j^R delivers the first κ-message m from ω_i^S. Therefore, ω_j^R must have received $2t + 1$ messages of the form $\langle \text{order } m, 0, i \rangle$ from different orderers when $c_j = 0$. Because of the bc-Relay property of ARcast, all correct receivers receive the same order messages from the orderers. By Lemma 1 it is not possible that a correct receiver $\omega_{j'}^R$ delivered a κ-message other than m, and therefore $c_{j'} = 0$ when $\omega_{j'}^R$ receives the order messages. Thus $\omega_{j'}^R$ will also deliver m.

Now assume the theorem holds for the first c κ-messages sent by ω_i^S. Say some correct receiver ω_j^R delivers the $(c+1)^{\text{st}}$ κ-message m from ω_i^S. Therefore, ω_j^R must have received $2t+1$ messages of the form $\langle \text{order } m, c, i \rangle$ from different orderers when $c_j = c$. Because of the bc-Relay property of ARcast, all correct receivers receive the same order messages from the orderers. Because of the induction hypothesis, the correct receivers deliver the first c κ-messages. By Lemma 1 it is not possible that a correct receiver $\omega_{j'}^R$ delivered a κ-message other than m, and therefore $c_j = c$ when $\omega_{j'}^R$ receives the order messages. Thus $\omega_{j'}^R$ will also deliver m.   □

Lemma 3. *Say m is the cth message that an honest receiver ω_j^R delivers from ω_i^S, and m' is the cth message that another honest receiver $\omega_{j'}^R$ delivers from ω_i^S. Then $m = m'$ (even if h_i is Byzantine).*

Proof. Say not. ω_j^R must have received $2t + 1$ messages of the form $\langle \text{order } m, c - 1, i \rangle$ from different orderers, while $\omega_{j'}^R$ must have received $2t + 1$ messages of the form $\langle \text{order } m', c - 1, i \rangle$ from different orderers. As there are only $3t + 1$ orderers, at least one correct orderer must have sent one of each, which is impossible as correct orderers increment their sequence numbers for each new message.   □

Theorem 4. *OARcast satisfies bc-Ordering.*

Proof. Corollary of Lemma 3.   □

Theorem 5. *OARcast satisfies bc-FIFO.*

Proof. Evident from the FIFOness of messages from senders to orderers and the sequence numbers utilized by orderers and receivers.   □

B   Correctness of Translation

We prove correctness of the Translation mechanism assuming the bc-properties. In particular, we show that the collection of coordinators and slave replicas that use the Translation mechanism preserves the α-properties: α-*Persistence*, α-*Authenticity*, α-*FIFO*, and α-*Validity*, for the master replicas $\{\alpha_i^i\}$.

For convenience, we combine bc-Relay and bc-Ordering to state that coordinators on correct hosts deliver the same sequence of κ-messages from any κ_k, even if h_k is Byzantine. This is put more formally in the following lemma:

Lemma 4. *For any i, j, and k, if h_i and h_j are correct, then κ_i and κ_j deliver the same sequence of messages from κ_k.*

Proof. bc-Relay guarantees that κ_i and κ_j deliver the same set of messages from κ_k. bc-Ordering further guarantees that the delivery order between any two messages is the same at both κ_i and κ_j.   □

In the proof we need to be able to compare states of hosts. We represent the state of host h_i by a vector of counters, $\Phi_i = (c_i^1, \ldots, c_i^n)$, where each c_i^k is the number of messages that (the local) actor α_i^k has delivered. As shown below, within an execution of the protocol, replicas of the same actor deliver the same sequence of messages. Thus from c_i^k and c_j^k we can compare progress of replicas of α_k on hosts h_i and h_j.

Lemma 5. *Given are that hosts h_i and h_j are correct, α_i^k delivers $m_1, \ldots, m_c$, and α_j^k delivers $c' \le c$ messages. Then the messages that α_j^k delivers are $m_1, \ldots, m_{c'}$.*

Proof. By the Translation mechanism, the first c' messages that α_i^k and α_j^k deliver are the contents of the first c' κ-messages that κ_i and κ_j delivered from κ_k, resp. By Lemma 4, the two κ-message sequences are identical. This and the fact that links from coordinators to actors are FIFO imply that the first c' messages that α_i^k and α_j^k deliver are identical.   □

In the remaining proof we use the following definitions and notations:

- h_i *reaches* $\Phi = (c_1, \ldots, c_n)$, denoted $h_i \rightsquigarrow \Phi$, if $\forall_j\, c_i^j \ge c_j$;
- $\Phi = (c_1, \ldots, c_n)$ *precedes* $\Phi' = (c_1', \ldots, c_n')$, denoted $\Phi < \Phi'$, if $(\forall_i\, c_i \le c_i') \wedge (\exists_j\, c_j < c_j')$;
- $\Phi = (c_1, \ldots, c_n)$ *produces* m if $m \in \bigcup_{i=1}^{n} \bigcup_{c=1}^{c_i} (F^i(m_c^i, s_{c-1}^i).\texttt{output})$, where m_c^i is the cth message to α_i and s_{c-1}^i is the state of α_i after it processes the first $c - 1$ input messages.

Corollary 1. *If Φ produces m on a correct host, Φ produces m on all correct hosts that reach Φ.*

Proof. By Lemma 5 and because replicas of the same actor start in the same state and are deterministic, if Φ produces m on a correct host, Φ produces m on all correct hosts that reach Φ.   □

We now show that if a correct host *is* in a particular state then all other correct hosts will *reach* this state.

Lemma 6. *If there is a correct host h_i in state Φ, then, eventually, all correct hosts reach Φ.*

Proof. By induction on Φ. All correct hosts start in state $\Phi^0 = (0, \ldots, 0)$, and $\forall \Phi \ne \Phi^0 : \Phi^0 < \Phi$.
Base case: All correct hosts reach Φ^0 by definition.
Inductive case: Say that correct host h_i is in state $\Phi = (c_1, \ldots, c_n)$, and the lemma holds for all $\Phi' < \Phi$ (Induction Hypothesis). We need to show that any correct host h_j reaches Φ.

Consider the last message m that some actor replica α_i^p delivered. Thus, m is the c_p^{th} message that α_i^p delivered. The state of h_i prior to delivering this message is $\Phi' = (c_1, \ldots, c_p - 1, \ldots, c_n)$. It is clear that $\Phi' < \Phi$. By the induction hypothesis $h_j \rightsquigarrow \Phi'$.

By the Translation mechanism we know that $\langle tag\ m, p \rangle$ (for some tag) is the c_p^{th} κ-message that κ_i delivers from κ_p. Lemma 4 implies that $\langle tag\ m, p \rangle$ must also be the c_p^{th} κ-message that κ_j delivers from κ_p. Since $h_j \rightsquigarrow \Phi'$, α_j^p delivers the first $c_p - 1$ α-messages, and thus κ_j must have removed those messages from Q_j^p. Consequently, m gets to the head of Q_j^p. $\hspace{1cm}$ (1)

Now there are two cases to consider. If m is external, then κ_j will directly remove m from Q_j^p and enqueue m on the link to α_j^p. Because α_i^p delivered m after delivering the first $c_p - 1$ messages (Lemma 5), and α_i^p and α_j^p run the same function F^p, α_j^p will eventually deliver m as well, and therefore $h_j \rightsquigarrow \Phi$.

Consider the case where m is internal. By definition, $\Phi' = (c_1, \ldots, c_p - 1, \ldots, c_n)$ *produces* m at host h_i. By Corollary 1, Φ' produces m at host h_j. Thus, eventually κ_j places the message in the message bag B_j. $\hspace{1cm}$ (2)

(1) and (2) provide the matching condition for κ_j to enqueue m on its link to α_j^p. Using the same reasoning for the external message case, $h_j \rightsquigarrow \Phi$. $\hspace{1cm}$ □

We can now show the first two communication properties. (The proof for α-FIFO has been omitted for lack of space.)

Theorem 6. (α-*Persistence.*) *If two hosts h_i and h_j are correct and α_i^i sends m to α_j, then α_j^j delivers m from α_i.*

Proof. Suppose h_i is in state Φ_i when α_i^i sends m to α_j. By Lemma 6, $h_j \rightsquigarrow \Phi_i$. Thus, α_j^i sends m to α_j as well. By the Translation mechanism, κ_j places m in B_j and OARcasts $\langle$internal $m, j\rangle$. By bc-Persistence, κ_j delivers $\langle$internal $m, j\rangle$ (from itself) and places m on its queue Q_j^j. $\hspace{1cm}$ (1)

By the Translation Mechanism, each external message at the head of Q_j^j is dequeued and delivered by α_j^j. $\hspace{1cm}$ (2)

Let us consider an internal message m' at the head of Q_j^j. Since h_j is correct, the Translation mechanism ensures that κ_j has delivered $\langle$internal $m', j\rangle$ (the κ-message containing m' and from κ_j). bc-Authenticity ensures that κ_j has indeed sent the κ-message. By the Translation mechanism, κ_j always puts a copy of m' in B_j before sending $\langle$internal $m', j\rangle$. Thus, m' in Q_j^j is matched with a copy in B_j, and α_j^j delivers m'. This together with (2) show that α_j^j delivers all internal messages in Q_j^j. $\hspace{1cm}$ (3)

(1) shows that m sent by α_i^i arrives in Q_j^j, and (3) shows that α_j^j delivers all internal messages in Q_j^j. Together they show that α_j^j delivers m from α_i. $\hspace{1cm}$ □

Theorem 7. (α-*Authenticity.*) *If two hosts h_i and h_j are honest and α_i^i does not send m to α_j, then α_j^j does not deliver m from α_i.*

Proof. Assume α_j^j delivers m from α_i, but α_i^i did not send m to α_j. By the Translation mechanism, a necessary condition for α_j^j to deliver m from α_i is that κ_j delivers $\langle$internal $m, i\rangle$. By bc-Authenticity of OARcast, κ_i must have OARcast $\langle$internal $m, i\rangle$. Then by the Translation mechanism, α_i^i must have sent m, contradicting the assumption. $\hspace{1cm}$ □

We introduce a lemma that helps us show α-*Validity*:

Lemma 7. *Actor replicas on honest hosts only send valid messages.*

Proof. Suppose not. Let m sent by α_j^i be the first invalid message sent by an actor replica on an honest host. Since h_j is honest, there must be a sequence of messages $m_1^i, \ldots, m_c^i$ that α_j^i delivered, such that

$$m \in F^i(m_c^i, F^i(m_{c-1}^i, F^i(\ldots, F^i(m_1^i, s_0^i).\texttt{next}\ldots).\texttt{next}).\texttt{next}).\texttt{output}$$

Since m is the first invalid message sent by an actor replica, all internal messages in the sequence $m_1^i, \ldots, m_c^i$ must be valid. Moreover, external messages are valid by definition. Thus, all messages $m_1^i, \ldots, m_c^i$ are valid. But then, m is valid by definition, contradicting the assumption.   □

Theorem 8. *(α-Validity.) If h_i is honest and α_i^i delivers m from α_j, then m is valid (even if $j \neq \perp$ and h_j is faulty.)*

Proof. If m is an external message, then it is valid and unforgeable by definition.

If m is an internal message, the fact that α_i^i delivers m from α_j implies that α_i^j has sent m to α_i. By Lemma 7, m is valid.   □

Maximizing the Number of Broadcast Operations in Static Random Geometric Ad-Hoc Networks*

Tiziana Calamoneri[1], Andrea Clementi[2], Emanuele G. Fusco[1], and Riccardo Silvestri[1]

[1] Dipartimento di Informatica
Università di Roma "La Sapienza"
{calamoneri,fusco,silver}@di.uniroma1.it
[2] Dipartimento di Matematica
Università Tor Vergata di Roma
clementi@mat.uniroma2.it

Abstract. We consider static ad-hoc wireless networks where nodes have the same initial battery charge and they may dynamically change their transmission range at every time slot. When a node v transmits with range $r(v)$, its battery charge is decreased by $\beta \times r(v)^2$ where $\beta > 0$ is a fixed constant.

The goal is to provide a range assignment schedule that maximizes the number of broadcast operations from a given source (this number is denoted as the *length* of the schedule). This maximization problem, denoted as MAX LIFETIME, is known to be NP-hard and the best algorithm yields worst-case approximation ratio $\Theta(\log n)$, where n is the number of nodes of the network [5].

We consider *random geometric* instances formed by selecting n points independently and uniformly at random from a square of side length $\sqrt{n}$ in the Euclidean plane.

We first present an efficient algorithm that constructs a range assignment schedule having length, with high probability, not smaller than $1/12$ of the optimum.

We then design an efficient distributed version of the above algorithm where nodes initially know n and their own position only. The resulting schedule guarantees the same approximation ratio achieved by the centralized version thus obtaining the first distributed algorithm having *provably-good* performance for this problem.

1 Introduction

Range assignments in ad-hoc networks. In static ad-hoc radio networks (in short, ad-hoc networks), nodes have the ability to vary their transmission ranges (and, thus, their energy consumption) in order to provide good network connectivity and low energy consumption at the same time. More precisely, the transmission ranges determine a (directed) communication graph over the set V of nodes. Indeed, a node v, with range r, can transmit to another node w if and only if w belongs to the *disk* centered in v and of radius r. The transmission range of a node depends, in turn, on the energy power

---

* Research partially supported by the European Union under the Project IP-FP6-015964
AEOLUS.

E. Tovar, P. Tsigas, and H. Fouchal (Eds.): OPODIS 2007, LNCS 4878, pp. 247–259, 2007.

supplied to the node. In particular, the power P_v required by a node v to correctly transmit data to another station w must satisfy the inequality (see [22])

$$\frac{P_v}{\text{dist}(v,w)^2} \geq \eta \tag{1}$$

where $\text{dist}(v,w)$ is the Euclidean distance between v and w while η is a constant that, wlog, can be fixed to 1.

In several previous theoretical works [1,9,16,21], it is assumed that nodes can arbitrarily vary their transmission range over the set $\{\text{dist}(v,w) \mid v,w \in V\}$ However, in some network models (like sensor networks), the adopted technology allows to have only few possible transmission range values. For this reason, we will assume that nodes have the ability to choose their transmission range from a finite set $\Gamma = \{0, r_1, r_2 \dots, r_k\}$ (with $0 < r_1 < r_2 < \dots < r_k$) that depends on the particular adopted technology (see [7,8,22]). Further technical constraints on Γ will be given and discussed in Subsection 1.1.

A fundamental class of problems, underlying any phase of a dynamic resource allocation algorithm in ad-hoc wireless networks, is the one known as *range assignment problems*. In these problems the goal is to find a transmission range assignment $r : V \to \Gamma$ such that (1) the corresponding communication graph satisfies a given connectivity property Π, and (2) the overall energy power cost$(r) = \sum r(v)^2$ required to deploy the assignment is minimized (see for example [16,21]). Clearly, the maximal range value r_k in Γ must be sufficiently large to guarantee that at least one feasible solution exists.

Several research works [1,9,16] have been devoted to the case where Π is defined as follows: *Given specific source $s \in V$, the transmission graph has to contain a directed spanning tree rooted at s (a broadcast tree from s).* The relevance of this problem (denoted as MIN ENERGY BROADCAST) is due to the fact that any communication graph satisfying the above property allows the source to perform a *broadcast* operation. Broadcast is a task initiated by the source that wants to transmits a message to all nodes. This task constitutes a basic and thus fundamental operation in real life multi-hop radio networks [2,3,16]. As for the worst-case complexity, MIN ENERGY BROADCAST is known to be NP-hard [9] (even when $|\Gamma| = 3$ and r_1 is a small positive constant) and a series of constant-factor approximation algorithms are available in [1,4,9,18]. The best known approximation factor is close to 4 and it is given in [6]. In [5], a more general version of MIN ENERGY BROADCAST is given where not uniform *node efficiency* is considered. In this version, a function $e : V \to R^+$ is given and the energy cost, required to transmit from node v to w, is $d(v,w)^2/e(v)$. This non-symmetric version of MIN ENERGY BROADCAST seems to be harder: the best known algorithm yields approximation ratio $\Theta(\log n)$ [5].

The MAX LIFETIME problem. The above power assignment problems do not consider important ad-hoc network scenarios where nodes are equipped with batteries of limited charge and the goal is to maximize the number of broadcast operations. This important (*maximization*) range assignment problem has been first analytically studied in [5] and it is the subject of our paper.

The goal is to maximize the *lifetime* of the network while having, at any *time period* t, a broadcast tree from a given source. Formally, each node is initially equipped with a battery charge [1] $B > 0$ that, at every time period t, is reduced by amount $\beta \times r_t(v)^2$ where $r_t(v)$ denotes the range assigned to node v during t and $\beta > 0$ is a fixed constant depending of the adopted technology. In this paper, we assume $\beta = 1$, however, all our results can be easily extended to any $\beta > 0$. A *range assignment schedule* is a set of functions $\{r_t : V \rightarrow \Gamma, t = 1, \ldots, m\}$. A range assignment schedule is said to be *feasible* if, at any time period t, r_t yields a broadcast tree from s and, for any $v \in V$, it holds that

$$\sum_{t=1}^{m} r_t(v)^2 \leq B$$

Then, the MAX LIFETIME problem is to find a feasible range assignment schedule of maximal length m.

In [5], MAX LIFETIME is shown to be NP-hard. In the same paper, by means of a rather involved reduction to MIN ENERGY BROADCAST with non uniform node efficiency, a polynomial time algorithm is provided yielding approximation ratio $\Theta(\log n)$. This positive result also holds when the initial node battery charges are not uniform.

A static version of MAX LIFETIME has been studied in [20]: the broadcast tree is fixed during the entire schedule and the quality of solutions returned by the MST-based algorithm is investigated. Such results and techniques are clearly not useful for our (dynamic) MAX LIFETIME problem.

Several other problems concerning network lifetime have been studied in the literature [7,8,20]. Their definitions vary depending on the particular node technology (i.e. fixed or adjustable node power) and on the required connectivity or covering property. However, both results and techniques (mostly of them being experimental) are not related to ours.

Our results. To the best of our knowledge, previous *analytical* results on MIN ENERGY BROADCAST and MAX LIFETIME concern worst-case instances only. Some *experimental* studies on MIN ENERGY BROADCAST have been done on *random geometric instances* [10,18]. Such input distributions turn out to be very important in the study of range assignment problems. On one hand, they represent the most natural random instance family where greedy heuristics (such as the MST-based one - see [16]) have a bad behaviour [18]. On the other hand, random geometric distributions is a first good way to model well-spread networks located on flat 2-dimensional regions [7,8,16,20].

We study MAX LIFETIME in random geometric instances of arbitrary size: set V is formed by n nodes selected uniformly and independently at random from the 2-dimensional square of side length $\lfloor \sqrt{n} \rfloor$. Such instances will be simply denoted as *random sets*. Notice that the maximal Euclidean distance among two nodes in random sets is $\sqrt{2n}$, so the maximal range value r_k can be assumed to be not larger than $\sqrt{2n}$.

A natural and important open question is thus to establish whether efficiently-constructible range assignment schedules exist for MAX LIFETIME having *provably-good* length on random sets. Moreover, the design of efficient *distributed* implementations of such schedules is of particular relevance in ad-hoc networks.

---

[1] So we here assume that, at the very beginning, all nodes are in the same energy situation.

To this aim, we first provide an upper bound on the length of optimal (i.e. maximal) range assignment schedules for *any* finite set V in the 2-dimensional plane. So this upper bound holds in the *worst-case*. Then, we present an efficient algorithm that, on any instance (V, s), returns a feasible schedule. Furthermore, when V is a random set, we prove the schedule length is, with high probability[2] (in short, *w.h.p.*), not smaller than $1/12$ of the optimum. The algorithm is centralized and works in $O(n^2 + nT)$ time where T is the number of broadcast operations yielded by the schedule.

In Section 4, we modify our centralized algorithm in order to design a distributed protocol for MAX LIFETIME on random sets. The protocol assumes that every node initially knows n and its Euclidean position only. This assumption is reasonable in *static* ad-hoc networks since node position can be either stored in the set-up phase or it can locally computed by every node by using GPS systems. This operation is not too expensive in terms of energy consumption since it is performed *once and for all* in the set-up phase.

We then show that the resulting scheduling is equivalent to that yielded by the centralized version and, hence, it achieves w.h.p. a constant approximation ratio as well. We thus get the first distributed protocol for MAX LIFETIME having provably good performance.

The protocol performs, somewhat in parallel, two tasks: (1) It constructs a broadcast communication subgraph starting from the source and (2) transmits the source message along this subgraph to all nodes. We emphasize that all node costs due to both the above tasks are taken into account: whenever a node transmits any message with range r, its battery charge is decreased by r^2.

Our analysis thus evaluates the number of broadcast operations achieved by our protocol. This suffices for bounding the approximation ratio. However, we also analyze the *amortized completion time* of single broadcast operations produced by our protocol. To this aim, we consider the *synchronous* model of communication [2,3,12,11,14] and take care of the MAC layer too: in fact, we also consider time delays due to avoid *collisions*.

Node communications thus work in synchronous *time-slots* and the *amortized completion time* of a protocol, yielding T broadcast operations, is the overall number of elapsed time slots divided by T.

It turns out that our protocol has amortized completion time

$$O\left(\frac{r_2 n \sqrt{n}}{T} + r_2^2 + \frac{\sqrt{n}}{r_2}\right)$$

Since our protocol w.h.p. returns an almost maximal number T of broadcast operations, we can point out some interesting facts.

Assume that $r_2 \in \Gamma$ is close to the *connectivity threshold* of *random geometric graphs* [15,19,23,24], i.e., $r_2 = \Theta(\sqrt{\log n})$ (this setting is relevant in our random input - see Subsection 1.1). Then, the worst scenario for our protocol is when the initial battery charge B is very small so that T is as well small, say $T = O(1)$. In fact, we get an amortized completion time $O(n\sqrt{n \log n})$ that is a factor $\sqrt{n \log n}$ larger than the best-known distributed broadcasting time [15], i.e., $O(n)$.

---

[2] Here and in the sequel the term *with high probability* means that the event holds with probability at least $1 - \frac{1}{n^c}$ for some constant $c > 0$.

However, those optimal-time distributed protocols [15] do not care about *node energy* costs and, thus, about the lifetime of the network. Our protocol, instead, somewhat trades global network lifetime with completion time of each single broadcast operation. This fact clearly arises whenever B is large enough to allow $T = \Omega(\sqrt{n})$ number of broadcast operations: in this case, we get $O(n\sqrt{\log n})$ amortized completion time, thus very close to the best-known distributed broadcasting completion time.

1.1 Preliminaries

A *random set* V is formed by n nodes selected uniformly and independently at random from the square Q of side length $\lfloor\sqrt{n}\rfloor$. The source node s can be any node in V. The length of a maximal feasible range assignment schedule (in short, schedule) for an input (V, s) is denoted as $\text{opt}(V, s)$.

Given a set V of n nodes in the 2-dimensional Euclidean space and a positive real r, the *disk graph* $G(V, r)$ is the symmetric graph where two nodes in V are linked if $d(v, w) \leq r$. When V is a random set, the resulting disk graph distribution is known as *geometric random graphs* that are the subject of several important studies related to wireless networking [15,19,23,24]. In particular, it is known that, for sufficiently large n, a random geometric graph $G(V, r)$ is w.h.p. connected if and only if $r \geq \mu\sqrt{\log n}$, where $\mu = 1 + \epsilon$ for any constant $\epsilon > 0$ [19,23,24] . The value $\text{CT}(n) = \mu\sqrt{\log n}$ is known as the *connectivity threshold* of random geometric graphs.

Assumptions on range set Γ. As for set

$$\Gamma = \{0, r_1, r_2 \ldots, r_k\}, \quad \text{with } 0 < r_1 < r_2 < \ldots < r_k \leq \sqrt{2n}$$

we make the following assumptions that are motivated by our choice of studying random sets.

The first positive value in Γ, i.e. r_1, is assumed to be $1 \leq r_1 < \text{CT}(n)$. Observe that if $r_1 \geq \text{CT}(n)$ then MAX LIFETIME on random sets admits a trivial schedule which is, w.h.p., a constant factor approximation: indeed the source must transmit at every time period with range at least r_1 and so all other nodes can transmit with the same range at every time period.

All other values in Γ can be arbitrarily fixed in input provided that all of them are *not smaller* than $\text{CT}(n)$ and at least one of them is larger than $2\sqrt{2}c\sqrt{\log n}$, where $c > \mu$ is a small constant that will be defined in Lemma 2. Informally speaking, we require that *at least* one value in Γ is a bit larger than the connectivity threshold. This is reasonable and relevant in energy problems related to random geometric wireless networks since this value is the *minimal* one achieving w.h.p. global connectivity. Further discussion on such assumptions can be found in Section 5.

2 The Upper Bound

In this section, we provide an upper bound on the length of any feasible range assignment schedule for a set V.

Consider the disk graph $G(V, r_1)$ and let k_1 be the size of the connected component C_s of G containing source s.

Lemma 1. *Given a set V and a source $s \in V$, it holds that $\mathrm{opt}(V, s) \leq \frac{B}{r_1^2}$. Furthermore, if $k_1 < n$ then*

$$\mathrm{opt}(V, s) \leq \min\left\{\frac{B}{r_1^2}, \frac{B}{r_2^2}(k_1 r_2^2 + r_1^2 - k_1 r_1^2)\right\}$$

Proof. Since the source must transmit with range at least r_1 at any time period, the first upper bound follows easily.

If $k_1 < n$ then consider any feasible range assignment schedule S. Let l_1 and l_2 be the number of time periods where the source transmits with range r_1 and *at least* r_2, respectively. It must hold that

$$l_1 r_1^2 + l_2 r_2^2 \leq B$$

Since $k_1 < n$ then, in each of the l_1 time periods of S, there is at least one node in C_s but s having radius at least r_2. This yields

$$l_1 r_2^2 \leq (k_1 - 1)B$$

By simple calculations, from the above two inequalities, we derive an upper bound on the number of time periods of S, i.e.

$$l_1 + l_2 \leq \min\left\{\frac{B}{r_1^2}r, \frac{B}{r_2^4}(k_1 r_2^2 + r_1^2 - k_1 r_1^2)\right\}$$

$\square$

Notice that if V is a random set then, since $r_1 < \mathrm{CT}(n)$, it holds w.h.p. $k_1 < n$.

3   The Algorithm

In this section we present a simple and efficient algorithm for MAX LIFETIME and then we analyze its performance. For the sake of simplicity, in this extended abstract we restrict ourselves to the case $r_2 \geq c\sqrt{\log n}$. Nevertheless, it is easy to extend all our results to the more general assumption described in Section 1.1.

In order to prove the approximation ratio achieved by the schedule returned by our algorithm, we will use the following result that is a simple consequence of Lemma 1 in [17].

Lemma 2. *Constants $c > 0$ and $\gamma > 0$ exist such that the following holds. Given a random set $V \subseteq Q$ of n nodes, consider the partition of Q into square cells of side length ℓ where $c\sqrt{\log n} \leq \ell \leq \sqrt{n}$. Then, w.h.p., every cell contains at least $\gamma \ell^2$ nodes. The constants can be set as $c = 12$ and $\gamma = 5/6$.*

Theorem 1. *Let $V \subseteq Q$ be a random set of n nodes and $s \in V$ be any source node. Then, w.h.p., the range assignment schedule returned by BS is feasible and it has length at least $\beta\mathrm{opt}(V, s)$, where $\beta = 1/12$.*

Proof. From Lemma 2, every cell contains w.h.p. a Pivot (transmitting with range r_2) at every time period. At every time period, there is a Pivot in W_s. This implies that, at any time period, the set of Pivots w.h.p. forms a strongly-connected subgraph that

---

Algorithm 1. BS (Broadcast Schedule)

1: Input: Set $V \subseteq Q$ of n nodes; a source $s \in V$; a battery charge $B > 0$; the range set $\Gamma = \{0, r_1, r_2 \ldots, r_k\}$

2: Partition Q into square *cells* of side length $r_2/(2\sqrt{2})$; For any cell Q_j, let V_j be the set of nodes in Q_j; construct an arbitrary ordering in V_j

3: Let C_s be the connected component in $G(V, r_1)$ that contains s

4: **if** $|C_s| \leq r_2^2$ **then**

5:    $W_s \leftarrow C_s$

6: **else**

7:    W_s is defined as any connected subgraph of C_s such that it contains s and $|W_s| = r_2^2$

8: **end if**

9: Construct an arbitrary ordering of W_s

10: **for** any time period $t = 1, \ldots,$ **do**

11:    **if** node with index $t \bmod |W_s|$ in W_s has remaining battery charge at least r_2^2 **then**

12:       it is selected as *Pivot* and range r_2 is assigned to it

13:    **else**

14:       The algorithm stops

15:    **end if**

16:    **for** any cell Q_j **do**

17:       **if** node with index $t \bmod |V_j|$ in Q_j has remaining battery charge at least r_2^2 **then**

18:          it is selected as *Pivot* and range r_2 is assigned to it

19:       **else**

20:          The algorithm stops

21:       **end if**

22:    **end for**

23:    All nodes in W_s not selected in lines 11 and 17 have radius r_1

24:    All nodes in $V \setminus W_s$ not selected in line 17 have range 0

25: **end for**

---

covers all nodes in V and s is connected to one of such Pivots. Moreover, BS assigns, to every node, an energy power which is never larger than the current battery charge of the node.

We now evaluate the length T of the scheduling produced by BS, so T is the last time period of the BS's run on input (V, s). Let w be any node in $V \setminus W_s$ then, from Lemma 2, in its cell there are w.h.p. at least $(\gamma r_2^2)/8$ nodes. So, w spends at most energy

$$\left(\frac{8T}{\gamma r_2^2}\right) r_2^2 \qquad (2)$$

From (2), T can be any value such that

$$T \leq \frac{\gamma B}{8} \qquad (3)$$

During the schedule, every node v in W_s will have range r_1 or r_2. Let $|W_s| = k$, then the energy spent by v is at most

$$\left(\frac{T}{k} + \frac{8T}{\gamma r_2^2}\right) r_2^2 + T r_1^2 \qquad (4)$$

Notice that in (4) we have considered the fact that a node in W_s can have range r_2 because it has been selected as Pivot of its cell (Line 17) or as Pivot of W_s (Line 11). Now, two cases may arise.

- If $k \geq \left(\frac{r_2}{r_1}\right)^2$, since $r_1 \geq 1$, from (4) the amount of spent energy is at most $Tr_1^2 (2 + 8/\gamma)$. So, T can be any value such that

$$T \leq \frac{B}{r_1^2 (2 + 8/\gamma)} \tag{5}$$

Observe that every value T that satisfies 5, it also satisfies Eq. 3. So T can assume value $\frac{B}{r_1^2(2+8/\gamma)}$ and, from Lemma 1, we have that

$$T \geq \frac{\text{opt}(V, s)}{2 + 8/\gamma}$$

- If $k < \left(\frac{r_2}{r_1}\right)^2$, according to the definition of W_s, we have $k = k_1$. From (4) and some simple calculations, the energy spent by $v \in W_s$ is at most

$$T \frac{r_2^4 + k_1 r_1^2 r_2^2 + (8/\gamma)k_1 r_2^2}{r_2^2 k_1 + r_1^2 - k_1 r_1^2}$$

where we used the fact that $r_1^2 - k_1 r_1^2 \leq 0$. Observe also that since $k_1 < \left(\frac{r_2}{r_1}\right)^2$ and $r_1 \geq 1$, we get

$$k_1 r_1^2 r_2^2 + (8/\gamma)k_1 r_2^2 \leq r_2^4 \left(1 + \frac{8}{\gamma r_1^2}\right) \leq r_2^4 \left(1 + \frac{8}{\gamma r_1^2}\right)$$

It thus follows that the energy spent by v is at most

$$T \frac{r_2^4 + k_1 r_1^2 r_2^2 + (8/\gamma)k_1 r_2^2}{r_2^2 k_1 + r_1^2 - k_1 r_1^2} \leq T \frac{r_2^4(2 + 8/\gamma)}{r_2^2 k_1 + r_1^2 - k_1 r_1^2}$$

It follows that T can be any value such that

$$T \leq \frac{r_2^2 k_1 + r_1^2 - k_1 r_1^2}{r_2^4(2 + 8/\gamma)} B \tag{6}$$

Finally, by combining (3), (6), and Lemma 1, we get again

$$T \geq \frac{\text{opt}(V, s)}{2 + 8/\gamma}$$

So, the Theorem is proved for $\beta = 1/(2 + 8/\gamma) > 1/12$.   □

4   The Distributed Version

In this section, we present a distributed version of BS. As mentioned in the Introduction, we adopt the synchronous model of node communication: the protocol acts in homogeneous *time slots*.

The resulting protocol is non spontaneous and assumes that every node v knows the number n of nodes, its own position (w.r.t. an absolute coordinate system) and, clearly, Γ.

In what follows, the eccentricity of source s in W_s (i.e. the maximal distance between s and a node in W_s) is denoted as $h(W_s)$ and the t-th message sent by the source is denoted as m_t. We assume that m_t contains the value of time period t.

Protocol: DBS (Distributed Broadcast Schedule)

Preprocessing: /* Construction of $W_s \subseteq C_s$ such that $h(W_s) \leq r_2^2$. */

- *One-to-All.* Starting from s, use round robin among nodes and range transmission r_1 to inform all nodes in C_s that are at most within r_2^2 hops from s: such nodes will form W_s. The one-to-all operation induces a spanning tree Tree of W_s rooted at s.
- *All-to-One.* By a simple bottom-up process on Tree and using round robin on each level, s collects all node labels and the structure of Tree.
- *Initialization.* Every node sets a local counter counter $= -1$. Furthermore, each node has a local array P of length $(\gamma/8)r_2^2$ where it will store the ordered list of the first $(\gamma/8)r_2^2$ labels belonging to its own cell. This array is initially empty.

Let us observe that at the end of the Preprocessing phase, source s has full knowledge of W_s.

Broadcast operations:

- For $t = 0, 1, \ldots$ /* time periods */
  Execute Procedure BROADCAST(m_t)

Procedure BROADCAST(m_t)

Nodes in W_s only:

- Source s selects the $(t \bmod \min\{|W_s|, r_2^2\})$-th node in W_s as *Pivot* (range r_2 will be assigned to it);
  s transmits, with range r_1, $\langle m_t, P \rangle$ where P is the path in Tree from s to the Pivot.
- When a node in W_s receives $\langle m_t, P \rangle$, it checks whether its label is the first in P. If this is the case, it transmits, with range r_1, $\langle m_t, P' \rangle$ where P' is the residual path to the Pivot.
- When the selected Pivot p of W_s receives $\langle m_t, P = (p) \rangle$, it transmits, with range r_2, $\langle m_t, i \rangle$ where i is the index of its cell.

All nodes:

- If $(t \leq (\gamma/8)r_2^2)$ then
  - When a node v receives, for the first time w.r.t. time period t, $\langle m_t, i \rangle$ from the Pivot of a neighbor cell i, it becomes active.

- An active node, at every time slot, increments counter by one and checks whether its label is equal to the value of its counter. If this is the case, it becomes the Pivot of its cell and transmits, with range r_2, $\langle m_t, i \rangle$ where i is the index of its cell.
- When an active node in cell i receives $\langle m_t, i \rangle$, it (so the Pivot as well) records in $P[t]$ the current value of counter c, i.e. the label of the Pivot, and becomes inactive.
- else (i.e. $(t > (\gamma/8)r_2^2)$)
  - When a node v receives, for the first time w.r.t. time period t, $\langle m_t, i \rangle$ from the Pivot of a neighbor cell i, it checks if its label is equal to $P[t \bmod (\gamma/8)r_2^2]$. If this is the case, it becomes the Pivot of its cell and transmits, with range r_2, $\langle m_t, j \rangle$ where j is the index of its cell.

The above protocol has the following properties that are a key-ingredient in the performance analysis.

Fact 2. *Even though they initially do not known each other, all nodes in the same cell are activated (and disactivated) at the same time slot, so their local counters share the same value at every time slot. Furthermore, after the first $(\gamma/8)r_2^2$ broadcast operations, all nodes in the same cell know the set P of Pivots of that cell.*

More precisely, if $l_0 < l_1 < l_2 < \cdots$ are the labels of the nodes in a cell, then, during the first $(\gamma/8)r_2^2$ broadcast operations (i.e. time periods), the Pivot of the cell at time period t will be node having label l_t.

Lemma 3. *Given a random set $V \subseteq Q$ and any source $s \in V$, if the length of the broadcast schedule yielded by BS is T, then the length of the broadcast schedule yielded by DBS is at least $T - 2$.*

Proof. Notice that, the only difference in terms of power consumption between BS and DBS lies in the Preprocessing phase required by the latter. In that phase, at most two messages with range r_1 are sent by a node to discover W_s. Indeed, thanks to Fact 2, the if branch of the Broadcast procedure for nodes in V spends *time* instead of *power* in order to discover the set of Pivots of each cell. Hence, in the worst case, the distributed version performs two broadcasts less than the centralized algorithm. $\square$

Corollary 1. *Let $V \subseteq Q$ be a random set of n nodes and $s \in V$ be any source node. Then, w.h.p., the range assignment schedule returned by DBS is feasible and it has a length at least $\beta\mathrm{opt}(V, s) - 2$ where $\beta = 1/12$.*

Proof. Direct consequence of Theorem 1 and Lemma 3. $\square$

We now evaluate message and time complexity of DBS.

Lemma 4. *The overall number of node transmissions (i.e. the message complexity) of DBS is $O(|W_s| + T \cdot ((n/r_2^2) + r_2^2))$, where T is the length of the schedule.*

Sketch of the proof. Observe that in the Preprocessing phase only nodes in C_s can exchange messages. In particular, s and all nodes within r_2^2 hops from s send only one message; all other nodes within 1 and $r_2^2 - 1$ hops from s send two messages. So, the message complexity of the Preprocessing phase is $\Theta(|W_s|)$. Thanks to Fact 2, during each broadcast, exactly one message per cell is sent, so globally $O(8n/r_2^2)$ messages are exchanged; to this number of messages, we have to add those sent by the nodes of path P in W_s: this value is bounded by r_2^2.   □

Theorem 3. *The overall number of time slots required by* DBS *to perform T broadcast operations is w.h.p.*

$$O(r_2 n\sqrt{n} + T \cdot (r_2^2 + \sqrt{n}/r_2))$$

Sketch of the proof. For a single broadcast operation performed by DBS, we define the *delay* of a cell as the number of time slots from its activation time and the selection of its Pivot. Observe that the sum of delays introduced by a cell during the first $(\gamma/8)r_2^2$ broadcasts is at most n. Then, the delay of any cell becomes 0 for all broadcasts after the first $(\gamma/8)r_2^2$ ones. Moreover, a broadcast can pass over at most $O(\sqrt{n}/r_2)$ cells. By assuming that a maximal length path (this length being $\Theta(\sqrt{n}/r_2)$) together with maximal cell delay can be found in each of the first $\min\{(\gamma/8)r_2^2, T\}$ broadcasts, we can bound the maximal overall delay with

$$O(r_2 n\sqrt{n}) \tag{7}$$

In the Preprocessing phase, DBS uses round robin to avoid collisions. During the All-to-One phase, each node needs to collect all messages from its children before sending a message to its parent in `Tree`. Hence, the whole phase is completed in

$$O(nr_2^2) \tag{8}$$

time slots as the height of `Tree` is bounded by r_2^2.

Finally, the number of time slots required by every broadcast without delays and Preprocessing time is

$$O(r_2^2 + \sqrt{n}/r_2) \tag{9}$$

since r_2^2 is the upper bound on $h(W_s)$ and the length of any path on the broadcast tree outside W_s is $O(\sqrt{n}/r_2)$.

By combining (7), (8), and (9), we get the theorem bound without considering collisions among cell Pivots. In order to avoid such collisions, we further organize DBS into iterative phases: in every phase, only cells with not colliding Pivot transmissions are active. Since the number of cells that can interfere with a given cell is constant, this further scheduling will increase the overall time of DBS by a constant factor only. This iterative process can be efficiently performed in a distributed way since every node knows n and its position, so it knows its cell.   □

From Theorem 3, the amortized completion time of a single broadcast operation performed by DBS is

$$O\left(\frac{r_2 n\sqrt{n}}{T} + r_2^2 + \frac{\sqrt{n}}{r_2}\right)$$

5 Open Problems

In this paper, we have studied the MAX LIFETIME problem on random sets. Further interesting future studies should address other basic operations than broadcasting: for instance, the gossiping operation which is known to be NP-hard too [5]. A more technical problem, left open by our research, is the study of MAX LIFETIME when Γ contains more than one *positive* values *smaller* than the connectivity threshold $CT(n)$ of random geometric graphs. This case seems to be very hard since it concerns the size and the structure of the connected components of such random graphs *under* the threshold connectivity [19,23].

References

1. Ambuehl, C.: An optimal bound for the MST algorithm to compute energy efficient broadcast trees in wireless networks. In: Caires, L., Italiano, G.F., Monteiro, L., Palamidessi, C., Yung, M. (eds.) ICALP 2005. LNCS, vol. 3580, pp. 1139–1150. Springer, Heidelberg (2005)
2. Bar-Yehuda, R., Goldreich, O., Itai, A.: On the time-complexity of broadcast in multi-hop radio networks: An exponential gap between determinism and randomization. JCSS 45, 104–126 (1992)
3. Bar-Yehuda, R., Israeli, A., Itai, A.: Multiple communication in multi-hop radio networks. SICOMP 22(4), 875–887 (1993)
4. Calinescu, G., Li, X.Y., Frieder, O., Wan, P.J.: Minimum-Energy Broadcast Routing in Static Ad Hoc Wireless Networks. In: Proc. of 20th IEEE INFOCOM, pp. 1162–1171 (April 2001)
5. Calinescu, G., Kapoor, S., Olshevsky, A., Zelikovsky, A.: Network lifetime and power assignment in ad hoc wireless networks. In: Di Battista, G., Zwick, U. (eds.) ESA 2003. LNCS, vol. 2832, pp. 114–126. Springer, Heidelberg (2003)
6. Caragiannis, I., Flammini, M., Moscardelli, L.: An exponential improvement on the MST heuristic for the minimum energy broadcast problem. In: Arge, L., Gachin, C., Jurdzinshi, T., Taoledci, A. (eds.) ICALP 2007. LNCS, vol. 4596, pp. 447–458. Springer, Heidelberg (2007)
7. Cardei, M., Du, D.-Z.: Improving wireless sensor network lifetime through power organization. Wireless Networks 11, 333–340 (2005)
8. Cardei, M., Wu, J., Lu, M.: Improving network lifetime using sensors with adjustable sensing ranges. Int. J. Sensor Networks 1(1/2), 41–49 (2006)
9. Clementi, A., Crescenzi, P., Penna, P., Rossi, G., Vocca, P.: On the Complexity of Computing Minimum Energy Consumption Broadcast Subgraphs. In: Ferreira, A., Reichel, H. (eds.) STACS 2001. LNCS, vol. 2010, pp. 121–131. Springer, Heidelberg (2001), http://www.dia.unisa.it/~penna
10. Clementi, A., Huiban, G., Penna, P., Rossi, G., Verhoeven, Y.C.: On the Approximation Ratio of the MST-based Heuristic for the Energy-Efficient Broadcast Problem in Static Ad-Hoc Radio Networks. In: Proc. of IPDPS 2003, p. 222 (2003)
11. Clementi, A.E.F., Monti, A., Silvestri, R.: Distributed broadcast in radio networks of unknown topology. Theor. Comput. Sci. 302(1-3), 337–364 (2003)
12. Chrobak, M., Gasieniec, L., Rytter, W.: Fast broadcasting and gossiping in radio networks. J. Algorithms 43(2), 177–189 (2002)
13. Chu, W., Colbourn, C.J., Syrotiuk, V.R.: The effects of synchronization on topology transparent scheduling. Wireless Networks 12, 681–690 (2006)
14. Czumaj, A., Rytter, W.: Broadcasting algorithms in radio networks with unknown topology. J. Algorithms 60(2), 115–143 (2006)

15. Dessmark, A., Pelc, A.: Broadcasting in geometric radio networks. Journal of Discrete Algorithms (2006)
16. Ephremides, A., Nguyen, G.D., Wieselthier, J.E.: On the Construction of Energy-Efficient Broadcast and Multicast Trees in Wireless Networks. In: Proc. of 19th IEEE INFOCOM, pp. 585–594 (2000)
17. Flaxman, A.D., Frieze, A.M., Vera, J.C.: On the average case performance of some greedy approximation algorithms for the uncapacitated facility location problem. In: Proc. of the 37-th ACM STOC 2005, pp. 441–449 (2005)
18. Flammini, M., Navarra, A., Perennes, S.: The Real Approximation Factor of the MST Heuristic for the Minimum Energy Broadcast. In: Nikoletseas, S.E. (ed.) WEA 2005. LNCS, vol. 3503, pp. 22–31. Springer, Heidelberg (2005)
19. Gupta, P., Kumar, P.R.: Critical power for asymptotic connectivity in wireless networks. In: Stochastic Analysis, Control, Optimization and Applications, Birkhauser, Boston, MA, pp. 547–566 (1999)
20. Kang, I., Poovendran, R.: Maximizing network lifetime of wireless broadcast ad hoc networks. J. of ACM Mobile Networks and Applications (6) (2005)
21. Kirousis, L.M., Kranakis, E., Krizanc, D., Pelc, A.: Power Consumption in Packet Radio Networks. Theoretical Computer Science 243, 289–305 (2000)
22. Pahlavan, K., Levesque, A.: Wireless Information Networks. Wiley-Interscience, Chichester (1995)
23. Penrose, M.: Random Geometric Graphs. Oxford University Press, Oxford (2003)
24. Santi, P., Blough, D.M.: The Critical Transmitting Range for Connectivity in Sparse Wireless Ad Hoc Networks. IEEE Trans. on Mobile Computing 2, 25–39 (2003)

N-Consensus is the Second Strongest Object for $N + 1$ Processes

Eli Gafni[1] and Petr Kuznetsov[2]

[1] Computer Science Department, University of California, Los Angeles
eli@ucla.edu
[2] Max Planck Institute for Software Systems
pkouznet@mpi-sws.mpg.de

Abstract. Objects like queue, swap, and test-and-set allow two processes to reach consensus, and are consequently "universal" for a system of two processes. But are there deterministic objects that do not solve 2-process consensus, and nevertheless allow two processes to solve a task that is not otherwise wait-free solvable in read-write shared memory?

The answer "no" is a simple corollary of the main result of this paper: Let A be a deterministic object such that no protocol solves consensus among $n+1$ processes using copies of A and read-write registers. If a task T is wait-free solvable by $n + 1$ processes using read-write shared-memory and copies of A, then T is also wait-free solvable when copies of A are replaced with n-consensus objects. Thus, from the task-solvability perspective, n-consensus is the second strongest object (after $(n+1)$-consensus) in deterministic shared memory systems of $n+1$ processes, i.e., there is a distinct gap between n- and $(n + 1)$-consensus.

We derive this result by showing that any $(n+1)$-process protocol P that uses objects A can be emulated using only n-consensus objects. The resulting emulation is non-blocking and relies on an *a priori* knowledge of P. The emulation technique is another important contribution of this paper.

1 Introduction

Consensus [1] (n-consensus object) is a fundamental abstraction that allows n processes to agree on one of their input values. Consensus is *n-universal*: every object shared by n processes can be *wait-free implemented* using n-consensus objects (and read-write registers), i.e., the object can be "replaced" with n-consensus objects, so that the external observer cannot detect the replacement [2].

But which aspects of the universality of n-process consensus remain valid in a system of $n+1$ processes? Ideally, one would wish to show that, in a system of $n+1$ processes, every object that does not allow for $(n + 1)$-process consensus (to be called an object of *consensus power* less than $n + 1$) can be wait-free implemented from n-consensus objects. This would imply that every problem that can be solved by $n + 1$ processes using objects of consensus power less than $n + 1$ can also be solved using n-consensus objects.

In this paper, we address an easier question: whether every deterministic object of consensus power less than $n + 1$ can be replaced with n-consensus objects, so that the

E. Tovar, P. Tsigas, and H. Fouchal (Eds.): OPODIS 2007, LNCS 4878, pp. 260–273, 2007.

replacement is not detectable *in a given* $(n + 1)$-*process protocol P*. Thus, we consider the classical *emulation* problem: given a protocol P designed for a system with objects from a set $\mathcal{C}$, how to *emulate* P in a system with objects from a set $\mathcal{C}'$.

We show that every protocol for $n+1$ processes using read-write registers and objects A of consensus power less than $n + 1$ can be emulated using only read-write registers and n-consensus objects. Our emulation is *non-blocking* [2]: at least one active process is guaranteed to take infinitely many (emulated) steps of P. Even though the emulation does not ensure progress for *every* active process, it helps in answering the following question: is there a *decision task T* [3] for $n + 1$ processes that can be solved by objects of consensus power less than $n + 1$ but *cannot* be solved using n-consensus objects? The answer is "no": our non-blocking emulation implies that every *terminating* protocol for $n + 1$ processes using objects A of consensus power less than $n + 1$ can be wait-free emulated using n-consensus objects. Thus, from the task-solvability perspective, n-consensus is the strongest object for systems of $n + 1$ processes in which $(n + 1)$-process consensus is unachievable, i.e., in a strict sense, there are no objects between n- and $n + 1$-consensus.

The emulation technique presented in this paper is novel and interesting in its own right. It is based on the fundamental *inseparability* property which we show to be inherent for all $(n + 1)$-process protocols that use registers and objects of consensus power less than $n + 1$. Inseparability generalizes the concept of connectivity used in classical characterizations of distributed computing models (e.g., [1,2,4]) and it captures the very essence of the inability of a collection of shared objects to solve consensus.

Note that the aforementioned emulation does not answer the question of *robustness* of (deterministic) consensus hierarchy posed by Jayanti [5]. Our protocol does not imply that a protocol using a *composition* of deterministic objects A and B, each of consensus power n, can be emulated using only registers and n-consensus objects. Proving or refuting this statement is left for future work.

The paper is organized as follows. In Section 2, we describe the system model. In Section 3, we introduce the key notions of our result: inseparability and non-separating paths. Section 4 presents our emulation protocol and Section 5 concludes the paper.

2   Preliminaries

In this section, we describe the system model, and introduce some key notions. Missing details of the model can be found in [2,5,6].

Processes. We consider a set Π of $n + 1$ ($n \geq 1$) asynchronous processes $p_1, p_2, \ldots, p_{n+1}$ that communicate using atomic shared *objects*. Every object is characterized by a set of *ports* that it exports, a set of *states* the object can take, a set of *operations* that can be performed on the object, a set of *responses* that these operations can return, and a relation known as the *sequential specification* of the type that defines, for every state, port, and applied operation, the set of possible resulting states and returned responses. We assume that objects are *deterministic*: the sequential specification of a deterministic object is a function that carries each state, port, and operation to a new state and a corresponding response. In particular, we assume that processes have access to read-write shared memory.

Protocols. A *protocol* P is a collection of deterministic state machines $P_1, \ldots P_{n+1}$, one for each process. For every i, P_i maps every local state of p_i to the next operation it has to perform on a shared object (if any). Since all protocols and shared objects we consider are deterministic, we can model an *execution* of a protocol as an *initial* system state and a sequence of process identifiers, specifying the order in which processes take steps in the execution. To simplify the presentation, our emulation assumes that a protocol has only one initial state. In Section 4.3, we show how our emulation can be extended to protocols with multiple initial states.

We also distinguish between *terminating* and *non-terminating* protocols. In a terminating protocol, every process that takes sufficiently many steps reaches an irrevocable *final* view (we say that the process *terminates*). Without loss of generality, we consider protocols in which a terminated process keeps taking *null* steps, i.e., we focus on protocols in which every active process takes infinitely many steps.

States and views. Every finite execution is regarded as a *state of* P, unambiguously defining states of all shared objects and local states of processes (to be called *views*) that result after the execution completes.

There is a natural ancestor/descendant relation between states of P: we say that state x' is a *descendant* of state x (x is an *ancestor* of x'), and we write $x \rightarrow x'$, if x is a prefix of x'. We also say that a (finite or infinite) execution e *extends* a state x if x is a prefix of e.

We say that a view v of a process p_i *appears* in a state x (of P) if the local state of p_i in x is v. Let $view_i(x)$ denote the view of process p_i that appears in state x. We say that a view v is *compatible with a state* x if v appears in x or an ancestor of x.

For an execution e and a process p_i, $e|i$ denotes the sequence of distinct views of p_i (resulting after p_i takes its steps in e) that appear in prefixes of e (in the order of appearance). For two distinct views v and v' of the same process p_i, we say that v' is a descendant of v (or v precedes v'), and we write $v \rightarrow v'$, if there is an execution e such that v precedes v' in $e|i$.

For two views v and v' of the same process p_i such that $v \rightarrow v'$, $next(v, v')$ denotes the earliest view u such that (i) $v \rightarrow u$, and (ii) $u = v'$ or $u \rightarrow v'$. We say that v immediately precedes v' if $v \rightarrow v'$ and $v' = next(v, v')$.

Consensus. The *consensus* problem [1] is one in which a set of processes need to reach an agreement on one of their *proposed* values. More precisely, every process starts with an initial proposal in $\{0, 1\}$ and it is required that: (Termination) Every process that takes sufficiently many steps eventually decides on a value; (Agreement) No two processes decide on different values; (Validity) If a process decides on a value v, then v was proposed by some process.

It is sometimes convenient to relate the consensus problem among m processes to the m-*consensus object*. The object exports m ports and can be accessed with the *propose*() operation that takes a value as a parameter and returns one of the proposed values, so that no two *propose*() operations return different values.

We say that an object A *solves m-process consensus* if there exists an m-process protocol that solves consensus using read-write registers and copies of object A.[1] The *consensus power* of A, denoted $cons(A)$, is the largest m such that A solves m-process consensus [2]. If no such largest m exists, then $cons(A) = \infty$. Further, if $cons(A) = n$, then $cons(\{A, n\text{-}consensus\})$, the consensus power of the composition of A and n-process consensus, is n, i.e., $(n + 1)$-process consensus cannot be solved using copies of an object of consensus power n and n-consensus objects [4].

Team consensus is a form of consensus in which processes are divided a priori into two non-empty teams and which satisfies Validity, Termination, and *Team Agreement*: no two processes decide on different values, under the condition that processes on the same team propose the same value. Consensus is, in a precise sense, equivalent to *team consensus*: if A can solve m-process team consensus, then A can solve m-process consensus [8,9].

Approximate agreement. Though it is impossible to reach non-trivial agreement using only read-write registers [1,10], we can achieve *approximate* agreement [11] that guarantees that all decided values are sufficiently *close*. Formally, the ε-agreement task (where $\varepsilon \in [0, 1]$ is a specified parameter) is defined for two processes, q_0 and q_1, as follows. Every process q_i ($i = 0, 1$) outputs a value $x_i \in [0, 1]$ such that (1) if q_i is the only participant, then q_i outputs i, and (2) $|x_0 - x_1| \le \varepsilon$. It is known that, for all $\varepsilon \in (0, 1]$, the 2-process ε-agreement task is wait-free solvable using read-write registers [11].

Protocol emulation. We address the following problem: given a protocol P that uses objects in a set $\mathcal{C}$, design a protocol that *emulates* P using objects in a set $\mathcal{C}'$. In the emulation, processes start from their views in an initial state of P, and every active (not yet terminated) process may periodically output a new view that results after the process takes one more step of P.

On the safety side, the emulation must guarantee that all views output by the processes are compatible with *some* execution of P. On the liveness side, a *non-blocking* emulation ensures that either every participating process eventually reaches a final view, or at least one participant obtains infinitely many distinct views. Clearly, if P is terminating, then any non-blocking emulation of P is also *wait-free*: every participant eventually reaches a final view.

3   Inseparability

The following observation generalizes the arguments of most valence-based asynchronous impossibility proofs (e.g., [1,2,4]). Let P be any protocol using objects of collective consensus power n, and let x be any state of P. Then the immediate descendants of x are, in a strict sense, connected. More precisely, for every non-empty partitions Π_0 and Π_1 of Π, there exists an execution e of P going through x in which some process p_i takes infinitely many steps, without being able to decide whether the first step of e extending x was taken by a member of Π_0 or a member of Π_1.

---

[1] The protocol designer is allowed to initialize the shared objects to any (reachable) states: this ability does not affect the consensus power of deterministic objects [7].

Formally, let P be any protocol, and e_0 and e_1 be executions of P. We say that e_0 and e_1 are i-*confusing* if (1) p_i takes infinitely many steps in both e_0 and e_1, and (2) $e_0|i = e_1|i$. In other words, p_i cannot distinguish e_0 and e_1, even by taking infinitely many steps of P.

Let x_0 and x_1 be any two states of P. We say that x_0 and x_1 are *inseparable* (by P), and we write $x_0 \sim x_1$, if there exist $p_i \in \Pi$ and e_0 and e_1, extending x_0 and x_1, respectively, such that e_0 and e_1 are i-confusing and either $view_i(x_0) = view_i(x_1)$, or $view_i(x_0)$ immediately precedes $view_i(x_1)$, or vice versa.

Lemma 1. *Let x_0 and x_1 be any two states of a protocol P, such that $x_0 = x_1$ or $x_0 \rightarrow x_1$ and some process $p_i \in \Pi$ takes at most one step in x_1 after x_0. Then $x_0 \sim x_1$.*

Proof. Indeed, since p_i takes at most one step in x_1 after x_0, either $view_i(x_0) = view_i(x_1)$ or $view_i(x_0)$ immediately precedes $view_i(x_1)$. Let e be any execution extending x_1 in which p_i takes infinitely many steps. Then $e_0 = e$ and $e_1 = e$ are i-confusing, and, thus, $x_0 \sim x_1$. □

3.1 Inseparably Connected Sets of States

Let $\approx$ denote the transitive closure of the $\sim$ relation. We say that a set of states is *inseparably connected* if, for every two states x_0 and x_1 in the set, $x_0 \approx x_1$.

Let x be any state of P. An *immediate descendant* of x is a one-step extension of x, i.e., a state that results after some process applies exactly one step to x. Note that if $x_0 = x_1$ or x_0 is an immediate descendant of x_1, then, by Lemma 1, $x_0 \sim x_1$, and if x_0 is a descendant of x_1, then $x_0 \approx x_1$. Let $G(x)$ denote the set of all $n+1$ immediate descendants of x. We say that a protocol P is *inseparably connected* if for every state x of P, $G(x)$ is inseparably connected.

Theorem 1. *Let A be any deterministic object of consensus power less than $n+1$ and P be any protocol among $n+1$ processes using copies of A and read-write registers. Then P is inseparably connected.*

Proof. Suppose, by contradiction, that there exists a state x of P, such that $G(x)$, the set of all $n+1$ immediate descendants of x, is not inseparably connected. We establish a contradiction by presenting a protocol that solves (team) consensus among $n+1$ processes using objects A and read-write registers.

Since $G(x)$ is not inseparably connected, it can be partitioned into two non-empty sets, G_0 and G_1, such that for all $x_0 \in G_0$ and $x_1 \in G_1$, $x_0 \nsim x_1$. Let processes whose steps applied to x result in G_0 constitute team Π_0 and the rest constitute team Π_1. Clearly, $\Pi_0 \cup \Pi_1 = \Pi$.

Assume that all objects used by P are initialized to their states in x. Let R_0 and R_1 be two shared registers, initially $\perp$. Every process p_i first writes its proposal in a shared register R_j such that $p_i \in \Pi_j$. Then p_i takes steps of P starting from its view in x. Note that the views obtained by the processes are compatible with some execution of P extending x. The process stops when, for some $k \in \{0, 1\}$, its view cannot appear in any descendant of any state in G_{1-k}. At this point, the process returns the value read in R_k.

Suppose, by contradiction, that the Termination property of consensus is violated: assume, without loss of generality, that P has an execution e_0 passing through a state $x_0 \in G_0$, in which p_i takes infinitely many steps, and every view obtained by p_i in e_0 could have been obtained in an execution e_1 passing through a state $x_1 \in G_1$. Thus, e_0 and e_1 are i-confusing. Moreover, since x_0 and x_1 are immediate descendants of the same state x, $view_i(x_0) = view_i(x_1)$, or $view_i(x_0)$ immediately precedes $view_i(x_1)$, or vice versa. Thus, $x_0 \sim x_1$ — a contradiction.

Now suppose that a process gets a view that is only compatible with descendants of states in G_k ($k \in \{0, 1\}$). Thus, the current execution e extends a state in G_k, and the process that took the first step in e after x has previously written its proposal in R_k. By the algorithm, the process returns the value read in R_k and, thus, Validity is satisfied. Since e extends a state in G_k, no process can ever obtain a view (in e) that is only compatible with executions extending a state in G_{1-k}. Thus, no process ever returns a value read in R_{1-k}. Now assume that processes on the same team (Π_0 or Π_1) propose the same value. Thus, no two different non-$\perp$ can be read in R_k — Team Agreement is ensured.

Hence, object A solves $(n + 1)$-team consensus and, therefore, $(n + 1)$-consensus — a contradiction.   □

3.2 Non-separating Paths

In every phase of our emulation protocol, processes try to reconcile their (possibly different) estimates of the emulated system state and the views to be output. Since we can use only registers and n-consensus objects, $n+1$ participants can only be guaranteed to reach *approximate* agreement. The approximate agreement is solved along a *path* connecting the concurrent estimates.

Formally, let P be a protocol, and (v_0, x_0) and (v_1, x_1) be tuples such that for $i = 0, 1$, x_i is a non-initial state of P, and v_i is a view that is compatible with x_i. Let $prec_i(x_0, x_1)$ ($i = 0, 1$) be defined as follows. If $x_0 \sim x_1$, then $prec_i(x_0, x_1) = x_i$. Otherwise, $prec_i(x_0, x_1)$ is the immediate predecessor of x_i.

We say that a sequence $(u_0, y_0), \ldots, (u_\ell, y_\ell)$, where each u_j is a view of P and each y_i is a state of P, is a *non-separating path connecting* (v_0, x_0) *and* (v_1, x_1) if:

(1) $(u_0, y_0) = (v_0, x_0)$ and $(u_\ell, y_\ell) = (v_1, x_1)$.
(2) $\forall j = 0, \ldots, \ell - 1$, u_j and u_{j+1} are both compatible with both y_j and y_{j+1}.
(3) $\forall j = 0, \ldots, \ell - 1$, $y_j \sim y_{j+1}$.
(4) $\forall j = 1, \ldots, \ell - 1$, $\exists i \in \{0, 1\}$, such that (i) $prec_i(x_0, x_1) \rightarrow y_j$ and (ii) either $u_j = v_i$ or u_j is not compatible with $prec_i(x_0, x_1)$.

Property (2) stipulates that the views of every two neighbors in a non-separating path must be compatible with both corresponding states. Intuitively, we need this property to ensure that all views produced by our emulation appear in some execution of the emulated protocol, i.e., the emulation is *safe*.

Property (3) requires that the states of every two neighbors in a non-separating path must be inseparable. Thus, it makes sure that competing state estimates produced by our emulation protocol are, in a strict sense, connected, so we could inductively extend the emulation. Property (4) implies that, for every view u_j on the path, there exists $i \in \{0, 1\}$ such that, unless $u_j = v_i$, u_j appears in a descendant of $prec_i(x_0, x_1)$ and does not appear in $prec_i(x_0, x_1)$. In other words, view u_j is "fresh" with respect to $prec_i(x_0, x_1)$. Intuitively, we need properties (3) and (4) to ensure that our emulation indeed makes progress, i.e., in each phase of the emulation, at least one participating process manages to perform one more step of P and obtain a new view.

If x_0' and x_1' are inseparable, then any two tuples (v_0, x_0) and (v_1, x_1) where each x_i $(i = 0, 1)$ is x_i' or one of x_i''s immediate descendants and v_i is compatible with x_i can be connected via a non-separating path. Moreover the *length* of this path (the number of hops) is bounded by $10(2n + 1)$.

Lemma 2. *Let P be any inseparably-connected protocol. Let x_0' and x_1' be non-initial states of P such that $x_0' \sim x_1'$. Then for all (v_0, x_0) and (v_1, x_1) such that $\forall i = 0, 1$, $x_i \in \{x_i'\} \cup G(x_i')$ and v_i is compatible with x_i, there exists a non-separating path connecting (v_0, x_0) and (v_1, x_1) the length of which does not exceed $\mathcal{L} = 10(2n + 1)$.*

Proof. There are three possible cases:

(a) Assume that $x_0 \sim x_1$ and, thus, $prec_j(x_0, x_1) = x_j$, $j = 0, 1$.

Let i be the smallest process identifier such that there exists i-confusing executions e_0 and e_1 that extend x_0 and x_1, respectively, and either $view_i(x_0) = view_i(x_1)$, or $view_i(x_0)$ immediately precedes $view_i(x_1)$, or $view_i(x_1)$ immediately precedes $view_i(x_0)$.

Let z_j $(j = 0, 1)$ be the shortest prefix of e_j in which p_i obtains a view that is compatible *neither* with x_0 *nor* with x_1. Note that, since e_0 and e_1 are i-confusing, $view_i(z_0) = view_i(z_1) = v$, and, since $view_i(x_0)$ and $view_i(x_1)$ are either identical or one of them immediately precedes the other, for each $j = 0, 1$, p_i takes at most two steps from x_j to reach view v.

Let y_j $(j = 0, 1)$ be the shortest prefix of e_j in which p_i takes at least one step after x_j (note that y_j can be equal to z_j). Let $u_j = view_i(y_j)$ (note that u_j can be equal to v).

Now we construct the non separating path connecting (v_0, x_0) and (v_1, x_1) as follows (Figure 1 (a)): (v_0, x_0), (v_0, y_0), (u_0, y_0), (u_0, z_0), (v, z_0), (v, z_1), (u_1, z_1),

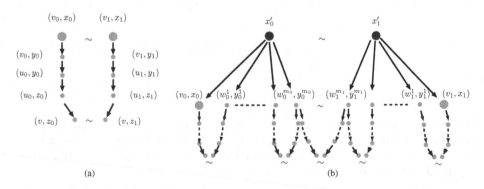

Fig. 1. Non-separating path connecting (v_0, x_0) and (v_1, x_1): (a) $x_0 \sim x_1$, (b) $x_0 \in G(x_0')$ and $x_1 \in G(x_1')$

(u_1, y_1), (v_1, y_1), (v_1, x_1). Trivially, property (1) of non-separating paths are satisfied. Note that, by construction, e_0 and e_1 extend z_0 and z_1, respectively, and $view_i(z_0) = view_i(z_1) = v$. Since e_0 and e_1 are i-confusing, $z_0 \sim z_1$. By Lemma 1, $x_j \sim y_j$ and $y_j \sim z_j$ ($j = 0, 1$). Thus, property (3) is satisfied.

For each internal vertex (u, y) in the path, u is compatible with the states of both its neighbors and, unless $u \in \{v_0, v_1\}$, u is not compatible with $x_j = prec_j(x_0, x_1)$ ($j = 0, 1$). Finally, each internal state in the path (y_j or z_j) is a descendant of $x_j = prec_j(x_0, x_1)$. Thus, properties (2) and (4) are satisfied. The length of the path is 9.

(b) Now assume that $x_0 \nsim x_1$, $x_0 \in G(x'_0)$ and $x_1 \in G(x'_1)$, and, thus, $prec_i(x_0, x_1)$ is the immediate ancestor of x_i, $i = 0, 1$. Recall that $x'_0 \sim x'_1$. Let i be the smallest process identifier such that there exists i-confusing executions e_0 and e_1 that extend x'_0 and x'_1, respectively, and $view_i(x'_0)$ and $view_i(x'_1)$ are either identical or one of them precedes the other.

Let, for $j = 0, 1$, y'_j be the state resulting after the first step of e_j is applied to x'_j. Clearly, $y'_0 \in G(x'_0)$ and $y'_1 \in G(x'_1)$. Note that since executions e_0 and e_1 are i-confusing executions for x'_0 and x'_1, they are also i-confusing executions for y'_0 and y'_1. Let u'_j denote the last view of the process taking the last step in y'_j, $j = 0, 1$.

Similarly to case (a), let y_j ($j = 0, 1$) denote the shortest prefix of e_j in which p_i takes exactly one step after x'_j, and z_j denote the shortest prefix of e_j in which p_i obtains a view that is compatible neither with x'_0 nor with x'_1. Let u_j and be the last view of p_i in y_j. Note that since $x'_0 \sim x'_1$, $view_i(z_0) = view_i(z_1) = v$. Thus, $Z = (u'_0, y'_0)$, (u'_0, y_0), (u_0, y_0), (u_0, z_0), (v, z_0), (v, z_1), (u_1, z_1), (u_1, y_1), (u'_1, y_1), (u'_1, y'_1) is a non-separating path connecting (u'_0, y'_0) and (u'_1, y'_1).

Recall that P is inseparably connected, so $G(x'_0)$ and $G(x'_1)$ are each inseparably connected. Thus, for all $j = 0, 1$, there is a sequence of states $y^0_j, \ldots, y^{m_j}_j$ of $G(x'_j)$ such that $y^0_j = x_j$, $y^{m_j}_j = y'_j$, and, for each $k = 0, \ldots, m_j - 1$, $y^k_j \sim y^{k+1}_j$. Let w^k_j denote the last view of the process taking the last step in y^k_j.

Now let, for each $j = 0, 1$ and $k = 0, \ldots, m_j - 1$, Z^k_j denote the non-separating path, constructed as described above in case (a), connecting (w^k_j, y^k_j) and (w^{k+1}_j, y^{k+1}_j).

Now consider the concatenation of paths $Z^0_0, Z^1_0, \ldots, Z^{m_0-1}_0, Z^{m_0}_0, Z, Z^{m_1}_1, Z^{m_1-1}_1, \ldots, Z^1_1, Z^0_1$ (Figure 1 (b)). Inductively, this is a non-separating path connecting (v_0, x_0) and (v_1, x_1). Since paths Z^k_j and Z are bounded by 9 and $m_j \leq n$ ($j = 0, 1$), the total length of the non-separating path is bounded by $9(2n + 1) + 2n < 10(2n + 1)$.

(c) Finally, assume that $x_0 \nsim x_1$, $x_0 = x'_0$ and $x_1 \in G(x'_1)$. Let x''_0 be the state in $G(x_0)$ such that there exists $x''_1 \in G(x'_1)$ and $x''_0 \sim x''_1$ (since P is inseparably connected, such x''_0 and x''_1 do exist). Let v''_j denote the last view of the process taking the last step in x''_j, $j = 0, 1$.

By employing the reasoning of case (b), we construct a non-separating path Z connecting (v''_0, x''_0) and (v_1, x_1). Since x''_0 and x''_1 are inseparable, the path does not "travel" through states in $G(x_0)$, and the length of Z is bounded by $9(n + 1) + n$.

Then the non-separating path connecting (v_0, x_0) and (v_1, x_1) is obtained by adding (v_0, x_0), (v_0, x''_0) to the beginning of Z. The case $x_0 \in G(x'_0)$ and $x_1 = x'_1$ is symmetric. The length of the resulting path is bounded by $10(2n + 1)$.   □

3.3   P-reconciliation

To reconcile possibly conflicting estimates of the system state and the view to promote, our emulation of a protocol P uses a subroutine called P-reconciliation. In the 2-process P-reconciliation task, every process q_i ($i = 0, 1$) has an input (v_i, x_i), where v_i is a view of P and x_i is a state of P such that v_i is compatible with x_i. If both q_0 and q_1 participate, and there exists a non-separating path connecting (v_0, x_0) and (v_1, x_1) of length at most $\mathcal{L}$ (let γ be the shortest such path), then each q_i outputs a tuple (U_i, z_i) where U_i is a set of at most two views and y_i is a state of P, such that:

(1) $U_0 \cap U_1 \neq \emptyset$, and
(2) there exist two neighbors (u_0, y_0) and (u_1, y_1) in γ such that $\{z_0, z_1\} \subseteq \{y_0, y_1\}$ and $U_0 \cup U_1 \subseteq \{u_0, u_1\}$.

Otherwise, if q_i is the only participant in the task or no such path γ exists, then q_i outputs $(\{v_i\}, x_i)$.

Shared variables :
    R_0, R_1, initially $\bot$

upon P-reconcile(v_i, x_i):

```
1:    R_i := (v_i, x_i)
2:    s := ε-agreement()    {ε = 1/(2L) where L = 10(2n + 1)}
3:    if R_{1-i} = ⊥ then    {If q_i goes solo }
4:        return ({v_i}, x_i)
5:    (v_{1-i}, x_{1-i}) := R_{1-i}    {Fetch the competing proposal}
6:    if (v_0, x_0) and (v_1, x_1) cannot be connected via a non-separating path of length ≤ L then
7:        return ({v_i}, x_i)
8:    let (u_0, y_0), (u_1, y_1) ..., (u_ℓ, y_ℓ) be the shortest non-separating path
          connecting (v_0, x_0) and (v_1, x_1)
9:    let j ∈ {0, ..., ℓ} be such that s ∈ ((j − 1/2)/ℓ, (j + 1/2)/ℓ]
10:   z := y_j
11:   if s ∈ ((j − 1/4)/ℓ, (j + 1/4)/ℓ] then    {If s belongs to 1/4ℓ-vicinity of j/ℓ}
12:       U = {u_j}
13:   else if s < j/ℓ    {s belongs to the mid-half of [(j − 1)/ℓ, j/ℓ]}
14:       U = {u_{j−1}, u_j}
15:   else    {s belongs to the mid-half of [j/ℓ, (j + 1)/ℓ]}
16:       U = {u_j, u_{j+1}}
17:   return (U, z)
```

Fig. 2. 2-process P-reconciliation task: code for every process q_i, $i = 0, 1$

Lemma 3. *P-reconciliation is wait-free solvable using read-write registers.*

Proof. A P-reconciliation algorithm is presented in Figure 2. In the algorithm, every process q_i first registers its proposal (v_i, x_i) in the shared memory (line 1). Then it runs ε-agreement with $\varepsilon = 1/(2\mathcal{L})$ ($\mathcal{L} = 10(2n + 1)$). Let $s \in [0, 1]$ be the value returned by ε-agreement. Then q_i reads R_{1-i} (line 3). If $R_{1-i} = \bot$ or there does not exist a non-separating path γ of length $\ell \leq \mathcal{L}$ connecting the two proposals, then q_i returns $(\{v_i\}, x_i)$ (lines 4 and 7). Otherwise, q_i computes a tuple (U_i, z_i), based on the output of ε-agreement (s), as follows (the procedure is summarized in Figure 3):

   – Let $j \in \{0, \ldots, \ell\}$ be such that s belongs to a $1/(2\ell)$-neighborhood of j/ℓ, i.e., $s \in ((j - 1/2)/\ell, (j + 1/2)/\ell]$. Then p_i sets $z_i = y_j$.

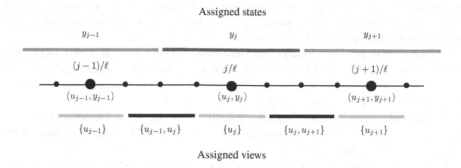

Fig. 3. Mapping the output of ε-agreement to views U_i and states y_i

- If s belongs to the $1/(4\ell)$-neighborhood of j/ℓ, i.e., $s \in ((j-1/4)/\ell, (j+1/4)/\ell]$ then p_i sets $U_i = \{u_j\}$.
- Otherwise, if $s < j/\ell$, i.e., s belongs to the middle half-interval of $[(j-1)/\ell, j/\ell]$, then p_i sets $U_i = \{u_{j-1}, u_j\}$. Else, if s belongs to the middle half-interval of $[j/\ell, (j+1)/\ell]$, then p_i sets $U_i = \{u_j, u_{j+1}\}$.

Since $\varepsilon = 1/(2\mathcal{L})$ and $\ell \leq \mathcal{L}$, the values s_0 and s_1 returned by ε-agreement at q_0 and q_1, respectively, are within $1/(2\ell)$ from each other.

By inspecting Figure 3 and taking into accound that $|s_0 - s_1| \leq 1/(2\ell)$, we observe that the following cases are only possible.

If q_0 and q_1 return the same state y_j (s_0 and s_1 both belong to the $1/(2\ell)$-neighborhood of some j/ℓ), then either U_0 and U_1 are equal to the same non-empty set of views ($U_0 = U_1 \in \{\{u_{j-1}, u_j\}, \{u_j\}, \{u_j, u_{j+1}\}\}$), or U_0 and U_1 are related by containment ($\{U_0, U_1\} \subseteq \{\{u_{j-1}, u_j\}, \{u_j\}\}$ or $\{U_0, U_1\} \subseteq \{\{u_j, u_{j+1}\}, \{u_j\}\}$). In both cases, the set of all returned views is either a subset of $\{u_{j-1}, u_j\}$ or or a subset of $\{u_j, u_{j+1}\}$, and the properties of P-reconciliation are satisfied.

If q_0 and q_1 return different states, then the two states can only be some y_j and y_{j+1} (neighbors in γ). Furthermore, either q_0 and q_1 both return $\{u_j, u_{j+1}\}$ as the sets of views, or one of them returns $\{u_j, u_{j+1}\}$, and the other — $\{u_j\}$ or $\{u_{j+1}\}$, and the properties of P-reconciliation are satisfied.   □

4   Protocol Emulation

Let P be any inseparably connected $(n + 1)$-process protocol. In Figure 4, we present a non-blocking emulation of P that uses only n-consensus objects and read-write registers.

4.1   Overview

In the emulation, every process periodically outputs views, called *converged views*. The emulation guarantees that at every moment of time, there exists an execution of P that is compatible with the sequence of views output locally at every process, and either every participating process eventually reaches a final view, or at least one participant outputs infinitely many views.

The emulation proceeds in asynchronous *phases*. The participants of a phase first split into two teams, q_0 and q_1. If $n = 1$, then p_i is assigned to team q_i, $i = 0, 1$. If $n \geq 2$, then every process dynamically chooses its team using a sequence of n **test-and-set** objects.[2] Every process that wins one of the test-and-set objects joins the first team, denoted q_0, and the left-out process constitutes the second team, denoted q_1. Note that if $n \geq 2$ and n or less processes participate in a phase, then there can be at most active team in that phase — q_0.

Each team q_j then agrees on the estimate of the emulated system state and a "fresh" view of a member of q_j that q_j is willing to promote in the current phase (in case $n \geq 2$, team q_0 uses an n-consensus object for this).

Shared variables :
    n-consensus objects $C[\,][\,]$ {*An array of consensus objects for every phase*}

Important local variables at p_i :
    x_i, initially $\bar{x}$ {*Current system state estimate ($\bar{x}$ is the initial system state)*}
    v_i, initially $view_i(\bar{x})$ {*The last converged view of p_i*}

```
1:   k := 0
2:   repeat
3:       k := k + 1
4:       if v_i = view_i(x_i) then
5:           z_i := the state after p_i applies its step to x_i
6:       else
7:           z_i := x_i
8:       w_i := next(v_i, view_i(z_i))    {Choose the next view of p_i to promote}
9:       join a team q_j (j = 0, 1)    {If n ≥ 2, first n join q_0 using test-and-set objects,}
                                       {and the last joins q_1; if n = 1, p_i joins team q_i i = 0, 1}
10:      (w, z) := agree with q_j on (w_i, z_i)    {If n ≥ 2, then q_0 uses n-consensus}
11:      (U, y) := P-reconcile_k(w, z)    {On behalf of team q_j, using n-consensus}
12:      x_i := y
13:      if ∃u ∈ U, v_i ⇀ u then    {A view of p_i has converged in phase k}
14:          v_i := next(v_i, u)    {Compute the next view of p_i toward u}
15:          output v_i
16:  until v_i is final
```

Fig. 4. The emulation protocol: code for every process p_i, $i = 1, \ldots, n + 1$

The two teams then act as processes q_0 and q_1 in an instance of P-reconciliation task which they use to reconcile on how to make progress. If $n \geq 2$, then in every instance of P-reconciliation, multiple processes in team q_0 use a series of n-consensus objects (distinct for every instance of P-reconciliation) to act as a single process. Team q_0 is associated with an $(n + 1)$-array of registers T_0, and q_1 is associated with a register T_1. To write a value v in executing the ε-agreement protocol, every process in q_0 increments its local sequence number and updates its slot in T_n with v, equipped with the monotonically increasing sequence number, while q_1 simply writes the value in T_1. To perform a read operation, processes in q_0 read T_1 and use n-process consensus to agree

---

[2] Test-and-set objects can be wait-free implemented from 2-process consensus objects and thus from objects of consensus power 2 [12].

on the read value, while q_1 reads all slots in T_0 and returns the value with the largest sequence number.

Let the *P-reconcile*$_k(w, z)$ procedure return a tuple (U, y) at process p_i (line 11). Then p_i adopts y as its state estimate, and if U contains a view u of p_i, then p_i outputs the next view toward u (line 15). We demonstrate below that, inductively, all views output up to phase k are compatible with every state estimate computed at the end of phase k. Furthermore, by the properties of P-reconciliation, all views in U are "fresh", i.e., they extend views output in previous phases. Since the sets of views returned by P-reconciliation have a non-empty intersection, at least one process p_i participating in every phase is guaranteed to output a new view at the end of the phase. Thus, the resulting simulation is both safe and live.

4.2 Correctness

Theorem 2. *Every inseparably connected $(n+1)$-process protocol P can be emulated in a nonblocking manner using n-consensus objects and read-write registers.*

Proof. Consider the protocol in Figure 4. We show first that the protocol preserves the following invariants:

(P1) In each phase k, there exist two inseparable states $\tilde{x}_0$ and $\tilde{x}_1$ of P such that each system state estimate x_i computed at the end of phase k is in $\{\tilde{x}_0, \tilde{x}_1\}$, and all views output up to phase k are compatible with both $\tilde{x}_0$ and $\tilde{x}_1$.

(P2) At the end of each phase k, at least one process p_i *that participated in the phase* (i.e., reached line 9 in Figure 4 in phase k) succeeds in taking one more emulated step of P and outputs a new view.

Initially, all processes agree on the initial state of P, denoted $\bar{x}$, and the initial views of all processes are compatible with $\bar{x}$. Inductively, suppose that P1 holds at the end of phase $k - 1$. In phase k, every process p_i chooses the next state z_i and the next view w_i (that p_i obtains if it is chosen to make a new step of P), based on its current view v_i and its current system state estimate x_i (lines 5 and 8). Note that each $z_i \in \{\tilde{x}_0, \tilde{x}_1\} \cup G(\tilde{x}_0) \cup G(\tilde{x}_1)$, and w_i is compatible with z_i. Since $\tilde{x}_0 \sim \tilde{x}_1, prec_j(z_0, z_1) \in \{\tilde{x}_0, \tilde{x}_1\}$ $(j = 0, 1)$.

Let $(\tilde{w}_j, \tilde{z}_j)$ denote the tuple proposed by team q_j $(j = 0, 1)$ to the P-reconciliation procedure in line 10, and let (U_j, y_j) be the value returned by *P-reconcile*$_k(\tilde{w}_j, \tilde{z}_j)$. By Lemma 2, there exists a non-separating path connecting $(\tilde{w}_0, \tilde{z}_0)$ and $(\tilde{w}_1, \tilde{z}_1)$ of length $\leq \mathcal{L}$. By the properties of P-reconciliation, (U_0, y_0) and (U_1, y_1) correspond to some neighbors in such a path (let us denote it γ).

Thus, by the properties of non-separating paths, y_0 and y_1 are inseparable, and every view $U_0 \cup U_1$ is compatible with both y_0 and y_1. Further, each y_j extends $\tilde{x}_0$ or $\tilde{x}_1$, and each $u \in U_0 \cup U_1$ is *not* compatible with some $\tilde{x}_0$ or $\tilde{x}_1$, unless $u \in \{\tilde{w}_0, \tilde{w}_1\}$. Thus, every view that is compatible with both $\tilde{x}_0$ and $\tilde{x}_1$ is also compatible with both y_0 and y_1. Since each $p_i \in q_j$ sets x_i to y_j (line 12) and outputs a new view only if it belongs to U_j (line 14), P1 is inductively preserved.

Now, since $U_0 \cap U_1 \neq \emptyset$, there is at least one view that is seen by every process that completes the phase. Thus, at least one process p_i will find its view in U_j. Thus, at least one process will output a new view in line 15. Note that if n or less process participate in phase k (which can happen only if some process crashes in phase $k-1$ or earlier), then only one team (if $n \geq 2$, then it can only be q_0) takes part in P-reconciliation and, thus, the participants of phase k agree on the state and the view proposed by one of them. Otherwise, if all $n+1$ processes participate in phase k, *some* process in Π gets a new view. In both cases, some process *participating* in phase k obtains a new view. Thus, P2 is preserved.

Finally, P1 and P2 ensure that in every execution of our emulation, all output views are compatible with some execution of P, and, at least one active process keeps making progress by outputting new views. Thus, our protocol indeed emulates P in a non-blocking manner.   □

Theorems 1 and 2 imply the following results:

Corollary 1. *Let A be a deterministic object of consensus power less than $n+1$. Every protocol using copies of A and registers can be emulated in a non-blocking manner using n-consensus objects and registers.*

Corollary 2. *Let A be a deterministic object of consensus power less than $n+1$. There is no task T that can be wait-free solved using copies of A and registers, but cannot be wait-free solved using n-consensus objects and registers.*

4.3 Multiple Initial States

The emulation protocol presented in the previous section can be easily extended to protocols with multiple initial states that differ only in inputs of processes. (This seems to be the case for most protocols.) Indeed, in our emulation, a team q_i needs to know the initial states of other processes only if, in a given phase k, it faces a competition with the other team q_{1-i}, i.e., only if q_i reaches line 5 of the P-reconcile algorithm in Figure 2. If this never happens, then q_i only needs to know the (estimated) states of shared objects to be able to make progress. But such a competition between q_0 and q_1 can only happen if all $n+1$ processes participate in phase k (otherwise, only one team would be "populated"). Thus, we can easily extend our emulation to the case of multiple initial states: every process registers its input in the shared memory before participating in the first phase of the emulation protocol. When q_i faces the competition with the other team (q_i reaches line 5 in Figure 2), q_i can compute an estimate of the current state of P using all $n+1$ registered inputs. ¿From this point on, the emulation will run as described in Figure 4.

5 Conclusion

We formalized one outcome of the intuition that n processes using n-process consensus are tantamount to a single process. Hence $n+1$ processes with n-process consensus are like two processes. It is easy to see why there is no task between read-write shared memory and 2-process consensus: A task's *output complex* [3] is either connected - then the two process can solve the task using reads and writes - or it is disconnected - in which case the task amounts to consensus. In generalizing this intuition we encountered certain difficulties: we only managed to equate n processes with one when a protocol was given ahead of time, and we could derive only a non-blocking emulation of the protocol. We conjecture that these limitations are inherent. We also conjecture that our results can be extended from $n + 1$ to any number of processes between $n + 1$ and $2n$: any deterministic object of consensus power less than $n + 1$, when used to solve a task T for k processes, $n + 1 \leq k \leq 2n$, can be replaced with n-consensus objects.

Acknowledgments

Special thanks should go to Rachid Guerraoui for the observation that our emulation establishes the distinction between n- and $(n + 1)$-consensus in determinstic shared memory models.

References

1. Fischer, M.J., Lynch, N.A., Paterson, M.S.: Impossibility of distributed consensus with one faulty process. Journal of the ACM 32(3), 374–382 (1985)
2. Herlihy, M.: Wait-free synchronization. ACM Transactions on Programming Languages and Systems 13(1), 124–149 (1991)
3. Herlihy, M., Shavit, N.: The topological structure of asynchronous computability. Journal of the ACM 46(6), 858–923 (1999)
4. Chandra, T.D., Hadzilacos, V., Jayanti, P., Toueg, S.: Generalized irreducibility of consensus and the equivalence of t-resilient and wait-free implementations of consensus. SIAM J. Comput. 34(2), 333–357 (2004)
5. Jayanti, P.: On the robustness of Herlihy's hierarchy. In: Proceedings of the 12th Annual ACM Symposium on Principles of Distributed Computing (PODC), pp. 145–158 (August 1993)
6. Attiya, H., Welch, J.L.: Distributed Computing: Fundamentals, Simulations and Advanced Topics, 2nd edn. Wiley, Chichester (2004)
7. Borowsky, E., Gafni, E., Afek, Y.: Consensus power makes (some) sense! In: Proceedings of the 13th Annual ACM Symposium on Principles of Distributed Computing (PODC), pp. 363–372 (August 1994)
8. Neiger, G.: Failure detectors and the wait-free hierarchy. In: Proceedings of the 14th Annual ACM Symposium on Principles of Distributed Computing (PODC), pp. 100–109 (August 1995)
9. Ruppert, E.: The Consensus Power of Shared-Memory Distributed Systems. PhD thesis, University of Toronto (1999)
10. Loui, M.C., Abu-Amara, H.H.: Memory requirements for agreement among unreliable asynchronous processes. Advances in Computing Research, 163–183 (1987)
11. Dolev, D., Lynch, N.A., Pinter, S.S., Stark, E.W., Weihl, W.E.: Reaching approximate agreement in the presence of faults. J. ACM 33(3), 499–516 (1986)
12. Afek, Y., Weisberger, E., Weisman, H.: A completeness theorem for a class of synchronization objects (extended abstract). In: Proceedings of the 12th Annual ACM Symposium on Principles of Distributed Computing (PODC), pp. 159–170 (1993)

Non-Searchability of Random Power-Law Graphs

Philippe Duchon[1], Nicole Eggemann[2], and Nicolas Hanusse[1,*]

[1] LaBRI, CNRS, Univ. Bordeaux, 351, cours de la Libération, F-33405 Talence
duchon,hanusse@labri.fr
[2] Dept. of Mathematics, Brunel University, UK
eggemann@brunel.ac.uk

Abstract. We investigate the complexity of searching for a given vertex in a scale-free graph, using only locally gathered information. In such graphs, the number of nodes of degree x is proportional to $x^{-\beta}$ for some constant $\beta > 0$. We consider two random scale-free graph models: the Chung-Lu model and the Móri model (a generalization of the Barabási-Albert model) proving two lower bounds of $\Omega(n/\log^{\Theta(\beta)} n)$ and $\Omega(n^{1/2})$ on the expected time to find the worst-case target, under a restrictive model of local information.

Keywords: Distributed Algorithm, Routing, Random graphs.

1 Introduction

In this paper, we investigate the efficiency of local search algorithms for some relatively unstructured networks. By local search, we mean that each vertex knows its very close neighborhood, typically the identities, degrees and possibly the contents. Assuming there is no preprocessing, we are interested in seeking a vertex of a given identity starting from any vertex. The time complexity of searching is expressed as the number of vertices to explore before reaching the target or a neighbor of the target. For an arbitrary graph and a worst-case choice of vertices, time complexity can be of the same order as the size of the graph itself. However, there is some hope that for large classes of graphs, the size of the exploration sequence would drastically decrease.

Recent literature exhibits non trivial properties shared by the topologies of numerous real-world distributed networks: the combination of a low diameter, a specific degree distribution of the vertices and a sparse network are typically representative of a *small-world* topology. The degree distribution of the vertices tends to follow a power-law distribution, that is the number of vertices of degree x is proportional to $n \left(\frac{1}{x} \right)^{\beta}$ for an n-vertex graph and β a constant strictly greater than one. Graphs having this property are often called *scale-free graphs*. Moreover, it has been observed that for real-life networks, β tends to belong to the range $[2, 3]$.

In this paper, we focus on the navigability property of scale-free graphs. Roughly speaking, a labeled graph is f-*navigable* if a distributed algorithm, using only the labels of the visited vertices (or its neighborhood), is able to route a message for any

* The first and third authors were supported by the French Ministry of Research and project Navgraphe of ACI Masses de données. The second author was supported by the European Union Community under a Marie Curie Host Fellowship for Early Stage Researchers Training.

E. Tovar, P. Tsigas, and H. Fouchal (Eds.): OPODIS 2007, LNCS 4878, pp. 274–285, 2007.

source and any target along a path of $O(f)$ vertices. This concept has been introduced in a seminal paper of Kleinberg [22] (see also the excellent survey [23] and recent extensions [17,18,30,19,1]) showing the ability of a user or a mobile agent to route along shorts paths within graphs built from a deterministic graph (2D-grid) augmented by one random extra edge per node. Kleinberg gives some condition on the design of the random extra edges to get $\log^2(n)$-navigable graphs and proves that many augmentation processes lead to graphs that are not $n^{1/3}$-navigable even if the diameter is polylogarithmic (See Nguyen and Martel [28]). However, graphs in the Kleinberg model are not scale-free and it turns out that labels are very informative since the underlying subgraph is a 2D-grid and labels represent coordinates.

We show in this paper that random graphs built in different scale-free models are not n^c-navigable for explicit constants c.

Keep in mind that these lower bounds hold for *local distributed algorithms*. All local[1] distributed search algorithms presented in the literature work as follows: given the set of visited vertices, one should choose the next vertex to explore. The process stops as soon as the target is reached. In the following, the underlying network is a random scale-free labeled graph of n nodes whose identities belong to the range $[1, n]$. Each vertex knows its own identity and its degree and we study two models of local knowledge: each node either knows the labels of its neighbors (*strong model*) or it does not (*weak model*). The first model is the more realistic; the second model is mostly a technical tool to prove lower bounds, which are then extended to the strong model using known results on the maximum degree.

Recall that we are interested in the time complexity of the search. For an arbitrary graph (for instance, a chain), the time complexity is clearly linear. Due to the common properties of scale-free graphs (low diameter and existence of large degree vertices), one might hope that the time complexity for the strong model could be very small, sublinear and possibly polylogarithmic.

Such a claim can be found in different studies dealing with economic search strategies in scale-free networks (see [2,21,29]) in the strong knowledge model. In these papers, the authors start from different random graph models whose degree distributions follow power laws and provide heuristics to reach a target vertex. Simulations and mean-field analysis are used to claim that on average, the target can be reached in $O(n^c)$ steps, for constant $c < 1$, using simple greedy algorithms. To our knowledge, it is still an open problem to know if these scale-free graphs are *navigable* in the polylogarithmic sense. In this paper, we answer this question negatively for two specific models of random scale-free graphs: the first one deals with random graphs with a fixed degree distribution whereas the second one is based upon preferential attachment processes. In both models, we prove polynomial lower bounds on the number of vertices that *any local distributed algorithm* is likely to visit before reaching the target, for a worst-case choice of target[2] In the following, we develop the important difference between the two models.

---

[1] A distributed algorithm is *local* if vertices only know information on a close neighboorhood.

[2] It is assumed that the target label is chosen prior to determining the random graph; thus, our result is about the maximum, over the possible choices of targets, of the expected number of vertices the algorithm will visit.

1.1   Related Works

Scale-free models. In this section, we summarize models of scale-free graphs which are related to our work. One can distinguish two families of scale-free models: *pure random graphs* and *random evolving graphs*.

In the pure random graph models, a random graph is built from a fixed degree distribution [25] (or possibly expected degree sequence in [9,11]). In such a model, it is important to notice that the degrees of neighbors are *independant*. Aiello *et al.* [3,9] focus on the power-law distribution and show the emergence of a huge component under some condition, proving that the largest component can have linear size and a logarithmic diameter. However, the pure random graph models do not explain how a graph comes to have a power law degree sequence. The random evolving models attempt to explain this emergence of a power law distribution.

In the evolving models, one starts from a fixed small graph (a single vertex, loop, or edge) and at successive time steps, new vertices and edges are added. The target of a new edge is chosen randomly, either uniformly (*uniform attachment*) or with probability proportional to the current degree of the target (*preferential attachment*). The simplest models add a single vertex and edge per time step. Variants with higher degree can be obtained either by adding more edges per time step, or, say, by building an nd-vertex graph and merging every d consecutive vertices into one; this results in a graph with n vertices and nd edges, so that the average degree is d. In these models, the degree and age of a vertex are positively correlated. In particular, the degrees of neighbors are *not independant*, and mean-field analysis of the models should not be used for random evolving graphs. This will make a real difference with the pure random graph models whenever we aim at analysing a search process.

Most of the models based on preferential attachment and their properties can also be found in the work of Bollobás and Riordan [5]. To our knowledge, Barabási and Albert [4] first proposed the preferential attachment model with out-degree 1 in order to get a power law distribution. In [6] (see also [5],[7]) Bollobás and Riordan gave a mathematically precise description of the Barabási-Albert model (BA model). In [7] it was shown rigorously that the proportion $P(x)$ of vertices with degree x asymptotically obeys a power law for $x \leq n^{1/15}$, where n is the number of vertices. Furthermore, in [6] it was proved for $d \geq 2$ that the graph is connected with high probability and that the diameter is asymptotically $\log(n)/\log\log(n)$ while for $d = 1$ the diameter is approximately $\log(n)$ (see also [5]). Other variants of the BA model have been proposed [8,31,15,16] and in all of them, scale-free random graphs are obtained.

Extensions to more general models combining uniform and preferential attachment have been studied in [26,27,12,24]. In these papers, each new vertex chooses with respective probabilities p and $1 - p$ whether to use uniform or preferential attachment. Depending on the value of parameter p, the power law distribution can be observed and is proved by Cooper and Frieze [12] (in a very general model in which extra links between old vertices can also be added) or by Móri [26,27]. In these last models, the authors also give the asymptotic limit of the maximum degree, which tends to be of order n^c for some explicit constant c depending on the model parameters (but not equal to what one would obtain by extrapolating the power-law up to $P(d) = 1/n$).

To sum up, many differences exist between graphs built in the pure random scale-free graphs models and in the random evolving models:

- the degree distributions are not the same for high degree nodes in both models. For the maximum degree, we get $\Theta(\sqrt{n})$ for the Barabási and Albert models and $o(\sqrt{n})$ for the pure random graph models with a constant average degree;
- the degree distribution in evolving graphs is typically not well known for high degrees. This makes the analysis of the search process more complicated;
- for the evolving models, there is a correlation between the age, which is a natural label of a node, and its degree. It is one reason why one might have hoped that the routing task could be done quickly using only knowledge of the neighboring labels.

Distributed search in scale-free graphs. As an input, Adamic *et al.* [2] takes random graphs in the random power law model whose exponent β is strictly between 2 and 3. They propose two strategies: a pure random walk and a search process based on high degree vertices. This last distributed algorithm works as follows: at each step, the next visited vertex is the highest degree neighbor of the set of visited vertices. Using a mean-field analysis of this greedy algorithm, the authors prove that the target is reached on average in $O(n^{2(1-2/k)})$ steps whereas for a pure random walk, the time complexity becomes $O(n^{3(1-2/k)})$ steps. The article also provides simulations on random graphs and sampling of the peer-to-peer network Gnutella confirming the tendancy of the theoretical analysis. However, this article lacks a well-defined random graph model, which means that comparison to our work is difficult. For instance, the underlying graph seems to be connected whereas it is not the case for the rigourous pure scale-free random graphs (Chung-Lu for instance). The reader can also refer to [29,20] for distributed search protocols dedicated to scale-free graphs in a Peer-to-peer context.

In [21], the authors deal with a similar high degree search process as in [2], using the BA model for the underlying topology. The article contains simulations indicating that after visiting a sublinear, though polynomial, number of vertices, a path of logarithmic length can be found between the source and target vertices. Note that all of these articles deal with the average time complexity on all pairs of sources and targets.

1.2 Our Contribution

We focus on two models of random scale-free graphs: the Chung-Lu model belongs to the pure random graph models whereas the Móri graph is an evolving model mixing preferential and uniform attachment. Actually, the Móri model is extremely close to a properly defined variant of the Barabási-Albert model, which we rephrase to use *indegree* of vertices instead of total degree (this makes it possible to explore a wider range of parameters; in both models edges come with a natural orientation).

Our results are summarized in Table 1 and show the difference between different scale-free models. A precise description of the random graph models and local search models is given in Section 2. Note that the upper bound holds for a non well-defined scale-free graph (using mean-field analysis) and gives a bound on the average number of vertices to visit for *a random* target whereas our lower bounds consider the *worst-case* target. Our main results are as follows:

Theorem 1. *In the Chung-Lu model with n vertices, power-law parameter $2 < \beta < 3$ and average degre d, for constant $d > 4/e$, no searching algorithm:*

– *operating in the weak model, can find a path to vertex n with an expected number of requests less than $\Omega(n \log^{-\beta} n)$.*
– *operating in the strong model, can find a path to vertex n with an expected number of requests less than $\Omega\left(n \log^{-\frac{\beta(\beta-1)}{\beta-2}}(n)\right)$.*

Theorem 2. *For any $d \geq 1$, in the Móri graph $G_N^{(d)}$ with parameters[3] d and p ($0 < p \leq 1$), no searching algorithm operating in the weak model can find a path to vertex $n \leq N$ with an expected number of requests less than $\Omega(n^{1/2})$.*

For $p < 1/2$, no searching algorithm operating in the strong model can find a path to vertex n with an expected number of requests less than $\Omega(n^{1/2-p-\epsilon})$, for any $\epsilon > 0$.

Due to space limitations, proofs of Theorem 1 and Theorem 2 are only sketched in Sections 4 and 5. Note that our result, at least for the basic BA model ($p = 1/2$ in our indegree-based model), may appear to be a consequence of Cooper *et al.*'s result [13] that the dominating number of the BA graph of size n is $\Omega(n)$, but it is not clear how one could rigorously argue that searching for the worst-case target requires (with positive probability) visiting a positive proportion of a dominating set; the search algorithm is provided with some information in the form of vertex labels indicating their age.

Table 1. Lower bounds on search time are result of this paper

Type	Scale-free models	Knowledge model	Lower Bounds	Upper Bounds
Pure random	?	Strong		$O(n^{2(1-2/k)})$ [2]
	Chung-Lu	Weak	$\Omega\left(\frac{n}{\log^\beta n}\right)$	
	Chung-Lu	Strong	$\Omega\left(\frac{n}{\log^{\frac{\beta(\beta-1)}{\beta-2}}(n)}\right)$	
Evolving	d-out Móri	Weak	$\Omega(n^{1/2})$	
	d-out Móri	Strong	$\Omega(n^{1/2-p-\epsilon})$	

2   Models

In this section, we describe more precisely both the random graph models we study, and the class of possible searching processes over which our lower bound results hold. We concentrate on models for which rigorous degree distribution results are known.

All graphs are constructed as directed graphs, but searching always takes place in the corresponding undirected graph.

In previous literature, preferential attachment models are described in terms of total degree. In this paper, we prefer to use *indegree* instead; the advantage is that selecting an existing vertex for preferential attachment is equivalent to selecting a uniform existing edge and copying its destination.

---

[3] Móri's papers use a parameter $\alpha > -1$; correspondence with our indegree-based model is through the change of parameter $p = 1/(2 + \alpha)$, which lets p be interpreted as a probability.

2.1 Graph Models: The Chung-Lu Model

The Chung-Lu model of *random graphs with a fixed sequence of expected degrees*[9,11] is a pure random graph model which can be used to produce graphs with a power-law degree distribution.

In the $G(\mathbf{w})$ model, $\mathbf{w} = (w_1, w_2, \ldots, w_n)$ is a vector of nonnegative weights, and one obtains a random graph where vertex i has expected degree exactly w_i by including an edge (i, j) with probability $p_{i,j} = w_i w_j / \sum_k w_k$. Thus, each degree is a sum of independent Bernoulli random variables, which ensures that a node with high expected degree is extremely likely to have a degree within ratio close to 1 of its expectation. Thus, by using an expected degree sequence $\mathbf{w}$ which matches a power-law distribution, one obtains a graph whose degrees closely follow the distribution, with high probability.

We consider the graphs obtained with a sequence of the form

$$w_i = \left\lfloor ci^{-\frac{1}{\beta-1}} \right\rfloor, \quad i_0 \leq i < i_0 + n,$$

where $c = \frac{\beta-2}{\beta-1} dn^{\frac{1}{\beta-1}}$ and $i_0 = n \left(\frac{d(\beta-2)}{m(\beta-1)} \right)^{\beta-1}$ are defined as in [9,10] to achieve prescribed average degree $d > 1$, maximum degree $m = o(\sqrt{nd})$ and exponent $2 < \beta < 3$ for the power law.

2.2 Graph Models: The Móri Model

The Móri model G_t of random trees starts, at time $t = 2$, with two vertices $1, 2$ and a single edge between them; then, at each later time, a new vertex t is added, together with a single outgoing edge to an older vertex u which is chosen with probability

$$p_t(u) = \frac{d'_t(u) + \alpha}{2(t-1) + t\alpha},$$

where $\alpha > -1$ is some fixed parameter and $d'_t(u)$ denotes the total degree of vertex u at time t. Setting $p = \frac{1}{2+\alpha}$ and noticing that the indegree $d_t(u)$ is simply $d'_t(u) - 1$, we rephrase this as

$$p_t(u) = \frac{pd_t(u) + (1-p)}{t - 2p}.$$

(Note that the equality $d_t(u) = d'_t(u) - 1$ is not true for the root 1, which has outdegree 0; the correct formula for $p_t(1)$ is $(pd_t(1) + 1)/(t - 2p)$.)

Thus, each new vertex can flip a biased coin and, with probability p, select its neighbor preferentially (based on indegree), or, with probability $1 - p$, uniformly (except that the root 1 has a "weight" $1/(1 - p)$ instead of 1, and is thus slightly more likely to be chosen). Note that $p = 0$ corresponds to a uniform attachment process whereas $p = 1/2$ corresponds exactly to the Barabási-Albert model.

So far our random graph is a tree; to get the d-out Móri graph of size n (with average degree $2d$), $G_n^{(d)}$, take the Móri tree of size nd and, for each $1 \leq i \leq n$, merge vertices $d(i - 1) + 1$ to $d.i$ into a new vertex i; this may result in outdegrees lower than d for a few vertices if multiple edges and loops are removed. It is proved in [26,27] that the resulting graph has a power law degree distribution with exponent $\beta = \alpha + 3$ and maximum degree $\Theta(n^p)$.

2.3 Modeling the Searching Process

We aim at proving lower bounds on the complexity of searching for a given vertex in a random graph, using only local information. For this, we consider two models of local knowledge, which differ in the information gained when a vertex is visited for the first time. At each time step, the searching process can try to discover a new vertex by making a request. The process can stop and output the description of a path from the starting vertex to the target vertex; our *measure of its performance* is the number of requests it made prior to stopping.

- In the *weak* model, a request is in the form of a pair (u, e), where u is an already discovered vertex, and e is an edge incident to u. The answer to the request is the identity v of the other endpoint of edge e, together with the list of all edges incident to v.
- In the *strong* model, a request is in the form of a vertex u that is adjacent to an already discovered vertex, and the answer consists of the list of vertices adjacent to u.

Our lower bound proofs rely on the weak model; results on the more realistic strong model come from known upper bounds on the degrees of the studied graphs.

Note that we do not impose restrictions on the sequence of requests. If modeling a search by a mobile agent, one would require at least that each request be about a vertex adjacent to the previous one, even if it meant re-issuing a previous request, so as to model the movement from one known vertex to another. We are also not making any assumptions on the computing power or memory requirements of the searching process. Since we are working on lower bounds, any results are valid under more restrictive assumptions.

3 Vertex Equivalence

Our proofs of lower bounds are based on a probabilistic notion of vertex equivalence. Intuitively, vertices are equivalent if their identities can be exchanged without modifying the probability distribution on graphs. In this section, we make this notion precise, and show how it can be used to prove lower bounds on the complexity of searching processes.

Definition 1. *Let G be some graph on the vertex set $[[1, n]] = \{1, \ldots, n\}$, and $\sigma \in S_n$ some permutation of $[[1, n]]$. We write $\sigma(G)$ for the graph on the same vertex set that is obtained by applying permutation σ on the vertices of G.*

Definition 2. *Let G be some random graph model on the vertex set $[[1, n]]$, and $V \subset [[1, n]]$; that is, we assume that a probability space Ω is given, where a graph-valued random variable is defined with the appropriate probability distribution.*

We say that the vertices in V are (probabilistically) equivalent if, for any $\sigma \in S_V$, the random graphs G and $\sigma(G)$ have the same probability distribution.

If $\mathcal{E}$ is some event, we say that the vertices in V are equivalent conditioned on $\mathcal{E}$ if, for all $\sigma \in S_V$, G and $\sigma(G)$ have the same probability distribution, conditioned on $\mathcal{E}$.

We do not require that $\mathcal{E}$ be G-measurable – that is, when looking at a possible realization g of the graph, or even at a possible realization of the graph process $g_1, \ldots, g_t$, it might not be possible to decide whether $\mathcal{E}$ occurred. We only have to find, in a suitable (faithful) model for the construction of our random graph, an event $\mathcal{E}$ (which will be measurable with respect to the construction process) with a large enough probability such that our equivalence property holds conditioned on $\mathcal{E}$.

The following lemma is the key to our lower bounds.

Lemma 1. *If a set V of vertices is equivalent conditioned on some event $\mathcal{E}$, then any search process operating in the weak model, starting from any vertex u and searching for any vertex $v \in V$ ($v \neq u$), has an expected complexity of at least $|V|\mathbb{P}(\mathcal{E})/2$.*

Proof. The whole proof is a formalization of the intuitively obvious fact that, conditioned on $\mathcal{E}$, the vertices in V are visited by the searching process in a uniform random order until the target is found, which implies that, on expectation, half of the vertices in V are visited before the target.

Let $\mathcal{A}$ denote some searching strategy in the weak model; that is, $\mathcal{A}$ defines, for each size n, starting vertex u and target vertex v, and each finite sequence of searching requests and possible answers to these requests, the next request that the searching process should make (or, if the searching process is itself randomized, a *probability distribution* for the next request). For each possible realization g of the random graph, $\mathcal{A}$ thus defines a (finite or infinite) sequence $\mathcal{A}(g)$ of requests and answers; thus, on the probability space Ω for the random graph, it defines a stochastic searching process $(R_t, A_t)_{t \geq 0}$ (here R_t is the t-th request, and A_t is the answer to it). We are concerned with the length of this process, that is, the first index t for which the visited vertex (specified in A_t) is the target v. If this length is not finite with probability 1, then its expectation is infinite and the lemma holds; thus, in the remaining of this proof, we assume that, with probability 1, the searching process does visit its target at some point.

Let σ be a uniform random permutation of the vertices of V, independent of the random graph G and of $\mathcal{E}$. We now define a new searching process $(R'_t, A'_t)_{t \geq 0}$ as follows: for any element $\omega \in \Omega$ of the probability space,

- if $\omega \notin \mathcal{E}$, $(R'_t, A'_t)(\omega) = (R_t, A_t)(G(\omega))$ (that is, if $\mathcal{E}$ does not occur, the new searching process is pointwise identical to the original);
- if $\omega \in \mathcal{E}$, $(R'_t, A'_t)(\omega) = (R_t, A_t)(\sigma(G(\omega)))$ (that is, if $\mathcal{E}$ occurs, the new searching process is obtained by running strategy $\mathcal{A}$ on the permuted graph $\sigma(G)$).

Obviously, the probability distribution of (R'_t, A'_t) conditioned on $\overline{\mathcal{E}}$ is exactly that of (R_t, A_t) conditioned on $\overline{\mathcal{E}}$ (the two are identical); and, thanks to the conditional equivalence, the same is true for the processes conditioned on $\mathcal{E}$. Thus, the two processes (R_t, A_t) and (R'_t, A'_t) have the same probability distribution.

Now, on $\mathcal{E}$, the order in which (R'_t, A'_t) discovers the vertices of V is uniformly random (that is, conditioned on the first k of them that X' visits, the $k+1$-st is uniformly distributed among the $|V| - k$ remaining); thus, the rank among them of target v is uniformly distributed, and the expected rank for v is thus $(1 + |V|)/2$. Removing the conditioning, the expected number of vertices in V that the search process (R'_t, A'_t) visits until it finds v (an obvious lower bound on the expected number of requests) is at least $(1 + |V|)\mathbb{P}(\mathcal{E})/2$. Since (R'_t, A'_t) and (R_t, A_t) have the same distribution, this completes the proof of the lemma.

4   The Chung-Lu Graph

An example of a random graph model where vertices are naturally equivalent according to our definition is the Chung and Lu model of *random graphs with given expected degrees*.

In this model, it is clear that any vertices with the exact same weight w_i are (unconditionally) equivalent, since their incident edges are decided by independent collections of Bernoulli random variables with the same distribution.

Though such graphs are not connected, it is proved in [9] that, with high probability, they have only one "giant" component of linear size, which contains all vertices of degree a least $C \log_d(n)$ for suitable C. For an integer $k = \Theta(\log(n))$, the number of *equivalent vertices* with expected degree k is $\Theta(n/\log^\beta(n))$.

Now consider some searching algorithm on this model, where we arbitrarily set the cost of searching for some vertex in a different connected component to 0 (that is, we assume that some oracle tells us "for free" if the target is in a different component). Lemma 1 yields a lower bound of $\Omega(n/\log^\beta(n))$ in the weak model, and $\Omega(n/m\log^\beta(n))$ in the strong model if m is the (high probability) maximum degree; a more careful analysis, using the sum of the largest degrees (an algorithm operating in the strong model and using N requests, can be simulated in the weak model with a number of requests at most equal to the sum of the N largest degrees in the graph), would give an almost linear bound of $\Omega(n/\log^{\frac{\beta(\beta-1)}{\beta-2}}(n))$, when the target is a vertex of expected degree $\Theta(\log(n))$.

5   The Móri Graph

In this section, we follow a similar approach to prove Theorem 2. Contrary to the Chung-Lu case where we had unconditional equivalence, we need conditional equivalence.

5.1   Conditional Equivalence in the Móri Tree

Lemma 2. *For any integers a, b, n with $a \leq b \leq n$, in G_n, the vertex set $V = [[a+1, b]]$ is equivalent conditioned on the event*

$$\mathcal{E}_{a,b} = \bigcap_{a < k \leq b} \{N_k \leq a\},$$

where N_k denotes the father of vertex k (that is, the destination of its outgoing edge).

We are now ready to prove our main result on this model; all we need is to prove that, for suitable choices of a and b, $|V|$ and $\mathbb{P}(\mathcal{E}_{a,b})$ are both large enough.

Lemma 3. *Let $b = a + \lfloor (a-1)^{1/2} \rfloor$. Then $\mathbb{P}(\mathcal{E}_{a,b}) \geq e^{-(1-p)}$.*

5.2 Proof of Theorem 2

Combining Lemmas 2 and 3, we see that, in G_t (for $t \geq n + \sqrt{n-1}$), the vertices in $[[n, n + \sqrt{n-1}]]$ are equivalent conditioned on an event of probability bounded away from 0. Going from G_t to $G_{t/d}^{(d)}$, we also get the same equivalence result for vertices in $[[n/d, (n + \sqrt{n-1})/d]]$ conditioned on the same event (permuting the vertices in $G_{t/d}^{(d)}$ corresponds to only permuting the vertices in G_t in such a way as too keep together blocks of d consecutive vertices; this corresponds to invariance under the action of a subgroup where we have proved invariance under the action of the whole group). Lemma 1 then concludes the proof for the weak model.

The strong model case then follows from Móri's result [27] that the maximum degree in graph G_t is of order t^p, which implies that, with high probability, this maximum degree is less than $t^{p+\epsilon}$ (Móri's result does not apply for $p = 0$, which is the uniform attachment model; in this case, the maximum degree is logarithmic, as proved in [14]). Any algorithm operating in the strong model can be simulated in the weak model by replacing each request about vertex u by requests about all edges incident to u. This gives a slowdown factor of at most the maximum degree. As a consequence, the weak model lower bound of $\Omega(n^{1/2})$ translates to $\Omega(n^{1/2-p-\epsilon})$ in the strong model.   □

6 Conclusion and Open Problems

We have proved, in our weak model of local information (and in the strong model, for the Chung-Lu graphs), a polynomially high lower bound on the time required to find a given vertex in the considered model of scale-free graphs. This is in contrast with all proved upper bound results on the *diameter* of such graphs, which is at most logarithmic in expectation and with high probability. That is, these random graph models cannot be searched in time polynomial in their diameter. Thus, these graph models do not have the "small world" easy searchability property as exhibited by several authors in different models of random graphs. The technique we used seems broad enough to be adapted to other models of growing random graphs (Cooper-Frieze).

For the evolving graph model, our results carry over somehow weakly to the (arguably more realistic) strong model of local information, whenever the maximum degree can be proved to be significantly smaller than $n^{1/2}$ (like in the BA model). Note that though our results are mostly stated as "worst-case expected time", taking the average over all source and target pairs is easy, and the same asymptotic lower bound holds: $\Omega(n^{1/2})$ requests on average.

References

1. Abraham, I., Gavoille, C.: Object location using path separators. In: ACM Symp. on Principles of Distributed Computing (PODC), pp. 188–197 (2006)
2. Adamic, L., Lukose, R., Puniyani, A., Huberman, B.: Search in power law networks. Physical Reviews E 64(046135), 1–8 (2001)
3. Aiello, W., Chung, F., Lu, L.: A random graph model for massive graphs. In: STOC 2000: Proceedings of the thirty-second annual ACM symposium on Theory of computing, pp. 171–180. ACM Press, New York (2000)

4. Barabási, A.-L., Albert, R.: Emergence of scaling in random networks. Science 286(5439), 509–512 (1999)
5. Bollobás, B., Riordan, O.: Mathematical results on scale-free random graphs. In: Handbook of graphs and networks, pp. 1–34. Wiley-VCH, Berlin (2003)
6. Bollobás, B., Riordan, O.: The diameter of a scale-free random graph. Combinatorica 24(1), 5–34 (2004)
7. Bollobás, B., Riordan, O., Spencer, J., Tusnády, G.: The degree sequence of a scale-free random graph process. Random Structures and Algorithms 18(3), 279–290 (2001)
8. Buckley, P.G., Osthus, D.: Popularity based random graph models leading to a scale-free degree sequence. Discrete Mathematics 282(1-3), 53–68 (2004)
9. Chung, F., Lu, L.: Connected components in random graphs with given degree sequences. Annals of Combinatorics 6, 125–145 (2002)
10. Chung, F., Lu, L.: The average distance in random graphs with given expected degrees. Internet Mathematics 1(1), 91–114 (2003)
11. Chung, F., Lu, L.: The volume of the giant component of a random graph with given expected degrees. SIAM J. Discret. Math. 20(2), 395–411 (2006)
12. Cooper, C., Frieze, A.M.: A general model of web graphs. Random Struct. Algorithms 22(3), 311–335 (2003)
13. Cooper, C., Klasing, R., Zito, M.: Lower bounds and algorithms for dominating sets in web graphs. Internet Mathematics 2(3), 275–300 (2005)
14. Devroye, L., Lu, J.: The strong convergence of maximal degrees in uniform random recursive trees and dags. Random Structures and Algorithms 6, 1–14 (1995)
15. Dorogovtsev, S.N., Mendes, J.F., Samukhin, A.N.: Structure of growing networks with preferential linking. Physical Review Letters 85(21), 4633–4636 (2000)
16. Drinea, E., Enachescu, M., Mitzenmacher, M.: Variations on random graph models for the web. Technical report, Harvard U., Dept. of Computer Science (2001)
17. Duchon, P., Hanusse, N., Lebhar, E., Schabanel, N.: Could any graph be turned into a small-world? Theor. Comput. Sci. 355(1), 96–103 (2006)
18. Duchon, P., Hanusse, N., Lebhar, E., Schabanel, N.: Towards small world emergence. In: Gibbons, P.B., Vishkin, U. (eds.) SPAA, pp. 225–232. ACM Press, New York (2006)
19. Fraigniaud, P.: Greedy routing in tree-decomposed graphs. In: Brodal, G.S., Leonardi, S. (eds.) ESA 2005. LNCS, vol. 3669, pp. 791–802. Springer, Heidelberg (2005)
20. Fraigniaud, P., Gauron, P., Latapy, M.: Combining the use of clustering and scale-free nature of user exchanges into a simple and efficient p2p system. In: Cunha, J.C., Medeiros, P.D. (eds.) Euro-Par 2005. LNCS, vol. 3648, pp. 1163–1172. Springer, Heidelberg (2005)
21. Kim, B.J., Han, C.N.Y.S.K., Jeong, H.: Path finding strategies in scale-free networks. Physical Review E, 65(0227103) (2002)
22. Kleinberg, J.: The small-world phenomenon: An algorithmic perspective. In: Proceedings of the ACM Symposium on Theory of Computing (STOC), pp. 163–170 (2000)
23. Kleinberg, J.: Complex networks and decentralized search algorithms. In: Proceedings of the International Congress of Mathematicians (ICM) (2006)
24. Li, Z., Lai, Y.-C., Ye, N., Dasgupta, P.: Connectivity distribution and attack tolerance of general networks with both preferential and random attachments. Physics Letters A 303, 337–344 (2002)
25. Molloy, M., Reed, B.: A critical point for random graphs with a given degree sequence. Random Structures and Algorithms 6(2-3), 161–179 (1995)
26. Mri, T.F.: On random trees. Studia Sci. Math. Hungar. 39, 143–155 (2003)
27. Mri, T.F.: The maximum degree of the Barabsi-Albert random tree. Combinatorics, Probability and Computing 14, 339–348 (2005)

28. Nguyen, V., Martel, C.: Analyzing and characterizing small-world graphs. In: SODA 2005: Proceedings of the sixteenth annual ACM-SIAM symposium on Discrete algorithms, pp. 311–320.
29. Sarshar, N., Boykin, O., Roychowdhury, V.P.: Percolation search in power law networks: Making unstructured peer-to-peer networks scalable. In: Proc. of the IEEE International Conference on Peer-to-Peer Computing (P2P 2004), pp. 2–9 (2004)
30. Slivkins, A.: Distance estimation and object location via rings of neighbors. In: 24th ACM Symp. on Principles of Distributed Computing (PODC), pp. 41–50 (2005)
31. Yao, X., Zhang, C.-S., Chen, J.-W., Li, Y.-D.: On the formation of degree and cluster-degree correlations in scale-free networks. Physica A 353, 661–673 (2005)

$O(\log n)$-Time Overlay Network Construction
from Graphs with Out-Degree 1

James Aspnes[1] and Yinghua Wu[1,*]

Yale University Department of Computer Science,
51 Prospect St, New Haven CT 06511, USA
Tel.: +1 203 432-1239, Fax.: +1 203 432-0593
aspnes@cs.yale.edu, y.wu@yale.edu

Abstract. A fast self-stabilizing algorithm is described to rapidly construct a balanced overlay network from a directed graph initially with out-degree 1, a natural starting case that arises in peer-to-peer systems where each node attempts to join by contacting some single other node. This algorithm constructs a balanced search tree in time $O(W + \log n)$, where W is the key length and n is the number of nodes, improving by a factor of $\log n$ on the previous bound starting from a general graph, while retaining the properties of low contention and short messages. Our construction includes an improved version of the distributed Patricia tree structure of Angluin *et al.* [1], which we call a *double-headed radix tree*. This data structure responds gracefully to node failures and supports search, predecessor, and successor operations in $O(W)$ time with smoothly distributed load for predecessor and successor operations. Though the resulting tree data structure is highly vulnerable to disconnection due to failures, the fast predecessor and successor operations (as shown in previous work) can be used to quickly construct standard overlay networks with more redundancy.

Keywords: Overlay network, balanced search tree, pipeline, randomization, self-stabilizing, fault tolerance.

1 Introduction

Much work has been done recently on rapidly building a peer-to-peer system with a ring or line structure such as Chord [2] or skip graphs [3]. The naive approach of sequential insertion performs quite poorly for large networks: the time complexity is $\Theta(n \log^2 n)$ for Chord and $\Theta(n \log n)$ for skip graphs. So there is an incentive to find ways to exploit the parallelism of the system to build a network more quickly. Such a fast construction algorithm could allow rapid deployment of overlay networks or serve as a substitute for more complex self-repair mechanisms.

Several heuristic algorithms have been proposed that appear to converge in time $O(\log n)$ [4,5,6,7]. But it is difficult to prove that this bound in fact holds, and the question of obtaining theoretical results justifying the observed practical performance remains open.

---

* Corresponding author.

E. Tovar, P. Tsigas, and H. Fouchal (Eds.): OPODIS 2007, LNCS 4878, pp. 286–300, 2007.

In previous work [1], we showed how to quickly sort nodes in a weakly-connected graph of bounded degree d with a provable time bound $O(W \log n)$, where n is the number of nodes and W is the length of node identifiers. This running time, which is $O(\log^2 n)$ under the reasonable assumption that $W = O(\log n)$, is much higher than both the lower bound of $\Omega(d + \log n)$ shown in the same paper and the observed behavior of practical methods. The algorithm contains three components: a randomized pairing algorithm that constructs a distributed matching from a degree-d weakly-connected graph; a distributed merging algorithm for combining balanced trees of nodes, i.e., distributed Patricia trees; and a supernode simulation that allows a tree to simulate a single supernode in the pairing algorithm. In each iteration, the output of the pairing algorithm is used to join nodes/supernodes into larger supernodes that then participate in subsequent iterations of the pairing algorithm, until a single supernode remains. The ultimate supernode is actually a distributed Patricia tree consisting of all the nodes, which supports efficient search, predecessor and successor operations. As observed in [1], having fast predecessor and successor operations can then be used to quickly construct other more robust distributed data structures, such as Chord rings or skip graphs.

In this paper, we present an even faster algorithm with expected time complexity of only $O(W + \log n)$ (which is $O(\log n)$ if node identifiers are small) and expected message complexity of $O(n \log n)$, which preserves the properties of low contention and short messages in our previous work [1]. The algorithm assumes that it starts with a directed graph initially with out-degree 1, an important special case that arises in practice. For example, a node joining an overlay network will typically connect to a single existing node, yielding a directed tree. If we relax the restriction that nodes attempt to connect to nodes already in the network, then in full generality we get a graph with out-degree 1, which may contain a cycle. Producing a sorted list quickly in this model then allows the construction of more complex data structures as in [1].

Despite the possibility of having a cycle, we use tree terminology: each node points to a parent, and we assume that each node also knows its children, which can be achieved by children's initial probes. There is no restriction on the diameter of the input structure, and unlike the output tree, children in the input graph are unordered. Our algorithm first restructures the input graph into a child-sibling graph, which can be viewed as consisting of a network of horizontal links (the sibling pointers) and vertical links (the parent and child pointers). By using a randomized pairing algorithm alternately along the horizontal and vertical links, we quickly pair off nodes and merge them to form distributed tree structures called **double-headed radix trees** (DHR trees), ultimately obtaining a single DHR tree.

What is important and different from our previous work [1] is that tree merges are pipelined, so when the roots of any pair of DHR trees start to merge, the lower layers of these trees may not be fully formed yet. This eliminates the overhead of internal communication within supernodes as in [1] and explains the reduction in cost from the previous algorithm by a factor of $O(W)$. The degree limitation on the input graph is carefully maintained to ensure that no supernode is given more than a constant number of outgoing edges so that merges will not create high contention.

Double-headed radix trees can be thought of as radix trees in which the leaves have been removed (with their keys propagated up to some ancestor) and the root has been split into a left and right root (the "double head"); these changes eliminate the need to allocate new internal nodes during merges and allow DHR trees to respond more gracefully to node failures than the distributed Patricia trees of [1] from which they are ultimately derived. From the point of view of network construction, the key property is that despite these optimizations they continue to support the fast predecessor and successor operations needed to extract (for example) a sorted ring.

The paper is organized as the following: we first introduce our model in Section 2 and then double-headed radix trees in Section 3. Section 4 gives the synchronous contraction algorithm. We show how our algorithm can be adapted to an asynchronous environment in Section 5. Finally, we conclude our work in Section 6.

1.1 Other Related Work

In addition to work specifically aimed at building overlay networks, there are several strains of work in the literature on problems that are similar to the fast construction problem. These include **resource discovery** [8,9,10,11,12], **leader election** [13], and **parallel sorting** [14], which will be described briefly below; for a detailed discussion of the relation between these problems and the fast construction problem see the discussion in [1].

The Resource Discovery Problem was introduced by Harchol-Balter *et al.* [8], in which all the processes in an initial weakly connected knowledge graph learn the identities of all the other processes. The problem was then relaxed to require that one process becomes the leader with the knowledge of all the other process identities, and the leader's identity is known to the whole system. In the related papers [8,9,10,11,12] addressing this problem, the final knowledge graph usually contains a star on all the vertices and messages may contain the whole list of all the processes. Cidon *et al.* [13] gave a deterministic algorithm for leader election in an initially connected knowledge graph with $O(n)$ messages and time $O(n)$, in which each non-leader must finally have an identified path to its leader, rather than a direct edge.

Goodrich *et al.* [14] introduced a parallel sorting algorithm for a parallel pointer machine that may be the closest work to ours. It builds a binary tree over nodes and then merges components according to the tree. Consecutive merging phases are pipelined to give an $O(\log n)$ total time. However, our algorithm achieves this time complexity in a far more difficult and dynamic distributed environment.

2 Model

We assume that in the initial state, n processes form a directed graph G with maximum out-degree 1, with each process running as a node in G. Such a graph naturally forms a tree, and each node u in G knows the identifier of its unique parent $u.parent$, which can be *null* if u is a root, and also the identifiers of its (set of) children $u.children$ learned from children's initial probes, which will be the empty set if u is a leaf. Using tree terminology, we will describe edges as parent and child pointers instead of incoming and outgoing edges. Furthermore, we assume the initial graph G has a maximum in-degree $d = O(\log n)$.

Following [1], we assume throughout that a process u can only send a message to another process v if u knows v's identifier, i.e., if v is in $u.parent \cup u.children$. Formally, we assume that messages are of the form (s, t, σ) or (s, t, σ, u), where s is the sender, t is the receiver, σ is a message type, and u (if present) is a *single* process identifier.

We first assume that our algorithms run in a synchronous model. The computation proceeds in rounds, and all messages sent to a process s in round i are delivered simultaneously in round $i + 1$. In other words, we assume the standard synchronous message-passing model with the added restrictions that processes can only communicate with known processes and can only send $O(1)$ messages per round. This follows the synchronous model used in [1]. Though this assumption might seem to limit the applicability of our results, we show (in Section 5) that a suitably adapted synchronizer will allow our algorithm to run in an asynchronous environment without introducing too much additional cost.

3   Double-Headed Radix Trees

We first introduce an improved version of the distributed Patricia tree structure of Angluin *et al.* [1], which we call a **double-headed radix tree** or **DHR tree**. A DHR tree with at least two nodes has two roots: a left root and a right root. (For a singleton, there is only one root, which we think of as being both the left and right root.) Its height is bounded by the length of a node identifier, W, and any node has at most two children. Each internal node stores the longest common prefix of the subtree of which it is the root and pointers to its parent and children. The two roots also store pointers to each other.

An example is shown in Figure 1(a). The node identifiers are listed in the table, and their prefixes within parentheses. To support searching, the tree must have the following property:

Property 1. The left and right roots have incomparable prefixes, as do the two children of any node.

This property guarantees the correctness of searching. While searching for a particular node identifier, we start from the roots and follow the path that leads to longer prefix match. If the node with such an identifier exists somewhere in the DHR tree, its prefix has been stored in all its ancestors. Since Property 1 holds, the searching path is uniquely determined.

We also define a **single-headed radix tree** (SHR tree) to facilitate merging procedures. A DHR tree can be transformed into a SHR tree by promoting its left root to a new super-root with only one child and the children of the two roots are assigned to the former right root. The corresponding SHR tree of Fig. 1(a) is shown in Fig. 1(b). We can also think of the left and right trees of a DHR tree as SHR trees.

The procedure to merge two DHR trees to form a larger DHR tree is quite straightforward. Any merge of two DHR trees can be reduced to merging two corresponding SHR trees, since any DHR tree can be transformed into a SHR tree. The prefixes of

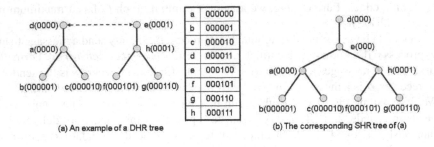

(a) An example of a DHR tree   (b) The corresponding SHR tree of (a)

Fig. 1. An example of a DHR tree and its corresponding SHR tree

the two merging roots are compared and the new root can be determined immediately, i.e. in time $O(1)$, which means that the new root can represent the combined DHR tree without waiting for the whole merge to be finished. Details of the merging procedures are given in Appendix A.2.

Given multiple DHR trees, pipelined merges to combine all these trees into a single tree can be viewed as multiple merging waves that propagate down the tree, with each consecutive wave following a few steps later. A partially complete tree can participate in another merge as soon as its root is determined, so that the extra time cost for an additional merge is constant. The result is that a tree of merges of maximum depth k can be completed in $O(W + k)$ time.

For the pairing algorithm given in Section 4, the depth k is given by the number of rounds of pairing, which is $O(\log n)$ with high probability. It follows that the running time of the full construction algorithm is $O(W + \log n)$.

4   Algorithms

This section contains a family of algorithms for quickly constructing an overlay network starting with a directed graph with maximum out-degree 1 and bounded in-degree d. The structure of our algorithm is as follows:

1. In the **pre-stage**, described in Section 4.1, the initial graph is converted into a child-sibling graph we call the **contraction graph**. Each node in the contraction graph is always the left root of some DHR (initially all singleton trees).
2. In the **merging stage**, described in Section 4.2, we alternate between contracting the child-sibling graph vertically (along the parent-child axis) and horizontally (along the sibling axis). Each contraction involves merging two DHR trees and replacing their left roots in the contraction tree with the single left root of the combined tree. An additional fix-up procedure is used to prevent each merged node from ending up with more than one child (or right sibling), by "kicking" such extra neighbors into the list of siblings (or descendants) one level down on the child-parent axis (or on the sibling axis) of the graph.

The pre-stage takes $O(d)$ time to construct the child-sibling graph, where we assume $d = O(\log n)$. It uses a total of $O(n)$ messages of length $O(W)$.

The merging stage, described in Section 4.2, takes advantage of pipelined merges of DHR trees to allow each merging operation to appear to complete in $O(1)$ time from the point of view of the contraction graph. This is the time needed to merge the top layers of two DHR trees and obtain the identifier of the new roots. Though the first merge operation continues to propagate downwards and will not finish for an additional $O(W)$ time, it is nonetheless possible to start a new merge operation immediately (which will then propagate through the merged trees behind the first merge operation). This pipelining means that each additional layer of merging adds only $O(1)$ time to the $O(W)$ cost of the first merge. The total cost of the merging stage is $O(W + \log n)$ with high probability, with a total of $O(n \log n)$ messages of size $O(W)$ each. This dominates the cost of the pre-stage and gives the overall asymptotic complexity of the algorithm.

4.1 Pre-stage

In the pre-stage, the original graph G is transformed into a child-sibling graph C. For each node u in G, it sequences the nodes in $u.children$ in arbitrary order and notifies each of its children $v \in u.children$ of v's left sibling and right sibling, denoted as $v.leftsibling$ and $v.rightsibling$ respectively. At the end, u only keeps a child pointer to its leftmost child, denoted as $u.child$. Figure 2 gives an example of how an ordinary graph (in this case a tree) can be transformed into a child-sibling graph. The pre-stage takes $O(d)$ rounds, as each node can notify only one of its children per round. At round $(d + 1)$, all the nodes will proceed to the merging stage as described in Section 4.2. Note that this description assumes that the in-degree bound d is a fixed parameter of the algorithm known to all nodes.

The child-sibling graph C can be thought as a graph of many crossing directional links embedded in two dimensions. In Figure 2(b), rightward arrows indicate horizontal links generated by sibling pointers and downward arrows indicate vertical links generated by child pointers. The child-sibling graph will have a root if and only if there is some node with out-degree 0. Conversely, if there is a cycle in this graph, it can only appear as a vertical cycle along the (rootless) child-parent axis.

4.2 Merging Stage

The merging stage consists of a sequence of contraction operations that alternate between contracting horizontal and vertical links generated by the pre-stage. We start

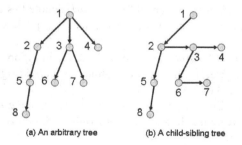

(a) An arbitrary tree   (b) A child-sibling tree

Fig. 2. Pre-stage: Transform a tree into a child-sibling tree

with a *horizontal contraction* operation (in Section 4.2) along all horizontal links and then a *vertical contraction* operation (in Section 4.2) along all vertical links, and then repeat the procedure until only a single DHR tree is left. Some care must be taken during the contractions to ensure that all nodes maintain bounded degree; this is done by having the nodes push extra edges down towards their children (or rightward towards their right siblings). If the graph is a tree, this pushes extra edges toward the leaves. If instead the graph contains a cycle, it instead shuffles the extra edges between levels. The main purpose of pushing downwards is not so much to grab extra space (since there is none in the cycle case) as it is to prevent extra edges from piling up as the root contracts downward in the tree case.

Horizontal Contraction. A horizontal contraction operation proceeds in two parts.

First, we do a pairing, which consists of (a) using a randomized algorithm to pair off nodes along horizontal links; (b) merging each pair of paired nodes (both being the left roots of two DHR trees) to form a new DHR tree; and (c) replacing each such pair in the contraction graph with the new left root of the resulting DHR tree.

Second, we move edges within the contraction graph. After merging some node may contain two child pointers with each coming from the previously paired nodes, so we must readjust the contraction graph C to retain the child-sibling property.

In detail, the horizontal contraction operation proceeds as follows:

> For each node u, so long as u is still within the contraction tree, it performs:
> *Pairing*:
> **round i:** Let *chosen* be picked uniformly from $\{u.\text{leftsibling}, u.\text{rightsibling}\}$; if *chosen* is *null*, choose another value; if still *null*, wait for Vertical Contraction.
> **round $i + 1$:** Send $(u, chosen, \text{pair})$ to *chosen*.
> **round $i + 2$:** **Upon** receiving (v, u, pair) from v **do**:
> > If $v = chosen$, send (u, v, accept) to v;
> > otherwise, send (u, v, reject) to v.
> **round $i + 3$:** **Upon** receiving (v, u, accept) from v **do**:
> > u merges with v and w.l.o.g, assume u becomes the new left root and v disconnects from the contraction graph.
> > **Upon** receiving (v, u, reject) from v **do**:
> > > Do nothing.
>
> *Readjusting*:
> **round $i + 4$:** If either $u.\text{rightsibling} \neq null$, denoted as u_1, or u has a second child from previous round, denoted as c_1, u pushes both u_1 and c_1 to a lower level:
> > 1. If $u.child$ is *null*, let $u.child = u_1$ (as in Figure 3 (a));
> > 2. otherwise, if u has only one child, let $u.child$.rightsibling $= u_1$ (as in Figure 3 (b));
> > 3. otherwise, u has two children c and c_1. Assume u keeps c as $u.child$.
> > > (a) If $u.\text{rightsibling} \neq null$, let c.rightsibling $= u_1$ and u_1.rightsibling $= c_1$ (as in Figure 3 (c));
> > > (b) otherwise, let c.rightsibling $= c_1$ (as in Figure 3 (d)).

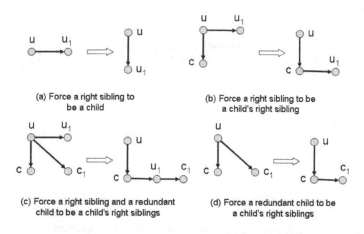

(a) Force a right sibling to
be a child

(b) Force a right sibling to be
a child's right sibling

(c) Force a right sibling and a redundant
child to be a child's right siblings

(d) Force a redundant child to be
a child's right siblings

Fig. 3. Possible adjustments after a horizontal contraction

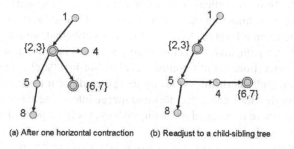

(a) After one horizontal contraction   (b) Readjust to a child-sibling tree

Fig. 4. Merging stage: Horizontal contraction operation and its postadjustment

In round $i + 3$, u takes over v's outgoing edges, and v is disconnected from the contraction graph and no longer participates in subsequent pairing procedures. Since all of these operations can be finished in one round, we can take advantage of pipelining to force every newly generated root to enter the next round of the pairing procedure at once, which is depicted in Section 3 as pipelined merges.

After a horizontal contraction operation, the graph C may not be a child-sibling graph any more. But notice that (as long as the previous graph is a child-sibling graph) the worst case is that some nodes have two children. We only need to do a local adjustment to retain the child-sibling structure as in round $i + 4$. Here all the nodes simultaneously push their right siblings to a lower level (to be their children or to be their children's right siblings) so that each node still keeps a constant number of outgoing edges.

Figure 4 shows a possible merging result from the contraction graph C in Figure 2(b). Here, a double-circled node indicates that a pair of nodes have merged with each other. The subsequent edge readjustment is shown in Figure 4(b).

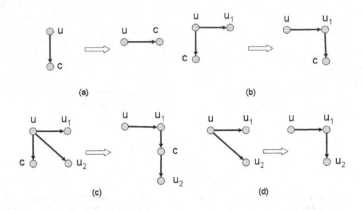

Fig. 5. Possible adjustments after a vertical contraction

Vertical Contraction. A vertical contraction operation is executed in exactly the same way as a horizontal contraction operation, except that it uses vertical rather than horizontal links. The main effects of this are (a) it is possible that we may have to contract a cycle rather than a path, and (b) so the pairing and pushing directions are switched.

Horizontal contractions do not contract cycles, but just "kick" edges along the cycles. Vertical contractions shrink cycles by merging adjacent nodes; when the cycle is reduced to two nodes, they can detect this and merge into a single node. Aside from this last optimization, there is no need to distinguish cycles from paths during the merging stage.

In pairing steps, for each node u, *chosen* is picked uniformly from $\{u.parent, u.child\}$, and merging is carried out along vertical links. In readjusting steps, u first pushes its child rightward to be either u.rightsibling's child or just its right sibling, and then u pushes its second right sibling (if any) to be either u.rightsibling's child or the child of u.rightsibling.*child*. These adjustments are shown in Figure 5.

It is not hard to see that the algorithm does not partition the graph, so as long as it continues to merge nodes, there will be only one DHR tree left. The time complexity of the contraction algorithm is given in the theorem below. The proof appears in Appendix A.1.

Theorem 1. *The contraction algorithm finishes in $O(W + \log n)$ rounds on average and with high probability.*

4.3   Fault Tolerance Issues

In this section, we assume the underlying network is reliable and there is no message loss, but that nodes are subject to crash failures that can be detected by the node's neighbors. We give a very brief sketch of how DHR trees respond to node failures and how the contraction algorithm can be used to reconnect fragmented DHR trees.

When a node u in a DHR tree fails, the tree will separate into at most three well-formed DHR or SHR trees. The tree containing u's parent is a valid DHR tree itself even if u's ancestors may not store the longest prefixes of their subtrees any more. But this tree can still correctly perform searching and merging operations. Each of u's subtrees can become a valid DHR tree by promoting one of its root's own children to be the other root, an operation that takes $O(1)$ time. If these two trees need to connect back to the contraction tree after being separated, only their roots will try to repair these connections.

Since network partitions are irreversible in the absence of extra edges, we make a reasonable assumption that every node will keep information about several other nodes, although it chooses only one as its initial outgoing edge in the contraction graph. Thus, whenever some node fails, the root of a separated tree will try to contact nodes still in the contraction graph through its unused links. These contacts are propagated up through the DHR trees (possibly merging with other incoming contacts as they propagate up). Since two trees T_1 and T_2 may simultaneously attempt to join each other, this may lead to a cycle in the contraction graph. But since our algorithm can gracefully handle cycles, after node failures stop and the contraction graph correctly reforms, our algorithm will ultimately stabilize.

5 Extension to an Asynchronous Model

So far we have assumed a synchronous model, which (a) simplifies the analysis of the contraction algorithm, (b) allows extra edges to be pushed down through the contraction tree without piling up, and (c) eliminates the need for explicit coordination of changes between nodes. The price of this assumption may, however, be too high in a practical setting, and it makes it difficult to compare our algorithm with previous algorithms (such as that of [1]) that work in asynchronous environments.

To address this issue, we show how the α synchronizer of [15] can be adapted to our setting. Details are given in the full paper. The result is:

Theorem 2. *Starting from an initial tree with consistent parent and child pointers, the tree contraction algorithm running under an α synchronizer produces a single DHR containing all nodes in $O(W + \log n)$ time using $O(n(W + \log n))$ messages with high probability in an asynchronous system.*

6 Conclusion

We have described a fast self-stabilizing algorithm to rapidly construct a balanced overlay network from a directed graph initially with out-degree 1. This algorithm organizes all the nodes in the network into a novel balanced search tree data structure that responds gracefully to node failures and supports quick search, predecessor and successor operations. And by applying predecessor and successor operations, the nodes can quickly form into a sorted link, which turns out to be a fundamental structure for many linear overlay networks. Our analysis shows that the expected running time of the algorithm is $O(W + \log n)$, which improves by a factor $\log n$ on our previous work [1], while still preserving low contention and using messages with length proportional to the length W of node identifiers.

Our algorithm is designed for in a synchronous model, but applying a synchronizer can extend the algorithm to work in an asynchronous environment. The key difficulty here is how to incorporate late arriving nodes into the ongoing procedure; more work needs to be done in this area.

In building our data structure, we developed methods for pushing extra edges downward to maintain small degree and for pipelining sequential merges efficiently. It is an interesting open problem whether these tools may be applied to algorithms for more general classes of initial graphs.

References

1. Angluin, D., Aspnes, J., Chen, J., Wu, Y., Yin, Y.: Fast construction of overlay networks. In: SPAA 2005. Proceedings of the 17th ACM Symposium on Parallelism in Algorithms and Architectures, Las Vegas, NV, USA (July 2005)
2. Stoica, I., Morris, R., Liben-Nowell, D., Karger, D.R., Kaashoek, M.F., Dabek, F., Balakrishnan, H.: Chord: A Scalable Peer-to-peer Lookup Service for Internet Applications. IEEE/ACM Transactions on Networking 11(1), 17–32 (2003)
3. Aspnes, J., Shah, G.: Skip Graphs. In: SODA. Proceedings of the Fourteenth Annual ACM-SIAM Symposium on Discrete Algorithms, Baltimore, MD, USA, pp. 384–393 (January 2003) (submitted to a special issue of Journal of Algorithms dedicated to select papers of SODA 2003)
4. Onus, M., Richa, A., Scheideler, C.: Linearization: Locally self-stabilizing sorting in graphs. In: Proceedings of the Workshop on Algorithm Engineering and Experiments (ALENEX) (to appear, 2007)
5. Jelasity, M., Babaoglu, O.: T-Man: Gossip-based overlay topology management. In: Brueckner, S.A., Serugendo, G.D.M., Hales, D., Zambonelli, F. (eds.) ESOA 2005. LNCS (LNAI), vol. 3910, pp. 1–15. Springer, Heidelberg (2006)
6. Jelasity, M., Montresor, A., Babaoglu, O.: The bootstrapping service. In: Proceedings of the 26th International Conference on Distributed Computing Systems Workshops (ICDCS WORKSHOPS): International Workshop on Dynamic Distributed Systems (IWDDS) (2006)
7. Montresor, A., Jelasity, M., Babaoglu, O.: Chord on demand. In: P2P 2005. Proceedings of the Fifth IEEE International Conference on Peer-to-Peer Computing, pp. 87–94. IEEE Computer Society Press, Los Alamitos (2005)
8. Harchol-Balter, M., Leighton, T., Lewin, D.: Resource discovery in distributed networks. In: Proceedings of the eighteenth annual ACM symposium on Principles of distributed computing, pp. 229–237. ACM Press, New York (1999)
9. Kutten, S., Peleg, D., Vishkin, U.: Deterministic resource discovery in distributed networks. In: Proceedings of the thirteenth annual ACM symposium on Parallel algorithms and architectures, pp. 77–83. ACM Press, New York (2001)
10. Law, C., Siu, K.Y.: An O(logn) randomized resource discovery algorithm. In: Brief Announcements of the 14th International Symposium on Distributed Computing, Technical University of Madrid, Technical Report FIM/110.1/DLSIIS/, pp. 5–8. (October 2000)
11. Kutten, S., Peleg, D.: Asynchronous resource discovery in peer to peer networks. In: SRDS 2002. 21st IEEE Symposium on Reliable Distributed Systems October 13–16, 2002, pp. 224–231 (2002)
12. Abraham, I., Dolev, D.: Asynchronous resource discovery. In: Proceedings of the twenty-second annual symposium on Principles of distributed computing, pp. 143–150. ACM Press, New York (2003)

13. Cidon, I., Gopal, I., Kutten, S.: New models and algorithms for future networks. IEEE Transactions on Information Theory 41(3), 769–780 (1995)
14. Goodrich, M.T., Kosaraju, S.R.: Sorting on a parallel pointer machine with applications to set expression evaluation. J. ACM 43(2), 331–361 (1996)
15. Awerbuch, B.: Complexity of network synchronization. J. ACM 32(4), 804–823 (1985)
16. Awerbuch, B., Sipser, M.: Dynamic networks are as fast as static networks (preliminary version). In: 29th Annual Symposium on Foundations of Computer Science, 24-26 October 1988, White Plains, New York, USA, pp. 206–220. (1988)
17. Karp, R.M.: Probabilistic recurrence relations. In: STOC 1991. Proceedings of the twenty-third annual ACM symposium on Theory of computing, pp. 190–197. ACM Press, New York (1991)

A   Appendix

A.1   Analysis of Time Complexity

Since the contraction graph C has at most n edges, there is a one-to-one mapping between each edge and some merge, except for the last merge that collapses the possible vertical cycle, which may consume two antiparallel edges. Thus after every successful merge, the total number of edges is reduced by one. In the following analysis, we will show that after one horizontal and vertical contraction operations, a constant fraction of edges will be eliminated on average.

Assume before the ith contraction operations there are A_{i-1} horizontal edges and B_{i-1} vertical edges(e.g. $A_0 + B_0 = n - 1$ or n).

Lemma 1. *After the ith horizontal and vertical contraction operations,* $\mathrm{E}[A_i + B_i] \leq \frac{7}{8}(A_{i-1} + B_{i-1})$.

Proof. Let H be the number of horizontal edges and V the number of vertical edges removed by the ith horizontal and vertical contraction operations. Since the probability of choosing any edge is at least $1/4$, we have $\mathrm{E}[H] \geq \frac{1}{4}A_{i-1}$.

After the horizontal contraction operation, we readjust the contraction graph to retain the child-sibling property. This adjustment may change some vertical edges to horizontal edges. But the number of such edges is no more than $B_{i-1}/2$, because such an adjustment happens only if a (consolidated) node has two children. Removing these edges leaves $B_{i-1}/2$ vertical edges to participate in the i-th vertical contraction, and so $\mathrm{E}[V] \geq \frac{1}{4}(B_{i-1}/2) = \frac{1}{8}B_{i-1}$. So we have

$$\mathrm{E}[A_i + B_i] = (A_{i-1} + B_{i-1}) - \mathrm{E}[H] - \mathrm{E}[V] \leq \frac{7}{8}(A_{i-1} + B_{i-1}) \ . \qquad (1)$$

$\square$

We use a classic theorem regarding probabilistic recurrence relations, due to Karp [17]. If a process can be described as $T(x) = a(x) + T(h(x))$, where x is a nonnegative real variable, $a(x)$ is a nonnegative real-valued function of x and $h(x)$ is a random variable ranging over $[0, x]$ and having expectation less than or equal to $m(x)$, where m is a nonnegative real-valued function, then the following theorem holds.

Theorem 3 ([17]). *Suppose there is a constant d such that $a(x) = 0$, $x < d$ and $a(x) = 1$, $x \geq d$. Let $c_t = \min\{x | u(x) \geq t\}$. Then, for every positive real x and every positive integer w, $\Pr[T(x) \geq u(x) + w] \leq \left(\frac{m(x)}{x}\right)^{w-1} \frac{m(x)}{c_{u(x)}}$,*

in which $u(x)$ denotes the least nonnegative solution of $\tau(x) = a(x) + \tau(m(x))$, a deterministic counterpart of the above process. $u(x)$ is uniquely given by the formula $u(x) = \sum_{i=0}^{\infty} a(m^{[i]}(x))$, where $m^{[0]}(x) = x$ and $m^{[i]}(x) = m(m^{[i-1]}(x))$ for $i = 1, 2, \ldots$.

Our contraction algorithm can be illustrated in the form of Theorem 3 as in [17]: $m(x) = \frac{7}{8}x$, $a(x) = 0, x < 1$, $a(x) = 1, x \geq 1$ for the time cost of each horizontal and vertical contraction operation is $O(1)$. Then $u(x) = 0$ for $x < 1$, $u(x) = \lfloor \log_{8/7}(x) \rfloor + 1$ for $x \geq 1$ and $c_t = \left(\frac{8}{7}\right)^{t-1}$. Then Theorem 3 gives the following result when we substitute x with $n - 1, n \geq 3$ and let $w = \lceil c \log_{8/7}(n-1) \rceil$ for any fixed constant c:

$$\Pr[T(n-1) \geq \lfloor \log_{8/7}(n-1) \rfloor + w + 1] \leq \left(\frac{7}{8}\right)^{w-1} \frac{n-1}{\left(\frac{8}{7}\right)^{\lfloor \log_{8/7}(n-1) \rfloor + 1}} \leq \frac{1}{(n-1)^{c-1}} .$$

$$(2)$$

Therefore, with high probability we will only need $O(\log n)$ rounds to reduce all the edges. If this bound fails, we are left with a contraction graph which again collapses to a single node in an additional $O(\log n)$ rounds w.h.p. It follows that the expected number of rounds to contract all the edges is also $O(\log n)$.

To this must be added the (deterministic) time cost $O(W)$ for the final DHR tree to finish all the pipelined merges. We thus obtain the total time cost for our algorithms $O(W + \log n)$, and thus prove Theorem 1.

A.2   Merging Two DHR Trees

Here we describe the merging procedure for a pair of DHR trees. Denote a DHR tree as T_D, and similarly a SHR tree as T_S. When the distinction is not necessary, both a DHR tree and a SHR tree can be denoted as T and called a radix tree. We adopt the following definitions:

- For u and v, $T_D(u, v)$ indicates a DHR tree with left root u and right root v; $T_S(u)$ indicates a SHR tree rooted at u. When there is no possibility of confusion, $T(u)$ means a radix subtree rooted at u.
- For a node u, its identifier is denoted as $u.id$ and its prefix as $u.prefix$. For a radix tree T, its prefix means the longest common prefix of all the node identifiers in T, denoted as $T.prefix$.
- For two prefixes x and y, we use $x = y$ to indicate that x is equal to y, $x \neq y$ that x is incomparable to y, and $x \sqsubset y$ that y is a short prefix of x respectively.

Any merge of two DHR trees can be reduced to merging two corresponding SHR trees, since any DHR tree can be transformed into a SHR tree. Assume T_1 is merging

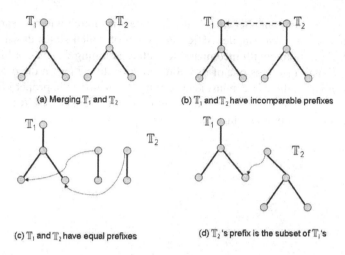

(a) Merging $\mathbb{T}_1$ and $\mathbb{T}_2$ (b) $\mathbb{T}_1$ and $\mathbb{T}_2$ have incomparable prefixes

(c) $\mathbb{T}_1$ and $\mathbb{T}_2$ have equal prefixes   (d) $\mathbb{T}_2$'s prefix is the subset of $\mathbb{T}_1$'s

Fig. 6. Merging two DHR trees T_1 and T_2

with T_2 as in Fig. 6(a) and let b be the first bit position at which $T_1.prefix$ differs from $T_2.prefix$. There are only three cases categorized by the relationship of T_1 and T_2's prefixes.

1. If $T_1.prefix \neq T_2.prefix$, we combine these two SHR trees into one DHR tree. The tree with the b-th bit equal to 0 will become the left tree of the merged DHR tree while the other becomes the right tree, as in Fig. 6(b).
2. If $T_1.prefix = T_2.prefix$, we can break the tie by choosing the tree with a head of a smaller node identifer, e.g. T_1, and another tree T_2 is decomposed into two smaller SHR trees, i.e. its left and right trees, which slide down along T_1 and carry on further merges with subtrees of T_1, as in Fig. 6.
3. If $T_1.prefix \subset T_2.prefix$ or $T_2.prefix \subset T_1.prefix$, e.g. as in Fig. 6 (d), the tree with shorter prefix keeps its root while the other slides down for further merges.

When a SHR tree is sliding down another tree, it either further decomposes into smaller SHR trees or settles down somewhere deep in the tree. For example, as in Fig. 7,

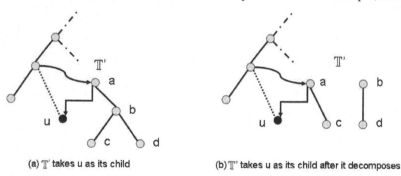

(a) $\mathbb{T}'$ takes u as its child   (b) $\mathbb{T}'$ takes u as its child after it decomposes

Fig. 7. T' is sliding down along another tree

T' is sliding down along another tree. If it encounters a subtree with the same prefix, it just decomposes into two smaller SHR trees, each of which slides down along the proper branch. If a subtree with incomparable prefix, assuming $T(u)$ as in Fig. 7(a), is encountered, T' will take u as one of its child and substitute $T(u)$ in the original tree. If $T' \subset T(u).prefix$, then T' can just keep sliding down along the proper branch. But if $T(u).prefix \subset T'$, T' needs to first decompose into two smaller SHR trees, one of which replaces u's position and takes u as its child while the other slides down, as in Fig. 7(b).

On the Self-stabilization of Mobile Robots in Graphs

Lélia Blin[1], Maria Gradinariu Potop-Butucaru[2,3], and Sébastien Tixeuil[2,4]

[1] IBISC, Universite d'Evry, CNRS, France
[2] Univ. Pierre & Marie Curie - Paris 6, LIP6-CNRS UMR 7606, France
[3] INRIA REGAL, France
[4] INRIA Grand Large, France

Abstract. Self-stabilization is a versatile technique to withstand any transient fault in a distributed system. Mobile robots (or agents) are one of the emerging trends in distributed computing as they mimic autonomous biologic entities. The contribution of this paper is threefold. First, we present a new model for studying mobile entities in networks subject to transient faults. Our model differs from the classical robot model because robots have constraints about the paths they are allowed to follow, and from the classical agent model because the number of agents remains fixed throughout the execution of the protocol. Second, in this model, we study the possibility of designing self-stabilizing algorithms when those algorithms are run by mobile robots (or agents) evolving on a graph. We concentrate on the core building blocks of robot and agents problems: naming and leader election. Not surprisingly, when no constraints are given on the network graph topology and local execution model, both problems are impossible to solve. Finally, using minimal hypothesis with respect to impossibility results, we provide deterministic and probabilistic solutions to both problems, and show equivalence of these problems by an algorithmic reduction mechanism.

1 Introduction

A large panel of recent research in Distributed Computing focused on solving problems using mobile entities, often denoted by the term of *robots* or *agents*. Those entities typically evolve in the network (that comprises a fixed set of nodes forming a particular topology) to provide services, either to the user of the network or to its core components. With the advent of large-scale networks that involve a total number of components in the order of the million, two particular issues were stressed: *(i)* the resources used by the agents should be kept to a minimum given a particular problem (see *e.g.* [15]), and *(ii)* the fault and attack tolerance capabilities are of premium importance. Most of the works on fault and attack tolerance with mobile agents deals with *external* threats, *i.e.* the faulty part of the system or the attacker is not an agent itself. For example, several papers (*e.g.* [9]) investigate the black hole search problem, where mobile entities must cooperate to find a hostile node of the network that destroys every mobile entity traversing it. In an orthogonal manner, decontamination and graph searching papers (*e.g.* [14]) consider the chasing of hostile mobile entities that are harmful to the nodes but not to the agents.

In this paper, we consider the novel problem of dealing with faults and attacks that hit the mobile entities themselves, that is, the threat is *internal*. More precisely, we

E. Tovar, P. Tsigas, and H. Fouchal (Eds.): OPODIS 2007, LNCS 4878, pp. 301–314, 2007.
© Springer-Verlag Berlin Heidelberg 2007

consider that an arbitrary transient fault or attack hits the system (both nodes and mobile entities), and devise algorithmic solutions to recover from those faults and attacks. The faults and attacks are *transient* in the sense that there exists a point from which they don't appear any more. In practice, it is sufficient that the faults and attacks are sporadic enough for the network to provide useful services most of the time. In this context, *self-stabilization* [10] is an elegant approach to forward recovery from transient faults and attacks as well as initializing a large-scale system. Informally, a self-stabilizing system is able to recover from any transient fault or attack in finite time, without restricting the nature or the span of those faults and attacks.

Related works. Mobile (software) agents on graphs were studied in the context of self-stabilization *e.g.* in [16,17,6,11], but the implicit model is completely different from ours. In the aforementioned works, agents are software entities that are exchanged through messages between processes (that are located in the nodes of the network), and thus can be destroyed, duplicated, and created at will. In [16,6], a single agent is assumed at a given time, and this agent is responsible for stabilizing a simultaneously running (classical *aka* non-stabilizing) distributed algorithm. In [17], exactly n agents are supposed to traverse a n sized tree network infinitely often, by means of a *swap* primitive that swaps agents located at two neighboring nodes. In [11], the authors consider dynamic evolving networks and rely on random walks to ensure proper agent traversal; again, the purpose of the agent protocol is to ensure that a single agent stabilizes the system. By contrast, in this paper, we focus on the self-stabilization of the agents themselves, and our model keeps the number of agents fixed for the whole life of the network.

Self-stabilizing mobile (hardware) robots in 2-dimensional space were recently studied in *e.g.* [19,18,13]. Here a fixed set of k mobile robots are able to move unconstrained, yet are not able to communicate other than by viewing the relative position of other robots. The presented algorithms are oblivious in the sense that between any two activations of a particular robot, the previous state of the robot is cleared. As such, those algorithms are inherently self-stabilizing, since any scheduling for execution will reset the state of a robot. In this model several problems have been studied under different assumptions on the environment (schedulers, fault-tolerance, robots visibility, accuracy of compasses): circle formation, pattern formation, gathering, leader election, scattering. However, the lack of digital communication between the robots somewhat limits the kind of problems that can be solved and a broad class of impossibility results have been obtained [19,18,13,7,1]. In this paper, we introduce non-oblivious robots (agents) in the context of self-stabilization and enable digital communication between robots (either because they are located at the same node or by using so-called whiteboards) to solve more elaborate tasks (*e.g.* naming and leader election), yet we restrict the motion capabilities of the robots (only edges of a given graph can be followed).

A third related model in the area of self-stabilization is that of Population Protocols (see *e.g.* [4,5,3]). In this model, finite-state agents interact in pairs chosen by an adversary, with both agents updating their state according to a joint transition function. For each such transition function, the resulting population protocol is said to stably compute a predicate on the initial states of the agents if, after sufficiently many interactions in a fair execution, all agents converge to having the correct value of the predicate. It was proved that this model permits to compute problems that can be expressed through Presburger arithmetic. Our model permits as well to express joint transition functions between agents located at the same node, but also (indirectly) between agents that are hosted by the same node at different moments through the whiteboard abstraction.

Our contribution. The contribution of this paper is threefold. First, we present a new model for studying mobile entities in networks subject to transient fault. Our model differs from the classical robot model because robots have constraints about the paths they are allowed to follow, and from the classical agent model because the number of agents remains fixed throughout the execution of the protocol. Second, in this model, we study the possibility of designing self-stabilizing algorithms when those algorithms are run by mobile robots (or agents) evolving on a graph. We concentrate on the core building blocks of robot and agents problems: naming and leader election. Not surprisingly, when no constraints are given on the network graph topology and local execution model, both problems are impossible to solve. Finally, using minimal hypotheses with respect to impossibility results, we provide deterministic and probabilistic solutions to both problems, and show equivalence of these problems by an algorithmic reduction mechanism. From a theoretical perspective, our results complement the widely known possible *vs.* impossible problems in anonymous distributed systems (see *e.g.* [21,22]). From a practical perspective, our symmetry breaking algorithm enables to solve other problems such as gathering (see [8]) that have known solutions when mobile entities have unique identifiers.

Outline. In Section 2, we present the computing model that is introduced in this paper. Section 3 provides impossibility results that justify the assumptions made in subsequent sections. Section 4 presents a deterministic algorithm for naming in acyclic networks with half-duplex links, while Section 5 provides a probabilistic naming algorithm for general networks. Section 6 shows that the naming and leader election problem are equivalent (by reduction of one problem to the other). Concluding remarks are presented in Section 7.

2   Model

The network is modeled as a connected graph $G = (V, E)$, where V is a set of nodes, and E is a set of edges. We assume that nodes have local distinct labels for links, but no assumption is made about the labeling process. Nodes also maintain a so-called *whiteboard* which can store a fixed amount of information. We distinguish between *acyclic* networks (*i.e.* trees) and *cyclic* networks (*i.e.* that contain at least one cycle).

   Agents (or *robots*) are entities that move between neighboring nodes in the network. A link is *full-duplex* if two agents located at neighboring nodes can exchange their position at the same time, crossing the same link in opposite directions. A link is *half-duplex* if only one direction can be used at a given time. We assume that k agents are present in the network at any time. Also, each agent is modeled by an automata whose state space is sufficient to hold a identifier that is unique in the network (*i.e.* the state space is at least k states). An agent may move from one node to one of the node's neighbors based on the following information: *(i)* the current state of the agent, *(ii)* the current state of other agents located at the same node, *(iii)* the local link labels of the current node (and possibly the label of the incoming link used by the agent to reach the node), and *(iv)* the memory stored at the node (the whiteboard).

A *configuration* of the system is the product of all agents locations and states and all whiteboards contents. The behavior of the system is essentially *asynchronous*, in the sense that there is no bound on the number of moves that an agent can make between any two moves of another agent. There is one notable exception: when two (or more) agents are at the same node, the execution order is decided by the host node. In the following we assume that no two agents located at the same node execute their actions concurrently. However, agents located at different nodes may execute their actions concurrently. So, in any configuration of the system, the scheduler may choose any subset of nodes that hold at least one agent: then, in one atomic step all chosen nodes execute the code of all their host agents. The pseudo-code of each node (unless otherwise stated) is formally presented as Algorithm 1.

Algorithm 1. Pseudo-code at node i

```
foreach agent on node
  agent.execute()
end foreach
```

We assume that the scheduler is *fair* in the sense that if a node holds at least one agent, it is eventually scheduled for execution by the scheduler. A *round* starting from configuration c is the minimum time until all nodes that hold at least one agent in c have been activated by the scheduler. We now define the naming and leader election problems that we focus on in this paper:

Definition 1 (Naming). *Let S be a system with k agents. The system S satisfies the naming specification if all k agents eventually have an unique identifier (no two agents in S share the same identifier).*

In the leader election problem agents have either the leader role or the follower role.

Definition 2 (Leader Election). *Let S be a system with k agents. The system S satisfies the leader election specification if an unique agent eventually has the leader role and all the agents have the follower role.*

Our goal is to withstand transient failures. For this purpose, we assume that every "changing" aspect of the network can be arbitrarily modified in the initial configuration of the system. These "changing" aspects include: *(i)* the agent states, *(ii)* the agent positions, *(iii)* the whiteboard states.

Definition 3 (Self-stabilizing Problem). *Let S be a system with k agents. The system S satisfies the naming or the leader election specification in a self-stabilizing way if Definition 1 and Definition 2 respectively are verified in spite of an arbitrary initial configuration.*

3   Impossibility Results

The results in this section are negative. We consider networks where agents have infinite memory, and nodes have whiteboards with infinite memory. Also, the scheduling is constrained in the sense that at every step, all nodes that hold at least one agent are scheduled for execution. With our assumptions, the initial memory of every agent is supposed to be identical, and the initial content of each whiteboard is supposed to be identical as well. Agents are anonymous and deterministic.

Theorem 1. *Deterministic naming or leader election of mobile agents is impossible in cyclic networks, even assuming synchronous scheduling, and infinite memory for each agent and whiteboard.*

Proof (Sketch): Assume the topology of the network is a cycle. The proof idea follows the lines of impossibility results found in [2]. Intuitively, assume a cyclic network in a symmetric initial configuration with two agents. Assume the agents have both the same identifier (or leader) variable and all the whiteboards in the network are initialized with the same arbitrary values. Since agents execute the same deterministic algorithm, there exists an execution of the system refereed in the following as e such that all configurations appearing in this execution are symmetrical with respect to the agents view. Since a configuration solving the naming problem is asymmetrical with respect to the agents view, and the fact that e does not contain asymmetrical configurations, there exists an execution of the system that never reaches a naming or leader election configuration.

In the following we construct a symmetric execution e with respect to the agents view. Without restraining the generality assume only two agents in the network placed such that agents have exactly the same view and the same initial state s_0. Since the two agents have the same view, start in identical states, and execute the same deterministic algorithm, they execute the same action. So, both agents will reach exactly the same state s_0 (in case the agents do not change their state) or $s_1 \neq s_0$. In the new state the agents have the same view of the network and the same state so they execute again the same action. Either, the two agents keep the same state or they both change to a new state s_2. The agents can repeat this game infinitely often. Overall, there is an infinite execution where the two agents pass exactly through the same states in the same time $(s_0)^*(s_1)^*(s_2)^* \ldots$ and the system never reaches an asymmetrical configuration.   □

Theorem 2. *Deterministic naming or leader election of mobile agents is impossible in acyclic networks with full-duplex links, even assuming synchronous scheduling, and infinite memory for each agent and whiteboard.*

Proof (Sketch): Consider a network consisting of two nodes u and v linked by edge e. Assume that there is an agent at each node. Initially all agents are in the same state, and all nodes whiteboards are in the same state. Also, the local labeling of edges is the same at each node. So, the network is completely symmetric, from an agent point of view. Now, each time an agent is scheduled for execution, it may update its own state, update the whiteboard, or (inclusive) move to the other node. Now assume that the scheduling of the agents is synchronous, this means that at every step, the state of each agent remains identical, the state of each whiteboard remains identical, and the relative position of each agent with respect to the view of the other agent remains the same. Overall, symmetry can not be broken by a deterministic agent algorithm, and naming or leader election can not be achieved.   □

4   Self-stabilizing Deterministic Naming in Acyclic Networks with Half-Duplex Links

In the following we propose a deterministic self-stabilizing algorithm for agents naming in acyclic networks with half-duplex links. In networks with k agents the algorithm uses $O(\log(k))$ bits memory per agent and $O(k\log(\Delta k))$ per node, where Δ is the maximum degree of the network.

Each agent has a state that includes a software identifier id ("software" meaning that this identifier can be corrupted), that is represented by some integer. Each node has a whiteboard (that can be corrupted as well) that can store up to k 2-tuples $\langle$id, edge$\rangle$. The id part of the 2-tuple denotes the integer identifier of an agent, and the edge part of the 2-tuple denotes a local edge identifier. This whiteboard is meant to represent the identifiers of the latest k agents with distinct identifiers that visited the node, along with the corresponding outgoing edge they took last time they visited the node. Each node provides to the agents that visit the node some helper functions to access the whiteboard:

- edge(i) returns the edge that is associated to i if i is present in the whiteboard, and *nil* if i is not in the whiteboard.
- visit(i, j) sets the edge j to be associated to agent i if i is in the whiteboard, or adds the entry (i, j) to the whiteboard if i is not present. If the whiteboard already contains k tuples with distinct identifiers, the least recently updated one is dropped from the whiteboard. After updating the whiteboard, the agent exits the node through port j.
- new returns a new identifier that does not exists in the whiteboard.

When arriving at a node, an agent checks whether the node has its identifier in its whiteboard. If it is not present, it adds its identifier and erases one of the identifiers if there are more than k identifiers on the node's whiteboard (assuming FIFO order). If it is present, then either there is another agent with the same identifier at the current node, or the agent is the only one with its identifier. In the first case, the first agent to be executed by the node simply picks up a new identifier, and initiates a Eulerian traversal. In the second case, the agent checks if the last outgoing edge followed by an agent with its identifier is the same as the current incoming edge. In the case it points to another edge (which means there is a discrepancy, whatever its cause), the node simply follows the path corresponding to its identifier, trying to confront the other agent with the same identifier (if such agent exists). Finally, when an agent enters a node through the expect ed edge, it continues performing a Eulerian tour of the tree, *e.g.* by choosing the outgoing edge that is next in the Eulerian tour, *i.e.* edge $(j + 1) \bmod \delta$, if j was the incoming edge. Formally, the algorithm that is executed by each agent is presented as Algorithm 2.

We prove self-stabilization by defining a predicate for *legitimate* configurations, then proving *(i)* every computation starting from a legitimate configuration is correct (see

---

Algorithm 2. Deterministic agent code for tree networks

```
id: integer
execute() {
  if ( edge(id) == nil )
       visit( id, 0 ) // add self, will exit through port 0 by default
  else if ( exists agent j on node i such that j.id == id )
    id = new // Not present or somebody else has the same id
       visit( id, 0 ) // add self, will exit through port 0 by default
  else if ( edge(id) != incoming edge ) )
       visit( id, edge( id ) ) // Follow possible conflicting agent
  else
    visit( id, edge( id ) + 1 mod delta ) // continue Eulerian traversal
}
```

Appendix), and *(ii)* every computation starting from an arbitrary configuration eventually reaches a legitimate configuration.

Definition 4 (Legitimate configuration). *A legitimate configuration for Algorithm 2 satisfies the three following properties:* (i) *all agents have distinct "software" identifiers,* (ii) *all whiteboards tuples contain only actual agent identifiers, and* (iii) *all whiteboards tuples are consistent with actual agent locations.*

Lemma 1 (Correctness). *Every computation of Algorithm 2 that starts from a legitimate configuration satisfies the Naming problem specification.*

Proof (Sketch): Since all k agents have distinct identifiers, and all k identifiers are present in all whiteboards, the whiteboards do not contain any spurious identifier information. So, an agent arriving at a node always finds its own identifier, with proper incoming edge. As a result, agents never change identifier, whiteboards never drop existing identifiers, and edge information is kept accurate, so that every agent performs Eulerian traversal of the tree forever.   □

In the following we prove that starting from any configuration, the system converges to a legitimate configuration.

Lemma 2. *An agent with identifier i eventually visits every node infinitely often.*

Proof (Sketch): Assume the contrary, *i.e.* there exists a time in the execution where at least one node u never gets visited by any agent with identifier i. In turn, this means that for every neighbor v of u, either v is never visited by an agent with identifier i (and the argument can be repeated on the neighbors of v), or v is visited infinitely often but the agent never takes the edge toward u (shortened as e_u). The only way for an agent a with identifier i not to take e_u is *(i)* to exit through edge number 0 (and that edge is not e_u), *(ii)* to follow the path of a (supposedly) other agent with identifier i that did not take e_u, or *(iii)* to never take e_u by performing a Eulerian traversal of the graph (*i.e.* the agent never arrives by port ($e_u - 1$ mod δ)). Cases *(i)* and *(ii)* can be executed only a finite number of times (since there are k agents), so this implies that the node is visited infinitely often by agents that properly execute the $(\text{edge}(i) + 1 \bmod \delta)$ rule and never exit through e_u. Since the network is acyclic, this last case is impossible. $\square$

Lemma 3. *If two agents have the same identifier they eventually meet within $O(m)$ rounds, where m is the number of edges of the graph.*

Proof (Sketch): Note that a node that keeps its identifier either follows the apparent path of a supposed other node, or performs a Eulerian traversal of the tree. Intuitively, the proof goes as follows. The apparent path may be either fake (it leads to a node that does not have identifier i in its whiteboard, or that does not contain another agent with identifier i) or real (the path leads to an agent whose identifier is i). If the path is fake, it is nevertheless finite, and the agent will perform only a finite number of steps to reach the end of the path and realize it is fake. When an agent realizes a path is fake, it executes the Eulerian traversal algorithm. When a node switches to the Eulerian traversal algorithm, its path becomes real. Now, if the path is real, the agent chases a real agent in an acyclic network, and the path information is correct. Since the network is acyclic and the links are half duplex, the two agents are bound to meet each other.

An agent follows a fake path when the information on whiteboards erroneously indicates the presence of another agent with the same identifier. In order to check and correct the information in the whiteboards and agents, in the worst case, has to visit every node in network. In order to perform the traversal, each edge is visited at most twice. Hence the complexity of the traversal is $O(m)$. $\square$

Note that after an agent visited each node of the graph at least once, all whiteboards are coherent with the agent direction and identifier.

Lemma 4 (Convergence). *Starting from any arbitrary initial configuration with k agents, any computation eventually reaches a legitimate configuration in $O(km)$ rounds.*

Proof (Sketch): First, we observe that no identifier that is initially present in the network on some agent is ever removed from the network. This is due to the fact that an agent only changes its identifier when observing that another agent at the same node has the exact same identifier. Since agents execute their code sequentially (activated by nodes), the first activated agent with a conflicting identifier changes its identifier, and the other agent remain unchanged (unless there are more that two agents at the same node with the same identifier).

Now, we prove that starting from any initial configuration, the number of distinct identifiers only increases until it reaches k. Initially the number of distinct identifiers is at least 1. Suppose that there exists some integer j ($1 \leq j < k$) such that there exists j distinct identifiers in the network. Now, after finite time, $O(jm)$, all j identifiers are present in each whiteboard in the network (see Lemma 3). Since $j < k$, there exist at least two agents with the same identifier. By the above argument, two agents with the same identifier are to meet within finite time, $O(m)$. When this is done, one of the agents will change its identifier to a new identifier. Since all j identifiers are on the whiteboards and are regularly refreshed, a new identifier (not in the existing j set) will be solicited by the agent, and the number of total identifiers in the network rises to $j + 1$. By induction hypothesis, the number of distinct identifiers eventually reaches k after $O(km)$ rounds.

When all agents have distinct identifiers, they all traverse all the network infinitely often (see Lemma 2). When each of them has traversed the network at least once, the paths to the agents are all correct with respect to their current position. As a consequence, the configuration is legal.   □

5   Probabilistic Naming in Arbitrary Networks

In this section we assume an weaker model where agents cannot communicate via whiteboard and the network is arbitrary with full-duplex links. Theorems 1 and 2 provide impossibility results related to deterministic naming in this model. In the following we show the possibility of probabilistic naming. The idea is to make every agent randomly move in the network. Anytime two agents that are located at the same node have the same identifier, each agent randomly chooses a new identifier. If there are several agents at the same node with distinct identifiers, the random walk is continued.

Each node provides to the agents that visit the node some helper functions:

- random(S) returns a random element from set S.
- visit(j) makes the agent exit the node through port j.

Algorithm 3. Probabilistic agent code executed at node i for arbitrary networks

```
id: integer
execute() {
    if (there exists agent a such that a.id = id at node i)
        id := random( 1..k )
    else
        visit( random( 0..degree(i) ))
}
```

Algorithm 3 presents the core of our algorithm for probabilistic agent naming. In the presentation, a random value for the identifier is assumed to be between 1 and k, but an upper bound on k may also be used to boost stabilization time (*e.g.* k^2). The proof of correctness can be found in the appendix.

Definition 5 (Legitimate configuration). *A configuration is legitimate if and only if all agents have distinct identifiers.*

Lemma 5 (Correctness). *Every computation of Algorithm 3 that starts from a legitimate configuration satisfies the naming problem specification.*

Proof (Sketch): Assume all identifiers are distinct for all agents, then the "if" clause is never falsified, so the identifier of the agent is never changed. As a result, the configuration remains legitimate.   □

Lemma 6 (Convergence). *Starting from an arbitrary initial configuration, the network eventually reaches a legitimate configuration. The expected stabilization time is $O(kn^3)$ where k is the number of agents in the network.*

Proof (Sketch): We first make the two following observations:

1. when two agents with two different identifiers meet at the same node in the network, their random walk is unaffected by the meeting;
2. when two agents with the same identifier meet at the same node in the network, they stop moving until at least one of them randomly picked a new identifier.

In an arbitrary initial configuration, a pair of agents (u, v) in the network may share the same identifier. We consider occurrences of meetings of two agents or more at the same node in the network. When random walks are unbiased, the meeting time between any two agents is $O(n^3)$, [20]. Here we do not consider the meeting time between agents with different identifiers. Instead we consider the first occurrence of a meeting involving two or more agents of the same color. When this occurs, the two agents draw a random coin and get a random identifier. With probability at least $\frac{1}{k}$, the drawn fresh random identifier is unique in the whole network. So, anytime two agents with the same identifier meet, there is a positive probability that they both get a unique identifier in the system. Anytime this happens, the number of agents who share their color with at least one other agent decreases by one. As a result, with probability one, a configuration where all agents have unique identifiers is reached, and remains thereafter. The stabilization time $O(kn^3)$. □

6 Naming and Leader Election

In this section, we consider the relationship between the aforementioned naming problem, and the leader election problem, where the network must eventually reach a configuration where exactly one agent is elected and all others are non-elected.

6.1 From Naming to Leader Election

We first observe that given a naming of k robots in the network, it is easy to come up with a leader election protocol.

1. In our deterministic protocol, whiteboards are used to register all identifiers used in the system by the agents. When an agent arrives at some node, it checks from the whiteboard if its identifier is maximum in the whiteboard, and becomes elected if so. If its identifier is not maximum in the node's whiteboard, the agent becomes non-elected. After stabilization of the naming algorithm, all whiteboards contain the exact identifiers used in the network, which means that all whiteboards contain the same identifiers in the system. So, if an agent has maximal identifier on one whiteboard, it has maximum identifier on all whiteboards. This guarantees the correctness of the leader election protocol.
2. In our probabilistic protocol, eventually all nodes have distinct identifiers in the network. If the exact value of k was used in the algorithm, then a node can simply checks its identifier against k to detect if it is the leader or not. If only an upper bound on k was used, then a more complicated process is required. The procedure is as follows: each node stores the identifiers of the last $k - 1$ distinct agents it last

saw; then if its identifier is maximum among those identifiers, it becomes elected, and remains non-elected otherwise. The leader status is updated anytime the list of the $k - 1$ distinct encounters is modified. After stabilization of the naming algorithm, all identifiers are distinct, so a non-biased random walk is performed by each agent. Then each agents meets every other agent regularly within polynomial time. Overall, after polynomial time, every agent has met every other agent and stored their identifiers in its local memory. When every agent has all other agent identifiers in its local memory, the leader status remains correct and unchanged. The memory cost of the algorithm is $O(k \log(k))$ per agent and the time complexity is polynomial.

An alternative to this algorithm is as follows. Each agent performs a random walk in the network (at each node the agent chooses with equal probability (1/node degree) the next edge to visit). In [12] it is proved that the expected time for a random walk to cover all nodes of a graph is $O(n \log(n))$. Each time an agent visits a node it marks in the node table its identifier if it is not present. If the agent identifier is the maximum in the table then the agent is the leader otherwise it keeps the follower status. The memory complexity of the algorithm is $O(k \log(k))$ per node and the expected time complexity is $O(kn \log(n))$.

6.2   From Leader Election to Naming

Now consider the reverse problem of solving the naming problem given a leader in the group of agents. Our solution is presented as Algorithms 4 and 5. For simplicity, we assume that the leader agent is identified by a special symbol that is not in the domain on non-leader agents identifiers and which can be recognized by the node as the leader mark. First we assume that each node, when activating agents, gives lower priority to the leader agent (*i.e.* the code of the leader agent, if present on the node, is executed last). The intuition of the algorithm is as follows: the leader agent simply performs a Eulerian traversal of the tree, and is not influenced by the other nodes. On its way during each traversal, the leader leaves in the edge variable of each traversed whiteboard the outgoing edge it used to exit last time it visited the node. In a legitimate situation, those edge variables constitute a tree pointing toward the current location of the leader. The rationale for the non-leader nodes is as follows: *(i)* when the leader is not present on the same node, the non-leader node simply follows the edge left by the leader, trying to reach it, and *(ii)* when the leader is present on the same node, the non-leader agent first checks against duplicate identifiers of non-leader agents located at the same leader-based node, and pick up a new fresh identifier if needed, then they take the same outgoing edge as the leader, in order to always remain at the same node as the leader agent. Since the network is acyclic and the links are half-duplex, every non-leader node eventually meets the leader, and once met, they never leave the leader. So, eventually, the leader agent collects all non-leader agents at its current location. When all agents are co-located at the same node and check that no duplicate identifiers exist, the naming process is finished.

Definition 6 (Legitimate configuration). *A configuration of the network is legitimate if it satisfies the following properties:* (i) *all non-leader agents have distinct identifiers,*

Algorithm 4. Deterministic agent code for naming in tree networks
---

```
id: integer
execute() {
  if ( leader )
    edge := edge + 1 mod delta // follow the Eulerian traversal
    visit( edge )
  else
    if ( leader is present on the same node )
      if (id is conflicting among present agents on the node)
        id := new // take fresh identifier
      visit( edge + 1 mod delta ) // take same exit as that of the lead
    else
      visit( edge ) // follow leader
}
```

Algorithm 5. Deterministic node code for naming in tree networks
---

```
foreach non-leader agent on node
  agent.execute()
end foreach
leader.execute()
```

(ii) *all agents are located in the same node, and* (iii) *all* edge *whiteboards point toward the node that contain all agents.*

Lemma 7 (Correctness). *Starting from a legitimate configuration, the naming problem is solved.*

Proof (Sketch): In a legitimate configuration, all agents have distinct identifiers. From the code of the algorithm, an agent may change its identifier only when discovering that it shares the same identifier with another agent. As a result, an agent never changes its identifier onwards, and the naming problem is solved.   □

Lemma 8 (Convergence). *Starting from an arbitrary initial configuration, a legitimate configuration is eventually reached.*

Proof (Sketch): We first prove that eventually, all edge whiteboards point toward the node that contain the leader. We observe that the leader behavior does not depend on the behavior of the non-leader agents. Second, when the leader leaves a node (whatever the initialization of the whiteboard of this node may be), the edge whiteboard of this node will always point toward the leader agent onwards (the network is acyclic, so the leader agent may only come back though this edge), and the next time the edge whiteboard is modified, it will advertise the current last taken edge by the leader agent. Our second observation is that whatever the initialization of the whiteboards, the leader agent always perform a Eulerian traversal of the network. As a result, all nodes are eventually visited by the leader node, and when all nodes have been visited at least once, all edge whiteboards are pointing toward the leader agent.

The second step of the proof is to show that any non-leader agent eventually meets the leader agent. Since the `edge` whiteboards all point toward the leader agent, and that non-leader agents that are not located on the same node as the leader simply follow the `edge` whiteboards, they always move toward the leader agent. Since the network is acyclic and the links are half-duplex, the leader agent and any non-leader agent are bound to meet within $O(m)$ rounds. Now, when a non-leader agent meets the leader agent, their moving behavior remains the same hereafter (*i.e.* the leader and the non-leader agents follow exactly the same path at the same moment–when the node they are both located on is activated). So, eventually, within $O(km)$ rounds all agents are located at the same node at a given moment, and remain located at the same node hereafter (though the node they are located changes anytime it is scheduled for execution).

When all agents are gathered at the same node, non-leader nodes (that are executed in sequence when the node is activated) simply choose different identifiers. After one such node activation, all agents have distinct identifiers, are gathered at the same node, and all `edge` whiteboards are pointing to them. As a consequence, the configuration is legitimate. □

7 Concluding Remarks

In this paper, we introduced the problem of self-stabilizing mobile robots in graphs, and presented deterministic and probabilistic solutions to the problems of naming, and leader election among robots. From a practical point of view, the main difference between the two solutions is that the deterministic solution uses a whiteboard (*i.e.* a local memory available at every node that the agents can use to communicate with others) while the probabilistic one does not. An interesting open question that is raised by this work is the trade-off between whiteboard availability and randomness capabilities. In addition, it would be of theoretical interest to prove that the computational power of our model is strictly greater (in terms of predicates that can be computed) than the Population Protocol model.

References

1. Agmon, N., Peleg, D.: Fault-tolerant gathering algorithms for autonomous mobile robots. In: Proc. 15th Annual ACM-SIAM Symposium on Discrete Algorithms (SODA 2004), pp. 1070–1078, New Orleans, LA, USA (January 2004)
2. Angluin, D.: Local and global properties in networks of processors (extended abstract). In: STOC, pp. 82–93. ACM (1980)
3. Angluin, D., Aspnes, J., Diamadi, Z., Fischer, M.J., Peralta, R.: Computation in networks of passively mobile finite-state sensors. In: PODC, pp. 290–299 (2004)
4. Angluin, D., Aspnes, J., Diamadi, Z., Fischer, M.J., Peralta, R.: Computation in networks of passively mobile finite-state sensors. Distributed Computing 235–253 (March 2006)
5. Angluin, D., Aspnes, J., Fischer, M.J., Jiang, H.: Self-stabilizing population protocols. In: Anderson, J.H., Prencipe, G., Wattenhofer, R. (eds.) OPODIS 2005. LNCS, vol. 3974, pp. 103–117. Springer, Heidelberg (2005)
6. Beauquier, J., Herault, T., Schiller, E.: Easy Stabilization with an Agent. In: Datta, A.K., Herman, T. (eds.) WSS 2001. LNCS, vol. 2194, pp. 35–51. Springer, Heidelberg (2001)

7. Défago, X., Gradinariu, M., Messika, S., Parvédy, P.R.: Fault-tolerant and self-stabilizing mobile robots gathering. In: DISC, pp. 46–60 (2006)
8. Dessmark, A., Fraigniaud, P., Kowalski, D.R., Pelc, A.: Deterministic rendezvous in graphs. Algorithmica 46(1), 69–96 (2006)
9. Dobrev, S., Flocchini, P., Prencipe, G., Santoro, N.: Searching for a black hole in arbitrary networks: optimal mobile agent protocols. In: PODC, pp. 153–161 (2002)
10. Dolev, S.: Self-stabilization. MIT Press, Cambridge (2000)
11. Dolev, S., Schiller, E., Welch, J.: Random walk for self-stabilizing group communication in ad-hoc networks.In: Reliable Distributed Systems, 2002. Proceedings. 21st IEEE Symposium on, pp. 70–79 (2002)
12. Feige, U.: A tight upper bound on the cover time for random walks on graphs. Random Struct. Algorithms 6(1), 51–54 (1995)
13. Flocchini, P., Prencipe, G., Santoro, N., Widmayer, P.: Distributed coordination of a set of autonomous mobile robots. IVS, 480–485, (2000)
14. Fomin, F.V., Fraigniaud, P., Nisse, N.: Nondeterministic Graph Searching: From Pathwidth to Treewidth. In: Jedrzejowicz, J., Szepietowski, A. (eds.) MFCS 2005. LNCS, vol. 3618, pp. 364–375. Springer, Heidelberg (2005)
15. Fraigniaud, P., Ilcinkas, D., Rajsbaum, S., Tixeuil, S.: The Reduced Automata Technique for Graph Exploration Space Lower Bounds. In: Goldreich, O., Rosenberg, A.L., Selman, A.L. (eds.) Theoretical Computer Science. LNCS, vol. 3895, pp. 1–26. Springer, Heidelberg (2006)
16. Ghosh, S.: Agents, distributed algorithms, and stabilization. In: Du, D.-Z., Eades, P., Sharma, A.K., Lin, X., Estivill-Castro, V. (eds.) COCOON 2000. LNCS, vol. 1858, pp. 242–251. Springer, Heidelberg (2000)
17. Herman, T., Masuzawa, T.: Self-Stabilizing Agent Traversal. In: Datta, A.K., Herman, T. (eds.) WSS 2001. LNCS, vol. 2194, pp. 152–166. Springer, Heidelberg (2001)
18. Prencipe, G.: Corda: Distributed coordination of a set of autonomous mobile robots.In: Proc. ERSADS, pp. 185–190, (May 2001)
19. Suzuki, I., Yamashita, M.: Distributed anonymous mobile robots—formation and agreement problems.In: Proceedings of the 3rd International Colloquium on Structural Information and Communication Complexity (SIROCCO 1996), Siena, Italy, (June 1996)
20. Tetali, P., Winkler, P.: On a random walk problem arising in self-stabilizing token management. In: PODC, pp. 273–280 (1991)
21. Yamashita, M., Kameda, T.: Computing on anonymous networks: Part i-characterizing the solvable cases. IEEE Trans. Parallel Distrib. Syst. 7(1), 69–89 (1996)
22. Yamashita, M., Kameda, T.: Computing on Anonymous Networks: Part II-Decision and Membership Problems. IEEE Trans. Parallel Distrib. Syst. 7(1), 90–96 (1996)

Peer to Peer Multidimensional Overlays: Approximating Complex Structures*

Olivier Beaumont[1], Anne-Marie Kermarrec[2], and Étienne Rivière[2,3]

[1] LaBRI/INRIA Futurs, Bordeaux France
obeaumon@labri.fr
[2] INRIA Rennes Bretagne Atlantique, France
{akermarr,eriviere}@irisa.fr
[3] IRISA/Université de Rennes 1, France

Abstract. Peer to peer overlay networks have proven to be a good support for storing and retrieving data in a fully decentralized way. A sound approach is to structure them in such a way that they reflect the structure of the application. Peers represent objects of the application so that neighbours in the peer to peer network are objects having similar characteristics from the application's point of view. Such structured peer to peer overlay networks provide a natural support for range queries. While some complex structures such as a Voronoï tessellation, where each peer is associated to a cell in the space, are clearly relevant to structure the objects, the associated cost to compute and maintain these structures is usually extremely high for dimensions larger than 2.

We argue that an approximation of a complex structure is enough to provide a native support of range queries. This stems from the fact that neighbours are important while the *exact* space partitioning associated to a given peer is not as crucial. In this paper, we present the design, analysis and evaluation of RayNet, a loosely structured Voronoï-based overlay network. RayNet organizes peers in an approximation of a Voronoï tessellation in a fully decentralized way. It relies on a Monte-Carlo algorithm to estimate the size of a cell and on an epidemic protocol to discover neighbours. In order to ensure efficient (polylogarithmic) routing, RayNet is inspired from the Kleinberg's small world model where each peer gets connected to close neighbours (its approximate Voronoï neighbours in Raynet) and shortcuts, long range neighbours, implemented using an existing Kleinberg-like peer sampling.

1 Introduction

Structure versus search expressiveness. Plethora of peer to peer overlay networks have been proposed in the past years to manage data collection at a large-scale. Peer to peer overlays organize peers in a logical network and are characterized by their underlying structure. As far as data management is concerned, they differentiate each other by the expressiveness and efficiency of the search functionalities they support. The expressiveness of search relates to the way data can be accessed: *(i)* exact search is used to access data objects identified by a unique identifier; *(ii)* attribute-based search enables

---

* This work was supported in part by French ANR "Masse de données" ALPAGE.

E. Tovar, P. Tsigas, and H. Fouchal (Eds.): OPODIS 2007, LNCS 4878, pp. 315–328, 2007.
© Springer-Verlag Berlin Heidelberg 2007

to access data using a set of attribute, value pairs; *(iii)* in range queries, the attribute values are specified for a given range At one end of the spectrum lie unstructured overlays in which each peer gets connected to a set of arbitrary neighbours. Such networks rely on constrained flooding techniques to search for data [21]. This provides a way to implement all types of search but such approaches often suffer from lack of efficiency. A query may need to ultimately visit the whole network to ensure exhaustive results. Fully structured overlays lie at the other end of the spectrum. In such networks, peers are organized along a precise structure such as a ring. In DHT-based networks [20], each object gets associated to a given peer. Such networks provide an efficient support for a DHT functionality. However, their expressiveness is naturally limited by the exact-match interface they provide.

We argue that, in order to improve upon the efficiency of expressive queries, the structure of the peer to peer overlay should reflect the application's one. Peers are then application objects and get connected to neighbours (*i.e.* sharing similar characteristics from the application point of view). Such a logical organization provides a natural support for nearest neighbours and range queries. Such peer to peer overlays then support *natively* complex queries. Examples of such approaches are : Sub-2-Sub [26] and Meghdoot [10] for content-based publish and subscribe or Skip-graph based overlays [1,9]. Those structures are however sometimes extremely complex to maintain accurately. For example, maintaining a Voronoï tessellation as in [4] involves a high overhead when the dimension is larger than 2 [6], and is prone to high levels of calculation degeneracy.

Weakening the structure. In this paper we argue that a loose structure is actually enough from the search perspective. What really matters is that each peer gets connected to carefully chosen neighbours, so that the graph can be exhaustively visited. The exact logical structure is not as crucial, provided that its estimation enables correct routing for all requests. In this paper, we propose a general approach based on a Monte-Carlo algorithm to approximate a complex structure, in order to build a loosely structured overlay network. More precisely, we propose an algorithm to approximate the size of Voronoï cells, upon which we build neighbourhood relations.

Contributions. The contributions of this paper are the following. First, we propose a general approach based on a Monte-Carlo method to approximate the size of a Voronoï cell. Then we propose the design and evaluation of RayNet, a weakly structured overlay network, achieving an approximation of a Voronoï tessellation. Following the generic approximation method, each peer in RayNet relies on an epidemic-based protocol to discover its neighbours. Using such a protocol, the quality of the estimation gradually improves to eventually achieve a close approximation of a Voronoï tessellation. This protocol ensures that each peer gets connected to its Voronoï-like neighbours while avoiding the need to accurately compute the exact Voronoï cells, thus keeping the overall overhead low. Each peer in RayNet also maintains a set of long-range links (also called shortcuts) to implement a small-world topology. Efficient (poly-logarithmic) routing in RayNet is achieved by choosing the shortcuts according to a distribution advocated by Kleinberg in [17]. Both links are created by gossip-based protocols. Finally, we evaluate the performance of RayNet through simulations and investigate its performance both in terms of bootstrapping time and routing performance. Note that implementing the query algorithm is actually out of the scope of this paper, and that we focus on the creation of the overlay itself.

2   Design Rationale

System model. We consider a system composed of n nodes, and a set of objects. We assume that each object is stored on the node that has created it. The overlay is actually linking objects themselves, rather than computing entities. This design choice is similar to the one made for Skip-Graphs based systems [1,9]. Nodes can maintain a set of objects. Although the mapping of objects to physical nodes may be investigated to improve performance, the scope of this paper is to present the object-to-object overlay and its capabilities. Leveraging the presence of multiple objects per node or proposing mapping algorithms of objects to physical nodes that provides better scalability, fault tolerance or performance is therefore left for future work.

We consider a d dimensional attribute space. Each object is exactly identified by a value for each attribute. The attribute values of an object represent the coordinates of the object in the attribute space. This may obviously lead to skewed distribution of objects in the naming space.

We assume that each peer maintains a partial view of the network, called its *view* and consisting of a list of neighbours (IP addresses and coordinates).

Structuring the network using Voronoï diagrams. Figure 1 describes coarsely the targeted structure for a two dimensional data set. A set of objects (black points) is maintained in the distributed application naming space. To achieve a structure that permits nearest neighbour and range queries possibilities, peers having *close* attribute values should be linked in the overlay. Figure 1 shows such links for a sample object o_i. Our general goal for the creation of these links is as follows: for any point p_{target} belonging to the application naming space, for a query that passes through an object o_i, either o_i is the nearest to p_{target} and is the solution, or o_i knows a peer o_j that is nearer to the destination. This property ensures that greedy routing always succeeds, since the distance to the destination point is reduced at each step during the query propagation process.

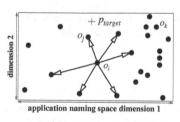

application naming space dimension 1

Fig. 1. *Target structure*

A structure that ensures this property is the Delaunay graph, which is the dual of the Voronoï diagram. The Voronoï diagram of a set of generators points $\{p \in \mathbb{R}^d\}$ is a tessellation of $\mathbb{R}^d$ into disjoint cells. Each cell $vc(p_x)$ is composed of all points that are closer to p_x than to any other generator in the set. The links we aim at creating are adjacencies relations between objects cells, and compose the Delaunay graph.

We have already successfully used Voronoï diagrams in the context of routing mechanisms [4] in a structured object-to-object overlay, This overlay provides a native support for range queries and nearest neighbour queries for datasets over two dimensions naming spaces. However, maintaining accurately this structure is extremely costly when the dimension goes over 2 [6]. First, the number of neighbours an object needs to handle is growing exponentially with the dimension.

Second, the maintenance cost to keep *exactly* all these links consistent in spite of nodes and links failure increases accordingly.

However, defining the exact Voronoï cells is more than what is actually needed to ensure that greedy routing succeeds in such a network. What matters is actually the fact that each peer gets connected to its "close" neighbours *along all directions*. Also, imposing a fixed size set of neighbours at each object is desirable for scalability and load balancing purposes.

We base our design on the following observation: *for an object o with neighbourhood consisting of objects whose Voronoï cell shares a boundary with o's cell, the volume of o's cell in the tessellation of all objects is the same as o's cell volume in the Voronoï tessellation of only o and its neighbours.* We are thus interested in discovering neighbours (partial view of the network) $o.view$ for each object o in the system, for which the volume of o's cell in the tessellation of $o \cup o.view$ is minimal. We use a fixed size set of neighbours, and each object exchanges its current view of the network by means of a gossip-based protocol. Figure 2 presents the principle of this evolution: the more peers an object detects, the more opportunities of choosing a peer configuration it encounters to improve its zone approximation. In the following section, we highlight the principles of gossip-based protocols used for overlay construction, presents the biased peer-sampling protocol we use to provide small world characteristics to the overlay (especially for routing efficiency purposes). We then describe the core of our protocol, that is gossip-based construction of *coverage and closeness* at each peer, and the mechanisms that permit this construction, Monte-Carlo Voronoï cell size estimation.

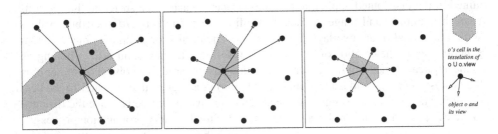

Fig. 2. Desired evolution of an object's neighbourhood: convergence towards the smallest (estimated) Voronoï cell. From random connections (left) to smallest possible zone (right).

3 Approximation Through Gossip

In this paper, we use gossip-based protocols to create and maintain the peer to peer overlay network. Although the focus of this paper is to approximate the neighbourhood at each peer, ultimately routing efficiently (in poly-logarithmic time) through the structure is an important concern. A small-world topology is created to achieve this. In this section we provide some background on small-world networks and gossip-based protocols. We then describe an existing gossip-based protocol that approximates a small-world topology. Finally, we present how we extend the generic gossip-based protocol framework to build the neighbourhood of each peer.

3.1 Small-World Networks

Small-world network models were introduced to investigate the inherent routing capabilities of human relations networks. In such network models, each peer is connected to its closest neighbours in a topology as well as additional long-range contacts, also called shortcuts. Watts and Strogatz [27] introduce such a small-world topology where shortcuts are picked uniformly at random. In 2000, Kleinberg [17] demonstrated that poly-logarithmic routing could be achieved using a greedy algorithm if such shortcuts were chosen according to a specific distribution (d-harmonic). In his work, Kleinberg consider a $n \times n$ grid where every vertex has edges to its four direct neighbours and k (typically one) long-range neighbour(s). This long-range neighbour is chosen with a probability proportional to $\frac{1}{l^d}$, where d is the dimension and l is the Euclidean distance between the vertex and its remote neighbour. These results can be extended to more general topologies and higher dimensions [3,4]

3.2 Gossip-Based Overlay Construction

Gossip-based protocols, first introduced to reliably disseminate events in large systems, have now been recognized as a scalable and reliable basic building block to instantiate and maintain peer to peer overlay networks. Their scalability stems from their simplicity, their ability to capture system dynamics and the emergent properties they lead to. They have been successfully applied to a large number of settings from reliable broadcast [5] to overlay maintenance [8,12,23,25], and from aggregation [15] to system size estimation [22] and are now turned into a generic and sound substrate for building and maintaining large-scale overlay networks [24].

A gossip-based protocol relies on a periodic exchange of information between peers. Such a period is called a *cycle*. Each peer keeps a (usually fixed-size) set of peers, called its *view*. Periodically, each peer picks a target from its view of the system, exchanges some information with it and processes the received information. If the information exchanged relates to neighbourhood, such a protocol creates an overlay network. We focus on such protocols in this paper. A gossip-based protocol is characterized by the following three parameters:

- **Peer selection policy:** each peer p_i chooses periodically a gossip target from its view $p_i.view$;
- **State exchanged:** the state exchanged between peers is membership information and consists of a list of peers (subset of their views);
- **State processing:** upon receipt of the list, the receiving peer merges the list of peers received with its own view to compose a new list of neighbours.

It turns out that these parameters can be tuned so that the resulting graph exhibit properties which are extremely close to those of a random graph [8,12,25], providing a *Peer Sampling Service*: each peer's view contains a set of randomly drawn other peers from the network and this view changes at each cycle. More generally, it has been shown that arbitrary structures can be maintained this way, including fully structured peer to peer overlay networks [11,23,26].

For instance, it has been shown in [7] that peer sampling protocol can be biased in order to approximate the distribution advocated by Kleinberg to improve routing in small-world networks. This can be achieved by simply adapting the *state processing* phase, to keep in the view, a set of peers that exhibits a Kleinberg-like long link length distribution. We use this protocol, called *small-world peer sampling* in the remaining of this document, as the substrate of our protocol, to achieve efficient routing.

3.3 Approximating the Close Neighbourhood: Coverage and Closeness

It has been shown in [11,25] that the same generic gossip protocol can be used to enable each peer to create links to its closest neighbours according to a given proximity metric. The peer selected to gossip with is then chosen as the closest from the view, and the state processing keeps the closest peers from the union of the local and received views. Such a clustering protocol is usually run concomitantly with a peer sampling service in order to ensure connectivity and to leave peers with the ability to cluster nodes[1].

In this paper, we propose to use a generalization of such a protocol to approximate the neighbourhood of a given peer. However, minimizing distances to each peer independently is not sufficient to ensure that the routing will succeed in all directions. Thus, instead of optimizing each item of the view independently, our approach is to decide on a new view as a whole. That means that, at each gossip cycle, set of peers are examined as *configurations* (potential new views) and not independently. To the best of our knowledge, this is the first time such an approach of generalization of gossip-based overlay construction protocols is proposed.

We denote as the *utility* of a new configuration the metric that permits us to decide whether a configuration is better than the current view or not. This utility is the estimation of the Voronoï cell size, as decided by our Monte-Carlo estimation algorithm (see Section 4.1). This metric ensures that (1) closeness is achieved, which means that eventually a peer will get to know peers that are as close as possible to itself and (2) coverage is ensured, *i.e.* eventually each portion of the space surrounding a peer is covered by a neighbour, if such a peer exists in the system.

4   Protocol Details

In this section we provide the details of building and maintaining RayNet. RayNet is based on a gossip-based approach: at each cycle, an object o chooses a gossip partner o_d from its current view (or a subset of its view) of the system to gossip with. After the state is exchanged, o then evaluates if there exists a new view (configuration of objects) that ensures better coverage and closeness. The candidate configurations have thus to be considered as a whole, and peer objects cannot be selected independently.

4.1   View Evolution Using Voronoï Cell Size Estimation

Size of the view. To ensure coverage and closeness, an object uses the estimated volume of its Voronoï cell based on its set of neighbours. Effectively, greedy routing succeeds if

---

[1] Obviously non uniform topologies would be prone to create disconnected clusters otherwise.

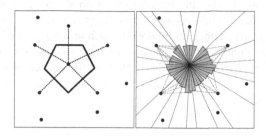

Fig. 3. Illustration of the Monte Carlo method (o is the central point)

o knows neighbours in each possible direction (to get closer to any other target object) and close neighbours (when the target object is close to o). If the volume of the Voronoï cell at o is bounded, then o knows Delaunay neighbours in all directions and if the volume of this cell is the smallest possible one, then these peers are among o's closest neighbours. In general, $2d + 1$ neighbours are enough to get a bounded Voronoï cell. In order to keep extra close neighbours, we set the size c of objects views to $c = 3d + 1$. Moreover, we assume that peers exchange their entire view during a gossip operation.

Monte-Carlo cell volume estimation. Once views have been exchanged, object o needs to estimate the volume of its Voronoï cell, for every possible configuration (on a naive basis; we show in the following Sections that examining *all possible* configurations is not mandatory). The volume of the cell is computed for each configuration. That is, given a set of objects $o.view \cup o_d.view = \{o_1, \ldots, o_n\}$, for each possible configuration $\{o_{i_1}, \ldots, o_{i_c}\}$ of size c, we estimate the volume of the Voronoï cell of o in the tessellation of points $o \cup \{o_{i_1}, \ldots, o_{i_c}\}$. Then, if a new configuration is found, for which the volume of the cell of object o is reduced, this configuration is used as o's new view.

There is no need to effectively compute the cell itself, which would be computationally expensive and prone to high levels of calculation degeneracy. Instead, we propose a new Monte-Carlo method for estimating this volume. Figure 3 presents an illustration of this approach in a two dimensional space. Note that this approach scales to higher dimensions.

A set of R *rays* is created, whose starting point is o and directions are drawn uniformly at random on the unit hyper-sphere. To this end, we use the method described in [18] that provides uniform probability distribution of points on the hyper-sphere. Algorithm 1.left describes the method. Rays (dashed lines starting from o on Figure 3) will act as *probes*, for which we discover the closest intersection point p_{int} lying on the ray r with a (virtual) Voronoï cell of another object in the configuration, this object being the object o_2 for which $\lambda = ||p_{int}, o|| = ||p_{int}, o_2||$ is minimal. For this, the function compDistOnRay() in Algorithm 1.left computes λ for each point. Distances $\lambda = ||p_{int}, o_2||$ are represented by discontinuous lines from o_2 to the intersection p_{int} on Figure 3. Lines (a) to (b) of Algorithm 1.left present the selection of the closest peers for each ray. We keep all λ values for each ray (set Λ), and use them to compute the estimation of the cell volume as follows (line (c) of Algorithm 1.left). Each ray r is associated to a *ball* of radius λ_r whose volume is given by $(BallVol \times (\lambda_r)^d)/R$, where

BallVol is the volume of the unit ball in dimension d. The volume of the estimated cell is the average value, for all rays, of volumes of such balls (the contribution for each ray is represented as grey cones on Figure 3). Such an estimator of the volume of the Voronoï cell is clearly unbiased, so that the estimated volume converges to the volume of the Voronoï cell when $R \to +\infty$. Nevertheless, the convergence strongly depends on the shape of the Voronoï cell, thus imposing the use of a large enough R (10^3 in the current implementation).

```
calcVolume()
parameters      : config (SET[objects])
begin
        SET[double] Λ ← ∅
        o.rays ← createRays(R)
(a)     for double[] r ∈ o.rays do
            double λ ← ∞
            for object oⱼ ∈ config do
                double l ← compDistOnRay(r,oⱼ)
                if l < dist then
                    λ ← l
(b)         Λ ← Λ ∪ λ
        /* BallVol contains the unit Ball volume in dimension
        d */
(c)     return   BallVol×Σ_{λ∈Λ}(λ^d)
                 ─────────────────────
                          R
end
```

```
update_naive()
parameters      : o_d.view (SET[objects])
Local variables:
        S : SET[objects]
        vol : double
begin
        o.current_vol ← calcVolume(o.view)
        foreach S ∈ P_c(view ∪ o_d.view) do
            vol ← calcVolume(S)
            if vol < o.current_vol then
                o.view ← S
                o.current_vol ← vol
end
```

Algorithm 1. Monte-Carlo algorithm for estimating the volume of the cell for object o (left) and naive update algorithm for o receiving $o_d.view$ (right).

4.2 Discovery of a New Configuration: Naive Approach

We describe in this section and in Algorithm 1.right the naive approach to select a new view for an object o upon reception of the view $o_d.view$. In order to determine the best view among the set of candidates, we need to estimate the volume of the Voronoï cell of o for the subgraph $S \bigcup o$ for each possible set S of c peer objects in the augmented view. That is, each possible subset of size c among $o.view \cup o_d.view$ shall be evaluated for replacement of $o.view$.

Evaluating all $C_{2c}^c = O(c!)$ possible configurations would provide exhaustive and accurate results, though at an unaffordable price. Therefore, we propose in the next Section a more realistic algorithm significantly reducing the overall complexity to a cost that is linear in the space dimension d.

4.3 Discovery of a New Configuration: Efficient, Linear Time Approach

Algorithm 2 presented in this section requires rays for a given object to be chosen once and for all upon creation of the object, in order to save information between configurations' associated cell volumes. Each peer o maintains a bipartite graph *best* containing on one side peers objects of $o.view$, and on the other side the rays $o.rays$. We denote by $best_O(r)$ the Voronoï neighbour o_p of o according to ray r: it is the node o_p such that a ray issued from o and whose direction is r first reaches the Voronoï cell of o_p (this entry is never empty). Similarly, we denote by $\{best_R(o_p)\}$ the set of rays for which o_p is the current Voronoï neighbour of o (this set may be empty).

The objective is as follows: to compute o's new view, for each object o_p in $o_d.view \cap \overline{o.view}$ (i.e. all peers for which $\{best_R(o_p)\}$ does not contain any information), we determine the set of rays for which o_d is the Voronoï neighbour of o in the augmented view Voronoï diagram. This operation is described by lines (a) to (b) of Algorithm 2. Peers found to be a Voronoï neighbour of o for a given ray are stored in the set $improve$, which has the same semantic as $best_O$, except that entries for some rays can be empty.

On line (c), either $improve$ or $best_O$ has information, for each ray, about which peer in the augmented view is a Voronoï neighbour of o. The next step is to compute to which extent each peer is needed in the new configuration. More precisely, given a peer o_x, we compute the volume of the cell of o with all peers *but* o_x (lines (c)-(d)). If the volume of the cell increases dramatically, that means that peer o_x was mandatory to ensure closeness and proximity. On the other hand, if the volume remains the same, then peer o_x has no contribution to coverage nor closeness.

Note that, unlike the naive method (Algorithms 1), it is not necessary to iterate through all peers of the tested configuration to find the peer with the smallest λ value. This information is usually contained in either $best_O$, if such a peer lies in $o.view$, or in $improve$, if such a peer is a candidate peer from the distant view. The only case when one needs to iterate through all peers is when the best known peer for a given ray is o_x, the currently ignored peer.

Volumes associated to each peer (*i.e.* the volume without that peer in the configuration) are stored in the map $volumes$. This map is then sorted by decreasing volume values : starting from entries of peers that contributes highly to coverage and closeness, to entries of peers that have no or few contribution to coverage and closeness. The new

---

update()
parameters   : $o_p.view$ (SET[objects]) /* distant view */
Local variables:
　　improve (map ray $\rightarrow$ object) init $\emptyset$ /*improve has the same semantic as $best_O$ */
　　volumes (list of pairs (object,volume)) init $\emptyset$
begin

(a) ㅤ**foreach** *ray* $r \in o.rays$ **do**
ㅤㅤ　double $best_\lambda = \bot$
ㅤㅤ　object $imp = \bot$
ㅤㅤ　**foreach** *object* $o_j \in (o_d.view \cap \overline{o.view})$ **do**
ㅤㅤㅤ　$\lambda \leftarrow$ distOnRay(r, o_j)
ㅤㅤㅤ　**if** $\lambda < \begin{cases} best_O(r) & \text{if } best_\lambda = \bot \\ best_\lambda & \text{if } best_\lambda \neq \bot \end{cases}$ **then**
ㅤㅤㅤㅤ　$imp \leftarrow o_j$
ㅤㅤㅤㅤ　$best_\lambda = \lambda$

ㅤㅤ　**if** $best_\lambda \neq \bot$ **then**
(b) ㅤㅤ　ㅤimprove[r] $= imp$

(c) ㅤ**foreach** *object* $o_x \in o.view \cup (o_d.view \cap \overline{o_i.view})$ **do**
(d) ㅤㅤ　volumes $\leftarrow$ volumes $\cup$ pair(o_x.calcVolumeImproved($best \cup improve, (o_d.view \cap \overline{o_i.view}) \setminus o_x$))
ㅤ　sort volumes by decreasing volume
ㅤ　$o.view \leftarrow \{volumes_1.o, \dots, volumes_c.o\}$
ㅤ　update $best_O$ and $best_R$
end

Algorithm 2. Update of object's view $o.view$: efficient approach. Sets $best_O$ and $best_R$ are constructed and coherent i.r.t. the current $o.view$ when starting the algorithm.

configuration is built from the c peers that presents the maximum contribution, *i.e.* peers of the first c entries of *volume*.

The cost of the approach is as follows: there are up to $(r \times c)$ calls to method distOnRay(), if all c candidates were unknown to the current peer, and up to $(2 \times c)$ calls to calcVolume(). Each call to distOnRay() has cost 1: it is a fixed size set of scalar products. Each call to calcVolume() takes $r \times (1 + \frac{2 \times c - 1}{2 \times c})$ operations, where the term $\frac{2 \times c - 1}{2 \times c}$ stands for the few cases where the "best" peer is the currently ignored peer o_x (on average, $\frac{1}{2 \times c}$ occurrences per call). The overall cost is thus $\simeq 5(r \times c)$ operations, where r is a constant and c only depends on the dimension of the naming space d, *i.e.* $c =$O(d). The overall cost of the improved update algorithm is thus O(d) operations.

5   Experimental Evaluation

In this section, we evaluate RayNet along two metrics: (1) the time needed by a chaotic system to converge towards an overlay where all routes succeed and (2) when such an overlay is created, how many steps are required by greedy routing from any object to the nearest object of a target point, as a function of system size. Expected results are respectively: (1) a fast convergence and self-organization towards full success for routing requests and (2) a poly-logarithmic evolution of the route size according to the size of the system, thanks to the small-world peer sampling layer.

We developed a simulator using Java, and ran simulations for populations of objects ranging from 500 to 7.000 objects. The dimension of the object naming space d ranges from 2 to 6. All objects points are drawn uniformly at random in this space. For all experiments, $r = 10^3$ rays were used to estimate cell volumes, and $3 \times d + 1$ neighbours are kept at each object. At each cycle, two exchanges take place, one for the small-world peer sampling layer (8 peers out of 20 maintained peers are sent), the other for the coverage and closeness layer (exchange of views). Also, for the first two cycles, each peer selects randomly 10 peers from the small-world peer sampling layer and assess them for potential inclusion in a new configuration to bootstrap the coverage and closeness level.

Bootstrapping the overlay. First, we evaluate the time RayNet takes to converge towards an overlay state where every routing request succeed. The overlay is initialized to a random graph for the small-world peer sampling layer, and no peer for the coverage and closeness layer. This makes sense as bootstrapping from a chaotic state is the worst case for gossip-based overlay construction mechanisms. More, following the proposal of [16] (with successful instantiations such as [13,23,26]), this represents the case where a distributed application needs the rapid instantiation of a routing substrate on top of a peer sampling layer. This experiment shows that our proposal fits perfectly in this scope, while being obviously applicable to long-term runs.

Figure 5 presents the results for all dimensions, and for different object population sizes. *Hit ratio* denotes the proportion of routes that succeed onto exactly the object that is nearest to the query destination. At each cycle, 20.000 random (object, destination point) pairs are tested. As expected, the hit ratio increases with the number of exchanges. In addition, perfect routing is achieved within at most 30 to 35 cycles, regardless of the dimension. Note that the cycle period is to be defined by the application,

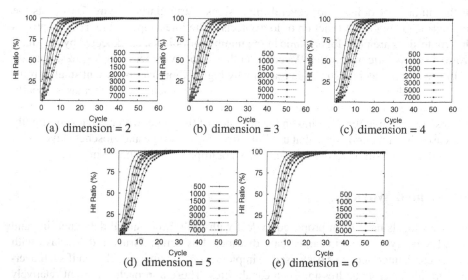

Fig. 4. Evolution of routes *hit ratio* for dimensions 2 to 6

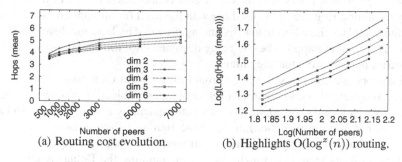

Fig. 5. Routing efficiency (data for (a) and (b) is the same)

and depends on the trade-off between quality of service and cost on computing entities. It is possible however to bootstrap faster by using shorter periods at the beginning and to decrease it when steady state has been reached. In a dynamic scenario, objects would join gradually, and each object can use several short-term gossip exchanges to insert themselves faster in the overlay. The hit ratio converges slightly slower if there are more nodes. Note that this does impact neither the time a node would need to join an already constructed overlay, nor the complexity of local self-organization of the structure. Figure 5 shows that approximating the structure does not impact routing correctness.

Routing efficiency. The second evaluation metric is the routing efficiency: how many routing steps are needed on average to route between a source object an a destination point. This metric is directly impacted by the performance of the small-world peer sampling substrate as well as the quality of the close neighbourhood. It has a great impact on the efficiency of search mechanisms that can be proposed over the RayNet overlay. Figures 5.(a) and 5.(b) present the evolution of the routing costs as a function of the number of objects, for several dimensions. Particularly, Figure 5.(b) plots the log log(mean hops) as a function of log(objects). The line shape of Figure 5.(b) proves that route sizes are poly-logarithmic in the number of objects, as expected by the small world characteristic of RayNet. We consider this property as being the key to scalability of future search mechanisms. The reason why higher dimensions present smaller routing paths is due to the fact that the size of the view at each objects increases linearly with the dimension d: for final steps (where small world links are not used), more possibilities are available for deciding on the next step of the route, which obviously slightly decreases the number of steps that use links from the coverage and closeness layer. This shows that approximating the structure does not impact routing performance.

6 Related Works

Other protocols have been proposed to deal with multidimensional data querying and complex query support in large scale distributed systems. Structured overlays with exact-search interface have been used to implement range queries [2] even if such overlays are not *natively* addressing such capabilities. These approaches present relatively high costs of maintenance of the structures: either a second indexing mechanism based on objects rather than nodes is built, whose cost is added to the cost of the structured overlay itself, or a single index is used but with the need for an implicit load balancing algorithm to replace the inherent load balancing provided by hash mechanisms. RayNet steps away from these approaches by being designed with the native support for complex queries in mind from the beginning.

The authors previously used *exact* Voronoï diagram (in dimension 2 only) for the design of VoroNet [4]. This structured overlay organizes objects in an overlay that, like RayNet, reflects exactly the application semantic space, by using the *exact* Delaunay graph (and not an approximation) as the basic routing substrate along with explicit small-world construction. Using such exact structures, while providing efficient search and routing, suffers from two drawbacks: (1) maintaining the Delaunay complex for higher dimensions would be too costly and (2) maintenance in two dimensions in face of churn is a difficult (yet not unsolvable) problem. RayNet addresses these two problems by (1) using an estimation of Voronoï cells as the basis for the construction of a subset of the Delaunay complex and (2) using Gossip-Based, self-organizing protocols that embed both protocol construction and re-organization in the same protocol, relieving the need for explicit fault tolerance mechanisms.

Skip-Webs [1] are multidimensional data structures that enable querying of data on a large scale, with multidimensional attributes. Nonetheless, maintaining such a structure in presence of churn may have a tremendous cost. Note that using Gossip-based techniques to construct this "Skip-List-like" structure could benefit from Gossip-based overlay construction protocols, such as the ones used for uni-dimensional data in GosSkip [9].

7 Conclusion

In this paper, we presented a new approach to create overlays that reflect a distributed application shared objects naming space. Organizing application objects in a distributed data structure based on the Delaunay graph of object points is sound but costly. We show that accuracy is not crucial and that reasonable approximation does not impact routing in such a structure. This paper presents the design and evaluation of RayNet, a peer to peer overlay that links objects in a multi-dimensional naming space, where each object's view is drawn according to an estimation of its Voronoï cell size using a Monte-Carlo algorithm. Gossip-based protocols are extensively used to provide self-organization properties and routing efficiency. Simulation results convey the soundness and efficiency of the approach.

Next steps in this research are the following. First, we would like to investigate complex queries mechanisms for which RayNet was designed to be the support. At the moment, range queries are implemented by using constraint flooding; refined mechanisms can be proposed by carrying some state on the query dissemination messages. We would like to investigate the scalability to higher dimensions of the mechanisms provided by [19]. Second, although gossip-based protocols are inherently resilient to nodes failures, little research has been done on securing such protocols. Following the early proposal of [14], we would like to investigate mechanisms to make our protocol resilient to adversary behaviours and detect malicious peers.

Acknowledgments. We would like to thank François Bonnet, who helped us to integrate the gossip-based small-world peer sampling in RayNet [7] and Philippe Duchon, whose comments and expertise helped us on early stages of this work.

References

1. Arge, L., Eppstein, D., Goodrich, M.T.: Skip-webs: efficient distributed data structures for multi-dimensional data sets. In: PODC 2005, pp. 69–76 (2005)
2. Aspnes, J., Kirsch, J., Krishnamurthy, A.: Load balancing and locality in range-queriable data structures. In: PODC 2004, pp. 115–124 (2004)
3. Barrière, L., Fraigniaud, P., Kranakis, E., Krizanc, D.: Efficient routing in networks with long range contacts. In: Welch, J.L. (ed.) DISC 2001. LNCS, vol. 2180, pp. 270–284. Springer, Heidelberg (2001)
4. Beaumont, O., Kermarrec, A.-M., Marchal, L., Rivière, É.: VoroNet: A scalable object network based on voronoi tessellations. In: IPDPS 2007 (March 2007)
5. Birman, K.P., Hayden, M., Ozkasap, O., Xiao, Z., Budiu, M., Minsky, Y.: Bimodal multicast. ACM Transactions on Computer Systems 17(2), 41–88 (1999)
6. Boissonnat, J.-D., Yvinec, M.: Algorithmic Geometry. Cambridge University Press, Cambridge (1998)
7. Bonnet, F., Kermarrec, A.-M., Raynal, M.: Small-world networks: From theoretical bounds to practical systems. In: Tovar, E., Tsigas, P., Fouchal, H. (eds.) OPODIS 2007. LNCS, vol. 4878, pp. 315–328. Springer, Heidelberg (2007)
8. Eugster, P.T., Guerraoui, R., Handurukande, S.B., Kouznetsov, P., Kermarrec, A.-M.: Lightweight probabilistic broadcast. ACM Transactions on Computer Systems 21(4), 341–374 (2003)
9. Guerraoui, R., Handurukande, S.B., Huguenin, K., Kermarrec, A.-M., Fessant, F.L., Rivière, É.: Gosskip, an efficient, fault-tolerant and self organizing overlay using gossip-based construction and skip-lists principles. In: IEEE P2P, Cambridge, pp. 12–22. IEEE Computer Society Press, Los Alamitos (2006)

10. Gupta, A., Sahin, O.D., Agrawal, D., Abbadi, A.E.: Meghdoot: content-based publish/ subscribe over p2p networks. In: Jacobsen, H.-A. (ed.) Middleware 2004. LNCS, vol. 3231, pp. 254–273. Springer, Heidelberg (2004)
11. Jelasity, M., Babaoglu, O.: T-man: Gossip-based overlay topology management. Engineering Self-Organising Systems 1(15) (2005)
12. Jelasity, M., Guerraoui, R., Kermarrec, A.-M., van Steen, M.: The peer sampling service: experimental evaluation of unstructured gossip-based implementations. In: Jacobsen, H.-A. (ed.) Middleware 2004. LNCS, vol. 3231, pp. 79–98. Springer, Heidelberg (2004)
13. Jelasity, M., Kermarrec, A.-M.: Ordered slicing of very large-scale overlay networks. In: IEEE P2P, Cambridge, pp. 117–124 (September 2006)
14. Jelasity, M., Montresor, A., Babaoglu, O.: Towards secure epidemics: Detection and removal of malicious peers in epidemic-style protocols. Technical Report UBLCS-2003-14, University of Bologna, Department of Computer Science, Bologna, Italy (November 2003)
15. Jelasity, M., Montresor, A., Babaoglu, O.: Gossip-based aggregation in large dynamic networks. ACM Transactions on Computer Systems 23(3), 219–252 (2005)
16. Jelasity, M., Montresor, A., Babaoglu, O.: The bootstrapping service. In: ICDCSW 2006: Proceedings of the 26th IEEE International ConferenceWorkshops on Distributed Computing Systems, Lisboa, Portugal, p. 11 (July 2006)
17. Kleinberg, J.: The small-world phenomenon: An algorithmic perspective. In: Proceedings of the 32nd ACM Symposium on Theory of Computing, Portland, OR, USA, pp. 163–170 (May 2000)
18. Knuth, D.E.: Seminumerical Algorithms. In: The Art of Computer Programming, vol. 2, Addison-Wesley, Reading, Massachusetts (1981)
19. Liebeherr, J., Nahas, M.: Application-layer multicast with delaunay triangulations. IEEE Journal on Selected Areas in Communications, Special Issue on Network Support for Multicast Communication 40(8), 1472–1488 (2002)
20. Lua, E.K., Crowcroft, J., Pias, M., Sharma, R., Lim, S.: A survey and comparison of peer-to-peer overlay network schemes. In: IEEE Communications survey and tutorial (March 2004)
21. Lv, Q., Cao, P., Cohen, E., Li, K., Shenker, S.: Search and replication in unstructured peer-to-peer networks. In: ICS 2002: the 16th international conference on Supercomputing, New York, pp. 84–95 (2002)
22. Merrer, E.L., Kermarrec, A.-M., Massoulié, L.: Peer to peer size estimation in large and dynamic networks: A comparative study. In: 15th IEEE HPDC, Paris, pp. 7–17 (June 2006)
23. Montresor, A., Jelasity, M., Babaoglu, O.: Chord on demand. In: IEEE P2P, Washington, pp. 87–94 (2005)
24. Rivière, É., Baldoni, R., Li, H., Pereira, J.: Compositional gossip: a conceptual architecture for designing gossip-based applications. ACM SIGOPS Operating Systems Review, special issue on Gossip-based Networking (October 2007)
25. Voulgaris, S.: Epidemic-Based Self-Organization in Peer-to-Peer Systems. PhD thesis, Vrije Universiteit, Amsterdam (November 2006)
26. Voulgaris, S., Rivière, É., Kermarrec, A.-M., van Steen, M.: Sub-2-sub: Self-organizing content-based publish and subscribe for dynamic and large scale collaborative networks. In: IPTPS, Santa Barbara (February 2006)
27. Watts, D.J., Strogatz, S.H.: Collective dynamics of small world networks. Nature 393, 440–442 (1998)

Secretive Birds:
Privacy in Population Protocols

Carole Delporte-Gallet[1], Hugues Fauconnier[1],
Rachid Guerraoui[2], and Eric Ruppert[3]

[1] LIAFA, University Paris 7-Denis Diderot
[2] School of Computer and Communication Sciences, EPFL
[3] Department of Computer Science and Engineering, York University

Abstract. We study private computations in a system of tiny mobile agents. We consider the mobile population protocol model of Angluin *et al.* [2] and ask what can be computed without ever revealing any input to a curious adversary. We show that any computable predicate of the original population model can be made private through an obfuscation procedure that exploits the inherent non-determinism of the mobility pattern. In short, the idea is for every mobile agent to generate, besides its actual input value, a set of wrong input values to confuse the curious adversary. To converge to the correct result, the procedure has the agents eventually eliminate the wrong values; however, the moment when this happens is hidden from the adversary. This is achieved without jeopardizing the tiny nature of the agents: they still have very small storage size that is independent of the cardinality of the system. We present three variants of this obfuscation procedure that help compute respectively, *remainder*, *threshold*, and *or* predicates which, when composed, cover all those that can be computed in the population protocol model.

A little bird has whispered a secret to me. [10]

1 Introduction

Despite the large amount of recent work on mobile systems, very little theoretical research has been devoted to modelling such systems. A notable exception is the work of Angluin *et al.* [2]: they introduced the population protocol model to describe systems of very simple mobile agents. The model has totally asynchronous agents, only a constant amount of memory per agent, no system infrastructure, and no assumptions about the mobility patterns of the agents, except for a fairness guarantee that ensures (for example) that agents cannot be forever disconnected from the others. The model was illustrated with a set of sensors, each strapped to a bird. Pairs of sensors could communicate when their host birds were close together, and the sensor network would provide aggregated information about the flock.

The population protocol model, along with some variations, has been studied in a series of papers [1,2,3,4,5,6,8]. In particular, the class of decision problems that can be solved by the population protocol model has been characterized precisely. Angluin *et al.* [2] gave several examples of predicates that can be computed in the population

E. Tovar, P. Tsigas, and H. Fouchal (Eds.): OPODIS 2007, LNCS 4878, pp. 329–342, 2007.

protocol model, and it was later shown that no others are computable [4]. This gave a characterization of computable predicates in the model: those that can be expressed in Presburger arithmetic [11]. This is essentially first-order arithmetic, using the symbols $+, 0, 1, \wedge, \vee, \neg, \forall, \exists, =, <, (,)$ and variables.

Computability in the population protocol model is defined in terms of eventually stabilizing to the correct output value. This is an essential property of the model, since there are no assumptions about the mobility pattern of the agents, beyond the weak fairness guarantee. In particular, an individual agent may have no interactions at all for an arbitrarily long prefix of a computation, so in general, one can never be certain that the final output value has been computed.

A key aspect of the population model is anonymity: there is no way to distinguish any two agents. One motivation for such an assumption is the lack of infrastructure and the mass production that might render it difficult to assign unique identifiers to agents or to programme them individually. Another motivation is for the agents to preserve their privacy. An agent might simply not want to reveal who it is, when it met which other agent or where it was. The first motivation underlying anonymity is sometimes questionable. Indeed, it takes only a small number of bits to store a huge collection of agent identifiers and a simple randomized procedure can generate distinct identifiers with very high probability. The second motivation seems generally more relevant, for there are many reasons a mobile agent might not like to leave its identifier wherever it goes or share it with whomever it meets.

In this work, we explore the privacy aspect of these anonymous mobile systems. That is, not only do we consider algorithms where agents never reveal their identifiers but we also seek for them to hide their input values from one another while computing some function of those inputs. In general, we say an algorithm is private if an honest but curious agent cannot learn any information about the inputs to the system (including even the number of inputs) beyond what can be deduced from its own input and the output value that must be computed. (This requirement would enforce anonymity, even if the agents had identifiers: otherwise one could deduce a lower bound on the number of participating agents.) Here, we focus on ensuring privacy in any finite prefix of a computation. This, together with the fact that population protocols are only required to eventually stabilize to the correct output value, allows us to strengthen the notion of privacy: we require that an honest but curious agent cannot definitively learn *anything* about the inputs of agents at any point in the computation, yet the algorithm must still correctly stabilize to the correct output value.

Consider a simple example of determining which of two candidates is the winner of an election by the agents. Assume each agent has input value 1 if it votes for the first candidate and 2 if it votes for the second candidate. There is a simple protocol to achieve this computation [2]: when two agents with different votes meet, they cancel each other. Once an agent has had its vote cancelled, it remembers the last non-cancelled vote that it has seen to determine its output. (Some extra care must be taken to deal with the possibility of a tie vote.) This protocol, however, provides no privacy. In fact, the unpredictability of the mobility pattern might allow a single curious agent to meet *all* others in their initial state and deduce the exact input vector of the entire population, discovering exactly how many agents voted for each candidate. In this paper, we ask what predicates can be computed without letting any curious agent, at any point of its computation, determine any information about the input (or output) values of any other agent. Following the specific example above, this means we would like a curious agent to be unable to determine at any point of its computation how many agents voted for a candidate, the width of the margin by which one candidate won, whether the number of voters was even or odd, and so on.

In a sense, we study a variant of secure multi-party computations [9] in the context of population protocols. We consider a passive adversary that can read the state of one agent but cannot corrupt it. However, there are several ways in which our work differs from the usual notion of secure multi-party computation. The tiny nature of the devices we consider precludes the use of expensive cryptographic protocols. The anonymity of the system means that signature schemes cannot be used. Our algorithms do not use randomization, instead relying on the inherent non-determinism of the mobility pattern. Interestingly, in our model, the curious agent can see the entire state of any other agent it interacts with, so no secret keys can be used to achieve privacy.

We prove that any predicate that can be computed in the original population protocol model, namely any predicate that can be expressed in Presburger arithmetic, can be computed privately. Our result holds even if the curious agent can store an unbounded amount of information, namely the states of all agents it has interacted with from the beginning of the computation to the present. At the heart of our result lies the idea of an *obfuscation procedure* which heavily relies on the non-determinism of the mobility pattern. We use this procedure in different forms, according to whether we compute a *remainder*, a *threshold* or an *or* predicate. (The composition of these covers all predicates computable by population protocols.) Basically, we make agents change their input values without changing the overall output, in a way designed to confuse any curious agent. In the context of the voting example, this would, roughly speaking, mean that every agent would generate, besides its own vote several votes that cancel each other. The procedure is devised such that (a) the confusing values are eventually cancelled, without any curious agent knowing when that happens, and (b) the correct result is indeed computed, while making sure that the size of the memory of every agent is fixed, independent of the size of the system.

The rest of the paper is organized as follows. We first recall the original population protocol model and introduce our definition of private computation in this context. Then we show how to compute any *remainder* or *threshold* predicate, and then how to compute Boolean combinations of such predicates, deriving our general result about what can be computed in a private way. We conclude by discussing several research directions for private mobile computing.

2   Private Population Protocols

Our formalization of the population protocol model is based on the work of Angluin *et al.* [2]. For a population of n agents, $\mathcal{P}_n = \{p_0, \ldots, p_{n-1}\}$ denotes the set of agents. (The subscripts are for convenience only, and are not visible to the agents themselves: they do not have any effect on an execution.) Each agent in the system is modelled as a finite state machine, and algorithms must be *uniform*: each finite state machine is "programmed" identically and the programming does not depend on the number of agents in the system. This makes the model strongly *anonymous*, since there is not enough space in the state to give each agent a unique identifier.

Let Σ be a finite input alphabet and Y be a finite output alphabet. Each agent p_i has an input drawn from Σ. The input for a population protocol for n agents is a vector $I = (\sigma_0, \ldots, \sigma_{n-1})$ of elements of Σ, where σ_i is the input of agent p_i. Let $\mathcal{D}$ be the set of all vectors on Σ of length at least two. The goal of an algorithm is to compute a function $f : \mathcal{D} \to Y$. Each agent must eventually output the value of this function for the input that was initially provided to the agents. Here we restrict ourselves to compute only *predicates*: the output alphabet is the set $\{0, 1\}$.

We now describe how to specify a population protocol. A population protocol is defined by a finite set Q of possible agent states, an input assignment $\iota : \Sigma \to Q$, a transition relation $\delta \subseteq Q \times Q \times Q \times Q$, and an output assignment $\omega : Q \to Y$. If two agents in states q_1 and q_2 encounter each other, they can change into states q_1' and q_2', respectively, where $(q_1, q_2, q_1', q_2') \in \delta$. We sometimes use the notation $q_1, q_2 \to q_1', q_2'$ to describe the elements of δ.

A *configuration* is a mapping $C : \mathcal{P}_n \to Q$ specifying the state of each agent. Let C and C' be configurations, u, v be distinct agents and t be a transition. We say that C goes to C' with *interaction* $e = ((u, v), t)$, denoted $C \xrightarrow{e} C'$, if $t = (C(u), C(v), C'(u), C'(v))$ belongs to δ and $C'(w) = C(w)$ for all $w \in \mathcal{P}_n - \{u, v\}$. We say that C goes to C' in one step, denoted $C \to C'$, if $C \xrightarrow{e} C'$ for some interaction $e = ((u, v), t)$; in this case e is called the interaction associated with this step, t is the transition of this step and agent u and agent v are *involved* in this step.

An *execution* of the protocol on input $I \in \mathcal{D}$ is an infinite sequence of configurations, $C_0, C_1, C_2, \ldots$ such that (1) C_0 is the initial assignment for I: if $I = (\sigma_0, \ldots, \sigma_{n-1})$ then, for all i such that $0 \leq i \leq n - 1$, $C_0(p_i) = \iota(\sigma_i)$ and (2) $C_i \to C_{i+1}$ for all i. An *execution fragment* is a contiguous portion of an execution. The output of an agent in state q is $\omega(q)$. We say that the execution *stably outputs* $v \in Y$ if every agent eventually outputs v and never changes its output thereafter. Formally, this means that there is an i such that for all agents p and for all $j > i$, $\omega(C_j(p)) = v$.

If every sequence of interactions were considered to be a possible execution in the model, then isolated agents might never interact with one another. Thus, the model must incorporate a fairness guarantee. In a *fair* execution, if a configuration C occurs infinitely often and $C \to C'$, then C' occurs infinitely often. If, for example, we associate probabilities with different interactions, then an execution will be fair with probability 1. A protocol *stably computes* a function $f : \mathcal{D} \to Y$ if, for every input $I \in \mathcal{D}$, every fair execution on input I stably outputs $f(I)$. In the following, all executions are assumed to be fair.

Given an execution $E = C_0, C_1, C_2, \ldots$ and an agent u, the *history of interactions* for agent u in E, denoted $H_u(E)$ is the sequence of states and transitions of interactions associated with each step of E in which u is involved. More precisely $H_u(E) = (q_0, t_0), \ldots (q_i, t_i) \ldots$ where t_i is the transition of the i-th interaction in which p_i is involved and q_i is the state of agent u when this interaction occurs. The history of interactions for agent u in E up to T is the initial segment of length T of $H_u(E)$ if T is greater than the length of $H_u(E)$ and $H_u(E)$ otherwise.

We now define the notion of privacy for a population protocol. If some agent encounters another agent, we assume that it learns both the current state of the other one and what transition is chosen. Then, intuitively, the protocol has the privacy property if no agent can learn anything about the current input from any initial sequence of the history of interactions in which it is involved. Let I_1 and I_2 be two inputs in $\mathcal{D}$ where some agent p gets the same input value. The agent p is able to distinguish I_1 from I_2 if, for at least one execution E_1 on input I_1, the history of interactions for p in E_1 up to some T cannot be an initial segment of a history of interactions of agent p for any execution on input I_2. A population protocol has the *output-independent privacy* property if no agent is able to distinguish any pair of sufficiently large input vectors in which it has the same input value. More formally, a population protocol has this property if and only if there is a constant n_0 such that for any agent p and any inputs I_1 and I_2 of size at least n_0 in which p has the same input, and any execution E_1 on input I_1, and any T, there exists an execution E_2 on input I_2, such that the histories of p's interactions up to T are identical in E_1 and E_2. Thus, if the protocol is private, at no time in the execution E_1 on input I_1 can an agent p deduce with certainty that the input vector of the execution was not I_2. In other words, there is no time when p can rule out any possible input vector (of size at least n_0).

3   Computing Predicates Privately

Our goal is to show that all predicates computable in the population protocol model are computable privately. We shall show that all computable predicates can be computed by a protocol satisfying several properties, and that those properties are sufficient for output-independent privacy. We label the curious agent p_0. (Since the identities of agents cannot be used in the protocols themselves, the arguments below are not affected by this convention.)

Consider a population protocol with state set Q. Fix some collection $\mathcal{G}$ of system configurations, which we shall call *good* configurations. A transition $q, r \to s, t$ of the protocol is called $\mathcal{G}$-*imitable* if, from any configuration $C_0 \in \mathcal{G}$ with p_0 in state q or r, there exists an execution fragment $C_0 \to C_1 \to \cdots \to C_m$ such that $C_m \in \mathcal{G}$ and agent p_0 participates in exactly one interaction during the fragment and that interaction's transition is $q, r \to s, t$. (This property should hold both for the case where p_0 is playing the role of the agent that changes from state q to s and for the case where p_0 changes from r to t.)

The following theorem, which will be proved in Sections 3.1, 3.2 and 3.3, will yield protocols that have output-independent privacy.

Theorem 1. *Let P be any predicate that is computable in the population protocol model (without privacy). Then there exist a protocol A that computes P, a constant n_0 and a set $\mathcal{G}$ of configurations of A such that*

1. *for any initial configuration with at least n_0 agents, there is an execution fragment of A that contains no interactions involving p_0 and ends in a configuration of $\mathcal{G}$,*
2. *every transition of A is $\mathcal{G}$-imitable,*

3. *for any states q_1 and q_2, there is a sequence of interactions between two agents that start in states q_1 and q_2 and end in states q_2 and q_1, respectively, and*
4. *for any states q_1 and q_2, the "null" transition $q_1, q_2 \rightarrow q_1, q_2$ is permitted.*

We now show that the first two properties of the preceding theorem are sufficient for privacy.

Theorem 2. *Any population protocol that satisfies Properties 1 and 2 of Theorem 1 has output-independent privacy.*

Proof. Consider any execution prefix E, starting from an initial configuration C_0. Let C_0' be any initial configuration that has at least n_0 agents. We must construct an execution prefix E', starting from C_0', such that p_0 undergoes the same sequence of interactions in E and E'. We begin E' with the execution fragment that satisfies Property 1, which does not include any interactions involving p_0 and leaves the system in a good configuration.

Then, for each interaction involving p_0 in E, we append an execution fragment to the end of the constructed execution using the definition of $\mathcal{G}$-imitability. Each fragment includes exactly one interaction that involves p_0, and that interaction's transition is the same as in p_0's next interaction in E, and the fragment leaves the system in a good configuration. The existence of such a fragment is guaranteed by Property 2.

When all of these fragments have been appended, we obtain the required execution E'. The history of interactions for p_0 is the same in E and E', by construction. $\square$

The following corollary follows immediately from Theorems 1 and 2.

Corollary 1. *Every predicate that can be computed in the population protocol model (without privacy) can be computed with output-independent privacy.*

Although Properties 3 and 4 of Theorem 1 are not required for privacy, they are crucial for our proof, in Sect. 3.3, that Boolean combinations of privately computable predicates are also privately computable.

3.1 Computing Remainder Predicates

Let Σ be an input alphabet. Let c_σ be an integer constant for each $\sigma \in \Sigma$ and let m and r be integer constants such that $0 \le r < m$. The predicate $P(I)$ that is 1 on input $I = (\sigma_0, \ldots, \sigma_{n-1})$ if and only if $\sum_{i=0}^{n-1} c_{\sigma_i} \equiv r(\mathrm{mod}\ m)$ is called a *remainder predicate*. In this section, we show that any remainder predicate can be computed in a way that satisfies the properties of Theorem 1.

There is a fairly straightforward way to compute the predicate $P(I)$ if there is no need for privacy [2]. Each agent stores a value, initially c_σ, where σ is the input symbol of the agent. When two agents with values v_1 and v_2 meet, one agent gives its value to the other: they change their values to 0 and $v_1 + v_2$. All arithmetic is done modulo m. The algorithm maintains the sum of the values of all agents as an invariant. Eventually, the sum is stored in a single agent, which can then determine the output value and disseminate it to all other agents.

To ensure privacy, we must add transitions that allow agents to disguise their input values. When agents in states v_1 and v_2 meet, one can give the other *part* of its value: the agents change their values to $v_1 + 1$ and $v_2 - 1$. This preserves the sum of the agents' values as an invariant. However, this modification, by itself, would prevent the protocol from converging to the correct output. To avoid this problem, we introduce a mechanism that ensures that this transition is only applied a finite (but unbounded) number of times. This will be sufficient to obscure the inputs from the adversary, while still ensuring that the sum is eventually gathered into a single agent to produce the output value. This mechanism is implemented by giving each agent a flag that is initially 1 and is eventually changed to 0. The transitions in which one agent shifts part of its value to the other are enabled only while the flags are 1. The algorithm is described more precisely in the following proof.

Proposition 1. *Any remainder predicate can be computed by a protocol satisfying the properties of Theorem 1.*

Proof. We give the protocol that computes the predicate $\sum_{i=0}^{n-1} c_{\sigma_i} \equiv r(\mathrm{mod}\ m)$. The state of each agent is a pair (v, f) comprised of a value $v \in \{\bot_0, \bot_1, 0, 1, \ldots, m-1\}$ and a Boolean flag f. Let Q be the set of all such pairs (v, f). The values $\bot_0$ and $\bot_1$ are used to indicate that the agent has given its value to another agent and is no longer active in exchanging values; the subscript indicates the agent's output value. The initial state of an agent with input σ is $(c_\sigma \bmod m, 1)$. The output for states $(r, 0)$ and $(\bot_1, 0)$ is 1. The output for all other states is 0. The transitions M1 to M10 are given below, where v_1 and v_2 are any values in $\{0, 1, \ldots, m-1\}$, i is any value in $\{0, 1\}$ and q_1 and q_2 are any states. All arithmetic is done modulo m. An asterisk ($*$) is used as a wildcard to match any value, and indicates that part of the state is not changed by the transition.

$$(v_1, 1), (v_2, 1) \rightarrow (v_1 + 1, 1), (v_2 - 1, 1) \tag{M1}$$

$$(*, 1), (*, *) \rightarrow (*, 0), (*, *) \tag{M2}$$

$$(*, 0), (*, 1) \rightarrow (*, 1), (*, 1) \tag{M3}$$

$$(v_1, 0), (v_2, 0) \rightarrow (v_1 + v_2, 0), (0, 0) \tag{M4}$$

$$(v_1, 0), (0, 0) \rightarrow (v_1, 0), (\bot_0, 0) \tag{M5}$$

$$(\bot_i, *), (*, 1) \rightarrow (0, 0), (*, 1) \tag{M6}$$

$$(r, 0), (\bot_i, 0) \rightarrow (r, 0), (\bot_1, 0) \tag{M7}$$

$$(v_1, 0), (\bot_i, 0) \rightarrow (v_1, 0), (\bot_0, 0), \text{if } v_1 \neq r \tag{M8}$$

$$q_1, q_2 \rightarrow q_2, q_1 \tag{M9}$$

$$q_1, q_2 \rightarrow q_1, q_2 \tag{M10}$$

Transition M1 is the crucial one for privacy: it conceals inputs by shifting part of an agent's value to another agent, and can be invoked as long as the agents' flags are 1. Transitions M2 and M3 control the flags. Transition M4 gathers the sum into a single agent once the flags are 0, and Transition M5 ensures that exactly one agent ends up with a non-$\bot$ value. Transition M6 allows the $\bot$ values to be turned back to 0, reversing the effect of Transition M5 as long as flags are 1. Transitions M7 and M8 spread the output value from the (eventually unique) agent with a non-$\perp$ value to all other agents. Finally, Transitions M9 and M10 are included to satisfy Properties 3 and 4 of Theorem 1.

We first argue that this protocol correctly computes the predicate $P(I)$. Transition M2 ensures that, from any configuration, there is always a reachable configuration in which all flags are 0. Thus, any fair execution will eventually enter a configuration in which all flags are 0. After that point, all flags will remain 0 forever. Then, Transition M4 ensures that every agent except one will have a value that is either 0 or $\perp$. Transition M5 ensures that, eventually, exactly one agent will have a value different from $\perp$. (Transition M6 cannot be applied since all flags are 0.) Since the sum of the non-$\perp$ values stored in all agents (modulo m) is left invariant by all of the transitions, the one remaining non-$\perp$ value will be $\left(\sum_{i=0}^{n-1} c_{\sigma_i} \right) \bmod m$, so it will have the correct output value. Transitions M7 and M8 ensure that all other agents eventually stabilize with output $P(I)$ also.

We now show that the protocol satisfies the properties of Theorem 1. We choose $n_0 = 5$ and we define a configuration to be in $\mathcal{G}$ if and only if it has at least five agents, and agents $p_1, \ldots, p_4$ each have flag 1 and non-$\perp$ values. Any initial configuration with at least n_0 agents is good, so Property 1 of Theorem 1 is trivially satisfied. Property 3 is satisfied, since the protocol includes Transition M9, which allows any pair of agents to swap states in a single interaction. Property 4 is also satisfied, since the protocol includes Transition M10.

It remains to show that every transition of the protocol is $\mathcal{G}$-imitable. Consider any transition to be imitated. Suppose the curious agent interacts with an agent in state (v, f) in this transition. Let $C_0 \in \mathcal{G}$. We show how to drive agent p_1 into state (v, f), starting from configuration C_0. We consider two cases.

If v is a non-$\perp$ value, p_1 and p_2 meet repeatedly using Transition M1 until p_1 has value v. Then, if $f = 0$, p_1 sets its flag to 0 using Transition M2. At this point, p_1 has state (v, f).

If v is $\perp_0$ or $\perp_1$, p_1 and p_2 meet repeatedly using Transition M1 until p_1 has value 0. Then agents p_1 and p_2 set their flags to 0 using Transition M2, and meet once more using Transition M5 to set p_1's state to $(\perp_0, 0)$. If $v = \perp_1$, p_3 and p_4 meet using Transition M1 until p_3's state is $(r, 1)$, p_3 sets its flag to 0 using Transition M2, and then p_3 meets p_1 using Transition M7 to set p_1's state to $(\perp_1, 0)$. At this point, p_1's state is $(v, 0)$. If $f = 1$, then p_1 meets p_4 using Transition M3 to set its flag to 1. Then, p_1 will be in state (v, f).

Once the agent p_1 has been driven into state (v, f), it has the necessary interaction with p_0. After that, the system can be returned to a good configuration as follows. The above procedure leaves p_4 with a non-$\perp$ value and flag 1. Thus any of p_1, p_2, p_3 that have values $\perp_0$ or $\perp_1$ can meet p_4 using Transition M6 to enter state $(0, 1)$. Then any of p_1, p_2, p_3 that have flag 0 can meet p_4 using Transition M3 to set their flags to 1. The resulting configuration is good.   □

3.2 Computing Threshold Predicates

Let Σ be an input alphabet. Let c_σ be an integer constant for each $\sigma \in \Sigma$ and let k be an integer constant. The predicate $P(I)$ that is 1 on input $I = (\sigma_0, \ldots, \sigma_{n-1})$ if and only if $\sum_{i=0}^{n-1} c_{\sigma_i} \geq k$ is called a *threshold predicate*. In this section, we show that any threshold predicate can be computed privately. We begin with the special case where the threshold k is positive.

Proposition 2. *Any threshold predicate with a positive threshold k can be computed by a protocol satisfying the properties of Theorem 1.*

Proof. The general approach used to construct this algorithm is similar to the one used in Sect. 3.1 to compute remainder predicates privately. Each agent stores a value and a flag bit, and while flags are 1, the agents can shift parts of their values to each other. Eventually, the flags will all be set to 0, and the algorithm will compute the sum.

For remainder predicates, the sum (modulo m) could be stored in a single agent. For threshold predicates, we cannot use modular arithmetic, so the sum may end up spread across several agents. Let $m = 2 \cdot \max(\{|c_\sigma| : \sigma \in \Sigma\} \cup \{k\})$. Each agent will store a value between $-m$ and m. If the sum is positive, eventually, some number of agents (possibly 0) have the value m, at most one other agent has a positive value, and the remaining agents have value 0. On the other hand, if the sum is negative, all agents eventually have non-positive values.

Because the sum is not collected into a single agent, distributing the output value to all agents is more complicated than in Sect. 3.1. Each agent stores an output bit. As long as the agent's flag is 1, its output bit is meaningless, so by convention we require it to be 0. Once an agent's flag is 0, the value of the output bit behaves as follows. If an agent's value is at least k, its output bit must be 1. If an agent's value is negative, its output bit must be 0. Otherwise, an agent's output bit can be either 0 or 1: in this case, the agent will determine its output bit from its interactions.

We now give a full description of the algorithm. The state of each agent is a triple (v, o, f) where $-m \leq v \leq m$, and o and f are Boolean values representing the output bit and flag bit, respectively. As described above, not all triples are legal states: the output bit can take values 0 and 1 only when $f = 0$ and $0 \leq v < k$. Initially, the state of an agent with input symbol σ is $(c_\sigma, 0, 1)$. The transitions T1 to T8 are given below, where v_1 and v_2 are any values between $-m$ and m and q_1 and q_2 are any states. (The notation $[v_1 \geq k]$ in Transition T2 indicates that the output bit should be set to 1 if and only if $v_1 \geq k$.)

$$(v_1, 0, 1), (v_2, 0, 1) \rightarrow (v_1 + 1, 0, 1), (v_2 - 1, 0, 1), \text{ if } v_1 < m \text{ and } v_2 > -m \qquad \text{(T1)}$$

$$(v_1, 0, 1), (*, *, *) \rightarrow (v_1, [v_1 \geq k], 0), (*, *, *) \qquad \text{(T2)}$$

$$(*, *, 0), (*, 0, 1) \rightarrow (*, 0, 1), (*, 0, 1) \qquad \text{(T3)}$$

$$(v_1, *, 0), (v_2, *, 0) \rightarrow \begin{cases} (m, 1, 0), (v_1 + v_2 - m, 1, 0) & \text{if } m \leq v_1 + v_2 \leq 2m \\ (v_1 + v_2, 1, 0), (0, 1, 0) & \text{if } k \leq v_1 + v_2 < m \\ (v_1 + v_2, 0, 0), (0, 0, 0) & \text{if } -m \leq v_1 + v_2 < k \end{cases}, \qquad \text{(T4)}$$
$$\text{if } v_1 \cdot v_2 \neq 0$$

$$(v_1, 1, 0), (v_2, 0, 0) \rightarrow (v_1, 1, 0), (v_2, 1, 0), \text{ if } v_1 \geq k \text{ and } 0 \leq v_2 < k \qquad \text{(T5)}$$

$$(v_1, 0, 0), (v_2, 1, 0) \rightarrow (v_1, 0, 0), (v_2, 0, 0), \text{ if } v_1 < k \text{ and } 0 \leq v_2 < k \qquad \text{(T6)}$$

$$q_1, q_2 \rightarrow q_2, q_1 \qquad \text{(T7)}$$

$$q_1, q_2 \rightarrow q_1, q_2 \qquad \text{(T8)}$$

Transitions T1, T2 and T3 play the same role as Transitions M1, M2 and M3 in Sect. 3.1. Values are collected into a smaller number of agents using Transition T4. The output value is distributed using Transitions T5 and T6. Transitions T7 and T8 are included to satisfy Properties 3 and 4 of Theorem 1.

The proof that this protocol correctly computes $P(I)$ is similar to the proof of Proposition 1 but a little more complicated. The details can be found in [7].

We now show that the protocol satisfies the properties of Theorem 1, which are sufficient for privacy. We choose n_0 to be 12. We define a configuration to be in $\mathcal{G}$ if and only if it has at least 6 agents, the flags of agents $p_1, \ldots, p_5$ are all 1, and the sum of the values of agents $p_0, \ldots, p_5$ is equal to 0.

First we establish Property 1 of Theorem 1. Consider any initial configuration that has at least 12 agents. We describe how to drive the system into a good configuration without using any interactions involving p_0. For $i = 1, 2, 3, 4, 5$, agents p_i and p_{i+5} interact using Transition T1 until each of the agents $p_1, \ldots, p_5$ have value 0. Then, p_5 interacts with p_{11} using Transition T1 until its value is the negation of p_0's value. The resulting configuration is good.

Next, we show that the protocol satisfies Property 2 of Theorem 1. Consider any transition to be imitated. Suppose the curious agent interacts with an agent in state (v, o, f) in this transition. Let C_0 be any good configuration. We show how to drive agent p_1 into state (v, o, f), starting from C_0. First, $p_1, \ldots, p_5$ meet using Transition T1 until p_1, p_2, p_3 and p_4 each have value 0. (This is possible, since the sum of values of $p_1, \ldots, p_5$ in configuration C_0 is equal to the opposite of the value of p_0, so the sum is between $-m$ and m.) Next, p_1 and p_2 meet repeatedly, using Transition T1 until p_1 has value v. If $f = 0$, p_1 and p_2 meet again, this time using Transition T2, to change p_1's flag to 0. If, at this point, p_1's output bit differs from o, we must have $0 \le v < k$ and $o = 1$. In this case, p_3 and p_4 meet repeatedly using Transition T1 until p_3's value is k, then once more to change p_3's flag to 0 using Transition T2, and then p_3 and p_1 meet using Transition T5 to change p_1's output bit to 1. When all of these interactions have occurred, p_1 is in state (v, o, f).

Next, p_0 and p_1 have their interaction. Now, we must restore the system to a good configuration. In C_0, the sum of the values of $p_0, \ldots, p_5$ was 0, since $C_0 \in \mathcal{G}$. All interactions since C_0 have been among agents $p_0, \ldots, p_5$ and every transition preserves the sum of the values of the two interacting agents. Thus, the sum of the values of agents $p_0, \ldots, p_5$ is still 0. The interactions since C_0 may have changed at most three agents' flags from 1 to 0. Since $p_1, \ldots, p_5$ all had flag 1 in C_0, there is at least one agent whose flag is still 1. If any of $p_1, \ldots, p_5$ have flag 0, those agents meet an agent whose flag is 1 using Transition T3 to set their flags back to 1. The resulting configuration is good.

Properties 3 and 4 of Theorem 1 are trivial, since the protocol has Transitions T7 and T8.   □

Corollary 2. *Any threshold predicate can be computed by a protocol satisfying the properties of Theorem 1.*

Proof. We have already described how to compute any threshold predicate with a positive threshold k. To compute a threshold predicate with a threshold $k \le 0$, notice that $\sum_{i=0}^{n-1} c_{\sigma_i} \ge k$ if and only if $\sum_{i=0}^{n-1} (-c_{\sigma_i}) \not\ge -k + 1$. Since $-k + 1 > 0$, we can compute the threshold predicate $\sum_{i=0}^{n-1}(-c_{\sigma_i}) \geq -k+1$ as described in the proof of Proposition 2 and negate the result. $\qquad\qquad\square$

3.3 Computing All Semilinear Predicates

To complete the proof of Theorem 1, we show that the properties of the theorem can be preserved when computing Boolean combinations of predicates.

Theorem 3. *If predicates P^1 and P^2 can be computed by population protocols which satisfy the properties of Theorem 1, then there are population protocols that compute $\neg P^1$ and $P^1 \vee P^2$, also satisfying the properties of Theorem 1.*

Proof. The required population protocol for $\neg P^1$ is obtained by simply negating the output map of the protocol for P^1.

We now construct a population protocol for computing $P^1 \vee P^2$. Let $A^1 = (Q^1, \delta^1, \iota^1, \omega^1)$ and $A^2 = (Q^2, \delta^2, \iota^2, \omega^2)$ be the population protocols for P^1 and P^2, respectively. The protocol for $P^1 \vee P^2$ is quite straightforward: it simply runs the algorithms A^1 and A^2 in parallel. Each agent's state will contain two components, one representing the state of the agent in each of the two algorithms. Whenever two agents meet, they have an interaction from the first algorithm, using the first components of their states, and an interaction from the second algorithm, using the second components of their states.

More formally, this protocol has the form $A = (Q, \delta, \iota, \omega)$, where:

$$Q = Q^1 \times Q^2,$$
$$\iota(\sigma) = (\iota^1(\sigma), \iota^2(\sigma)),$$
$$\omega(q) = \omega^1(q) \vee \omega^2(q), \text{ and}$$
$$\delta = \{((q^1, q^2), (r^1, r^2), (s^1, s^2), (t^1, t^2)) : (q^1, r^1, s^1, t^1) \in \delta^1 \text{ and}$$
$$(q^2, r^2, s^2, t^2) \in \delta^2\}.$$

Since A^1 and A^2 satisfy Property 4 of Theorem 1, this definition of δ allows two agents who have an interaction to update the first or second halves of their states according to the transition relation of A^1 or A^2, respectively, while leaving the other halves of their states unchanged. Similarly, because A^1 and A^2 satisfy Property 3, this definition of δ allows two agents to swap the first halves or the second halves of their states while leaving the other halves unchanged. These facts are useful in some of the constructions we give below. If $C = ((q_1^1, q_1^2), (q_2^1, q_2^2), \ldots, (q_n^1, q_n^2))$ is a configuration of algorithm A, we use the notation C^1 for $(q_1^1, q_2^1, \ldots, q_n^1)$ and C^2 for $(q_1^2, q_2^2, \ldots, q_n^2)$. Also, we write $C = (C^1, C^2)$.

We first argue that this algorithm A stably computes the predicate $P^1 \vee P^2$. Consider any fair execution $E = (C_0^1, C_0^2), (C_1^1, C_1^2), (C_2^1, C_2^2), \ldots$ of A on some input I of size n. We show that $E^1 = C_0^1, C_1^1, C_2^1, \ldots$ is a fair execution of A^1. By the definition of A, C_0^1 is the initial configuration of A^1 on input I, and for all i, $C_i^1 \to C_{i+1}^1$, according to the transition relation of A^1. To see that E^1 is fair, suppose some configuration C^1 appears infinitely often in the execution and $C^1 \to D^1$ is a possible transition of A^1.

Since there are only a finite number of possible configurations of A^2 with n agents, some configuration (C^1, C^2) must appear infinitely often in E. Because A^2 satisfies Property 4 of Theorem 1, $(C^1, C^2) \rightarrow (D^1, C^2)$ is a possible transition of A. Since E is fair, (D^1, C^2) must appear infinitely often in E. Thus, D^1 appears infinitely often in E^1, as required. A symmetric argument proves that $C_0^2, C_1^2, C_2^2, \ldots$ is a fair execution of A^2. Thus, after some point, if any agent is in state (q^1, q^2), we must have $\omega^1(q^1) = P^1(I)$ and $\omega^2(q^2) = P^2(I)$, so $\omega(q^1, q^2) = \omega^1(q^1) \vee \omega^2(q^2) = P^1(I) \vee P^2(I)$.

In the remainder of this proof, we show that A satisfies the properties of Theorem 1. Choose n_0^1 and $\mathcal{G}^1$ to satisfy the properties of Theorem 1 for A^1. Choose n_0^2 and $\mathcal{G}^2$ to satisfy the properties of Theorem 1 for A^2. Let $n_0 = \max(n_0^1, n_0^2)$. Let $\mathcal{G}$ be the set of configurations C where the first components of the elements of C form a configuration in $\mathcal{G}^1$ and the second components of elements of C form a configuration in $\mathcal{G}^2$. (I.e., $\mathcal{G} = \{(C^1, C^2) : C^1 \in \mathcal{G}^1 \text{ and } C^2 \in \mathcal{G}^2\}$.) We shall show that n_0 and $\mathcal{G}$ satisfy the properties of Theorem 1 for A.

First, we show that A has Property 1. Consider any initial configuration $C_0 = (C_0^1, C_0^2)$ for algorithm A that has size at least n_0. Then, C_0^1 is an initial configuration of A^1 with at least $n_0 \geq n_0^1$ agents. There exists an execution fragment of A^1 that starts from C_0^1 and leads to a configuration $C^1 \in \mathcal{G}^1$. Thus, there is an execution fragment of A that starts from (C_0^1, C_0^2) and leads to (C^1, C_0^2). Since C_0^2 is an initial configuration of A^2 with at least $n_0 \geq n_0^2$ agents, there is also an execution fragment of A^2 that starts from C_0^2 and leads to a configuration $C^2 \in \mathcal{G}^2$. Thus, there is an execution fragment of A that starts from (C^1, C_0^2) and leads to $(C^1, C^2) \in \mathcal{G}$. Concatenating the two execution fragments of A establishes Property 1 of Theorem 1 for protocol A.

Next, we show that A has Property 2. Consider any transition $(q^1, q^2), (r^1, r^2) \rightarrow (s^1, s^2), (t^1, t^2)$. Let $C = (C^1, C^2)$ be any good configuration of A in which p_0 has state (q^1, q^2). Then, $C^1 \in \mathcal{G}^1$ and $C^2 \in \mathcal{G}^2$.

Since p_0 is in state q^1 in C^1, there is an execution fragment of A^1 starting from C^1 and ending in a good configuration G^1 during which p_0 has just one interaction, which has transition $q^1, r^1 \rightarrow s^1, t^1$. Let p_i be the agent that p_0 interacts with. Let D^1 and F^1 be the configurations immediately before and after p_0's interaction. Then, there is an execution fragment α_1 of A starting from (C^1, C^2) and ending in (D^1, C^2) during which p_0 has no interactions. (In α_1, interactions affect only the first components of agents' states.)

Since p_0 is in state q^2 in C^2, there is an execution fragment of A^2 starting from C^2 and ending in a good configuration G^2 during which p_0 has just one interaction of the form $q^2, r^2 \rightarrow s^2, t^2$. Let p_j be the agent that p_0 interacts with. Let D^2 and F^2 be the configurations immediately before and after p_0's interaction. Then, there is an execution fragment α_2 of A starting from (D^1, C^2) and ending in (D^1, D^2) during which p_0 has no interactions. (In α_2, interactions affect only the second components of agents' states.)

If $i \neq j$, let β_1 be an execution fragment starting from (D^1, D^2) in which p_i and p_j swap the second components of their states. (Otherwise, let β_1 be an empty execution fragment.) At the end of β_1, agent p_i is in state (r^1, r^2). Let β_2 be an execution fragment starting from the end of β_1 consisting of a single interaction between p_0 and p_i, applying the transition $(q^1, q^2), (r^1, r^2) \rightarrow (s^1, s^2), (t^1, t^2)$. If $i \neq j$, let β_3 be an execution fragment starting from the final configuration of β_2 in which p_i and p_j swap the second components of their states. (Otherwise, let β_3 be an empty execution fragment.) Then, at the end of $\beta_1 \cdot \beta_2 \cdot \beta_3$, the configuration of the system is (F^1, F^2).

There is an execution fragment γ_1 of A starting from (F^1, F^2) and ending in (G^1, F^2) during which p_0 has no interactions. (The interactions in γ_1 affect only the first halves of agents' states.) There is also an execution fragment γ_2 of A starting from (G^1, F^2) and ending in (G^1, G^2) during which p_0 has no interactions. (The interactions in γ_2 affect only the second halves of agents' states.)

Putting these fragments together, we obtain the fragment $\alpha_1 \cdot \alpha_2 \cdot \beta_1 \cdot \beta_2 \cdot \beta_3 \cdot \gamma_1 \cdot \gamma_2$ of A, which starts from configuration (C^1, C^2), ends in $(G^1, G^2) \in \mathcal{G}$, and during which p_0 has exactly one interaction, which has transition $(q^1, q^2), (r^1, r^2) \rightarrow (s^1, s^2), (t^1, t^2)$. Thus, this transition is $\mathcal{G}$-imitable. This completes the proof of Property 2 for A.

Next, we establish Property 3 for A. Let (q_1^1, q_1^2) and (q_2^1, q_2^2) be any two states of Q. There is a sequence of interactions of A^1 between two agents that start in states q_1^1 and q_2^1 and end in states q_2^1 and q_1^1, respectively. Thus, there is a sequence of interactions of A between two agents that start in states (q_1^1, q_1^2) and (q_2^1, q_2^2) and end in states (q_2^1, q_1^2) and (q_1^1, q_2^2), respectively. Also, there is a sequence of interactions of A^2 between two agents that start in states q_1^2 and q_2^2 and end in states q_2^2 and q_1^2, respectively. So there is a sequence of interactions of A between two agents that start in states (q_2^1, q_1^2) and (q_1^1, q_2^2) and end in states (q_2^1, q_2^2) and (q_1^1, q_1^2), respectively. Concatenating the two sequences of interactions of A yields the required sequence that starts with two agents in states (q_1^1, q_1^2) and (q_2^1, q_2^2) and ends with the agents in states (q_2^1, q_2^2) and (q_1^1, q_1^2), respectively. Thus, A satisfies Property 3 of Theorem 1.

Finally, Property 4 of Theorem 1 for A follows trivially from the definition of δ and the fact that both A^1 and A^2 have this property.   □

Putting together all of the preceding results yields a proof of Theorem 1. It is known that every predicate computable in the population protocol model can be expressed as a Boolean combination of remainder and threshold predicates [4]. It follows from Proposition 1, Corollary 2 and Theorem 3 that all such predicates can be computed by a protocol that satisfies the properties of Theorem 1. (Notice that in no case do we ever choose a value of n_0 that is greater than 12, so the choice of n_0 does not depend on the predicate to be computed.)

4   Concluding Remarks

Although we restricted attention to computing predicates, the techniques can be applied to any function. Let $f : \mathcal{D} \rightarrow Y$ be any function that is computable by a population protocol without privacy. Then, for each $y \in Y$, define a predicate $P_y(x)$ to be 1 if and only if $f(x) = y$. This predicate can be computed, and can therefore be computed privately. All of the (finitely many) predicates P_y can be computed in parallel using the same approach as in Sect. 3.3 to yield a private protocol for computing f.

This work is a first step toward studying private mobile computing. Several directions for future research are appealing. Some seem fairly accessible. For instance, one could show that our obfuscation procedure can also be effective against a dynamic adversary that can control several agents on the fly. None of these agents will be able to determine the input values of the other agents, either individually or collectively. Other problems appear more difficult. It is not clear whether it is possible to devise an obfuscation procedure that would work if the adversary need only eventually converge toward gaining knowledge of the inputs of other agents, without necessarily knowing when the correct input values have been discovered. We restricted attention to problems where all agents produce the same output, but one could also consider problems that require agents to output different values. Some papers have altered the basic model of population protocols by putting a probability distribution on the possible transitions. Can we design protocols that would protect privacy with high probability, even if the adversary knows the probability distribution? It would also be intriguing to see how the agents should be strengthened to hide their inputs from an active adversary, who can cause agents to diverge from the protocol.

Acknowledgements. This research was supported in part by the Natural Sciences and Engineering Research Council of Canada.

References

1. Angluin, D., Aspnes, J., Chan, M., Fischer, M.J., Jiang, H., Peralta, R.: Stably computable properties of network graphs. In: Prasanna, V.K., Iyengar, S., Spirakis, P.G., Welsh, M. (eds.) DCOSS 2005. LNCS, vol. 3560, pp. 63–74. Springer, Heidelberg (2005)
2. Angluin, D., Aspnes, J., Diamadi, Z., Fischer, M.J., Peralta, R.: Computation in networks of passively mobile finite-state sensors. Distributed Computing 18(4), 235–253 (2006)
3. Angluin, D., Aspnes, J., Eisenstat, D.: Fast computation by population protocols with a leader. In: Dolev, S. (ed.) DISC 2006. LNCS, vol. 4167, pp. 61–75. Springer, Heidelberg (2006)
4. Angluin, D., Aspnes, J., Eisenstat, D., Ruppert, E.: The computational power of population protocols. Distributed Computing (to appear)
5. Angluin, D., Aspnes, J., Fischer, M.J., Jiang, H.: Self-stabilizing Population Protocols. In: Anderson, J.H., Prencipe, G., Wattenhofer, R. (eds.) OPODIS 2005. LNCS, vol. 3974, pp. 103–117. Springer, Heidelberg (2006)
6. Delporte-Gallet, C., Fauconnier, H., Guerraoui, R., Ruppert, E.: When birds die: Making population protocols fault-tolerant. In: Gibbons, P.B., Abdelzaher, T., Aspnes, J., Rao, R. (eds.) DCOSS 2006. LNCS, vol. 4026, pp. 51–66. Springer, Heidelberg (2006)
7. Delporte-Gallet, C., Fauconnier, H., Guerraoui, R., Ruppert, E.: Secretive birds: Privacy in population protocols. Technical Report hal-00175536, CNRS, France (2007)
8. Fischer, M., Jiang, H.: Self-stabilizing leader election in networks of finite-state anonymous agents. In: Shvartsman, A.A. (ed.) OPODIS 2006. LNCS, vol. 4305, pp. 395–409. Springer, Heidelberg (2006)
9. Goldreich, O.: Foundations of Cryptography, ch. 7, vol. 2. Cambridge University Press, Cambridge (2004)
10. Marryat, F.: Peter Simple, vol. 3, ch. I. Saunders and Otley (1834)
11. Presburger, M.: Über die Vollständigkeit eines gewissen Systems der Arithmetik ganzer Zahlen, in welchem die Addition als einzige Operation hervortritt. In: Comptes-Rendus du I Congrès de Mathématiciens des Pays Slaves, pp. 92–101, Warszawa (1929)

Self-stabilizing and Byzantine-Tolerant Overlay Network[*]

Danny Dolev[1], Ezra N. Hoch[1], and Robbert van Renesse[2]

[1] School of Engineering and Computer Science
The Hebrew University of Jerusalem, Israel
{dolev,ezraho}@cs.huji.ac.il
[2] Dept. of Computer Science
Cornell University, Ithaca, NY
rvr@cs.cornell.edu

Abstract. Network overlays have been the subject of intensive research in recent years. The paper presents an overlay structure, *S-Fireflies*, that is self-stabilizing and is robust against permanent Byzantine faults. The overlay structure has a logarithmic diameter with high probability, which matches the diameter of less robust overlays. The overlay can withstand high churn without affecting the ability of active and correct members to disseminate their messages. The construction uses a randomized technique to choose the neighbors of each member, while limiting the ability of Byzantine members to affect the randomization or to disturb the construction. The basic ideas generalize the original *Fireflies* construction that withstands Byzantine failures but was not self-stabilizing.

1 Introduction

Network overlays have become a basic technique for routing among a dynamic set of participants. The literature studies various efficiency measures and availability issues. Recent papers address the issues of stabilization [1,2,3] and overcoming Byzantine faults [4,5,6]. In the current paper we extend the *Fireflies* construction [6], making it self-stabilizing. We call the resulting system *S-Fireflies*, for "stabilizing" *Fireflies*. *S-Fireflies* provides robust support (middleware) for various peer-to-peer and distributed applications, including Distributed Hash Tables ([7,8]) and reliable broadcast. For example, *Fireflies* has been used for Byzantine video streaming [9] and secure dissemination of software patches [10], and *S-Fireflies* can make the same applications significantly more robust.

S-Fireflies provides a *dissemination structure* along which members can exchange messages. The structure is an overlay graph among currently active members, having logarithmic diameter and adapting to churn (members coming and going). It overcomes

---

[*] This material is based in part upon work supported by ISF, ISOC, by the AFOSR under Award No. FA8750-06-2-0060, FA9550-06-1-0019, FA9550-06-1-0244, and by the National Science Foundation under Grant No. 0424422. Any opinions, findings, and conclusions or recommendations expressed in this publications are those of the author(s) and do not necessarily reflect the views of the AFOSR, NSF or ISF.

E. Tovar, P. Tsigas, and H. Fouchal (Eds.): OPODIS 2007, LNCS 4878, pp. 343–357, 2007.

Byzantine members who may try to prevent correct members from reliably communicating, or to cause them to send a large amount of useless messages. We assume that the networking facility underneath the overlay allows any two correct and active members to establish a communication channel, resembling networking over the Internet.

Each member maintains communication channels to a subset of the active members. The dissemination structure is composed of a dynamic number of "random subgraphs" that determine neighboring members with whom a member communicates. The sequence of subgraphs is used also for constructing additional structures that monitor availability of neighboring members.

Members may leave or crash, some may be Byzantine, and some or all may face transient faults that arbitrarily change values stored in their memory. *S-Fireflies* guarantees that the system will maintain its robustness as long as the number of correct and active members is sufficiently larger than the number of Byzantine members and the number of members that have recently recovered. Moreover, if the system loses the required ratio among correct and failed members, it will converge to a robust overlay once the ratio is restored and remains so for a long enough period of time.

When the system recovers from a transient fault members may not know which are the currently active members. Moreover, it may be that the system may find itself in several disjoint components. In [1] the authors assume the existence of some failure detection subsystem, and when instability is identified, members flood the network to form a new stable membership. In [3] a gossiping style is used, with members occasionally probing potential neighbors to identify whether they are active or not. Our technique resembles this later one, though we reduce the ability of Byzantine members to probe all members all the time.

A significant challenge of overcoming churn and facing Byzantine failures is to find ways to limit the ability of faulty members to take advantage of high churn to destroy the system's structure. Mechanisms that deal with churn and transient faults may make the system prone to replay attacks by Byzantine members. A typical use of counters becomes problematic in the environment we envision, and special care need be given to the use of digital signatures. While we address these issues in the *S-Fireflies* system, the technique presented in this paper is general and can be applied to improve the robustness of other overlay networks. Our protocols use randomization and the results are achieved with high probability (whp).

1.1 Related Work

The structures that we create are intended to simulate random graphs, in contrast to ring-based Distributed Hash Tables (DHTs) like Chord [7]. In Chord, members are organized in a single ring, with each member having $\log N$ "fingers" pointing across the ring that provide routing shortcuts. Instead, in *S-Fireflies* each member has $\log N$ pseudo-random neighbors, from which we construct the various structures. In both cases members end up with $\log N$ neighbors, but an important difference is that in *S-Fireflies* the neighbor relation is easily verifiable, preventing a Byzantine member from claiming to be a neighbor of an arbitrary other member.

[4] describes defenses against various Byzantine behavior for Pastry [8], another ring-based DHT. The paper suggest remedial approaches to impersonation [11], as well

as to attacks on overlay routing table maintenance and message forwarding. An *eclipse attack* is an attack where malicious members isolate correct members by filling the neighbor table of a correct member with addresses of malicious members. [5] suggests thwarting this attack by enforcing bounds on the in- and out-degrees of P2P members. None of these approaches consider self-stabilization however.

There has been a variety of work on Byzantine-tolerant epidemic protocols, apparently starting with [12]. These protocols consider the problem of correct members not accepting any malicious updates without using unforgeable signatures, and use a form of voting instead.

Drum [13] is a DoS-resistant multicast protocol. It uses a combination of gossip techniques, resource bounds for certain operations, and random UDP ports in order to fight DoS attacks, especially those directed against a small subset of the correct members. These techniques are orthogonal to the ones used by *S-Fireflies*.

The issue of self-stabilization was studied in the context of group membership [1]. That work assumes that there is failure detection—once the system detects failure it switches to a stabilization phase. The main objective is to reduce communication overhead. The paper does not deal with permanent presence of Byzantine faults.

One observation in the current paper is that in order to overcome Byzantine members there is a need for a high connectivity underlying graph. One could consider using Harary graphs, or even Logarithmic Harary Graphs [14]. Unfortunately, despite its high connectivity, such structures are fragile and cannot be built on-the-fly in the presence of Byzantine members.

2   The Model

The system consists of a set $\mathcal{P}$ of members. Each member, m, has an identifier $m.id \in \mathcal{P}$, that is randomly assigned by a central authority (CA). To simplify notations we assume that all identifiers are in $[1, \ldots, |\mathcal{P}|]$, and we use the convention $m \in \mathcal{P}$. Members can be *active* or *passive*. An active member participates in the protocol; a passive one may be dead or detached. Some of the active members may be *Byzantine*. Members may go through transient periods resulting in an arbitrary state of the various variables, though the protocols (consisting of code and constants) are hard-coded and unaffected by transient faults. We assume that members may dynamically fail; failed members may recover and need to be re-integrated into the system.

We assume the existence of a public key cryptography scheme that allows each member to verify the signature of each other member. We further assume that non-Byzantine members never reveal their private keys,[1] such that faulty members cannot forge signatures. Member identifiers and their keys are part of their hard-coded state. The keys (as well as the signed identifier) are acquired via a trusted CA.

We assume that after going through a transient failure period the system eventually recovers, and at steady state the probability of an active member being Byzantine is bounded by p_{byz}.[2] We also assume that the communication network allows any two

---

[1] A Byzantine member that reveals its private key can never recover and be considered correct.

[2] One can assume that this holds only when the number of active members is more than some small n_0. One may generalize p_{byz} to be a distribution over the number of active members.

active members to establish a secure communication channel. Moreover, there is a constant δ that bounds, with high probability, the time it takes messages among active members to reach their destination. Informally, we are interested in establishing an overlay among a given set of members over the Internet.

Correct members have internal timers that run at a bounded drift from real time, which enable them to measure periods of time with relative precision. We do not require clock values to be synchronized.

Members that face transient failure may find themselves in an arbitrary state. Therefore it may take some time to integrate them back into the system.

Definition 1. *An* active member *is* non-faulty *if it follows its protocols, processes messages in no more than π real-time units and has a bounded drift of its internal timer. An active member that is* not *non-faulty* is considered *Byzantine.*

A member will be called *faulty* or Byzantine, interchangeably.

Definition 2. *A* member *is* correct *if it has been* non-faulty *for* Δ_{memb}.

The value of Δ_{memb} is determined in Theorem 2. The communication network itself may face periods of time during which it deviates from its assumed properties.

Definition 3. *A* communication network *is* non-faulty *if messages arrive at their destination within δ real-time, and the content of the messages as well as the identity of the sender are not tampered with.*

Definition 4. *A* communication network *is* correct *if it has been* non-faulty *for* Δ_{net} *real-time.*

The value of Δ_{net} is chosen such that all messages that were sent before t_1 or were forged due to transient faults in the network are removed by $t_1 + \Delta_{net}$.

Definition 5. *A* system *is* coherent *if there is group $\mathcal{G}$ of correct members, such that $|\mathcal{G}| \geq N \cdot (1 - p_{byz})$, where N is the number of the currently active members, and the network connecting the members in $\mathcal{G}$ is correct.*

In the following, we will discuss only members from $\mathcal{G}$, thus, when stating "correct member m," we actually mean "correct member m s.t. $m \in \mathcal{G}$."

Once the system is coherent, a message between any two correct members is sent, received, and processed within d real-time units, where d includes δ, π, and drifts of local timers. For simplicity we will assume that $\Delta_{net} = 2d$, though one can choose different values.

3   The BSS Overlay Service Specification

Each correct member has a *view*, $m.view$, which is a subset of all members, $\mathcal{P}$. Informally, $m_2 \in m_1.view$ means that m_1 believes that m_2 is, at least until recently, neither stopped nor exhibiting Byzantine behavior. Conversely, $m_2 \notin m_1.view$ means that m_1

believes that m_2 is stopped or faulty.[3] The subset $m.neighbors$ of a member's view represents its *neighbors*.

An *overlay* G, $G = (V, E)$, is a directed graph whose members, $V \subseteq \mathcal{P}$, are the active members and $E = \{(m_i, m_j) | m_i, m_j \in V, m_j \in m_i.neighbors\}$. A *Byzantine-Self-Stabilizing (BSS) overlay* G, is an *overlay* G that is Byzantine-tolerant and self-stabilizing. Thus, a BSS-overlay forms a usable routing substrate among the active members that is highly robust. We refer to the graph spanned by the BSS-overlay in which each directed edge is replaced by an undirected one as *underlying-BSS-overlay*. For maintaining the BSS-overlay each member has an additional list: $m.detect$ contains members used for failure detection.

Our goal is to design a protocol that guarantees that when the system is coherent the following properties hold with high probability:[4]

P1: There is a directed path in the BSS-overlay from any correct member to any other correct member composed of only correct members;
P2: The diameter of the underlying-BSS-overlay is bounded by $O(\log(V))$;

Our aim is to develop protocols that converge from any arbitrary initial state, once the system stabilizes and there are enough correct members; i.e., the protocols spans a BSS-overlay among the active members satisfying the properties above. Moreover, we wish to reduce the time it takes for the system to converge and for a recovering member to be considered correct, i.e., to obtain Δ_{memb} as small as possible.

4 Data Structures

4.1 The Sequence of Subgraphs

The randomization used in the various structures of *S-Fireflies* are derived from a sequence of permutations. Each member m has a list $m(r_1), \ldots, m(r_j)$ of permutations, where $m(r_i)$ is a permutation over $\mathcal{P} - \{m\}$. For each permutation m should connect to the first member in that permutation, and if that member is down, m will connect to the next member in the permutation, and so on.

The solution proposed in this paper requires the list of permutations to be chosen independently and uniformly at random. This list should have at least $|\mathcal{P}| \cdot log(|\mathcal{P}|)$ permutations in it, since each member should have at most $\log N$ neighbors. According to experiments done by [6], a collision-resistant hash function can provide the required "randomization".[5] Therefore, we will assume the existence of a hash function

$$\mathcal{H} : (\mathcal{P}, \mathcal{N}) \to permutations([1, \ldots, |\mathcal{P}|]),$$

where $\mathcal{N}$ is the set of natural numbers and $permutations()$ is the set of all permutations over some group, such that for each member and subgraph index there is a permutation over the set $\mathcal{P}$. It is assumed that each member knows all permutations.

---

[3] We do not provide Virtual Synchrony properties such as consensus on views.

[4] The probabilities can be tuned to any desired probability.

[5] One can have the CA randomly select the permutations and send them to each member, exchanging practical performance with theoretical robustness.

Table 1. Additional View Lists

List	Description	Duration	Action
rcnt_suspected	members that were recently suspected	2Δ	remove from $m.view$ move to rcnt_removed
rcnt_removed	members that were recently removed	Δ	remove
to_be_joined	recently accepted members	Δ	move to $m.view$

Members are aware of their successors and predecessors on the various subgraphs, where a successor m of m' on the ith subgraph is the first active member along the r_i permutation of m' as perceived by the view of m'; if m is a successor of m' then m' is the predecessor of m (on subgraph i). The actual number of subgraphs that a member uses may differ in different structures and will be specified for each one accordingly. On subgraph i:

$$succ_i(m) = \min_j \{m(r_i)_j | m(r_i)_j \in m.view\} \ ,$$

$$pred_i(m) = \{m' | m \in succ_i(m')\} \ ,$$

Recall that $m \notin m(r_i)$. Note that $pred_i(m)$ might contain several members. When the specific subgraph is clear from context we omit the subscript i. Our notations resembles those of [2].

We introduce operators that represent the segment of potential successors or predecessors of a member in a subgraph:

$$seg\_succ_i(m) = \{m(r_i)_j | j < location(succ_i(m), m(r_i))\} \ ,$$
$$seg\_pred_i(m) = \{m' | m' = succ_i(m), location(m', m(r_i)) \neq 1)\} \ ,$$

where $location(m, perm)$ returns the index of m in the permutation $perm$. Observe that these operators depend on the current view of the member, and different members might have different views.

4.2   The Views

High churn in the system and uncertainty about the time at which various members update their views require that each member maintains temporary lists of additional members, as described in Table 1. *S-Fireflies* members gossip on the BSS-overlay *dissemination structure* (Section 5), and the connectivity is chosen so with high probability all members learn of new gossip within Δ time units.

A member that is suspected as failed (as described in Section 6) is listed on the rcnt_suspected list and if it does not rejoin within 2Δ (as described in Section 7) it is removed from $m.view$ (and from rcnt_suspected). During the uncertainty period members in this list are still considered as potentially connected. The process of joining is also a double step. A joiner that will be accepted (as described in Section 7) is first placed in the to_be_joined list, and will be integrated into $m.view$ only after being in the list for Δ time units, giving the rest of the members a chance to identify the new addition.

S-Fireflies does not reach agreement on views, therefore views can always differ. At steady state the difference among the views of two correct members is due to the lists above and due to Byzantine behavior. To accommodate for that flexibility, when a member m considers its view, $m.view$, to check whether m' is allowed to connect to m, it will actually consider *rcnt_removed*'s and *to_be_joined*'s effect on $m.view$; that is, m will accept m' to connect to it if there is an update of $m.view$ with members from *rcnt_removed* $\cup$ *to_be_joined* such that $m' \in pred_i(m)$ (for some $i \leq r'_m$, as defined in Section 5). In such a case we say that the view of m' is close to the view of m. However, when m considers which members to connect to, it will consider $m.view$ only. Such a behavior will allow the required flexibility for m and m' to connect to each other in the presence of joining and leaving members.

4.3 The Epoch and Epoch List

The assumed existence of digital signatures reduces the ability of Byzantine members to mislead correct members. But since members may fail and recover, Byzantine members can replay old signed messages. In a self-stabilizing environment it is challenging to identify replayed messages.

In order to reduce the ability of Byzantine members to perform a convincing replay attack, a member needs a mechanism that produces some randomization to its new identity when it recovers. To achieve that, a member chooses periodically (and during recovery) a new random incarnation number. A new *epoch* of a member is the signed pair (*prev_inc, new_inc*), where *prev_inc* is its previous incarnation value and *new_inc* is its new incarnation value. The incarnation values are random numbers from a large enough space (much larger than the memory space of the faulty members), so that the probability that a member repeats the pair (*prev_inc, new_inc*) is negligible, and the ability of a faulty member to replay such a pair is even smaller. We will ignore this small probability of error.

The introduction of a random epoch is similar to choosing a random id. Therefore, in our protocols, whenever a member sends a signed message it should include its current epoch. We assume that members send signed messages, and members ignore any message that is not signed properly or does not carry the matching epoch. We will ignore these details when describing the protocols.

Each member maintains as part of its view the latest epoch of each member in the view ("the epoch list"). A receiver of a signed message will consider the message *current* only if the epoch matches the last epoch the receiver knows of. If the recent epoch was received less than Δ ago, it can still accept signed messages containing the previous epoch value. The message is current also when the member did not receive the new epoch yet, but its latest copy of the epoch matches the *prev_inc* part of the epoch of the received message. When a member m_1 updates its epoch (done once in Δ_{epoch}) it will send a special message containing the new epoch; this message is disseminated the same as other messages in the system. If a member m_2 receives such a message and m_2's current epoch is equal to m_1's *prev_inc* then m_2 updates its view of m_1's epoch.

5   The Dissemination Structure

The dissemination structure is defined according to the neighbor relations induced by the set of subgraphs as determined by the size of the views of individual active members. Let $N_m = |m.view|$ and define g_m, the number of active members m establishes a connection to, as

$$g_m = g_0 + \lceil \frac{1}{1 - p_{byz}} \ln N_m \rceil,$$

where g_0 is a minimal number of neighbors (defined in Theorem 1). Member m establishes a secure channel with the g_m different members of $m.view$ that are $succ(m)$ in one of the first $r(m.view)$ subgraphs, where $r(m.view)$ is the minimal number of such subgraphs satisfying

$$r_m(m.view) = \min_i (|\bigcup_{j \leq i} \{m'|m' = succ_j(m)\}| = g_m)$$

$r(m.view)$ and r_m will also be used. These g_m members are the members of the $m.neighbors$ set, and member m will gossip its messages along these channels. Note that whp $r_m = g_m$.

Since views of different members may differ, member m accepts a connection request from each active member m' who is $pred(m)$ in one of r'_m permutations of m', defined as:

$$r'_m = r(m.view \cup rcnt\_removed \cup to\_be\_joined) \cdot (1 + p_{byz}).$$

Thus, m estimates the number of subgraphs of m' within which it appears as a $succ(m')$ in order to accept the connection. In such a case we say that the view of m' is *close* to the view of m. This notion of "close" intends to allow for two correct members to differ by the potential presence of current Byzantine members and view changes that are in transit. As in [6], if the request arrives from a member that is not $pred(m)$, a message is returned containing an update.

The dissemination structure that defines the BSS-overlay is composed of the active members and the secure channels they establish with their neighbors. Each member m has g_m outgoing links.

Theorem 1. *A gossip protocol over* BSS-*overlay completes with high probability within* $\Delta = (\ln N + c_0) \cdot d$, *where* N *is the number of currently active and correct members and* c_0 *is a constant that depends on the probability of message loss and on* p_{byz}.

Proof. Sketch: Kermarrec et al. [15] show that it is possible to build effective gossip protocols if each member only has a small set of uniformly chosen members it gossips with. In the dissemination structure, each member m effectively gossips with some g_m *neighbors* from its view uniformly at random, where g_m is large enough to create a connected graph of correct members; if we have k neighbors, then $p_{byz} \cdot k$ neighbors will by Byzantine (in expectation), hence we would like to have $(1 + p_{byz}) \cdot k$ neighbors; now we have an additional $p_{byz}^2 \cdot k$ Byzantine neighbors, and so on. Using $\sum_{i=0}^{\infty} p_{byz}^i = \frac{1}{1 - p_{byz}}$, we obtain the definition of g_m.

Detection of a Crashed Member   /* executed at member m */
                        /* others members act upon receiving appropriate message */
                                       /* all gossip along the BSS-overlay */

Monitoring m:
  If suspects crashing of $m' = succ_i(m)$ then
      add m' to rcnt_suspected;
      disseminate "suspect$(m, epoch_m, m', epoch_{m'})$",
          where $epoch$ is m's epoch and $epoch_{m'}$ is m'''s;
Member m'':
  when received "suspect$(m, epoch_m, m', epoch_{m'})$" from m and $m' \neq m''$ do
      if $epoch_m$ and $epoch_{m'}$ current and $m = pred(m')$ and $m \notin banned(m')$ then
          add m' to rcnt_suspected;
          disseminate "suspect$(m, epoch_m, m', epoch_{m'})$",
  when received "suspect$(m, epoch_m, m', epoch_{m'})$" from m and $m' = m''$ do
      if $epoch_m$ and $epoch_{m'}$ current and $m = pred(m')$ then
          add m to $banned(m'')$
          if $|banned(m'')| > f_{m''}$ then $banned(m'') = \perp$
          invoke a new incarnation of m''

Fig. 1. Handling Suspicions

A classic result of Erdös and Rényi [16] shows that in a graph of n members, if the probability of two members being connected is $p_n = (\log n + c + o(1))/n$, then the probability of the graph being connected goes to $\exp(-\exp(-c))$. The proof follows this line of arguments, using the potential difference between views of different members, their additional lists, and their estimate of the number of currently active members. The value of g_0 is determined by c and the initial n for which the estimates hold.   □

6 Membership Maintenance

The membership maintenance draws upon ideas presented in [6]. The basic idea is that members exchange accusations regarding suspected misbehavior of other members. They keep track of other members using the detection structure (defined below) and gossip their accusations using the dissemination structure.

In the *detection structure*, each member maintains outgoing links (some of which may overlap with the links of other structures) with its successors in a number of subgraphs such that each member in its view has g_m different $pred(m)$ members. The number of detection subgraphs that an active member considers is determined as follows: Increase the number of subgraphs until for every $m' \in m.view$ there exist at least g_m different members of $m.view$ as their predecessors on the different subgraphs. More formally:

$$detect(m) = \min_r(|\bigcup_{i \leq r}\{pred_i(m)\}| \geq g_m).$$

Each member maintains secure channels with the set of its successors along these subgraphs. When a member is requested to establish a secure channel it checks that the requester is in *pred* for one of the subgraphs implied by that view (while considering *to_be_joined* and *rcnt_removed*).

The detection structure is the graph spanning the active members and all channels to their successors in one of the detection subgraphs, as defined above. Member m monitors $succ_i(m)$, for each $i \leq detect(m)$, and is expected to be monitored by $pred_i(m)$.

We use the pinging techniques of [6]. If a member suspects that the member it monitors fails, it gossips along the dissemination structure an accusation message as defined in [6], except that each such message carries the epoch as defined above. Observe that the pinging technique does not have long term state and therefore introduces no difficulty to stabilization of the system.

To prevent faulty members from continuously sending accusation messages about correct and active members, each member maintains a list *banned-members* flagging up to f_m of its predecessors as disabled. A predecessor that is disabled cannot disseminate any accepted accusation of a member. Figure 1 presents the schematic protocol that handles crash detection.

The view of each member includes not only the identities of members it assumes to be active and correctly operating, but also for each member the latest signed epoch and the vector of disabled predecessors.

Observe that the detection structure does not need to use the technique of skipping across accused members, used in [6], in order to guarantee that each member has a monitoring member. Our detection structure has that property by construction.

Members also track the activities of other members and if they can prove Byzantine behavior they can disseminate such a proof and members can remove the faulty member. We will not elaborate on that optimization.

Lemma 1. *A crashed member will be removed from the view of every correct and active member within 3Δ, whp.*

Proof. When the system becomes coherent correct members exchange messages within Δ whp. A crashed member has at least one correct and active predecessor that is not in its banned-members list. That member will detect the crash and will be able to disseminate that to all correct and active members whp. Within Δ it will reach all correct and active members, and within an additional 2Δ those members will update their views.

$\square$

7 Recovery of Members

Due to the self-stabilizing requirement, the system must cope with transient faults. Members can be subject to such faults, and may be able to identify them via inconsistencies in their internal state, or they may realize that other members suspect them as failed. In such cases, the member needs to recover and integrate back into the system.

Observe that the new epoch cannot be disseminated as is because simple gossiping will enable faulty members to gossip about past values, thus enabling replay attacks. The first step of recovering a member is to ensure it has an updated epoch list.

Sending epochs and views to all members   /* executed at member m
                                                            every $\Delta_1/|\mathcal{P}|$ time units */
Member m:
    Send epoch and $m.view$ to member i;
    $i := i + 1(mod\ |\mathcal{P}|)$;
Member m':
    upon receiving epoch and view from m, update epoch list with m's epoch, and update
$m'.view$ with $m.view$

Fig. 2. Background process: sending epochs and views to all members

7.1 Epoch Renewal and Epoch List Stabilization

The usage of signatures handicaps Byzantine members to some degree; however, the Byzantine members may replay signed messages. To prevent this, each member p has a counter that it includes in each message and increments for each message. Receiving members will not accept a message from a member with a lower counter than expected. Due to transient faults, members in the system may have invalid values for these counters. Moreover, Byzantine members may replay messages of higher counters in case of a transient fault that caused the correct members to think that there are lower counter values.

To overcome both these issues a member should select a new epoch every so often (depending on the system security requirements); with each new epoch the message counter is reset. However, there might be a mismatch between a receiving members' value of $prev\_inc$ of p and p's value of $prev\_inc$; this will lead to members not accepting the new incarnation.

We consider two scenarios: The first is a scenario in which a majority of correct members have undergone transient faults, and their epoch lists are not valid anymore; in the second scenario only a small portion of members have undergone transient faults (this is likely the more common case in practice).

To solve the first case – when many members have undergone transient faults – we use a background process that periodically sends the epoch and view to each member (see Figure 2). The second case is solved by contacting the immediate neighbors and updating the list of epochs and views according to their majority agreement (see Figure 3).

Transient faults may disturb other data structures as well as the epoch list. If the value of $m.view$ is too far off to even connect to other members to gather information about the epoch list then m has to wait Δ_1 time for the algorithm in Figure 2 to update its epoch list. In case $m.view$ approximately represents which members are up and which not then the algorithm in Figure 3 will operate correctly and "re-update" the epoch list of m within $\Delta_{1'}$ time.

In Figure 3, the size of the group to request the epoch list from (N_{epoch}) affects tolerance to multiple transient failures. To increase tolerance this size can be increased. Let p_{trans} be the probability of having a transient fault at some member. If $(p_{byz} + p_{trans}) < 1/2$ then the larger $\mathcal{G}_{epoch}$ is, the higher the probability of "hitting" enough

Getting epoch list   /* executed at member m every Δ_1, time units */
Member m:
    $\mathcal{G}_{epoch}$:=randomly select N_{epoch} active members from $m.view$;
    request epoch list and view from all members in $\mathcal{G}_{epoch}$;
    upon receiving responses (wait at most $2d$ to collect responses):
        for each member, select the epoch that appears most often.
        for each member, select the state that appears most often.

Fig. 3. Background process: getting epoch list and views from members

Choosing a new epoch
Member m:
    either once every Δ_{epoch} **or** if m has been accused:
        randomly select a new epoch;
        disseminate the new epoch;
Member m':
    upon receiving information about a new epoch of member m, if m' epoch list contains
m's *prev_inc* then update the epoch list with the current epoch of m;

Fig. 4. Background process: choosing a new epoch

correct members in the search for epoch lists. Moreover, if $m.view$ was subject to some transient faults, then the larger $\mathcal{G}_{epoch}$ is, the larger group out of $m.view$ is examined, which increases the probability of reaching enough correct members.

Assume that each member renews its epoch to ensure that the epoch is always fresh every Δ_{epoch} period (as specified in the next subsection).

Lemma 2. *Starting from any state, each correct member has an updated epoch list within $\Delta_1 + \Delta_{epoch}$.*

Note that from this point on correct members can communicate safely among each other; also, Byzantine members cannot use replay attacks because all epochs have been changed.

7.2   Periodical Epoch Update

A member m creates a new epoch every Δ_{epoch} and disseminates the message among all members (see Figure 4).

Lemma 3. *An active and correct member that renews its epoch in less than Δ from the time the first correct and active member suspects it as failed succeeds to do so before it is removed from the view of any correct and active member, whp.*

Proof. Sketch: The renewal message carries the new epoch that matches the last epoch at all active and correct members in its previous view. Since dissemination takes less than Δ, whp, its renewal message reaches and is accepted by each such member before it is removed from the *rcnt_suspected* list of any such member. Note that the renewal message may reach members that are not aware of the suspicion. If an old suspicion message will be received in such a case its epoch will not match and the message will be ignored.   □

Note that the lemma also claims that a member that renews its epoch without it being in *rcnt_suspected* of any correct member also has its epoch accepted by all correct members within Δ whp.

Lemma 4. *A correct and active member will not enter the rcnt_suspected list of any correct and active member as long it remains active, whp.*

7.3   Stabilization of the Overlay Network Structures

In Section 7.1 it was shown that all correct members eventually agree on their epoch list. However, due to transient failures, members might disagree on the dissemination structures.

In the following the self-stabilization of the overlay network structures is considered (assuming the epoch list has stabilized). Consider all correct members in the system to be in an arbitrary state. That is, a member m has arbitrary values for $m.view$, *rcnt_suspected*, etc. By the algorithm in Figure 2 after Δ_1 all members will have similar view sizes; hence they will agree on the value of g_m.

Since each member continuously monitors the members in seg_succ_i (for all $i \leq r_m$) and in seg_pred_i (for all $i \leq r'_m$), then eventually each member will have connections with the members it should be connected too. (Note that the lists *rcnt_suspected*, *rcnt_removed*, *to_be_joined*, and *banned* are cleared when the items in them are old enough.)

From this point on all disseminations are performed correctly, as messages are sent and received along the "correct" connections; however, members still do not have valid views of all the network, and it will take time for this view to become consistent. Note that this view inconsistency is not an issue, as it only affects new connections in case some member leaves the overlay network and since seg_succ and seg_pred are always monitored, such failures will be detected.

In addition, members' states are continuously disseminated along the network (for example, due to periodic distribution of new epochs described in Section 7.2). Since each active member is connected to the overlay, once the overlay network has its connections set each member will disseminate its sate. Hence, after an additional Δ time units all members will receive each such dissemination and will have up-to-date views of the status of all other correct members.

Note that this stabilization will take no more than $O(\Delta + \Delta_{scan})$ time whp (where Δ_{scan} is the interval for scanning seg_pred and seg_succ, and is also the rate at which members refresh their *banned-members* list). Define the stabilization period $\Delta_2 = O(\Delta + \Delta_{scan})$.

Theorem 2. *Starting from an arbitrary state, each disjoint set of the system converges within $\Delta_{memb} = \Delta_{epoch} + \Delta_1 + \Delta_2$.*

Proof. Sketch: Starting from an arbitrary state, after $\Delta_{epoch} + \Delta_1$ time all non-faulty and active members agree on each other's epochs. From this step on, secure communication can commence. In addition, all members agree (approximately) on the view size. Hence, they all consider the same g_m which leads to the construction of a working overlay network; after an additional Δ_2 time, all correct members will have up-to-date overlay structures in their connected subgraph.   □

Theorem 3. *The* BSS-*overlay with the detection and the integration structure satisfies properties P1 and P2, with high probability.*

Proof. *Sketch:* We prove that once the system is coherent the system converges from an arbitrary state to a safe state and that once it is in a safe state it remains in such a state unless the system becomes incoherent.

Let $\mathcal{G}$ be the set of members that are active and non-faulty for $\Delta_{epoch} + \Delta_1 + \Delta_2$. Within $\Delta_{epoch} + \Delta_1$ after the system becomes coherent each one of them will go through its subgraphs and will end up learning about all possible connected components. Within Δ_2 each member m will connect to at least g_m members. Observe that in these bi-lateral exchanges members add to their view each member they found active.

Within Δ each one will establish connections with g_m and will connect the BSS-overlay. Members that crash disappear from views and correct and active members remain in views.   □

8 Conclusion

The paper presents a robust and self-stabilizing overlay network. In order to establish self-stabilization while overcoming Byzantine faults some unique techniques are developed. These techniques can help turn other constructions into self-stabilizing systems that withstand Byzantine faults. The basic techniques are: 1) the use of randomization to create permutations of the list of members; 2) the use of a pair of random numbers to form a member's epoch, instead of an ordinal number; 3) the introduction of integration and detection structures that enable dealing with high churn without the need to reconstruct the overlay network when members fail and recover.

References

1. Dolev, S., Schiller, E.: Communicaiton adaptive self-stabilizing group membership service. IEEE Transactions on Parallel and Distributed Systems 14(7), 709–720 (2003)
2. Ghodsi, A., El-Ansary, S., Krishnamurthy, S., Haridi, S.: A self-stabilizing network size estimation gossip algorithm for peer-to-peer systems. Technical Report Technical Report T2005:16, SICS (2005)
3. Shafaat, T., Ghodsi, A., Haridi, S.: Handling network partitions and mergers in structured overlay networks. In: Proc. of the Seventh IEEE International Conference on Peer-to-Peer Computing, Galway, Ireland (September 2007)
4. Castro, M., Druschel, P., Ganesh, A., Rowstron, A., Wallach, D.S.: Secure routing for structured peer-to-peer overlay networks. In: Proc. of the 5th Usenix Symposium on Operation System Design and Implementation (OSDI), Boston, MA (December 2002)

5. Singh, A., Castro, M., Druschel, P., Rowstron, A.: Defending against Eclipse attacks on overlay networks. In: Proc. of the 11th European SIGOPS Workshop, Leuven, Belgium, ACM, New York (2004)
6. Johansen, H., Allavena, A., van Renesse, R.: Fireflies: Scalable support for intrusion-tolerant network overlays. In: Eurosys 2006, Leuven, Belgium (2006)
7. Stoica, I., Morris, R., Karger, D., Kaashoek, M.F.: Chord: A scalable peer-to-peer lookup service for Internet applications. In: Proc. of the 1995 Symp. on Communications Architectures & Protocols, Cambridge, MA, ACM SIGCOMM (August 1995)
8. Rowstron, A., Druschel, P.: Pastry: Scalable, distributed object location and routing for large-scale peer-to-peer systems. In: Guerraoui, R. (ed.) Middleware 2001. LNCS, vol. 2218, Springer, Heidelberg (2001)
9. Haridasan, M., van Renesse, R.: Defense against intrusion in a live streaming multicast system. In: 6th IEEE International Conference on Peer-to-Peer Computing (P2P 2006), Cambridge, UK (September 2006)
10. Johansen, H., Johansen, D., van Renesse, R.: Firepatch: Secure and time-critical dissemination of software patches. In: IFIP International Information Security Conference (IFIPSEC 2007), Sandton, South-Africa (May 2007)
11. Douceur, J.: The Sybil attack. In: Proc. of the 1st Int. Workshop on Peer-to-Peer Systems, Cambridge, MA (March 2002)
12. Malkhi, D., Mansour, Y., Reiter, M.K.: On diffusing updates in a Byzantine environment. In: Symposium on Reliable Distributed Systems, Lausanne, Switzerland, pp. 134–143 (October 1999)
13. Badishi, G., Keidar, I., Sasson, A.: Exposing and eliminating vulnerabilities to Denial of Service attacks in secure gossip-based multicast. In: Proc. of the International Conference on Dependable Systems and Networks (DSN), pp. 201–210 (2004)
14. Jenkins, K., Demers, A.: Logarithmic harary graphs. In: Proceedings of the 21st International Conference on Distributed Computing Systems, ICDCSW (2001)
15. Kermarrec, A.-M., Massoulié, L., Ganesh, A.J.: Probabilistic reliable dissemination in large-scale systems. IEEE Transactions on Parallel and Distributed Systems, 14(3), (March 2003)
16. Erdös, P., Rényi, A.: On the evolution of random graphs. Magyar Tud. Akad. Mat. Kutato Int. Közl 5(17), 17–61 (1960)

Separability to Help Parallel Simulation of Distributed Computations*

Philippe Mauran, Gérard Padiou, and Philippe Quéinnec

Institut de Recherche en Informatique de Toulouse, UMR CNRS 5505
Université de Toulouse
ENSEEIHT, 2 rue Camichel, BP 7122, F-31071. Toulouse cedex 7
Tel.: +33 (0)5 58 82 34, Fax: +33 (0)5 61 58 83 06
{mauran,padiou,queinnec}@enseeiht.fr

Abstract. We consider the parallel simulation of distributed systems based upon the notion of separability. We define a model of distributed systems that integrates a limited set of temporal properties, from which we deduce specific parallel simulation strategies avoiding rollback and dynamic scheduling which are often necessary to obtain an optimal rate of parallelism in parallel and/or distributed simulations. In particular, we present strategies that enable to compute the simulation schedule in advance, or even statically.

This approach appears to be relevant for a large class of distributed computations, inasmuch as it relies upon a limited set of temporal properties of the simulated systems.

Keywords: parallel discrete event simulation, causality, scheduling, separability.

1 Introduction

The design of distributed algorithms and systems is intrinsically and notably hard, due to the lack of global time, the impossibility of having an instant global knowledge of the system state, and the open and dynamic nature of such systems. Our aim is to study efficient and scalable models and mechanisms, that are fitted to simulating such systems, for analysis and validation purposes. More precisely, our goal is to enable the (application or simulation) programmer to take advantage of simulation features, which are not available in a distributed setting:

- the existence of a global view of the simulated system, that can be used for debugging, or, more generally, for observing global predicates;
- the ability to predict forthcoming events in the simulated system, which is useful for the control of the simulation itself, but could also be a means to provide theoretical properties that cannot be implemented in a real distributed environment, such as oracles.

---

* This research was supported by CNES grant R-S06/VF-001-058, in collaboration with the Spacebel company.

E. Tovar, P. Tsigas, and H. Fouchal (Eds.): OPODIS 2007, LNCS 4878, pp. 358–371, 2007.

By its problematics, our approach departs from the field of distributed or parallel simulation [1], where the core problem is the parallel or distributed implementation of the simulator itself, regardless of the simulated system.

The simulation of a system involves three notions of time, that should be clearly set apart [1]:

- the *physical time*, which is the time in the system that is the target of the simulation. For example, if the simulation models the activity of an airport during one day, the physical time bounds of the simulation could be from 6.00 GMT July 8, 1969 to 6.00 GMT July 9, 1969.
- the *simulation time*, which is the (internal) representation of time used and managed by the simulator to order the simulation events.
- the *wallclock time*, which is the time related to a given run of the simulation. For example, the previous airport simulation may have been run in 55 minutes, from 10.15 GMT to 11.10 GMT, on September 5, 2007.

The control of a simulation, that is the scheduling of the simulation actions, can be characterized by the way in which the relationship between the physical time and the other times is handled (or not). Numerous works in the field of distributed simulation focus on the synchronization between the components of the simulation, at runtime. In other words, these works focus on the relationship between the wallclock time and other times, and especially the physical time. Different kinds of consistencies have thus been defined, allowing to state various constraints:

- the *causal consistency* of a distributed simulation run is usually enforced by building a global virtual time [2,3,1,4], such as in the HLA framework which ensures the interoperability of simulators and a global ordering of interactions between simulators [5,6,7];
- *multi-player real-time games* provide a classic example of application where the wallclock time is to be integrated in the scheduling of the simulation events [8].

On the other hand, the use of the specificities of a class or model of simulated systems, in order to optimize the scheduling of a simulation has little been explored, to the best of our knowledge. Thus, for example, although some proposals have attempted at increasing parallelism [9], the lack of assumptions on the simulated system in HLA leads to runs that can be inefficient, as a global order on the simulation events has to be built.

This work comes within the latter direction. Specifically, we consider the simulation of a a specific class of distributed systems, where physical time, relating to components and their interactions, is explicit, and is an integral part of the model. In particular, the distributed system model relies on a temporal characterization of the components' behavior (i.e. whether they are sporadic, periodic, or aperiodic), and of their interactions.

The scheduling of the simulation aims mainly at:

- reducing the *overhead* induced by the management of the simulation:
  - either in terms of context switching between the simulation activities or in terms of synchronization barriers;
  - by taking advantage of the temporal properties of the system, namely: the frequency, the jitter and the delay of the interactions.

In this perspective, one of the key ideas of this paper is to characterize and determine the *separable* CPU bursts of the simulation's components, that is the computation slices that are causally independent, and can thus be run concurrently. This separability analysis is based on the temporal aspects of the simulated system, and exploits the global view of the system which is available to the simulator.

– *supervising* the simulation, which leads to *relate the simulation time to the other times*. A centralized model appears to be the most convenient user model for supervision purposes. Hence, it seems interesting to relate a distributed model (which is the simulated system's model) to a centralized model (which is the simulation's model) and, in particular to provide the means to build:

- a global time, a pace that corresponds to the simulation's pace;
- consistent snapshots, corresponding to state observations, required for the monitoring of the simulation.

To this end, our approach is to construct a synchronous run, out of an asynchronous one, along the lines of the general pattern provided by synchronizers [10]. This pattern will prove to be well fitted, in terms of efficiency, for the setting that we consider in the remainder of this paper, where the simulation tasks are periodic.

Section 2 presents the context of this study, and introduces the (classic) distributed system model used by simulations. Then, we elaborate this model, in order to introduce the temporal properties on which the separability analysis is based. Lastly, we state a necessary and sufficient condition to ensure the consistency of separate and concurrent computations. Section 3 presents an evaluation of consistent computation slices based on communication delays, while Section 4 analyses separability from communication frequencies. Section 5 concludes the paper.

2   Separability in Distributed Computations

We first present the general context of this study. Then, we present our definitions of distributed computations. Lastly, separability leads to express a criterion for dividing a computation into causally consistent steps and to define a corresponding static scheduling of the simulation.

2.1   Context of the Study

The starting point of this study is the notion of separability proposed by Pierre Keller in the field of space systems [11]. The simulation of space systems is complex and costly. Furthermore, space systems are becoming increasingly complex, as they involve more and more components and satellites, which raises the problem of the scalability of their simulation.

In order to tackle these difficulties, the notion of separability brings in a methodology and a heuristics for decomposing these systems, based on their interactions. This approach aims at enabling a sequential or parallel simulation of the behavior of separable systems, at introducing of a physical logic for subsystems initialization, and at

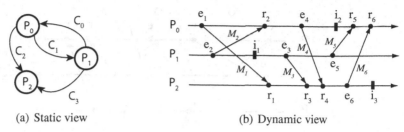

(a) Static view   (b) Dynamic view

Fig. 1. Distributed Computation

reducing of the size of the state vector of separated subsystems, which will correlatively reduce the time and space complexity of the simulation.

Separability assumes that subsystems:

- have an interface that can be described by discrete interactions[1];
- have sporadic interactions, i.e. the frequency of their interactions has an upper bound;
- may have drifting clocks.

These assumptions transpose straightforwardly into the setting of distributed computations, which provide a basis to reason about behavioral aspects of such systems. The study of separability in this formal framework enables to define dedicated efficient scheduling strategies for the simulation of these systems.

2.2 Distributed Computation Model

We start from the standard model of distributed computations [12,13]. In this model, a distributed computation is abstracted as a set of communicating processes. A static view as in Figure 1(a) consists in a graph in which vertices are processes and edges are communication channels.

A dynamic view of the computation consists in a timing diagram in which each process generates a sequence of events. A distributed computation is described as a set of events and a partial order capturing the causal relationship between events [14]. For instance, Figure 1(b) illustrates the dynamic behavior of three processes $\{P_0, P_1, P_2\}$ exchanging messages. Each send event e_i precedes causally the corresponding receive event r_i, and all the events of each process (internal events, send events or receive events) are totally ordered.

This event-oriented abstraction allows to specify various properties about distributed computations. For instance, the notion of cut allows to verify whether a global snapshot of a distributed computation is consistent [15].

The notion of separability leads to define a more structured description of distributed computations. More precisely, events are grouped into so-called *slices* of computation[2].

---

[1] Separable subsystems can be submitted to continuous interactions, such as gravity, which are handled and simulated autonomously by each subsystem, but are not relevant for the scheduling of the simulation.

[2] This notion of slice is not related to the notion of slice developped by Garg [13]. The later is an abstraction of a cut used to compute a global predicates.

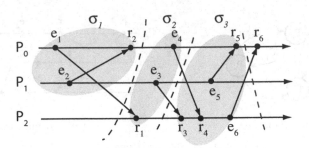

Fig. 2. Computation Slices

Figure 2 illustrates this notion: the distributed computation is structured as a sequence of event sets (slices) σ_k:

$$\sigma_1 = \{e_1, e_2, r_2\} \quad \sigma_2 = \{e_3, e_4, r_1\} \quad \sigma_3 = \{e_5, e, r_3, r_4, r_5\} \ldots$$

Definition 1 (Slice-Oriented Computation). *Any distributed computation can be described as a sequence of slices* $\sigma = \sigma_1\sigma_2 \ldots$ *such that the following properties are verified:*

- *Each slice* σ_i *is a finite set of events;*
- *Events belonging to slices preceding a given slice* σ_i *precede causally at least one event of* σ_i:

$$\forall i, \forall k < i, \forall e \in \sigma_k, \exists e' \in \sigma_i : e \prec e'$$

- *Events belonging to slices following a given slice* σ_i *are causally preceded by at least one event of* σ_i:

$$\forall i, \forall k > i, \forall e \in \sigma_k, \exists e' \in \sigma_i : e' \prec e$$

In other words, a slice defines a buffer between the past and the future of a distributed computation.

For parallel simulation purposes, we aim at determining slice-oriented compositions of a distributed computation. Each slice will delineate a parallel simulation unit during which each process performs a simulation step. Our main goal consists in defining the longest periods of simulation steps in any slice without resulting in causal inconsistencies or rollback steps.

With respect to these constraints, a parallel slice of simulation will be safe if, at the beginning of its execution, all the messages to be received during this slice have already been sent during an earlier slice and, consequently, are ready to be received during this current slice or any future one. In other words, each process is allowed to perform its simulation step in an independent way without any constraints about its execution speed because all the messages to be received during this step are already pending at the beginning of the slice execution.

This principle leads to define the following separability criterion and execution patterns for the parallel simulation of distributed computations.

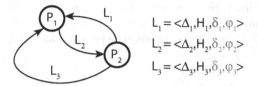

Fig. 3. Revisited Static View of a Distributed Computation

2.3 Separability Criterion

The definition of the separability criterion relies upon the notion of slice defined in 2.2. However, for the slice to be safe (i.e. separable), its set of events must satisfy a more restrictive property.

Definition 2 (Separability Criterion). *A distributed computation can be described as a sequence of separable slices* $\sigma = \sigma_1 \ldots \sigma_i \ldots$ *verifying the following separability property: for any slice* σ_i, *if a send event of a message* m *exists in the slice, then the corresponding receive event does not belong to this slice* σ_i. *In other words, this receive event can only belong to a later slice* $\sigma_k, k > i$ *and the message can be considered as in transit with respect to the slice* σ_i. *More formally, this property can be stated by:*

$$\forall m, i : e(m) \in \sigma_i \Rightarrow r(m) \notin \sigma_i (\equiv \exists k > i : r(m) \in \sigma_k)$$

2.4 Distributed Computation Model for Parallel Simulation

According to the previous assumptions, the scheduling of the parallel simulation of a distributed computation relies upon the evaluation of slice durations. Thus, we need an abstract model of distributed computations that allows to express the required temporal parameters. We extend the static view given in Figure 1(a) by interpreting the edges as message *links*. A link is defined as a unidirectional point-to-point communication channel, and may have the following attributes:

- a minimal delay Δ: this parameter specifies the lower bound of message transfer, that is, the time interval between the send event and the corresponding receive event;
- a frequency H: this parameter states the frequency of the messages; the corresponding period $T = \frac{1}{H}$ can also be used;

When the message frequency is known, two other parameters can be specified:

- a jitter δ: we consider this jitter as an uncertainty upon the reception date. This uncertainty comes as well from variations in the communication delay as from an uncertainty in the send event date. Strictly speaking, a system with jitter is not periodic. However, if the jitter is small enough (which is a reasonable assumption), it can still be considered as periodic.

– a phase φ: even in a periodic system, all subsystems may not start sending messages at the same date. A fixed frequency link can have a different phasing from the others. This phase is noted φ. On a link with period T and phase φ, the n-th message is sent at date $n * T + \varphi$.

Figure 3 describes an example with two processes. Several links can be defined from a source process to a destination process: for instance, two links are specified from P_1 to P_2. However, at the implementation level, the same communication channel can be used to transfer the messages associated to different links connecting the same processes.

2.5   Scheduling of a Parallel Simulation

The slicing of a distributed computation allows to simulate a distributed computation as a sequence of slices. A slice execution only begins when the previous one is terminated, namely, when all the processes have performed their simulation step in the current slice. Moreover, all messages sent during a simulation step by a process must be recorded because their receive dates can only belong to a latter slice according to the separability criterion (Definition 2).

3   Parallel Simulation Using Delays

In this section, we show how to compute the simulation step intervals for each process, when each link is only characterized by a minimal communication delay.

3.1   An Example of Separability Analysis

We consider a small system with only two processes. We assume the following parameters: process P_1 sends messages to P_2 with a minimal delay Δ_1 and process P_2 sends messages to P_1 with a minimal delay Δ_2.

In such a case, the separability can only be derived from the delays. Initially, the available lookahead[3] for each process is equal to the minimal transmission delay of messages sent by the other processes. In other words, the process P_1 can perform a first simulation step during (simulation) time interval $[0, \Delta_2[$. In parallel, process P_2 can perform a step during (simulation) time interval $[0, \Delta_1[$. From the simulation point of view, the *frontier* of each slice, i.e. the set of the maximal events (for the causal order) of the slice, acts as a synchronization barrier (see Figure 4(b)). Thus, the distributed computation is simulated as a sequence of separable slices, and the frontier of each slice is a consistent cut. After this first slice execution, each process begins a new step simulation: for process P_1, this new step will last for Δ_1 and, for process P_2, it will last for Δ_2.

Figure 4(a) illustrates this behavior. During its first step (1), each process will not receive any message: the messages sent by other processes during this step will not be received before the second step, due to transmission delays. Then, during the next

---

[3] That is: the maximal duration for which a given process can be run (or simulated) concurrently, without interacting (and thus synchronizing) with other processes.

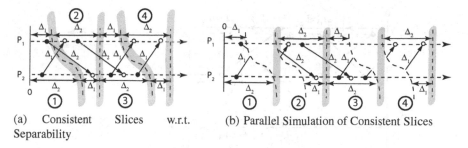

(a) Consistent Slices w.r.t.   (b) Parallel Simulation of Consistent Slices
Separability

Fig. 4. Running Consistent Slices

slice simulation (2), they receive messages sent during the previous slice and may send other messages which will be received in following slices, slice (3) for instance. The simulations of slices 3 and 4 follow the same pattern and have the same properties with respect to the separability criterion: no message is ever sent *and* received during the *same* slice simulation.

Figure 4(b) describes the synchronization of parallel simulation steps. In this particular case, each process executes steps alternating Δ_1 and Δ_2 continuous periods. Process P_1 starts with a Δ_2 period and process P_2 with a Δ_1 period.

3.2 Slicing in the General Case

We consider the general case, when a set of processes $\mathcal{P} = P_i, 0 < i \leq N$ exchange messages. Any pair $(P_i, P_j), i \neq j$ can communicate through different message links. Let Δ_{ij} be the minimal transmission delay for the set of links from P_i to P_j. This delay measures the minimal transfer time of a message sent by a process P_i to the process P_j, for all links from P_i to P_j. If no communication occurs, we assume the minimal delay is infinite: $\Delta_{ij} = +\infty$ iff P_i does not send any message to P_j.

The evaluation of slices relies upon the following principle: an initial slice is first determined and, then, a sequence of repeated slices is computed.

The initial slice of the parallel simulation consists in running the processes in parallel during a period equal to the minimal transfer delay of messages received by this process from other processes. The initial step duration Γ_i for a process P_i is equal to:

$$\Gamma_i = \min_{k \neq i} \Delta_{ki}$$

Without loss of generality, we change the numbering of the processes according to their Γ_i value in ascending order. This numbering ensures the property: $\forall i : \Gamma_i \leq \Gamma_{i+1}$

Proposition 1. *Step Interval Evaluation. The duration of the simulation steps of all processes can be evaluated statically. More precisely, the parallel simulation of N processes ordered according to their Γ_i attribute can execute steps of the following periods:*

- *The sequence of steps of the first process P_1 is assigned the values*[4]*: $(\Gamma_1; \Gamma_2)^*$*
- *The sequence of steps of all other processes is assigned the values: $\Gamma_p; (\Gamma_1; \Gamma_2)^*$*

---

[4] The regular expression $(a; b)^*$ defines an undefined number of iterations of the basic sequence $a; b$.

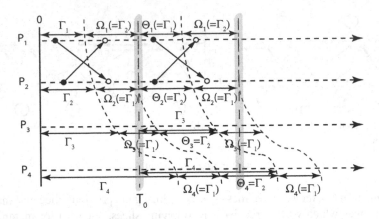

Fig. 5. Simulation Slices for N Processes

Proof. After the execution of the first slice, all processes are allowed to start running a second slice. In order to enforce separability, its duration (Ω_i for process P_i) must be at most equal to the minimal step duration of the initial slice of the other processes:

$$\Omega_i = \min_{k \neq i} \Gamma_k$$

The evaluation of the Ω_i durations is straightforward: thanks to the process renumbering, we have the following property:

- for the first process P_1: $\Omega_1 = \min_{k \neq 1} \Gamma_k = \Gamma_2$
- for the other processes P_i, $i > 1$: $\Omega_i = \min_{k \neq i} \Gamma_k = \Gamma_1$

Therefore, during the second slice, the process P_1 is run during a Γ_2 interval and all the other processes run during a Γ_1 interval.

When all processes have terminated this second slice, they can start a third slice during which a process P_i will perform a simulation step of Θ_i duration. The evaluation of these intervals relies upon the following remark: the processes P_1 et P_2 which receive their messages with the shortest delays, have been running during the same $\Gamma_1 + \Gamma_2$ interval. All the other processes $P_i, i > 2$ have been running during a longer interval:

$$\forall i > 2 : \Gamma_i + \Gamma_1 \geq \Gamma_1 + \Gamma_2$$

The instant $t_0 = \Gamma_1 + \Gamma_2$ (see Figure 5) sets up a frontier from which the assumptions of the initial point are valid again: each process P_i is allowed to run during Γ_i. For the two first processes, since they are stopped at point t_0, they can actually continue during respectively Γ_1 and Γ_2. The other processes are ahead in time: they are allowed to run until the instant $t_0 + \Gamma_i$, but they have already performed an interval equal to $\Gamma_i + \Gamma_1$. Therefore, they can only run during the following Θ_i duration intervals:

$$\forall i > 2 : \Theta_i = (t_0 + \Gamma_i) - (\Gamma_i + \Gamma_1)$$

But, from $t_0 = \Gamma_1 + \Gamma_2$, we deduce:

$$\forall i > 2 : \Theta_i = (\Gamma_1 + \Gamma_2 + \Gamma_i) - (\Gamma_i + \Gamma_1) = \Gamma_2$$

Indeed, all the processes, except P_1, are allowed to run during an interval equal to Γ_2 in parallel with the process P_1 which is only allowed to run during an interval equal to Γ_1. Then, the simulation can continue with a fourth slice identical to the second one: the process P_1 runs during a Γ_2 interval and all the others run during a Γ_1 interval.

3.3 Performance

With respect to parallelism, the simulation performance exclusively depends on the two processes receiving their messages with the shortest delays. Their parameters Γ_1 et Γ_2 determine the simulation steps. If we do not consider the first slice, the execution time to simulate a period $\Gamma_1 + \Gamma_2$ of the actual system is $2 * \Gamma_2$. Therefore, the rate between the simulation speed and the actual system execution is:

$$\frac{\Gamma_1 + \Gamma_2}{2 * \Gamma_2} = \frac{1}{2}(1 + \frac{\Gamma_1}{\Gamma_2})$$

As $\Gamma_1 \leq \Gamma_2$, we also obtain:

$$\frac{1}{2} \leq \frac{1}{2}(1 + \frac{\Gamma_1}{\Gamma_2}) \leq 1$$

In the worst-case, parallel simulation is twice slower than the actual distributed computation.

3.4 Conclusion

In a distributed computation with known minimal communication delays between processes, static lookahead steps can be computed leading to a parallel execution at worst twice slower than the actual system. Moreover, if the two processes which communicate the most rapidly (i.e. P_1 and P_2) satisfy $\Gamma_1 = \Gamma_2$, then the parallelism is optimal.

Moreover, message frequencies are not involved in this computation, as the scheduling of the simulation step intervals described in Proposition 1 solely relies upon the Γ_i attributes, and thus on message delays. Therefore, any sending behavior is allowed.

In the following section, we analyze how knowledge about message frequencies allow to decrease the number of synchronization barriers during a parallel simulation.

4 Parallel Simulation Using Frequencies

4.1 Principle

We consider a system where all communications are periodic. Each communication link is used at a fixed frequency. Actually, communication can happen less often than the fixed frequency, by missing some slots. However, the delay between two sendings must always be a multiple of the frequency.

A simulation run is split into slices. Our goal is to achieve an optimal degree of parallelism for the simulation, that is to find a simulation where each step has the same duration for all subsystems. However, consecutive slices do not have to be of the same duration. In doing so, time loss only occurs because of the duration of a subsystem simulation step (upon which the simulation scheduler has no influence) and, for a small part, because of the required synchronization at the end of each step.

To ensure the separability requirement, we must choose a duration slice so that no message is both sent and received in the same slice. A solution is to choose a slice duration such that the global system advances strictly until the next reception. All processes advance in parallel by this duration. Once each process has reached this same date, a new slice, which includes the effective reception, is done. Thus, the message has been sent in a previous slice and received in a different slice.

The choice of the duration is improved by using the transmission delay: when we are seeking the next reception, transmission delay can be used to assure that the message was not sent in the current slice but in a previous slice; if so, it does not induce a frontier and can be ignored.

If all communication frequencies are fixed and known, we can a priori determine the duration of each slice, yielding a sequence of slices. Except for a fixed prefix of slices, this sequence is *periodic*: it cycles after a duration which is the *least common multiple* of the communication periods. For instance, if a system has three communication links with periods of 5 s, 8 s and 12 s, we get a sequence of 40 slices whose cumulated duration is 120 s. After that duration, the sequence of slices starts over again.

Proposition 2. *If all communication frequencies are fixed, there exists a periodic sequence of slices which ensures separability. The total duration of this sequence is the least common multiple of the communication periods.*

Let us consider a cut at any large enough date t. This date t must be such that a message has been sent and received on all links, that is: $t \geq \max_{l \in \mathcal{L}}(l.phase + l.delay)$. At date t+lcm of the periods, every process has made an integer number of slices, and is in the same configuration (with regard to communication) as at date t. So the whole system is in the same configuration.

4.2 Jitter

Let us note δ the reception jitter. If we consider a communication link having period T, delay Δ, jitter δ and first emission date (phase) φ, the n-th message is received at a date included in $[n * T + \varphi + \Delta - \delta, n * T + \varphi + \Delta + \delta]$.

Jitter introduces two problems:

- an early message could be received before the frontier and invalidate the separability criterion. To avoid this, the frontier is set at the earliest date, δ before the date given by the frequency;
- a message can be ignored if we are sure that it was sent in a previous slice. As the exact sent date is unknown, we choose the latest date, δ after the date given by the frequency.

To ensure that, on a given link, a send event is never considered to happen after its corresponding receive event, the jitter must be less than half the transmission delay Δ.

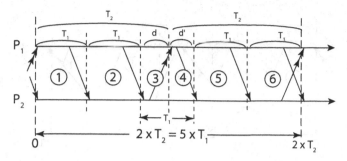

Fig. 6. Frequency Use, Base Case

4.3   Algorithm

For a link l, we consider all the parameters introduced in the model: its transmission delay Δ, its period T, its jitter δ and its phase φ.

At time t, the date of the next message which will be received on link l is at least[5]:

$$\text{nextDate}(t, l) \triangleq (t + l.T - l.\Delta - l.\varphi) \div l.T * l.T + l.\Delta + l.\varphi - l.\delta$$

At time t, the link l causes the next frontier if:

$$\text{nextDate}(t, l) = \min_{l' \in \mathcal{L}} \text{nextDate}(t, l')$$

but this message can be ignored if we know that it comes from a previous slice, that is:

$$\text{nextDate}(t, l) - l.\Delta + 2 * l.\delta \geq \text{previous frontier}$$

If the message is not ignored, $\text{nextDate}(t, l)$ is the new frontier and a slice of duration $\text{nextDate}(t, l) - \text{previous frontier}$ is run.

4.4   Example

We consider a system with two subsystems and two links. The periods are such that $T_2 = \frac{5}{2}T_1$. The least common multiple is $5T_1$ and we generate a sequence of slices whose cumulated duration is $5T_1$. Three cases are considered, based on different transmission delays. For the sake of simplicty, we have chosen a common start date of 0 where the two subsystems start with the reception of a message on their links.

- If the delays are small enough (Figure 6), all messages induce a frontier and the sequence is $(T_1, T_1, \frac{1}{2}T_1, \frac{1}{2}T_1, T_1, T_1)^*$.
- If the delay of a double-arrow message (period T_2) is greater than $\frac{1}{2}T_1$ (Figure 7), the double-arrow message which is received at date $\frac{5}{2}T_1$ has necessarily been sent in the previous slice. It can be ignored and the sequence is $(T_1, T_1, T_1, T_1, T_1)^*$
- if the delay of a single-arrow message (period T_1) is greater than $\frac{1}{2}T_1$ (Figure 8), the third single-arrow message has necessarily been sent in slice 3 and can be ignored. The sequence is $(T_1, T_1, \frac{1}{2}T_1, \frac{3}{2}T_1, T_1, T_1)^*$.

---

[5] The operator $\div$ is the integer division.

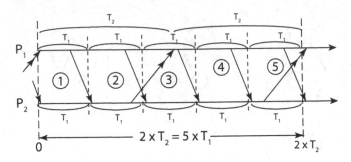

Fig. 7. Frequency Use: a T_2 Message Is Ignored

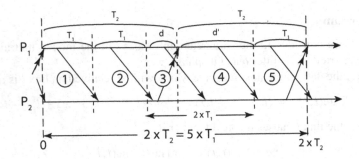

Fig. 8. Frequency Use: a T_1 Message Is Ignored

5   Conclusion

We have proposed a parallel execution pattern for simulating distributed computations. This approach avoids complex and dynamic synchronization of simulators (including dynamic look-ahead computation, rollback or dead-reckoning) and allows an a priori evaluation of simulation step intervals of processes. Moreover, this static schedule provides a simple means to assess the overhead and the degree of parallelism of the simulation. In this respect, the implementation of a simulation engine is currently being developped in the field of space systems and will illustrate the theoretical results of our study. However, the constraints to cope with the message frequencies can be too rigid. We are currently extending our parallel simulation model to introduce more flexibility and enable dynamic commutation of frequencies:

- upon exceptional asynchronous events (failures, reconfiguration of the system for instance);
- to handle clock drifts, which may result in a discernible change in the links' phase or frequency, over time.

These commutations divide the global simulation into long periods during which step intervals are statically known. However, a commutation occurrence leads to reevaluate step intervals according to the updated, new or disappeared links and their parameter values.

Our approach must also be confronted with simulations involving testbeds and consequently real-time constraints. The static features of our strategy seems a propitious property insofar as simulated step intervals are perfectly known.

Acknowlegments. We thank Bernard Delatte and Pierre Keller from CNES, and Fernand Quartier from the Spacebel company who brought us their expertise in the field of the simulation of spacial embedded systems, and whose contributions have greatly helped us to improve and complete this work.

References

1. Fujimoto, R.M.: Time management in the High Level Architecture. Simulation 171(6), 377–420 (1998)
2. Jefferson, D.R.: Virtual time. ACM Trans. Program. Lang. Syst. 7(3), 404–425 (1985)
3. Mattern, F.: Efficient Algorithms for Distributed Snapshots and Global Virtual Time Approximation. Journal of Parallel and Distributed Computing 18(4), 423–434 (1993)
4. Bauer, D., Yaun, G., Carothers, C.D., Yuksel, M., Kalyanaraman, S.: Seven-O'Clock: A New Distributed GVT Algorithm Using Network Atomic Operations. In: PADS 2005: Proc. of the 19th Workshop on Principles of Advanced and Distributed Simulation, pp. 39–48. IEEE Computer Society Press, Los Alamitos (2005)
5. Open HLA: Sourceforge.net http://sourceforge.net/projects/ohla
6. CERTI: Département Traitement de l'Information et Modélisation. ONERA (Office National d'Études et de Recherches Aérospatiales) http://savannah.nongnu.org/projects/certi/
7. RTI: NetLab : Networking & Simulation Lab. George Mason University http://netlab.gmu.edu/rti/#RTI
8. Mauve, M., Vogel, J., Hilt, V., Effelsberg, W.: Local-lag and Timewarp: Providing Consistency for Replicated Continuous Applications. IEEE Transactions on Multimedia 6(1), 47–57 (2004)
9. Fujimoto, R.M.: Exploiting Temporal Uncertainty in Parallel and Distributed Simulations. In: PADS 1999: Proc. of the 13th Workshop on Parallel and distributed simulation, pp. 46–53. IEEE Computer Society Press, Los Alamitos (1999)
10. Awerbuch, B.: Complexity of Network Synchronization. Journal of the ACM 32(4), 804–823 (1985)
11. Keller, P.: Séparabilité. Enveloppe Solau number 273002, INPI (October 2006)
12. Garg, V.K.: Principles of Distributed Systems. Kluwer Academic Publishers, Dordrecht (1996)
13. Garg, V.K.: Elements of Distributed Computing. John Wiley & Sons, Inc, Chichester (2002)
14. Lamport, L.: Time, Clocks and the Ordering of Events in a Distributed System. Communications of the ACM 21(7), 558–565 (1978)
15. Raynal, M.: Synchronisation et état global dans les systèmes répartis. Collection Direction Études-Recherches EDF. Edition Eyrolles (1992)

Small-World Networks:
From Theoretical Bounds to Practical Systems

François Bonnet, Anne-Marie Kermarrec, and Michel Raynal

IRISA, Campus de Beaulieu, 35042 Rennes Cedex, France

Abstract. In small-world networks, each peer is connected to its closest neighbors in the network topology, as well as to additional long-range contact(s), also called shortcut(s). In 2000, Kleinberg provided asymptotic lower bounds on routing performances and showed that greedy routing in an n-peer small-world network performs in $\Omega(n^{\frac{1}{3}})$ steps when the distance to shortcuts is chosen uniformly at random, and in $\Theta(\log^2 n)$ when the distance to shortcuts is chosen according to a harmonic distribution in a d-dimensional mesh. Yet, we observe through experimental results that peer to peer gossip-based protocols achieving small-world topologies where shortcuts are randomly chosen, perform reasonably well in practice.

Kleinberg results are relevant for extremely large systems while systems considered in practice are usually of smaller size (they are typically made up of less than one million of peers). This paper explores the impact of Kleinberg results in the context of practical systems and small-world networks. More precisely, based on the observation that, despite the fact that the routing complexity of gossip-based small-world overlay networks is not polylogarithmic (as proved by Kleinberg), this type of networks ultimately provide reasonable results in practice. This leads us to think that the asymptotic big $O()$ complexity alone might not always be sufficient to assess the practicality of a system whose size is typically smaller that what the one theory targets. The paper consequently proposes a refined routing complexity measure for small-world networks (namely, a recurrence formula that can be easily computed). Yet, given that Kleinberg proved that the distribution of shortcuts has a strong impact on the routing complexity (when extremely large networks are considered), arises the question of leveraging this result to improve upon current gossip-based protocols. We show that gossip-based protocols (designed for less than one million of peers) can benefit from a good approximation of Kleinberg-like small-world topologies (designed for extremely large networks). Along, are presented simulation results that demonstrate the relevance of the proposed approach.

1 Introduction

Distributed systems have experienced a dramatic scale shift over the past decade. Peer to peer (P2P) overlay networks have been at the center of distributed systems research both in the theoretical and practical communities, often in a fully de-correlated manner though. The research yields rather different expectations whether theory or practice is considered. On one hand, practical implementations target effectiveness for the most frequent cases, potentially at the price of lack of theoretical "worst-case" guarantees.

E. Tovar, P. Tsigas, and H. Fouchal (Eds.): OPODIS 2007, LNCS 4878, pp. 372–385, 2007.

On the other hand, theoretical analysis provides asymptotic bounds for extremely large systems, without always being used to design solutions viable in practice. Routing is one of the main issues encountered in these systems. Focusing on the cost of routing in 2-dimensional torus topologies, this paper is an attempt to (i) consider both theory and practice in the context of small-world overlay networks, where each peer is connected to its closest neighbors in the topology and additional long-range contact(s) (shortcut(s)), and (ii) leverage both areas to provide provably-efficient systems. Its main contributions are the following.

- Asymptotic bounds are relevant for extremely large systems. Yet, systems considered in practice are typically smaller, usually under a million. Considering such practical systems and a greedy routing strategy, the paper first confronts asymptotic bound results with the efficiency achieved using practical epidemic (also called gossip-based) protocols. We observe through simulations that the expected gap in the routing performance between the two approaches to select shortcuts is not entirely reflected in such practical systems. Based on this observation, we argue that the asymptotic complexity analysis alone is not sufficient to assess the practicality of a small-world topology. The paper refines consequently this analysis and characterizes the cost of routing, in terms of the average number of hops in both the grid and uniform topologies. This cost is expressed by a recurrence formula that can easily be computed[1].
- According to the previous results, the paper provides a fresh look at epidemic-based overlay networks and argue that they can achieve small-world topologies. We investigate the improvement of epidemic-based small-world networks to fully leverage Kleinberg's results in practical settings[2]. More specifically, we provide the design and preliminary results of a gossip-based protocol, biasing the peer sampling component used to create shortcuts, so that it provides a good approximation of Kleinberg's harmonic distribution.

The table below summarizes methods to analyze algorithms/systems. This paper is mainly concerned with "Recurrence Formula" and "Simulations".

Theory	$O(\ )$ Formula	Describe asymptotic behaviors for all pb instances
	Recurrence Formula	
Experiments	Simulations	Give exact results for each pb instance
	Real Experiments	

Small-World Networks and Kleinberg's Result. Small-world networks have been introduced as an analytical way of understanding and exploiting the *six degrees of*

---

[1] As shown in the paper, the number of hops provided by the formula and the number of hops provided by simulation experiments are practically the same. The advantage (with respect to a simulation) of having a recurrence formula lies in its generality, the fact that it can easily be computed, and the fact that computing a formula is much more efficient than running a simulation. (Finding a corresponding closed form formula remains an open problem.)

[2] "Practical setting" means here "a network with no more than one million of nodes". So, we are mainly interested in distributions suited to "small" grids/topologies when we adopt a "big $O(\ )$ point of view".

separation stating that two random individuals are separated by small chains of acquaintances [13]. When applied to computing networks, this can be achieved by each node in a mesh, knowing its closest neighbors and having additional shortcuts in the graph. While Watts and Strogatz [18] considered shortcuts as picked up uniformly at random, Kleinberg refined this result, demonstrating that meshes augmented with shortcuts provide a polylogarithmic routing and navigation under a greedy routing protocol, as long as the distances from the peers to their shortcuts follow a specific distribution (d-harmonic) [11,12]. One of the main results of Kleinberg's work is the determination of the magnitude order of the routing complexity in such networks (this model is further detailed in Section 2). This result has been of the utmost importance in the community, leading to a full range of works improving upon the routing complexity based on an increase knowledge of the system or a slightly different greedy algorithm (e.g., [1,8,14]). Yet, those results consider extremely large system sizes.

Epidemic-Based Overlay Networks. Epidemic-based (or gossip-based) protocols were first introduced to reliably disseminate data in large-scale networks [2,4]. In the practical world, epidemic-based protocols have received an increasing attention as a scalable and reliable solution to build and maintain P2P overlay networks of arbitrary structure [9,10]. Their convergence properties, reliability and simplicity make them however attractive for much more than data dissemination [6]. More specifically, they have been applied in a wide variety of settings and are now turned into a generic tool to build and maintain large-scale overlay networks. It turns out that depending on the peer locally chosen for the interaction and the information exchanged, gossip-based protocols can be used to build overlay networks ranging from fully random-like unstructured networks to fully (DHT-like) structured networks (e.g., [7]). In this paper, we take a fresh look at overlay networks based on epidemic protocols and consider them with respect to small-world networks.

Epidemic protocols may be used to construct P2P overlay networks achieving graph properties very close to those of random graphs [5,10,15]. Typically, a gossip-based peer sampling service provides each peer with a set of long range contacts in a large-scale overlay network [10]. Resulting graphs are extremely robust and remain connected even in the presence of a large number of failures. In the context of this paper, we consider such a peer sampling service to be a way to implement randomly chosen shortcuts of small-world networks. Gossip-based protocols have also been used to create overlays optimized with respect to application-specific metric (e.g., clustering peers according to a proximity metric). It is actually relatively straightforward to use such gossip-based clustering protocols [16,17] to choose the local neighbors in a small-world network.

Motivation. The paper focuses on systems provided with *(i)* an underlying peer sampling gossip-based protocol that provides each peer with a random sample of the system (i.e., each peer is provided with shortcuts randomly chosen), and *(ii)* a gossip-based clustering protocol that provides each peer with a set of close neighbors (according to the considered underlying topology). Such a combination creates therefore a small-world topology according to the Watts and Strogatz model [18].

While, as proved by Kleinberg [12], the routing expectation (expected number of hops) is $\Omega(n^{\frac{1}{3}})$ (n being the total number of peers), it appears that performance results

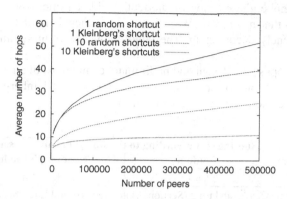

Fig. 1. Choice of shortcuts: random choice vs Kleinberg's model choice

in practical settings turn out to be reasonable and follow the exponential convergence time of epidemic-based protocols, thus qualifying such networks for efficient routing. On another side, should the peer sampling service provide a sample following the distribution as defined in the Kleinberg model [12], the routing cost should greatly improve to $\Theta(\log^2 n)$.

The previous observations constitute the starting point of our work. Simulating a system whose size ranges from 5000 to 500, 000 peers, using six close neighbors and 1 or 10 shortcut(s) in a uniform topology, we first compared the random selection of shortcuts against Kleinberg's selection, and computed the average number of hops between any pair of peers in the system (this is depicted on the Fig. 1). It appears that (as expected) the average number of hops between two peers is significantly improved when using the latter choice. The discrepancy increases with the size of the system and the number of shortcuts. These results show however that a random selection of neighbors keeps the average number of hops within reasonable bounds. This gives the motivation of our work, namely, while Kleinberg results are obviously relevant for extremely large systems, to the best of our knowledge, no one looked at the impact of those results on smaller size systems such as the ones encountered in practiced. In this paper, we show that the impact is not as striking as expected between random and Kleinberg-like shortcuts but important enough so that the practical systems should try to benefit from small-world network theory.

Contribution. Kleinberg's results were obtained on a d-dimensional grid topology. As such a topology is not always encountered in practice, we consider in this paper a topology where peers are randomly and uniformly distributed. Accordingly, the paper refers to the *uniform topology*.

Based on the observed results, we argue that relying on the magnitude order of the complexity analysis is not sufficient to draw conclusions on the practicality of an approach. Using random shortcuts, the first contribution provides a refinement of the analysis of the routing cost in the uniform topology. This analysis provides us with a way to compute the expected routing performance in small-world networks. Simulations results demonstrate the good accuracy of the number of hops provided by the proposed analysis. As Kleinberg's selection of shortcuts yields an improved routing, we apply our approach to that model too. We have also conducted simulations, the results of which are extremely encouraging. The table below the right summarizes the paper contributions.

Finally, we propose the design and preliminary evaluations of a gossip-based protocol leveraging the theory to achieve an approximation of a Kleinberg-like small-world network. More developments can be found in [3].

| Topology | Routing cost according to the way shortcuts are selected | |
	Random	Kleinberg's model
Grid	$\Omega(n^{\frac{1}{3}})$	$\Theta(\log^2 n)$
Uniform	$\Omega(n^{\frac{1}{3}})$ and Eq 2 (Section 3.1)	$\Theta(\log^2 n)$ and Eq 5 (Section 3.2)

2   System Model and Simulation Setup

This section describes the system models considered in the paper. Dealing with failures is out of the scope of this paper. Network dynamic is also left out for this study and left for future work (robustness in face of high dynamics is one of the main strengths of epidemic-based protocols and we are confident that resulting protocols should sustain high dynamic).

In this paper, we consider a uniform topology. We also conducted the analysis in the context of the Grid topology; details can be found in [3]. The uniform topology considered is based on a 2-dimensional torus. In the following, a peer A is denoted by its name or its coordinates in the corresponding topology. The positions of the n peers are chosen uniformly at random in a 2-dimensional torus $[0 : 1] \times [0 : 1]$. More precisely, the pair of coordinates (A_x, A_y) associated with a peer A are chosen from the set $[0 : 1]$ following a uniform random distribution. In this topology, the distance between two peers located at (i_1, j_1) and (i_2, j_2) is the classical Euclidean distance, i.e.,

$$d_e = \sqrt{\min(|i_2 - i_1|, 1 - |i_2 - i_1|)^2 + \min(|j_2 - j_1|, 1 - |j_2 - j_1|)^2}.$$

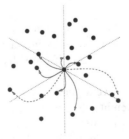

Fig. 2. Uniform topology ($n = \ell^2 = 25$)

2.1 Neighbor Selection

In a small-world network, each peer, fully characterized by its location in the torus, maintains a *view* of the system. That view is made up of two sets of neighbors: a set of *local neighbors* (or *local contacts*), which are close neighbors in the graph and a set of long-range neighbors, called *shortcuts*, chosen according to a selection distribution.

We consider a *greedy routing* algorithm to navigate a small-world network. This means that, at each hop, a message is routed to a peer, the position of which is *closer* to the destination thus ensuring that the distance to the destination always decreases as the routing process progresses. At each routing peer, the neighbors from these two sets are considered to select the peer to which a message has to be routed.

Local Contact Selection. To allow for a greedy routing, each peer must know at least six of its closest neighbors, one in each wedge of the space as shown in the figure above. (If a node does not have a contact belonging to one of these wedges, it can easily been shown that the greedy routing may fail [19] [3].) Partitioning evenly the space around each peer into 60° wedges, and assigning a local contact belonging to each of these wedges ensures that the greedy routing can be implemented using only local contacts.

Shortcut Selection. Shortcuts are added to the view of each peer to speed up the routing process, providing them with candidates to perform "large" routing steps. The complexity achieved by a greedy routing is highly sensitive to the way such shortcuts are chosen. We consider two selection algorithms in this paper, providing each peer with q shortcuts. In the figure above, we have $q = 2$, and the two shortcuts are depicted with dashed lines.

- **Random selection:** As introduced in the Watts and Strogatz model [18] and implemented using the peer sampling protocol in the context of epidemic-based algorithms, the selection is done uniformly at random. Each peer A is provided with q shortcuts by choosing q peers uniformly at random from the set of all the peers of the network that are not local contacts of A.
- **Kleinberg's selection:** As proposed in [12], shortcuts can be added according to a non-uniform distribution. Selecting shortcuts this way has proven to significantly reduce the cost of a greedy routing, achieving polylogarithmic complexity. In Kleinberg's model, a peer A selects a peer B as a shortcut with a probability proportional to the value $\delta(B) = \frac{1}{d(A,B)^2}$ ($d()$ denotes the Euclidean distance). More precisely, a peer B is chosen by a peer A with probability $\frac{\delta(B)}{\sum_{B' \in S} \delta(B')}$ where S denotes the set of all the peers that are not a local contact of A. In the following, this selection mode will be referred as *Kleinberg's selection*.

2.2 Simulation Setup

Due to page limitation, the simulation setup is not described in detail. The results are illustrated by comparing analytical results against simulation results obtained using the

---

[3] In practice, there is no need of this condition if the algorithm takes enough local contacts. It is possible to show that the probability of these special cases is then close to 0.

simulator PeerSim [20]. This simulator allows us to choose the topology, the number of nodes, the number of local contacts p, and the number of shortcuts q. For each generated network, a high number (500, 000 if not specified otherwise) of pairs of peers have been randomly selected to evaluate the cost of the routing. The simulator also implements the gossip-based protocols evaluated in Section 4.

3   Routing Analysis in Small-World Overlay Networks

3.1   Small-Worlds with Randomly Selected Shortcuts

As already noticed, studying the complexity of greedy routing in a grid topology in [12], Kleinberg proved that a random selection of shortcuts in a small-world network gives rise to a routing cost with an expected number of hops that is at least $\alpha n^{\frac{1}{3}}$, where n denotes the number of peers and α is a coefficient -not explicitly determined- that is independent of n.

The good performance achieved in small-world networks by epidemic protocols (and more specifically by the random selection of shortcuts achieved by peer sampling protocols), led us to think that knowing the value of α is actually interesting. The idea here is that knowing more precisely that value enables us to analyze efficient implementations, and allows consequently for a better understanding of why gossip-based protocols are practically efficient. Although Kleinberg's study is only on the grid topology, we are confident that the same kind of results can be extended to the uniform topology. We checked this experimentally [3] and consider only the uniform topology in this paper.

In a uniform topology, distances are real numbers in $[0, \frac{\sqrt{2}}{2}]$ (let us recall that the nodes are on a $[0 : 1] \times [0 : 1]$ torus). Let us define $f(d)$, a function that gives the average number of routing hops between any two peers that are at distance d. p denotes the number of local contacts and q denotes the number of (randomly chosen) shortcuts. Local contacts are defined from a radius; let us estimate the corresponding radius r_p. As the torus $[0 : 1] \times [0 : 1]$ represents an area of 1 unit, the average surface is $\frac{p}{n}$ when considering p peers. If a disk is used to approximate that area, its radius is $r_p = \sqrt{\frac{p}{n\pi}}$.

$d_q(i)$ denotes the density of probability that the best shortcut is at distance i of the destination. The function $d_1()$ is as follows (details can be found in [3]):

$$0 \leq i \leq \tfrac{1}{2} : \quad d_1(i) = 2\pi i,$$
$$\tfrac{1}{2} < i \leq \tfrac{\sqrt{2}}{2} : d_1(i) = -2\pi i + 8i \arcsin\left(\tfrac{1}{2i}\right).$$

The other functions $d_q()$ can be computed recursively from $d_1()$ (the derivative symbol dk is omitted in order not to overload the formulas):

$$d_q(i) = d_{q-1}(i)\left(1 - \int_{k=0}^{i} d_1(k)\right) + \left(1 - \int_{k=0}^{i} d_{q-1}(k)\right) d_1(i). \tag{1}$$

Taking into account these modifications, we obtain the following recurrence formula for the uniform topology:

$$0 < d \leq r_p : \qquad f(d) = 1,$$

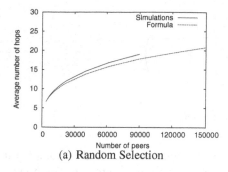

(a) Random Selection

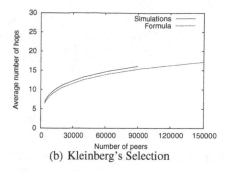

(b) Kleinberg's Selection

$$\forall d > r_p : \qquad f(d) = 1 + \left(\int_{i=0}^{d-r_p} d_q(i) f(i) \right) + \left(1 - \int_{i=0}^{d-r_p} d_q(i) \right) f(d - r_p). \quad (2)$$

Figure 3(a) compares simulations wrt the formula for networks of size ranging from $4,000$ up to one million. Each peer knows $p = 20$ local contacts and $q = 2$ random shortcuts are chosen. We observe a slight discrepancy between our formula and the simulation results. This comes from the fact we always consider that a local contact is located on the circle of radius r_p, and consequently the distance to the destination is reduced by r_p each time a local contact is used. In a real setting, as a local contact may be within the disk of radius r_p, the gain may be smaller (it would actually be possible to take this fact into account at the price of a much more complicated formula).

3.2 Small-Worlds with Shortcuts According to Kleinberg's Distribution

In this section, we analyze the performance of routing algorithms based on Kleinberg's shortcut selection

Local Contacts Analysis. The effect of the p local contacts on the routing performance is the same, be the q shortcuts selected randomly or according to Kleinberg's distribution. So, in our analysis, the study of locals contacts remains the same, namely, there is an estimated radius $r_p = \sqrt{\frac{p}{n\pi}}$ which corresponds to the area approximately covered by the local contacts.

Distribution of Shortcut Locations. Since the shortcuts are no longer chosen following the uniform distribution, that distribution becomes more complex. As described in Section 2, a shortcut B is selected by a peer A following a probability proportional to the inverse of the square of the distance between A and B. We already know the distribution of the distance between two peers, that is expressed by the function $d_1()$. We consequently obtain the density of probability $dist()$ that the shortcut B is at distance i from A from the following formula (defined only for $i > r_p$ since shortcuts can not be taken amongst local contacts);

$$\forall r_p < i \le \frac{\sqrt{2}}{2} : \qquad dist(i) = \frac{\frac{d_1(i)}{i^2}}{\int_{k=r_p}^{\frac{\sqrt{2}}{2}} \frac{d_1(k)}{k^2}}. \quad (3)$$

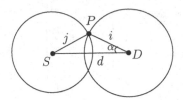

Fig. 3. Best shortcut

Expected Number of Hops. As in the previous analysis, we need to compute the probability for a peer to use one of its shortcuts in the routing process. The previous recurrence formulas remain correct if the function $d()$ is appropriately adapted. Let us start with only one shortcut ($q = 1$). We are looking for the density of probability $d_1'()$ that the shortcut is at distance i to the destination.

Figure 3 depicts the following situation: S is the source node, D the destination, and P the shortcut; d, i, and j denotes the distances SD, DP, and SP, respectively. From a geometrical analysis we conclude that $j = \sqrt{d^2 + i^2 - 2di\cos(\alpha)}$. Summing all the possible positions of P over the circle gives:

$$d_1'(d, i) = i \int_{\alpha=0}^{2\pi} \frac{dist\left(\sqrt{d^2 + i^2 - 2di\cos(\alpha)}\right)}{2\pi\sqrt{d^2 + i^2 - 2di\cos(\alpha)}}.$$

Let us notice that the function $d_1'()$ depends not only on i, but also on a second parameter measuring the Euclidean distance d between the source and the destination. More generally, the function $d_q'()$, for more shortcuts $q > 1$, can be computed from the value of $d_1'()$. We then obtain the following value:

$$d_q'(d, i) = d_{q-1}'(d, i) * \left(1 - \int_{k=0}^{i} d_1'(d, k)\right) + \left(1 - \int_{k=0}^{i} d_{q-1}'(d, k)\right) d_1(d, i). \quad (4)$$

Finally, similarly to Equation 2 the routing cost can be computed with the following recurrence:

$$\forall d > r_p: \qquad f(d) = 1 + \left(\int_{i=0}^{d-r_p} d_q'(d, i) f(i)\right) + \left(1 - \int_{i=0}^{d-r_p} d_q'(d, i)\right) f(d - r_p). \quad (5)$$

Figure 3(b) compares simulations wrt the formula for networks of size ranging from $4,000$ up to $150,000$. Each peer knows $p = 20$ local contacts and $q = 2$ Kleinberg's shortcuts are chosen. We observe again a slight discrepancy between our formula and the simulation results. This come from the same fact as described for the Figure 3(a), namely, the use of a local contact always reduces the distance to the destination by the distance r_p.

Figure 4 shows the impact of the number of shortcuts on the average number of hops in a $200,000$ peer system and compares the random shortcut selection against the Kleinberg's one. As expected, the routing performance improves with the number of shortcuts regardless of the shortcuts selection. However, we observe that the routing

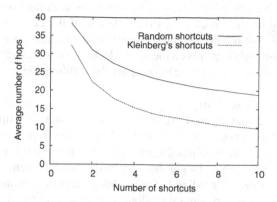

Fig. 4. Impact of the number of shortcuts on the routing performance in a 200,000 peer system

performance decreases faster with Kleinberg's selection: with one shortcut only, Kleinberg's selection improves the number of hops of 16% with one shortcuts and 48% with 10 shortcuts. Although the average number of hops is less than 20 in a 200,000 peer system using randomly selected shortcuts, and therefore qualify for a practical system, there is still room for improvement by leveraging the Kleinberg's selection method in practice.

4   Kleinberg-Like Epidemic-Based Small-World Networks

Gossip-based protocols have been recognized as a sensible and efficient paradigm for building peer to peer overlay networks of arbitrary structure. Current gossip-based protocols can achieve already small-world topologies with random shortcuts. This section presents the design of a gossip-based protocol implementing a small-world overlay network where shortcuts are selected according to an approximation of Kleinberg's selection.

A Generic Gossip-Based Protocol. Let us consider a system made up of n peers uniquely defined by their coordinates[4]. Each peer maintains a set of neighbors (IP address of other peers in the system) called its *view*, reflecting its knowledge of the membership of the system[5]. This creates a connection graph, where an edge between two peers A and B means that each of them belongs to the view of the other one. Each peer executes an active thread and a passive thread. The size of a view is c (c being a parameter of the system). Periodically each peer A runs the active thread: *(i)* it selects from its view a peer B to gossip with, (ii) sends a message to B containing a subset of its view, and *(iii)* merges its own view with the information received from B, truncating its view back to c. The passive thread on A *(i)* sends to B a subset of its view upon receiving

---

[4] Peers could join and leave the system dynamically although we do not consider dynamics in our experiments.

[5] As, in this paper, we consider the use of gossip-protocols for overlay maintenance only, the state of a peer is fully represented by its view.

a gossip message from B and *(ii)* merges its own view with the information received from B, truncating its view back to c. (Many details of the protocol are omitted due to space limitations, but full details can be found in [10].) It turns out that the resulting connection graph strongly depends on the peer selection, the state exchanged during the gossip and the processing of the state to compute the resulting view.

Local Contact Selection. Using the generic protocol described above, a clustering gossip-based protocol may be used to create the local contacts in a small-world. Let us consider the uniform topology case. As shown in Figure 2, each peer needs to maintain a peer in each of the six wedges attached to each peer (recall that each wedge covers $60°$). In such a context, a gossip-based algorithm may easily be implemented as follows. *Peer selection*: the closest peer, according to the Euclidean distance, in one of the wedge of the circle, is chosen to gossip with (at random if several candidates). *State exchanged*: in this preliminary version, the whole views are exchanged. *State processing*: the closest peers, according to the Euclidean distance and optimizing along all directions, are kept. (In a dynamic system, such a clustering protocol might be run in parallel with a random peer sampling protocol.)

Random Shortcuts. It has been shown in [10] that such a gossip-based protocol can be used to provide a random sample to each peer. (Running the Cyclon [15] protocol for example results in a graph, the properties of which are close to those of random graphs with respect to the average path length, clustering coefficient and diameter.) Therefore, this gossip-based protocol can be run together with the clustering protocol mentioned above in a straightforward manner, thereby implementing the random shortcuts of a small-world random graph. For the purpose of comparison, we use the Cyclon protocol in our simulations of gossip-based random small-world overlays (Figure 5).

Creating Kleinberg's Shortcuts. In order to leverage the potential of the d-harmonic distribution as defined in [11], we bias the peer sampling service in order to approximate the distribution advocated by Kleinberg. To that end, we propose to change the nature of the state exchanged between peers upon gossip, in order to match as closely as possible this distribution. The algorithm on peer A is implemented as follows. *Peer selection*: a peer B is chosen uniformly at random from A's view (of size c). *State exchanged*: $\frac{c}{2}$ peers are chosen in A's view to reflect the Kleinberg's distribution. More specifically, a peer A keeps a peer C from its view with a probability proportional to $\delta(C)$ (as defined in 2.1, i.e., $\delta(C) = \frac{1}{d(A,C)^2}$ where d is the distance separating A and C). The remaining $\frac{c}{2}$ peers are sent to B during the gossip operation. This enables to minimize the loss of information during the gossip operation. *State processing*: the view is replaced by the $\frac{c}{2}$ non chosen entries from the view, sent over during the gossip operation.

We illustrate this protocol through an example. Both Cyclon and the proposed protocol follow the same pattern. They differ only in the way a peer selects the set of peers it sends to another peer during a round (steps denoted (2) and (3) in the following). While these peers are randomly selected in Cyclon, they are selected according to their distance in the proposed protocol.

The behavior of each protocol is explained through the following example. Let A and B be two peers whose views (of size $c = 6$) are $v_A = \{B, C, D, E, F, G\}$ and $v_B = \{U, V, W, X, Y, Z\}$, respectively.

A round in the random peer sampling protocol

1 A randomly selects a peer from its view (say B).
2 A randomly selects $\frac{c}{2} - 1$ other peers from its view, say C and E, and sends to B the set $A\_to\_B = \{A, C, E\}$.
3 When B receives the set A_to_B from A, it randomly selects $\frac{c}{2}$ peers from it view (e.g., the set $B\_to\_A = \{U, W, Z\}$), and sends it to A. It executes $v_B \leftarrow (v_B \setminus B\_to\_A) \cup A\_to\_B$ to obtain its new view. So, the view of B is now $v_B = \{A, V, C, X, Y, E\}$.
4 Finally, when A receives the set B_to_A from B, it executes $v_A \leftarrow (v_A \setminus (\{B\} \cup A\_to\_B)) \cup B\_to\_A$ to obtain its new view, that becomes $v_A = \{U, W, D, Z, F, G\}$.

A round in the Kleinberg-like sampling protocol

1 A randomly selects a peer from its view (say B).
2 Among the other peers in A's view ($v'_A = v_A \setminus \{B\} = \{C, D, E, F, G\}$), A chooses $\frac{c}{2}$ peers to be kept in its view and sends the other peers to B. The peer selection is done according to Kleinberg's distribution. A computes the value $\frac{1}{d(A,x)^2}$ for each peer $x \in v'_A$. Then A keeps a peer in its view according to a probability proportional to the previous value. More precisely, a peer x is chosen with probability

$$\frac{\frac{1}{d(A,x)^2}}{\sum_{y \in v'_A} \frac{1}{d(A,y)^2}}.$$

For example A keeps the peers $\{D, E, F\}$ and then sends to B the set $A\_to\_B = \{A, C, G\}$.
3 When B received the set A_to_B from A, it keeps $\frac{c}{2}$ peers in its view (according to Kleinberg's distribution), e.g., the set $\{U, V, Z\}$, and sends the remaining peers to A, i.e., the set $B\_to\_A = \{W, X, Y\}$ to A. It finally executes $v_B \leftarrow (v_B \setminus B\_to\_A) \cup A\_to\_B$ to update its view, that becomes $v_B = \{U, V, A, C, G, Z\}$.
4 Finally, when A receives the set B_to_A from B, it executes $v_A \leftarrow (v_A \setminus (\{B\} \cup A\_to\_B)) \cup B\_to\_A$ to update its view, that becomes $v_A = \{W, X, D, E, F, Y\}$.

Figure 5 compares the routing performance in the uniform topology of a gossip-based protocol implementing an approximation of Kleinberg distribution against a gossip-based protocol implementing the random selection (peer sampling service). In addition we compared those simulations with the hypothetical ideal simulation mode [6]. Those preliminary results confirm that gossip-based protocols can be used to achieve in a fully decentralized way a close approximation of Kleinberg-like small-world overlay networks. We are currently investigating a broader exploration of the parameter space.

---

[6] In this mode, all nodes are considered in the simulator to select the shortcuts.

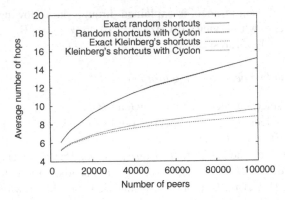

Fig. 5. Ideal versus gossip-based selection of random and Kleinberg shorcuts in small-world over-lay networks

5   Conclusion

This work has been motivated by the observation that, despite theoretical evidence that a random selection of shortcuts in small-world networks is not optimal from a greedy routing point of view, such systems are reasonably efficient in practice (i.e., systems where the number of nodes does not usually go beyond one million). To have a better understanding of this observation, we (i) precisely analyzed the average number of routing hops (required in a greedy routing strategy), both in the grid topology and the uniform topology, and (ii) compared the random selection and Kleinberg's selection of shortcuts. Not surprisingly, this analysis confirms the superiority of Kleinberg's selection, but nonetheless demonstrates that a random selection of shortcuts is not practically irrelevant. Simulation results show that there is an almost perfect match between the results observed in practice and the recurrence formula provided by our analysis. As practical small-world topologies (i.e., when the number of nodes remain "reasonably small") can already be implemented using a two layer gossip-based protocol, we proposed a gossip-based protocol whose peer sampling service is modified to benefit from an approximation of Kleinberg selection of shortcuts, thereby leveraging theory results to improve practical protocols. Further investigation is now needed to refine the biased gossip-based protocol, explore arbitrary topologies, apply such techniques to other routing strategies and consider dynamic settings.

Acknowledgment

We would like to thank Pierre Fraigniaud, Cyrille Gavoile, Rachid Guerraoui and Etienne Rivière for their constructive comments on a draft of this paper.

References

1. Barrière, L., Fraigniaud, P., Kranakis, E., Krizanc, D.: Efficient Routing in Networks with Long Range Contacts. In: Welch, J.L. (ed.) DISC 2001. LNCS, vol. 2180, pp. 270–284. Springer, Heidelberg (2001)

2. Birman, K.P., Hayden, M., Ozkasap, O., Xiao, Z., Budiu, M., Minsky, V.: Bimodal Multicast. ACM Transactions on Computer Systems 17(2), 41–88 (1999)
3. Bonnet, F., Kermarrec, A.-M., Raynal, M.: Small-World Networks: Is there a mismatch between theory and practice. In: Research Report IRISA #1849 (2007)
4. Demers, A.J., Greene, D.H., Hauser, C., Irish, W., Larson, J.: Epidemic Algorithms for Replicated Database Maintenance. In: Proc. 6th ACM Symposium on Principles of Distributed Computing (PODC 1987), pp. 1–12 (1987)
5. Eugster, P.T., Guerraoui, G., Handurukande, B., Kermarrec, A.-M., Kouznetsov, P.: Lightweight Probabilistic Broadcast. ACM TOCS 21(1), 341–374 (2003)
6. Eugster, P.T., Guerraoui, G., Kermarrec, A.-M., Massoulié, L.: Epidemic Information Dissemination in Distributed Systems. IEEE Computer 37(5), 60–67 (2004)
7. Fraigniaud, P., Gauron, P., Latapy, M.: Combining the Use of Clustering and Scale-free Nature of User Exchanges into a Simple and Efficient P2P System. In: Proc. European Conf. on Parallelism (EUROPAR 2005) (2005)
8. Fraigniaud, P., Gavoille, C., Paul, C.: Eclecticism Shrinks even Small Worlds. In: Fraigniaud, P., Gavoille, C., Paul, C. (eds.) Proc. 23th ACM Symposium on Principles of Distributed Computing (PODC 2004), pp. 169–178. ACM Press, New York (2004)
9. Jelasity, M., Babaoglu, O.: T-Man: Gossip-based Overlay Topology Management. In: Proc. Engineering Self-Organising Applications (ESOA 2005) (2005)
10. Jelasity, M., Guerraoui, G., Kermarrec, A.-M., van Steen, M.: The Peer Sampling Service: Experimental Evaluation of Unstructured Gossip-based Implementations. In: Proc. 5th ACM/IFIP/USENIX Int'l Conference on Middleware. Lecture Notes in Computer Science, pp. 79–98. Springer-Verlag, Heidelberg (2004)
11. Kleinberg, J.: Navigation in a Small World. Nature 845(406) (2000)
12. Kleinberg, J.: The Small-World Phenomenon: an Algorithmic Perspective. In: Proc. 32nd ACM Symposium on Theory of Computing, pp. 163–170. ACM Press, New York (2000)
13. Milgram, S.: The Small-World Problem. Psychology Today 61(2), 60–67 (1967)
14. Naor, M., Wieder, U.: Know The Neighbor's Neighbor: Better Routing for Skip-Graphs and Small Worlds. In: IPTPS 2004. LNCS, vol. 3279, pp. 269–277. Springer, Heidelberg (2005)
15. Voulgaris, S., Gavidia, D., van Steen, M.: CYCLON: Inexpensive Membership Management for Unstructured P2P Overlays. Journal of Network and Systems Management 13(2), 197–217 (2005)
16. Voulgaris, S., Rivière, E., Kermarrec, A.-M., van Steen, M.: Sub-2-Sub: Self-Organizing Content-Based Publish and Subscribe for Dynamic and Large Scale Collaborative Networks. In: Proc. 5th Workshop on Peer-to-Peer Systems (2006)
17. Voulgaris, S., van Steen, M.: Epidemic-style Management of Semantic Overlays for Content-Based Searching. In: RSCTC 2000. LNCS (LNAI), vol. 2005, Springer, Heidelberg (2001)
18. Watts, D.J., Strogatz, S.H.: Collective Dynamics of Small-World Networks. Nature 393, 440–442 (1998)
19. Yao, A.C.C.: On Constructing Minimum Spanning Trees in k-dimensional Space and Related Problems. SIAM Journal of Computing 11, 721–736 (1982)
20. http://peersim.sourceforge.net/

The Anonymous Consensus Hierarchy and Naming Problems

Eric Ruppert

York University

Abstract. This paper investigates whether the assumption of unique identifiers is essential for wait-free distributed computing using shared objects of various types. Algorithms where all processes are programmed identically and do not use unique identifiers are called anonymous. We study the anonymous solvability of two key problems, consensus and naming. These problems are used to define measures of a type T's power to solve problems anonymously. These measures provide a significant amount of information about whether anonymous implementations of one type from another are possible. We compare these measures with one another and with the consensus numbers defined by Herlihy [13].

1   Introduction

It is routinely assumed, in the literature on distributed computing, that processes have unique identifiers or, equivalently, that each process can be given a different programme to follow. Such a system is called *eponymous* [21]. In contrast, in an *anonymous* system, processes do not have unique identifiers and are programmed identically. This paper studies the differences between anonymous and eponymous systems in the context of wait-free shared-memory computation.

Unique identifiers are used in many ways. They are incorporated into timestamps to ensure that no two timestamps are identical. A process can announce information in a register that it alone is allowed to write, and that information will never be overwritten by another process. Processes can access a compare&swap object with their own identifiers and determine which process accessed it first. These uses of unique identifiers (and many others) are useful tools in solving problems. But are they truly essential? This paper studies how the answer to this question depends on the types of objects that are being used.

Our primary motivation is foundational: it is crucial to understand the significance of each assumption that is made when defining a model of distributed computing. In the widely-studied model of asynchronous, shared-memory computing where algorithms are designed to tolerate failures, the ubiquitous assumption of unique identifiers has received scant attention. One reason for this is the availability of identifiers in most real systems (although handing out those names can be tricky, particularly in systems where nodes frequently arrive and leave). It is worth knowing whether anonymous algorithms exist, even when identifiers *are* available, because processes accessing shared objects may not want to divulge their identifiers for reasons of privacy. Processes may not want other processes, or even the server housing the shared memory, to know who is

E. Tovar, P. Tsigas, and H. Fouchal (Eds.): OPODIS 2007, LNCS 4878, pp. 386–400, 2007.

performing operations on the shared data, or even whether two operations are being invoked by the same process. If it is possible to implement any required algorithms anonymously, then processes can maintain this kind of privacy. (If a process wishes to keep its identity secret even from the data server, a trusted third party can be used as an anonymizer to forward messages between a process and the server.)

This paper focusses on asynchronous shared-memory systems, where n processes communicate with one another using linearizable shared objects. In keeping with the anonymous theme, we consider only *oblivious* types, where the behaviour of the object in response to an operation cannot depend on the identity of the invoking process. Any number of processes may experience crash failures; algorithms that work correctly in such an environment are called *wait-free* [13].

Herlihy [13] defined the consensus number of type T, denoted $cons(T)$, to be the maximum number of processes that can solve wait-free consensus using objects of type T and registers. If no such maximum exists, then $cons(T) = \infty$. This classifies objects into the *consensus hierarchy*: a type T is at level k of the hierarchy if $cons(T) = k$. The consensus number of a type is an effective measure of its power in eponymous systems for two reasons. Firstly, consensus is *universal*: if $cons(T) \geq k$ then there is a wait-free eponymous implementation (for k processes) of *every* object from objects of type T and registers. Secondly, if $cons(T_1) < cons(T_2)$, then objects of type T_1 (and registers) cannot implement an object of type T_2 for more than $cons(T_1)$ processes.

A key problem for studying anonymous systems is the *naming problem*, where each process must output a distinct natural number. If naming can be solved, then many techniques from eponymous algorithms can be used in the system too. A naming algorithm may choose arbitrarily large names. In the *strong naming problem*, the n processes must output distinct names from $\{1, 2, \ldots, n\}$. We shall see that this version is strictly harder to solve. These naming problems address the question of whether the identifiers that are used by so many algorithms can be assigned within the system model or whether they must be pre-assigned. If the strong naming problem can be solved, then any eponymous algorithm can be run: processes first choose identifiers and then run the code of that process.

The following assumptions are widely used and are, in particular, used in defining $cons(T)$: (1) an unlimited number of objects of type T are available, (2) an unlimited number of registers are available, (3) algorithms are deterministic, (4) objects can be initialized by the algorithm designer, (5) n (or an upper bound on n) is known, (6) processes have unique identifiers, and (7) the identifiers are $1, 2, \ldots, n$. Variants of the hierarchy were defined by altering assumptions (1) and (2) [15], but it was ultimately agreed that these assumptions are indeed natural. Without assumption (3), the consensus hierarchy collapses because randomized algorithms can solve consensus among any number of processes using only registers [8]. Assumption (4) is essentially redundant for deterministic objects [5], although the proof of this requires unique identifiers. Algorithms that work without assumption (5) have been widely studied in eponymous systems [1].

Here, we retain assumptions (1) to (5) to study the importance of (6) and (7). (In [25] we also briefly consider the effect of dropping assumption (5).) The significance of assumption (6) was questioned by Buhrman *et al.* [7], who showed it is crucial for

Herlihy's universality result: a system equipped with registers and black-box objects that solve consensus cannot solve the naming problem. We continue this line of research by studying arbitrary types of shared objects. The goals of this paper include understanding what the consensus hierarchy would look like without assumption (6), and whether (7) is an essential addition to (6).

The *anonymous consensus number* of a type T, denoted $acons(T)$, is the maximum number of processes that can solve *anonymous* wait-free consensus using objects of type T and registers. If there is no such maximum, then $acons(T) = \infty$. A type T is at level k of the *anonymous consensus hierarchy* if $acons(T) = k$. The *strong naming number* of a type T, denoted $snaming(T)$ is the maximum number of processes for which there exists an anonymous wait-free strong naming algorithm using objects of type T and registers. If there is no such maximum, then $snaming(T) = \infty$. There is no need to define a corresponding hierarchy for the ordinary naming problem, since we shall prove that any type that can solve naming among two processes can solve naming among any number of processes. In the end, it may turn out that the strong naming hierarchy similarly collapses into two levels (1 and ∞): it is an open question whether there exist types at other levels of the strong naming hierarchy.

In eponymous systems, a type T is universal for k processes if and only if $cons(T) \geq k$ [13]. The same result does not hold for anonymous systems. The *universal number* of a type T, denoted $univ(T)$, is the maximum number of processes for which every type of object can be *anonymously* implemented from objects of type T and registers. If no such maximum exists, then $univ(T) = \infty$. We show that, if the system can solve *strong* naming for two processes, then $univ(T) = cons(T)$. On the other hand, if the system cannot solve strong naming for two processes, then $univ(T)$ is clearly 1. The classification of types T according to $acons(T)$, $univ(T)$ and their ability to solve naming provides a lot of information about whether anonymous implementations are possible.

This paper proves the following facts about these new measures.

- A type is at level 1 of the anonymous consensus hierarchy if and only if it is at level 1 of the (standard) consensus hierarchy (Theorem 2).
- For types T at level $x \geq 2$ of the consensus hierarchy, $acons(T)$ can take any value between 2 and x, inclusive (Proposition 4).
- If $acons(T) < cons(T)$ then objects of type T (and registers)cannot solve naming (Theorem 5).
- We characterize types that can solve naming, showing that if 2-process naming can be solved, then naming can be solved for any number of processes.
- If strong naming and consensus can be solved for two processes, then strong naming can be solved for any number of processes (Corollary 1).
- Strong naming is strictly harder than naming (Theorem 6).
- Strong naming is equivalent in difficulty to naming in systems where 2-process (eponymous) consensus can be solved (Theorem 4).

The main results are combined in Sect. 6 to show every type belongs to a row of Table 1. It is unknown whether any types belong to row 3; we give example types for all others. All deterministic types belong to rows 1, 5 and 6.

Table 1. Classification of types by their ability to solve consensus and naming

Example types T	$cons(T)$	$acons(T)$	Solves naming?	$snaming(T)$	$univ(T)$
register	1	1	No	1	1
weak-name	1	1	Yes	1	1
?	1	1	Yes	$z \in \{2,3,\dots\}$	1
strong-name	1	1	Yes	∞	1
$T_{x,y}$	$x \in \{2,3,\dots,\infty\}$	$y \in \{2,3,\dots,x\}$	No	1	1
$acons_x$	$x \in \{2,3,\dots,\infty\}$	x	Yes	∞	x

Related Work. Asynchronous anonymous computation in *failure-free* models has been studied previously. Johnson and Schneider gave leader-election algorithms [16]. Attiya, Gorbach and Moran characterized tasks solvable using only registers [3]. Aspnes, Fich and Ruppert looked at models with other types of shared objects, such as counters [2]. Several randomized algorithms using registers are known for naming [9,18,19,26], which was introduced by Lipton and Park [19].

There is also some work on fault-tolerant anonymous computing, which is closer to the topic of this paper. Panconesi *et al.* [24] gave a *randomized* wait-free naming algorithm. It is not purely anonymous since it uses single-writer registers, which give the system some ability to distinguish between different processes' actions. Randomized naming is known to be impossible if only multi-writer registers are available [7,9,18]. However, consensus is solvable in this randomized model [7]. Thus, naming is strictly harder than consensus in the randomized setting. This also implies that the anonymous consensus hierarchy collapses if randomization is permitted, just like the ordinary consensus hierarchy.

Guerraoui and Ruppert investigated what can be implemented deterministically in an anonymous asynchronous system using only registers if processes may crash [12]. In addition to giving algorithms for basic problems, they characterized the types that have obstruction-free implementations. Herlihy and Shavit [14] characterized decision tasks that have wait-free eponymous solutions using only registers, and extended the characterization to systems with a kind of anonymity: processes have identifiers but are only allowed to use them in very limited ways. Merritt and Taubenfeld considered uniform algorithms (where processes do not know the size of the system) in a failure-free model where processes have identifiers but can only use them in a limited way: identifiers can be compared with one another but cannot be used, for example, to index into an array [22].

2 Preliminaries

We briefly describe the model of computation, which is fairly standard except for the assumption of anonymity. An object type is described by a *sequential specification*, which is comprised of a set of possible states Q, a set of operations OP, a set of responses to operations RES and a transition function $\delta : Q \times OP \to \mathcal{P}(Q \times RES) - \emptyset$. ($\mathcal{P}(S)$ denotes the power set of S.) If $(q',r) \in \delta(q,op)$, it means that when a process applies op to an object in state q, the object may return response r and switch to state q'. An object type is *deterministic* if $|\delta(q, op)| = 1$ for all q, op. An object type has *finite non-determinism* if $|\delta(q, op)|$ is finite for all q, op. The behaviour of an object when accessed concurrently is governed by the constraint that it is linearizable. The most basic shared type is the *register* which stores a value and provides READ and WRITE operations.

A distributed algorithm is a (deterministic) sequential programme for each process, $P_1, \ldots, P_n$. The subscripts $1, \ldots, n$ are used for convenience to reason about the system; the algorithm cannot make use of them. The programme can do standard (Turing-computable) steps on the process's local memory, and perform operations on shared objects. If the programmes assigned to all processes are identical, the algorithm is called *anonymous*. A *step* of an algorithm is described by (P_i, op, X, res, q), which indicates that process P_i accesses object X using operation op, receiving result res and causing X to enter the state q. The step also includes any local computation by the process, which is not represented explicitly. An *execution* of an algorithm is a sequence of steps satisfying two constraints: the subsequence performed on each object X conforms to X's sequential specification, and the subsequence performed by each process P_i conforms to P_i's programme. A *solo execution* by P_i is an execution where only P_i takes steps. A *configuration* describes the state of all shared objects and the local state of all processes.

We consider two types of problems in this paper: one-shot tasks and (long-lived) implementations. In a *one-shot task*, each process receives an input (possibly null) and must produce an output. The problem specification describes which outputs are legal for each possible assignment of inputs to processes. In an *implementation*, the goal is to implement or simulate an object X of type T. A solution gives a programme (for each process) for each operation that can be applied to X and specifies the initial state of all shared objects used in the implementation for each possible initial state of X. The implementation must be linearizable. *Wait-freedom* requires that no process can take an infinite number of steps in any execution without completing its programme.

The consensus problem allows inputs from an arbitrary set. In the *binary* consensus problem, inputs must be 0 or 1. The two problems are equivalent: If there is an anonymous binary consensus algorithm for k processes using objects of type T and registers, then $acons(T) \geq k$. The proof of this is identical to the proof of Proposition 8 in [12], where the output of consensus is agreed upon bit-by-bit. We therefore consider only binary consensus. We denote $1 - x$ by $\overline{x}$.

Some proofs below use valency arguments, introduced by Fischer, Lynch and Paterson [11]. We generalize their definitions slightly to take advantage of anonymity. Fix some (binary) consensus algorithm. Let $\mathcal{T}$ be a tree with the following properties. Each node represents a configuration of the algorithm. One configuration may be represented by several nodes. The root of $\mathcal{T}$ represents an initial configuration. If a node v has a child u, then the configuration u is reachable from v. An example of such a tree is the complete execution tree, in which each node v has one child for each configuration that is reachable from v by a single step. A branch in $\mathcal{T}$ corresponds to an execution. If, during the execution from the root to a node, a process outputs a value, label that node with that value. If no descendant of a node is labelled by $\overline{v}$, that node is called *v-valent in $\mathcal{T}$*. A node is *univalent in $\mathcal{T}$* if it is 0- or 1-valent in $\mathcal{T}$; otherwise it is *multivalent in*

$\mathcal{T}$. When $\mathcal{T}$ is the complete execution tree, we omit the phrase "in $\mathcal{T}$" for these terms and the definitions correspond to the original ones [11].

Wait-freedom does not require a bound on the number of steps before termination. However, the following application of König's Lemma [17] was observed in [4,6]. (We assume finite non-determinism throughout the rest of this paper.)

Proposition 1. *Consider a wait-free algorithm for a one-shot task. If the algorithm uses only objects with finite non-determinism then, for any input, the algorithm has a finite execution tree.*

3   Anonymous Consensus Numbers

Here, we study the anonymous consensus hierarchy. (See [25] for details omitted due to lack of space.) We begin with easy consequences of the definition of *acons* and the fact that an anonymous algorithm can run in an eponymous system.

Observation 1. For all types T, $acons(T) \le cons(T)$.

Proposition 2. *If $acons(T_1) < acons(T_2)$, then objects of type T_1 and registers cannot implement T_2 in an anonymous system of more than $acons(T_1)$ processes.*

Proof (sketch). If T_2 can be implemented anonymously from T_1 objects and registers, then T_1 objects and registers can simulate any consensus algorithm that uses T_2 objects and registers.   □

The anonymous consensus hierarchy is *full*: it has types at every level. A register has consensus number one [8,20], so $acons(\text{register}) = 1$, by Observation 1. Herlihy gave a consensus algorithm for any number of processes using a compare&swap object [13]. That algorithm is anonymous, so $acons(\text{compare\&swap})$ is ∞. For $2 \le k < \infty$, consider the type $acons_k$, which has one operation, PROPOSE(x) for $x \in \{0, 1\}$, that returns the argument of the first PROPOSE operation to each of the first k PROPOSE operations performed on it. After the kth PROPOSE, it returns to its initial state. To solve k-process anonymous consensus, each process proposes its input value to an $acons_k$ object and outputs the value the object returns. A simple valency argument proves that the type cannot solve consensus among more processes. Thus, we have the following result.

Proposition 3. *For $2 \le k < \infty$, $acons(acons_k) = cons(acons_k) = k$.*

Observation 1 says that anonymous consensus is no easier than consensus. Here, we show that anonymous consensus is strictly harder: it is possible for $acons(T)$ to be strictly smaller than $cons(T)$. We define an object type $T_{x,y}$ that has $cons(T) = x$ and $acons(T) = y$, for any x and y satisfying $2 \le y \le x \le \infty$. The type $T_{x,y}$ will, of necessity, be somewhat artificial, since we wish to construct an example for all possible values of x and y. (A more natural example type T with $acons(T) < cons(T)$ is given in [25].) A process accesses an object of type $T_{x,y}$ either anonymously, using a PROPOSE($value$) operation, or eponymously using a PROPOSE($value, id$) operation. Intuitively, an object, initially in state $\perp$, solves consensus by returning to each operation the first value proposed to it, but does so only if it is accessed anonymously by at most y processes and by at most $y - x$ additional processes that use unique identifiers. If more than y processes access it anonymously or if two processes use the same identifier, then the object changes to the UPSET state and returns useless random results to all further accesses. To implement this functionality, the state of the object stores the value first proposed to it, the number of anonymous accesses that have taken place and the set of identifiers that have been used by the eponymous accesses.

Proposition 4. *For* $2 \leq y \leq x \leq \infty$, $cons(T_{x,y}) = x$ *and* $acons(T_{x,y}) = y$.

Proof. If $x < \infty$, there is a simple eponymous consensus algorithm for x processes that uses a single object of type $T_{x,y}$, initialized to state $\perp$. For $1 \leq i \leq y$, the ith process performs a PROPOSE($input$) operation on the object and outputs the result. For $y < i \leq x$, the ith process performs a PROPOSE($input, i$) operation on the object and outputs the result. If $x = \infty$, then this algorithm can be used with any number of processes. Thus, $cons(T_{x,y}) \geq x$.

If $y < \infty$, y processes can solve consensus anonymously as in the previous paragraph: each process performs a PROPOSE($input$) operation on an object initialized to $\perp$ and returns the result. If $y = \infty$, then this algorithm can be used for any number of processes. Thus, $acons(T_{x,y}) \geq y$.

If $x < \infty$, a straightforward valency argument proves $cons(T_{x,y}) \leq x$ [25].

Finally, we show $acons(T_{x,y}) \leq y$. To derive a contradiction, suppose there is an anonymous consensus algorithm for $y + 1$ processes, denoted $P_0, \ldots, P_y$, using only objects of type $T_{x,y}$ and registers. We use a valency argument. Consider a tree T, where each node represents a configuration C such that process $P_1, \ldots, P_y$ have the same local state in C, constructed as follows. The root is the initial configuration where process P_0 has input 0 and processes $P_1, \ldots, P_y$ have input 1. If C is any configuration in the tree where P_0 has not terminated, we add *left children* of C to represent the configurations that can be reached from C by a single step of process P_0. Similarly, if C is any configuration in the tree where P_1 has not terminated, we add *right children* of C to represent the configurations that can be reached from C by a sequence of y steps where each of the processes $P_1, \ldots, P_y$ take an identical step. There is at least one such extension because a sequence of WRITES to a register will all return a null response, a sequence of READS of a register will all return identical responses, and a sequence of operations on an object of type $T_{x,y}$ *can* always all return identical responses.

All leaves of T are univalent in T. The root is multivalent in T, since the executions where only P_0 takes steps must produce output 0 and the executions where P_0 takes no steps must produce output 1. There must be a node C such that C is multivalent in T and C's children are all univalent in T; otherwise there would be an infinite path of nodes that are multivalent in T, which is impossible in a wait-free algorithm. Then there must be a left child C_{left} of C that is v-valent in T and a right child C_{right} of C that is $\bar{v}$-valent in T.

If P_0 and P_1 either access different objects or if they both read the same register in their first steps after C then a right child of C_{left} and a left child of C_{right} are identical configurations, contradicting the fact that they have opposite valencies. If, in their next steps after C, P_0 writes a register R and P_1 accesses R, then P_0 cannot distinguish C_{left} from a left child of C_{right}, which is again a contradiction. A symmetric argument applies if P_0 reads a register R and P_1 writes to R in their next steps after C. Thus, P_0

and P_1 must both access the same object, X, in their next steps after C and X must be of type $T_{x,y}$.

Let α be a solo execution by P_0, starting from configuration C and passing through C_{left}. In α, P_0 must output v. If an object of type $T_{x,y}$ (in any state) has the same operation applied to it y times, it will end up in the state UPSET (since $y \geq 2$). Thus, in C_{right}, X's state must be UPSET. The local state of P_0 and the state of every object except X are the same in C and C_{right}. Thus, the execution α is also legal starting from C_{right}, since the sequence of responses that P_0 receives from X in α can also occur if the execution is started from C_{right}, where X is upset. So, C_{right} has a descendant in $\mathcal{T}$ that outputs v. However, C_{right} is $\bar{v}$-valent in $\mathcal{T}$. This contradiction proves that $acons(T_{x,y}) \leq y$. $\qquad \square$

Although the consensus hierarchy and the anonymous consensus hierarchy are quite different, the division between levels one and two coincide.

Theorem 2. *For any type T, $cons(T) = 1$ if and only if $acons(T) = 1$.*

Proof. The "only if" direction follows from Observation 1. To prove the converse, we show that $cons(T) \geq 2$ implies $acons(T) \geq 2$. Assume $cons(T) \geq 2$. Let $\text{PROPOSE}_0(x)$ and $\text{PROPOSE}_1(x)$ be the code that is executed by two processes to solve consensus eponymously. Let B be a bound on the maximum number of steps a process must do while executing either of these routines. Proposition 1 guarantees the existence of such a bound, since there are only two possible inputs to each of the two processes in the binary consensus algorithm. The following anonymous 2-process consensus algorithm uses two registers R_0 and R_1 (initially $\perp$), in addition to any shared objects used by PROPOSE_0 and PROPOSE_1.

$\text{PROPOSE}(x)$
    if a READ of $R_{\bar{x}}$ returns $\top$ then return $\bar{x}$
    else
        WRITE($\top$) in R_x
        run $\text{PROPOSE}_x(x)$ until it halts or B steps of it have been taken
        let r be the result of the preceding line (if the subroutine halts)
        if a READ of $R_{\bar{x}}$ returns $\top$ then output r
        else output x

The algorithm is clearly wait-free. It is necessary to include the "time limit" of B steps in calling the subroutine $\text{PROPOSE}_x(x)$ because, when both processes call $\text{PROPOSE}_0(0)$ or both call $\text{PROPOSE}_1(1)$, there is no guarantee that those subroutines will halt. If both processes have the same input x, then $R_{\bar{x}}$ is always $\perp$, so outputs can only be x. We now prove that if the two processes have different inputs and both produce outputs, those outputs are equal. Consider two cases.

If one process P with input x sees $\top$ when first reading $R_{\bar{x}}$, then the value of R_x remains $\perp$ throughout the execution. Thus, the other process, Q, can only output its own input value, $\bar{x}$. Process P also can only return $\bar{x}$.

If each process sees $\perp$ in its first READ, then one process runs $\text{PROPOSE}_0(0)$ and the other process runs $\text{PROPOSE}_1(1)$. This means that the subroutines will both terminate within B steps and will both produce the same output r. If both processes output r, agreement is guaranteed. However, if one process P sees $\perp$ in its second READ of $R_{\overline{x}}$, then it outputs its own input x. In this case, P has completed running PROPOSE$_x(x)$ before the other process Q started running PROPOSE$_{\overline{x}}(\overline{x})$, so r must be equal to x, and Q must return x also. $\square$

4   Naming

In this section, we study the ability of anonymous systems to solve the naming problem using different types of shared objects. First, we see in Theorem 3 that, in contrast to the consensus problem, the number of processes in the system has no effect on whether the naming problem is solvable. This theorem also gives an exact characterization of the types of objects that can be used to solve the naming problem, using the following definition of Aspnes, Fich and Ruppert [2].

Definition 1. *An operation is* idemdicent *if, for every starting state, every operation, and every choice of operands for that operation, it is possible that two consecutive invocations of the operation with these operands return identical responses. A type is* idemdicent *if every operation defined on it is idemdicent.*

Intuitively, an object is idemdicent if it is incapable of breaking symmetry between two processes. Examples include registers, snapshot objects, resettable consensus objects, counters (with separate READ and INCREMENT operations, the latter of which returns a null result), and the type $T_{x,y}$ of Sect. 3.

Theorem 3. *For any type T and any $n \geq 2$, the following are equivalent.*
(1) *Naming can be solved for n processes using objects of type T.*
(2) *Naming can be solved for n processes using objects of type T and registers.*
(3) *Naming can be solved for two processes using objects of type T.*
(4) *Naming can be solved for two processes using objects of type T and registers.*
(5) *T is not idemdicent.*

Proof. Trivially, we have $(1) \Rightarrow (2) \Rightarrow (4)$ and $(1) \Rightarrow (3) \Rightarrow (4)$.

(4) $\Rightarrow$ (5): Suppose two processes can solve naming using objects of type T and registers. To derive a contradiction, assume T is idemdicent. Consider an execution of the naming algorithm where the two processes alternate taking steps, both performing the same sequence of operations and getting the same sequence of responses. This is possible, since the algorithm is anonymous and every time the two processes perform the same operation on an object, that object can return the same response to both, by the definition of idemdicence. In this execution, both processes produce the same output, a contradiction.

(5) $\Rightarrow$ (1): Assume (5). Suppose two successive invocations of operation op on an object in state q cannot return the same response. Let $\mathcal{R}$ be the set of possible responses that can be returned if up to n successive invocations of op are applied to an object initially in state q. Let $d = |\mathcal{R}|$. Since T has finite non-determinism, d is finite. An algorithm for the naming problem among n processes can be constructed using objects

of type T as a weak kind of splitter [23]. The naming algorithm uses a tree data structure of height $n - 1$, where every internal node has d children. Each node has an associated object of type T, initialized to state q. The edges leading from a node v to its d children are labelled by the elements of $\mathcal{R}$. The leaves of the tree are labelled by distinct natural numbers.

To run the naming algorithm, each process starts at the root of the tree and follows a path towards a leaf. For each internal node v that the process visits, it applies the operation op to the associated object. When it receives a response r, the process advances to a child of v along the edge labelled by r. When the process reaches a leaf, it outputs the label of that leaf. If m processes access a node v, the first two processes must receive different responses and proceed to different children of v. Thus, at most $m-1$ processes will visit any child of v. It follows by induction on k that at most $n - k$ processes will visit any node at depth k in the tree. Thus, at most one process will reach any leaf, and this guarantees that the names produced by the algorithm are distinct.   □

5 Strong Naming

We now consider the strong naming problem, where processes must return distinct names from the range $\{1, \ldots, n\}$. In Corollary 1, we obtain a result analogous to Theorem 3. However, it applies only to object types whose consensus numbers are at least two. It is an open problem whether the result also holds for objects at level one of the consensus hierarchy. The following proposition shows that, if the system is capable of solving consensus among two processes, the naming and strong naming problems are equivalent.

Theorem 4. *If $cons(T) \geq 2$ then, for any n, objects of type T and registers can solve n-process naming if and only if they can solve n-process strong naming.*

Proof. The claim is trivial for $n = 1$. For $n \geq 2$, the "if" part of the claim is trivial. For the converse, suppose naming is solvable for n processes using objects of type T and registers. By Theorem 3, T is not idemdicent. By Proposition 1, the tree of possible executions of the naming algorithm is finite, and therefore the set of possible names is finite. Let M be the maximum possible name.

The following algorithm solves the strong naming problem for n processes. It uses a data structure that consists of n binary trees, numbered 1 to n, each with M leaves, to implement a renaming algorithm that reduces the size of the name space. Each internal node of each tree is associated with a different instance of two-process eponymous consensus, which is implemented from objects of type T and registers. Each process first obtains a name $i \in \{1, 2, \ldots, M\}$ using the naming algorithm. It then accesses the first binary tree, starting from the ith leaf and moving along the path from that leaf to the root. At each internal node, it proposes *left* or *right* to the instance of the two-process eponymous consensus algorithm associated with the node. If the process arrived at the node from its left child, it proposes *left*, using the consensus algorithm for process 1, and if it arrived from the right child, it proposes *right*, using the consensus algorithm for process 2. The process continues towards the root only if the result returned is equal to the value it proposed. In this case, we say that the process *wins* at that node. A process that does not receive its own input as the output of consensus at some node is said to *lose* at that node. If it ever loses at some node, it stops accessing the tree and switches to the next tree. It accesses this tree in exactly the same way, again moving on to the next one if it ever loses at some node. The process continues accessing trees until it wins at the root of one of the trees. If the process wins at the root of the jth tree, it outputs j as its name and halts.

The consensus algorithm associated with a node is run by at most one process for each of the two children of the node, namely the process that either started at that child (if the child is a leaf) or won at that child (if the child is an internal node). Thus, the algorithm will correctly solve consensus. At most one process will win at the root of any tree, and it follows that all names produced will be distinct elements of the set $\{1, 2, \ldots, n\}$. To prove that processes terminate, we observe that if r processes access nodes at some level of a tree $\mathcal{T}$, at least $\lceil r/2 \rceil$ of them either win or experience a halting failure. So, if any processes access tree $\mathcal{T}$, at least one process either wins at the root of $\mathcal{T}$ or fails at some time during its accesses to $\mathcal{T}$. Thus, if k processes access a tree, at most $k - 1$ processes access the next tree. It follows that every process eventually produces a name.   □

Combining Theorem 3 and Theorem 4 yields the following corollary.

Corollary 1. *If* $cons(T) \geq 2$ *and* $n \geq 2$, *the following are equivalent.*
(1) *Objects of type* T *and registers can solve n-process strong naming.*
(2) *Objects of type* T *and registers can solve 2-process strong naming.*
(3) T *is not idemdicent.*

Corollary 1 reveals the following connection between consensus and naming.

Theorem 5. *If* T *is not idemdicent,* $acons(T) = cons(T)$.

Proof. To derive a contradiction, suppose T is not idemdicent but $acons(T) \neq cons(T)$. By Observation 1, $acons(T) < cons(T)$. Thus, $cons(T) \geq 2$ and $acons(T) \neq \infty$. Since T is not idemdicent, strong naming can be solved for $acons(T) + 1$ processes using objects of type T and registers, by Corollary 1. Then, $acons(T) + 1$ processes can solve consensus anonymously using objects of type T and registers by first solving strong naming and then running an eponymous consensus algorithm. This contradicts the definition of $acons(T)$.   □

Theorem 4 showed that naming and strong naming are equivalent if the underlying system can solve two-process consensus. However, if this is not the case, strong naming is strictly harder than naming. We now define a type that can solve naming for any number of processes but cannot solve strong naming even for two processes. The *weak-name* object has one operation, GETNAME. The first two GETNAME operations non-deterministically return any two distinct names from $\{1, 2, 3\}$. If any further GETNAME operations are performed, the object non-deterministically chooses any value from $\{1, 2, 3\}$ to return. More formally, the state set is $\{\bot, 1, 2, 3, \text{UPSET}\}$. The transition function is given by $\delta(\bot, \text{GETNAME}) = \{(i, i) : i \in \{1, 2, 3\}\}, \delta(i, \text{GETNAME}) = \{(\text{UPSET}, j) : j \in \{1, 2, 3\} - \{i\}\}$, and $\delta(\text{UPSET}, \text{GETNAME}) = \{(\text{UPSET}, j) : j \in \{1, 2, 3\}\}$.

Theorem 6. *Weak-name objects can solve naming for n processes, for all n. Weak-name objects and registers cannot solve strong naming for two processes.*

Proof. If a weak-name object is in state $\perp$, the first two accesses must return different results. By Theorem 3, it can solve naming for any number of processes.

Assume that weak-name objects and registers can solve strong naming for two processes. To derive a contradiction, we shall use a reduction involving the renaming problem. The *renaming* problem is to design an anonymous algorithm such that, in any execution where processes receive distinct inputs from $\{1, \dots, M\}$, they output distinct values from $\{1, \dots, m\}$. We describe how to build a two-process renaming algorithm for $M = 3$ and $m = 2$ using only registers. This was shown to be impossible by Herlihy and Shavit [14].

To solve the renaming problem, each of the two processes runs the strong naming algorithm. Each weak-name object X used in the naming algorithm is simulated without doing any accesses to shared memory as follows. We consider several cases, depending on how X is initialized. First, suppose X is initially $\perp$. When a process with input i is supposed to first access X, it pretends that the response from X was i. If the process does any subsequent accesses to X, it pretends X's response was $i \bmod 3 + 1$. Note that, in any execution, the first two simulated responses from X will be distinct, whether those two accesses are by the same process or by different processes. If X initially has state i, then all accesses to X return the response $i \bmod 3 + 1$. If X is initially UPSET, then all accesses to X return the response 1. This simulation of the algorithm requires only registers. Because this is a faithful simulation of the strong naming algorithm, the two processes will output distinct values from $\{1, 2\}$, thereby solving the renaming problem, which is impossible.   □

Corollary 2. *The type weak-name has consensus number 1.*

Proof. By Theorem 6, weak-name objects can solve the naming problem for two processes. If $cons$(weak-name) were bigger than one, then, by Theorem 4, strong naming for two processes could be solved using weak-name objects and registers, but this would contradict Theorem 6.   □

6   Summary

The preceding results provide enough information to give a fairly complete picture of the classification of object types according to their ability to solve consensus and naming, and their universal numbers.

Theorem 7. *Every type T belongs to one of the rows in Table 1. (The fourth column describes whether naming can be solved for any number of processes greater than 1 using objects of type T and registers.)*

Proof. We first show that every type T belongs to some row in Table 1, ignoring the last column for now.

Suppose $cons(T) = 1$. By Observation 1, $acons(T) = 1$. If T is idemdicent, it cannot solve naming (even with registers), by Theorem 3, so its strong naming number is 1. Thus, T belongs to row 1. If T is not idemdicent, then it can solve naming, so it belongs to row 2, 3 or 4, depending on its strong naming number.

Now suppose $cons(T) = x > 1$. If T is idemdicent, then objects of type T (and registers) cannot solve naming, by Theorem 3. Therefore, they cannot solve strong naming, even for two processes, either. The anonymous consensus number of T must be at least two, by Theorem 2, and at most x, by Observation 1. Thus T belongs to row 5 of Table 1. If T is not idemdicent, then $acons(T)$ is also x, by Proposition 5. Objects of type T can solve naming, by Theorem 3. Objects of type T and registers can solve strong naming for any number of processes, by Proposition 1. Thus, T belongs to row 5 of Table 1.

Finally, we show that the value given for $univ(T)$ is correct for each row. For the first 4 rows, $univ(T) = 1$, since objects of type T and registers cannot implement 2-process consensus. For row 5, $univ(T)$ must be 1, since objects of type T and registers cannot solve 2-process strong naming. For types in row 6, $univ(T) \leq x$, since objects of type T and registers cannot implement consensus for $x + 1$ processes. To see that $univ(T) = x$, x processes can anonymously implement any object using objects of type T and registers by first solving strong naming and then applying Herlihy's universal construction [13]. □

It is unknown whether any types belong to row 3 of Table 1, so it is possible that this row could be removed from the table, or additional constraints on the value of z could be included. We now show that the rest of the classification cannot be improved: we give examples for each other row in Table 1.

A register has consensus number 1 [8,20] and is idemdicent, so it belongs to row 1. The weak-name object is in row 2, by Theorem 6 and Corollary 2.

For row 4, we define a new *strong-name* type. It provides one operation, GETNAME(k) where k is a positive integer, that returns a positive integer. If processes perform up to k GETNAME operations with the same argument k, the object returns distinct responses from $\{1, 2, \ldots, k\}$. If processes access the object in a different way, the object becomes upset and returns non-deterministic results. The following proposition, proved in [25], shows that this type occupies line 4 of Table 1. The proof that it has consensus number 1 shows that there is an eponymous implementation for two processes that does not use shared memory.

Proposition 5. $snaming(strong\text{-}name) = \infty$ and $cons(strong\text{-}name) = 1$.

For $2 \leq y \leq x \leq \infty$, the type $T_{x,y}$, defined in Sect. 3 has $cons(T_{x,y}) = x$ and $acons(T_{x,y}) = y$, by Proposition 4. It is easy to verify that $T_{x,y}$ is idemdicent. Thus, there are types in row 5 of Table 1 for all possible values of x and y.

The final row of Table 1 contains the $acons_x$ type, defined in Sect. 3, for $2 \leq x < \infty$. Two successive invocations of PROPOSE(1) starting from state $(0, x - 1)$ return 0 and 1, so this type is not idemdicent, and can solve naming. The compare&swap type is also in the final row of Table 1, with $x = \infty$.

6.1 Deterministic Types

If we restrict attention to deterministic types only, then the classification of Theorem 7 can be refined. The objects given above as examples for rows 1 and 6 of Table 1 are deterministic. The following proposition rules out the possibility of any deterministic types in rows 2, 3 and 4 of Table 1.

Proposition 6. *If T is deterministic and not idemdicent, then $acons(T) \geq 2$.*

Proof. If T is deterministic and not idemdicent, there is a state q and an operation op such that two successive invocations of op return results r_1 and r_2 with $r_1 \neq r_2$. The following anonymous algorithm solves two-process consensus using one object X of type T, initialized to q, and two registers R_0 and R_1, initialized to $\perp$. A process can output only the input of the process that accesses X first.

PROPOSE(x)
>WRITE($\top$) in R_x
>if applying op to X returns r_2 and a READ of $R_{\overline{x}}$ returns $\top$ then return $\overline{x}$
>else return x □

There are deterministic types in row 5 of Table 1. For example, standard consensus objects have consensus number ∞, but are idemdicent. Whether there is a deterministic type in row 5 for all x and y is an open question.

Acknowledgements. This research was supported by NSERC and was partly done during a visit to the École Polytechnique Fédérale de Lausanne.

References

1. Aguilera, M.K.: A pleasant stroll through the land of infinitely many creatures. ACM SIGACT News. 35(2), 36–59 (2004)
2. Aspnes, J., Fich, F., Ruppert, E.: Relationships between broadcast and shared memory in reliable anonymous distributed systems. Distributed Computing 18(3), 209–219 (2006)
3. Attiya, H., Gorbach, A., Moran, S.: Computing in totally anonymous asynchronous shared memory systems. Info. and Comp. 173(2), 162–183 (2002)
4. Bazzi, R.A., Neiger, G., Peterson, G.L.: On the use of registers in achieving wait-free consensus. In: Proc. 13th ACM Symp. on Principles of Distributed Computing, pp. 354–362. ACM Press, New York (1994)
5. Borowsky, E., Gafni, E., Afek, Y.: Consensus power makes (some) sense! In: Proc. 13th ACM Symp. on Principles of Distributed Computing, pp. 363–372. ACM Press, New York (1994)
6. Brit, H., Moran, S.: Wait-freedom vs. bounded wait-freedom in public data structures. Journal of Universal Computer Science 2(1), 2–19 (1996)
7. Buhrman, H., Panconesi, A., Silvestri, R., Vitanyi, P.: On the importance of having an identity or, is consensus really universal? Distributed Computing 18(3), 167–176 (2006)
8. Chor, B., Israeli, A., Li, M.: On processor coordination using asynchronous hardware. In: Proc. 6th ACM Symp. on Princ. of Dist. Comp., pp. 86–97. ACM Press, New York (1987)
9. Eğecioğlu, O., Singh, A.K.: Naming symmetric processes using shared variables. Distributed Computing 8(1), 19–38 (1994)
10. Fich, F., Ruppert, E.: Hundreds of impossibility results for distributed computing. Distributed Computing 16(2-3), 121–163 (2003)
11. Fischer, M.J., Lynch, N.A., Paterson, M.S.: Impossibility of distributed consensus with one faulty process. J. ACM 32(2), 374–382 (1985)

12. Guerraoui, R., Ruppert, E.: Anonymous and fault-tolerant shared-memory computing. Distributed Computing. To appear
13. Herlihy, M.: Wait-free synchronization. ACM Trans. Prog. Lang. Syst. 13(1), 124–149 (1991)
14. Herlihy, M., Shavit, N.: The topological structure of asynchronous computability. J. ACM 46(6), 858–923 (1999)
15. Jayanti, P.: On the robustness of Herlihy's hierarchy. In: Proc. 12th ACM Symp. on Principles of Distributed Computing, pp. 145–157. ACM Press, New York (1993)
16. Johnson, R.E., Schneider, F.B.: Symmetry and similarity in distributed systems. In: Proc. 4th ACM Symp. on Princ. of Distributed Comp. pp. 13–22. ACM Press, New York (1985)
17. König, D.: Über eine Schlussweise aus dem Endlichen ins Unendliche. Acta. Litterarum ac Scientiarum Regiae Universitatis Hungaricae Francisco-Josephinae: Sectio Scientiarum Mathematicarum 3, 121–130 (1927)
18. Kutten, S., Ostrovsky, R., Patt-Shamir, B.: The Las-Vegas processor identity problem (How and when to be unique). J. Algorithms 37(2), 468–494 (2000)
19. Lipton, R.J., Park, A.: The processor identity problem. Process. Lett. 36(2), 91–94 (1990)
20. Loui, M.C., Abu-Amara, H.H.: Memory requirements for agreement among unreliable asynchronous processes. In: Preparata, F.P. (ed.) Advances in Computing Research, vol. 4, pp. 163–183. JAI Press, Greenwich, Connecticut (1987)
21. Mavronicolas, M., Michael, L., Spirakis, P.: Computing on a partially eponymous ring. In: Proc. 10th Intl Conf. on Princ. of Distributed Systems, pp. 380–394 (2006)
22. Merritt, M., Taubenfeld, G.: Computing with infinitely many processes under assumptions on concurrency and participation. In: Distributed Computing, 14th International Conference, pp. 164–178 (2000)
23. Moir, M., Anderson, J.H.: Wait-free algorithms for fast, long-lived renaming. Science of Computer Programming 25(1), 1–39 (1995)
24. Panconesi, A., Papatriantafilou, M., Tsigas, P., Vitányi, P.: Randomized naming using wait-free shared variables. Distributed Computing 11(3), 113–124 (1998)
25. Ruppert, E.: The anonymous consensus hierarchy and naming problems. In: Technical Report CSE-2006-11. Dept of Comp. Sci. and Engineering, York University (2006)
26. Teng, S.-H.: Space efficient processor identity protocol. Inf. Process. Lett. 34(3), 147–154 (1990)

The Baskets Queue

Moshe Hoffman[1], Ori Shalev[1], and Nir Shavit[1,2]

[1] The School of Computer Science, Tel Aviv University, Israel
[2] Sun Microsystems Laboratories
moshe.hoffman@gmail.com, orish@post.tau.ac.il,
shanir@post.tau.ac.il

Abstract. FIFO Queues have over the years been the subject of significant research. Such queues are used as buffers both in a variety of applications, and in recent years as a key tool in buffering data in high speed communication networks.

Overall, the most popular dynamic-memory lock-free FIFO queue algorithm in the literature remains the MS-queue algorithm of Michael and Scott. Unfortunately, this algorithm, as well as many others, offers no more parallelism than that provided by allowing concurrent accesses to the head and tail. In this paper we present the Baskets Queue - a new, highly concurrent lock-free linearizable dynamic memory FIFO queue. The Baskets Queue introduces a new form of parallelism among enqueue operations that creates *baskets* of mixed-order items instead of the standard totally ordered list. The operations in different baskets can be executed in parallel. Surprisingly however, the end result is a linearizable FIFO queue, and in fact, we show that a basket queue based on the MS-queue outperforms the original MS-queue algorithm in various benchmarks.

Keywords: CAS, Compare and Swap, Concurrent Data Structures, FIFO queue, Lock-free, Non-blocking, Synchronization.

1 Introduction

First-in-first-out (FIFO) queues are among the most basic and widely used concurrent data structures. They have been studied in a static memory setting [1,2] and in a dynamic one [3,4,5,6,7,8,9,10,11,12,13,14,15,2]. The classical concurrent queue is a linearizable structure that supports enqueue and dequeue operations with the usual FIFO semantics. This paper focuses on queues with dynamic memory allocation.

The best known concurrent FIFO queue implementation is the lock-free queue of Michael and Scott [16] which is included in the Java^{TM} Concurrency Package [17]. Its key feature is that it maintains, in a lock-free manner, a FIFO ordered list that can be accessed disjointly through head and tail pointers. This allows enqueue operations to execute in parallel with dequeue operations.

A later article by Ladan-Mozes and Shavit [7] presented the *optimistic queue* that in many cases performs better than the MS-queue algorithm. The optimistic doubly-linked list reduces the number of compare-and-swap (CAS) operations necessary to perform an enqueue and replaces them with simple stores. However, neither algorithm allows more parallelism then that allowed by the disjoint head and tail.

E. Tovar, P. Tsigas, and H. Fouchal (Eds.): OPODIS 2007, LNCS 4878, pp. 401–414, 2007.

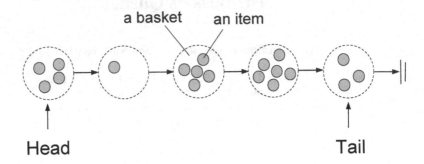

Fig. 1. The abstract Baskets Queue

In an attempt to add more parallelism, Moir et. al [18] showed how one could use elimination as a back-off scheme to allow pairs of concurrent enqueue and dequeue operations to exchange values without accessing the shared queue itself. Unfortunately, in order to keep the correct FIFO queue semantics, the enqueue operation cannot be eliminated unless all previous inserted nodes have been dequeued. Thus, the *elimination backoff queue* is practical only for very short queues.

In this paper we present a new approach that allows added parallelism in the design of concurrent shared queues. Our approach, which we apply to the MS-queue [16], can also be applied to the optimistic queue [7]. In our new "basket" approach, instead of the traditional ordered list of nodes, the queue consists of an ordered list of groups of nodes (baskets). The order of nodes in each basket need not be specified, and in fact, it is easiest to maintain them in LIFO order. Nevertheless, we prove that the end result is a linearizable FIFO queue. The benefit of the basket technique is that, with little overhead, it introduces a new form of parallelism among enqueue operations by allowing insertions into the different baskets to take place in parallel.

1.1   The Baskets Queue

Linearizability was introduced by Herlihy and Wing [4] as a correctness condition for concurrent objects. For a FIFO queue, an execution history is linearizable if we can pick a point within each enqueue or dequeue operation's execution interval so that the sequential history defined by these points maintains the FIFO order.

We notice that the definition of linearizability allows overlapping operations to be reordered arbitrarily. This observation leads to the key idea behind our algorithm: a group of overlapping enqueue operations can be enqueued onto our queue as one group (basket), without the need to specify the order between the nodes. Due to this fact, nodes in the same basket can be dequeued in any order, as the order of enqueue operations can be "fixed" to meet the dequeue operations order. Moreover, nodes from different groups may be inserted in parallel.

A concise abstraction of the new queue is a FIFO-ordered list of baskets where each basket contains one or more nodes (see Fig. 1). The baskets fulfill the following basic rules:

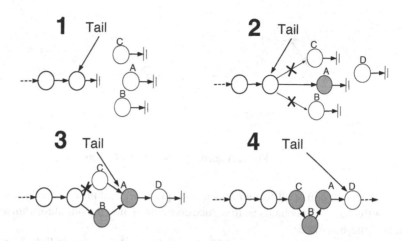

Fig. 2. (1) Each thread checks that the tail-node's next field is null, and tries to atomically change it to point to its new node's address. (2) Thread A succeeds to enqueue the node. Threads B and C fail on the same CAS operation, hence both of them will retry to insert into the basket. (3) Thread B was the first to succeed to enqueue, at the same time thread D calls the enqueue operation, and finishes successfully to enqueue onto the tail. (4) thread C finishes successfully.

1. Each basket has a time interval in which all its nodes' enqueue operations overlap.
2. The baskets are ordered by the order of their respective time intervals.
3. For each basket, its nodes' dequeue operations occur after its time interval.
4. The dequeue operations are performed according to the order of baskets.

Two properties define the FIFO order of nodes:

1. The order of nodes in a basket is not specified.
2. The order of nodes in different baskets is the FIFO-order of their respective baskets.

The basic idea behind these rules is that setting the linearization points of enqueue operations that share an interval according to the order of their respective dequeues, yields a linearizable FIFO-queue.

How do we detect which enqueue operations overlap, and can therefore fall into the same basket? The answer is that in algorithms such as the MS-queue or optimistic queue, threads enqueue items by applying a Compare-and-swap (CAS) operation to the queue's tail pointer, and all the threads that fail on a particular CAS operation (and also the winner of that CAS) overlap in time. In particular, they share the time interval of the CAS operation itself. Hence, all the threads that fail to CAS on the tail-node of the queue may be inserted into the same basket. By integrating the basket-mechanism as the back-off mechanism, the time usually spent on backing-off before trying to link onto the new tail, can now be utilized to insert the failed operations into the basket, allowing enqueues to complete sooner. In the meantime, the next successful CAS operations by enqueues allow new baskets to be formed down the list, and these can be filled concurrently. Moreover, the failed operations don't retry their link attempt on the new tail, lowering the overall contention on it. As we will show, this leads to a queue

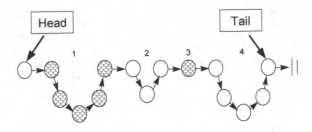

Fig. 3. A queue composed of 4 baskets

algorithm that unlike all former concurrent queue algorithms requires virtually no tuning of the backoff mechanisms to reduce contention, making our algorithm an attractive out-of-the-box queue.

In order to enqueue, just as in MS-Queue, a thread first tries to link the new node to the last node. If it failed to do so, then another thread has already succeeded. Thus it tries to insert the new node into the new basket that was created by the winner thread (see Fig. 2). To dequeue a node, a thread first reads the head of the queue to obtain the oldest basket. It may then dequeue any node in the oldest basket.

As we noted earlier, the implementation of the Baskets Queue we present here is based on Michael and Scott's MS-queue. Our algorithm maintains a linked list of nodes logically divided into baskets (see Fig. 3). Although, as the reader will see, in our implementation the baskets have a stack-like behavior, any concurrent pool object that supports the add and the remove operations, can serve as a basket. The advantage of such objects is that they can deliver more scalability than the stack-like baskets.

1.2 Performance

We compared our new lock-free queue algorithm to the lock-free MS-queue of Michael and Scott [16], and to the Optimistic-Queue by Ladan-Mozes and Shavit [7]. The algorithms were implemented in the C programming language and were executed on a 16 processors Sun Fire 6800 running the Solaris 9 operating system.

As our empirical results show, the new algorithm scales better under high contention due to the simultaneous successful enqueue operations. We believe that as the number of processors running the basket queue increases, it will be possible to replace the stack-like baskets with more scalable data-structures based on diffracting-trees [19] or counting-networks [20], that will make the Baskets Queue even faster.

2   The Baskets Queue

We now describe our algorithm in detail. Since we employ CAS operations in our algorithm, ABA issues arise [16,15]. In Section 2.2, we describe the enqueue and dequeue operations ignoring ABA issues. The tagging mechanism we added to overcome the ABA problem is explained in Section A. The code in this section includes this tagging mechanism.

```
struct pointer_t {
  <ptr, deleted, tag>: <node_t *, boolean, unsigned integer>
};
```

```
struct node_t {                          struct queue_t {
  data_type value;                         pointer_t tail
  pointer_t next;                          pointer_t head
};                                       };
```

```
void init_queue(queue_t* q)
I01: node_t* nd = new_node()       # Allocate a new node
I02: nd->next = <null, 0, 0>       # next points to null with tag 0
I03: q->tail = <nd, 0, 0>;         # tail points to nd with tag 0
I04: q->head = <nd, 0, 0>;         # head points to nd with tag 0
```

Fig. 4. Types, structures and initialization

Although the nodes of the same basket need not be ordered, we insert and remove them in a stack-like manner, one by one. It is a subject for further research to determine if it feasible to exploit weaker orders to make the queue more scalable.

2.1 Data Structures

Just as in the MS-queue, our queue is implemented as a linked list of nodes with head and tail pointers. The tail points either to a node in the last basket, or in the second to last basket. In contrast to the MS-queue, we use pointer marking [10] to logically delete nodes. The queue's head always points to a dummy node, which might be followed by a sequence of logically deleted (marked) nodes.

2.2 The Baskets Queue Operations

The FIFO queue supports two operations: enqueue and dequeue. The enqueue method inserts a value into the queue and the dequeue method deletes the oldest value from the queue.

To enqueue a new node into the list, the thread first reads the current tail. If the tail is the last node (E07) it tries to atomically link the new node to the last node (E09). If the CAS operation succeeded the node was enqueued successfully, and the thread tries to point the queue's tail to the new node (E10), and then returns. However, if the thread failed to atomically swap the Null value, it means that the thread overlaps in time with the winner of the CAS operation. Thus, the thread tries to insert the new node to the basket (E12-E18). It re-reads the next pointer that points to the first node in the basket, and as long as no node in the basket has been deleted (E13), it tries to insert the node at the same list position. If the tail did not point to the last node, the last node is searched (E20-E21), and the queue's tail is fixed.

To prevent a late enqueuer from inserting its new node behind the queue's head, a node is dequeued by setting the deleted bit of its pointer so that a new node can only

```
E01: nd = new_node()
E02: nd->value = val
E03: repeat:
E04:     tail = Q->tail
E05:     next = tail.ptr->next
E06:     if (tail == Q->tail)):
E07:         if (next.ptr == NULL):
E08:             nd->next = <NULL, 0, tail.tag+2>
E09:             if CAS(&tail.ptr->next, next, <nd, 0, tail.tag+1>):
E10:                 CAS(&Q->tail, tail, <nd, 0, tail.tag+1>
E11:                 return True
E12:             next = tail.ptr->next
E13:             while((next.tag==tail.tag+1) and (not next.deleted)):
E14:                 backoff_scheme()
E15:                 nd->next = next
E16:                 if CAS(&tail.ptr->next, next, <nd, 0, tail.tag+1>):
E17:                     return True
E18:                 next = tail.ptr->next;
E19:         else:
E20:             while ((next.ptr->next.ptr != NULL) and (Q->tail==tail)):
E21:                 next = next.ptr->next;
E22:             CAS(&Q->tail, tail, <next.ptr, 0, tail.tag+1>)
```

Fig. 5. The enqueue operation

be inserted adjacently to another unmarked node. As the queue's head is only required as a hint to the next unmarked node, the lazy update approach of Tsigas and Zhang [1] can be used to reduce the number of CAS operations needed to update the head.

To dequeue a node, a thread reads the current state of the queue (D01-D04) and re-checks it for consistency (D05). If the head and tail of the list point to the same node (D06), then either the list is empty (D07) or the tail lags. In the latter case, the last node is searched (D09-D10) and the tail is updated(D11). If the head and the tail point to different nodes, then the algorithm searches for the first unmarked node between the head and the tail (D15-D18). If a non-deleted node is found, its value is first read (D24) before trying to logically delete it (D25). If the deletion succeeded the dequeue is completed. Before returning, if the deleted node is far enough from the head (D26), the free_chain method is performed (D27). If while searching for a non-deleted node the thread reached the tail (D21) the queue's head is updated (D22). See Fig. 7 for an illustration.

The free_chain procedure tries to update the queue's head (F01). If it successful, it is safe to reclaim the deleted nodes between the old and the new head (F02-F05).

3   Performance

We compared the performance of our FIFO queue to the best performing dynamic memory FIFO-queue algorithms. The algorithms were compiled in the C programming language with Sun's "CC" compiler 5.8 with the flags "-XO3 -xarch=v8plusa". The

```
const MAX_HOPS = 3 # constant

data_type dequeue(queue_t* Q)

D01: repeat
D02:     head = Q->headf
D03:     tail = Q->tail
D04:     next = head.ptr->next
D05:     if (head == Q->head):
D06:         if (head.ptr == tail.ptr)
D07:             if (next.ptr == NULL):
D08:                 return 'empty'
D09:             while ((next.ptr->next.ptr != NULL) and (Q->tail==tail)):
D10:                 next = next.ptr->next;
D11:             CAS(&Q->tail, tail, <next.ptr, 0, tail.tag+1)
D12:         else:
D13:             iter = head
D14:             hops = 0
D15:             while ((next.deleted and iter.ptr != tail.ptr) and (Q->head==head)):
D16:                 iter = next
D17:                 next = iter.ptr->next
D18:                 hops++
D19:             if (Q->head != head):
D20:                 continue;
D21:             elif (iter.ptr == tail.ptr):
D22:                 free_chain(Q, head, iter)
D23:             else:
D24:                 value = next.ptr->value
D25:                 if CAS(&iter.ptr->next, next, <next.ptr, 1, next.tag+1>):
D26:                     if (hops >= MAX_HOPS):
D27:                         free_chain(Q, head, next)
D28:                     return value
D29:                 backoff-scheme()
```

Fig. 6. The dequeue operation

different benchmarks were executed on a 16 processor Sun Fire™ 6800 running the Solaris™ 9 operating system.

3.1 The Benchmarked Algorithms

We compared our FIFO-queue algorithm to the lock-free queue of Michael and Scott [16], and to the Optimistic Queue of Ladan-Mozes and Shavit [7]. To expose the possible effects of our use of logical deletions, a variation of the MS-Queue with logical deletions was added as a control. The set of compared queue implementations was:

1. Baskets Queue - the new algorithm implementation.
2. Optimistic Queue - the pre-backoff version of the Optimistic FIFO-queue.
3. MS-queue - the lock-free version of the Michael and Scott's queue.
4. MS-queue lazy head - This is a variation of MS-Queue where dequeues are performed by logically deleting the dequeued node. Therefore, following Tsigas and Zhang's technique [1], the queue's head may be updated only once for several dequeues.

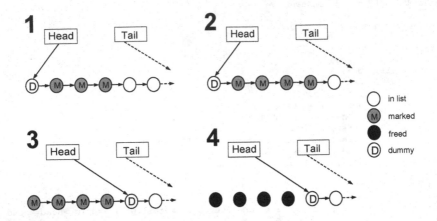

Fig. 7. (1) three nodes are logically deleted. (2) the first non-deleted node is deleted (3) the head is advanced (4) the chain of deleted nodes can be reclaimed.

```
void free_chain(queue_t* q, pointer_t head, pointer_t new_head)

F01: if CAS(&Q->head, head, <new_head.ptr, 0, head.tag+1>):
F02:     while (head.ptr != new_head.ptr):
F03:         next = head.ptr->next
F04:         reclaim_node(head.ptr)
F05:         head = next
```

Fig. 8. The free_chain procedure

3.2   The Benchmarks

We chose to use the same benchmarks as in the optimistic queue article [7].

- 50% Enqueues: each process chooses uniformly at random whether to perform an enqueue or a dequeue, creating a random pattern of 50% enqueue and 50% dequeue operations.
- Enqueue-Dequeue Pairs: each process alternately performs an enqueue or a dequeue operation.
- Grouped Operations: each process picks a random number between 1 and 16, and performs this number of enqueues or dequeues. The process performs enqueues and dequeues alternately as in the Enqueue-Dequeue Pairs benchmark.

The total number of enqueue and dequeue operations is not changed, they are only executed in a different order.

3.3   The Experiments

We ran the specified benchmarks measuring the total time required to perform one million operations as a function of the number of processes. For each benchmark and

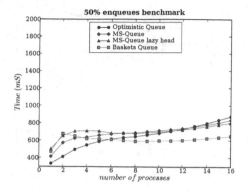

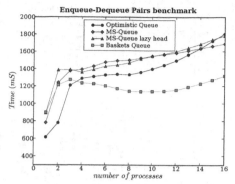

Fig. 9. The 50 % enqueues benchmark

Fig. 10. The Enqueue-Dequeue pairs benchmark

algorithm we chose the exponential backoff delays that optimize the maximal latency (the maximal time required to complete an operation).

To counteract transient startup effects, we synchronized the start of the processes (i.e: no process started before all others finished their initialization phase).

3.4 Empirical Results

Figures 9, 10 and 11 show the results of the three different benchmarks. It can be seen that high levels of concurrency have only moderate effects on the performance of the Baskets Queue. The Baskets Queue is up to 25% faster than the other algorithms. This can be explained by the load on the tail of all the data-structures but the baskets queue, whereas in the baskets queue the contention on the tail is distributed among several baskets. However, at lower concurrency levels, the optimistic approach is superior because the basket-mechanism is triggered upon contention.

When we optimized the exponential backoff delays of the algorithms for each benchmark, we found that for the Basket Queue the optimal backoff delays of all three benchmark is identical. In contrast, for the other algorithms, no single combination of backoff-delays was optimal for all benchmarks. This is due to the fact that the exponential backoff is used only as a secondary backoff scheme when inserting into the baskets, thus it has only a minor effect on the performance.

To further test the robustness of our algorithm to exponential backoff delays, we conducted the same benchmark test without using exponential backoff delays. As seen in figures 12, 13 and 14, in this setting the Baskets Queue outperforms the other algorithms by a large factor. This robustness can be explained by the fact that the basket-mechanism plays the role of the backoff-mechanism by distributing concurrent enqueue operations to different baskets.

To gauge the effectiveness of the basket-mechanism on our 16 processor machine, we took snapshots of the list of baskets. Figure 15 shows a typical snapshot of the Baskets Queue on the 50% enqueues benchmarks. The basket sizes vary from only 1 to 3 nodes. In the average case, an enqueue operation will succeed to enqueue after at

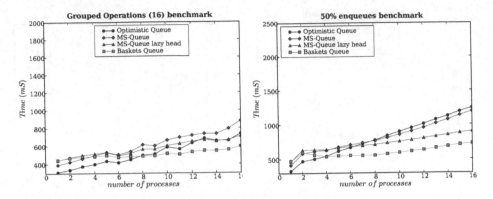

Fig. 11. The grouped operation benchmark

Fig. 12. The 50% enqueues benchmark without backoff

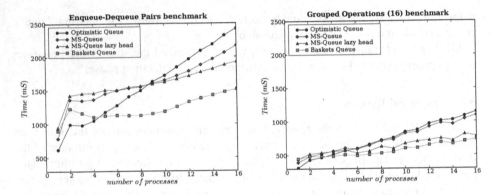

Fig. 13. The Enqueue-Dequeue pairs benchmark without backoff

Fig. 14. The Grouped operations benchmark without backoff

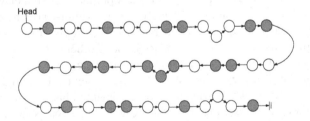

Fig. 15. A typical snapshot of the queue (16 processes)

most 3 failed CAS operations. The baskets sizes are smaller than 8 nodes as one would expect them to be, because the elements are inserted into the baskets one by one. This unnecessary synchronization on the nodes of the same basket imposes a delay on the last nodes to be inserted.

In addition to the robustness to exponential backoff delays, this snapshot confirms that when in use, the backoff-mechanism inside each basket needs only to synchronize at most 3 concurrent enqueues, if any. Therefore, it has only a minor effect on the overall performance. We believe that for machines where exponential backoff techniques are crucial for performance, this robustness makes our algorithm a natural solution as an out-of-the-box queue, to be used without the requirement of fine tuning.

Acknowledgement

We thank Edya Ladan Mozes for useful conversations and suggestions.

References

1. Tsigas, P., Zhang, Y.: A simple, fast and scalable non-blocking concurrent FIFO queue for shared memory multiprocessor systems. In: Proceedings of the 13th annual ACM symposium on Parallel algorithms and architectures, Crete Island, Greece, pp. 134–143. ACM Press, New York (2001)
2. Valois, J.: Implementing lock-free queues. In: Proceedings of the 7th International Conference on Parallel and Distributed Computing Systems. 64–69 (1994)
3. Gottlieb, A., Lubachevsky, B.D., Rudolph, L.: Basic techniques for the efficient coordination of very large numbers of cooperating sequential processors. ACM Trans. Program. Lang. Syst. 5(2), 164–189 (1983)
4. Herlihy, M., Wing, J.: Linearizability: A Correctness Condition for Concurrent Objects. ACM Transactions on Programming Languages and Systems 12(3), 463–492 (1990), doi:10.1145/78969.78972
5. Hwang, K., Briggs, F.A.: Computer Architecture and Parallel Processing. McGraw-Hill, New York (1990)
6. Lamport, L.: Specifying Concurrent Program Modules. ACM Transactions on Programming Languages and Systems 5(2), 190–222 (1983)
7. Ladan-Mozes, E., Shavit, N.: An Optimistic Approach to Lock-Free FIFO Queues. In: In: Proceedings of Distributed computing, Amsterdam, Netherlands, pp. 117–131. Springer, Heidelberg (2004)
8. Mellor-Crummey, J.M.: Concurrent queues: Practical fetch-and-ϕ algorithms. Technical Report Technical Report 229, University of Rochester(November 1987)
9. Prakash, S., Lee, Y.H., Johnson, T.: Non-blocking algorithms for concurrent data structures. Technical Report 91–002, Department of Information Sciences, University of Florida(1991)
10. Prakash, S., Lee, Y.-H., Johnson, T.: A non-blocking algorithm for shared queues using compare-and-swap. IEEE Transactions on Computers 43(5), 548–559 (1994)
11. Sites, R.: Operating Systems and Computer Architecture. In: Stone, H. (ed.) Introduction to Computer Architecture, 2nd edn. (1980)
12. Stone, H.S.: High-performance computer architecture. Addison-Wesley Longman Publishing Co., Inc (1987)
13. Stone, J.: A simple and correct shared-queue algorithm using compare-and-swap. In: Proceedings of the 1990 conference on Supercomputing, pp. 495–504. IEEE Computer Society Press, Los Alamitos (1990)
14. Stone, J.M.: A Nonblocking Compare-and-Swap Algorithm for a Shared Circular Queue. In: Parallel and Distributed Computing in Engineering Systems, pp. 147–152. Elsevier Science B.V, Amsterdam (1992)

15. Treiber, R.K.: Systems programming: Coping with parallelism. Technical Report RJ 5118, IBM Almaden Research Center(April 1986)
16. Michael, M., Scott, M.: Nonblocking Algorithms and Preemption-Safe Locking on Multi-programmed Shared - Memory Multiprocessors. Journal of Parallel and Distributed Computing 51(1), 1–26 (1998)
17. Lea, D.: The java concurrency package (JSR-166),
   lhttp://gee.cs.oswego.edu/dl/concurrency-interest/index.html
18. Moir, M., Nussbaum, D., Shalev, O., Shavit, N.: Using elimination to implement scalable and lock-free FIFO queues. In: SPAA 2005: Proceedings of the 17th annual ACM symposium on Parallelism in algorithms and architectures, pp. 253–262. ACM Press, New York, NY, USA (2005)
19. Shavit, N., Zemach, A.: Diffracting Trees. ACM Transactions on Computer Systems 14(4), 385–428 (1996)
20. Herlihy, M., Lim, B., Shavit, N.: Scalable Concurrent Counting. ACM Transactions on Computer Systems 13(4), 343–364 (1995)
21. Moir, M.: Practical implementations of non-blocking synchronization primitives. In: Proceedings of the 16th Annual ACM Symposium on Principles of Distributed Computing, pp. 219–228. ACM Press, New York (1997)
22. Cormen, T., Leiserson, C., Rivest, R., Stein, C.: Introduction to Algorithms, 2nd edn. MIT Press, Cambridge, MA (2001)

A   Memory Management

Our memory manager is similar to the memory manager of the optimistic queue [7]. It consists of a shared pool of nodes. Each thread possesses a list of pointers to nodes in the shared pool, ready for its exclusive allocation. When a thread physically removes a node from the queue, it adds the node's pointer to its list of available allocations.

Although the memory manager is rather simple, the algorithm can be easily adapted to interact with more sophisticated memory schemes as well as garbage collected languages.

A.1   The Tagging Mechanism and the ABA Problem

As our algorithm is based on CAS operations, it suffers from the known ABA problem [16,15]. To overcome it we use the standard tagging-mechanism approach [16,21]. A portion of each pointer address is used to timestamp changes of the pointer, where the pointer and the tag are manipulated atomically using a single CAS operation.

B   Correctness Proof

Due to lack of space, the correct set semantics and lock-free proofs are omitted.

B.1   Linearizability of Our Algorithm

If by ordering the operations in the order of their linearization points the queue behaves as the abstract sequential queue, then the queue is linearizable to the abstract FIFO-queue.

Definition 1. *A sequential FIFO queue as defined in [22] is a data structure that supports two operations:* enqueue *and* dequeue. *The state of the queue is a sequence* $<e_1, ..., e_k>$ *of items. The queue is initially empty. The semantics of* enqueue *and* dequeue *operations on a given state* $<e_1, ..., e_k>$ *is described as follows:*

- enqueue(n) - *inserts n to the end of the queue yielding the new state* $<e_1, ..., e_k, n>$
- dequeue() - *if the queue is empty, the operation returns "empty" and does not change the state. Otherwise, it deletes and returns the oldest value from the queue, yielding a new state* $<e_2, ..., e_k>$

Definition 2. *The linearization point of a* dequeue *operation that returned a value is the successful pointer marking at line D23.*

Definition 3. *The linearization point of a* dequeue *operation that returned "empty" is when reading the* dummy *node's next null pointer at line D04.*

Definition 4. *The linearization points of the* enqueue *operations of a basket are set inside the basket's shared time interval in the order of their respective dequeues. In other words, the linearization points of the enqueues are determined only once the items are dequeued.*

Lemma 1. *The* enqueue *operation of the same basket overlap in time.*

Proof. An enqueue operation tries to insert a node into a basket only if it failed to CAS on the tail of the list (E09). Before trying to CAS, the enqueue operation checks that the next pointer of the tail-node is null. Thus, all the failed enqueue operations overlap the time interval that starts at some point when the next pointer of the tail-node is null, and ends when it points to a new node. The winner of the CAS overlap the same interval too.   □

Lemma 2. *The baskets are ordered according to the order of their respective time intervals.*

Proof. A basket is created by a successful enqueue operation on the tail of the queue. The enqueue operations that failed to enqueue, retry to insert their nodes at the same list position. Therefore, the first node of a basket is next to the last node of the previous basket, and the last node of a basket is the winner of the CAS operation.   □

Lemma 3. *The linearization points of the* dequeue *operations of a basket come after the basket's shared time interval.*

Proof. In order for a dequeue operation to complete, the node must be in the list. A basket's first node is linked into the list only after the CAS operation on the tail is completed. The completion of this CAS operation is also the end of the shared time interval of the basket. Thus nodes can be marked only after the basket's time interval.   □

Lemma 4. *The nodes of a basket are dequeued before the nodes of later (younger) baskets.*

Proof. The nodes are dequeued according to their sequential order in the list (which is logically divided into baskets). In addition, since the nodes are deleted by pointer marking, once all the nodes of a basket are dequeued, no more nodes are allowed to be enqueued into it.   □

Lemma 5. *The linearization point of a dequeue operation that returned "empty" comes exactly after an equal number of enqueue and dequeue operations.*

Proof. If the `next` pointer of the dummy node is null then all the enqueued nodes had been removed from the list. Since nodes are removed from the list only after they are marked, the linearization point of an "empty" dequeue comes after equal number of enqueue and dequeue linearization points.   □

Theorem 1. *The FIFO-queue is linearizable to a sequential FIFO queue.*

Proof. Ignoring for a moment dequeues that return "empty", from lemmas 2 and 4, the order in which baskets are dequeued is identical to the order in which baskets are enqueued. From lemma 3 the `enqueue` operations of a basket preceed its dequeues. Lemma 1 guarantees that the construction of definition 4 is possible. Thus the order of the `enqueue` operations of a basket is identical to the order of its `dequeue` operations, and the queue is linearizable.

From lemma 5 the queue is linearizable also with respect to dequeue operations that returned "empty".   □

The Cost of Monotonicity in Distributed Graph Searching

David Ilcinkas[1], Nicolas Nisse[2,*], and David Soguet[2]

[1] Université du Québec en Outaouais, Canada,
[2] LRI, Université Paris-Sud, France
{ilcinkas,nisse,soguet}@lri.fr

Abstract. Blin *et al.* (2006) proposed a distributed protocol that enables the smallest number of searchers to clear any unknown asynchronous graph in a decentralized manner. *Unknown* means that the searchers are provided no *a priori* information about the graph. However, the strategy that is actually performed lacks of an important property, namely the monotonicity. That is, the clear part of the graph may decrease at some steps of the execution of the protocol. Actually, the protocol of Blin *et al.* is executed in exponential time. Nisse and Soguet (2007) proved that, in order to ensure the smallest number of searchers to clear any n-node graph in a monotone way, it is necessary and sufficient to provide $\Theta(n \log n)$ bits of information to the searchers by putting short labels on the nodes of the graph. This paper deals with the smallest number of searchers that are necessary and sufficient to monotoneously clear any graph in a decentralized manner, when the searchers have no a priori information about the graph.

The distributed graph searching problem considers a team of searchers that is aiming at clearing any connected contaminated graph. The clearing of the graph is required to be *connected*, i.e., the clear part of the graph must remain permanently connected, and *monotone*, i.e., the clear part of the graph only grows. The *search number* $\mathbf{mcs}(G)$ of a graph G is the smallest number of searchers necessary to clear G in a monotone connected way in centralized settings. We prove that any distributed protocol aiming at clearing any unknown n-node graph in a monotone connected way, in decentralized settings, has *competitive ratio* $\Theta(\frac{n}{\log n})$. That is, we prove that, for any distributed protocol $\mathcal{P}$, there exists a constant c such that for any sufficiently large n, there exists a n-node graph G such that $\mathcal{P}$ requires at least $c \frac{n}{\log n} \mathbf{mcs}(G)$ searchers to clear G. Moreover, we propose a distributed protocol that allows $O(\frac{n}{\log n}) \mathbf{mcs}(G)$ searchers to clear any unknown asynchronous n-node graph G in a monotone connected way.

Keywords: Graph searching, Monotonicity, Competitive ratio.

1 Introduction

In graph searching [6,17], a team of *searchers* is aiming at capturing an invisible arbitrarily fast fugitive hidden in a graph (see [3] for a survey). Equivalently, an undirected

---

* Additional supports from the project FRAGILE of the ACI Sécurité Informatique, and from the project GRAND LARGE of INRIA.

E. Tovar, P. Tsigas, and H. Fouchal (Eds.): OPODIS 2007, LNCS 4878, pp. 415–428, 2007.

connected graph is thought as a system of tunnels contaminated by a toxic gas. In this setting, the searchers are aiming at clearing the graph. The *search problem* has been widely studied in the design of distributed protocols for clearing a network in a decentralized manner [5,7,8,9,16]. Initially, all edges are contaminated. The searchers stand at the vertices of the graph and move along the edges. An edge is *cleared* when it is traversed by a searcher. A clear edge e is *recontaminated* as soon as there exists a path P between e and a contaminated edge such that no searchers are occupying any vertex or any edge of P. A *search strategy* is a sequence of moves of the searchers along the edges of the graph, such that, initially, all the searchers are placed at a particular vertex of the graph, called the *homebase*. Moreover, this sequence of moves must satisfy that *recontamination* never occurs, that is, a clear edge always remains clear. A search strategy is aiming at clearing the whole network. Given a graph G and a homebase $v_0 \in V(G)$, the search problem consists in designing a distributed protocol that allows the smallest number of searchers to clear G starting from v_0. The search strategy must be computed online by the searchers themselves.

Note that, by definition, a search strategy satisfies two important properties. First, a search strategy is *monotone* [4,13]. That is, the contaminated part of the graph never grows. This ensures that the clearing of the graph can be performed in polynomial time. Secondly, a search strategy is *connected* [1,2], in the sense that, at any step of the strategy, the clear part of the graph induces a connected subgraph. This latter property ensures safe communications between the searchers. In the following, the *search number* $\mathbf{mcs}(G, v_0)$ of a graph G with homebase $v_0 \in V(G)$ denotes the smallest number of searchers required to clear the graph in a monotone connected way, starting from v_0, in centralized settings.

Several distributed protocols have been proposed to solve the search problem [1,5,7,8,9,14,16]. Two main approaches have been proposed in the previous works. On one hand, Blin *et al.* proposed a distributed protocol that enables $\mathbf{mcs}(G, v_0) + 1$ searchers to clear any *unknown* asynchronous graph G, starting from any homebase $v_0 \in V(G)$, in a connected way [5]. That is, the clearing of the graph is performed without the searchers being provided any information about the graph. However, the search strategy that is actually performed is not monotone and may be performed in exponential time, which is not surprising since the problem of computing $\mathbf{mcs}(G, v_0)$ is NP-complete [15]. On the other hand, the distributed protocols that are proposed in [7,8,9,14,16] enable $\mathbf{mcs}(G, v_0) + 1$ searchers to monotoneously clear a graph G, starting from a homebase v_0, such that the searchers are given some *a priori* information about it. In this paper, we consider the problem from another point of view. More precisely, we address the problem of the minimum number of searchers permitting to solve the search problem (again, the performed strategy must be connected and monotone) without any *a priori* information about the graph.

1.1 Model and Definitions

The searchers are modeled by synchronous autonomous mobile computing entities with distinct IDs. A network is modeled by a synchronous undirected connected simple graph. The network is anonymous, that is, the nodes are not labelled. The $\deg(u)$ edges incident to any node u are labelled from 1 to $\deg(u)$, so that the searchers can distinguish the different edges incident to a node. These labels are called *port numbers*. Every node of the network has a zone of local memory, called *whiteboard*, in which searchers can read, erase, and write symbols. It is moreover assumed that searchers can access these whiteboards in fair mutual exclusion.

A *search protocol* $\mathcal{P}$ is a distributed protocol that solves the search problem, i.e., for any connected graph G and any homebase $v_0 \in V(G)$, a team of searchers executing $\mathcal{P}$ can clear G in a connected monotone way, starting from v_0. In these settings, the searchers do not know in advance in which graph they are launched. The number of searchers used by $\mathcal{P}$ to clear G is the maximum number of searchers that stand at the vertices of G over all steps of the execution of $\mathcal{P}$. The quality of a search protocol $\mathcal{P}$ is measured by comparing the number of searchers it used to clear a graph G to the search number $\mathbf{mcs}(G, v_0)$ of G. This ratio, maximized over all graphs and all starting nodes, is called the *competitive ratio* $r(\mathcal{P})$ of the protocol $\mathcal{P}$.

1.2 Our Results

We prove that any search protocol for clearing n-node graphs has competitive ratio $\Omega(\frac{n}{\log n})$. Moreover, we propose a search protocol that has competitive ratio $O(\frac{n}{\log n})$. More precisely, we prove that for any distributed protocol $\mathcal{P}$, there exists a constant c such that for any sufficiently large n, there exists a n-node graph G with a homebase $v_0 \in V_G$, such that $\mathcal{P}$ requires at least $c\frac{n}{\log n}\,\mathbf{mcs}(G, v_0)$ searchers to clear G, starting from v_0. On the other hand, we propose a search protocol that uses at most $O(\frac{n}{\log n})\,\mathbf{mcs}(G, v_0)$ searchers to clear any connected graph G in a connected monotone way, starting from any homebase $v_0 \in V(G)$. Moreover, our protocol performs clearing of n-node graphs using searchers with at most $O(\log n)$ bits of memory, and whiteboards of size $O(n)$ bits.

1.3 Related Work

In connected graph searching [1,2,10], the clear part must remain connected during all steps of the search strategy. This property is very useful as soon as we want to ensure the communications between the searchers to be secured. Contrary to the classical, i.e., non-connected, graph searching [4,13,17], the monotonicity has a cost in terms of number of searchers. Indeed, Alspash *et al.* proved that *recontamination does help* in the case of connected graph searching [18] (see also [11]). That is, they describe a class of graphs for which the smallest number of searchers required to clear these graphs is strictly less than the number of searchers necessary to clear them in a monotone connected way. This result has an important impact since it is not known whether the decision problem corresponding to the connected search number of a graph, i.e., the smallest number of searchers required to clear a graph in a connected way, belongs to NP. Moreover, monotone strategies are of particular interest in decentralized settings since, first, they perform in polynomial time, and second, it is *a priori* difficult to design non-monotone search strategies.

Several distributed protocols have been proposed to solve the search problem for particular graph's topologies. More precisely, Barrière *et al.* designed protocols for clearing trees [1], Flocchini, Luccio and Song considered tori [7] and meshes [8], Flocchini, Huang and Luccio considered hypercubes [9], and Luccio dealt with Sierpinski's graphs [14]. Assuming the searchers know the topology of the graph G they must clear, these protocols enable $\mathbf{mcs}(G, v_0) + 1$ searchers to clear G in a monotone connected way, starting from any homebase $v_0 \in V(G)$. The extra searcher, compared to the centralized case, is necessary and due to the asynchrony of the network [8]. In [5], Blin *et al.* proposed a distributed protocol that allows $\mathbf{mcs}(G, v_0) + 1$ searchers to clear any unknown asynchronous graph G in a connected way, starting from any homebase $v_0 \in V(G)$. In this case, the searchers do not need any *a priori* information about the graph in which they are placed. However, the search strategy that is actually performed is not monotone and may be performed in exponential time. In [16], Nisse and Soguet proposed to give to the searchers some information about the graph by putting short labels on the nodes of the graph. They proved that $\Theta(n \log n)$ bits of information are necessary and sufficient to solve the search problem for any n-node asynchronous graph G, using $\mathbf{mcs}(G, v_0) + 1$ searchers and starting from a homebase v_0.

2   Lower Bound

This section is devoted to prove a lower bound on the competitive ratio of any search protocol. For this purpose, we consider a game between an arbitrary search protocol and an adversary. Roughly, the adversary gradually builds the graph, which is actually a ternary tree, as the search protocol clears it in a monotone connected way. The role of the adversary is to force the protocol to use the maximum number of agents to clear the graph. The fact that the adversary can build the graph during the execution of the search protocol is possible since the searchers have no information concerning the graph they are clearing.

We need the following definition. A *partial graph* is a simple connected graph which can have edges with only one end. Edges with one single end (resp., two ends) are called *half-edges* (resp., *full-edges*). Let $G = (V, H, F)$ be a partial graph, where V is the vertex-set of G, H its set of half-edges and F its set of full-edges. Let G^- be the graph (V, F). Let G^+ be the graph obtained by adding a degree-one end to any half-edge of G.

Let us give some definitions and results that will be used in the following. A ternary tree is a tree whose internal vertices have degree at most three. A search strategy that is not constrained to satisfy neither the connected property, nor the monotone property is simply a sequence of moves of the searchers along the edges of a graph that results in clearing the whole graph. $\mathbf{s}(G)$ denotes the smallest number of searchers that are necessary to clear a graph G in such a way. The class of trees has particularly been studied regarding graph searching. In particular, the following results have been proved.

Theorem 1. *Let T be a tree with $n \geq 2$ vertices,*
   $\mathbf{s}(T) \leq 1 + \log_3(n - 1)$ **(Megiddo *et al.* [15])**
   *For any $v_0 \in V(T)$, $\mathbf{mcs}(T, v_0) \leq 2\mathbf{s}(T) - 1$ (**Barrière *et al.* [2]**)*

The remaining part of this section is devoted to the proof of Theorem 2.

Theorem 2. *Any search protocol for clearing n-node graphs has competitive ratio* $\Omega(\frac{n}{\log n})$.

Proof. Let $\mathcal{P}$ be any search protocol. We prove that there exists a constant $c > 0$, such that for any $n \geq 5$, there exists a n-node ternary tree T (actually, if n is odd, T has exactly one internal vertex of degree two, and none otherwise), such that $\mathcal{P}$ uses at least k searchers to clear T in a monotone connected way, starting from any homebase $v_0 \in V(T)$, with $k \geq c \frac{n}{\log n} \mathbf{mcs}(T, v_0)$.

Let $n \geq 5$. We consider an unknown ternary tree T, that $\mathcal{P}$ has to clear starting from $v_0 \in V(T)$. Let us describe the game executed turn by turn by $\mathcal{P}$ and the adversary $\mathcal{A}$. Initially, the partial graph T_p consists of a single vertex, the homebase v_0, incident to three half-edges. All searchers are placed at v_0. Then, $\mathcal{P}$ and $\mathcal{A}$ play alternatively, starting with $\mathcal{P}$. At each round, $T_p = (V, H, F)$ corresponds to the part of T that $\mathcal{P}$ currently knows. $\mathcal{P}$ chooses a searcher and it moves this searcher along an edge e of T_p if it does not imply recontamination. Such a move is always possible since $\mathcal{P}$ is a search protocol, and thus, it eventually clears T. Note that e may be a half-edge or a full-edge. If e is a full-edge, then $\mathcal{A}$ skips its turn. Otherwise, two cases must be considered. Either $|V(T_p^+)| < n - 1$, or $|V(T_p^+)| = n - 1$. In the first case, $\mathcal{A}$ adds a new end v to e such that v is incident to two new half-edges f and h. That is, the partial graph becomes $T_p = (V \cup \{v\}, H_{new}, F_{new})$, with $H_{new} = (H \setminus \{e\}) \cup \{f\} \cup \{h\}$ and $F_{new} = F \cup \{e\}$. In the latter case, $\mathcal{A}$ adds a new end v to e such that v is incident to only one new half-edge f. Again, this is possible since $\mathcal{P}$ does not know the graph in advance. The game ends when $|V(T_p^+)| = n$. At such a round, $\mathcal{A}$ decides that the graph T is actually T_p^+.

Let us consider the last round, that is when $|V(T_p^+)| = n$. We show that at this round the number k of vertices of T_p^+ occupied by searchers is at least $k \geq n/4$. Let us first do the following easy remarks. At each round of the game, T_p^- is a ternary tree, and T_p^+ is a ternary tree with at least $(n + 2)/2$ leaves (this can be easily prove by induction on the number of rounds). Moreover, T_p^- is exactly the clear part of T at this step of the execution of $\mathcal{P}$. In other words, the half-edges of T_p corresponds to the contaminated edges that are incident to the clear part of T. Since the execution of $\mathcal{P}$ ensures that the strategy performed is monotone, it follows that, at any round of the game, the vertices incident to at least one half-edge are occupied by a searcher. From the previous remarks, it follows that T_p^+ is a ternary tree with at least $(n+2)/4$ vertices occupied by a searcher. Indeed, every parent of a leaf in T_p^+ must be occupied by a searcher, and every node is parent of at most two leaves. Thus, $\mathcal{P}$ uses at least $k \geq n/4$ searchers. By Theorem 1, $\mathbf{mcs}(T, v_0) \leq 2(1 + \log_3(n - 1))$. Therefore,

$$k \geq \mathbf{mcs}(T, v_0) \times \frac{n}{8(1 + \log_3(n - 1))} .$$

It follows easily that there is a constant $c > 0$ such that for any $n \geq 5$ we have

$$k \geq c \frac{n}{\log n} \mathbf{mcs}(T, v_0) ,$$

which concludes the proof the theorem. □

3 Upper Bound

In this section, we propose a search protocol mc_search (for monotone connected search) with competitive ratio $O(\frac{n}{\log n})$ for any n-node graph. Combining with the lower bound proved in section 2, it shows that $\Theta(\frac{n}{\log n} \mathbf{mcs}(G, v_0))$ searchers are necessary and sufficient to clear any unknown n-node graph G in a monotone connected way, starting from any homebase v_0 and in decentralized settings.

Before describing the search protocol mc_search, we need some definitions. In the following, the depth of a rooted tree T is the maximum length of the paths between the root and any leaf of T. Let $v \in V(T)$ that is not the root. Let u be the parent of v, then the edge $\{u, v\}$ is called the *parent-edge* of v. A *complete ternary tree* is defined as follows. The complete ternary tree T_0 of depth 0 consists of a single vertex, called its root. For any $k \geq 1$, a complete ternary tree T_k of depth k is a ternary tree in which all internal vertices have degree exactly three, and there exists a vertex, called its root, that is at distance exactly k from all leaves.

Theorem 3. (Barrière *et al.* [2])

For any $k \geq 0$, $\mathbf{mcs}(T_k) = k + 1$.

A graph H is a *minor* of a graph G if H is a subgraph of a graph obtained by a succession of edge contractions* of G. A well known result is that, for any graph G and any minor H of G, $\mathbf{s}(G) \geq \mathbf{s}(H)$. Note that this result is not valid for the search number $\mathbf{mcs}$, i.e., there exist some graph G, and H minor of G such that $\mathbf{mcs}(H) > \mathbf{mcs}(G)$ [2].

3.1 Idea of Protocol mc_search

Let us roughly describe the search protocol mc_search. Let G be a connected n-node graph and $v_0 \in V(G)$. The main issue of mc_search is to maintain two dynamic rooted trees T and S. At each step, T is a subtree of the clear part of G, and S is a minor of T with same root. Intuitively, S represents the current positions of the searchers in G, and T enables the searchers to move in the clear part of the graph by performing a DFS of T. Initially, $S = T = \{v_0\}$ and all searchers are at v_0.

Roughly speaking, at each step, Protocol mc_search tries to clear an edge of G that is chosen such that S becomes as close as possible to a complete ternary tree. If the chosen edge e reaches a new vertex, i.e., a vertex that is not occupied by a searcher yet, e is added to S and labelled *Minor*. Otherwise, e is labelled *Removed*, meaning that e has been cleared but it does not belong to S nor T.

At some step of the execution of Protocol mc_search, it might happen that some vertices of S are not "useful" to let S be the densest possible ternary tree. Such vertices are those vertices of S with degree two or less in S, and whose all incident edges (in G) have been cleared. Let v be such a vertex and e its parent-edge. Protocol mc_search is aiming at "contracting" e. There are two cases according whether v is a leaf of S or not. In the first case, e is labelled *Removed*. In the latter case, e will be used by the searchers to circulate between the different components of S in G. For this purpose, e is labelled *Tree*. As a consequence, edges labelled *Minor* and *Tree* induce a tree T that enables the searchers to circulate in the clear part of G, by performing a DFS. Especially, T enables the searchers to reach all vertices of S.

We will show in the next sections that Protocol mc_search eventually clears G in a monotone connected way, starting from v_0, and using $N > 0$ searchers. Moreover,

---

* The *contraction* of the edge e with endpoints u, v is the replacement of u and v with a single vertex whose incident edges are the edges other than e that were incident to u or v.

mc_search organizes the moves of the searchers in such a way that the following three properties are satisfied at any step. These three properties enable to show that $N = O(\frac{n}{\log n} \times \textbf{mcs}(G, v_0))$.

1. T and S have maximum degree three,
2. the vertex-set of S is the set of vertices of G occupied by a searcher at this step, and
3. S has depth $k \geq 1$ only if there exists a previous step when S was the complete ternary tree T_{k-1}.

Let us consider k to be the maximum depth of S during the clearing of G. By properties **1,2** and **3**,

$$N \leq |V(T_k)| = \frac{|V(T_k)|}{\log |V(T_k)|} \times \log |V(T_k)|.$$

Moreover, by property **3**, T_{k-1} is minor of G, thus $\textbf{s}(T_{k-1}) \leq \textbf{s}(G) \leq \textbf{mcs}(G, v_0)$ and $|V(T_{k-1})| \leq 2|V(G)|$. By Theorems 1 and 3, $\log |V(T_k)| = O(k) = O(\textbf{mcs}(T_{k-1})) \leq O(\textbf{s}(T_{k-1})) \leq O(\textbf{s}(G)) \leq O(\textbf{mcs}(G, v_0))$. Finally, since the function $\frac{x}{\log x}$ is strictly increasing, and $|V(T_k)| = 3 |V(T_{k-1})| + 1 \leq 3 |V(G)| + 1 = 3 n + 1$, we obtain:

$$N = O(\frac{n}{\log n} \times \textbf{mcs}(G, v_0)).$$

3.2 Protocol mc_search

In this section, we describe the main features of protocol mc_search that is described in Figure 1. For the purpose of simplifying the presentation, we assume in this figure that searchers are able to communicate by exchanging messages of size $O(\log n)$ bits. This assumption can be implemented by an additional searcher. This extra searcher will be used to schedule the moves of the other searchers and to transmit few information between the searchers. For this purpose, the extra searcher performs a DFS of the tree T that enables it to reach any other searcher. First, we describe the data structure used by mc_search.

Every searcher has a state variable $level \in \{0, \cdots, n\}$. Roughly, this variable indicates the distance between the vertex currently occupied by the searcher and the root, in the tree S. Initially, any searcher has $level = 0$.

The whiteboard of every vertex $v \in V(G)$ contains one vector $status_v$. For any edge $e \in E(G)$ incident to v, $status_v[e]$ takes a value in $L = \{Contaminated, Removed, Tree, Minor\}$. Initially, for any vertex v and any edge e, $status_v[e] = Contaminated$. To simplify the presentation, we assume that each edge $e = \{u, v\} \in E(G)$ has only one label $\ell(e) = status_v[e] = status_u[e] \in L$. This also may be implemented by the extra searcher. Moreover the whiteboard of every vertex v contains a boolean $root_v$ which is either true if v is the current root of S or false.

The protocol is divided in $O(|E(G)|)$ phases. At each phase, at least an edge is relabelled. Note that any edge labelled $Contaminated$ (resp., $Minor$, resp., $Tree$) can be labelled $Minor$ or $Removed$ (resp., $Tree$ or $Removed$, resp., $Removed$). The edges labelled $Removed$ are not relabelled, which proves that Protocol mc_search terminates.

Let us define some notations. At any step, T is the subgraph of G induced by the edges labelled $Minor$ or $Tree$. In the next section, we prove that T is indeed a tree. S is the minor of T obtained by contracting all edges labelled $Tree$. Initially, T is rooted at v_0. Finally, for any vertex $v \in V(G)$, m_v, t_v, r_v, c_v denote the number of edges incident to v that are respectively labelled $Minor, Tree, Removed, Contaminated$.

Let us describe a phase of the execution of Protocol mc_search. A phase starts by the election of the searcher that will perform the move or the labelling of an edge. The elected searcher is an arbitrary searcher with minimum $level$ and that occupies a vertex $v \in V(G)$ satisfying one of the following four conditions, that we detail below. **Case a:** $t_v + m_v \leq 2$ and $c_v \geq 1$, **Case b:** $m_v = 1, t_v = 0$ and $c_v = 0$, **Case c:** $m_v + t_v = 2$, $m_v > 0$, $c_v = 0$ and v is not the root, **Case d:** $m_v + t_v = 2$, $c_v = 0$ and v is the root. We prove below that, while the graph is not clear, at least one vertex occupied by a searcher satisfies one of these conditions.

We will prove that, at any phase, any searcher actually occupies a vertex of S. Therefore, this election can easily be implemented by the extra searcher performing a DFS of T. Moreover, that can be done with $O(\log n)$ bit of memory, since the extra searcher only needs to remember the minimum $level$ of a searcher satisfying one of the above conditions that it meets during this DFS.

Once the extra searcher has performed this DFS and has gone back to the root, let k be the minimum $level$ satisfying one of the conditions, it has met. Then, the extra searcher performs a new DFS to reach a searcher A with $level = k$ at a vertex $v \in V(G)$ satisfying one of the conditions. We consider the four cases.

Case a. $t_v + m_v \leq 2$ and $c_v \geq 1$. That is, v has degree at most two in T and it is incident to a contaminated edge e. This case is aiming at adding an edge to T and S for letting S to be as close as possible to a complete ternary tree.

In this case, the extra searcher has led another searcher B from the root to v during its second DFS. The searcher B, followed by the extra searcher, clears e and reaches its other end $u \in V(G)$. Either there is an other searcher at u, i.e., u belongs to S, or not, i.e., $u \notin V(T)$. In the first case, the extra searcher labels e with $Removed$, i.e. e is clear but it does not belong to T. Then, B and the extra searcher goes back to the root. In the second case, the extra searcher labels e with $Minor$, i.e. e is added to S and T. Then, B remains at u to guard it, and B takes $level = k + 1$.

Case b. $m_v = 1$, $t_v = 0$ and $c_v = 0$. That is, v has degree one in T and S, and it is incident to no contaminated edge. This case is aiming at removing a leaf from S and T, because no other edge incident to this vertex might be added to T. This corresponds to relabelling $Removed$ the edge e incident to v in S that was labelled $Minor$. Moreover, let P be the maximal-inclusion path in T, such that v is an end of P, all edges of P are labelled $Tree$ and all internal vertices in P have degree two in T, then all these edges are relabelled $Removed$, which corresponds to removing all the vertices of P from T.

In this case, searcher A traverses the edge e labelled $Minor$, labelling it $Removed$. Let u be the other end of e. Once e has been removed from T, if u has degree one in T and its incident edge f in T has label $Tree$, f is removed in a similar way. This process is done recursively while it is possible. Note that

u cannot be incident to a contaminated edge, otherwise, the protocol ensures that another searcher with $level < k$ would have stand at u. To conclude this case, the extra searcher and searcher A go back to the root and takes $level = 0$. Again, it is possible thanks to a DFS of T.

Case c. $m_v + t_v = 2$, $m_v > 0$, $c_v = 0$ and v is not the root. That is, v has degree two in T and at least one in S and it is incident to no contaminated edge. This case is aiming at contracting an edge e in S. That corresponds to relabelling $Tree$ an edge incident to v in S that was labelled $Minor$. We prove that the parent-edge of such vertex is actually labelled $Minor$.

In this case, searcher A traverses the edge e labelled $Minor$, labelling it $Tree$. Then, searcher A goes back to the root and takes $level = 0$. Since, this case correspond to the contraction of e in S, we need to update, i.e., to decrease by one, the level of any searcher standing at a descendant of v. For this purpose, the extra searcher can perform a DFS of T_v the subtree of T rooted in v. Finally, the extra searcher goes back to the root.

Case d. $m_v + t_v = 2$, $c_v = 0$ and v is the root. That is, v has degree two in T and it is incident to no contaminated edge. This case is aiming at contracting an edge in S. There are two cases according whether v is incident to an edge labelled $Minor$, or not. If v is incident to an edge labelled $Minor$, let e be this edge. Otherwise, let w be the vertex that is one of the two vertices closest to v in T and such that $m_w > 0$, let e be the edge labelled $Minor$ incident to w, and let u be the other end of e. Note that we will prove that such a vertex w has degree two in T and is incident to exactly one edge labelled $Minor$. This case is aiming at contracting the edge e in S. That corresponds to relabelling the edge e with $Tree$. This case also modifies the position of the root.

In this case, all searchers standing at v (the root) are aiming at traversing the edge e and at labelling it $Tree$. If e is incident to v, it can easily be done. Otherwise, the searchers choose one of the two edges incident to v and traverse all edges labelled $Tree$ that they meet until reaching a vertex incident to an edge labelled $Minor$, i.e., the vertex w. Then, they traverse $e = \{w, u\}$ and relabelled it $Tree$. In both cases, the searchers reach the vertex u that becomes the new root, i.e., the booleans $root_v$ and $root_u$ are updated. Again, we need to update, i.e., to decrease by one, the level of any searcher standing at a descendant of v in the subtree containing u. This can be done by the extra searcher as in the previous case. Finally, the extra searcher goes back to the new root.

3.3   Correctness of Protocol `mc_search`

This section is devoted to prove the following theorem.

Theorem 4. *Let G be a connected n-node graph and $v_0 \in V(G)$. Protocol* `mc_search` *enables $O(\frac{n}{\log n} \mathbf{mcs}(G, v_0))$ searchers to clear G in a monotone connected way, starting from v_0.*

Proof. The difficult part of the proof consists in showing that not too many searchers are used. Thus, let us first prove that Protocol `mc_search` clears G in a monotone

Initially all searchers stand at v_0 with $level = 0$. $T = (v_0, \emptyset)$ with v_0 as root.
During the execution of mc_search, T is the tree that consists of edges labelled $Tree$ or $Minor$.

Description of the execution of any phase of Protocol mc_search.

While there exists an edge labelled $Contaminated$ **do**

1. Election of a searcher A occupying a vertex v, with minimum $level$, say L, such that one of the four
   following cases is satisfied.
   (Case a) $t_v + m_v \leq 2, c_v \geq 1$
   (Case b) $m_v = 1, t_v = 0, c_v = 0$
   (Case c) $m_v + t_v = 2, m_v > 0, c_v = 0$ and v is not the root
   (Case d) $m_v + t_v = 2, c_v = 0$ and v is the root

2. **(Case a)**
   > A searcher B standing at the root is called and goes to v.
   > Let e be an edge incident to v and labelled $Contaminated$;
   > B clears e; Let u be the other end of e;
   > **if** u is occupied by another searcher **then**
   > > Label e $Removed$;
   > > Searcher B goes to the root;
   >
   > **else** Label e $Minor$; Searcher B takes $level = L + 1$; **endif**

   (Case b)
   > Let e be the edge incident to v labelled $Minor$.
   > Label e $Removed$ and let u its other end;
   > **if** v is the root **then** u becomes the new root;
   > > all searchers standing at v go to u; **endif**
   >
   > **While** $m_u = 0, t_u = 1, c_u = 0$ **do**
   > > Let f be the edge incident to u labelled $Tree$.
   > > Label f $Removed$; Let u' the other end of f and A goes to u';
   > > **if** u is the root **then** u' becomes the new root
   > > > and all searchers standing at u go to u'; **endif**
   > >
   > > $u \leftarrow u'$;
   >
   > **EndWhile**
   > Searcher A goes to the root;

   (Case c)
   > Let e be the parent-edge of v and u its other end;
   > Label e with $Tree$;
   > Let T_v be the subtree of T obtained by removing e and containing v;
   > Any searcher occupying a vertex of T_v decreases its $level$ by one;
   > Searcher A goes to the root;

   (Case d)
   > Let e be an edge that is closest to v in T such that e is labelled $Minor$;
   > Let u be the vertex such that e is its parent-edge;
   > Label e with $Tree$;
   > Let T' be the subtree of T obtained by removing e and that does not contain v;
   > Any searcher occupying a vertex of T' decreases its $level$ by one;
   > u becomes the new root;
   > All searchers that were standing at v go to u;

endWhile

Fig. 1. Protocol mc_search

connected way. Initially, all edges are labelled $Contaminated$ and the label of an edge
e becomes $Minor$ or $Removed$ as soon as e is traversed by a searcher. Moreover, after this traversal, each of its ends is occupied by a searcher (Case a). The strategy is

obviously monotone since a searcher is removed from a vertex v if either v is occupied by an other searcher (Case a), or no contaminated edge is incident to v, i.e. $c_v = 0$, (Cases b, c and d). Therefore, the strategy is monotone and connected since it is monotone and starts from a single vertex v_0. Finally, Protocol mc_search eventually clears G. Indeed, at each step, an edge is labelled, and any edge is relabelled at most three times: $Minor, Tree$, and $Removed$ in this order. Thus, no loop can occur. Moreover, we prove below that T is a tree. Therefore, at any step, at least the searchers occupying its leaves satisfy the conditions of the cases a, b, c, or d. Thus, while there remains a contaminated edge, a searcher will eventually be called to clear this edge.

The remaining part of the section is devoted to prove that Protocol mc_search uses at most $O(\frac{n}{\log n} \mathbf{mcs}(G, v_0))$ searchers. For this purpose, it is sufficient to prove the three properties described in section 3.1. More precisely, we prove the following lemma.

Lemma 1. *Let us consider a phase of the execution of Protocol* mc_search. *Let T be the subgraph of G induced by the edges labelled $Minor$ or $Tree$. Let S be the minor of T when all edges labelled $Tree$ have been contracted.*

1. *T and S are rooted trees with maximum degree at most three,*
2. *the vertex-set of S is the set of vertices of G occupied by a searcher at this phase, and*
3. *S has depth $k \geq 1$ only if there exists a previous step when S was the complete ternary tree T_{k-1}.*

The proof is by induction on the number of phases of the execution of Protocol mc_search. Initially, the result is obviously valid. Let $p > 0$ be a phase of the execution of mc_search and let us assume that the result is valid for any previous phase. Let T' be the subgraph of G induced by the edges labelled $Minor$ or $Tree$ after phase $p - 1$, and S' the minor corresponding to the contraction of edges labelled $Tree$.

First we prove that S and T are acyclic. Note that, by definition, for any vertex $v \in V(G)$, $m_v + t_v$ is the degree of v in T'. According to the induction hypothesis, T' is a tree with maximum degree at most three. Let v be a vertex incident to at least one edge labelled $Contaminated$ and that is not occupied by a searcher. By monotonicity of the strategy, all edges incident to v are labelled $Contaminated$. Thus, such a vertex does not belong to T'. Let us show that after phase p, T is a tree with maximum degree three. We consider the four cases (a),(b),(c) and (d).

Case a. Either an edge $e = \{v, u\}$ is added to T', i.e., $T = (V(T') \cup \{u\}, E(T') \cup \{e\})$, or T' remains unchanged, i.e., $T = T'$. Since, $v \in V(T')$ and $u \notin V(T')$, T is a tree in both cases. Moreover, $m_v + t_v \leq 2$, thus v has degree at most two in T'. Thus T has maximum degree at most three.

Case b. $m_v + t_v = 1$, thus v is a leaf of T. Let $u' \in V(T')$ be the neighbor of v and $e = \{u', v\}$ that is labelled $Minor$. First e is relabelled $Removed$, thus v is removed from T'. Then, if u' is of degree one in $T' \setminus \{v\}$ and its incident edge f in $T' \setminus \{v\}$ is labelled $Tree$, f is relabelled $Removed$, i.e. u' is removed from $T' \setminus \{v\}$. This process is repeated recursively. Thus, T is a tree obtained from T' by recursively removing leaves of T'. Hence, the maximum degree of T is at most three.

Cases c and d. At most one edge of T' is relabelled $Tree$, thus $T' = T$. In the proof of the Claim (see above) we prove that exactly one edge of T' is relabelled $Tree$.

It follows that T is a tree with maximum degree at most three. Since S is a minor of T, S is a tree.

Before proving that the maximum degree of S is three, we prove the second property. We prove by induction on p that the vertices occupied by a searcher are exactly: the root, and those vertices the parent-edge of which is labelled $Minor$.

Initially, the result is obviously valid. Let $p > 0$ be a phase of the execution of mc_search and let us assume that the result is valid for any previous phase. We consider the four cases a, b, c and d. Let V'_M be the set of vertices such that their parent-edge are labelled $Minor$ after the phase $p - 1$.

Case a. An edge $e = \{v, u\}$ labelled $Contaminated$ is the only edge to be relabelled. It is relabelled either $Removed$ or $Minor$. In the first case, $S = S'$ and the searchers occupy exactly the same vertices than after the phase $p - 1$, thus the property holds. In the second case, u is a leaf of T, and e is the parent edge of u. Thus $S = (V(S') \cup \{u\}, E(S') \cup \{e\})$. Moreover the vertices occupied by a searcher are exactly $V(S') \cup \{u\}$. Thus the property holds.

Case b. Let $e = \{v, u\}$ be the edge adjacent to v labelled $Minor$. e is the only edge relabelled from $Minor$ to $Removed$. All the other relabelled edges are labelled from $Tree$ to $Removed$. Thus $V_M = V'_M \setminus \{v\}$. Indeed note that if the root changes, the parent-edge of each vertex in $V'_M \setminus \{v\}$ does not change. If the root does not change, then $S = (V(S') \setminus \{u\}, E(S') \setminus \{e\})$. Moreover the vertices occupied by a searcher are exactly $V(S)$ and the property holds. If the root changes to w, $S = (V_M \cup \{w\}, E(S') \setminus \{e\})$, the vertices occupied by a searcher are exactly $V(S)$ and the property holds.

Case c. The parent-edge e of the vertex v is the only edge relabelled, and according to induction hypothesis it is relabelled from $Minor$ to $Tree$. Thus $S = (V(S') \setminus \{v\}, E(S') \setminus \{e\})$. Moreover the vertices occupied by a searcher are exactly $V(S)$, thus the property holds.

Case d. Let e be an edge that is closest to v in T' such that e is labelled $Minor$. We will prove in the next proof that such an edge always exists. If this edge does not exist nothing happens and the property holds.

Let u be the vertex such that e is its parent-edge. The edge e is the only edge relabelled, it is relabelled from $Minor$ to $Tree$. Thus $V_M = V'_M \setminus \{u\}$. Indeed the root changes such that the parent-edge of each vertex in V_M does not change and u is the new root. The root changes to u, thus $S = (V_M \cup \{u\}, E(S') \setminus \{e\})$. Moreover the vertices occupied by a searcher are exactly $V_M \cup \{u\}$ and the property holds.

Thus, at phase p, the vertex-set of S is the set of vertices of G occupied by a searcher at this phase.

In order to prove that S has maximum degree at most three, we need the following claim:

Claim. Let $v \in V(T)$ incident to an edge e labelled $Tree$, and such that e is not its parent-edge. Let T_v be the subtree of T obtained by removing e from T and that does not contain v. There exists an edge $f = \{u, w\}$ labelled $Minor$, such that f is the parent edge of w, u has degree two in T, and the subtree P of T_v obtained by removing f from T_v and that contains u consists of a path of edges labelled $Tree$.

Obviously, T_v contains at least one edge labelled $Minor$ because all leaves of T are labelled $Minor$. Indeed, when a leaf is added to T, its incident edge is labelled $Minor$ (Case a) and, when a leaf and its incident edge e labelled $Minor$ are removed, the whole path of edges labelled $Tree$ at which e is attached are removed (Case b).

We now prove that, for any vertex $u \in V(T)$ that is not the root, such that all its incident edges in T are labelled $Tree$, u has degree two in T. Since we have proved that a leaf can only be incident to an edge labelled $Minor$, u has degree at least two in T. For purpose of contradiction, let us assume that u has degree three in T. Let us consider the phase of the execution of mc_search such that the last edge incident to u and labelled $Contaminated$ has been relabelled. From this phase, the degree of u in T might only have decreased. It follows that this vertex cannot have satisfied conditions corresponding to Cases b,c, or d. Thus, u has never been the root otherwise it would still be the case. Moreover, the parent-edge of u has never been relabelled contradicting the fact that it is labelled $Tree$. Hence, such a vertex u has degree exactly two in T.

Let f be the edge labelled $Minor$ that is the closest to v in T_v. Let u be the end of f that is closest to v. Obviously, u is not the root and its parent-edge is labelled $Tree$. It only remains to prove that u has degree exactly two in T. Similarly to the previous paragraph, we assume, for purpose of contradiction, that u has degree three in T. Again, this leads to the fact that its parent-edge could not have been relabelled, a contradiction. Thus, u has degree two and it is incident to an edge labelled $Minor$ and another edge labelled $Tree$. Moreover, all internal vertices of the path between u and v have degree two in T and they are incident to edges labelled $Tree$. This concludes the proof of the Claim.   ◇

Now, let us prove that S has maximum degree at most three. According to the induction hypothesis, S' has maximum degree at most three. To prove that the maximum degree of S is at most three, the four cases a, b, c and d must be considered by taking into account the previous claim. Indeed using the Claim, we get that the degree in S of a node v is actually equal to $m_v + t_v$, i.e., its degree in T. The induction consists to prove that at the end of the phase p, for all node $v \in S$, $m_v + t_v \leq 3$ according to the case a, b, c and d. The formal proof is omitted due to lack of space and can be found in [12].

To conclude the proof of the lemma, let us prove the third property. First, for any searcher occupying a vertex v of S, its level is the distance between v and the root. Let $k \geq 1$ and let us consider the first phase p at which the depth of S becomes k. The phase p consists of the clearing of a contaminated edge $e = \{u, v\}$ with $u \in V(S)$ occupied by a searcher with level $k - 1$, and $v \in V(G) \setminus V(T)$. Since the move performed at phase p is executed by the searcher with smallest level, it means that no searcher with level less than $k - 1$ can move. That is, all internal vertices of S have degree three and S has depth $k - 1$, i.e. $S = T_{k-1}$. This concludes the proof of the lemma and of the theorem.   □

References

1. Barrière, L., Flocchini, P., Fraigniaud, P., Santoro, N.: Capture of an intruder by mobile agents. In: 14th ACM Symp. on Parallel Algorithms and Architectures (SPAA), pp. 200–209. ACM Press, New York (2002)
2. Barrière, L., Fraigniaud, P., Santoro, N., Thilikos, D.: Connected and Internal Graph Searching. In: Bodlaender, H.L. (ed.) WG 2003. LNCS, vol. 2880, pp. 34–45. Springer, Heidelberg (2003)
3. Bienstock, D.: Graph searching, path-width, tree-width and related problems (a survey) DIMACS Ser. in Discrete Mathematics and Theoretical Computer Science, 5, pp. 33–49 (1991)
4. Bienstock, D., Seymour, P.: Monotonicity in graph searching. Journal of Algorithms 12, 239–245 (1991)
5. Blin, L., Fraigniaud, P., Nisse, N., Vial, S.: Distributing Chasing of Network Intruders. In: Flocchini, P., Gasieniec, L. (eds.) SIROCCO 2006. LNCS, vol. 4056, pp. 70–84. Springer, Heidelberg (2006)
6. Breisch, R.: An intuitive approach to speleotopology. Southwestern Cavers 5, 72–78 (1967)
7. Flocchini, P., Luccio, F.L., Song, L.: Decontamination of chordal rings and tori. In: Proc. of 8th Workshop on Advances in Parallel and Distributed Computational Models (APDCM) (2006)
8. Flocchini, P., Luccio, F.L., Song, L.: Size Optimal Strategies for Capturing an Intruder in Mesh Networks. In: Proceedings of the 2005 International Conference on Communications in Computing (CIC), pp. 200–206 (2005)
9. Flocchini, P., Huang, M.J., Luccio, F.L.: Contiguous search in the hypercube for capturing an intruder. In: Proc. of 18th IEEE Int. Parallel and Distributed Processing Symp (IPDPS), IEEE Computer Society Press, Los Alamitos (2005)
10. Fraigniaud, P., Nisse, N.: Connected Treewidth and Connected Graph Searching. In: Correa, J.R., Hevia, A., Kiwi, M. (eds.) LATIN 2006. LNCS, vol. 3887, pp. 470–490. Springer, Heidelberg (2006)
11. Fraigniaud, P., Nisse, N.: Monotony properties of connected visible graph searching. In: Fomin, F.V. (ed.) WG 2006. LNCS, vol. 4271, pp. 229–240. Springer, Heidelberg (2006)
12. Ilcinkas, D., Nisse, N., Soguet, D.: The cost of monotonicity in distributed graph searching. Technical Report, LRI-1475, University Paris-Sud, France (September 2007)
13. LaPaugh, A.: Recontamination does not help to search a graph. Journal of the ACM 40(2), 224–245 (1993)
14. Luccio, F.L.: Intruder capture in Sierpinski graphs. In: Crescenzi, P., Prencipe, G., Pucci, G. (eds.) FUN 2007. LNCS, vol. 4475, pp. 249–261. Springer, Heidelberg (2007)
15. Megiddo, N., Hakimi, S., Garey, M., Johnson, D., Papadimitriou, C.: The complexity of searching a graph. Journal of the ACM 35(1), 18–44 (1988)
16. Nisse, N., Soguet, D.: Graph searching with advice. In: Prencipe, G., Fales, S. (eds.) SIROCCO 2007. 14th Colloquium on Structural Information and Communication Complexity. LNCS, vol. 4474, pp. 51–67. Springer, Heidelberg (2007)
17. Parson, T.: Pursuit-evasion in a graph. In: Parson, T. (ed.) Theory and Applications of Graphs. Lecture Notes in Mathematics, pp. 426–441. Springer, Heidelberg (1976)
18. Yang, B., Dyer, D., Alspach, B.: Sweeping Graphs with Large Clique Number. In: Fleischer, R., Trippen, G. (eds.) ISAAC 2004. LNCS, vol. 3341, pp. 908–920. Springer, Heidelberg (2004)

Timed Quorum Systems for Large-Scale and Dynamic Environments

Vincent Gramoli[1,2,*] and Michel Raynal[2]

[1] INRIA Futurs,
Parc Club Orsay Université, 91893 Orsay, France
vgramoli@irisa.fr
[2] Université de Rennes 1 and INRIA Research Centre Rennes,
Campus de Beaulieu, 35042 Rennes, France
raynal@irisa.fr

Abstract. This paper presents Timed Quorum System (TQS), a quorum system for large-scale and dynamic systems. TQS provides guarantees that two quorums, accessed at instances of time that are close together, intersect with high probability. We present an algorithm that implements TQS at its core and that provides operations that respect atomicity with high probability. This TQS implementation has quorums of size $O(\sqrt{nD})$ and expected access time of $O(\log \sqrt{nD})$ message delays, where n measures the size of the system and D is a required parameter to handle dynamism. This algorithm is shown to have complexity sub-linear in size and dynamism of the system, and hence to be scalable. It is also shown that for systems where operations are frequent enough, the system achieves the lower bound on quorum size for probabilistic quorums in static systems, and it is thus optimal in that sense.

Keywords: Time, Quorums, Churn, Scalability, Probabilistic atomicity.

1 Introduction

The need of resources is a main motivation behind distributed systems. Take peer-to-peer (p2p) systems as an example. A p2p system is a distributed system that has no centralized control. The p2p systems have gained in popularity with the massive utilization of file-sharing applications over the Internet, since 2000. These systems propose a tremendous amount of file resources. More generally, there is an increasing amount of various computing devices surrounding us: IDC predicts that there will be 17 billions of traditional network devices by 2012. In such a context, it is common knowledge that scalability has become one of the most important challenges of today's distributed systems.

The scale-shift of distributed systems modifies the way computational entities communicate. Energy dependence, disconnection, malfunctioning, and environmental factors affect the availability of various computational entities independently. This translates into irregular periods of activity during which an entity can receive messages

---

* Corresponding author: ASAP Research Group, INRIA Futurs, 3-4 rue Jacques Monod, 91893 Orsay, France; fax: +33 1 74 85 42 42.

E. Tovar, P. Tsigas, and H. Fouchal (Eds.): OPODIS 2007, LNCS 4878, pp. 429–442, 2007.

or compute tasks. As a result of this independent and periodic behaviors, these systems are inherently highly dynamic.

Quorum system is a largely adopted solution for communication in message-passing system. Despite the interest for emulating shared-memory in dynamic systems [1,2,3,4], there is no scalable solution due to the cost of their failure handling mechanism or their operation complexity.

This paper describes a Timed Quorum System (TQS) for large-scale dynamic systems. TQS provides guarantees that two quorums, accessed at instances of time that are close together, intersect with high probability. We propose an algorithm that implements TQS and that verifies probabilistic atomicity: a consistency criterion that requires each operation to respect atomicity with high probability. This algorithm is analyzed to show scalability in terms of complexity. More precisely, the expected time complexity is $O(\log \sqrt{nD})$ message delays, where n measures the size of the system and D is a required parameter to handle dynamism. It is also shown that for systems where operations are frequent enough, the algorithm achieves a lower bound, $O(\sqrt{n})$, on quorum size for probabilistic quorum in static systems, and it is thus optimal in that sense. In addition, we show that our solution does not need a reconfiguration mechanism to tolerate the dynamic and fault-prone environment for which it is designed due to the integration of a replication mechanism on top of the operations performed on the replicated object.

Related Work. Dynamic quorum systems are a very active research area. Some dynamic quorum systems rely on failure detectors where quorums are dynamically redefined according to failure detection, This adaption leads to a redefinition of the quorums [1,5] or to the replacement of the failed nodes in the quorums [6,7,8]. For example, in [7], a communication structure is continuously maintained to ensure that quorums intersect at all time (with high probability).

Other solutions rely on periodic reconfigurations [2,4] where the quorum systems are subsequently replaced. These solutions are different from the previous ones since the newly installed quorums do not need to intersect with the previous ones. In [3] a quorum abstraction is defined by two properties: (i) intersection and (ii) progress, in which the notion of time is introduced. First, a quorum of a certain type intersects the quorum of another type contacted subsequently. Second, each node of a quorum remains active between the time the quorum starts being probed and the time the quorum stopped being probed.

As far as we know, TQS is the first quorum system that expresses guarantees that are both timely and probabilistic. Time and probability relax the traditional intersection requirement of quorums. We present a scalable emulation of a probabilistic atomic memory where each operation is atomic with high probability and complexity is sublinear in both the size and the dynamism of the system.

Roadmap. Section 2 presents the model and describes the problem. Section 3 defines the Timed Quorum System. Section 4 presents a shared object by specifying read and write operations based on a TQS. Section 5 shows that this solution implements TQS and verifies probabilistic atomicity, and analyses the complexity of the algorithm. Finally, Section 6 concludes the paper.

2   System Model and Problem Definition

2.1   Model

The computation model is very simple. The system consists of n nodes. It is dynamic in the following sense. Every time unit, cn nodes leave the system and cn nodes enter the system, where c is an upper bound on the percentage of nodes that enter/leave the system per time unit and is called the *churn*; this can be seen as new nodes "replacing" leaving nodes. A node leaves the system either voluntarily or because it crashes. A node that leaves the system does not reenter it later. (Practically, this means that, when a node reenters the system, it is considered as a new node; all its previous knowledge of the system state is lost.) For the sake of simplicity, it is assumed that for any subset S of nodes, the portion of replaced nodes is $c|S|$. As explained below, the model can be made more complex. The *universe* U denotes all the nodes of the system, plus the ones that have already left the system and the ones that have not joined the system yet.

2.2   Problem

Most of the dynamic models assume that dynamic events are dependent from each other: only a limited number of nodes leave and join the system during a bounded period of time. For instance in [4], it is assumed that node departures are dependent: quorum replication ensures that all nodes of at least any two quorums remain active between the occurrence of two reconfigurations. However, in a real dynamic system, nodes act independently. Due to this independence, even with a precise knowledge of the past dynamic events, one can not predict the future behavior of a node. That is, putting this observation into the quorums context, it translates into the impossibility of predicting deterministically whether quorums intersect.

In contrast, TQS requires that quorums intersect with high probability. This allows to use a more realistic model in which there is a certain probability that nodes leave/join the system at the same time. That is, *the goal here is to measure the probability that any two quorums intersect as time elapses*. Observe that, realistically, the probability that k nodes leave the system increases as time elapses. As a result, the probability that a quorum $Q(t)$ probed at time t and that a quorum $Q(t')$ probed at time t' intersect decreases as the period $|t'-t|$ increases. In the following we propose an implementation of TQS where probability of intersection remains high.

More precisely, each quorum of our TQS implementation is defined for a given time t. Each quorum $Q(t)$ has a lifetime Δ that represents a period during which the quorum is *reachable*. Differently from availability defined in [5], reachability does not depend on the number of nodes that are failed in a quorum system because this number is unpredictable in dynamic systems. Instead, a $Q(t)$ quorum is reachable if at least one node of quorum $Q(t)$ is reached with high probability: if two quorums are reachable at the same time, they intersect with high probability. More generally, let two quorums $Q(t)$ and $Q(t')$ of a TQS be reachable during Δ time (their lifetime is Δ); if $|t-t'| \leq \Delta$ then $Q(t)$ and $Q(t')$ intersect with high probability.

2.3   Preliminary Notations and Definitions

This section defines several terms that are used in the algorithm description. Recall that a shared object is accessed through read operations, which return the current value of the object, and write operations, which modify the current value of the object. Initially, any object has a default value v_0 that is replicated at a set of nodes and V denotes the set of all possible values present in the system. An object is accessed by read or write operations initiated by some nodes i at time $t \in T$ that return or modify the object value v. (T is the set of all possible time instances.) If a node initiates an operation, then it is referred to as a *client*. All nodes of the system, including nodes of the quorum system, can initiate a read or a write operation, i.e., all nodes are potential clients and the multi-reader/multi-writer model is used. In the following we only consider a single object accessed by operations.

First, to clarify the notion of currency when concurrency happens, it is important to explain what are the up-to-date values that could be considered as current. We refer to the *last value* as the value associated with the largest *tag* among all values whose propagation is complete. We refer to the *up-to-date values* at time t as all values v that satisfies one of the following properties: *(i)* value v is the last value or *(ii)* value v is a value whose propagation is ongoing and whose associated tag is at least equal or larger to the tag associated with the last value.

Second, it is important to understand what is a successful phase. The goal of a consultation phase is to return an up-to-date value, whereas the goal of the propagation phase is to propagate an up-to-date value v so that v can be identified as an up-to-date value. Thus, we refer to a *successful phase* as a phase that achieves its goal. Observe that, if the consultation of an operation is unsuccessful, then the subsequent propagation phase of the same operation might propagate a new value with a small tag so that this value will not be identifiable as an up-to-date value. In this case, we say that both the consultation and propagation are unsuccessful phases. A more formal definition of the successful/unsuccessful phase follows.

Definition 1 (Successful Phase). *A consultation phase ϕ is* successful *if and only if it returns an up-to-date value $val(\phi)$. A propagation phase ρ is* successful *if and only if it propagates a tag $tag(\rho)$ largest than any of the tags that were in the system when ρ started. A phase is* unsuccessful *if it is not successful.*

We refer to successful operations as operations whose consultation phase and propagation phase are successful.

TQS ensures that two active quorums will intersect with high probability, however, if no quorum is active, then the value of an object does no longer persist. To ensure that new operations replicate the object value sufficiently, we assume that at last one operation is executed every period Δ. As previously explained this mechanism serves as a continuous replication and replaces the traditional reconfiguration mechanism to cope with accumulated failures.

2.4   Probabilistic Atomic Object

A probabilistic atomic object aims at emulating a memory that offers high quality of service despite large-scale and dynamism. For the sake of tolerating scale-shift and dynamism, we aim at relaxing some properties. However, our goal is to provide each client with a distributed shared memory emulation that offers satisfying quality of service. Quality of service must be formally stated by a consistency criterion that defines the guarantees the application can expect from the memory emulation. We aim at providing quality of service in terms of accuracy of read and write operations. In other words, our goal is to provide the clients with a memory that guarantees that each read or write operation will be successfully executed with high probability. We define the probabilistic atomic object as an atomic object where operation accuracy is ensured with high probability.

Let us first recall properties 2 and 4 of atomicity from Theorem 13.16 of [9] which require that any sequence of invocations and responses of read and write operations applied to x satisfies a partial ordering $\prec$ such that:

- (π_1, π_2)-*ordering*: if the response event of operation π_1 precedes the invocation event of operation π_2, then it is not possible to have $\pi_2 \prec \pi_1$;
- (π_1, π_2)-*return*: the value returned by a read operation π_2 is the value written by the last preceding write operation π_1 regarding to $\prec$ (in case no such write operation π_1 exists, this value returned is the default value).

The definition of probabilistic atomicity is similar to the definition of atomicity: only Properties 2 and 4 are slightly modified, as indicated below.

Definition 2 (Probabilistic Atomic Object). *Let x be a read/write probabilistic atomic object. Let H be a complete sequence of invocations responses of read and write operations applied to object x. The sequence H satisfies probabilistic atomicity if and only if there is a partial ordering $\prec$ on the operations such that the following properties hold:*

1. *For any operation π_2, there are only finitely many successful operations π_1, such that $\pi_1 \prec \pi_2$.*
2. *Let π_1 be a successful operation. Any operation π_2 satisfies (π_1, π_2)-ordering with high probability. (If π_2 does not satisfy it, then π_2 is unsuccessful.)*
3. *if π_1 is a successful write operation and π_2 is any successful operation, then either $\pi_2 \prec \pi_1$ or $\pi_1 \prec \pi_2$;*
4. *Let π_1 be a successful operation. Any operation π_2 satisfies (π_1, π_2)-return with high probability. (If π_2 does not satisfy it, then π_2 is unsuccessful.)*

Observe that the partial ordering is defined on successful operations. That is, either an operation π fails and this operation is considered as unordered or the operation succeeds and is ordered with respect to other successful operations.

Even though an operation succeeds with high probability, there might be a lot of unsuccessful operations in a long enough execution. However, our goal is to provide the operation requester (client) with high guarantee of success for each of its operation request.

3   Timed Quorum System

This section defines Timed Quorum Systems (TQS). Before being created or after its lifetime has elapsed, a quorum is not guaranteed to intersect with any other quorum, however, during its lifetime a quorum is considered as available: two quorums that are available at the same time intersect with high probability. In dynamic systems nodes may leave at any time, but this probability is bounded, thus it is possible to determine the intersection probability of two quorums.

Next, we formally define TQS that are especially suited for dynamic systems. Recall that the universe U contains the set of all possible nodes, including nodes that have not yet joined the system. First, we restate the definition of a *set system* as a set of subsets of a universe of nodes.

Definition 3 (Set System). *A set system S over a universe U is a set of subsets of U.*

Then, we define the timed access strategy as a probability distribution over a set system that may vary over time. This definition is motivated by the fact that an access strategy defined over a set S can evolve. To compare with the existing probabilistic dynamic quorums, in [7] the authors defined a dynamic quorum system using an evolving strategy that might replace some nodes of a quorum while its access strategy remains identical despite this evolution. Unlike the dynamic quorum approach, we need a more general framework to consider quorums that are different not only because of their structure but also because of how likely they can be accessed. The timely access strategy adds a time parameter to the seminal definition access strategy given by Malkhi et al. [10]. A timely access strategy is allowed to evolve over time.

Definition 4 (Timed Access Strategy). *A timed access strategy $\omega(t)$ for a set system S at time $t \in T$ is a probability distribution on the elements of S at time t. That is, $\omega : S \times T \to [0, 1]$ satisfies at any time $t \in T$: $\sum_{s \in S} \omega(s, t) = 1$.*

Informally, at two distinct instants $t_1 \in T$ and $t_2 \in T$, an access strategy might be different for any reason. For instance, consider that some node i is active at time t_1 while the same node i is failed at time t_2, hence it is likely that if $i \in s$, then $\omega(s, t_1) \neq 0$ while $\omega(s, t_2) = 0$. This is due to the fact that a node is reachable only when it is active.

Definition 5 (Δ-Timed Quorum System). *Let Q be a set system, let $\omega(t)$ be a timed access strategy for Q at time t, and let $0 < \epsilon < 1$ be given. The tuple $\langle Q, \omega(t) \rangle$ is a Δ-timed quorum system if for any quorums $Q(t_1) \in Q$ accessed with strategy $\omega(t_1)$ and $Q(t_2) \in Q$ accessed with strategy $\omega(t_2)$, we have:*

$$\Delta \geq |t_1 - t_2| \Rightarrow \Pr[Q(t_1) \cap Q(t_2) \neq \emptyset] \geq 1 - \epsilon.$$

4   Timed Quorum System Implementation for Probabilistic Atomic Memory

In the following, we present a structureless memory. The quorum systems this memory uses does not rely on any structure, that is, the quorum system is flexible. In contrast with using a logical structured overlay (e.g., [11]) for communication among quorum system nodes, we use an unstructured communication overlay [12]. The lack of structure presents several benefits. First, there is no need to re-adapt the structure at each dynamic event. Second, there is no need for detecting failure. Our solution proposes a periodic replication. To ensure the persistence of an object value despite unbounded leaves, the value must be replicated an unbounded number of times. The solution we propose requires periodic operations and an approximation of the system size. Although we do not focus on the problem of approximating the system size n, we suggest the use of existing protocols approximating closely the system size in dynamic systems [13].

4.1 Replicating During Client Operations

Benefiting from the natural primitive of the distributed shared memory, values are replicated using operations. Any operation has at its heart a quorum-probe that replicates value. On the one hand, it is natural to think of a write operation as an operation that replicates a value. On the other hand, in [14] a Theorem shows that "read must write", meaning that a read operation must replicates the value it returns. This raises the question: if operations replicate, why does a memory need additional replication mechanism? In large-scale systems, it is also reasonable to assume that shared objects are frequently accessed because of the large number of participants. Since operations provide replication and shared objects experience frequent operation requests in large-scale systems, frequent replications can be mainly ensured by client operations.

4.2 Quorum Probe

The algorithm is divided in three distinct parts that represent the state of the algorithm (Lines 1–12), the actions initiated by a client (Lines 13–42), and the actions taken upon reception of messages by a node (Lines 43–63), respectively. Each node i has its own copy of the object called its value val_i and an associated tag tag_i. Field tag is a couple of a counter and a node identifier and represents, at any time, the version number of its corresponding value val. We assume that, initially, there are q nodes that own the default value of the object, the other nodes have their values val set to $\perp$ and all their $tags$ are set to $\langle 0, 0 \rangle$.

Each read and write operation is executed by client i in two subsequent phases, each disseminating a message to $q = O(\sqrt{nD})$ nodes, where $D = (1 - c)^{-\Delta}$ represents the inverse of the portion of nodes that stayed in the system during period Δ. This dynamic parameter D is required to handle churn c during period Δ.[1] The two successive phases are called the *consultation phase* and the *propagation phase*. The consultation phase aims at consulting the up-to-date value of the object that is present in the system. (This value is identifiable because it is associated with the largest tag present in the system.) More precisely, client i disseminates a consultation message to q nodes so that each receiver j responds with a message containing value val_j and tag tag_j so that client i can update val_i and tag_i. In fact, i updates val_i and tag_i if and only if the tag_i has either a smaller counter than tag_j or it has an equal counter but a smaller identifier $i < j$ (node identifiers are always distinct); in this case we say $tag_i < tag_j$ for short (cf. Lines 51 and 53). Ideally, at the end of the consultation phase client i has set its value val_i to the up-to-date value. Read and write operations differ from the value and tag that are propagated by the client i. Specifically, in case of a read, client i propagates the value

---

[1] It is shown in [10] that $q = O(\sqrt{n})$ is sufficient in static systems.

Algorithm 1. Disseminating Memory at node i

1: **State of node i:**
2:    $q = \frac{\beta \sqrt{n}}{(1-c)^{\frac{\Delta}{2}}}$, the quorum size
3:    $\ell, k \in \mathbb{N}$ the disseminating parameters taken such that $\frac{k^{l+1}-1}{k-1} \geq q$
4:    $val \in V$, the value of the object, initially $\perp$
5:    tag, a couple of fields:
6:       $counter \in \mathbb{N}$, initially 0
7:       $id \in I$, an identifier initially i
8:    $marked$, an array of booleans initially false at all indices
9:    $sent\text{-}to\text{-}nbrs1$, $sent\text{-}to\text{-}nbrs2$ two sets of node identifiers, initially $\emptyset$
10:   $rcvd\text{-}from\text{-}qnodes$, an infinite array of identifier sets, initially $\emptyset$ at all indices
11:   $sn \in \mathbb{N}$, the sequence number of the current phase, initially 0
12:   $father \in I$, the id of the node that disseminated a message to i, initially i

13: **Read$_i$:**
14:   $\langle val, tag \rangle \leftarrow$ **Consult**()
15:   **Propagate**($\langle val, tag \rangle$)

16: **Write(v)$_i$:**
17:   $\langle *, tag \rangle \leftarrow$**Consult**()
18:   $tag.counter \leftarrow tag.counter + 1$
19:   $tag.id \leftarrow i$
20:   $val \leftarrow v$
21:   **Propagate**($\langle val, tag \rangle$)

22: **Consult$_i$:**
23:   $ttl \leftarrow \ell$
24:   $sn \leftarrow sn + 1$
25:   **while** ($|sent\text{-}to\text{-}nbrs1| < k$) **do**
26:      send$\langle$CONS, $val, tag, ttl, i, sn\rangle$ to
27:         a set J of $(k - |sent\text{-}to\text{-}nbrs1|)$ neighbors $\neq father$
28:      $sent\text{-}to\text{-}nbrs1 \leftarrow sent\text{-}to\text{-}nbrs1 \cup J$
29:   **end while**
30:   $sent\text{-}to\text{-}nbrs1 \leftarrow \emptyset$
31:   **wait until** $|rcvd\text{-}from\text{-}qnodes[sn]| \geq q$
32:   **return** ($\langle val, tag \rangle$)

---

and tag pair freshly consulted, while in the case of write, client i propagates the new value to write with a strictly larger tag than the largest tag that i has consulted so far. The propagation phase propagates the corresponding value and tag by dissemination among nodes.

Next, we focus on the dissemination procedure that is at the heart of the consultation and propagation phases. There are two parameters, ℓ, k, that define the way all consultation or propagation messages are disseminated. Parameter ℓ indicates the depth of the dissemination, it is used to set a time-to-live field ttl that is decremented at each intermediary node that participates in the dissemination; if $ttl = 0$, then dissemination is complete. Parameter k represents the number of neighbors that are contacted by each intermediary participating node. Together, parameters ℓ and k define the number of nodes that are contacted during a dissemination. This number is $\frac{k^{\ell+1}-1}{k-1}$ (Line 3) and

33: **Propagate**$((\langle \, val,t \, \rangle))_i$**:**
34:     $ttl \leftarrow \ell$
35:     $sn \leftarrow sn + 1$
36:     **while** $(|\,sent\text{-}to\text{-}nbrs1\,| < k)$ **do**
37:         send$\langle$PROP$, val, tag, ttl, i, sn\rangle$ to
38:             a set J of $(k - |\,sent\text{-}to\text{-}nbrs1\,|)$ neighbors $\neq father$
39:             $sent\text{-}to\text{-}nbrs1 \leftarrow sent\text{-}to\text{-}nbrs1 \cup J$
40:     **end while**
41:     $sent\text{-}to\text{-}nbrs1 \leftarrow \emptyset$
42:     **wait until** $|rcvd\text{-}from\text{-}qnodes[sn]| \geq q$

43: **Participate**$_i$ **(Activated upon reception of a message):**
44:     recv$\langle type, v, t, ttl, client\text{-}id, sn\rangle$ from j
45:     **if** $(marked[sn])$ **then**
46:         send$\langle type, v, t, ttl, client\text{-}id, sn\rangle$ to a neighbor $\neq j$
47:     **else**
48:         $marked[sn] \leftarrow$ true
49:         $father \leftarrow j$
50:         **if** $((type = $ CONS$))$ **then** $\langle v, t\rangle \leftarrow \langle val, tag\rangle$
51:         **if** $((type = $ PROP$))$ **then** $\langle val, tag\rangle \leftarrow \langle v, t\rangle$
52:         **if** $(type = $ RESP$)$ **then**
53:             **if** $(tag < t)$ **then** $\langle val, tag\rangle \leftarrow \langle v, t\rangle$
54:             $rcvd\text{-}from\text{-}qnodes[sn] \leftarrow rcvd\text{-}from\text{-}qnodes[sn] \cup \{j\}$
55:         $ttl \leftarrow ttl - 1$
56:         **if** $(ttl > 0)$ **then**
57:             **while** $(|\,sent\text{-}to\text{-}nbrs2\,| < k)$ **do**
58:                 send$\langle type, v, t, ttl, client\text{-}id, sn\rangle$ to
59:                     a set J of $(k - |\,sent\text{-}to\text{-}nbrs2\,|)$ neighbors $\neq father$
60:                     $sent\text{-}to\text{-}nbrs2 \leftarrow sent\text{-}to\text{-}nbrs2 \cup J$
61:             **end while**
62:             $sent\text{-}to\text{-}nbrs2 \leftarrow \emptyset$
63:         send $\langle$RESP$, val, tag, ttl, \perp, sn\rangle$ to $client\text{-}id$

represents the number of nodes in a balanced tree of depth ℓ and width k: each node having exactly k children. (This value is provable by recurrence on the depth ℓ of the tree.) Observe that ℓ and k are chosen such that the number of nodes that are contacted during a dissemination be larger than q as written Line 3.

There are three kinds of messages denoted by message $type$: CONS, PROP, RESP indicating if the message is a consultation message, a propagation message, or a response to any of the two other messages. When a new phase starts at client i, a time-to-live field ttl is set to ℓ and a sequence number sn is incremented. This number is used in message exchanges to indicate whether a message corresponds to the right phase. Then the phase proceeds in sending continuously messages to k neighbors waiting for their answer (Lines 25–29 and Lines 36–40). When the k neighbors answer, client i knows that the dissemination is ongoing. Then client i receives all messages until a large enough number q of nodes have responded in this phase, i.e., with the right sequence number (Lines 31, 42). If so, then the phase is complete.

Observe that during the dissemination, messages are simply marked (if they have not already been marked), responded (to client i), and re-forwarded to other neighbors (until ttl is null). Messages are marked by the node i that participates in a dissemination for preventing node i from participating multiple times in the same dissemination (Line 45). As a result, if node i is asked several times to participate, it first participates (Lines 48–63) and then it asks another node to participate (Lines 45–47). More precisely, if $marked[sn]$ is true, then node i re-forwards messages of sequence number sn without decrementing the ttl. Observe that phase termination and dissemination termination depends on the number of participants rather than the number of responses: it is important that enough participants participate in each dissemination for the phase to eventually end.

4.3 Contacting Participants Randomly

In order to contact the participants randomly, we implemented a membership protocol [12]. This protocol is based on Cyclon [15], thus, it is lightweight and fault-tolerant. Each node has a set of m neighbors called its view $\mathcal{N}_i$, it periodically updates its view and recomputes its set of neighbors. Our underlying membership algorithm provides each node with a set of $m \geq k + 1$ neighbors, so that phases of Algorithm 1 disseminate through a tree of degree $k + 1$. This algorithm shuffles the view at each cycle of its execution so that it provides randomness in the choice of neighbors. Moreover, it has been shown by simulation that the communication graph obtained with Cyclon is similar to a random graph where neighbors are picked uniformly among nodes [16].

For the sake of uniformity, the membership procedure is similar to the Cyclon algorithm: each node i maintains a view $\mathcal{N}_i$ containing one entry per neighbor. The entry of a neighbor j corresponds to a tuple containing the neighbor identifier and its age. Node i copies its view, selects the oldest neighbor j of its view, removes the entry e_j of j from the copy of its view, and finally sends the resulting copy to j. When j receives the view, j sends its own view back to i discarding possible pointers to i, and i and j update their view with the one they receive by firstly keeping the entries they received. The age of neighbor j entry denotes the time that elapsed since the last message from j has been received; this is used to remove failed neighbor from the list. This variant of Cyclon exchanges all entries of the view at each step like in [17].

5 Correctness Proof and Performance Analysis

Here, we show that Algorithm 1 implements a Timed Quorum System and that it emulates the probabilistic atomic object abstraction defined in Definition 2. The key points of this proof are to show that quorums are sufficiently re-activated by new operations to face dynamism and that subsequent quorums intersect with very high probability to achieve probabilistic atomicity. The proofs of Lemmas and Theorems can be found in [18].

5.1 Assumptions and Notations

First, we only consider executions starting with at least q nodes that own the default value of the object. In these executions, at least one propagation phase from a successful operation starts every Δ time units and let the time of any phase be bounded by δ time units. We assume that during a propagation that propagates a value v to q nodes and that executes between time t and $t + \delta$, there is at least one instant t' where the q nodes own value v simultaneously. This instant, t', can occur arbitrarily between time t and $t + \delta$. Even if this assumption may not seem realistic since propagation occurs in parallel of churn (i.e., at the time the propagation contacts the qth node the first contacted node may have left the system), our motivations for this assumption comes from the sake of clarity of the proof and we claim that the absence of this assumption leads to the same results.

Second, we assume that our underlying communication protocol provides each node with a view that represents a set of neighbors uniformly drawn at random among the set of all active nodes. This assumption is reasonable since, as already mentioned, the underlying algorithm is based on Cyclon that shuffles node views and provides communication graph similar to a random graph [16].

Next, we show that Algorithm 1 implements a probabilistic object. Observe that the liveness part of this proof relies simply on the activity of neighbors, and the fact that messages are eventually received. More precisely, by examination of the code of Algorithm 1, messages are gossiped among neighbors while neighbors are uniformly chosen. It is clear that operation termination depends on eventual message delivery. As a result, only the safety part of the proof follows. In the following, $val(\phi)$ (resp. $tag(\phi)$) denote, the value (resp. tag) consulted/propagated by phase ϕ.

5.2 Correctness Proof

First, we restate a Lemma appeared in [19] that computes the ratio of nodes that leave the system as time elapses, given a churn of c. The result is the ratio of nodes that leave and join, and helps computing the probability that up-to-date values remain reachable despite dynamism.

Lemma 1. *The ratio of initial nodes that have been replaced after τ time units is at most $C = 1 - (1 - c)^\tau$.*

The reader will find the proof of this Lemma 1 in [19]. The following Lemma gives a lower bound on the number of nodes that own the up-to-date value at any time in the system. (Recall that an up-to-date value is either the value with the largest tag and whose propagation is complete, or any value with a larger tag, but whose propagation is ongoing.)

Lemma 2. *At any time t in the system, the number of nodes that own an up-to-date value is at least $q(1 - c)^\Delta$, where Δ is the maximum period between two subsequent and successful propagation starting time instances, q is the quorum size, and c is the churn of the system.*

The following fact gives this well-known bound on the exponential function, provable using the Euler's method.

Fact 1. $(1 + \frac{x}{n})^n \le e^x$ *for* $n > |x|$.

Next Lemma lower bounds the probability that any consultation consults an up-to-date value v. Recall that sometime it might happen that a value v' is unsuccessfully propagated. This may happen when a write operation fails in consulting the largest tag just before propagating value v'. Observe that in any case, a successful consultation returns only successfully propagated values.

Lemma 3. *If the number of nodes that own an up-to-date value is at least* $q(1-c)^\Delta$ *during the whole period of execution of consultation* ϕ, *then consultation* ϕ *succeeds with high probability* $(\ge 1 - e^{-\beta^2}$, *with* β *a constant).*

This Corollary simply concludes the two previous Lemmas stating that any consultation executed in the system succeeds by returning an up-to-date value.

Corollary 1. *Any consultation* ϕ *succeeds with high probability* $(\ge 1 - e^{-\beta^2}$, *with* β *a constant).*

Proof. The result is straightforward from Lemma 2 and Lemma 3.   □ Last but not least, the two Theorems conclude the proof by showing that Algorithm 1 implements a Δ-TQS and verifies probabilistic atomicity.

Theorem 1. *Algorithm 1 implements a* Δ-*Timed Quorum System, where* Δ *is the maximum period between two subsequent and successful propagation starting time instances.*

Theorem 2. *Algorithm 1 implements a probabilistic atomic object.*

5.3   Performance Analysis

The following Lemmas show the performance of our solution: the first Lemma gives the expected message complexity of our solution while the second Lemma gives the expected time complexity of our solution. Observe first that operations complete provided that sent messages are reliably delivered. Building onto this assumption, an operation complete after contacting $O(\sqrt{nD})$ nodes. The following Lemma shows this result.

Lemma 4. *An operation completes after having contacted* $O(\sqrt{nD})$ *nodes.*

Proof. This is straightforward from the fact that termination of the dissemination process is conditioned to the number of distinct nodes contacted: $q = O(\sqrt{nD})$, with $D = (1-c)^{-\Delta}$ (cf. Line 2). Since there are two disseminating phases in each operation, an operation is executed after contacting $O(\sqrt{nD})$ nodes.   □

Next Lemma indicates that an operation terminates in $O(\log \sqrt{nD})$ message delays, in expectation.

Lemma 5. *If messages are not lost, the expected time of an operation is $O(\log \sqrt{nD})$ message delays.*

Proof. The proof relies on the fact that q' nodes are contacted uniformly at random with replacement. In expectation, the number q' that must be contacted to obtain q distinct nodes is $q' = q = O(\sqrt{nD})$. Since nodes are contacted in parallel along a tree of depth ℓ and width k, the time required to contact all the nodes on the tree is $\ell = O(\log_k q)$. That is, it is done in $\ell = O(\log_k \sqrt{nD})$ message delays. $\square$

6 Conclusion

This paper addressed the problem of emulating a distributed shared memory that copes with scalability and dynamism while being efficient. TQS ensures probabilistic intersection of quorums in a timely fashion. Interestingly, we showed that some TQS implementation verifies a consistency criterion weaker but similar to atomicity: probabilistic atomicity. Hence, any operation satisfies the ordering required for atomicity with high probability. The given implementation of TQS verifies probabilistic atomicity, provides lightweight ($O(\sqrt{nD})$ messages) and fast ($O(\log \sqrt{nD})$ message delays) operations, and does not require reconfiguration mechanism since periodic replication is piggybacked into operations.

Since we started tackling the problem that node can fail independently, we are now able to implement probabilistic memory into more realistic models. Previous solutions required that a very few amount of nodes could fail at the same time. More realistically, a model should allow node to act independently. Thus, an interesting question is: what probabilistic consistency can TQS achieve in such a more realistic model?

Acknowledgments

We are grateful to Anne-Marie Kermarrec, Achour Mostéfaoui for fruitful discussions about gossip-based algorithms and dynamic systems, and the anonymous referees for their helpful comments.

References

1. Herlihy, M.: Dynamic quorum adjustment for partitioned data. ACM Trans. Database Syst. 12(2), 170–194 (1987)
2. Lynch, N., Shvartsman, A.: RAMBO: A reconfigurable atomic memory service for dynamic networks. In: Malkhi, D. (ed.) DISC 2002. LNCS, vol. 2508, pp. 173–190. Springer, Heidelberg (2002)
3. Friedman, R., Raynal, M., Travers, C.: Two abstractions for implementing atomic objects in dynamic systems. In: Anderson, J.H., Prencipe, G., Wattenhofer, R. (eds.) OPODIS 2005. LNCS, vol. 3974, pp. 73–87. Springer, Heidelberg (2006)
4. Chockler, G., Gilbert, S., Gramoli, V., Musial, P., Shvartsman, A.: Reconfigurable distributed storage for dynamic networks. In: Anderson, J.H., Prencipe, G., Wattenhofer, R. (eds.) OPODIS 2005. LNCS, vol. 3974, pp. 214–219. Springer, Heidelberg (2006)

5. Naor, M., Wool, A.: The load, capacity, and availability of quorum systems. SIAM Journal on Computing 27(2), 423–447 (1998)
6. Nadav, U., Naor, M.: The dynamic and-or quorum system. In: Fraigniaud, P. (ed.) DISC 2005. LNCS, vol. 3724, pp. 472–486. Springer, Heidelberg (2005)
7. Abraham, I., Malkhi, D.: Probabilistic quorum systems for dynamic systems. Distributed Computing 18(2), 113–124 (2005)
8. Gramoli, V., Anceaume, E., Virgillito, A.: SQUARE: Scalable quorum-based atomic memory with local reconfiguration. In: SAC 2007. Proceedings of the 22nd ACM Symposium on Applied Computing, pp. 574–579. ACM Press, New York (2007)
9. Lynch, N.: Distributed Algorithms. Morgan Kaufmann, San Francisco (1996)
10. Malkhi, D., Reiter, M., Wool, A., Wright, R.: Probabilistic quorum systems. The Information and Computation Journal 170(2), 184–206 (2001)
11. Morris, R., Karger, D., Kaashoek, F., Balakrishnan, H.: Chord: A scalable peer-to-peer lookup service for internet applications. In: ACM SIGCOMM 2001, San Diego, CA (2001)
12. Ganesh, A.J., Kermarrec, A.M., Massoulié, L.: Peer-to-peer membership management for gossip-based protocols. IEEE Trans. Comput. 52(2), 139–149 (2003)
13. Ganesh, A.J., Kermarrec, A.M., Le Merrer, E., Massoulié, L.: Peer counting and sampling in overlay networks based on random walks. In: Distributed Computing (2007)
14. Attiya, H., Welch, J.: Distributed Computing. In: Fundamentals, Simulations, and Advanced Topics., McGraw-Hill, New York (1998)
15. Voulgaris, S., Gavidia, D., van Steen, M.: Cyclon: Inexpensive membership management for unstructured p2p overlays. Journal of Network and Systems Management 13(2), 197–217 (2005)
16. Iwanicki, K.: Gossip-based dissemination of time. Master's thesis, Warsaw University - Vrije Universiteit Amsterdam (2005)
17. Fernández, A., Gramoli, V., Jiménez, E., Kermarrec, A.M., Raynal, M.: Distributed slicing in dynamic systems. In: ICDCS 2007. Proceedings of the 27th International Conference on Distributed Computing Systems, IEEE Computer Society Press, Los Alamitos (2007)
18. Gramoli, V., Raynal, M.: Timed quorum system for large-scale dynamic environments. Technical Report 1859, INRIA Research Centre Rennes (2007)
19. Gramoli, V., Kermarrec, A.M., Mostefaoui, A., Raynal, M., Sericola, B.: Core persistence in peer-to-peer systems: Relating size to lifetime. In: Meersman, R., Tari, Z., Herrero, P. (eds.) On the Move to Meaningful Internet Systems 2006: OTM 2006 Workshops. LNCS, vol. 4278, pp. 1470–1479. Springer, Heidelberg (2006)

Worm Versus Alert: Who Wins in a Battle for Control of a Large-Scale Network?

James Aspnes[1,*], Navin Rustagi[2,**], and Jared Saia[2,***]

[1] Department of Computer Science, Yale University
aspnes@cs.yale.edu
[2] Department of Computer Science, University of New Mexico, Albuquerque, NM 87131-1386
Fax: (505) 277-6927
{navin, saia}@cs.unm.edu

Abstract. Consider the following game between a worm and an alert[1] over a network of n nodes. Initially, no nodes are infected or alerted and each node in the network is a special *detector* node independently with small but constant probability. The game starts with a single node becoming infected. In every round thereafter, every infected node sends out a constant number of worms to other nodes in the population, and every alerted node sends out a constant number of alerts. Nodes in the network change state according to the following four rules: 1) If a worm is received by a node that is not a detector and is not alerted, that node becomes infected; 2) If a worm is received by a node that is a detector, that node becomes alerted; 3) If an alert is received by a node that is not infected, that node becomes alerted; 4) If a worm or an alert is received by a node that is already infected or already alerted, then there is no change in the state of that node.

We make two assumptions about this game. First, that an infected node can send worm messages to any other node in the network but, in contrast, an alerted node can send alert messages only through a previously determined, constant degree overlay network. Second, we assume that the infected nodes are intelligent, coordinated and essentially omniscient. In other words, the infected nodes know everything except for which nodes are detectors and the alerted nodes' random coin flips i.e. they know the topology of the overlay network used by the alerts; which nodes are alerted and which are infected at any time; where alerts and worms are being sent; the overall strategy used by the alerted nodes; etc. The alerted nodes are assumed to know nothing about which other nodes are infected or alerted, where alerts or worms are being sent, or the strategy used by the infected nodes.

Is there a strategy for the alerted nodes that ensures only a vanishingly small fraction of the nodes become infected, no matter what strategy is used by the infected nodes? Surprisingly, the answer is yes. In particular, we prove that a simple strategy achieves this result with probability approaching 1 provided that the overlay network has good node expansion. Specifically, this result holds if

---

* This research was partially supported by NSF CNS 0435201.
** This research was partially supported by NSF CAREER Award 0644058 and NSF CCR-0313160.
*** Corresponding Author.
[1] Specifically, we consider self-certifying alerts[1], which contain short proofs that a security flaw exists and thereby eliminate false alerts.

E. Tovar, P. Tsigas, and H. Fouchal (Eds.): OPODIS 2007, LNCS 4878, pp. 443–456, 2007.
© Springer-Verlag Berlin Heidelberg 2007

$d \geq \alpha$ and $\frac{\alpha}{\beta(1-\gamma)} > \frac{2d}{c}$, where α and β represent the rate of the spread of the alert and worm respectively; γ is the probability that a node is a detector node; d is the degree of the overlay network; and c is the node expansion of the overlay network. Next, we give empirical results that suggest that our algorithms for the alert may be useful in current large-scale networks. Finally, we show that if the overlay network has poor expansion, in particular if $(1-\gamma)\beta > d$, then the worm will likely infect almost all of the non-detector nodes.

Keywords: Self-certifying alert, worm, overlay network, peer-to-peer, expander graphs, epidemic processes.

1   Introduction

Attacks on the Internet are characterized by several alarming trends: (i) increases in frequency: large-scale attacks are approximately doubling every year [2]; (ii) increases in speed: the recent slammer worm infected 90% of vulnerable hosts within 10 minutes [3]; and (iii) increases in severity: the slammer worm had many unforeseen consequences including failures of 911 emergency data-entry terminals, network outages, and canceled airline flights, [3,4,5,6]. In addition, there has been a broadening of motivations for attack to include extortion [7,8]; phishing [9,10,11]; sending anonymous spam [12,13]; and political reasons [14,15]. Modern computer worms simply propagate too quickly for human detection. Since attacks are now occurring at a speed which prevents direct human intervention, there is a need to develop automated defenses. Since the financial, social and political stakes are so high, we need defenses which are *provably good* against a worst case attacks.

A promising recent result in this direction is the development of self certifying alerts(SCAs)[1]. An SCA is a short, machine verifiable, automatically generated proof that a security flaw exists. Because an SCA is short, it is easily propagated through a network. Because an SCA is efficiently verifiable, false positives are eliminated. SCAs are generated by dedicated machines called detectors. Detectors run instrumented software to automatically detect a worm, determine which vulnerability the worm exploits, and then generate an SCA for the worm, i.e. a short proof that the vulnerability the worm exploits does in fact exist. After receiving and verifying an SCA, a machine can generate a filter that blocks infection by analyzing the exploit which the SCA proves exists. Because the SCA focuses on the security flaw exploited by a worm, rather than the textual content of the worm, SCAs can easily be created for polymorphic worms. Recent empirical results suggest that SCAs can be generated, checked and deployed efficiently. For example, the Vigilante system [16] takes 18 milliseconds to generate an SCA for the Slammer worm, the resulting SCA is 457 bytes long, the time to verify this SCA is 10 milliseconds, and the time to create a filter from the verified SCA is 24 milliseconds. These times for SCA generation, verification and filter creation are on the same scale as the time it takes a worm to infect a machine. Vigilante performs similarly for two other Internet worms, Code Red and Blaster.

Distribution of alerts in the Vigilante system is performed by the Pastry[17] peer-to-peer overlay network. It is shown empirically that a very small fraction of special detector nodes is enough to ensure that a worm infects no more than 5% of the vulnerable population. While these initial results are promising, several critical problems remain. First, Vigilante requires that the nodes participating in the overlay network all be resistant to infection. Second, Vigilante requires that the topology of the overlay network be hidden from the worm. These two assumptions may hold true for an overlay network owned and operated by a single company, but seem unlikely to hold for a large-scale open source peer-to-peer network. Finally, while the Vigilante systems performs well empirically against currently known worms, the system has no known theoretical guarantees against all worms. In this paper, we focus exclusively on the problem of distribution of alerts through an overlay network and address these three problems.

1.1   Our Model

We model our problem of alert distribution as a game between a worm and an alert over a synchronous network. Initially, no nodes are infected or alerted and each node in the network is a special *detector* node independently with fixed probability γ. The game starts with a single node becoming infected. In every round thereafter, every infected node sends out β worms to other nodes in the population, and every alerted node sends out α alerts for fixed constants α and β. Nodes in the network change state according to the following four rules: 1) If a worm is received by a node that is not a detector and is not alerted, that node becomes infected; 2) If a worm is received by a node that is a detector, it is not infected, instead it becomes alerted; 3) If an alert is received by a node that is not infected, that node becomes alerted; 4) If a worm or an alert is received by a node that is already infected or already alerted, then there is no change in the state of that node.

We make two assumptions about this game. First, an infected node can send worm messages to any other node in the network but, in contrast, an alerted node can send alert messages only through a previously determined, constant degree overlay network. In other words, the alert-spreading algorithm is "polite" in the sense that it does not bombard arbitrary nodes with alerts unless it knows that they are interested in receiving them. Since the worm is not required to be polite, it is not constrained by the overlay network, although a particularly sophisticated worm may exploit the structure of the overlay network for its own purposes. An edge in this overlay network represents an agreement between two nodes to accept SCAs from each other. Second, we assume that the infected nodes are intelligent, coordinated and essentially omniscient. In other words, the infected nodes know everything except for which nodes are detectors and the alerted nodes' random coin flips i.e. they know the topology of the overlay network used by the alerts; which nodes are alerted and which are infected at any time; where alerts and worms are being sent; the overall strategy used by the alerted nodes; etc. Moreover, the worm is unconstrained in which nodes it attacks. For example, it could always try to infect nodes which have never been infected before. The alerted nodes are assumed to know nothing about which other nodes are infected or alerted, where alerts or worms are being sent, or the strategy used by the infected nodes. Also the number of messages an alerted node can send is constrained by the degree of the graph.

1.2   Results

In our results, we make use of a d-regular overlay network with node expansion c. As a concrete example, a random d-regular graph has node expansion $c = d/5 - 1$ with high probability[2]. Throughout this paper, we use the phrase with high probability (w.h.p) to mean with probability at least $1 - 1/n^\epsilon$ for some fixed $\epsilon > 0$. Let RANDOM be the algorithm that has each alerted node in each round send out alerts to α nodes selected uniformly at random without replacement from its neighbors in the overlay. Our main theoretical results are stated below as the following two theorems which are proven in Sections 2 and 4 respectively.

Theorem 3: If $d \geq \alpha$ and $\frac{\alpha}{\beta(1-\gamma)} > \frac{2d}{c}$, then the algorithm RANDOM ensures that, w.h.p, only $o(n)$ nodes are ever infected.

Theorem 6: If the overlay network has bounded degree d and $\beta(1 - \gamma) > d$, then any alert algorithm in expectation will save a fraction of non-detector nodes that approaches 0 as n gets large

Our empirical results, presented in Section 3, show that if the overlay network is a d-regular random graph, as n grows large, the algorithm RANDOM saves an increasingly large fraction of the nodes against a worm that spreads uniformly at random. For example, for $n = 10^6, d = 100, \beta = 1, \alpha = 5$ and $\gamma = .02$, we were able to save 99% of the nodes on average.

1.3   Other Related Work

Several approaches for generating self-certifying alerts have been proposed recently (see e.g. [19,20,21], but few systems have been proposed for disseminating those alerts. The Vigilante system and its limitations have been discussed above. Zhou et al. [22] propose a system for distributing alerts over a network, but their system is focused on confronting worms that can spread only through the same overlay network through which the alert is spreading. Vojnovic and Ganesh [23] and Shakkottai and Srikant [24] perform exhaustive analytical and empirical studies of the effectiveness of different types of alert dissemination. However, their work focuses only on worms that spread uniformly at random in the network. In contrast, our work considers worms that may use smarter dissemination strategies.

2   Alert Versus Worm in an Expanding Overlay Network

In this section, we focus on d-regular graphs for our overlay network. We show that for a suitable choice of parameters and a particular type of overlay network, we are able to save most of the nodes from getting infected with high probability. More precisely, at the end of the process only $o(n)$ nodes get infected, and all other nodes get alerted.

The essential idea is that we want the long-run growth rate of the set of alerted nodes to be higher than the rate for the infected nodes. The rate for infected nodes is easy to

---

[2] See [18] for an algorithm for sampling from random d-regular overlay networks in a distributed manner.

calculate; assuming an optimal choice of targets, each infected node infects on average an additional $\beta(1 - \gamma)$ nodes per round. The rate for alerted nodes is trickier, as alerted nodes are limited by the structure of the overlay network. But we can get a lower bound on the expected rate during the early parts of the protocol by observing that A alerted nodes will between them have at most dA neighbors, of which at least cA will not already be alerted, where c is the expansion parameter of the network. It follows that each alerted node will attempt to alert on average at least $\alpha(c/d)$ unalerted nodes at each step. In the absence of the worm, this would give the growth rate of the alerted nodes; with M infected nodes, we must subtract these from the pool of new alerted nodes (using the simplifying assumption that the worm successfully concentrates itself on the boundary of the set A). Fortunately these lost infected nodes are compensated for somewhat by the boost of $\gamma\beta M$ new alerted nodes from triggered detectors.

This overview ignores two important details. Because we want a high-probability bound, it is not enough simply to consider expected growth rates. And because the expansion factor applies only for sets with $n/2$ or fewer elements, we must consider separately the case where the set of alerted nodes is larger. We handle both problems by dividing the execution into three phases. Phase I starts with a single infected node and ends when $\ln n$ worm messages have been received by nodes in the network. During this phase we ignore the spread of alerts and content ourselves with getting only the $\Theta(\gamma \ln n)$ alerted nodes that result from successful detections. Phase II starts at the end of of Phase I. During this phase we use the fact that the number of infected and alerted nodes are both $\Omega(\log n)$ to show that both the worm and the SCA propagate at close to the expected rate with high probability; the key point is that when the populations of both are large enough, Chernoff bounds apply to the increases. Phase II ends when n/d^2 nodes have been alerted by the SCA; at this point we can no longer rely on the expansion properties of the network and must resort to a different analysis. Note that there are expansion properties till the end of Phase II. For this analysis, done in Section 2.3, we show that in constant number of steps, we would alert n/2 nodes and then after c log(log(n)) further steps we would have only o(n) not alerted or not infected nodes. Thus we would have shown that only o(n) nodes could have been infected and $\theta(n)$ nodes have been alerted.

In the remainder of this section, all lemmas that bound a random variable's value for t rounds hold with probability greater than or equal to $1 - t/n^c$ for some fixed constant $c > 0$. Also for all the remaining lemma's in this section, $d \geq \alpha$.

2.1   Phase I

Let Z be the set of nodes that receive the first $\ln n$ worm messages; i.e., the set of nodes that receive worm messages in Phase I.

We write A_i for the number of nodes alerted at time t, counting from the end of Phase I; thus A_0 is the number of nodes alerted in Z.

Lemma 1. *At the end of Phase I, (a) the expected number of alerted nodes* $E[A_0]$ *is at least* $\gamma \ln n$; *and (b) for any* $c > 0$, *there exists a constant* $\delta \leq 1/2$, *such that with probability greater than* $1 - 1/n^c$, $(1 - \delta) E[A_0] \leq A_0$.

Proof. For each $v \in Z$, let X_v be the indicator random variable for the event that v is alerted in Phase I and let Y_v be the event that v is a detector node. While the X_v are not necessarily independent, we do have that $X_v \geq Y_v$ for all v, and thus $A_0 = \sum_{v \in Z} X_v \geq \sum_{v \in Z} Y_v$. It follows that $E[A_0] \geq \sum E[Y_v] = \gamma |Z| = \gamma \ln n$. The second part is an immediate application of Chernoff bounds.   ∎

It follows that A_0 is $\Theta(\ln n)$ with high probability.

2.2   Analysis of Phase II

For the second phase, begin by comparing the number of infected nodes in the actual process with the number of infected nodes in an infinite graph where the SCA has no effect on the spread of the worm. The process in the latter graph has the advantage of being much easier to analyze; and, as we show, it gives an upper bound on the outcome of the original process.

Formally, let M_t be the number of infected nodes at time t in the original graph, where as before we count rounds from the start of Phase II. Let M_t' be the number of infected nodes at time t in an infinite graph under the assumptions that (a) no alert messages are ever sent out by the detector nodes, even though they are alerted by worm messages, and (b) each infected node spreads the worm to β unique, previously uninfected nodes in the network at each round. Where no confusion will result, we also use M_t and M_t' to refer to the set of nodes infected in each case.

Observe that the assumptions for M_t' only increase the number of infected nodes; so that M_t' *stochastically dominates* M_t in the sense that $\forall\, k \geq 0$, $Pr(M_t' \geq k) \geq Pr(M_t \geq k)$, no matter what strategy the worm applies in the original graph.

Let M_0 and M_0' count the nodes infected by the end of Phase I, in their respective simulations. From Lemma 1, we have that $M_0 \leq |Z| - A_0 \leq \ln n$.

Lemma 2. *For all $t \geq 0$, the expected value of the random variable M_t' at time t is equal to $(1 + \beta(1 - \gamma))^t M_0$.*

Proof. By our assumption about the number of messages sent by the infected nodes and the fraction of detector nodes, the expected number of new infected nodes is $\beta(1 - \gamma)\, E[M_t']$, where $(1 - \gamma)$ is the probability that a given node is not a detector node. Hence the recurrence relation for $E[M_t']$ is $E[M_t'] = (1 + \beta(1 - \gamma))\, E[M_{t-1}']$. Hence $E[M_t'] = (1 + \beta(1 - \gamma))^t M_0$.   ∎

We now show that M_t' remains closely bounded around its expected value, thus giving an upper bound on the variable M_t. The proof of the following lemma is somewhat technical; it is omitted from this extended abstract due to space constraints.

Lemma 3. *For any $c > 0$ and fixed β and γ, there exists a constant k such that, for sufficiently large n and any t, it holds that $M_s' \leq k\, E[M_s']$ for all $s \leq t$*

We now turn to alerted nodes. Let A_t be the number of nodes that are in the alerted state at time t. For any set of vertices A, let $N(A)$ be the set of neighbors of nodes in A in the overlay network that are not themselves in A. Let the random variable Z_t be equal to the number of nodes in $N(A_{t-1})$ that receive an alert message at time step t.

Lemma 4. *For all* $t \geq 0$, $A_t \geq A_{t-1} + Z_t - M'_t$.

Proof. Out of the unalerted nodes which receive alert messages, at most M'_{t-1} nodes could be infected nodes. Hence the lower bound result holds true. ∎

Lemma 5. *For all* $t \geq 0$, $E(Z_t) \geq (c\alpha/d)A_{t-1}$.

Proof. Let S_{t-1} be the set of nodes that are alerted at time $t-1$ and let $n' = |N(S_{t-1})|$. Number the nodes in $N(S_{t-1})$ from 1 to n'. Let $X_{i,t} = 1$ if the i-th such node is alerted at time step t for the first time, and 0 otherwise. Then $Z_t \geq \sum_{i=1}^{n'} X_{i,t}$. By linearity of expectation, $E[Z_t] \geq \sum_{i=1}^{n'} E[X_{i,t}]$. Observe that each node counted in A_{t-1} sends an alert to fixed neighbor with probability α/d; it follows that for each node i in $N(S_{t-1})$, $\Pr[X_{i,t} = 1] \geq \alpha/d$. We thus have $E[Z_t] \geq n'\alpha/d \geq (c\alpha/d)A_{t-1}$, where c is the expansion factor. ∎

Lemma 6. *For all* $t \geq 0$ $A_t \geq A_{t-1} + (1/2)E(Z_t) - M'_t$.

Proof. We now imagine that the alerted nodes use the following process to decide where to send out their α alert messages. They randomly permute all of their neighbors and then send out alerts to the first alpha nodes in this random permutation. Imagine further that some alerted node j determines its random permutation by assigning a random variable $X_{j,i}$ to each node i that is a neighbor of j. This random variable takes on a value uniformly at random in the real interval between 0 and 1. The nodes that the alert is sent to are thus determined by finding the α random variables among the d whose outcomes are closest to 0. For each node i and j, there is a separate such random $X_{j,i}$ and we note that these random variables are all independent. Let f be a function such that $Z_t = f(X_{1,1}, X_{1,2}, \ldots, X_{m,d})$. We note that f satisfies the Lipchitz condition, i.e $|f(X_{1,1}, X_{1,2}, \ldots, X_{l,p}, \ldots, X_{m,d}) - f(X_{1,1}, X_{1,2}, \ldots, X'_{l,p}, \ldots, X_{m,d})| \leq 1$. This is the case since a change in the outcome of a single $X_{i,j}$ will at most cause one new node to receive an alert and one old node to not receive an alert. Hence we can use Azuma's Inequality to say that $\Pr(\ Pr(|Z_t - E(Z_t)| \geq (1/2)E(Z_t) \leq 2e^{-\frac{(1/4)E(Z_t)^2}{2A_{t-1}d}}$. Since by the previous lemma $E(Z_t) \geq (c\alpha/d)A_{t-1}$, the right hand side is less than or equal to $2e^{-\frac{((c\alpha/d)A_{t-1})^2}{8A_{t-1}d}}$ which is $O(1/n^{k'})$ for some constant $k' > 0$ since A_{t-1} is $\theta(\ln n)$. The lemma then follows by a simple Union bound. ∎

Let k be the multiplicative constant of the expectation, in the statement of lemma 3.

Lemma 7. *For all* $t \geq 0$, $A_t \geq (1 + (\alpha c)/(2d))A_{t-1} - k(1 + \beta(1 - \gamma))^t \ln n$

Proof. From Lemma 5 and Lemma 6 we get that the number of nodes alerted at round t follows the inequality $A_t \geq A_{t-1} + (1/2)((c\alpha/d)A_{t-1}) - M'_t$. Hence $A_t \geq (1 + (\alpha c)/(2d))A_{t-1} - M'_t$. By Lemma 2 and Lemma 3 we know that M'_t is no more than $k(1 + \beta(1 - \gamma))^t \ln n$ for t rounds, with probability at least $1-t/n^c$. Hence replacing the upper bound value of M_t in the above expression yields the inequality $A_t > (1 + (\alpha c)/(2d))A_{t-1} - k(1 + \beta(1 - \gamma))^t \ln n$. ∎

Let $p = (1 + (\alpha c)/(2d))$, $q = (1 + \beta(1 - \gamma))$. Hence the recurrence relation as given in the last lemma is $A_t \geq pA_{t-1} - kq^t$.

Lemma 8. *For all* $t \geq 0$, $A_t \geq p^t A_0 - k(q^t + pq^{t-1} + \ldots p^t)$

Proof. Proof is by induction on t. It is easy to see that the base case holds. Assume that the claim holds for all rounds less than or equal to t-1. Hence $A_t \geq p(p^{t-1}A_0 - k(q^{t-1} + \ldots p^{t-1})) - kq^t$. Expanding the algebraic expression, we get the expression in the claim. ∎

Let $\kappa = p/q$. Then $A_t \geq p^t \ln n - p^t k(1 + 1/\kappa + \ldots (1/\kappa)^t)$. Or

$$A_t \geq p^t(\ln n - k(1 + 1/\kappa + \ldots (1/\kappa)^t)). \tag{1}$$

2.3   Analysis of Phase III

In this phase, we make use of a graph with two types of expansion. We show below that a random d regular graph has the types of expansion that we need. The proof of the following two theorems are omitted from this extended abstract.

Theorem 1. *Let* $d \geq 30$ *and* $\epsilon > 0$, *then with high probability, a random d-regular graph G has the following properties*

1. *For any set S such that* $\epsilon \log n \leq |S| \leq \frac{n}{d^2}$, $|N(S)| \geq |S|(\frac{d}{5} - 1)$.
2. *For any set S such that* $\frac{n}{d^2} \leq |S| \leq \frac{n}{2}$, $|N(S)| \geq \frac{|S|}{2}$.

The following theorem assumes that the overlay network has expansion properties as given in the Theorem 1.

Theorem 2. *Assume that at some point, the number of alerted nodes is at least* n/d^2 *and that the number of infected nodes is no more than* $n^{1-\epsilon}$ *for some* $\epsilon > 0$. *Then w.h.p, at the end of the process, all but* $o(n)$ *nodes will be alerted.*

The next theorem is the main result of this section.

Theorem 3. *If* $d \geq \alpha$ *and* $\frac{\alpha}{\beta(1-\gamma)} > \frac{2d}{c}$, *then the algorithm RANDOM ensures that, w.h.p, only* $o(n)$ *nodes are ever infected.*

Proof. Since $\frac{\alpha}{\beta(1-\gamma)} > \frac{2d}{c}$, therefore $\frac{\alpha c}{2d} > \beta(1 - \gamma)$. Hence $1 + \frac{\alpha c}{2d} > 1 + \beta(1 - \gamma)$, or $p/q > 1$. From equation 1 it is clear that $A_t \geq p^t \ln n - 3k$. Hence $A_t \geq p^t$. Hence for $t \geq \log_p n$, $A_t \geq \Omega(n)$. Hence in Phase II, the process cannot last for more that $\log_p(n)$ steps. Hence from Lemma 3, we know that $M_{\log_p(n)} \leq k(1 + \beta(1 - \gamma))^{\log_p(n)}$ with probability greater than $1 - \log_p(n)/n^c$. Hence $M_{\log_p n} < k \, q^{\log_p(n)}$. Since $p > q$, clearly $M_t = o(n)$ at the end of Phase II. Further it is $O(n^{1-\epsilon})$. Now, from Theorem 2, we know that if we have $o(n^{1-\epsilon})$ infected nodes at the end of Phase II, we would have at most $o(n)$ infected nodes at the end of the Phase III. ∎

3 Empirical Results

We simulated the spread of a worm and an alert through a network to empirically determine the fraction of nodes saved.[3] We performed our experiment using a random d-regular graph as the overlay network and set each node in the network to be a detector node independently with probability γ. In addition, we fixed the worm strategy such that each infected node, in each round, sent out the worm to β unique nodes selected uniformly at random, and we fixed the alert strategy such that each alerted node sent out the alert to α unique nodes selected uniformly at random among its neighbors in the overlay network. We note that the worm strategy we used in these experiments is not necessarily the best possible worm strategy, but we selected this strategy for concreteness. Our d regular random graph was created using the configuration model method proposed in [25].

In each round we iterate through the set of vertices, allowing each infected or alerted node to send the worm or alert to the appropriate number of other nodes in the network. There are several possible strategies for resolving the status of a virgin (i.e. neither alerted or infected) node that gets both a worm message and an alert message in the same round. In our previous theoretical analysis, we assumed that if a node receives just one worm message it becomes infected. However, in our experiments, we used the somewhat more relaxed and realistic assumption that the probability that the node gets infected equals the number of worm messages received divided by the total number of messages received, and that the probability the node becomes alerted is 1 minus this quantity. We note that this assumption is equivalent to assuming that the messages all arrive in the node's message queue according to some random permutation.

Figure 1(a) illustrates our results when $\gamma = 0.1$, $\beta = 1$, $\alpha = 1$ and $d = 10$, where we varied the value of n from 2^{10} to 2^{20}, multiplying at each step by 2. To remove noise in the simulation, each data point represents the average over 100 trials. The best result we obtained was saving only 45% of the nodes for $n = 2^{20}$. Even though this final data point is somewhat disappointing, we do observe a clear increasing trend in the fraction saved as n increases.

Given these results, it seems for current network sizes, there is not much hope for the alert when $\alpha = \beta$. We thus next considered the case where $\alpha > \beta$. In practice, this condition may hold since the alerts are traveling through a predetermined overlay network and a technique such as throttling can ensure that alert messages received through the overlay are given priority over types of messages. To explore this scenario, we conducted experiments where we fixed β at 1. We then determined necessary values of γ for each α ranging from 2 to 10, that would ensure that we save 90%, 95% and 99% of the nodes (Figure 1(b)). The values of n and d used in the experiment were 10^6 and 100 respectively. The results of these experiments were much more encouraging. In particular, for $\alpha = 2$, we were able to save 99% of the nodes with $\gamma = .14$. When $\alpha = 5$, we required a γ of .018 to save 99% of the nodes, and when $\alpha = 10$, we required a γ of only .001 to save 99% of the nodes. These results suggest that our algorithms

---

[3] All of the code necessary to replicate these experiments is available at
http://www.cs.unm.edu/~navin/worm.html.

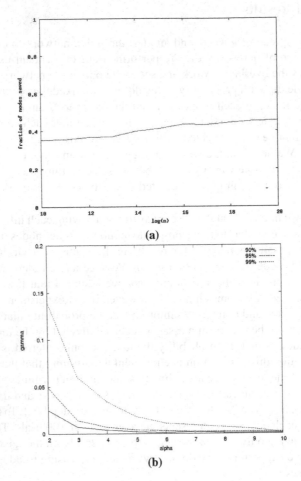

Fig. 1. (a) log of the network size versus fraction of nodes saved (b) contour plot of α versus γ required to save 99%, 95% and 90% of the nodes

for spreading alerts might be most effective in conjunction with other techniques (like throttling) that would enable the alerts to spread more quickly than the worm.

4   Is Expansion Necessary?

In this section, we consider what happens in graphs with poor expansion properties. In particular, we look at the growth rate of the number of nodes at distance k from some initial point of infection, and show that if this growth rate is small, the worm successfully infects almost every node that does not detect it itself.

For the purposes of this lower bound, we adopt a simplified deterministic version of the model. We proceed in a sequence of rounds starting from the time at which the worm is first detected, and think of the graph as organized in layers $V_0, V_1, \ldots$, where

V_0 contains the initial a_0 alerted and b_0 infected nodes, and each V_i is the set of nodes at distance i from this initial set.

We ignore the structure of the interconnections between layers; instead, we allow an SCA that has already alerted a_i nodes in layer V_i to alert any αa_i nodes in layer V_{i+1} in one round. Because the worm can spread without regard to the layer structure, we assume that it can attempt to infect these nodes first; a round thus consists of the worm attempting to infect nodes in layer V_{i+1} followed by the SCA attempting to alert any nodes that are left.

Let b_i be the total number of infected nodes in layer i after round i and let $B_i = \sum_{j=0}^{i}$ be the total number of infected nodes after round i without regard to what layer they are in. The worm can attempt to infect up to βB_i nodes in round $i + 1$; of these, $\gamma \beta B_i$ will trigger detectors.

If we similarly let a_i be the number of alerted nodes in layer V_i after round i, then the SCA can attempt to alert αa_i nodes in layer V_{i+1}. But because the worm goes first, there may not be any nodes left to alert.

The overall pattern in round $i + 1$ is thus:

1. The worm attempts to infect up to βB_i nodes in layer V_{i+1}, of which $(1 - \gamma)\beta B_i$ become infected and $\gamma\beta B_i$ become alerted.
2. The SCA spreads from layer V_i to layer V_{i+1}, yielding an additional $\min(\alpha a_i, |V_{i+1}| - \beta B_i)$ alerted nodes.

This gives us the recurrence

$$b_{i+1} = (1 - \gamma) \min (|V_{i+1}|, \beta B_i)$$
$$a_{i+1} = \gamma \min (|V_{i+1}|, \beta B_i) + \min (\alpha a_i, |V_{i+1}| - \beta B_i)$$

Theorem 4. *Define a_i, b_i, and V_i as above. Let $|V_0|, |V_1|, \ldots$ be such that, for all $i \geq 0$,*

$$|V_{i+1}| \leq \beta(1 - \gamma) \sum_{j=0}^{i} |V_i|.$$

Let $b_0 \geq (1 - \gamma)|V_0|$. Then $b_i \geq (1 - \gamma)|V_i|$ for all i.

Proof. Straightforward induction on i. The base case is given. For the induction step suppose the claim holds for i. Then we have

$$b_{i+1} = (1 - \gamma) \min (|V_{i+1}|, \beta B_i)$$
$$= (1 - \gamma) \min \left(|V_{i+1}|, \beta \sum_{j=0}^{i} b_j \right)$$
$$\geq (1 - \gamma) \min \left(|V_{i+1}|, \beta(1 - \gamma) \sum_{j=0}^{i} |V_j| \right)$$
$$= (1 - \gamma)|V_{i+1}|.$$

In other words, if the growth rate of the graph is small enough and the initial set of alerted nodes is small enough, then the SCA has no effect beyond the original detection sites.

For a large enough graph, a higher initial growth rate or lower initial worm numbers can be compensated for in the limit. For simplicity, we consider an *infinitely large* graph that is again organized into layers $V_0, V_1, \ldots$ as above.

Theorem 5. *Let a_i, b_i, V_i be as in Theorem 4. Let $b_0 > 0$ and let*

$$\limsup_{i \to \infty} \frac{|V_{i+1}|}{\sum_{j=0}^{i} |V_i|} < (1 - \beta)\gamma. \tag{2}$$

Suppose further that $|V_{i+1}| \geq |V_i|$ for all i. Then

$$\lim_{i \to \infty} \frac{b_i}{|V_i|} = (1 - \gamma).$$

Proof. We assume that α is sufficiently large that at the end of round i, any node in layer i that is not infected is alerted. This assumption only hurts the worm, so if the assumption is violated the result only improves.

From (2), there exists some ϵ, i_0 such that for all $i > i_0$, $|V_{i+1}| \leq (1 - \epsilon)(1 - \gamma)\beta \sum_{j=0}^{i} |V_j|$. Let $r_i = B_i / \sum_{j=0}^{i} |V_j|$ and compute, for $i > i_0$,

$$
\begin{aligned}
b_{i+1} &= (1 - \gamma) \min \left(|V_{i+1}|, \beta B_i \right) \\
&= (1 - \gamma) \min \left(|V_{i+1}|, \beta r_i \sum_{j=0}^{i} |V_i| \right) \\
&= \min \left((1 - \gamma)|V_{i+1}|, r_i \beta (1 - \gamma) \sum_{j=0}^{i} |V_i| \right) \\
&\geq \min \left((1 - \gamma)|V_{i+1}|, \frac{r_i}{1 - \epsilon} |V_{i+1}| \right) \\
&= \min \left(1 - \gamma, \frac{r_i}{1 - \epsilon} \right) |V_{i+1}|.
\end{aligned}
$$

Unless $r_i = 1 - \gamma$, we expect $b_{i+1}/|V_{i+1}|$ to be larger than r_i; in particular we have $b_{i+1}/|V_{i+1}| \geq \min((1 - \gamma), (1 + \epsilon)r_i)$. The new ratio r_{i+1} is a weighted average of r_i and b_{i+1}/V_{i+1}. Under the assumption that $|V_i|$ is nondecreasing, the weight on the second term is at least $1/(i + 1)$. Thus we have

$$r_{i+1} \geq \frac{i}{i+1} r_i + \frac{\min(1 - \gamma, \epsilon r_i)}{i + 1} = r_i + \frac{\min((1 - \gamma) - r_i, \epsilon r_i)}{i + 1}.$$

Observe that the first term in the minimum is decreasing and the second increasing. As long as $\epsilon r_i < (1 - \gamma)r_i$, we have $r_{i+1} \geq r_i \frac{\epsilon}{i+1}$. So $r_{i+k} \geq r_i \left(1 + \epsilon \sum_{j=i}^{k-1} \frac{1}{j+1} \right)$; as the series diverges, eventually r_{i+k} must be large enough that the first term takes over. But then let $s_i = (1 - \gamma) - r_i$, and compute $s_{i+1} = (1 - \gamma) - r_{i+1} \leq s_i - \frac{s_i}{i+1} = s_i \frac{i}{i+1}$, from which it follows via a telescoping product that $s_{i+k} \leq s_i \frac{i}{i+k}$, which goes to zero in the limit.   ∎

The proof of the following theorem follows directly from the above.

Theorem 6. *For a graph with bounded degree d, we have $|V_{i+1}| \leq d \sum_{j=1}^{i} |V_j| + 1$. So if $(1 - \gamma)\beta > d$ we expect almost no non-detector nodes to be alerted.*

5   Conclusion and Future Work

We have described a simple distributed algorithm for spreading alert messages through a network during a worm attack and have proven that this algorithm protects all but a vanishingly small fraction of the network provided that the alerts spread through an overlay network with sufficiently good node expansion. Our algorithm is provably good no matter what strategy the worm uses to spread through the network. We have demonstrated empirically that this algorithm works effectively against a randomly spreading worm under conditions that may be reasonable for modern computer networks. Finally, we have shown that if the overlay network has poor expansion, then the worm will likely infect almost all of the non-detector nodes in the network. Many open problems remain including: (1) tightening the upper and lower-bounds for the expansion needed in the overlay network to save almost all of the nodes; (2) developing other models for the spread of a dynamic process and its inhibitor over a network, and finding provably good strategies in these models; and (3) further empirical study to determine the efficacy of deploying our algorithm in a real network.

References

1. Costa, M., Crowcroft, J., Castro, M., Rowstron, A.: Can we contain internet worms? In: Proceedings of the 3rd Workshop on Hot Topics in Networks (HotNets-III) (2004)
2. Spafford, E.: Exploring Grand Challenges in Trustworthy Computing., http://digitalenterprise.org/seminar/spafford2.html
3. Moore, D., Paxson, V., Savage, S., Shannon, C., Staniford, S., Weaver, N.: Inside the Slammer Worm. IEEE Security and Privacy journal 1(4), 33–39 (2003)
4. Davis, A.: Computer Worm Snarls Web (2004), http://www.bayarea.com/mld/mercurynews/5034748.html
5. Lemos, R.: Slammer Attacks May Become Way of Life for the Net (2003), http://www.news.com/2009-1001-983540.html?tag=fd_lede2_hed
6. Jr., R.O.: Internet Worm Unearths New Holes (2003), http://www.securityfocus.com/news/2186
7. Sturgeon, W.: Denial-of-service-attack victim speaks out (2005), http://www.zdnetasia.com/insight/business/0,39044868,39233051,00.htm
8. Baker, S., Grow, B.: Gambling Sites, This Is A Holdup (2005), http://www.businessweek.com/magazine/content/04_32/b3895106_mz063.htm
9. Garvey, M.: Phishing Attacks Show Sixfold Increase This Year (2005), http://www.informationweek.com/story/showArticle.jhtml?articleID=164302582

10. Talbot, C.: Phishing Attacks Up More Than 200% in May, says IBM (2005), http://www.integratedmar.com/ecl-usa/story.cfm?item=19703
11. Leyden, J.: Phishers Tapping Botnets to Automate Attack (2004), http://www.theregister.co.uk/2004/11/26/anti-phishing_report/
12. Liet, D.: Most Spam Generated by Botnets, Says Expert (2004), http://news.zdnet.co.uk/internet/security/0,39020375,39167561,00.htm
13. Leyden, J.: ISPs urged to throttle spam zombies (2005), http://www.theregister.co.uk/2005/05/24/operation_spam_zombie/
14. Preatoni, R.: Prophet Mohammed protest spreads on the digital ground. In: Hundreds of cyber attacks against Danish and western webservers spreading rage in the name of Allah (2006)
15. Roberts, P.: Al-Jazeera hobbled by DDOS attack (2003), http://www.infoworld.com/article/03/03/26/HNjazeera_1.html
16. Costa, M., Crowcroft, J., Castro, M., Rowstron, A., Zhou, L., Zhang, L., Barham, P.: Vigilante: End-to-end containment of internet worms. In: Symposium on Operating System Principles (SOSP) (2005)
17. Rowstron, A.I.T., Druschel, P.: Pastry: Scalable, decentralized object location, and routing for large-scale peer-to-peer systems. In: Proceedings of the IFIP/ACM International Conference on Distributed Systems Platforms, Heidelberg, pp. 329–350 (2001)
18. Cooper, C., Dyer, M., Greenhill, C.: Sampling regular graphs and a peer-to-peer network. In: Proceedings of the Sixteenth Annual ACM-SIAM Symposium on Discrete algorithms (SODA) (2005)
19. Joshi, A., King, S., Dunlap, G., Chen, P.: Detecting past and present intrusions through vulnerability-specific predicates. In: Symposium on Operating System Principles (SOSP) (2005)
20. Liang, Z., Sekar, R.: Fast and automated generation of attack signatures: a basis for building self-protecting servers. In: Proceedings of the 12th ACM Conference on Computer and Communications Security (CCS), pp. 213–222 (2005)
21. Brumley, D., Newsome, J., Song, D., Wang, H., Jha, S.: Towards automatic generation of vulnerability-based signatures. In: Proceedings of the IEEE Symposium on Security and Privacy, 2–16 (2006)
22. Zhou, L., Zhang, L., McSherry, F., Immorlica, N., Costa, M., Chien, S.: A first look at peer-to-peer worms: Threats and defenses. In: Castro, M., van Renesse, R. (eds.) IPTPS 2005. LNCS, vol. 3640, Springer, Heidelberg (2005)
23. Vojnovic, M., Ganesh, A.: On the effectiveness of automatic patching. In: ACM Workshop on Rapid Malcode (WORM) (2005)
24. Shakkottai, S., Srikant, R.: Peer to peer networks for defense against internet worms. In: Proceedings of the 2006 workshop on Interdisciplinary systems approach in performance evaluation and design of computer and communications sytems (2006)
25. Bollobas, B.: Random Graphs. Academic Press, London (1985)

Author Index

Ammar, Mostafa   31
Anceaume, Emmanuelle   90
Arora, Anish   143
Aspnes, James   286, 443
Awerbuch, Baruch   48

Baduel, Laurent   1
Baker, Theodore P.   62
Baruah, Sanjoy   204
Beaumont, Olivier   315
Blin, Lélia   301
Bonnet, François   372

Calamoneri, Tiziana   247
Cirinei, Michele   62
Clementi, Andrea   247

Delporte-Gallet, Carole   90, 329
Dieudonné, Yoann   132
Dolev, Danny   232, 343
Duchon, Philippe   274

Eggemann, Nicole   274

Fauconnier, Hugues   90, 329
Fernández Anta, Antonio   119, 189
Fisher, Nathan   204
Flocchini, Paola   105
Fusco, Emanuele G.   247

Gafni, Eli   260
Gidenstam, Anders   217
Gradinariu Potop-Butucaru, Maria   301
Gramoli, Vincent   429
Groß, Christian   174
Guerraoui, Rachid   329

Hamouma, Moumen   76
Hanusse, Nicolas   274
Hermanns, Holger   174
Ho, Chi   232
Hoch, Ezra N.   343
Hoffman, Moshe   401
Hurfin, Michel   90

Ilcinkas, David   105, 415

Kermarrec, Anne-Marie   315, 372
Krumke, Sven O.   159

Kulathumani, Vinodkrishnan   143
Kumar, Rajnish   31
Kuznetsov, Petr   260

Matsuoka, Satoshi   1
Mauran, Philippe   358
Merz, Peter   159
Mohapatra, Dushmanta   31
Mostefaoui, Achour   76
Mosteiro, Miguel A.   119

Nisgav, Aviv   48
Nisse, Nicolas   415
Nonner, Tim   159

Padiou, Gérard   358
Papatriantafilou, Marina   217
Patt-Shamir, Boaz   48
Pedone, Fernando   16
Pelc, Andrzej   105
Petit, Franck   132
Pulungan, Reza   174

Quéinnec, Philippe   358

Ramachandran, Umakishore   31
Raynal, Michel   189, 372, 429
Rivière, Étienne   315
Rupp, Katharina   159
Ruppert, Eric   329, 386
Rustagi, Navin   443

Saia, Jared   443
Santoro, Nicola   105
Schmidt, Rodrigo   16
Shalev, Ori   401
Shavit, Nir   401
Shin, Junsuk   31
Silvestri, Riccardo   247
Soguet, David   415

Thraves, Christopher   119
Tixeuil, Sébastien   301
Trédan, Gilles   76

van Renesse, Robbert   232, 343

Widder, Josef   90
Wu, Yinghua   286

Lecture Notes in Computer Science

Sublibrary 1: Theoretical Computer Science and General Issues

For information about Vols. 1– 4510
please contact your bookseller or Springer

Vol. 4878: E. Tovar, P. Tsigas, H. Fouchal (Eds.), Principles of Distributed Systems. XIII, 457 pages. 2007.

Vol. 4873: S. Aluru, M. Parashar, R. Badrinath, V.K. Prasanna (Eds.), High Performance Computing – HiPC 2007. XXIV, 663 pages. 2007.

Vol. 4863: A. Bonato, F.R.K. Chung (Eds.), Algorithms and Models for the Web-Graph. X, 217 pages. 2007.

Vol. 4855: V. Arvind, S. Prasad (Eds.), FSTTCS 2007: Foundations of Software Technology and Theoretical Computer Science. XIV, 558 pages. 2007.

Vol. 4847: M. Xu, Y. Zhan, J. Cao, Y. Liu (Eds.), Advanced Parallel Processing Technologies. XIX, 767 pages. 2007.

Vol. 4846: I. Cervesato (Ed.), Advances in Computer Science – ASIAN 2007. XI, 313 pages. 2007.

Vol. 4838: T. Masuzawa, S. Tixeuil (Eds.), Stabilization, Safety, and Security of Distributed Systems. XIII, 409 pages. 2007.

Vol. 4835: T. Tokuyama (Ed.), Algorithms and Computation. XVII, 929 pages. 2007.

Vol. 4783: J. Holub, J. Žďárek (Eds.), Implementation and Application of Automata. XIII, 324 pages. 2007.

Vol. 4782: R. Perrott, B.M. Chapman, J. Subhlok, R.F. de Mello, L.T. Yang (Eds.), High Performance Computing and Communications. XIX, 823 pages. 2007.

Vol. 4771: T. Bartz-Beielstein, M.J. Blesa Aguilera, C. Blum, B. Naujoks, A. Roli, G. Rudolph, M. Sampels (Eds.), Hybrid Metaheuristics. X, 202 pages. 2007.

Vol. 4770: V.G. Ganzha, E.W. Mayr, E.V. Vorozhtsov (Eds.), Computer Algebra in Scientific Computing. XIII, 460 pages. 2007.

Vol. 4763: J.-F. Raskin, P.S. Thiagarajan (Eds.), Formal Modeling and Analysis of Timed Systems. X, 369 pages. 2007.

Vol. 4746: A. Bondavalli, F. Brasileiro, S. Rajsbaum (Eds.), Dependable Computing. XV, 239 pages. 2007.

Vol. 4743: P. Thulasiraman, X. He, T.L. Xu, M.K. Denko, R.K. Thulasiram, L.T. Yang (Eds.), Frontiers of High Performance Computing and Networking ISPA 2007 Workshops. XXIX, 536 pages. 2007.

Vol. 4742: I. Stojmenovic, R.K. Thulasiram, L.T. Yang, W. Jia, M. Guo, R.F. de Mello (Eds.), Parallel and Distributed Processing and Applications. XX, 995 pages. 2007.

Vol. 4739: R. Moreno Díaz, F. Pichler, A. Quesada Arencibia (Eds.), Computer Aided Systems Theory – EUROCAST 2007. XIX, 1233 pages. 2007.

Vol. 4736: S. Winter, M. Duckham, L. Kulik, B. Kuipers (Eds.), Spatial Information Theory. XV, 455 pages. 2007.

Vol. 4732: K. Schneider, J. Brandt (Eds.), Theorem Proving in Higher Order Logics. IX, 401 pages. 2007.

Vol. 4731: A. Pelc (Ed.), Distributed Computing. XVI, 510 pages. 2007.

Vol. 4726: N. Ziviani, R. Baeza-Yates (Eds.), String Processing and Information Retrieval. XII, 311 pages. 2007.

Vol. 4711: C.B. Jones, Z. Liu, J. Woodcock (Eds.), Theoretical Aspects of Computing – ICTAC 2007. XI, 483 pages. 2007.

Vol. 4710: C.W. George, Z. Liu, J. Woodcock (Eds.), Domain Modeling and the Duration Calculus. XI, 237 pages. 2007.

Vol. 4708: L. Kučera, A. Kučera (Eds.), Mathematical Foundations of Computer Science 2007. XVIII, 764 pages. 2007.

Vol. 4707: O. Gervasi, M.L. Gavrilova (Eds.), Computational Science and Its Applications – ICCSA 2007, Part III. XXIV, 1205 pages. 2007.

Vol. 4706: O. Gervasi, M.L. Gavrilova (Eds.), Computational Science and Its Applications – ICCSA 2007, Part II. XXIII, 1129 pages. 2007.

Vol. 4705: O. Gervasi, M.L. Gavrilova (Eds.), Computational Science and Its Applications – ICCSA 2007, Part I. XLIV, 1169 pages. 2007.

Vol. 4703: L. Caires, V.T. Vasconcelos (Eds.), CONCUR 2007 – Concurrency Theory. XIII, 507 pages. 2007.

Vol. 4700: C.B. Jones, Z. Liu, J. Woodcock (Eds.), Formal Methods and Hybrid Real-Time Systems. XVI, 539 pages. 2007.

Vol. 4699: B. Kågström, E. Elmroth, J. Dongarra, J. Waśniewski (Eds.), Applied Parallel Computing. XXIX, 1192 pages. 2007.

Vol. 4698: L. Arge, M. Hoffmann, E. Welzl (Eds.), Algorithms – ESA 2007. XV, 769 pages. 2007.

Vol. 4697: L. Choi, Y. Paek, S. Cho (Eds.), Advances in Computer Systems Architecture. XIII, 400 pages. 2007.

Vol. 4688: K. Li, M. Fei, G.W. Irwin, S. Ma (Eds.), Bio-Inspired Computational Intelligence and Applications. XIX, 805 pages. 2007.

Vol. 4684: L. Kang, Y. Liu, S. Zeng (Eds.), Evolvable Systems: From Biology to Hardware. XIV, 446 pages. 2007.

Vol. 4683: L. Kang, Y. Liu, S. Zeng (Eds.), Advances in Computation and Intelligence. XVII, 663 pages. 2007.

Vol. 4681: D.-S. Huang, L. Heutte, M. Loog (Eds.), Advanced Intelligent Computing Theories and Applications. XXVI, 1379 pages. 2007.

Vol. 4672: K. Li, C. Jesshope, H. Jin, J.-L. Gaudiot (Eds.), Network and Parallel Computing. XVIII, 558 pages. 2007.

Vol. 4671: V.E. Malyshkin (Ed.), Parallel Computing Technologies. XIV, 635 pages. 2007.

Vol. 4669: J.M. de Sá, L.A. Alexandre, W. Duch, D. Mandic (Eds.), Artificial Neural Networks – ICANN 2007, Part II. XXXI, 990 pages. 2007.

Vol. 4668: J.M. de Sá, L.A. Alexandre, W. Duch, D. Mandic (Eds.), Artificial Neural Networks – ICANN 2007, Part I. XXXI, 978 pages. 2007.

Vol. 4666: M.E. Davies, C.J. James, S.A. Abdallah, M.D. Plumbley (Eds.), Independent Component Analysis and Blind Signal Separation. XIX, 847 pages. 2007.

Vol. 4665: J. Hromkovič, R. Královič, M. Nunkesser, P. Widmayer (Eds.), Stochastic Algorithms: Foundations and Applications. X, 167 pages. 2007.

Vol. 4664: J. Durand-Lose, M. Margenstern (Eds.), Machines, Computations, and Universality. X, 325 pages. 2007.

Vol. 4661: U. Montanari, D. Sannella, R. Bruni (Eds.), Trustworthy Global Computing. X, 339 pages. 2007.

Vol. 4649: V. Diekert, M.V. Volkov, A. Voronkov (Eds.), Computer Science – Theory and Applications. XIII, 420 pages. 2007.

Vol. 4647: R. Martin, M.A. Sabin, J.R. Winkler (Eds.), Mathematics of Surfaces XII. IX, 509 pages. 2007.

Vol. 4646: J. Duparc, T.A. Henzinger (Eds.), Computer Science Logic. XIV, 600 pages. 2007.

Vol. 4644: N. Azémard, L. Svensson (Eds.), Integrated Circuit and System Design. XIV, 583 pages. 2007.

Vol. 4641: A.-M. Kermarrec, L. Bougé, T. Priol (Eds.), Euro-Par 2007 Parallel Processing. XXVII, 974 pages. 2007.

Vol. 4639: E. Csuhaj-Varjú, Z. Ésik (Eds.), Fundamentals of Computation Theory. XIV, 508 pages. 2007.

Vol. 4638: T. Stützle, M. Birattari, H. H. Hoos (Eds.), Engineering Stochastic Local Search Algorithms. X, 223 pages. 2007.

Vol. 4630: H.J. van den Herik, P. Ciancarini, H.H.L.M.(J.) Donkers (Eds.), Computers and Games. XII, 283 pages. 2007.

Vol. 4628: L.N. de Castro, F.J. Von Zuben, H. Knidel (Eds.), Artificial Immune Systems. XII, 438 pages. 2007.

Vol. 4627: M. Charikar, K. Jansen, O. Reingold, J.D.P. Rolim (Eds.), Approximation, Randomization, and Combinatorial Optimization. XII, 626 pages. 2007.

Vol. 4624: T. Mossakowski, U. Montanari, M. Haveraaen (Eds.), Algebra and Coalgebra in Computer Science. XI, 463 pages. 2007.

Vol. 4623: M. Collard (Ed.), Ontologies-Based Databases and Information Systems. X, 153 pages. 2007.

Vol. 4621: D. Wagner, R. Wattenhofer (Eds.), Algorithms for Sensor and Ad Hoc Networks. XIII, 415 pages. 2007.

Vol. 4619: F. Dehne, J.-R. Sack, N. Zeh (Eds.), Algorithms and Data Structures. XVI, 662 pages. 2007.

Vol. 4618: S.G. Akl, C.S. Calude, M.J. Dinneen, G. Rozenberg, H.T. Wareham (Eds.), Unconventional Computation. X, 243 pages. 2007.

Vol. 4616: A.W.M. Dress, Y. Xu, B. Zhu (Eds.), Combinatorial Optimization and Applications. XI, 390 pages. 2007.

Vol. 4614: B. Chen, M. Paterson, G. Zhang (Eds.), Combinatorics, Algorithms, Probabilistic and Experimental Methodologies. XII, 530 pages. 2007.

Vol. 4613: F.P. Preparata, Q. Fang (Eds.), Frontiers in Algorithmics. XI, 348 pages. 2007.

Vol. 4600: H. Comon-Lundh, C. Kirchner, H. Kirchner (Eds.), Rewriting, Computation and Proof. XVI, 273 pages. 2007.

Vol. 4599: S. Vassiliadis, M. Bereković, T.D. Hämäläinen (Eds.), Embedded Computer Systems: Architectures, Modeling, and Simulation. XVIII, 466 pages. 2007.

Vol. 4598: G. Lin (Ed.), Computing and Combinatorics. XII, 570 pages. 2007.

Vol. 4596: L. Arge, C. Cachin, T. Jurdziński, A. Tarlecki (Eds.), Automata, Languages and Programming. XVII, 953 pages. 2007.

Vol. 4595: D. Bošnački, S. Edelkamp (Eds.), Model Checking Software. X, 285 pages. 2007.

Vol. 4590: W. Damm, H. Hermanns (Eds.), Computer Aided Verification. XV, 562 pages. 2007.

Vol. 4588: T. Harju, J. Karhumäki, A. Lepistö (Eds.), Developments in Language Theory. XI, 423 pages. 2007.

Vol. 4583: S.R. Della Rocca (Ed.), Typed Lambda Calculi and Applications. X, 397 pages. 2007.

Vol. 4580: B. Ma, K. Zhang (Eds.), Combinatorial Pattern Matching. XII, 366 pages. 2007.

Vol. 4576: D. Leivant, R. de Queiroz (Eds.), Logic, Language, Information and Computation. X, 363 pages. 2007.

Vol. 4547: C. Carlet, B. Sunar (Eds.), Arithmetic of Finite Fields. XI, 355 pages. 2007.

Vol. 4546: J. Kleijn, A. Yakovlev (Eds.), Petri Nets and Other Models of Concurrency – ICATPN 2007. XI, 515 pages. 2007.

Vol. 4545: H. Anai, K. Horimoto, T. Kutsia (Eds.), Algebraic Biology. XIII, 379 pages. 2007.

Vol. 4533: F. Baader (Ed.), Term Rewriting and Applications. XII, 419 pages. 2007.

Vol. 4528: J. Mira, J.R. Álvarez (Eds.), Nature Inspired Problem-Solving Methods in Knowledge Engineering, Part II. XXII, 650 pages. 2007.

Vol. 4527: J. Mira, J.R. Álvarez (Eds.), Bio-inspired Modeling of Cognitive Tasks, Part I. XXII, 630 pages. 2007.

Vol. 4525: C. Demetrescu (Ed.), Experimental Algorithms. XIII, 448 pages. 2007.

Vol. 4514: S.N. Artemov, A. Nerode (Eds.), Logical Foundations of Computer Science. XI, 513 pages. 2007.

Vol. 4513: M. Fischetti, D.P. Williamson (Eds.), Integer Programming and Combinatorial Optimization. IX, 500 pages. 2007.